THE BARBOUR
COLLECTION
OF CONNECTICUT TOWN
VITAL RECORDS

THE BARBOUR COLLECTION
OF CONNECTICUT TOWN
VITAL RECORDS

CANAAN 1739–1852

CANTERBURY 1703–1850

Compiled by

Lorraine Cook White

INTRODUCTION

As early as 1640 the Connecticut Court of Election ordered all
magistrates to keep a record of the marriages they performed. In 1644 the
registration of births and marriages became the official responsibility of town
clerks and registrars, with deaths added to their duties in 1650. From 1660
until the close of the Revolutionary War these vital records of birth,
marriage, and death were generally well kept, but then for a period of about
two generations until the mid-nineteenth century, the faithful recording of
vital records declined in some towns.

General Lucius Barnes Barbour was the Connecticut Examiner of Public
Records from 1911 to 1934 and in that capacity directed a project in which
the vital records kept by the towns up to about 1850 were copied and
abstracted. Barbour previously had directed the publication of the Bolton
and Vernon vital records for the Connecticut Historical Society. For this
new project he hired several individuals who were experienced in copying
old records and familiar with the old script.

Barbour presented the completed transcriptions of town vital records to
the Connecticut State Library where the information was typed onto printed
forms. The form sheets were then cut, producing twelve small slips from
each sheet. The slips for most towns were then alphabetized and the
information was then typed a second time on large sheets of rag paper,
which were subsequently bound into separate volumes for each town. The
slips for all towns were then interfiled, forming a statewide alphabetized slip
index for most surviving town vital records.

The dates of coverage vary from town to town, and of course the
records of some towns are more complete than others. There are many cases
in which an entry may appear two or three times, apparently because that
entry was entered by one or more persons. Altogether the entire Barbour
Collection--one of the great genealogical manuscript collections and one of
the last to be published--covers 137 towns and comprises 14,333 typed
pages.

TABLE OF CONTENTS

ABBREVIATIONS

ae.------------age
b. ------------born, both
bd.------------buried
B. G.----------Burying Ground
d. ------------died, day, or daughter
decd.----------deceased
f.--------------father
h.--------------hour
J. P.------------Justice of Peace
m.--------------married or month
res.------------resident
s.--------------son
st.--------------stillborn
w. ----------wife
wid.----------widow
wk.----------week
y. ------------year

THE BARBOUR COLLECTION OF CONNECTICUT TOWN VITAL RECORDS

ADAMS, ADDAMS, ADAM, Abigail, 9th child of John & Abigail,
 b. Mar. 28, 1790; d. Apr. 19, 1790, ae 22 d.   A   44
Abigail, 10th child of John & Abigail, b. Apr. 21, 1791;
 d. July 21, 1791, ae 3 m.   A   44
Charles, m. Maria **LAWRENCE,** b. of Canaan, Sept. 21, 1846,
 by Rev. D. D. Francis   A   107
Francis Charlotte, d. [William & Charlotte], b. Aug. 31, 1830   A   53
James F., m. Julia **PECK,** b. of Sheffield, May 13, 1838,
 by H. H. Woodbridge   A   97
Jane E., m. William G. **PIERCE,** b. of Canaan, May 1, 1843,
 by Charles Kittridge   A   103
Jane Elizabeth, d. Leonard & Arabella, b. Nov. 16, 1815   A   53
John, b. Mar. 4, 1755, in Taunton, Mass.; m. Abigail
 FOORBES, Aug. 6, 1780, at her father's house   A   44
John & Abigail, had twin d. [   ], b. July 1, 1784; d. same day   A   44
John, 6th child of John & Abigail, b. June 22, 1785   A   44
John Quincy, s. Leonard & Arabella, b. Dec. 29, 1827   A   53
John Quincy, [s. Leonard & Arabella], d. Dec. 9, 1829   A   53
Jonathan, s. James & Submit, b. Sept. 20, 1765   A   11
Julia, of Litchfield, m. Joseph W. **CAKE** (?), of Harrisburg,
 Pa., Aug. 1, 1839, by Rev. Henry H. Woodbridge, of the
 2nd Cong. Ch. Int. Pub.   A   98
Julia M., of New Marlborough, Mass., m. John
 HUNGTINGTON, of Canaan, Dec. 16, 1845, by Rev. D.
 D. Francis   A   106
Leonard, 8th child of John & Abigail, b. Mar. 8, 1788   A   44
Leonard, s. John & Abigail, b. Mar. 8, 1788   A   53
Leonard, s. John & Abigail, m. Arabella **COOK,** d. Silas
 & Abigail, Nov. 7, 1811   A   53
Leonard Cook, s. Leonard & Arabella, b. Mar. 7, 1826   A   53
Lucius S., m. Eliza A. **PRENTICE,** Jan. 1, 1835, by Charles
 Prentice. Int. Pub.   A   94
Lucy, d. John & Abigail, b. May 20, 1781   A   44
Lucy M., m. Milton **JOSLIN,** Nov. 3, 1831   A   53
Lucy M:, of Canaan, m. Milton **JOSLIN,** of Southbridge,
 Mass., Nov. 3, 1831, by Pitkin Cowles   A   89
Lucy Mary, d. Leonard & Arabella, b. Jan. 8, 1813   A   53
Martin, s. James & Submit, b. Feb. 5, 1764   A   11
Milton Joslin, s. Leonard & Arabella, b. June 24, 1833   A   53
Polly, 11th child of John & Abigail, b. Feb. 9, 1794;
 d. Feb. 29, 1796, ae 2 y. 20 d.   A   44

	Vol.	Page
ADAMS, ADDAMS, ADAM, (cont.)		
Robert William, s. William & Charlotte, b. Sept. 28, 1825	A	53
Sally, m. Samuel **BECKLEY**, Jr., Sept. 20, 1801	A	53
Samuel Forbes, 3rd Child of John & Abigail, b. June 1, 1783	A	44
Sarah, 2nd d. John & Abigail, b. June 26, 1782	A	44
Sarah Walker, d. [William & Charlotte], b. Apr. 28, 1836	A	53
Thirza, d. James & Submit, b. Sept. 29, 1767	A	11
William, 7th child of John & Abigail, b. May 7, 1786	A	44
William, 7th child of John & Abigail, d. Oct. 28, 1791, ae 5 y. 5 m. 3 w.	A	44
William, 12th child & 5th s. of John & Abigail, b. Apr. 17, 1799	A	47
William, m. Charlotte **LAWRENCE**, Sept. 15, 1824, by Pitkin Cowles	A	83
William, s. Leonard & Arabella, b. Oct. 10, 1829	A	53
ADKINS, Sarah, of Southington, m. Zebulon **ANDRUSS**, of Canaan, Nov. [ ], 1747	LR1	426
ALLEN, [see also **ALLING & ALLYN**], Mary, wid. of Norfolk, m. Samuel **HOOD**, of Canaan, Oct. 8, 1820, by Pitkin Cowles	A	79
ALLING, [see also **ALLYN & ALLEN**], Maria, of Canaan, m. John **RUSSELL**, Jr., of Salisbury, Dec. 10, 1826, by Joshua Cornwall, J. P.	A	85
ALLYN, [see also **ALLING & ALLEN**], Erastus P., m. Altha A. **ROCKWELL**, May 21, 1832, by Pitkin Cowles	A	90
ANDREWS, ANDRUS, Amey, d. Hezekiah & Anne, b. Apr. 17, 1766	A	11
Chloe, m. Moses **MARSH**, Dec. 5, 1780	A	38
David, s. Hezekiah & Anne, b. Mar. 29, 1768	A	12
Elijah, m. Emma A. **ELTON**, July 4, 1825, by Rev. Samuel Eighmy, of the M. E. Ch.	A	84
Elisha, s. Hezekiah & Anne, b. July 15, 1760	A	11
Elvina, m. Frederick S. **BOTSFORD**, Mar. 9, 1851, by Rev. Zephaniah D. Scobey	A	108
Hezekiah, m. Anabel **HANCOX**, Apr. 11, 1754, by Rev. Mr. Farrand	LR2	227
Jonathan Hancox, s. Hezekiah & Anabel, b. June 17, 1757	LR2	227
Maria, of Canaan, m. Kellogg **RHOADES**, of New Marlborough, Mass., July 4, 1837, by Rev. H. H. Woodbridge, of the 2nd Cong. Ch.	A	96
Maria, of Norfolk, m. Edward **CHATFIELD**, of Killingworth, July 4, 1841, by Rev. H. H. Woodbridge, of the 2nd Cong. Ch. Int. Pub. in Norfolk	A	100
Mary, m. Timothy **BROWN**, Feb. 25, 1744/5	LR2	239
Pedy, d. Hezekiah & Anne, b. Oct. 7, 1763	A	11
Robert N., of Avon, m. Mary E. **BRIGGS**, Nov. 25, 1851, by Rev. Elisha Whittlesey	A	109
Zebulon, of Canaan, m. Sarah **ADKINS**, of Southington,		

	Vol.	Page
ANDREWS, ANDRUS, (cont.)		
Nov. [ ], 1747	LR1	426
Zubah, d. Zebulon & Sarah, b. Aug. 25, 1748	LR1	426
ARMSTRONG, Eliza, of Pine Plains, N. Y., m. John **TEN IKE**, of		
Canaan, Oct. 10, 1830, by Pitkin Cowles	A	88
Richard, of Salisbury, m. Mariah **DAVIS**, of Canaan, Dec.		
9, 1830, by Pitkin Cowles	A	88
ASHLEY, John, m. Desire **THATCHER**, Apr. 24, 1765	A	7
AUSTIN, Anna, d. Caleb & Martha, b. Feb. 18, 1783	A	41
Archibald, of Goshen, m. Almira **MORGAN**, of Canaan, Oct.		
21, 1821, by Pitkin Cowles	A	80
Aurelia, d. Caleb & Martha, b. Sept. 23, 1792	A	42
Caleb Hopkins, s. Caleb & Martha, b. Sept. 3, 1794	A	42
Emmeline, d. Caleb & Martha, b. Oct. 28, 1797	A	44
Flavia, d. Caleb & Martha, b. Aug. 28, 1781	A	36
Hiram, s. Samuel & Elizabeth, b. May 23, 1795	A	46
Hiram, of Perrysbury, N. Y., m. Electa **REED**, of Canaan,		
Nov. 17, 1831, by Charles Prentice	A	89
Laura, d. Caleb & Martha, b. May 12, 1785	A	41
Luther, s. Samuel & Elizabeth, b. Oct. 3, 1792	A	46
Martha, d. Caleb & Martha, b. Dec. 3, 1789	A	41
Prudence, m. Joseph **KELLOGG**, Jr., Mar. 10, 1774	A	27
Samantha, of Canaan, m. Luther **BROOKS**, Jr., of New		
Marlborough, Oct. 27, 1824, by Pitkin Cowles	A	83
Samuel, m. Elizabeth **HOSMER**, Nov. 27, 1791	A	46
Samuel, d. Aug. 28, 1797	A	46
Sarah, of Sheffield, Mass., m. Thomas **McMAHON**, of New		
Hartford, Nov. 19, 1840, by Rev. H. H. Woodbridge, of		
the 2nd Cong. Ch.	A	99
BABCOCK, Cyrus, s. Rufus & Zuriah, b. Jan. 25, 1789	A	41
Elijah, see James **BABCOCK**	A	29
James, s. Elijah & Sarah, b. June 4, 1778	A	28
James, youngest, s. Elijah & Sarah, had his name changed		
to Elijah, June 4, 1778, by the desire of his parents	A	29
Lydia, d. Elijah & Sarah, b. May 17, 1774	A	28
Mary F., of Hudson, N. Y., m. Dr. J. Edmund **SMITH**, of		
West Cornwall, Oct. 5, 1847, by Rev. D. D. Francis	A	107
Rufus, m. Zeruiah **MOSES**, May 24, 1781	A	36
Sarah, d. Elijah & Sarah, b. May 11, 1776	A	28
Timothy, s. Rufus & Zeruiah, b. Mar. 12, 1782	A	36
BACKUS, Charles Dyer, s. Simon & Gesia, b. Jan. 23, 1784	A	41
George, s. Simon & Gesia, b. July 15, 1788	A	41
Phebe, d. Simon & Gesia, b. Nov. 10, 1785	A	41
Simon, m. Gesia **CORMICK**, Apr. 17, 1783	A	41
BACON, Andrew, m. Elizabeth **DUNHAM**, Mar. 17, 1754	A	7
Andrew, s. Andrew & Elizabeth, b. Aug. 1, 1755; d. same		
month, 5th day	A	7
Andrew, s. Andrew & Elizabeth, b. Sept. 19, 1765	A	7

	Vol.	Page
BACON, (cont.)		
Andrew, m. Lucy UPSON, Dec. 29, 1788	A	41
Andrew, s. Andrew, Jr. & Lucy, b. Nov. 1, 1791	A	42
Andrew, s. Josiah & Mary, b. May 1, 1801	A	49
Andrew, s. Josiah & Mary, b. May 1, 1802	A	47
Charity, d. Samuel & Lydia, b. Nov. 20, 1781	A	43
Charlotte E., of Canaan, m. Caleb P. CONE, of Torrington, Aug. 21, 1843, by Charles Kettridge	A	103
Elizabeth, d. Andrew & Elizabeth, b. Mar. 14, 1763	A	7
Hervey, s. Josiah & Mary, b. Aug. 10, 1793	A	43
Josiah, s. Andrew & Elizabeth, b. Mar. 14, 1761; d. same month, 16th day	A	7
Josiah, s. Andrew & Elizabeth, b. June 16, 1770	A	43
Martha, d. Josiah & Mary, b. Mar. 13, 1799	A	45
Mary, w. Josiah, d. Oct. 5, 1809	A	50
Mary, w. Josiah, d. Oct. 5, 1811	A	48
Olive, d. William & Abigail, b. July 3, 17[ ]	A	41
Polly, d. Josiah & Mary, b. Jan. 7, 1797	A	43
Salathiel, s. Andrew & Elizabeth, b. Mar. 10, 1759; d. Jan. 10, 1760	A	7
Sally, d. Andrew & Lucy, b. Apr. 19, 1790	A	41
Samuel, s. Andrew & Elizabeth, b. Mar. 24, 1757	A	7
William, m. Abigail DOUGLASS, Sept. 15, 1768	A	41
BAILEY, BAILY, BALEY, Abiram, m. Harriet BROWN, Mar. 9, 1828, by Charles Prentice	A	86
Cyrus, m. Amelia M. ROOT, b. of Canaan, Sept. 4, 1848, by Rev. K. W. Keeler	A	105
Daniel, of Kent, m. Clarissa MUNS, of Sharon, Mar. 27, 1821, by Rev. Walter Smith, of Cornwall	A	80
Henry, s. Thomas & Elizabeth, b. May 4, 1765	A	8
Jerusha, m. Micajah BENEDICT, Dec. 22, 1822, by William Holobird, J. P.	A	82
Lawrence, s. Thomas & Elizabeth, b. Aug. 1, 1770	A	23
Lucretia, m. Sheldon DEAN, Oct. 4, 1826, by William Holobird, J. P.	A	85
Maria C., m. Edward R. BRIGHTMAN, b. of Canaan, July 30, 1848, by Rev. D. D. Francis	A	107
Mary, d. Thomas & Elizabeth, b. Mar. 19, 1767	A	10
BAIRD, Parks, s. Aaron & Lucy, b. Mar. [ ], 1779	A	34
BAKER, Elisha, s. Elisha & Elizabeth, b. Mar. 13, 1767	A	9
Elizabeth, w. Elisha, d. Sept. 5, 1769	A	12
Esther, d. Elisha & Elizabeth, b. Nov. 28, 1763	A	8
Jeremiah, m. Linne* STEPHENS, Mar. 4, 1773 *("Anne" overwritten)	A	24
Mary, d. Jeremiah & Anna, b. Jan. 14, 1774	A	24
Rebeckah, d. Elisha & Elizabeth, b. July 14, 1765	A	8
Robert H., d. Feb. 10, 1839, ae 67 y.	A	53
Robert Harris, s. Elisha & Barshua, b. Apr. 6, 1772	A	15

	Vol.	Page

BAKER, (cont.)

Sereno, s. Elisha & Elizabth, b. Apr. 4, 1761 — A — 8

Susannah, m. David **FELLOWS,** June 2, 1762; d. Apr. 5, 1763 — A — 21

Thankfull, of Middletown, m. William **MARSH,** May 3, 1759,
by Rev. Mr. Farand — LR2 — 228

William, s. Elisha & Elizabeth, b. Dec. 5, 1768 — A — 12

BALDWIN, John R., of Stamford, N. Y., m. Louisa A.
UNDERWOOD, of Canaan, Oct. 25, 1847, by Rev. D. D.
Francis — A — 107

William, of Barkhamsted, m. Minerva Ann **JAKWAY,** of
Canaan, Nov. 11, 1840, by Rev. H. H. Woodbridge, of the
2nd Cong. Ch. Int. Pub. — A — 99

BALL, Abner, s. Gideon & Jane, b. Jan. 18, 1757 — LR2 — 233

Sarah, d. Gideon & Jane, b. June 4, 1750 — LR2 — 233

Sophronia, m. Harmon **ROCKWELL,** Sept. 11, 1827, by
Pitkin Cowles — A — 86

Susannah, d. Gideon & Jane, b. Feb. 14, 1753 — LR2 — 233

BANCROFT, Anah, m. Joseph **BUEL,** b. of Canaan, Mar. 20, 1831,
by Rev. Aaron Pearce — A — 89

BARBER, Betsey, of Canaan, m. George C. **SMITH,** of Norfolk,
June 5, 1822, by Pitkin Cowles — A — 81

Betsey M., of Canaan, m. Henry D. **WARNER,** of Austerlitz,
N. Y., Oct. 27, 1825, by Pitkin Cowles — A — 84

BARNES, BARNS, Aaron, m. Abigail **HORSFORD,** July 25, 1771 — A — 19

Aaron, s. Aaron & Abigail, b. Aug. 31, 1773;
d. Mar. 6, 1773 (sic) — A — 19

Abigail, d. Aaron & Abigail, b. May 13, 1774 — A — 26

Abraham, m. Hannah **TUCKER,** July 24, 1804 — A — 47

Abram, s. Thomas & Anna. b. Apr. 15, 1787 — A — 40

Adira, s. Thomas & Anna, b. Dec. 19, 1789 — A — 41

Anne, d. Thomas & Anne, b. Aug. 30, 1772 — A — 20

Asa, s. Job & Eunice, b. Sept. 14, 1795 — A — 46

Asa, m. Lucinda **DEAN,** b. of Canaan, May 22, 1823, by
Rev. Charles Prentice — A — 82

Asahel Horsford, s. Thomas & Anne, b. Mar. 30, 178[ ] — A — 37

Aurelia, m. William **RICHARDSON,** b. of Canaan, Nov. 6,
1836, by Rev. H. H. Woodbridge, of the 2nd Cong. Ch. — A — 95

Calvin S., m. Anna **WARNER,** b. of Canaan, Dec. 19, 1837,
by Charles Prentice — A — 96

Diana, d. Aaron & Abigail, b. May 15, 1776 — A — 26

Elizabeth, d. Gideon, Jr. & Lucy, b. Mar. 16, 1768 — A — 11

Elizabeth, d. Thomas & Anne, b. Aug. 27, 1780 — A — 37

Esther, d. Thomas & Anne, b. Apr. 27, 1776 — A — 26

Esther, d. Job & Esther, b. Mar. 19, 1789 — A — 46

Gideon, Jr. m. Lucy **WAY,** of Meredan, Nov. 16, 1757,
by Rev. Mr. Hall — LR2 — 228

Gideon, d. Oct. 6, 1779 — A — 34

Gideon, s. Job & Hester, b. Feb. 1, 1781 — A — 34

	Vol.	Page
BARNES, BARNS, (cont.)		
Hannah Rebeckah, d. Gideon & Lucy, b. Dec. 10, 1777	A	35
Horace A., m. Anna **ROOT**, Nov. 28, 1824, by Charles		
Prentice	A	84
Israel, s. Gideon, Jr. & Lucy, b. June 12, 1760	LR2	227
Job, m. Esther **HORSFORD**, May 28, 1778	A	31
Job, s. Job & Hester, b. Apr. 11, 1779	A	34
Julia, of Canaan, m. Jeremiah **BEACH**, of Norfolk, June 5,		
1822, by Charles Prentice	A	81
Lucy, d. Gideon, Jr. & Lucy, b. Feb. 20, 1763	A	3
Lucy, d. Gideon & Lucy, d. Feb. 6, 1765	A	5
Lucy, d. Gideon & Lucy, b. Dec. 7, 1765	A	9
Lidiah, d. Gideon & Lucy, b. Sept. 20, 1758	LR2	228
Mehitabel, m. Jane **WALLING**, Jan. 11, 1813	A	51
Nancy, d. Job & Eunice, b. July 14, 1790	A	46
Phelinda, d. Gideon, Jr. & Lucy, b. Feb. 19, 1774	A	20
Polly, d. Job & Esther, b. Nov. 14, 1784	A	46
Salmon, s. Thomas & Anne, b. Jan. 23, 1771	A	15
Salome, d. Thomas & Anne, b. Dec. 23, 1782	A	37
Samuel, s. Job & Eunice, b. Apr. 8, 1793	A	46
Thomas, m. Anne **HORSFORD**, Apr. 24, 1770	A	15
Thomas, s. Thomas & Anne, b. June 8, 1778	A	29
Timothy, s. Aaron & Abigail, b. June 26, 1779	A	32
BARNEY, Rufus, of Bennington, Vt., m. Mary E. **CROSSMAN**, of		
Canaan, Apr. 19, 1835, by Charles Prentice	A	94
BARRY, John, m. Ellen **COLLINS**, b. in Ireland, now of		
Barrington, Mass., July 23, 1852, by Rev. John Smith	A	109
BARTLETT, Ephraim, m. Sarah **NEWELL**, Feb. 15, 1801	A	46
James, d. Aug. 18, 1801	A	47
BASS, Laura, of New Marlborough, Mass., m. Samuel **HINMAN**, of		
Canaan, June 18, 1823, by Rev. Charles Prentice	A	82
BATES, Jonathan, m. Eunice **DEAN**, b. of Canaan, Aug. 23, 1840,		
by Rev. Erastus Doty, of Colebrook	A	99
Parmelia S., m. Charles **HUNT**, Apr. 29, 1841, by Rev. H. H.		
Woodbridge, of the 2nd Cong. Ch.	A	100
BEACH, Jeremiah, of Norfolk, m. Julia **BARNES**, of Canaan, June		
5, 1822, by Charles Prentice	A	81
[BEAL] BEELE, [see also **BEEBE**], Daniel, s. John & Martha,		
b. May 27, 1744	LR1	424
Elisha, s. John & Martha, b. June 11, 1747	LR1	424
Hannah, d. John & Martha, b. Apr. 11, 1740	LR1	424
Martha, d. John & Martha, b. Dec. 27, 1745	LR1	424
BEARDSLEY, Marcus, of Goshen, m. Mary Ann **BELDEN**, of		
Canaan, June 13, 1833, by Charles Prentice	A	91
BECKLEY, BECKLY, Amanda M., m. Horatio N. **HOLOBIRD**, b.		
of Canaan, May 16, 1825, by Charles Prentice	A	84
Amanda Malvina, d. Luther & Jette, b. Aug. 4, 1804	A	49
Belle*, s. Samuel & Sarah, b. Aug. 29, 1773 *("Billa"?)	A	20

	Vol.	Page
BECKLEY, BECKLY, (cont.)		
Caroline, [d. Samuel, Jr. & Sally], b. Aug. 14, 1802	A	53
Caroline, m. Luther **MONSON**, Sept. 9, 1824	A	53
Caroline, m. Luther **MONSON**, Sept. 9,1824, by Pitkin Cowles	A	83
Charlotte E., m. Nelson **HOLCOMB**, Aug. 31, 1831, by		
Charles Prentice	A	89
Charlotte Eliza, d. Luther & Jette, b. July 27, 1810	A	49
Cloe, d. Joseph & Pedey, b. Mar. 25, 1755	LR2	233
Cloe, m. Elijah **WHITNEY**, Sept. 24, 1772	A	16
Chloe, d. Joseph & Jane, b. Sept. 6, 1780	A	35
David, s. Joseph & Jane, b. Feb. 29, 1772	A	19
Everit, s. Billa & Wealthy, b. Sept. 5, 1798	A	46
Harriet Anna, m. Asahel **KELLOGG**, b. of Canaan, Jan. 10,		
1838, by H. H. Woodbridge	A	97
Jane Webster, d. Luther & Jette, b. June 19, 1807	A	49
John A., m. Sarah D. **MUNSON**, May 4, 1836, by Charles		
Prentice. Int. Pub.	A	95
John Adam, [s. Samuel, Jr. & Sally], b. Sept. 2, 1808	A	53
Jonathan, s. Joseph, Jr. & Jane, b. May 29, 1775	A	28
Joseph, of Canaan, m. Peadey **HANCOX**, of Canaan, May [ ],		
1747	LR1	424
Joseph, s. Joseph & Fedy, b. May 3, 1749	LR1	424
Joseph, Jr., m. Jane **BUZZARD**, Jan. 5, 1769	A	19
Laura, [d. Samuel, Jr. & Sally], b. Sept. 5, 1815	A	53
Levi Washington, s. Luther & Jette, b. Jan. 2, 1812	A	49
Lucey A., m. Asahel **KELLOGG**, b. of Canaan, May 22, 1843,		
by Charles Kittridge	A	103
Luther, s. Samuel & Sarah, b. Dec. 31, 1779	A	39
Luther, m. Jette **BEEBE**, Oct. 13, 1803	A	49
Luther Beebe, s. Luther & Jette, b. Nov. 22, 1805	A	49
Oliver, [s. Samuel, Jr. & Sally], b. May 16, 1804	A	53
Pede, d. Joseph, Jr. & Jane, b. Jan. 29, 1777	A	28
Samuell, s. Joseph & Pedy, b. July 27, 1751	LR1	427
Samuel, m. Sarah **ROOT**, May 28, 1771	A	16
Samuel, s. Samuel & Sarah, b. June 15, 1776	A	27
Samuel, Jr., m. Sally **ADAM**, Sept. 20, 1801	A	53
Sarah, d. Billa & Wealthy, b. Apr. 9, 1797	A	46
Silas, s. Samuel & Sarah, b. Jan. 11, 1786	A	39
BEEBE, BEBEE, [see also **BEAL**], Abigail, d. David & Abigail,		
b. Feb. 14, 1753	LR2	238
Anne, d. Asahel & Rebeckah, b. Oct. 1, 1753	LR2	238
Asahel, m. Rebeckah **WRIGHT**, Dec. 21, 1752	LR2	239
Ashman, s. Elisha & Martha, b. Feb. 17, 1780	A	33
Charles, s. Isaac & Jette, b. Mar. 19, 1788	A	41
Charles S., b. Sept. 10, 1817	A	54
Charlotte, d. Elisha & Eleanor, b. Jan. 1, 1796:		
d. Nov. 13, 1797	A	46
Cloe, d. Asahel & Rebecah, b. Nov. 21, 1754	LR2	238

	Vol.	Page

BEEBE, BEBEE, (cont.)

	Vol.	Page
Cloe, d. Asahel & Rebeckah, d. Sept. 20, 1759	LR2	228
Chyren Z., b. Nov. 6, 1820	A	54
Cornelia, b. J[ ] 4, 1823	A	54
Daniel, s. Elisha & Eleanor, b. May 28, 1792	A	46
Daniel, Capt., d. Nov. 20, 1821, ae 77	A	52
Daniel F., m. Eliza DEAN, Aug. 29, 1826, by John Lovejoy	A	85
Daniel Forbes, s. Daniel, b. Feb. 5, 1804	A	47
David, m. Abigail DIBLE, Nov. 23, 1752	LR2	238
David, s. David & Abigail, b. Jan. 22, 1755	LR2	232
David Lewis, s. Elisha & Eleanor, b. Jan. 15, 1790;		
d. Oct. 28, 1798	A	46
Electa, d. Elisha & Martha, b. Sept. 30, 1783	A	37
Elisha, s. Elisha & Martha, b. Nov. 13, 1775	A	26
Elizabeth, d. William & Mary, b. Oct. 31, 1753	LR2	238
Elliss, d. David & Abigal, b. Jan. 17, 1757	LR2	232
Emeline, d. Isaac & Gette, b. Feb. 26, 1800	A	45
Emeline, of Canaan, m. Dr. Stephen REED, of Goshen, May		
20, 1829, by Charles Prentice	A	87
Helen E., m. Chauncey S. FOSTER, b. of Canaan, Dec. 25,		
1849, by Rev. Z. D. Scobey	A	105
Henry Smith, s. Asahel & Betsey, b. Sept. 4, 1811	A	49
Hester, d. Asahel & Rebeckah, b. July 9, 1758	LR2	228
Hester, d. Asahel & Rebeckah, d. Sept. 20, 1759	LR2	228
Homan, s. Elisha & Martha, b. Dec. 22, 1777	A	33
Horace, m. Julia MORRIS, Sept. 21, 1829, by Charles Prentice	2	87
Isaac, Jr., s. Isaac & Jette, b. Jan. 26, 17[ ]	A	37
Isaac, s. John & Martha, b. Jan. 8, 1752	LR2	238
Isaac, m. Jette BELDING, June 26, 1777	A	34
Isaac N., b. Aug. 7, 1834	A	54
James, s. Asahel & Rebeckah, b. July 26, 1756	LR2	228
James, s. Asahel & Rebeckah, d. Sept. 28, 1759	LR2	228
Jette, d. Isaac & Jette, b. Apr. 15, 1786	A	39
Jette, m. Luther BECKLY, Oct. 13, 1803	A	49
John, s. Elisha & Martha, b. Feb. 1, 1774	A	20
John, s. Elisha & Martha, b. Mar. 25, 1786	A	46
John, m. Lucy MANSFIELD, b. of Canaan, Nov. 18, 1838,		
by Simeon Higley, J. P.	A	98
John A., b. Dec. 7, 1828	A	54
Joseph, m. Christian DUTCHER, Nov. 9, 1777	A	27
Levi, s. Isaac & Gitte, b. Jan. 31, 1780	A	36
Levi S., b. June 4, 1826	A	54
Lewis, s. John & Martha, b. Mar. 10, 1749	LR2	238
Lucy, d. Asahel & Betsey, b. Jan. 29, 1813	A	51
Maria, of Canaan, m. Joseph HURLBURT, of Darien, Nov. 26,		
1835, by Charles Prentice	A	94
Martha, d. Isaac & Jette, b. Apr. 14, 1778	A	34
Martha, m. Joseph KELLOGG, Jr., Oct. 13, 1803	A	47

	Vol.	Page

BEEBE, BEBEE, (cont.)

Mary, w. William, d. May 23, 1757 — LR2 233

Rachel, m. John **DEAN**, Jan. 21, 1756 — LR2 228

Sally, m. Henry **BELDEN**, b. of Canaan, Nov. 1, 1820,
  by Rev. Charles Prentice — A 79

William, m. Mary **HANCOX**, Mar. 19, 1752 — LR2 238

William, s. William & Mary, b. Dec. 28, 1755 — LR2 233

BEECHER, John E., of Sheffield, Mass., m. Jemima **MOSES**, of
  Canaan, Feb. 12, 1843, by Charles Rittridge, of N. Canaan — A 102

BEELE, [see under **BEAL**]

BELDEN, BELDING, Abigail, d. Charles & Hannah, b. Nov 13,
  1752 — LR2 238

Abigail, d. Oliver & Abigail, b. Feb. 14, 1756 — LR2 233

Abigail, twin with Lois, d. Jonathan & Sarah, b. May 13, 1771 — A 18

Abigail, twin with Lois, d. Jonathan & Sarah, b. May 13, 1773 — A 22

Abigail, d. Jonathan & Sarah, d. Oct. 1, 1775 — A 23

Almira, d. Bartholomew & Tabithy, b. Nov. 1, 1785 — A 38

Anna, d. Jonathan & Sarah, b. June 15, 1775 — A 23

Anne, d. Oliver & Abigail, b. May 17, 1765 — A 7

Austin, s. Jeremiah & Elizabeth, b. Jan. 1, 1806 — A 50

Bartholomew, s. Charles & Hannah, b. Dec. 30, 1759 — A 1

Bartholomew, m. Tabithy **KELLOGG**, Jan. 11, 1780 — A 38

Betsey, of Canaan, m. Asahel **BENEDICT**, of Salisbury,
  [Nov. 22, 1825], by Charles Prentice — A 85

Charles, m. Hannah **HOGEBOON**, June 14, 1752 — LR1 427

Charles, s. Charles & Hannah, b. Aug. 31, 1754 — LR2 238

Charlotte, of Canaan, m. Fowler **BRADFORD**, of Cornwall,
  May 17, 1831, by Charles Prentice — A 89

Edmund, m. Elizabeth **BURRETT**, July 9, 1834, by Charles
  Prentice — A 93

Edward Porter, s. Edmund, b. Mar. 30, 1841 — A 54

Elizabeth, d. Jeremiah & Elizabeth, b. July 24, 1808 — A 50

Hannah, d. Charles & Hannah, b. Sept. 9, 1757 — LR2 228

Hannah, d. Jeremiah & Elizabeth, b. May 1, 1810 — A 50

Hannah, m. William **CHAPIN**, b. of Canaan, June 19, 1836,
  by Charles Prentice — A 95

Harriet Elizabeth, d. Edmund, b. Oct. 6, 1835 — A 54

Henry, m. Sally **BEEBE**, b. of Canaan, Nov. 1, 1820, by
  Rev. Charles Prentice — A 79

Henry, m. Cornelia **MUNSON**, b. of Canaan, Mar. 28, 1844,
  by Rev. Harley Goodwin — A 103

Jane, of Canaan, m. George **WATSON**, of Torrington, Sept.
  11, 1833, by Charles Prentice — A 91

Jante, d. Charles & Hannah, b. Apr. 20, 1756 — LR2 228

Jeremiah, s. Charles, b. Apr. 14, 1774 — A 46

Jeremiah, m. Elizabeth **KELLOGG**, Feb. 18, 1796 — A 46

Jeremiah, s. Jeremiah & Elizabeth, b. July 14, 1803 — A 50

Jeremiah, Jr., m. Ann **JACOBS**, Feb. 11, 1830, by Charles — A 88

	Vol.	Page
BELDEN, BELDING, (cont.)		
Prentice	A	88
Jette, m. Isaac **BEEBE**, June 26, 1777	A	34
Jonathan, m. Sarah **BELDING**, of Hartford, Mar. 22, 1759,		
by Rev. Joshua Bels, of Weathersfield	LR2	228
Jonathan, s. Jonathan & Sarah, b. June 18, 1760	A	3
Jonathan, s. Jonathan & Sarah, d. Oct. 1, 1772	A	16
Jonathan, d. Jan. 9, 1778, in the 41st y. of his age	A	27
Jonathan, s. Jonathan & Sarah, b. June 14, 1778	A	30
Joseph, s. Jeremiah & Elizabeth, b. June 15, 1799	A	50
Joseph, s. Jeremiah & Elizabeth, b. July 15, 1799	A	47
Joseph, of Canaan, m. Abigail C. **CLEMMENT**, of Rapert,		
Vt., Jan. 31, 1830, by Charles Prentice	A	88
Joshua, s. Charles & Hannah, b. Dec. 17, 1761	A	3
Joshua, Jr., m. Betsey E. **FENN**, b. of Canaan, Nov. 5,		
1839, by Rev. Henry H. Woodbridge, of the 2nd Cong.		
Ch.	A	98
Kellogg, s. Bartholomew & Tabithy, b. May 25, 1783	A	38
Lois, d. Jonathan & Sarah, b. Dec. 18, 1769	A	16
Lois, twin with Abigail, d. Jonathan & Sarah, b. May 13, 1771	A	18
Lois, twin with Abigail, d. Jonathan & Sarah, b. May 13, 1773	A	22
Martha, d. Jeremiah & Elizabeth, b. June 25, 1801	A	47
Martin Kellogg, s. Jeremiah & Elizabeth, b. Sept. 16, 1812	A	50
Mary, d. Charles & Hannah, b. Dec. 3, 1763	A	4
Mary Ann, of Canaan, m. Marcus **BEARDSLEY**, of Goshen,		
June 13, 1833, by Charles Prentice	A	91
Molle, d. Jonathan & Sarah, b. Oct. 17, 1765	A	7
Octabia, d. Bartholomew & Tabithy, b. Nov. 16, 1781	A	38
Oliver, m. Abigail **MERRELLS**, of Hartford, May 8, 1755,		
by Rev. Mr. Colton	LR2	233
Oliver, s. Oliver & Abigail, b. Mar. 13, 1762	A	7
Patience, d. Jonathan & Sarah, b. Feb. 18, 1764	A	4
Polly, 2nd, m. Ashbel **HOSMER**, Nov. 2, 1783	A	38
Polly, m. John **HOLABARD**, Feb. 21, 1788	A	40
Sarah, of Hartford, m. Jonathan **BELDING**, Mar. 22, 1759,		
by Rev. Joshua Bels, of Weathersfield	LR2	228
Sarah, d. Jonathan & Sarah, b. Jan. 18, 1762	A	3
Sarah, d. Dec. 26, 1777	A	27
Sarah Ann, m. Isaac **KELLOGG**, b. of Canaan, Feb. 6, 1833,		
by Charles Prentice	A	91
Silas, s. Jonathan & Sarah, b. Sept. 11, 1767	A	10
Thede, d. Oliver & Abigail, b. May 9, 1759	A	7
BELL, Ruth, of Cornwall, m. Nehemiah **MARSH**, June 10, 1795	A	45
BENEDICT, Almon, of Salisbury, m. Clarissa **BENEDICT**, of		
Canaan, Nov. 12, 1820, by Rev. Charles Prentice	A	79
Asahel, of Salisbury, m. Betsey **BELDEN**, of Canaan, [Nov.		
22, 1825], by Charles Prentice	A	85
Clarissa, of Canaan, m. Almon **BENEDICT**, of Salisbury,		

	Vol.	Page

BENEDICT, (cont.)

Nov. 12, 1820, by Rev. Charles Prentice — A 79

Hepsey, m. Joel Harris **DIMING,** b. of Canaan, Dec. 11, 1821,
by Pitkin Cowles — A 80

Joshua N., m. Phidelia **MOSES,** Nov. 30, 1843, by Thomas
Benedict — A 103

Mercy R., m. William R. **RUSSELL,** Jr., Apr. 26, 1829, by
Rufus Babcock, of Colebrook — A 87

Micajah, m. Jerusha **BALEY,** Dec. 22, 1822, by William
Holobird, J. P. — A 82

Moses, s. Benjamin & Mary, b. Sept. 4, 1782 — A 36

Moses, m. Lucy **PARTRIDGE,** b. of Canaan, Jan. 25, 1825,
by Pitkin Cowles — A 84

Phebe, m. Edmund **WILLCOX,** Jan. 1, 1824, by Rufus
Babcock, of Colebrook — A 83

Thomas, m. Betsey **PRINDLE,** on or about Feb. 15, 1824,
by William Holobird, J. P. — A 83

BENNETT, Harriet, of Canaan, m. Joseph W. **BOSTICK,** of
Pompey, N. Y., Nov. 8, 1830, by Pitkin Cowles — A 88

William, m. Clarrissa **MINOR,** b. of Canaan, Mar. 4, 1833,
by Charles Prentice. Int. Pub. — A 91

BENTON, Edward B., m. Mary **JACKSON,** b. of Sheffield, Mass.,
Jan. 28, 1850, by Rev. D. D. Francis — A 108

BETTIS, Edwin R., s. Solon E. & Sarah, b. May 20, 1828,
in South Canaan — A 54

Solon E., of Sandisfield, m. Sarah **PHELPS,** of Canaan,
July 26, 1825, by Charles Prentice — A 84

BIBBINS, Calvin, s. Samuel & Deborah, b. Mar. 1, 1773 — A 33

Luther, s. Samuel & Deborah, b. Jan. 24, 1771 — A 33

Susanna, d. Samuel & Deborah, b. Dec. 3, 1774 — A 33

BIDWELL, Chester, s. George & Sarah, b. Sept. 28, 17[ ] — A 37

David, s. David & Easther, b. Oct. 20, 1754 — LR2 237

Easther, d. David & Easter, b. May 6, 1750 — LR1 427

Jacob, s. David & Easther, b. Sept. 9, 1758 — LR2 228

BIGELOW, Asa, of Tyringham, Mass., m. Pharlee **LAWRENCE,**
of Canaan, Nov. 5, 1832, by Pitkin Cowles — A 90

Augustus, of New Lebanon, N. Y., m. Frances P. **FENN,** of
Canaan, Feb. 1, 1831, by Pitkin Cowles — A 88

BILLINGS, William, m. Minerva **DEAN,** Dec. 13, 1838, by Reuben
Hunt, J. P. — A 98

BINGHAM, Carstine, m. Edward P. **HUNT,** b. of Canaan, Sept. 24,
1833, by Charles Prentice — A 91

BISHOP, Mary, m. Judah **FULLER,** Feb. 11, 1766 — A 10

BISSELL, Benjamin, Jr., of Litchfield, m. Melisa **POST,** of
Canaan, Feb. 6, 1822, by Rev. Charles Prentice — A 80

BLACK, John G., m. Ann **McCOURT,** b. of Canaan, Nov. 2, 1840,
by Rev. H. H. Woodbridge, of the 2nd Cong. Ch. — A 99

Julia A., of Canaan, m. Peter **RAINSONEW (?),** of Great

	Vol.	Page

BLACK, (cont.)

Barrington, Mass., Jan. 9, 1842, by Rev. Adam Reed   A   101

BLAKE, Alma C., of Canaan, m. Adoniram **SUIDAM**, of Salisbury,
Feb. 26, 1824, by Charles Prentice   A   83

Anna, m. Oren **PERRY**, Oct. 18, 1826, by Charles Prentice   A   85

Herman, m. Julia Ann **REED**, b. of Canaan, Oct. 31, 1844,
by Harley Goodwin   A   104

Susan, of Canaan, m. John **BUMP**, Jr., of Salisbury, Oct.
15, 1834, by Rev. H. H. Woodbridge, of N. Canaan   A   93

BLAKESLEE, BLAKESLEY, BLAKELY, BLACKSLEE,
BLACKSLEY, BLATCHELY, Anna, d. Daniel & Elizaeth, b. Sept.
17, 1824   A   53

Charry, d. Daniel & Betsey, b. Aug. 12, 1813   A   52

Cherry Ann, m. Elisha H. **DEAN**, b. of Canaan, Mar. 31,
1833, by Charles Prentice   A   91

Daniel, m. Betsey **MUNRO**, Oct. 25, 1812   A   52

Hannah, d. Ithamer & Sarah, b. Mar. 12, 1774   A   18

Hannah, d. Ithamer, d. Aug. 21, 1776   A   26

Hannah, m. Hiram **DEAN**, Sept. 24, 1823   A   52

Ithamer, m. Sarah **SPRAGUE**, June 9, 1773   A   18

John Sprague, s. Ithamer & Sarah, b. Apr. 7, 1776   A   25

Sabra, m. Orton **BROWN**, b. of Canaan, May 2, 1838, by
James Wadsworth   A   97

Sabrina, d. Daniel & Betsey, b. July 8, 1815   A   52

Sarah, d. Ithamer & Sarah, b. Oct. 16, 1778   A   30

BLATCHELY, [see under **BLAKESLEE**]

BLIN, William, m. Julia **DEAN**, b. of Canaan, Dec. 15, 1835,
by Charles Prentice   A   94

BLODGET, BLOGIT, Lois, m. Seth **KENT**, Jan. 27, 1756   LR2   237

Martha, m. A. **CARRIER**, Sept. 11, 1831, by Charles Prentice   A   89

BOARDMAN, BORDMAN, Alfred, s. [Ozias & Lydia], b. May 11,
1782   A   38

Charles, s. [Ozias & Lydia], b. Mar. 17, 1780;
d. May [ ], 1780   A   38

Edward, s. William & Elizabeth, b. June 1, 1804   A   47

Elisha, s. [Ozias & Lydia], b. Jan. 23, 1773   A   38

Elizabeth, of Canaan, m. Cornelius **BROWN**, of Salisbury,
Jan. 11, 1835, by Charles Prentice. Int. Pub.   A   94

Harriet, m. Miles **MINOR**, b. of Canaan, Mar. 29, 1832, by
Charles Prentice   A   90

Henry, m. Corinthia **HOSKINS**, June 3, 1832   A   54

Henry, m. Corintha **HOSKINS**, June 3, 1832, by Charles
Prentice   A   90

Henry, s. Henry & Corinthia, [ ]   A   54

Isaac, s. [Ozias & Lydia], b. Dec. 31, 1773; d. Jan. [ ], 1776   A   38

Jacob. s. [Ozias & Lydia], b. June 4, 1785; d. June 23, 1785   A   38

Jerusha, of New Milford, m. Daniel **FARRAND** (Rev.), of
Canaan, Oct. 20, 1755   LR2   237

	Vol.	Page
BOARDMAN, BORDMAN, (cont.)		
Levi, s. [Ozias & Lydia], b. Dec. 1, 1777; d. Apr. 14, 1785	A	38
Lucy A., m. Lyman **BUNCE**, b. of Canaan, May 18, 1834, by Charles Prentice. Int. Pub.	A	93
Nathaniel, s. William & Elizabeth, b. Nov. 12, 1798	A	47
Ozias. m. Lydia **HINSDALE**, Apr. 23, 1772	A	38
Ozias, s. [Ozias & Lydia], b. Jan. 4, 1774	A	38
Ozias, d. Apr. 11, 1785	A	38
Philo, s. William & Elizabeth, b. Mar. 22, 1802	A	47
Samuel, s. Henry & Corinthia, b. May 22, 1834	A	54
Sarah, of Sheffield, m. Nehemiah **LAWRENCE**, of Canaan, Nov. 28, 1749	LR1	426
William, s. [Ozias & Lydia], b. June 16, 1776	A	38
William, s. William & Elizabeth, b. Dec. 7, 1800	A	47
BORDEN, Moses, of Norfolk, m. Melissa **WILLEY**, of Canaan, Feb. 16, 1846, by Rev. D. D. Francis	A	106
BOSTWICK, BOSTICK, Joseph W., of Pompey, N. Y., m. Harriet **BENNETT**, of Canaan, Nov. 8, 1830, by Pitkin Cowles	A	88
Mary A., of New Milford, m. William H. **KELLEY**, of Durham, Nov. 12, 1850, by Rev. Harley Goodwin	A	108
BOTSFORD, Frederick S., m. Elvina **ANDRUS**, Mar. 9, 1851, by Rev. Zephaniah D. Scobey	A	108
Jane, of Salisbury, m. Charles **McDANIELDS**, of Salisbury, Apr. 27, 1845, by Rev. Stephen J. Stebbins	A	104
BOWMAN, Godfrey, s. Joseph & Lydia, b. June 1, 1781	A	37
BRACKETT, Henry S., of Canaan, m. Matilda **KEELIER**, of Walkill, Orange Co., N. Y., Mar. 31, 1840, by Rev. H. H. Woodbridge, of the 2nd Cong. Ch.	A	99
BRADFORD, Fowler, of Cornwall, m. Charlotte **BELDEN**, of Canaan, May 17, 1831, by Charles Prentice	A	89
Uri, of Cornwall, m. Charlotte M. **HURLBURT**, of Canaan, Mar. 21, 1841, by Rev. Edward B. Emerson	A	100
BRADLEY Mary, d. Moses & Jane, b. Oct. 21, 1770	A	13
Sylvester, of Norfolk, m. Mariann **ENSIGN**, of Canaan, Apr. 20, 1831, by Pitkin Cowles	A	89
BRANCH, Simon, of Lebanon, m. Jane W. **BUCKLEY**, of Canaan, Jan. 7, 1830, by Charles Prentice	A	87
BRENMAN, Thomas, m. Alice **LANDON**, b. of Canaan, Jan. 3, 1836, by Charles Prentice. Int. Pub.	A	95
BRENTON, Nathaniel, of Salisbury, m. Harriet **HOSKINS**, of Canaan, May 22, 1836, by [ ]	A	95
BREWSTER, Daniel, of Canaan, m. Mary Ann G. **CANFIELD**, of Salisbury, Oct. 10, 1842, by Rev. Edward B. Emerson	A	102
Elizabeth S., of Canaan, m. William S. **MARSH**, of Winchester, June 15, 1836, by Charles Prentice	A	95
Jabez, m. Elizabeth **CLARK**, b. of Canaan, July 27, 1820, by Rev. Charles Prentice, of South Canaan	A	79
BRIGGS, Andis, m. Judith **DAY**, b. of Canaan, Dec. 6, 1846,		

	Vol.	Page
BRIGGS, (cont.)		
by Rev. D. D. Francis	A	107
Daniel, of Canaan, m. Mary **EVANS**, of Sheffield, Dec. 4, 1831, by Pitkin Cowles	A	89
Hiram, m. Alice Ann **DEAN**, b. of Canaan, Jan. 10, 1836, by Rev. H. H. Woodbridge, of the 2nd Cong. Ch.	A	95
Hiram, m. Jane **PECK**, b. of Canaan, Sept. 30, 1841, by Rev. H. H. Woodbridge, of the 2nd Cong. Ch.	A	101
Luther A., of Great Barrington, Mass., m. Elisa A. **WARNER**, Dec. 31, 1851, by Rev. Elisha Whittlesey	A	109
Mabel, m. Henry **DOOLITTLE**, b. of Canaan, Jan. 5, 1840, by Rev. H. H. Woodbridge, of the 2nd Cong. Ch.	A	99
Mary E., m. Robert N. **ANDREWS**, of Avon, Nov. 25, 1851, by Rev. Elisha Whittlesey	A	109
BRIGHTMAN, Edward R. m. Maria C. **BAILEY**, b. of Canaan, July 30, 1848, by Rev. D. D. Francis	A	107
BRINTON, Ebenezer, Jr., of Salisbury, m. Sarah **FLETCHER**, of Canaan, [ ], by Charles Prentice. Int. Pub. Recorded Sept. 30, 1835	A	94
Ormel K., m. Malissa **WATKINS**, Jan. 11, 1837, by Charles Prentice	A	96
BROOKINS, Hannah, m. Reuben **STEVENS**, Jan. 14, 1760	A	7
Sarah, m. Stephen **PATRIDGE**, Feb. 6, 1772	A	17
BROOKS, Luther, Jr., of New Marlborough, m. Samantha **AUSTIN**, of Canaan, Oct. 27, 1824, by Pitkin Cowles	A	83
BROWN, Amand[a], d. Jerediah & Eunice, b. Aug. 26, 1797	A	46
Anna, d. Jacob & Anna, b. Mar. 2, 1791	A	45
An[n]e, d. Jacob & Hannah, b. June 9, 1745	LR2	232
Asher, of Cornwall, m. Laura **DEAN**, Apr. 17, 1823, by Rev. Charles Prentice	A	82
Benajah, s. John & Sarah, b. May 14, 1786	A	45
Benajah, s. John & Sarah, d. Nov. 17, 1790	A	45
Betsey, d. Jacob & Anna, b. Apr. 12, 1795	A	45
Chauncey, s. Jerediah & Eunice, b. June 26, 1794	A	46
Cloe, d. Jacob & Hannah, b. Sept. 22, 1764	A	4
Chloe, m. Isaac **HANCHET**, b. of Canaan, Jan. 22, 1816*, by Charles Prentice *(Probably "1826")	A	85
Cornelius, of Salisbury, m. Elizabeth **BOARDMAN**, of Canaan, Jan. 11, 1835, by Charles Prentice. Int. Pub.	A	94
Daniel, s. Timothy & Mary, b. Nov. 19, 1745	LR2	239
Dorothy, d. Jerediah & Eunice, b. Nov. 17, 1785; d. Apr. 6, 1790	A	46
Emma, d. Jerediah & Eunice, b. Aug. 18, 1791	A	46
Erastus, s. Jacob & Hannah, b. May 4, 1771	A	14
Erastus, m. Esther **STODDARD**, Sept. 27, 1800	A	46
Erastus, m. Nancy **DEAN**, b. of Canaan, Jan. 23, 1834, by Charles Prentice	A	92
George H., s. Cornelius, b. Dec. 31, 1839	A	54

	Vol.	Page
BROWN, (cont.)		
Hannah, d. Jacob & Hannah, b. Jan. 8, 1762	A	3
Hannah, d. Jerediah & Eunice, b. May 11, 1787	A	46
Harriet, m. Abiram **BAILEY**, Mar. 9, 1828, by Charles		
Prentice	A	86
Harriet Elizabeth, d. Cornelius, b. Mar. 14, 1836	A	54
Jacob, of Canaan, m. Hannah **HURLBURT**, of Cornwall, Mar.		
5, 1752	LR1	427
Jacob, s. Jacob & Hannah, b. June 11, 1767	A	10
Jacob, m. Anna **DEAN**, Oct. 13, 1790	A	45
Jacob, d. Dec. 1, 1795	A	43
Jerediah, m. Febe **WAY**, of Wallingford, Aug. 9, 1753,		
by Rev. Mr. Farrand	LR2	239
Jerediah, s. Jerediah & Phebe, b. Oct. 25, 1764	A	5
Jerediah, Jr., m. Eunice **HARRIS**, Jan. 6, 1785	A	46
John, s. Jerediah & Febe, b. July 8, 1756	LR2	232
John, d. Mar. 30, 1767	A	10
John, m. Sarah **JACKWAYS**, d. Ebenezer, May 19, 1785	A	45
John, twin with Sally, s. John & Sarah, b. Sept. 30, 1787	A	45
John, s. John & Sarah, d. Nov. 19, 1790	A	45
Jonathan, s. Jacob & Hannah, b. Sept. 12, 1758	LR2	227
Lucy, d. Timothy & Mary, d. Aug. 22, 17[ ]	LR2	239
Lucy, d. Timothy & Mary, b. Sept. 3, 17[ ]	LR2	239
Luther, s. John & Sarah, b. May 25, 1789	A	45
Mary, d. Jedediah & Phebe, b. Mar. 15, 1754	LR2	237
Mary, of Stockbridge, m. Isaac **LAWRENCE**, Mar. 18, 1760	A	1
Mary, d. Jerediah & Eunice, b. Mar. 12, 1789	A	46
Mary, d. Jacob & Anna, b. June 16, 1797	A	45
Orton, m. Sabra **BLACKSLEE**, b. of Canaan, May 2, 1838,		
by James Wadsworth	A	97
Phebe, d. Jerediah & Eunice, b. Nov. 26, 1800	A	46
Sally, twin with John, d. John & Sarah, b. Sept. 30, 1787	A	45
Sarah, d. Timothy & Mary, b. Jan. 12, 1747/8	LR2	239
Sarah, d. Jacob & Hanah, b. Jan. 26, 1754	LR2	232
Timothy, m. Mary **ANDRUS**, Feb. 25, 1744/5	LR2	239
Timothy, s. Timothy & Mary, b. Apr. 8, 1753	LR2	239
William, s. Jacob & Anna, b. Mar. 10, 1793	A	45
BROWNELL, BROWNEL, Beriah Southworth, s. Edward &		
Susanna, b. Mar. 26, 1776	A	26
Chancey, s. Edward & Susannah, b. Mar. 27, 1782	A	37
Edward, m. Susanna **WELLS**, Jan. 27, 1774, by Rev.		
Asahel Hart	A	23
Hannah, d. Edward & Susannah, b. June 5, 1780	A	37
Harvey, s. Edward & Susanna, b. July 12, 1786	A	40
Ira, s. Edward & Susannah, b. Feb. 17, 1784	A	37
Mariett, m. Seth P. **CROFOOT**, b. of Canaan, [ ],		
by Rev. H. H. Woodbridge, of the 2nd Cong. Ch.	A	101
Samuel, s. Edward & Susannah, b. June 7, 1778	A	37

	Vol.	Page
BROWNELL, BROWNEL, (cont.)		
Samuel Aaron, s. Edward & Susanna, b. Dec. 10, 1774	A	23
Samuell Aaron, d. Aug. 6, 1776	A	26
BRYAN, Abiah, d. Augustine & Martha, b. June 16, 1772	A	15
John, s. Augustian & Martha, b. July 7, 1769	A	12
Joseph, s. Agustin & Mary, b. Jan. 6, 1748	LR1	426
Marah, d. Augustine & Martha, b. Oct. 25, 1770	A	13
Naomi, d. Augustian & Mary, b. Aug. 6, 1750	LR2	237
BUCKLEY, Emeline H., of Canaan, m. Siles A. **ST. JOHN,** of Ontario, N. Y., July 5, 1832, by Charles Prentice	A	90
Jane W., of Canaan, m. Simon **BRANCH,** of Lebanon, Jan. 7, 1830, by Charles Prentice	A	87
Luther B., m. Maritta **SAWYER,** b. of Canaan, Aug. 16, 1825, by Charles Prentice	A	84
Sarah, m. Isaac **WHITE,** b. of Canaan, Jan. 1, 1828, by C. Prentice	A	86
BUEL, BUELL, Benjamin, m. Harriet **ROWLSTON,** b. of Canaan, Nov. 24, 1831, by Pitkin Cowles	A	89
David, of Litchfield, m. Betsey **FELLOWS,** of Canaan, Jan. 14, 1846, by Rev. A. V. Warren	A	104
Joseph, m. Anah **BANCROFT,** b. of Canaan, Mar. 20, 1831, by Rev. Aaron Pearce	A	89
Martha Mariah, m. Edward **ROCKWELL,** b. of Canaan, Sept. 13, 1835, by Rev. Thomas Sparkes	A	94
Theophilus, m. Sally **MINOR,** Nov. 27, 1834, by Charles Prentice	A	93
BULL, Henriette, m. Linus **McKEAN,** b. of Canaan, Apr. 18, 1822, by Pitkin Cowles	A	81
BULLARD, Elijah, m. Lura **LAKE,** Nov. 5, 1822, by Bushnell Knapp, J. P.	A	82
BUMP, John, Jr., of Salisbury, m. Susan **BLAKE,** of Canaan, Oct. 15, 1834, by Rev. H. H. Woodbridge, of N. Canaan	A	93
BUNCE, Abraham, s. Jacob & Martha, b. Nov. 8, 1747	A	2
Anes, d. Jacob & Hope, b. June 9, 1761	A	2
Daniel, s. Jacob & Martha, b. July 8, 1749	A	2
Jacob, m. Hope **GRAVES,** Aug. 4, 1760, by John Beebe	A	2
Lyman, m. Lucy A. **BOARDMAN,** b. of Canaan, May 18, 1834, by Charles Prentice. Int. Pub.	A	93
Martha, w. Jacob, d. Dec. 19, 1759	A	2
BUNNELL, BUNNALL, Harvey, of Oxford, m. Eliza **HINMAN,** of Canaan, Jan. 11, 1824, by Pitkin Cowles	A	83
Joel, Jr., m. Fanny **PALMER,** Mar. 2, 1834, by Rev. Walter Smith, of the North Cong. Ch.	A	92
BURNHAM, Lucy, of Windsor, m. Jeremiah **HORSFORD,** May 26, 1757, by Roger Woolcot, Jr.	A	2
BURRALL, BURRELL, BURRALLS, Abigail, d. Charles & Abigail, b. Dec. 5, 1747	LR1	425
Abigail Dwight, d. Ovid & Lucy, b. May 18, 1805	A	47

	Vol.	Page
BURRALL, BURRELL, BURRALLS, (cont.)		
Charles, s. Charles & Abigail, b. Feb. 1, 1751	LR1	425
Charles, 3rd, s. Ovid & Lucy, b. July 12, 1784	A	39
Charles, had negro Joseph, s. Phebe, b. Aug. 25, 1796	A	43
Chloe, d. Charles & Abigail, b. Oct. 23, 1757	LR2	232
Delia, d. Ovid & Lucy, b. Jan. 13, 1788	A	40
Edward, s. Ovid & Lucy, b. May 2, 1786	A	39
Elizabeth, d. Samuell & Easther, b. Oct. 27, 1757	LR2	228
Erastus, s. Ovid & Lucy, b. Apr. 27, 1792	A	42
Frederick, s. Ovid & Lucy, b. Aug. 29, 1795	A	43
Joanna, d. Charles & Abigail, b. Dec. 20, 1745	LR1	425
Joanna, m. William **DOUGLASS**, Oct. 31, 1765	A	8
Jonathan, s. Charles & Abigail, b. Aug. 12, 1759	LR2	228
Jonathan, m. Charlotte **DAVIS**, Mar. 27, 1783	A	40
Lucy, d. Ovid & Lucy, b. June 27, 1800	A	45
Mary, d. Charles & Abigail, b. Jan. 28, 1755	LR2	232
Mary, d. Charles & Abigail, d. June 22, 1759	LR2	228
Mary, d. Charles & Abigail, b. Oct. 3, 1765	A	11
Oved, s. Charles & Abigail, b. July 23, 1761	A	4
Ovid, m. Lucy **WELLS**, Oct. 12, 1783	A	39
Ovid, s. Ovid & Lucy, b. May 29, 1797	A	43
Susan, m. John Ely **ENSIGN**, May 17, 1835, by Charles Prentice	A	94
Susanna, d. Charles & Abigail, b. May 1, 1753	LR2	232
Thomas Davis, s. Jonathan & Charlotte, b. June 2, 1786	A	40
Wealthyan, d. William & Elizabeth, b. Oct. 26, 17[ ]	A	40
William, s. William & Elizabeth, b. Aug. 23, 17[ ]	A	40
William, s. Charles & Abigail, b. July 18, 1749	LR1	425
William Davis, s. Jonathan & Charlotte, b. Apr. 7, 1784	A	40
BURRETT, Elizabeth, m. Edmund **BELDEN**, July 9, 1834, by Charles Prentice	A	93
BUSHNELL, Abraham, m. Molly **ENSIGN**, Jan. 9, 1770	A	13
Almira, d. Abraham & Molle, b. Jan. 23, 1783	A	40
Ensign, s. Abraham & Molle, b. Mar. 14, 1775	A	40
Jeremy, s. Abraham & Molle, b. Mar. 17, 1779	A	40
John, s. Abraham & Molle, b. Mar. 7, 1777	A	40
Laura, d. Abraham & Molle, b. May 14, 1781	A	40
Lois, d. Abraham & Molle, b. Jan. 24, 1786	A	40
Molly, d. Abraham & Molly, b. Dec. 23, 1770	A	13
Samuel, s. Abraham & Molly, b. May 9, 1773	A	19
Sedgwick, s. Abraham & Molle, b. Dec. 13, 1787	A	40
BUTLER, Calvin, of Cornwall, m. Maria **COLVIN**, of Canaan, Sept. 4, 1842, by Rev. Levi Warner	A	102
Charles Cotesworth **PINCKNEY**, s. Calvin & Rosanna, b. Nov. 12, 1800	A	45
Matilda, of Norfolk, m. John **WITHERELL**, of Canaan, Oct. 24, 1848, by Rev. D. D. Francis	A	107
BUZZARD, Jane, m,. Joseph **BECKLEY**, Jr., Jan. 5, 1769	A	19

Vol.   Page

CADY, Laura, of Canaan, m. Stephen **ROBBERTS**, of Goshen, July
17, 1842, by Rev. H. H. Woodbridge, of the 2nd Cong.
Ch. Int. Pub.   A   102

    Lucinda, of Canaan, m. William **PEET**, of Salisbury, Jan.
19, 1843, by Rev. Levi Warner   A   102

CAKE (?), Joseph W., of Harrisburg, Pa., m. Julia **ADAM**, of
Litchfield, Aug. 1, 1839, by Rev. Henry H. Woodbridge,
of the 2nd Cong. Ch. Int. Pub.   A   98

CALENDER, Mark, of Sheffield, m. Martha **ROOD**, of Canaan,
Oct. 15, 1829, by Pitkin Cowles   A   87

CAMFIELD, [see under CANFIELD]

CANDEE, CANDE, Isaac, s. Theophilus & Mary, b. Aug. 7, 1779   A   33

    Mary, m. Isaac **HOW**, Nov. 22, 1764   A   7

    Rebeckah, d. Theophilus & Mary, b. Sept. 3, 1782   A   36

    Samuel, s. Theophilus & Mary, b. Mar. 10, 1781   A   34

CANFIELD, CAMFIELD, Abigail, m. Jared **HUXLEY**, Jr., Nov. 1,
1764   A   10

    Carrie A., d. William J. & Fanny, b. July [ ], 1858;
m. Marvin A. **DEAN**, Dec. 31, 1876   A   133

    Mary Ann G., of Salisbury, m. Daniel **BREWSTER**, of
Canaan, Oct. 10, 1842, by Rev. Edward B. Emerson   A   102

CARD, George, of Anthram, N. Y., m. Mary **WITHERELL** , of
Canaan, Sept. 12, 1824, by Pitkin Cowles   A   83

CARPENTER, Dorcas, m. Benjamin **PHELPS**, Jr., Mar. 8, 1775,
by Elisha Baker   A   22

CARRIER, A., m. Martha **BLODGET**, Sept. 11, 1831, by Charles
Prentice   A   89

CARTER, Janett, m. Joel **DEMING**, Dec. 2, 1824, by Charles
Prentice   A   84

CATLIN, Martha, of Canaan, m. Henry **HUMPHREY**, of Goshen,
Oct. 11, 1832, by Charles Prentice   A   90

    Mindwell G., m. Joshua **ROOT**, Nov. 11, 1790   A   41

    Olivia, m. Sheldon **MANSFIELD**, b. of Canaan, Apr. 4, 1827,
by [ ]   A   86

    Sarah D., of Canaan, m. Albert **JOHNSON**, of Salisbury,
Apr. 17, 1834, by Rev. Aaron Hill   A   92

CHADWICK, Delia, m. Alva **WILLEY**, b. of Canaan, July 23,
1826, by Pitkin Cowles   A   85

CHAPEL, Dorothy S., ae 32, of Colebrook, m. Joel L.
ROCKWELL, ae 45, of North Canaan, Sept. 10, 1848,
by Rev. Charles W. Waterous   A   105

CHAPIN, Salome, m. Luther **DEAN**, Apr. 2, 1829, by Charles
Prentice   A   87

    William, m. Hannah **BELDEN**, b. of Canaan, June 19, 1836,
by Charles Prentice   A   95

CHASE, CHACE, George Clinton, s. Job & Rachel, b. May 31,
1810   A   48

    James H., of Washington, N. Y., m. Mary Ann **ROOT**, of

	Vol.	Page
CHASE, CHACE, (cont.)		
Canaan, Feb. 26, 1839, by H. H. Woodbridge	A	98
CHATFIELD, Edward, of Killingworth, m. Maria **ANDREWS,** of		
Norfolk, July 4, 1841, by Rev. H. H. Woodbridge, of the		
2nd Cong. Ch. Int. Pub. in Norfolk	A	100
CHURCH, Ensign, [s. Leman & Sally], b. July 15, 1820	A	53
George, [s. Leman & Sally], b. July 20, 1826	A	53
Leman, b. June 22, 1794; m. Sally **POMEROY,** Mar. 18, 1819	A	53
Mary, of Winchester, m. Harlow **DEAN,** of Canaan, Dec. 13,		
1836, by Charles Prentice	A	96
Nathaniel Porter, [s. Leman & Sally], b. Dec. 15, 1822	A	53
Nathaniel Porter, [s. Leman & Sally], d. Sept. 22, 1823	A	53
Ruth Ann, [d. Leman & Sally], b. July 19, 1824	A	53
William Pomeroy, [s. Leman & Sally], b. Dec. 23, 1833	A	53
CLARK, Benjamin, s. Samuel & Lucy, b. Aug. 20, 1776	A	30
Elizabeth, m. Jabez **BREWSTER,** b. of Canaan, July 27,		
1820, by Rev. Charles Prentice, of South Canaan	A	79
Elizabeth Lois, d. Rufus & Tryphena, b. Apr. 19, 1790	A	45
Elmira, of Jefferson, N. Y., m. Orrin **KING,** of Sheffield,		
Nov. 22, 1835, by Charles Prentice	A	94
Harvey, m. Amelia **HOSFORD,** June 3, 1837, by Erastus Doty	A	96
James Harvey, s. Rufus & Tryphena, b. Nov. 19, 1786	A	45
John Harmon, s. Rufus & Tryphena, b. July 27, 1788	A	45
Jonathan Lawrence, s. Samuel & Lucy, b. Mar. 16, 1774	A	24
Julia Anna, of New Marlborough, m. William **ROOD,** Jr.,		
of Canaan, Jan. 20, 1825, by Pitkin Cowles	A	84
Lucy, d. Samuel & Lucy, b. Dec. 15, 1771	A	24
Michael, m. Mary **McHALE,** b. of Salisbury, Jan. 23, 1852,		
by Rev. John Smith	A	109
Orlando, m. Melissa **RACE,** b. of Salisbury, Nov. 30, 1842,		
by Rev. Parmele Chamberlain. Witnesses: Miles Belden,		
Eliza Belden & Theo. S. Lodges	A	102
Rufus, m. Tryphena **JAKWAYS,** d. Ebenezer, Aug. 4, 1785	A	45
Samuel, s. Samuel & Lucy, b. Apr. 11, 1770	A	24
Susanna, d. William & Susanna, b. Sept. 2, 1770	A	14
Sibbal*, d. Samuel & Lucy, b. Oct. 12, 1778 *("Sybel")	A	30
Thomas, s. Rufus & Tryphena, b. Feb. 25, 1795	A	45
Tryphena, w. Rufus d. Nov. 2, 1798	A	45
Tryphena Salina, d. Rufus & Tryphena, b. Apr. 10, 1792	A	45
CLEMMENT, Abigail C., of Rapert, Vt., m. Joseph **BELDEN,** of		
Canaan, Jan. 31, 1830, by Charles Prentice	A	88
CLINTON, Samuel, m. Rachel **KNAPP,** Oct. 27, 1822, by B.		
Knapp, J. P.	A	81
COBB, Abigail, d. Elijah & Amy, b. Aug. 27, 1767	A	10
Anne, d. Elijah & Anne, b. Feb. 1, 1771; d. Feb. 21, 1771	A	20
Asenath, m. Allen **PERKINS,** of Goshen, Feb. 10, 1830, by		
Pitkin Cowles	A	87
Charity, d. Elijah William & Sarah, b. Dec. 5, 1793	A	47

	Vol.	Page
COBB, (cont.)		
Chloe, m. Leonard **LAWRENCE**, b. of Canaan, Oct. 6, 1824,		
by Pitkin Cowles	A	83
Daniel Johns, s. Elijah W. & Sarah, b. Oct. 18, 1795	A	43
Dolly, d. Elijah & Ame, b. July 16, 1763	A	4
Elijah, m. Amy **LAWRENCE**, Mar. 20, 1760	A	1
Elijah William, s. Elijah & Amy, b. Sept. 24, 1765	A	10
Elijah William, m. Sarah **WHITNEY**, Feb. 27, 178[ ]	A	39
James, s. Elijah & Anne, b. Nov. 4, 1773	A	20
James, s. Elijah & Ame, d. Mar. 11, 1807	A	47
Joshua, s. Elijah William & Sarah, b. Nov. 18, 1786	A	39
Lucy, m. Stephen **JACKWAY**, b. of Canaan, Oct. 8, 1828,		
by Pitkin Cowles	A	86
Lydia, d. Elijah & Anne, b. July 22, 1769; d. Jan. 6, 1770	A	20
Lydia, d. Elijah William & Sarah, b. Mar. 19, 1798	A	44
Permela, d. Elijah William & Sally, b. Jan. 18, 1791	A	41
Persis, d. Elijah & Ame, b. Nov. 21, 1761	A	4
COGGSELL, Martha, m. Samuel **DINSMORE**, Apr. 20, 1757	LR2	228
[COLLER], COLLOR, Mary, of New Marlborough, m. Nehemiah		
MARSH, Nov. 17, 1791	A	45
COLLINS, Ellen, m. John **BARRY**, both b. Ireland, now of		
Barrington, Mass., July 23, 1852, by Rev. John Smith	A	109
Laura Ann, of Canaan, m. Hiram **MILLS**, of Wis., May 7,		
1846, by Rev. D. D. Francis	A	106
Lucy, of Canaan, m. Marcus **HUNTLEY**, of Salisbury, July		
2, 1837, by Aaron Rogers	A	96
COLTON, Eliza, m. Dorrance **ROOD**, b. of Canaan, Nov. 29, 1820,		
by Pitkin Cowles	A	79
COLVIN, Maria, of Canaan, m. Calvin **BUTLER**, of Cornwall,		
Sept. 4, 1842, by Rev. Levi Warner	A	102
CONE, Caleb P., of Torrington, m. Charlotte E. **BACON**, of		
Canaan, Aug. 21, 1843, by Charles Kettridge	A	103
Julia Ann, m. John W. **TUTTLE**, Apr. 29, 1829, by Charles		
Prentice	A	87
COOK, Abiah, d. Silas & Abiah, b. Jan. 19, 1809	A	48
Arabella, d. Silas & Abiah, b. Jan. 13, 1793	A	48
Arabelle, d. Silas & Abigail, b. Jan. 13, 1793	A	53
Arabella, d. Silas & Abigail, m. Leonard **ADAM**, s. John		
& Abigail, Nov. 7, 1811	A	53
Caroline, twin with Rozina, d. Silas & Abiah, b. Mar. 30, 1798	A	48
Daniel, s. Silas & Abiah, b. June 16, 1802; d. Jan. 15, 1803	A	48
Ephraim, s. Silas & Abiah, b. Apr. 23, 1804	A	48
Pollyphene, d. Silas & Abiah, b. Dec. 13, 1795	A	48
Rozina, twin with Caroline, d. Silas & Abiah, b. Mar. 30, 1798	A	48
Silas, b. Jan. 1, 1772; m. Abiah **HEWIT**, July 8, 1792	A	48
Silas & Abiah, had child b. Nov. 23, 1794; d. Nov. 25, 1794	A	48
COON, James, s. John & Elizabeth, b. Mar. 11, 1744	A	4
COOPER, Annah Minerva, m. Benjamin Franklin **TOBEY**, b. of		

	Vol.	Page
COOPER, (cont.)		
Canaan, Oct. 31, 1832, by Rev. Harmon Ellis, of the 1st Bapt. Ch., Norfolk	A	90
Elizabeth A., of Canaan, m. Charles **HUMPHREY**, of Tolland, Nov. 29, 1835, by Rev. Thomas Sparkes	A	94
Sarah L., of Canaan, m. William **WHITE**, of Homer, N. Y., May 10, 1845, by Rev. Stephen J. Stebbins	A	104
Sylvia Ann, m. Pierce **DEAN**, b. of Canaan, Nov. 20, 1836, by Rev. Aaron Rogers, of South Canaan	A	95
CORMICK, Gesia, m. Simon **BACKUS**, Apr. 17, 1783	A	41
CORNALUS, Joshua J., colored, b. Aug. 17, 1797	A	51
CORNISH, Abigail, d. Gabrel & Marcy, b. Nov. 11, 1753	LR2	232
Andrew, s. Gabrel & Marcy, b. July 4, 1751	LR2	232
Gabrel, d. May 10, 1753	LR2	232
Hannah, d. Gabrel & Marcy, b. May 4, 1749	LR2	232
Jabez, m. Sarah **WHITING**, Jan 30, 1770	A	12
Jerusha, d. Jabez & Sarah, b. Nov. 22, 1770	A	12
Mary, d. Gabrel & Marcy, b. Nov. 2, 1746	LR2	232
Mary, m. Joshua **MUDGE**, Sept. 10, 1767	A	16
Silas, s. Gabrel & Sarah, b. Oct. 8, 1744	LR1	424
CORNWALL, Joshua, Dr., m. Surviah **DOUGLASS**, b. of Canaan, Aug. 22, 1820, by Rev. Charles Prentice of South Canaan	A	79
COTTERILL, Mary Ann, of Dover, N. Y., m. David **HALL**, of Canaan, Oct. 31, 1842, by Rev. Edward B. Emerson	A	102
COUCH, Emeline, of Canaan, m. Benjamin **SEARS**, of Sharon, Sept. 11, 1844, by Harley Goodwin	A	103
COWLES, Abiah, d. John & Ame, b. Aug. 3, 1769	A	37
Abigail, d. Daniel & Huldah, b. Jan. 13, 1751/2	LR1	427
Amos, 2nd, s. Joseph & Ruth, b. Nov. 15, 1757	LR2	228
Amy, d. Samuel & Mary, b. Jan. 9, 1761	A	1
Asa, s. Joseph & Ruth, b. Aug. 23, 1752	LR2	228
Bela, s. Timothy & Anne, b. May 30, 1773	A	19
Benjamin, s. Benjamin & Hannah, b. May 21, 1743	LR1	426
Daniel, m. Huldah **ROOT**, of Panthorn, Jan. 31, 1750	LR1	427
Daniel, s. Daniel & Huldah, b. Apr. 1, 1763	A	3
Darius N., m. Marcissa **LANE**, Mar. 7, 1822, by Pitkin Cowles	A	81
Eli, s. Benjamin & Hannah, b. June 29, 1739	LR1	426
Elizabeth, d. Benjamin & Hannah, b. July 21, 1740	LR1	426
Elizabeth, d. Samuel & Mary, b. Mar. 21, 1763	A	3
Elen*, s. Jason & Thankfull, b. Sept. 4, 1794 *(Perhaps "Eben" or "Elon")	A	42
Esther, d. Joseph & Ruth, b. Sept. 30, 1744	LR1	425
Frances A., m. Albert A. **WRIGHT**, b. of Canaan, May 17, 1831, by Pitkin Cowles	A	89
Frances Anne, d. Rev. Pitkin & Frances, b. Apr. 19, 1809	A	50
Hannah, d. Benjamin & Hannah, b. Feb. 22, 1742	LR1	426
Hulda, d. Daniel & Huldah, b. Sept. 21, 1754	LR2	238
Isaac, s. Joseph & Ruth, b. July 23, 1748	LR2	228

	Vol.	Page
COWLES, (cont.)		
Isaac, s. Isaac & Elizabeth, b. Sept. 28, 1765	A	19
Jabez, s. Joel & Susannah, b. Apr. 20, 1786	A	39
Jason, s. Joseph & Ruth, b. Mar. 17, 1762	A	13
Jemima, d. Daniel & Hulda, b. June 21, 1760	A	3
Joel, s. Joseph & Ruth, b. Apr. 3, 1765	A	13
Joel, m. Susannah **PHELPS**, Oct. 10, 1783	A	39
John, s. Benjamin & Hannah, b. May 9, 1745	LR1	426
Joseph, s. Joseph & Ruth, b. Oct. 7, 1755	LR2	228
Joseph, s. Jason & Thankfull, b. June 7, 1792	A	42
Levi, s. Daniel & Huldah, b. Nov. 3, 1757	LR2	228
Loes, d. Benjamin & Hannah, b. Mar. 13, 1752	LR1	426
Mary, d. Benjamin & Hannah, b. Jan. 9, 1737	LR1	426
Nathaniel, s. Benjamin & Hannah, b. Oct. 18, 1755	LR2	237
Olive, d. Jason & Thankfull, b. Dec. 25, 1789	A	42
Phebe, d. Benjamin & Hannah, b. Mar. 31, 1747	LR1	426
Rhoda, d. Samuell & Mary, b. Sept. 12, 1758	A	1
Rhoda Catharine, [d. Rev. Pitkin & Frances], b. Oct. 23, 1812	A	50
Roxanna, d. Timothy & Anna, b. Mar. 28, 1779	A	33
Ruth, d. Joseph & Ruth, b. Mar. 25, 1750	LR2	228
Sarah, d. Benjamin & Hannah, b. Mar. 11, 1749	LR1	426
Sarah, d. John & Ame, b. Nov. 21, 1767	A	37
Sarah Lee, d. Rev. Pitkin & Frances, b. Nov. 20, 1810	A	50
Solomon, s. Samuell & Mary, b. Apr. 2, 1756	LR2	233
Sylvester, s. Timothy & Anne, b. July 3, 1775	A	24
Thankful, d. Benjamin & Hannah, b. Feb. 23, 1738	LR1	426
Thankfull, m. Asa **JOHNSON**, of Canaan, Apr. 28, 1757,		
by Rev. Daniel Farrand	LR2	227
Theoda, s. Samuell & Mary, b. Jan. 29, 1754	LR2	238
Timothy, s. Joseph & Ruth, b. Apr. 22, 1746	LR1	425
Timothy, m. Anne **HATCH**, Dec. 11, 1770	A	15
William, s. Benjamin & Catharine, b. July 9, 1767	A	35
CRANDALL, Elias, of Goshen, m. Betsey **ROCKWELL**, of		
Canaan, Feb. 14, 1831, by Pitkin Cowles	A	88
CRITTENDEN, Henry, s. Levi & Clarina, b. July 6, 1782	A	39
Laura, d. Levi & Clarissee, b. Jan. 27, 1781	A	36
CROFOOT, CROWFOOT, Deborah Minerva, of Canaan, m.		
Ephraim **GLEASON**, of Austerlitz, N. Y., Apr. 25, 1833,		
by Rev. Harmon Ellis, of Bap. Ch., Norfolk	A	91
Sarah M., m. George **THOMPSON**, b. of Canaan, July 22,		
1845, by Rev. D. D. Francis	A	106
Seth P., m. Mariett **BROWNELL**, b. of Canaan, [ ], by Rev.		
H. H. Woodbridge, of the 2nd Cong. Ch.	A	101
CROSSMAN, Mary E., of Canaan, m. Rufus **BARNEY**, of		
Bennington, Vt., Apr. 19, 1835, by Charles Prentice	A	94
CROWELL, William, of Salisbury, m. Eliza **GRISWOLD**, of		
Canaan, Apr. 19, 1837, by Rev. H. H. Woodbridge, of the		
2nd Cong. Ch.	A	96

	Vol.	Page
CULVER, Elizabeth Ann, d. Philander & Prusha, b. Aug. 29, 1814	A	51
CUMMINGS, James V' B., m. Susan CURREY, b. of Canaan, June		
4, 1834, by Charles Prentice. Int. Pub.	A	93
CURREY, Martha Ann, m. Horace RUSSELL, b. of Canaan, July		
15, 1838, by Adam Reed	A	97
Susan, m. James V'B. CUMMINGS, b. of Canaan, June 4,		
1834, by Charles Prentice. Int. Pub.	A	93
CURTIS, CURTISS, CURTICE, Alanthus, s. Medad & Welthy, b.		
May 5, 1765	A	10
Almira, m. Rev. Elisha WHITTLESEY, Sept. 16, 1851, by		
Rev. Daniel Smith	A	109
Amasa, s. John & Deborah, b. Nov. 15, 1767	A	11
Asahel, s. John & Deborah, b. Sept. 23, 1765	A	9
Chester, of Goshen, m. Fann DORMAN, of Canaan, Jan. 3,		
1833, by Rev. George Carrington, of Goshen	A	90
Joel, s. Samuell & Elizabeth, b. July 9, 1753	LR2	239
Joel, s. Samuel & Elizabeth, d. July 12, 1753	LR2	239
John, s. Samuell & Elizabeth, b. Feb. 14, 1760	A	1
Josiah, s. Samuell & Elizabeth, b. Sept. 15, 1754	LR2	238
Josiah, s. Medad & Hannah, b. Aug. 22, 1767	A	10
Rhoda, m. Micah SHEFFIELD, Dec. 26, 1776	A	25
Seth, s. Medad & Welthy, b. Aug. 15, 1761	A	10
Solomon, s. John & Deborah, b. Jan. 15, 1764	A	9
DABALL, DAYBALL, Edna, b. Oct. 17, 1781, at Windsor	A	52
Edna, b. Oct. 17, 1781, at Windsor; m. John FELLOWS,		
Oct. 8, 1799	A	52
Eliza, of Canaan, m. Nathan M. DEBALL, of Groton, Nov.		
10, 1841, by Rev. H. H. Woodbrige, of the 2nd Cong. Ch.	A	101
Ezekiel, m. Laura FELLOWS, Jan. 14, 1813	A	49
Laura, of Canaan, m. William J. POTTER, of Salisbury,		
Sept. 9, 1841, by Rev. H. H. Woodbridge, of the 2nd		
Cong. Ch. Int. Pub.	A	100
Nathan M., of Groton, Centre, m. Eliza DABALL, of Canaan,		
Nov. 10, 1841, by Rev. H. H. Woodbridge, of the 2nd		
Cong. Ch.	A	101
DARLEY, Reuben, m. Linne SPAULDING, Oct. 27, 1779	A	34
Sybel, w. Reuben, d. Jan. 23, 1779	A	34
DARROW, Samuel, m. wid. Abigail HOLCOMB, Oct. 5, 1777	A	27
DAVIS, Batchley T., m. Elizabeth JAQUA, b. of Canaan, May 6,		
1827, by Pitkin Cowles	A	86
Charlotte, m. Jonathan BURRALL, Mar. 27, 1783	A	40
Mariah, of Canaan, m. Richard ARMSTRONG, of Salisbury,		
Dec. 9, 1830, by Pitkin Cowles	A	88
DAY, Elisa F., m,. Nehemiah S. STEVENS, b. of Canaan, Jan.		
1, 1846, by Rev. D. D. Francis	A	106
Jane C., m. Jay A. UNDERWOOD, Oct. 28, 1850, by Rev.		
Isaac H. Scott, of the M. E. Ch.	A	108
Judith, m. Andis BRIGGS, b. of Canaan, Dec. 6, 1846,		

	Vol.	Page
DAY, (cont.)		
by Rev. D. D. Francis	A	107
Lucy, m. Daniel **JACKWAY**, Jr., b. of Canaan, Jan. 21,		
1822, by P. Cowles	A	80
Rebecca, d. Zenas & Joanna, b. June 13, 1800	A	47
Samuel Younglove, s. Zenas & Joanna, b. July 10, 1802	A	47
Sarah, m. Solomon **WRIGHT**, Dec. 13, 1752	LR2	239
DEAN, Abiah, d. John & Rachal, b. May 26, 1767	A	11
Abigail, d. Nathaniel & Hannah, b. Feb. 9, 1771	A	16
Abigail, m. William **DEAN**, b. of Canaan, Feb. 12, 1830,		
by Rev. Silas Ambler	A	88
Abigail, of Canaan, m. Ransom **WICKWIRE**, of Cornwall,		
Oct. 23, 1836, by Charles Prentice	A	95
Adaline, m. William **DEAN**, b. of Canaan, May 1, 1823, by		
Rev. Charles Prentice	A	82
Alice Ann, m. Hiram **BRIGGS**, b. of Canaan, Jan. 10, 1836,		
by Rev. H. H. Woodbridge, of the 2nd Cong. Ch.	A	95
Alta, [child of Asa & Jain], b. Mar. 3, 1785	A	38
Anna, m. Jacob **BROWN**, Oct. 13, 1790	A	45
Anne, d. Oliver & Mary, b. June 6, 1773	A	17
Asa, s. Nathaniel & Hannah, b. Aug. 29, 1760	A	3
Asa, m. Jain **HURLBURT**, Feb. 27, 1783	A	38
Benajah, s. John & Rachel, b. Oct. 4, 1764	A	5
Betsey, m. Azanah **SMITH**, Apr. 6, 1828, by Charles Prentice	A	86
Charles, s. Nathaniel & Hanah, b. Jan. 19, 1754	LR2	238
Charles, s. Nathaniel, d. Mar. 17, 1772	A	16
Charles, s. Nathaniel, Jr. & Abigail, b. Nov. 12, 1779	A	33
Charles Belding, s. Roswel & Abigail, b. Feb. 23, 1782	A	38
Daniel Hiram, b. Apr. 27, 1837	A	54
Dwight Eli, s. [Henry & Almira], b. June 4, 1848	A	133
Electa, of Canaan, m. John **SILL**, of Bethany, Genessee		
Co., N. Y., Oct. 21, 1836, by Charles Prentice	A	95
Eli, s. John, 2nd & Rachel, b. Oct. 20, 1759	LR2	227
Elisha H., m. Cherry Ann **BLATCHELY**, b. of Canaan, Mar.		
31, 1833, by Charles Prentice	A	91
Eliza, m. Daniel F. **BEBEE**, Aug. 29, 1826, by John Lovejoy	A	85
Ellen E., d. Henry & Almira, b. Dec. 12, 1834	A	133
Ellen E., m. Eleezer Butler **MANLEY**, Nov. 1, 1857	A	133
Emma L., m. Asahel M. **DUNHAM**, Mar. 19, 1871	A	133
Emma Lucretia, d. [Henry & Almira], b. Nov. 8, 1843	A	133
Esther, d. Oliver & Mary, b. Nov. 6, 1784	A	37
Eunice, d. Oliver & Mary, b. Sept. 14, 1782	A	37
Eunice, d. Nathaniel & Hannah, b. Nov. 7, 1765	A	16
Eunice, m. Jonathan **BATES**, b. of Canaan, Aug. 23, 1840,		
by Rev. Erastus Doty, of Colebrook	A	99
Frances Almira, [d. Henry & Almira], b. Dec. 16, 1845	A	133
Francis, s. Roswell & Abigail, b. Oct. 20, 1786	A	40
Freelove, m. Edmund **DUNNING**, b. of Canaan, Oct. 14,		

	Vol.	Page
DEAN, (cont.)		
1845, by Grove Lawrence Brunnell	A	104
George Martin, b. June 1, 1834	A	54
Hannah, d. Nathaniel & Hannah, b. Jan. 30, 1758	LR2	228
Hannah, m. Jeremiah **HORSFORD**, Jr., Jan.1, 1784	A	37
Harlow, of Canaan, m. Mary **CHURCH**, of Winchester, Dec.		
13, 1836, by Charles Prentice	A	96
Harriet, d. David & Phebe, b. Mar. 14, 1799	A	47
Harriet, m. Nathan **PHILLIPS**, b. of Canaan, Apr. 17,		
1823, by Rev. Charles Prentice	A	82
Henry, s. Eli & Judeth, b. June 10, 1800; m. Almira		
MUNSON, d. Lyman & Comfort, Mar. 23, 1834	A	133
Henry, m. Almira **MUNSON**, b. of Canaan, Mar. 23, 1834,		
by Charles Prentice. Int. Pub.	A	92
Henry Johnson, s. Henry & Emma, b. Feb. 10, 1869, at		
Muscatine, Ia.	A	133
Henry M., m. Emma **JOHNSON**, June 28, 1866, at		
Philadelphia, Pa.	A	133
Henry Munson, s. [Henry & Almira], b. Nov. 8, 1836	A	133
Hiram,, s. Eli & Judeth, b. Jan. 22, 1798	A	52
Hiram, m. Hannah **BLAKESLEE**, Sept. 24, 1823	A	52
Irene, m. Nelson **HOWE**, Feb. 9, 1851, by Rev. Zephaniah		
D. Scobey	A	108
Isaac, s. Oliver & Mary, b. Dec. 1, 1766	A	10
Israel, s. Oliver & Marah, b. Jan. 16, 1771	A	14
Jette, d. Rosewell, & Abigail, b. Sept. 17, 1774	A	24
John, m. Rachel **BEEBE**, Jan. 21, 1756	LR2	288
John, 2nd, m. Rachel **JONES**, Mar. 1, 1759, by Rev. Mr.		
Farrand	LR2	227
John, 3rd, [s. David & Phebe], b. Aug. 28, 1800	A	47
John Milton, b. Aug. 31, 1836	A	54
Julia, m. William **BLIN**, b. of Canaan, Dec. 15, 1835, by		
Charles Prentice	A	94
Kezia, d. John & Rachel, b. Mar. 28, 1758	LR2	227
Laura, m. Asher **BROWN**, of Cornwall, Apr. 17, 1823, by		
Rev. Charles Prentice	A	82
Lee Maltbie, s. Lee P. & Seraph E., b. May 16, 1875	A	133
Lee P., m. Seraph Elizabeth **MALTBIE**, d. Dr. Charles B.		
& Elizabeth, May 27, 1874	A	133
Lee Parker, [s. Henry & Almira], b. Oct. 18, 1838	A	133
Lee Wallace, s. [Henry & Emma], b. Mar. 28, 1873, at		
Mascatine, Ia.	A	133
Lois, d. Nathaniel & Hannah, b. July 2, 1762	A	3
Love, [child of Asa & Jain], b. Oct. 10, 1783	A	38
Lucinda, m. Asa **BARNS**, b. of Canaan, May 22, 1823, by		
Rev. Charles Prentice	A	82
Lucinda, of Canaan, m. Theodore H. **PALMER**, of Otis,		
Sept. 2, 1834, by Rev. Julius Field	A	93

	Vol.	Page
DEAN, (cont.)		
Luther, m. Salome **CHAPIN**, Apr. 2, 1829, by Charles Prentice	A	87
Margaret, m. Recompence **WADSWORTH**, of Wolcott, N. Y., Apr. 18, 1821, by Rev. Charles Prentice, of the 1st Ch.	A	80
Maria, of Canaan, m. Himan **JACOBS**, of Salisbury, May 1, 1822, by Rev. Charles Prentice	A	81
Marvin A., m. Carrie A. **CANFIELD**, d. William J. & Fanny, Dec. 31, 1876	A	133
Marvin Ansel, [s. Henry & Almira], b. Nov. 13, 1852	A	133
Mary, of Canaan, m. Albert **HURD**, of Goshen, Dec. 11, 1831, by Charles Prentice	A	89
Mary Reed, d. Myron U. & Mary T., b. Dec. 6, 1869	A	133
Milla, d. Oliver & Mary, b. Jan. 18, 1769	A	11
Minerva. m. William **BILLINGS**, Dec. 13, 1838, by Reuben Hunt, J. P.	A	98
Myron U., m. Mary T. **REED**, d. James & Rhoda, Mar. 9, 1865	A	133
Myron Uriah, [s. Henry & Almira], b. Feb. 17, 1841	A	133
Nabby, d. Nathaniel, Jr. & Abigail, b. May 22, 1784	A	38
Nancy, m. Erastus **BROWN**, b. of Canaan, Jan. 23, 1834, by Charles Prentice	A · A	92
Nathaniel, m. Hannah **DIBBLE**, Nov. 29, 1750	LR2	239
Nathaniel, s. Nathaniel & Hannah, b. June 27, 1756	LR2	228
Nathaniel, Jr., m. Abigail **HOLCOMB**, June 11, 1778	A	33
Oliver, s. Oliver & Mary, b. Sept. 22, 1764	A	10
Patty Ann, d. Hiram & Hannah, b. Feb. 10, 1825	A	52
Pierce, m. Sylvia Ann **COOPER**, b. of Canaan, Nov. 20, 1836, by Rev. Aaron Rogers, of South Canaan	A	95
Ray Elbert, [s. Henry & Emma], b. [ ], 1876, at Muscatine, Ia.	A	133
Rozzel, s. Nathaniel & Hannah, b. Dec. 1, 1751	LR2	239
Ruth, d. John & Rachel, b. May 3, 1761	A	2
Sarah, d. John & Rachel, b. Jan. 7, 1757	LR2	228
Sebe, m. Maria **GIBBS**, May 6, 1821, by Rev. Asa Talmage, of Cornwall	A	80
Seth, s. Seth & Sarah, b. July 26, 1764	A	5
Sheldon, m. Lucretia **BALEY**, Oct. 4, 1826, by William Holobird, J. P.	A	85
Solomon, s. John & Rachel, b. Aug. 17, 1759	LR2	227
Thankfull, m. Jacob **WILLIAMS**, Feb. 23, 1769	A	13
William, m. Adaline **DEAN**, b. of Canaan, May 1, 1823, by Rev. Charles Prentice	A	82
William, m. Abigail **DEAN**, b. of Canaan, Feb. 12, 1830, by Rev. Silas Ambler	A	88
DELMAN, Ruth, d. Ichabod & Polly, b. Oct. 10, 1769	A	19
DEMING, DIMING, DEMMING, Abia A., m. Ezekiel S. **HOSKINS**, b. of Canaan, Mar. 7, 1839, by H. H. Woodbridge	A	98

	Vol.	Page

DEMING, DIMING, DEMMING, (cont.)

Belinda S., of Canaan, m. Lucius **WILCOX**, of Cornwall,
    July 24, 1834, by Charles Prentice. Int. Pub. — A — 93

Charles Dean, s. Daniel & Lois, b. Oct. 17, 1799 — A — 47

Daniel, s. Hezekiah & Hannah, b. Feb. 23, 1748 — LR2 — 232

Eunis, d. Hezekiah & Hannah, b. Jan. 28, 1739 — LR2 — 232

Hannah, d. Hezekiah & Hannah, b. Feb. 2, 1754 — LR2 — 232

Harmon, s. Roswell, b. Apr. 26, 1767 — A — 37

Harmon, m. Dorothy **NORTON**, July 12, 1792 — A — 46

Harmon, s. Harmon & Dorothy, b. Oct. 24, 1797 — A — 46

Harriet M., m. Joseph **JAMES**, b. of Canaan, [Mar. 1,
    1843], b. Rev. Edward B. Emerson — A — 103

Henry, s. Harmon, b. Feb. 7, 1804 — A — 48

Hezekiah, s. Hezekiah & Hannah, b. Mar. 24, 1741 — LR2 — 232

Hezekiah, d. Feb. 15, 1757 — LR2 — 232

Joel, s. Hezekiah & Hannah, b. Dec. 10, 1745 — LR2 — 232

Joel, m. Janett **CARTER**, Dec. 2, 1824, by Charles Prentice — A — 84

Joel Harris, m. Hepsey **BENEDICT**, b. of Canaan, Dec. 11,
    1821, by Pitkin Cowles — A — 80

John, s. Hezekiah & Hannah b. Jan. 8, 1735 — LR2 — 232

Lemuel, s. Hezekiah & Hannah, b. Sept. 17, 1751 — LR2 — 232

Levinus, s. Harmon, b. Oct. 12, 1808 — A — 48

Lucretia, d. Harmon & Dorothy, b. Apr. 19, 1793 — A — 46

Mary, m. Horatio N. **WETHERELL**, b. of Canaan, Dec. 24,
    1825, by Charles Prentice — A — 85

Pede, d. Roswel, b. Oct. 24, 1772 — A — 37

Phinehas, s. Hezekiah & Hannah, b. Jan. 26, 1750 — LR2 — 232

Polly, d. Daniel & Lois, b. Feb. 15, 1795 — A — 43

Polly, d. Harmon & Dorothy, b. May 9, 1795 — A — 46

Ralph, s. Heziekiah & Hannah, b. Nov. 18, 1737 — LR2 — 232

Roswell, s. Roswel, b. Apr. 16, 1768 — A — 37

Samuel, s. Joel & Mary, b. July 16, 1777 — A — 27

Sarah, d. Daniel & Sarah, b. May 17, 1770 — A — 19

Seymour, m. Clarissa **HUNT**, Jan. 8, 1828, by Charles Prentice — A — 86

Silvia, d. Daniel & Sarah, b. Oct. 29, 1775 — A — 36

Warren, s. Harmon, b. Nov. 8, 1801 — A — 48

William, s. Joel & Mary, b. May 22, 1770 — A — 27

William, m. Sarah **HOSFORD**, Mar. 9, 1851, by Rev.
    Zephaniah D. Scobey — A — 108

DENISSON, Susannah, d. Samuel & Martha, b. Oct. 10, 1763 — A — 34

DENSMORE, [see under **DINSMORE**]

DEWEY, Diame, d. Zenas & Joanna, b. Nov. 3, 1794 — A — 43

Dianna, d. Zenas & Joanna, b. Mar. 25, 1786 — A — 39

Isabelle, d. Zenas & Joanna, b. Feb. 12, 1779 — A — 35

Joanna, d. Zenas & Joanna, b. Oct. 31, 1790 — A — 41

Minerva, d. Zenas & Joanna, b. Aug. 8, 1798 — A — 45

Filo*, s. Zenas & Joanna, b. Feb. 15, 1784 *("Philo") — A — 39

Philo, s. Zenas & Joanna, b. Jan. 12, 1789 — A — 41

	Vol.	Page

DEMING, DIMING, DEMMING, (cont.)

Zenas, m. Joanna **ROOT**, Dec. 26, 1779 — A — 35

Zenas, s. Zenas & Joanna, b. Mar. 22, 1782 — A — 39

DIBBLE, DIBLE, Abigail, m. David **BEEBE**, Nov. 23, 1752 — LR2 — 238

Caroline, m. Gillitt **RICHARDSON**, Dec. 2, 1830, by James Fenn, J. P. — A — 88

Hannah, m. Nathaniel **DEAN**, Nov. 29, 1750 — LR2 — 239

DICKINSON, Phebe, d. Obadiah & Mary Thomas, b. Nov. 20, 1801 — A — 47

DINSMORE, DENSMORE, Anne, m. Samuel **HORSFORD**, June 22, 1783 — A — 37

David, s. Samuell & Martha, b. May 29, 1768 — A — 12

Martha, d. Samuell & Martha, b. July 1, 1770 — A — 12

Naoma, d. Samuell & Martha, b. Aug. 30, 1757 — LR2 — 228

Rebeckah, d. Samuel & Martha, b. May 9, 1761 — A — 2

Samuel, m. Martha **COGGSELL**, Apr. 20, 1757 — LR2 — 228

DIXON, Christian, m. Henry **DOOLITTLE**, b. of Canaan, Dec. 22, 1833, by Rev. Henry H. Woodbridge, of the 2nd Cong. Ch. — A — 92

DONEIGHY, David, s. William & [E]unice, b. Aug. 17, 1750 — LR1 — 425

DONOLDS, Betsey, of Canaan, m. Grove **GAYLORD**, of Norfolk, Jan. 1, 1852, by John Watson, J. P. — A — 109

Sophia, d. Jonathan & Prudence, b. Feb. 10, 1786 — A — 42

DOOLITTLE, Abigail, m. Henry W. **LAWRENCE**, b. of Canaan, Nov. 27, 1845, by Rev. D. D. Francis — A — 106

Henry, m. Mary **RICHARDS**, Dec. 29, 1812 — A — 49

Henry, m. Christian **DIXON**, b. of Canaan, Dec. 22, 1833, by Rev. Henry H. Woodbridge, of the 2nd Cong. Ch. — A — 92

Henry, m. Mabel **BRIGGS**, b. of Canaan, Jan. 5, 1840, by Rev. H. H. Woodbridge, of the 2nd Cong. Ch. — A — 99

William, m. Alma **KELLOGG**, b. of Canaan, Mar. 8, 1841, by Rev. H. H. Woodbridge — A — 100

DORMAN, Fann, of Canaan, m. Chester **CURTISS**, of Goshen, Jan. 3, 1833, by Rev. George Carrington, of Goshen — A — 90

Rhoda, m. Phabeus **HART**, b. of Canaan, Dec. 20, 1838, by Rev. Charles Stearnes, of the M. E. Ch. — A — 97

DOUGLASS, Abiah, d. William & Joanna, b. Aug. 21, 1767 — A — 11

Abigail, m. William **BACON**, Sept. 15, 1768 — A — 41

Abigail, d. Benajah & Marcy, b. May 8, 1771 — A — 13

Amelia, d. Benajah & Marcy, b. Jan. 10, 1782 — A — 39

Benajah, s. Benajah & Mercy, b. Jan. 30, 1773 — A — 20

Benajah & Marcy, had d. [ ], b. Jan. 6, 1781; d. Jan. 12, 1781 — A — 39

Benajah, d. Aug. 21, 1810, in the 73rd y. of his age — A — 47

Benajah, m. Lucretia **JOHNS**, Nov. 28, 1822, by Pitkin Cowles — A — 82

Benajah, d. Apr. 11, 1840, ae 67 — A — 54

Benjamin, s. Asa & Rebeckah, b. Dec. 3, 1760 — A — 5

Betsey, d. Benajah & Marcy, b. Mar. 12, 1784 — A — 39

Ellen, d. Benajah & Lucretia, b. Jan. 3, 1824 — A — 52

John, s. Asa & Rebeckah, b. Aug. 2, 1758 — A — 5

	Vol.	Page
DOUGLASS, (cont.)		
Jonathan, s. Asa & Rebeckah, b. Feb. 14, 1752	LR2	237
Lucy, d. Asa & Rebeckah, b. May 10, 1762	A	5
Marcy, w. Benajah, d. Nov. 22, 1804, ae 60 y. last July	A	47
Mary, d. Apr. 21, 1783	A	36
Mary, d. Benajah & Marcy, b. Mar. 29, 1790	A	41
Nathaniel, s. Asa & Rebeckah, b. Aug. 15, 1754	LR2	237
Sarah, m. Simon **WENTER**, May 8, 1754	LR2	237
Wheeler, s. Asa & Rebeckah, b. Apr. 10, 1750	LR2	237
William, m. Joanna **BURRALL**, Oct. 31, 1765	LR2	8
William, d. Jan. 12, 1769	A	11
William, s. Benajah & Mercy, b. Mar. 15, 1774	A	20
William, d. May 22, 1821	A	52
William, s. Benajah & Lucretia, b. May 18, 1825	A	52
Surviah*, d. Benajah & Marcy, b. Mar. 27, 17[ ] *("Zurviah")	A	39
Surviah, m. Dr. Joshua **CORNWALL**, b. of Canaan, Aug. 22,		
1820,by Rev. Charles Prentice,of South Canaan (Zurviah)	A	79
DRAKE, Rachel, m. Abiel **FELLOWS**, June 12, 1771	A	13
Solomon, m. Sarah **RICHARDS**, June 22, 1834, by Reuben		
Hunt, J. P.	A	93
DUELL, Julia, m. John Nelson **FOX**, b. of Canaan, May 29, 1844,		
by Harley Goodwin	A	103
DUNHAM, Alma, m. William **HAYS**, b. of Canaan, [ ], by		
Pitkin Cowles	A	85
Almira, of Canaan, m. George **WILLIAMS**, of Great		
Barrington, Dec. 14, 1824, by Pitkin Cowles	A	84
Asahel M., m. Emma L. **DEAN**, Mar. 19, 1871	A	133
Clara Emma, d. [Asahel & Emma L.], b. May 18, 1874	A	133
Cornelius, s. James & Dinah, b. Apr. 28, 1763	A	9
Cynthia, twin with Pamela, d. James & Dinah, b. Mar. 28, 1761	A	8
Desire, d. James & Dinah, b. Feb. 11, 1757; d. Dec. 9, 1758	A	8
Elizabeth, d. James & Dinah, b. Sept. 1, 1751	A	8
Elizabeth, m. Andrew **BACON**, Mar. 17, 1754	A	7
George Asa, s. Asahel & Emma L., b. Dec. 15, 1871, at		
Mt. Washington, Mass.	A	133
Isaac, s. James & Dinah, b. Feb. 23, 1765	A	9
James, s. James & Dinah, b. Nov. 24, 1754; d. Dec. 11, 1758	A	8
Jane, of Canaan, m. Dr. Ithamer H. **SMITH**, of Sheffield,		
Jan. 17, 1832, by Pitkin Cowles	A	90
Josephine A., [d. Asahel & Emma L.], b. Jan. 3, 1877;		
d. July 22, 1877	A	133
Pamela, twin with Cynthia, d. James & Dinah, b. Mar. 28, 1761	A	8
Salathiel, d. James & Dinah, b. Mar. 22, 1753	A	8
Theophilus, s. James & Dinah, b. Nov. 28, 1758;		
d. Dec. 28, 1758	A	8
DUNN, James, m. Rachel **MURRAY**, b. from Ireland, now of		
Norfolk, July 11, 1852, by Rev. John Smith, at Falls		
Village	A	109

	Vol.	Page
DUNNING, DUNING, Betsey, m. Harvey **LAWRENCE**, Nov. 24, 1812, by Rev. Pitkin Cowles	A	49
Edmund, m. Freelove **DEAN**, b. of Canaan, Oct. 14, 1845, by Grove Lawrence Brunnell	A	104
Ellen L., m. Jerome **HOLCOMB**, Nov. 26, 1851, by Rev. Elisha Whittlesey	A	109
Hawley, m. Sarah **PORTER**, June 10, 1821, by Pitkin Cowles. Int. Pub.	A	80
Maria Ann, d. Rufus B. & Roxa, b. Nov. 28, 1812	A	50
Mary, m. Leonard **LAWRENCE**, Oct. 26, 1835, by Rev. H. H. Woodbridge, of the 2nd Cong. Ch.	A	94
Rufus B., m. Roxa **FELLOWS**, Mar. 4, 1811	A	50
DUPEE, Hanah, d. Charles & Hanah, b. Oct. 23, 1758	LR2	228
James, s. Charles & Hannah, b. June 27, 1767	A	10
Nancy, d. Charles & Hannah, b. June 27, 1767	A	10
Samuel, s. Charles & Hannah, b. Nov. 25, 1761	A	2
DUTCHER, Catharine L., m. Duncan L. **STEWART**, Dec. 30, 1849, by Rev. William Atwell, of Christ Ch.	A	106
Christian, m. Joshua **STEVENS**, Oct. 27, 1767	A	11
Christian, m. Joseph **BEEBE**, Nov. 9, 1777	A	27
George W., of Salisbury, m. Phebe **FAXON**, of Canaan, Jan. 3, 1827, by Pitkin Cowles	A	86
Ruluff, had negro Tom, s. Gin, b. Nov. [ ], 1784	A	43
Ruluff, Capt. had negro Cata, s. Gin, b. Dec. [ ], 1787	A	43
DUTTON, Esther, m. William Solomon **LAWRENCE**, Oct. 12, 1780	A	37
ELLIOTT, Joseph, m. Sarah **WILLIAMS**, July 7, 1833, by Reuben Hunt	A	91
Mercy, d. Jan. 4, 1770	A	12
ELMORE, John, Jr., s. John & Elizabeth, b. Dec. 17, 1792	A	48
Julia, d. John & Elizabeth, b. Oct. 18, 1786	A	48
Phinehas, s. John & Elizabeth, b. Nov. 20, 1784	A	48
ELTON, Amanda, d. Solomon H. & Lydia, b. June 23, 1792	A	50
Eliza, d. Solomon & Lydia, b. Dec. 2, 1798	A	50
Emma A., m. Elijah **ANDREWS**, July 4, 1825, by Rev. Samuel Eighmy, of the M. E. Ch.	A	84
Honoria, d. Solomon & Lydia, b. Apr. 19, 1794	A	50
John A., of Tyringham, Mass., m. Mary **PIERCE**, of Canaan, Feb. 2, 1840, by Rev. H. H. Woodbridge, of the 2nd Cong. Ch.	A	99
Philena, m. Joseph **FELLOWS**, Jr., Nov. 25, 1789	A	41
Rhesa G., s. Solomon & Lydia, b. Nov. 13, 1800	A	50
Rhoda, d. Solomon & Lydia, b. Mar. 20, 1796	A	50
Salmon H., m. Abigail **SAGE**, b. of Canaan, Dec. 16, 1832, by Pitkin Cowles	A	90
ENSIGN, Eli, s. John, Jr. & Rhoda, b. Jan. 8, 1779	A	31
Elizabeth, s. John, Jr. & Rhoda, b. July 28, 1772	A	25
Harriet, m. Charles Theron **PRENTICE**, Apr. 28, 1835, by		

	Vol.	Page
ENSIGN, (cont.)		
Charles Prentice	A	94
John, s. John, Jr. & Rhoda, b. Mar. 26, 1777	A	27
John, s. John, Jr. & Rhoda, b. Mar. 26, 1777	A	28
John A., of Salisbury, m. Caroline M. **POPE**, of Canaan,		
Oct. 8, 1844, by Harley Goodwin	A	104
John Ely, s. Ely & Lucy, b. Mar. 13, 1812	A	50
John Ely, m. Susan **BURRALL**, May 17, 1835, by Charles		
Prentice	A	94
Lois, d. John, Jr. & Rhoda, b. Mar. 24, 1785	A	38
Love, d. John, Jr., & Rhoda, b. Mar. 22, 1783	A	38
Mariann, of Canaan, m. Sylvester **BRADLEY**, of Norfolk,		
Apr. 20, 1831, by Pitkin Cowles	A	89
Molly, m. Abraham **BUSHNELL**, Jan. 9, 1770	A	13
Molly, d. John, Jr. & Rhoda, b. Jan. 19, 1774	A	25
Rhoda, d. John, Jr. & Rhoda, b. Apr. 22, 1775	A	25
Sidney, s. Ely & Lucy, b. Sept. 4, 1807	A	50
Sidney, m. Clarinda H. **PRENTICE**, Jan. 13, 1833, by		
Charles Prentice	A	91
Sophia, s. John, Jr. & Rhoda, b. Mar. 3, 1781	A	34
Thankfull, d. Ely & Lucy, b. Apr. 16, 1810	A	50
EVANS, Mary, of Sheffield, m. Daniel **BRIGGS**, of Canaan, Dec.		
4, 1831, by Pitkin Cowles	A	89
EWELL, Patience, m. John **HARREY**, Aug. 19, 1848, by Lyman		
Lawrence, J. P.	A	105
FANNING, FANING, Anna, m. Elias **REED**, b. of Canaan, Jan. 24,		
1821, by Pitkin Cowles	A	79
Clarena, d. James & Sarah, b. Sept. 26, 1763	A	5
Erastus, s. James & Sarah, b. Apr. 14, 1770	A	15
Helen M., m. Gribeon G. **WHEELER**, b. of Barrington, Mass.,		
[Sept. 11, 1842], by Rev. Edward B. Emerson	A	102
James, m. Sarah **GILLIT**, Sept. 26, 1762	A	5
James Garliff, s. James & Sarah, b. Mar. 23, 1767	A	15
John Williams, s. James & Sarah, b. Aug. 11, 1765	A	15
Nancy, d. James & Sarah, b. Dec. 26, 1776	A	32
Orromel, s. James & Sarah, b. Dec. 13, 1768	A	15
Sarah, d. James & Sarah, b. Sept. 29, 1771	A	16
FARRAND, Anna, d. Daniel & Jerusha, b. Apr. 1, 1757	LR2	232
Daniel, Rev. of Canaan, m. Jerusha **BORDMAN**, of New		
Milford, Oct. 20, 1755	LR2	237
David Sherman, s. Rev. Daniel & Jerusha, b. Jan. 9, 1769	A	11
Esther, d. Daniel & Jerusha, b. Aug. 21, 1764	A	4
Jerusha, d. Rev. Daniel & Jerusha, b. Oct. 17, 1766	A	11
Nathaniel, s. Daniel & Jerusha, b. Mar. 30, 1774	A	21
Pamela, d. Daniel & Jerusha, b. Oct. 3, 1758	LR2	228
Urania, d. Rev. Daniel & Jerusha, b. Feb. 8, 1771	A	17
FAXON, Douglass, s. William & Wealthy, b. Nov. 27, 1794	A	44
Elizabeth, of Canaan, m. Albert **ROBBERTS**, of West		

	Vol.	Page
FAXON, (cont.)		
Stockbridge, Mass., Nov. 13, 1829, by Pitkin Cowles	A	87
Elvira, m. Fitch **FERRIS**, Feb. 28, 1819	A	52
John, s. William & Wealthy, b. Dec. 9, 1797	A	44
Phebe, of Canaan, m. George W. **DUTCHER**, of Salisbury,		
Jan. 3, 1827, by Pitkin Cowles	A	86
William, m. Wealthy **WATSON**, Mar. 23, 1794	A	44
FELLOWS, Abiel, m. Elizabeth **ROE**, Jan. 19, 1758, by Col.		
David Whitney	A	11
Abial, s. Abial & Elizabeth, b. Oct. 1, 1764	A	4
Abiel, s. Abiel & Elizabeth, b. Oct. 1, 1764	A	11
Abiel, m. Rachel **DRAKE**, June 12, 1771	A	13
Abiel, m. Sarah **HOWE**, Dec. 1, 1796	A	43
Abigail, m. Hezekiah **WATSON**, May 10, 1779	A	31
Abiram, s. Jose;h & Leah, b. Nov. 4, 1770	A	14
Adaline, d. Joseph, Jr. & Melona, b. Feb. 14, 1801	A	47
Allener, d. David & Lois, b. Oct. 22, 1772	A	22
Anne, d. Abiel & Elizabeth, b. Apr. 26, 1768	A	11
Asa, s. David & Lois, b. Jan. 31, 1768	A	21
Asahel, s. Abiel & Rachel, b. May 6, 1780	A	33
Asahel, [s. John & Edna], b. Nov. 23, 1803	A	52
Betsey, of Canaan, m. David **BUELL**, of Litchfield, Jan.		
14, 1846, by Rev. A. V. Warren	A	104
Chloe, d. Abiel & Rachal, b. Mar. 22, 1782	A	37
Chloe, [d. Jonathan & Betsey], b. Sept. 26, 1788	A	45
Cyrus, s. Joseph & Leah, b. Oct. 10, 1711* *("1771"?)	A	14
Daniel, s. Joseph & Leah, b. Feb. 19, 1777	A	26
David, m. Susannah **BAKER**, June 2, 1762	A	21
David, m. Lois **STEVENS**, Dec. 22, 1763, by Col. Whitney	A	4
Delana, d. Joseph & Leah, b. Jan. 2, 1759	A	4
Drake, s. Abiel & Rachal, b. Oct. 31, 1778	A	30
Edna Eliza, [d. John & Edna], b. Dec. 14, 1814	A	52
Edwin, [s. John & Edna], b. Sept. 1, 1805	A	52
Eliza, [d. John & Edna], b. Feb. 8, 1802; d. Aug. 15, 1803	A	52
Elizabeth, d. Abial & Elizabeth, b. Feb. 2, 1759	LR2	227
Elizabeth, w. Abiel, d. Sept. 26, 1770	A	12
Elizabeth, [d. Jonathan & Betsey], b. Sept. 14, 1791	A	45
Elizabeth, m. Ransom **MOORE**, Feb. 5, 1832, by James Fenn,		
J. P.	A	90
Ephraim, Jr., m. Anne **PALMER**, of Sheffield, May 11, 1749	LR1	423
Ephraim, s. Joseph & Leah, b. Nov. 2, 1761	A	4
Ephraim, s. Obil & Lois, b. July 6, 1774	A	22
Erastus, s. Abiel & Rachel, b. Apr. 2, 1776	A	25
Erastus, [s. Jonathan & Betsey], b. Dec. 14, 1799	A	45
Erastus, [s. John & Edna], b. July 31, 1800	A	52
Esther, d. Ephraim & Anne, b. Dec. 18, 1749; d. July 2, 1750	LR1	423
George, of Canaan, m. Jane **FURGESON**, of Sheffield, Dec.		
9, 1824, by Pitkin Cowles	A	84

	Vol.	Page
FELLOWS, (cont.)		
Henry, s. David & Lois, b. Mar. 24, 1770	A	21
Horace, [s. John & Edna], b. Aug. 31, 1808	A	52
Huldah, d. Jonathan & Mary, b. Oct. 31, 1754	LR2	238
Hulda, m. Daniel **RICHARDS**, Feb. 6, 1773	A	17
Huldah Ann, [d. John & Edna], b. Jan. 26, 1811	A	52
Isaac, s. Jonathan & Mary, b. June 19, 1753	LR2	238
Isaac, s. Jonathan & Mary, d. Oct. 17, 1754	LR2	238
Isaac, s. Thomas & Sarah, b. May 23, 1755	A	6
James, s. David & Lois, b. Sept. 13, 1765; d. Apr. 1, 1767	A	21
James, s. Obil & Lois, b. Mar. 24, 1771	A	22
Jena, d. Joseph & Leah, b. Dec. 22, 1763	A	4
Jerusha, of Edgemont*, m. Daniel **LAWRENCE**, of Canaan,		
Jan. 4, 1827, by Pitkin Cowles *("Egremont"?)	A	86
Joanna, d. William & Sarah, b. Mar. 10, 1748	LR1	424
Joanna, d. Joseph & Leah, b. Jan. 14, 1757	A	4
John, s. William & Sarah, b. May 15, 1749	LR1	424
John, s. Abiel & Rachel, b. June 30, 1774	A	19
John, s. Abiel & Rachel, b. June 30, 1774	A	52
John, m. Edna **DABALL**, Oct. 8, 1799	A	52
John Meret, [s. John & Edna], b. Mar. 12, 1821	A	52
Jonathan, m. Mary **RICHARDS**, of Norfolk, Sept. 13, 1752,		
by David Whitney	LR2	238
Jonathan, s. Abial & Elizabeth, b. Oct. 17, 1762	A	3
Jonathan, m. Betsey **ROOT**, Nov. 3, 1785	A	45
Jonathan, Jr., [s. Jonathan & Betsey], b. Apr. 12, 1790	A	45
Joseph, m. Leah **HUXLEY**, Mar. 7, 1754, by Rev. Mr. Farrand	A	4
Joseph, s. Joseph & Leah, b. May 28, 1768	A	14
Joseph, Jr., m. Philena **ELTON**, Nov. 25, 1789	A	41
Laura, m. Ezekiel **DAYBALL**, Jan. 14, 1813	A	49
Linus, s. Joseph, Jr. & Philena, b. July 21, 1790	A	41
Loes, d. Ephraim, Jr. & Anne, b. Jan. 24, 1750/1	LR1	423
Lorry, [s. Jonathan & Betsey], b. Sept. 17, 1786	A	45
Lucy, d. Abial & Elizabeth, b. Nov. 28, 1760	A	1
Lydia, m. Sherman **SMITH**, b. of Canaan, June 12, 1831,		
by Harmon Ellis, of Bap. Ch. Norfolk	A	89
Mary, m. Elisha **MERRELLS**, Apr. 17, 1760	A	6
Mary, wid., d. Dec. 16, 1774, in the 82nd y. of her age	A	21
Mary, [d. Jonathan & Betsey], b. Dec. 18, 1794	A	45
Melinda, m. Wheeler M. **SMITH**, b. of Canaan, May 9, 1821,		
by Pitkin Cowles	A	80
Mellona, d. Joseph, Jr. & Melona, b. Mar. 7, 1794	A	47
Meriam, d. Joseph & Leah, b. Apr. 24, 1773	A	26
Pheleana, d. Joseph, Jr. & Melona, b. July 17, 1797	A	47
Phileda, d. Joseph & Leah, b. May 26, 1766	A	14
Philemon, s. Obil & Lois, b. Apr. 29, 1768	A	22
Rachel, d. Thomas & Sarah, b. June 12, 1753	A	6
Rachel, d. Abiel & Rachal, b. June 12, 1772	A	15

	Vol.	Page
FELLOWS, (cont.)		
Rachal, b. June 12, 1772; m. Silas **FRANKLIN**, Sept. 26, 1790	A	47
Rachel, m. Silas **FRANKLIN**, Sept. 26, 1790	A	41
Roxa, m. Rufus B. **DUNING**, Mar. 4, 1811	A	50
Rozzle, s. Thomas & Sarah, b. Dec. 7, 1751	LR1	424
Sarah, d. Thomas & Sarah, b. May 17, 1759	A	6
Silas, s. Abiel & Elizabeth, b. Sept. 18, 1770	A	12
Stephen, s. William & Sarah, b. Feb. 21, 1751	LR1	424
Susannah, w. David, d. Apr. 5, 1763	A	21
Susanna, d. Abiel & Elizabeth, b. May 7, 1766	A	11
Susannah, d. David & Lois, b. June 30, 1776	A	30
Susanna, m. Stephen **KINGSBURY**, Aug. 30, 1784	A	41
Thomas, m. Sarah **LAWRENCE**, b. of Canaan, May 3, 1750	LR1	424
Vilette, d. Thomas & Sarah, b. May 4, 1762	A	6
William, of Canaan, m. Sarah **RICHARDS**, of Norfolk, Feb. 26, 1746/7	LR1	424
William, s. Thomas & Sarah, b. Apr. 30, 1757	A	6
Zilpha, d. Joseph & Leah, b. May 19, 1755	A	4
Zilpha, m. Thomas **GILBERT**, Mar. 9, 1775, by Elisha Baker	A	22
FENN, Betsey, of Canaan, m. John **MORSE**, of Litchfield, Feb. 23, 1831, by Pitkin Cowles	A	88
Betsey E., m. Joshua **BELDEN**, Jr., b. of Canaan, Nov. 5, 1839, by Rev. Henry H. Woodbridge, of the 2nd Cong. Ch.	A	98
Frances P., of Canaan, m. Augustus **BIGELOW**, of New Lebanon, N. Y., Feb. 1, 1831, by Pitkin Cowles	A	88
Frederick J., of Washington, m. Emeline **HOSKINS**, of Canaan, Dec. 11, 1823, by Charles Prentice	A	83
Frederick James, s. James & Louis, b. Sept. 22, 1796	A	50
Julia E., of Canaan, m. John **VAN BUREN**, of Schadoe, N. Y., Dec. 24, 1832, by Theodosius Clark	A	91
Theophilus, 2nd s. James & Louis, b. Dec. 18, 1800	A	50
FERGUSON, FURGESON, Catharine M., m. Charles **GILLETT**, b. of Canaan, Oct. 17, 1838, by H. H. Woodbridge. Int. Pub.	A	97
Jane, of Sheffield, m. George **FELLOWS**, of Canaan, Dec. 9, 1824, by Pitkin Cowles	A	84
Sally, m. Lyman **RAWLSON**, b. of Canaan, Dec. 10, 1826, by Pitkin Cowles	A	86
FERRIS, Elvira, w. Fitch, d. Dec. 22, 1837, ae 45 y.	A	53
Fitch, m. Elvira **FAXON**, Feb. 28, 1819	A	52
Fitch, m. Mary Ann **NOBLE**, Aug. 22, 1838	A	53
Margaret, d. Fitch & Elvira, b. July 1, 1833	A	53
Marilla, d. Fitch & Elvina, b. Dec. 28, 1829	A	53
Mary Elizabeth, d. [Fitch & Elvira], b. Sept. 12, 1823	A	52
Minerva, d. Fitch & Elvira, b. May 28, 1827	A	53
Minerva, of Canaan, m. John A. **HENRY**, of New York, Jan. 9, 1849	A	54

	Vol.	Page
FERRIS, (cont.)		
Minerva, m. John A. **HENRY**, Jan. 9, 1849, by Rev. William		
Atwell, of Christ Ch.	A	105
Reid, s. [Fitch & Elvira], b. Mar. 23, 1820	A	52
Reid, s. [Fitch & Elvira], d. Aug. 28, 1826	A	52
Walter, of Salisbury, m. Sarah E. **LAWRENCE**, of Canaan,		
Aug. 8, 1851, by Rev. Elisha Whittlesey	A	109
FIELD, Lucy, m. Anson S. **HILLS**, b. of Canaan, Jan. 14, 1822,		
by P. Cowles	A	80
FITCH, Sibel, m. Moses **MARSH**, Feb. 19,. 1767	A	13
FLETCHER, Sarah, of Canaan, m. Ebenezer **BRINTON**, Jr., of		
Salisbury [ ], by Charles Prentice. Int. Pub.		
Recorded Sept. 30, 1835	A	94
Silance, of Salisbury, m. Sam[ue]ll **LEE**, of Canaan, Mar.		
28, 1754, by David Whitney, J. P.	LR2	238
FOOT, Lucius H., of Wolcottville, m. Clarrissa T. **WICKWIRE**,		
of South Canaan, July 10, 1836 by Charles Prentice. Int.		
Pub.	A	95
FORBES, Abigail, b. June 19, 1755, in Canaan, m. John **ADAMS**,		
Aug. 6, 1780, at her father's house	A	45
Abisha, s. Elisha & Hannah, b. Nov. 9, 1762	A	9
Elisha, Jr., s. Elisha & Hannah, b. Aug. 26, 1756	A	9
Elisha, Jr., [s. Elisha & Hannah], d. Dec. 29, 1757	A	9
Elisha Norman, s. Elisha & Hannah, b. June 24, 1759	A	9
Hannah, d. Elisha & Hannah, b. July 11, 1764	A	9
John, s. Elisha & Hannah, b. Oct. 13, 1757	A	9
John, [s. Elisha & Hannah], d. Jan. 6, 1758	A	9
John, s. Elisha & Hannah, b. Jan. 10, 1761	A	9
Samuel, s. Elisha & Hannah, b. Aug. 25, 1766	A	9
FORD, Joel C., of New Marlborough, m. Mary B. **PARTRIDGE**, of		
Canaan, Feb. 16, 1834, by Rev. Julius Field	A	92
FOSTER, Chauncey S., m. Helen E. **BEEBE**, b. of Canaan, Dec.		
25, 1849, by Rev. Z. D. Scobey	A	105
Harriet Louisa, of Canaan, m. Peter **VAN DUSEN**, of		
Sheffield, Mass., Dec. 31, 1840, by Rev. H. H.		
Woodbridge, of the 2nd Cong. Ch.	A	100
Lucinda, of Canaan, m. Avery **SMITH**, of Norfolk, Jan.		
18, 1821, by Pitkin Cowles	A	79
Sally, m. Richard Price **STEVENS**, Mar. 27, 1818	A	52
FOX, Caroline, of New Marlborough, Mass., m. [ ] **WARNER**,		
of Canaan, Jan. 1, 1839, by Rev. Charles Stearnes	A	97
John Nelson, m. Julia **DUELL**, b. of Canaan, May 29, 1844,		
by Harley Goodwin	A	103
Olive, m. William **HUGG**, Feb. 16, 1776	A	24
FRANCIS, Eliza, of Salisbury, m. Charles **JACKSON**, of Canaan,		
July 18, 1824, by Pitkin Cowles	A	83
FRANKLIN, Abiah, s. John & Kezia, b. Mar. 17, 1762	A	8
Abigail, d. John & Kezia, b. Aug. 9, 1747	A	8

	Vol.	Page
FRANKLIN, (cont.)		
Billa, s. John & Kezia, b. Nov. 5, 1767	A	11
Charles, m. Jane **LAWRENCE**, b. of Canaan, Nov. 27, 1833,		
by Rev. Henry H. Woodbridge, of the 2nd Cong. Ch.	A	92
Charles Walker, s. Silas & Rachel, b. Sept. 12, 1806	A	48
Chloe, d. Silas & Rachal, b. Feb. 15, 1793	A	48
Edward Morgan, s. Silas & Rachel, b. Aug. 16, 1804	A	48
Fanny Smith, d. Silas & Rachel, b. Nov. 18, 1799	A	48
Flora Austin, d. Silas & Rachal, b. Sept. 3, 1797	A	48
John, m. Kezia **PIERCE**, Dec. 24, 1745	A	8
John, s. John & Kezia, b. Sept. 15, 1749	A	8
John, s. Silas & Rachal, b. Feb. 26, 1795	A	48
John, m. Betsey **LAWRENCE**, b. of Canaan, Nov. 4, 1823,		
by Pitkin Cowles	A	82
Lucy, d. John & Kezia, b. May 13, 1754	A	8
Lucy, m. Amos **ORMSBY**, May 25, 1775	A	40
Mary, d. John & Kezia, b. Feb. 2, 1757	A	8
Mary, d. Silas & Rachal, b. Jan. 20, 1801	A	48
Samuel, s. John & Kezia, b. May 10, 1759	A	8
Silas, s. John & Kezia, b. Apr. 24, 1765	A	8
Silas, b. Apr. 24, 1765; m. Rachal **FELLOWS**, Sept. 26, 1790	A	47
Silas, m. Rachel **FELLOWS**, Sept. 26, 1790	A	41
Susanna, d. John & Kezia, b. Dec. 6, 1751	A	8
Thomas, s. Silas & Rachel, b. July 27, 1809	A	48
FREEMAN, Anna, of Canaan, m. Samuel **MILLS**, of Watervliet(?),		
N. Y., Dec. 15, 1822, by Pitkin Cowles	A	82
Anne, w. Elisha, d. Feb. 13, 1768	A	18
Elisha, m. Cloe **STEVENS**, May 5, 1771	A	18
Ellranall, s. Elisha & Cloe, b. Feb. 2, 1772	A	18
Jette, d. Elisha & Rachel, b. Nov. 21, 1769	A	20
Obed, of Cornwall, m. Naoma **KAIN**, of Canaan, Apr. 6,		
1826, by Rev. Elbert Osborn	A	85
Sarah Anne, d. Elisha & Cloe, b. July 11, 1774	A	19
FRENCH, Isaac, m. Polly **LEMERLY**, b. of Canaan, Apr. 24, 1836,		
by Charles Prentice. Int. Pub.	A	95
Sarah Ann, m. Curtis B. **HATCH**, Nov. 1, 1847, by Rev.		
William Atwell, of Christ Ch.	A	105
Sarah R., of Canaan, m. Richard E. **JOSLIN**, of Pittsfield,		
N. Y., Nov. 16, 1846, by Rev. D. D. Francis	A	107
FRINK, Betsey, m. Eliphalet **LADD**, Jan. 29, 1794	A	43
FULLER, Anne, d. Judah & Mary, b. Apr. 20, 1771	A	14
Ebenezer, m. Hannah **TAYLOR**, Apr. 17, 1775, by Elisha		
Baker	A	22
Ezekiel, of Salisbury, m. Dolly **WHITE**, of Canaan, Jan.		
23, 1834, by Charles Prentice	A	92
Hannah, d. Judah & Mary, b. Mar. 22, 1767	A	10
John R., m. Fanny **PEET**, Nov. 27, 1844, at the house of		
Harmon Peet, by Rev. George Fash, of N. Canaan	A	104

	Vol.	Page
FULLER, (cont.)		
Judah, m. Mary **BISHOP**, Feb. 11, 1766	A	10
Samuel, s. Judah & Mary, b. Apr. 22, 176[ ]	A	12
GAINES, Charlotte D., of Canaan, m. Joseph L. **MERVIN**, of		
Goshen, Mar. 20, 1834, by Charles Prentice. Int. Pub.	A	92
GAMMONS, Rufus H., of Salisbury, m. Lucinda **PHILLIPS**, of		
Canaan, Apr. 27, 1836, by Charles Prentice	A	95
GAYLORD, Grove, of Norfolk, m. Betsey **DONOLDS**, of Canaan,		
Jan. 1, 1852, by John Watson, J. P.	A	109
Naoma, m. Asahel **KELLOGG**, Sept. 10, 1778	A	32
GEUTAN (?), Phebe, m. James **STEPHENS**, Jan. 19, 1768	A	12
GIBBS, Maria, m. Sebe **DEAN**, May 6, 1821, by Rev. Asa Talmage,		
of Cornwall	A	80
GILBERT, Ephraim, s. Thomas & Zilpha, b. Nov. 6, 1779	A	33
Phelomelia, m. George **MARVIN**, b. of Canaan, Oct. 16, 1845,		
by Rev. D. D. Francis	A	106
Polly, d. Thomas & Zilpah, b. Nov. 24, 1777	A	27
Thomas, m. Zilpha **FELLOWS**, Mar. 9, 1775, by Elisha Baker	A	22
GILLETT, GILLIT, GILLET, Abby, m. Horace **WEED**, of		
Sharon, Mar. 24, 1852, by Rev. Elisha Whittlesey	A	109
Abigail, m. Eber **YALE**, b. of Canaan, Feb. 10, 1839, by		
Reuben Hunt, J. P.	A	98
Ann, m. Gamaliel **WHITING**, b. of Canaan, June 18, 1752	LR1	427
Betsey Sophronia, d. Martin & Hannah, b. June 9, 1802,		
in Bethleham, Mass., Co. of Berkshire	A	51
Charles, m. Catharine M. **FERGUSON**, b. of Canaan, Oct.		
17, 1838, by H. H. Woodbridge. Int. Pub.	A	97
Elizabeth, m. Edward M. **HILL**, Sept. 15, 1852, by Rev.		
Elisha Whittlesey	A	109
Hannah, d. Martin & Hannah, b. Mar. 7, 1806	A	51
John, d. Feb. 29, 1764	A	6
Lawrence, m. Abigail **LAWRENCE**, b. of Canaan, Jan. 2,		
1839, by H. H. Woodbridge. Int. Pub.	A	98
Mary, d. Martin & Hannah, b. Aug. 26, 1809	A	51
Phebe, of Canaan, m. Lorenzo **HAKES**, of Nassau, N. Y.,		
Jan. 1, 1838, by H. H. Woodbridge	A	97
Sally Mariah, d. Martin & Hannah, b. May 15, 1804, in		
Bethleham, Mass.	A	51
Sarah, m. James **FANING**, Sept. 26, 1762	A	5
Sarah M., of Canaan, m. Edward **SMITH**, of Salisbury, Nov.		
7, 1849, by Rev. D. D. Francis	A	108
Serena B., b. Oct. 20, 1790; m. Abigail **LAWRENCE**, Dec.		
30, 1812, by Rev. Pitkin Cowles	A	49
GLEASON, Ephraim, of Austerlitz, N. Y., m. Deborah Minerva		
CROWFOOT, of Canaan, Apr. 25, 1833, by Rev.		
Harmon Elliss, of Bapt. Ch., Norfolk	A	91
Martin F., of Austerlitz, N. Y., m. Wealthy Ann **STEPHENS**,		
of Canaan, Jan. 18, 1849, by Rev. D. D. Francis	A	108

	Vol.	Page
GOODWIN, Lyman D., of Deerfield, N. Y., m. Phebe **LAWRENCE**, of Canaan, May 26, 1842, by Rev. H. H. Woodbridge	A	101
Submit, m. Jacob **HURLBURT**, Jan. 2, 1777	A	25
GORHAM, Levi M., m. Harriet **PRESTON**, b. of Sheffield, Mass., Mar. 7, 1841, by Rev. H. H. Woodbridge	A	100
GRACE, John, m. Julia **MULHALL**, b. lately from Ireland, June 27, 1852, by Rev. John Smith	A	109
GRAVES, Elizabeth, of Canaan, m. Henry **LOOMIS**, of Salisbury, Nov. 4, 1844, by Rev. Stephen J. Stebbins	A	104
Hope, m. Jacob **BUNCE**, Aug. 4, 1760, by John Beebe	A	2
GREEN, Asahel, s. Robert & Susanna, b. May 17, 1764	A	6
Bethany, d. Robert & Susanna, b. May 5, 1760	A	6
Bette, m. Jonathan **LAWRENCE**, May 24, 1756	A	1
Buel, of Sheffield, m. Harriet **PIERCE**, of Canaan, Jan. 21, 1822, by P. Cowles	A	80
Ellis, d. Robert & Susanna, b. Dec. 28, 1753	A	6
Eunice, w. Willard, d. Nov. 13, 1810	A	48
Hannah, d. Willard & Eunice, b. June 12, 1759	A	6
Huldah, d. Willard & Eunice, b. July 13, 1778	A	48
Louisa, d. Willard & Eunice, b. July 7, 1769	A	48
Louisa, of Sheffield, m. Joel A. **PHELPS**, of Middletown, Jan. 10, 1832, by Pitkin Cowles	A	90
Lidia, d. Robert & Susanna, b. June 23, 1758	A	6
Mary, d. Robert & Susanna, b. July 15, 1762	A	6
Mary, of Salisbury, m. Jethro **HATCH**, of Sherbourne, N. Y., Sept. 23, 1838, by Simeon Higley, J. P.	A	98
Polly, d. Samuel & Anna, b. Mar. 25, 1788	A	44
Rachel, of Canaan, m. Rodman **WILCOX**, of Goshen, June 12, 1832, by Charles Prentice	A	90
Ruth, d. Robert & Susanna, b. May 9, 1756	A	6
Samuel, s. Samuel & Anna, b. Jan. 25, 1780	A	44
Susanna, d. Samuel & Anna, b. Apr. 13, 1777	A	44
Sylvia, d. Willard & Eunice, b. Feb. 18, 1767	A	48
Wheeler, s. Willard & Eunice, b. Apr. 19, 1772	A	48
Willard, m. Eunice **LAWRENCE**, Mar. 1, 1759	A	6
Willard, s. Willard & Eunice, b. Mar. 18, 1762	A	6
William, s. Samuel & Anna, b. June 30, 1775	A	44
GRIMES, Christian, of Goshen, m. Moses **PRINDLE**, Mar. 22, 1749	LR1	427
GRISWOLD, GRISWOULD, Abigail, d. Benjamin & Susannah, b. July 8, 1754	LR2	233
Abraham, s. Marcus & Chloe, b. Nov. 33 [sic], 1774	A	22
Amy, d. Marcus & Chloe, b. Apr. 30, 1776	A	29
Benjamin, s. Benjamin & Susannah, b. Dec. 3, 1756	LR2	228
Eliza, of Canaan, m. William **CROWELL**, of Salisbury, Apr. 19, 1837, by Rev. H. H. Woodbridge, of the 2nd Cong. Ch.	A	96

	Vol.	Page
GRISWOLD, GRISWOULD, (cont.)		
Lucy, d. Manus* & Cloe, b. Dec. 21, 1772 *(Marcus"?)	A	17
Reuben, m. Mary **ROCKWELL**, Feb. 26, 1776	A	24
Warren, s. Marcus, d. Jan. 20, 1778	A	29
GRUNDY, Mary, d. Edmon & Mary, b. Jan. 30, 1774	A	22
Rachel, d. Edmon & Mary, b. July 26, 1772	A	22
GUNN, Mary, m. David **WHITNEY**, Jr., Sept. 23, 1739	LR2	238
HAKES, Lorenzo, of Nassau, N. Y., m. Phebe **GILLETT**, of		
Canaan, Jan. 1 1838, by H. H. Woodbridge	A	97
HALE, [see also **HALL**], Elizabeth, d. Nathan & Salome, b. Feb.		
18, 1779	A	30
Nathan, m. Wid. Salome **ROBBINS**, Apr. 26, 1778	A	30
HALL, [see also **HALE**], David, of Canaan, m. Mary Ann		
COTTERILL, of Dover, N. Y., Oct. 31, 1842, by Rev.		
Edward B. Emerson	A	102
Elias, s. John & Molly, b. Dec. 22, 1773	A	20
Eliza, of Canaan, m. Newman **WEBSTER**, of Kingsville, O.,		
Aug. 22, 1824, by Pitkin Cowles	A	83
John, s. John & Molly, b. Sept. 10, 1777	A	27
Roserline, of South Canaan, m. James **HICKS**, of North		
Goshen, Oct. 16, 1842, by Rev. Edward B. Emerson	A	102
HAMILTON, [see also **HAMLIN**], Esther, d. Ezekiel & Mary, b.		
Aug. 8, 1772	A	16
Ezekiel, m. Mary **STEPHENS**, Aug. 1, 1771	A	16
HAMLIN, [see also **HAMILTON**], Clarence, s. Giles & Eunice, b.		
Mar. 27, 1763	A	9
Filandia, d. Giles & [E]unice, b. Mar. 28, 1770	A	18
Giles, m. Eunice **KINGMAN**, May 20, 1762	A	9
Giles, s. Giles & [E]unice, b. Feb. 13, 1776	A	26
Phebe, d. Giles & Eunice, b. Sept. 18, 1765	A	9
Phebe, d. Giles & [E]unice, b. Nov. 6, 1767	A	19
Sarah, d. Giles & [E]unice, b. Dec. 24, 1773	A	19
HANCHET, Emeline, of Canaan, m. Franklin **SWEET**, of Cornwall,		
June 17, 1838, by H. H. Woodbridge	A	97
Isaac, m. Chloe **BROWN**, b. of Canaan, Jan. 22, 1816*; by		
Charles Prentice *(Probably "1826")	A	85
L. Sophia, of Canaan, m. Henry A. **TOBEY**, of New Bedford,		
Mass., Oct. 22, 1849, by Rev. D. D. Francis	A	108
HANCOX, Anabel, m. Hezekiah **ANDRUS**, Apr. 11, 1754, by Rev.		
Mr. Farrand	LR2	227
Jonathan, m. Sibel **KELLOGG**, Apr. 8, 1754, by Rev. Mr.		
Farrand	LR2	237
Jonathan, s. Daniel, d. Sept. 13, 1757	LR2	232
Mary, m. William **BEEBE**, Mar. 19, 1752	LR2	238
Mary, d. Jonathan & Sible, b. Feb. 17, 1757	LR2	233
Peadey, of Canaan, m. Joseph **BECKLEY**, of Canaan, May		
[ ], 1747	LR1	424
Rhoda, d. Jonathan & Sible, b. July 25, 1755	LR2	237

	Vol.	Page
HANCOX, (cont.)		
Sibel, m. Solomon **WRIGHT**, Jan. 23, 1759	A	1
Tabitha, m. Aaron **KELLOGG**, Apr. 22, 1762, by Rev. Mr. Farrand	A	3
HAMMER, Rhoda, m. Elizur **WRIGHT**, Jr., Oct. 28, 1784	A	38
HARLEY, Benjamin, m. Parnel **MOSES**, b. of Canaan, Apr. 8, 1834, by Rev. Harmon Ellis, of the Bap. Ch., Norfolk	A	92
HARREY*, John, m. Patience **EWELL**, Aug. 19, 1848, by Lyman Lawrence, J. P. *("HARVEY"?)	A	105
HARRIS, HARRISS, Abigail, m. Abiram **NORTH**, Nov. 20, 1826, by Rev. Samuel Eighmy, of the M. E. Ch.	A	85
Anne, d. Daniel & Submit, b. Nov. 21, 1766	A	27
Daniel, Jr., m. Submit **JOHNSON**, Feb. 23, 1764, by Rev. Mr. Farrand	A	4
Eunice, m. Jerediah **BROWN**, Jr., Jan. 6, 1785	A	46
George, m. Eleanor **LOWRY**, Apr. 23, 1829, by Charles Prentice	A	87
Lucy, d. Daniel & Submit, b. Apr. 16, 1765	A	27
HART, Deidamia, of Canaan, m. Luke **HUDSON**, of New Marlborough, Mass., Dec. 11, 1849, by Rev. Z. D. Scobey, of South Canaan	A	105
Henry, of Sheffield, Mass., m. Huldah M. **RICHARDSON**, of Canaan, Dec. 13, 1840, by Rev. H. H. Woodbridge, of the 2nd Cong. Ch.	A	99
Phabeus, m. Rhoda **DORMAN**, b. of Canaan, Dec. 20, 1838, by Rev. Charles Stearnes, of the M. E. Ch.	A	97
HASKEL, Anna, m. Alban **ROSE**, Dec. 12, 1801, by Elizur Wright	A	48
HATCH, Anne, m. Timothy **COWLES**, Dec. 11, 1770	A	15
Curtis B., m. Sarah Ann **FRENCH**, Nov. 1, 1847, by Rev. William Atwell, of Christ Ch.	A	105
James H., m. Julia **SPAULDING**, b. of Canaan, Dec. 27, 1829, by Rev. Noah Bigelow. Int. Pub.	A	87
Jethro, of Sherbourne, N. Y., m. Mary **GREEN**, of Salisbury, Sept. 23, 1838, by Simeon Higley, J. P.	A	98
HAYS, William, m. Alma **DUNHAM**, b. of Canaan, [ ], by Pitkin Cowles	A	85
HECTOR, Harmon, m. Sarah **WALLOW**, b. of Salisbury, Feb. 22, 1841, by Rev. H. H. Woodbridge, of the 2nd Cong. Ch.	A	100
Hariet, of Salisbury, m. Isaac **VAN NESS**, of Lenox, Mass., Sept. 5, 1842, by Rev. H. H. Woodbridge	A	102
HENIS, Mary A., m. Curtice **MUNGER**, b. of Canaan, Dec. 9, 1830, by Pitkin Cowles	A	88
HENRY, John A., of New York, m. Minerva **FERRIS**, of Canaan, Jan. 9, 1849, by [ ]	A	54
John A., m. Minerva **FERRIS**, Jan. 9, 1849, by Rev. William Atwell, of Christ Ch.	A	105
Mary, m. Marriner **ROOD**, Jr., Nov. 30, 1768	A	12
HENSDIL, [see under **HINSDALE**]		

	Vol.	Page
HERD, Mary, Mrs. of South Canaan, m. Marvin **TREADWAY**, of Torrington, Feb. 21, 1841, by Rev. Erastus Doty, of Colebrook	A	100
HERRICK, Sarah, m. Zebulon **STEVENS**, Jr., Mar. 28, 1779	A	31
HEWITT, HEWIT, Abiah, b. Aug. 9, 1772; m. Silas **COOK**, July 8, 1792	A	48
Abigail, d. Ephraim & Mary, b. Aug. 29, 1764	A	9
Abigail, d. Gorshom & Elizabeth, b. Oct. 8, 1773	A	51
Anna R., d. Gorshom & Elizabeth, b. Mar. 19, 1788	A	51
Asa, s. Ephraim & Mary, b. Dec. 5, 1750	A	9
Benjamin, s. Ephraim & Mary, b. May 23, 1749	A	9
Benjamin, m. Dorothy **ROS[S]**, Oct. 30, 1765	A	6
Benjamin, s. Gorshom & Elizabeth, b. May 7, 1778	A	51
Charlotte, d. Benjamin & Polly, b. Oct. 4, 1804	A	51
Clarre, d. Benjamin & Dorothy, b. Jan. 16, 1776	A	25
Daniel, s. Benjamin & Dorothy, b. Aug. 9, 1772	A	15
Diadame, d. Benjamin & Dorothy, b. Nov. 23, 1779	A	33
Elizabeth, d. Gorshom & Elizabeth, b. Apr. 12, 1776	A	51
Gorshom, s. Gorshom & Elizabeth, b. June 14, 1780	A	51
Hephzibah, d. Garshom & Elizabeth, b. Sept. 11, 1766	A	51
John, s. Ephraim & Mary, b. June 22, 1758	A	9
Joseph, s. Ephraim & Mary, b. Dec. 7, 1753	A	9
Mary, d. Ephraim & Mary, b. Aug. 3, 1762	A	9
Mary, d. Benjamin & Dorothy, b. Aug. 25, 1768	A	11
Nathaniel, s. Ephraim & Mary, b. Dec. 5, 1755	A	9
Oliver, s. Benjamin & Polly, b. Sept. 4, 1812	A	51
Philander, s. Ephraim & Mary, b. Aug. 9, 1769	A	13
Polly, d. Garshom & Elizabeth, b. Sept. 25, 1770	A	51
Randal, s. Ephraim & Mary, b. June 28, 1760	A	9
Richard, s. Benjamin & Dorothy, b. May 27, 1766	A	9
Sally, d. Gorshom & Elizabeth, b. Jan. 22, 1784	A	51
Sally, m. Anthony **HORSFORD**, Nov. 16, 1803	A	52
Walter, s. Gorshom & Elizabeth, b. June 17, 1795	A	51
HICKS, James, of North Goshen, m. Roserline **HALL**, of South Canaan, Oct. 16, 1842, by Rev. Edward B. Emerson	A	102
HIDE, Bettey Rebeckah, d. Samuel & Azubah, b. June 12, 1766	A	9
Bettey Rebeckah, d. Oct. 14, 1768	A	11
Bettey Rebeckah, d. Samuel & Azubah, b. Apr. 28, 1770	A	12
Hannah, d. Samuell & Azubah, b. Nov. 1, 1756	LR2	233
Lydah, d. Samuell & Azubah, b. July 25, 1754	LR1	427
Marian, d. Samuel & Asabah, b. Jan. 25, 1773	A	17
Mary, d. Samuel & Azubah, b. Aug. 16, 1764	A	4
Samuel, of Norwich, m. Azubah **LAWRENCE**, of Canaan, Oct. 25, 1750	LR1	423
Samuel, s. Samuel & Azubah, b. Sept. 13, 1768	A	11
Solomon, s. Samuel & Asabah, b. Apr. 20, 1777	A	28
Tryphena, d. Samuel & Azubah, b. June 10, 1762	A	3
Zenus, s. Samuell, b. July 10, 1752	LR1	427

	Vol.	Page
HIDE, (cont.)		
Zenas, s. Samuell & Azubah, d. May 21, 1756	LR2	233
[HIGBY], **HIGBE**, [see also **HIGLEY**], Elizabeth, m. Jeremiah		
LAWRENCE, July 6, 1773	A	21
John, s. John & Mindwell, b. June 1, 1757	LR2	228
Mindwell, s. John & Mindwell, b. Oct. 9, 1758	LR2	228
Sarah, d. John & Mindwell, b. May 26, 1760	A	3
Submit, d. John & Mindwell, b. Dec. 10, 1761	A	3
HIGLEY, [see also **HIBGY**], Simeon, Jr., m. Wealthy **NOBLES**, of		
Canaan, Feb. 20, 1822, by Rev. Charles Prentice	A	80
HILLAS, Silas, m. Eunice **PEARCE**, June 15, 1834, by Reuben		
Hunt, J. P.	A	93
HILLS, **HILL**, Abigail, m. Jonathan **NORTH**, Nov. 5, 1778	A	31
Anson S., m. Lucy **FIELD**, b. of Canaan, Jan. 14, 1822,		
by P. Cowles	A	80
Edward M., m. Elizabeth **GILLETT**, Sept. 15, 1852, by Rev.		
Elisha Whittlesey	A	109
HINES, Bennet H., m. Lucy **WILLEY**, Apr. 9, 1843, by Charles		
Kettridge	A	103
Joel, of Norfolk, m. Emily **SPAULDING**, of Canaan, Feb.		
24, 1844, by Rev. Harley Goodwin	A	103
HING, Amos S., m. Sarah **ROOD**, Jan. 13, 1833, by Pitkin Cowles	A	91
HINMAN, Anna, d. Moses & Lydia, b. June 27, 1801	A	50
Anne, d. Joseph & Mary, b. Feb. 7, 178[ ]	A	37
Benjamin, s. Joseph & Mary, b. Nov. 28, 1766	A	15
Clarisa, d. Moses & Lydia, b. June 17, 1805	A	50
Eliza, d. Moses & Lydia, b. June 4, 1803	A	50
Eliza, of Canaan, m. Harvey **BUNNALL**, of Oxford, Jan. 11,		
1824, by Pitkin Cowles	A	83
Hannah, d. Moses & Lydia, b. Jan. 9, 1800	A	50
Isaac, s. Joseph & Mary, b. June 30, 1777	A	31
John W., s. Moses & Lydia, b. June 13, 1807	A	50
Joseph, s. Joseph & Mary, b. Jan. 23, 1770	A'	15
Joseph, 3rd, s. Joseph, Jr. & Lydia, b. May 3, 1794	A	48
Lucy P., m. Joseph M. **ROOT**, of Norfolk, Mar. 18, 1830,		
by Charles Prentice	A	88
Lydia, d. Moses & Lydia, b. May 30, 1809	A	50
Mary Ann, d. Moses & Lydia, b. May 27, 1812	A	50
Moses, s. Joseph & Mary, b. June 11, 1775	A	24
Moses, m. Lydia **WHITNEY**, June 6, 1799	A	50
Samuel, of Canaan, m. Laura **BASS**, of New Marlborough,		
Mass., June 18, 1823, by Rev. Charles Prentice	A	82
William, s. Joseph & Mary, b. Oct. 2, 1772	A	18
William B., of Sheffield, Mass., m. Almira **ROSS**, of		
Canaan, Aug. 19, 1840, by Rev. Henry H. Woodbridge, of		
the 2nd Cong. Ch.	A	99
HINSDALE, **HENSDIL**, **HENSDELL**, Aaron, s. Joseph &		
Elizabeth, b. Mar. 23, 1764	A	42

	Vol.	Page

HINSDALE, HENSDIL, HENSDELL, (cont.)

Chloe, d. Joseph & Elizabeth, b. Dec . 17, 1769	A	42
Elizabeth, d. Joseph & Elizabeth, b. Dec. 15, 1756	A	42
Elizabeth, w. Joseph, d. Oct. 24, 1789, in the 63rd y. of her age	A	42
Harry, s. William & Sarah, b. May 9, 1785	A	38
Jacob, s. Joseph & Elizabeth, b. Mar. 23, 1766	A	42
Jacob, Jr., of Brewville, O., m. Alice LOVELAND, of Canaan, Oct. 18, 1837, by H. H. Woodbridge. Int. Pub.	A	96
Joseph, m. Elizabeth KELLOGG, of Hartford, Nov. 6, 1746	A	42
Joseph, s. Joseph & Elizabeth, b. Sept. 14, 1747	A	42
Lucy, d. Joseph & Elizabeth, b. Aug. 2, 1759	A	42
Lydia, twin with Mary, d. Joseph & Elizabeth, b. Mar. 12, 1749	A	42
Lydia, m. Ozias BOARDMAN, Apr. 23, 1772	A	38
Mary, twin with Lydia, d. Joseph & Elizabeth, b. Mar. 12, 1749	A	42
Moses, s. Joseph & Elizabeth, b. May 22, 1754	A	42
Strong, s. William & Sarah, b. July 31, 1783	A	38
William, m. Sarah STRONG, June 14, 1781	A	35

HOBART, Betsey, [d. Edmond & Mehitabel], b. Nov. 4, 1781

	A	43
Betsey, [d. Edmond & Mehitabel], d. Sept. 3, 1782	A	43
Bille, [s. Edmond & Mehitabel], b. Mar. 29, 1791	A	43
Charlotte, [d. Edmond & Mehitabel], b. Dec. 17, 1779	A	43
Edmund, m. Mehitabel PECK, Jan. 1, 1776	A	43
Edmon, see Edmon HUBBARD	A	24
Esther, [d. Edmond & Mehitabel], b. May 2, 1793	A	43
Isaac, [s. Edmond & Mehitabel], b. Sept. 29, 1788	A	43
Mille, [d. Edmond & Mehitabel], b. Mar. 12, 1786; d. Dec. 7, 1793	A	43
Prescoat, s. Edmond & Mehitabel, b. Oct. 24, 1777	A	43
Rodney, [s. Edmond & Mehitabel], b. Aug. 10, 1783	A	43

HOGEBOON, HUCKABOON, Elener, m. Elisha HURLBUT, Feb. 24, 1756

	A	2
Hannah, m. Charles BELDING, June 14, 1752	LR1	427

HOLABARD, HOLOBIRD, [see also HURLBURT], Amos B., m. Polly HUNT, b. of Canaan, Oct. 30, 1822, by Rev. Charles Prentice

	A	81
Charles, s. John & Polle, b. Dec. 16, 1788	A	41
Elizabeth, m. Aeneas MUNSON, b. of Canaan, May 30, 1838, by H. H. Woodbridge	A	97
Harlow C., m. Caroline HUNT, Dec. 2, 1822, by Rev. Charles Prentice	A	82
Harriet E., m. Gerrit KELLOGG, b. of Canaan, Dec. 10, 1828, by Charles Prentice	A	86
Horatio N., m. Amanda M. BECKLEY, b. of Canaan, May 16, 1825, by Charles Prentice	A	84
John, m. Polly BELDON, Feb. 21, 1788	A	40
Mary, d. John & Mary, b. Sept. 27, 1799	A	50
Nabby, d. John & Polly, b. Sept. 4, 1791	A	41

HOLCOMB, Abigail, d. David & Sarah, b. Dec. 13, 1758 A 4

	Vol.	Page
HOLCOMB, (cont.)		
Abigail, wid., m. Samuel **DARROW**, Oct. 5, 1777	A	27
Abigail, m. Nathaniel **DEAN**, Jr., June 11, 1778	A	33
Abraham, s. David & Sarah, b. June 20, 1753	LR2	238
Abraham, s. David & Fila, b. Feb. 14, 1762	A	28
Anne, d. David & Fila, b. Oct. 31, 1760	A	28
Anne, d. Elijah & Anna, b. Feb. 8, 1774	A	30
Bethany, d. Joel, Jr. & Sarah, b. Jan. 21, 1774	A	18
Betty, d. Abraham & Betty, b. June 25, 1780	A	38
Charles, s. Abraham & Betty, b. July 14, 1782	A	38
Cloe, d. Abraham & Bette, b. Oct. 10, 1778	A	30
David, s. David & Fila, b. Jan. 26, 1777	A	28
Davis, s. Elijah, Jr. & Hannah, b. Sept. 16, 1798	A	46
Doltha, m. Heman **HOWE**, Dec. 1, 1824, by Charles Prentice	A	84
Elias Slaughter, s. Noah & Hannah, b. Apr. 22, 1775	A	24
Elijah, s. Elijah & Anne, b. Oct. 9, 1769	A	18
Elijah, Jr., m. Hannah **WELLS**, Jan. 1, 1795	A	46
Eliza, d. Elijah, Jr. & Hannah, b. Sept. 1, 1800	A	46
Elizabeth, d. David & Fila, b. Nov. 23, 1763	A	28
Elizabeth, [d. David & Fila], d. June 27, 1769	A	28
Elizabeth, d. Elijah & Anne, b. Mar. 28, 1776	A	30
Esther, d. Timothy & Abigail, b. Aug. 10, 1767	A	16
Esther, d. Timothy & Abigail, d. Jan. 16, 1773	A	19
Esther, d. Timothy & Abigail, b. Apr. 1, 1773	A	19
Esther, d. Joel & Sarah, b. Apr. 18, 1777	A	26
Fila, [d. David & Fila], b. Jan. 4, 1768	A	28
Hannah, d. Noah & Hannah, b. Dec. 31, 1788	A	44
Harriet, d. Elijah, Jr. & Hannah, b. Mar. 26, 1797	A	46
Harriet, m. Russell **MORRIS**, b. of Canaan, [June] 27, 1820, by Rev. Charles Prentice, of South Canaan	A	79
Ira, s. Joel & Sarah, b. June 7, 1775	A	23
Isaac, s. David & Sarah, b. Feb. 11, 1755	LR2	237
Isabel, b. Nov. 22, 1832	A	54
Jerome, b. Oct. 12, 1830	A	54
Jerome, m. Ellen L. **DUNNING**, Nov. 26, 1851, by Rev. Elisha Whittlesey	A	109
Joel, Jr., m. Sarah **WHITNEY**, Mar. 4, 1773	A	17
Kellogg, s. Elijah, Jr. & Hannah, b. Nov. 28, 1795	A	46
Lauria, m. Heman **HOWE**, b. of Canaan, Mar. 29, 1835, by H. H. Woodbridge	A	94
Lewis, m. Lucy Ann **McKEAN**, b. of Canaan, Nov. 8, 1830, by Pitkin Cowles	A	88
Lois, d. Amasa & Lois, b. Feb. 11, 1780	A	39
Lucia, d. Elijah & Hannah, b. Mar. 11, 1804	A	47
Lucretia, d. David & Fila, b. June 21, 1770	A	28
Martin, m. Polly M. **ROOT**, b. of Canaan, Oct. 28, 1828, by Rev. Stephen Beach, of Salisbury	A	86
Mary, d. David & Sarah, b. Feb. 11, 1755	LR2	237

	Vol.	Page

HOLCOMB, (cont.)

Mary, d. Noah & Hannah, b. Mar. 14, 1778 — A 28

Mary, of Canaan, m. Horatio N. **SMITH**, of Sharon, June
26, 1828, by Rev. Silas Ambler — A 86

Merriam, d. Noah & Hannah, b. Jan. 12, 1780 — A 36

Miles*, m. Julia **HOTCHKISS**, May [ ], 1820, by Rev. Asa
Talmage, of the Bap. Ch., Litchfield *("Milo"?) — A 79

Milo*, s. Noah & Hannah, b. Mar. 12, 1793 *("Miles"?) — A 44

Nelson, m. Charlotte E. **BECKLEY**, Aug. 31, 1831, by
Charles Prentice — A 89

Noah, m. Hannah **MARSH**, Feb. 21, 1771 — A 24

Noah, s. Noah & Hannah, b. Nov. 3, 1773 — A 24

Olive, d. Noah & Hannah, b. July 25, 1781 — A 36

Olive, d. Noah & Hannah, b. July 25, 1781 — A 38

Orange, s. Abraham & Betty, b. July 16, 1784 — A 38

Rhoda, d. Elijah & Anne, b. Aug. 22, 1767 — A 18

Rhodan, b. Feb. 16, 1810 — A 49

Riley, s. Amasa & Lois, b. Jan. 9, 1786 — A 39

Roue, d. Noah & Hannah, b. Jan. 24, 1785 — A 38

Sabra, d. Joel & Sarah, b. May 29, 1766 — A 16

Sarah, w. David, d. Jan. 11, 1762, in the 44th y. of her age — A 3

Sarah, d. David & Fila, b. May 3, 1766 — A 28

Silvey, d. Joel & Sarah, b. Feb. 14, 1764 — A 16

Solomon, s. Timothy & Abigail, b. Oct. 29, 1770 — A 16

Solomon, s. David & Fila, b. Jan. 29, 1775 — A 28

Susanna, d. Elijah & Anne, b. Nov. 28, 1771 — A 18

Sybel, d. Elijah, Jr. & Hannah, b. June 20, 1802 — A 47

Timothy, m. Abigail **ROBBINS**, May 20, 1766 — A 16

Timothy, s. Timothy & Abigail, b. June 8, 1775;
d. Sept. 18, 1775 — A 23

Timothy, Jr., d. Dec. 3, 1775 — A 24

Timothy, s. Noah & Hannah, b. Oct. 5, 1776 — A 26

Titus, s. Noah & Hannah, b. Apr. 21, 1783 — A 38

Zilpha, d. Elijah & Anne, b. Dec. 2, 1778 — A 30

HOLDRIDGE, Dudley, m. Eunice **MARKHAM**, May 5, 1768, by
Rev. Daniel Farrand — A 15

Elizabeth, d. Dudley & Eunice, b. Sept. 16, 1771 — A 15

William, s. Dudley & Eunice, b. June 9, 1769 — A 15

HOLLENBECK, Abraham, s. John & Esther, b. Sept. 15, 1770 — A 25

Elizabeth, d. John & Esther, b. June 21, 1773 — A 25

Rachel, d. John & Esther, b. Aug. 5, 1775 — A 25

HOOD, Samuel, of Canaan, m. wid. Mary **ALLEN**, of Norfolk, Oct.
8, 1820, by Pitkin Cowles — A 79

HORSFORD, HOSFORD, Abigail, d. Timothy & Nancy, b. June
16, 1749 — LR1 423

Abigail, m. Aaron **BARNES**, July 25, 1771 — A 19

Amelia, m. Harvey **CLARK**, June 3, 1837, by Erastus Doty — A 96

Amme, s. Timothy & Mehitabel, b. Apr. 4, 1791 — A 44

	Vol.	Page

HORSFORD, HOSFORD, (cont.)

	Vol.	Page
Ann, d. Timothy & Nancy, b. June 25, 1747	LR1	423
Anna, d. Timothy & Mehitabell, b. Sept. 19, 1783	A	37
Anne, m. Thomas BARNS, Apr. 24, 1770	A	15
Anthony, s. Timothy & Mehitabell, b. Dec. 21, 1781	A	37
Anthony, m. Sally HEWIT, Nov. 16, 1803	A	52
Anthony Stevens, [s. Anthony & Sally], b. June 12, 1806	A	52
Ashel, s. Jeremiah & Lucy, b. Mar. 7, 1769	A	14
Aurellia, twin with Ordelia, d. Timothy & Mehitabel, b. Apr. 23, 1800	A	47
Benjamin Hewit, [s. Anthony & Sally], b. Dec. 22, 1811	A	52
Betsey, d. Timothy & Mehitabel, b. Jan. 18, 1788	A	41
Betsey Ann, [d. Anthony & Sally], b. Mar. 25, 1821	A	52
Cate, d. Jeremiah & Lucy, b. Jan. 10, 1711* *("1771"?)	A	14
Catharine, d. Solomon & Sarah, b. Sept. 17, 1801	A	52
Chancey, s. Jeremiah, Jr. & Hannah, b. Sept. 19, 17[ ]	A	37
Daniel, s. Daniel, Jr. & Marther, b. Oct. 2, 1749	LR2	228
Daniel, d. May 23, 1777	A	26
Daniel Solomon, s. Solomon & Sarah, b. Sept. 25, 1806	A	52
David, s. Timothy & Mehitabel, b. Feb. 23, 1802	A	47
Elizabeth, d. Timothy & Nancy, b. Jan. 8, 1752	LR1	425
Elizabeth, m. Isaac TUCKER, May 9, 1782	A	37
Esther, m. Job BARNES, May 28, 1778	A	31
[E]unice, d. Jeremiah, Jr. & Hannah, b. May 17, 1786	A	39
Hannah, d. Roger & Mary, b. July 2, 1779	A	34
Hannah, d. Jeremiah, Jr. & Hannah, b. May 24, 178[ ]	A	40
Hannah, [d. Anthony & Sally], b. Oct. 11, 1823	A	52
Harriet, [d. Anthony & Sally], b. Mar. 31, 1809	A	52
Hester, d. Timothy & Nancy, b. Dec. 26, 1754	LR1	425
Jeremiah, m. Lucy BURNHAM, of Windsor, May 26, 1757, by Roger Woolcot, Jr.	A	2
Jeremiah, s. Jeremiah & Lucy, b. Sept. 12, 1760	A	2
Jeremiah, Jr., m. Hannah DEAN, Jan. 1, 1784	A	37
Joel, s. Daniel & Martha, b. Jan. 13, 1751/2	LR1	427
John Laman, s. Solomon & Sarah, b. Feb. 27, 1805	A	52
Julius C., m. Esther M. WICKHAM, b. of Canaan, Aug. 22, 1831, by Charles Prentice	A	89
Lois, d. Timothy & Mehitabel, b. July 14, 1793	A	44
Lucy, d. Jeremiah & Lucy, b. Aug. 27, 1758	A	2
Luther, s. Samuell & Anne, b. Jan. 16, 1784	A	37
Marthar, d. Daniel, Jr. & Marthar, b. Oct. 14, 1758	LR2	228
Martha, d. Daniel & Martha, d. Oct. 16, 1759	LR2	228
Martha, d. Daniel & Martha, b. Nov. 4, 1762	A	3
Mehitabel, d. Timothy & Mehitabel, b. Feb. 23, 1797	A	44
Mehitabel, [d. Anthomy & Sally], b. June 21, 1813	A	52
Ordelia, twin with Aurellia, d. Timothy & Mehitabel, b. Apr. 23, 1800	A	47
Orilla, m. Joel ROOT, July 9, 1820, by Rev. Asa Talmage,		

	Vol.	Page
HORSFORD, HOSFORD, (cont.)		
of the Bap. Ch. Litchfield	A	79
Roger, s. Daniel, Jr. & Marthar, b. Jan. 21, 1754	LR2	228
Sally Ann, [d. Anthony & Sally], b. July 27, 1818	A	52
Samuell, s. Jeremiah & Lucy, b. Oct. 29, 1762	A	4
Samuel, m. Anne DENSMORE, June 22, 1783	A	37
Sarah, m. William DEMING, Mar. 9, 1851, by Rev.		
Zephaniah D. Scobey	A	108
Sarah Ann, d. Solomon & Sarah, b. Apr. 16, 1811	A	52
Selah, s. Jeremiah & Lucy, b. May 4, 1767	A	10
Solomon, s. Jeremiah & Lucy, b. Mar. 21, 1773	A	22
Susanna, d. Jeremiah & Lucy, b. Apr. 4, 1765	A	5
Timothy, s. Timothy & Nancy, b. Dec. 25, 1757	LR2	232
Timothy, m. Mehitabell ROOT, Dec. 25, 1780	A	37
Timothy, s. Timothy & Mehitabel, b. Sept. 17, 1795	A	44
Walter, [s. Anthony & Sally], b. Oct. 23, 1816	A	52
Zilpha, d. Timothy & Mehitabel, b. Feb. 17, 1786	A	40
HOSKINS, Almira, m. Elihu JOHNSON, b. of Canaan, Aug. 6,		
1826, by Rev. Epaphras Goodman	A	85
Ann, m. Roderick YALE, Nov. 13, 1826, by Charles Prentice	A	85
Charlotte Ann, m. Frederick H. LOWRY, b. of Canaan, Oct.		
1, 1823, by Rev. Charles Prentice	A	82
Corinthia, m. Henry BOARDMAN, June 3, 1832	A	54
Corintha, m. Henry BOARDMAN, June 3, 1832, by Charles		
Prentice	A	90
Emeline, of Canaan, m. Frederick J. FENN, of Washington,		
Dec. 11, 1823, by Charles Prentice	A	83
Ezekiel S., m. Abia A. DEMING, b. of Canaan, Mar. 7,		
1839, by H. H. Woodbridge	A	98
Harriet, of Canaan, m. Nathaniel BRENTON, of Salisbury,		
May 22, 1836, by [ ]	A	95
Hilpa, m. Henry POST, b. of Canaan, May 18, 1831, by		
Charles Prentice	A	89
Julia, m. John B. REED, Feb. 20, 1828, by Charles Prentice	A	86
Sarah G., of Canaan, m. Theodore PRENTICE, of Bridgeport,		
[Oct. 31, 1841], by Rev. Edward B. Emerson, of the 1st		
Cong. Ch.	A	101
HOSMER, Amelia, d. Thomas & Hannah, b. Jan. 23, 1795	A	43
Ashbel, m. Polly BELDING, 2nd, Nov. 2, 1783	A	38
Ashbel Alfred, s. Ashbel & Polly, b. Mar. 9, 1786	A	42
Elizabeth, [d. Thomas & Elizabth], b. Nov. 22, 1782,		
at Winchester	A	36
Elizabeth, m. Samuel AUSTIN, Nov. 27, 1791	A	46
Hannah, [d. Thomas & Hannah], b. June 27, 1782	A	36
Jonathan Belden, s. Ashbel & Polly, b. Feb. 4, 1792	A	42
Lydia, d. Ashbel & Polly, b. Apr. 24, 1790	A	42
Nabby, d. Ashbel & Polly, b. Mar. 10, 1788	A	42
Polly, d. Ashbel & Polly, b. Aug. 8, 1784	A	38

	Vol.	Page

HOSMER, (cont.)

Sherman, s. Thomas & Hannah, b. Sept. 20, 1786 — A 40

Thomas, [s. Thomas & Elizabeth], b. Oct. 12, 1767,
at Winchester — A 36

Tryphena, [d. Thomas & Elizabeth], b. Dec. 13, 1769,
at Winchester — A 36

Weltha, [d. Thomas & Hannah], b. Apr. 27, 1778 — A 36

HOTCHKISS, Julia, m. Miles **HOLCOMB**, May [ ], 1820, by
Rev. Asa Talmage, of the Bap. Ch., Litchfield — A 79

HOWD, HOUD, Henry, m. Agatha **LANDON**, b. of Canaan, Nov.
26, 1825, by Charles Prentice — A 85

Orie, of Canaan, m. James **WOODWORTH**, of Litchfield,
Nov. 13, 1821, by Rev. Charles Prentice — A 80

HOWE, HOW, HOWES, Abigail, d. Samuel, Jr. & Mary, b. Sept.
10, 1764* *(Written below, "Aug. 10, 1764") — A 5

Alice, of Canaan, m. Alexander **NORTON**, Jr., of Goshen,
Jan. 30, 1827, by Charles Prentice — A 86

Baits Hait, s. Samuel, 2nd & Lydia, b. Oct. 15, 1776 — A 27

Bowers, s. Samuel & Lydia, b. Mar. 26, 1769 — A 18

George, m. Abigail J. **KNAPP**, Oct. 24, 1822, by Pitkin
Cowles — A 81

Heman, m. Doltha **HOLCOMB**, Dec. 1, 1824, by Charles
Prentice — A 84

Heman, m. Lauria **HOLCOMB**, b. of Canaan, Mar. 29, 1835,
by H. H. Woodbridge — A 94

Isaac, m. Mary **CANDE**, Nov. 22, 1764 — A 7

Jacob, s. Samuell & Martha, b. Aug. 12, 1750 — A 3

James, s. Samuell & Martha, b. June 8, 17[5]2 — A 3

James, s. Samuel, 2nd & Lydia, b. Mar. 26, 1775 — A 27

Jeremiah, s. Jeremiah & Martha, b. Apr. 18, 1769 — A 14

Josiah, s. Samuel & Mary, b. Aug. 7, 1763 — A 5

Judeth, d. Jeremiah & Martha, b. Aug. 8, 1765 — A 7

Keziah, d. Samuell & Martha, b. Mar. 18, 1755 — A 3

Lois, twin with Lydia, d. Samuel & Lydia, b. June 12, 1771 — A 18

Lydia, twin with Lois, d. Samuel & Lydia, b. June 12, 1771 — A 18

Martha, d. Samuell & Martha, b. Aug. 17, 1757 — A 3

Martha, d. Jeremiah & Martha, b. Jan. 16, 1767 — A 10

Mary, d. Samuell & Martha, b. June 6, 1762 — A 3

Mary, w. Samuel, Jr., d. Dec. 15, 1766 — A 18

Nathaniel, Jr., m. Eleanor **WARNER**, of Suffield,
Nov. 10, 1768 — A 11

Nelson, m. Irene **DEAN**, Feb. 9, 1851, by Rev. Zephaniah
D. Scobey — A 108

Phebe, m. John **STEVENS**, Jan. 2, 1759 — LR2 228

Philip, s. Samuell & Martha, b. Feb. 20, 1759 — A 3

Samantha, m. Edwin **JUDD**, b. of Canaan, Mar. 19, 1837,
by Rev. H. H. Woodbridge, of the 2nd Cong. Ch. — A 96

Samuel, Jr., m. Mary **TURNER**, Sept. 29, 1763 — A 5

	Vol.	Page

HOWE, HOW, HOWES, (cont.)

Samuel, Jr., m,. Lydia **PAIN**, June 30, 1768 — A — 18

Sarah, w. Nathaniel, d. Oct. 21, 1778 — A — 29

Sarah, m. Abiel **FELLOWS**, Dec. 1, 1796 — A — 43

Sarah Ann, of Canaan, m. Milo **TOLLMADE**, of Lee, Mass.,
Dec. 23, 1829, by Charles Pentice — A — 87

Solomon, s. Jeremiah & Martha, b. July 7, 1771 — A — 14

Solomon M., m. Jane E. **YALE**, b. of Canaan, Nov. 3, 1840,
by Rev. H. H. Woodbridge, of the 2nd Cong. Ch. Int.
Pub. — A — 99

HOWEL, Sarah, d. Benjamin & Dorothy, b. July 29, 1778 — A — 29

HUBBARD*, Edmon, m. Mehetabel **PECK**, Jan. 1, 1776
*("**HOBART**" overwritten) — A — 24

Jane E., of Salisbury, m. John **PARKER**, of Essex, Apr.
7, 1850, by Rev. D. D. Francis — A — 108

HUBBELL, Maria, of Salisbury, m. Whiting H.
KNICKERBOCKER, of Canaan, Jan. 26, 1834, by Rev.
Henry H. Woodbridge, of the 2nd Cong. Ch. — A — 92

HUCKABOON, [see under **HOGEBOON**]

HUDSEL, Cynthia, m. William **PERKINS**, b. of Marlborough, Feb.
17, 1833, by Theodosius Clark — A — 91

HUDSON, Luke, of New Marlborough, Mass., m. Deidamia
HART, of Canaan, Dec. 11, 1849, by Rev. Z. D. Scobey,
of S. Canaan — A — 105

HUGG, Daniel, s. William & Margrit, b. Jan. 25, 1770 — A — 14

Isaac, d. William & Margret, b. May 9, 1757 — LR2 — 233

John, s. William & Margaret, b. Nov 8, 1767 — A — 14

Margaret, w. William, d. Mar. 9, 1772 — A — 18

Thankfull, d. William & Margret, b. May 29, 1762 — A — 14

William, m. Margaret **JOHNSON**, July 14, 1756, by Rev.
Mr. Farrand — LR2 — 233

William, s. William & Margrit, b. Dec. 18, 1764 — A — 14

William, m. Olive **FOX**, Feb. 16, 1776 — A — 24

HUMPHREY, Charles, of Tolland, m. Elizabeth A. **COOPER**, of
Canaan, Nov. 29, 1835, by Rev. Thomas Sparkes — A — 94

Henry, of Goshen, m. Martha **CATLIN**, of Canaan, Oct. 11,
1832, by Charles Prentice — A — 90

HUNT, Amos, s. Robert & Rebeckah, b. July 14, 1754 — A — 5

Amos, s. Russell & Lydia, b. May 6, 1774 — A — 23

Betsey, d. Salmon & Ruby, b. Mar. 7, 1791 — A — 47

Caroline, m. Harlow C. **HOLOBIRD**, Dec. 2, 1822, by Rev.
Charles Prentice — A — 82

Charles, m. Parmelia S. **BATES**, Apr. 29, 1841, by Rev. H.
H. Woodbridge, of the 2nd Cong. Ch. — A — 100

Charles, his w. [ ], d. [ ], 1842 — A — 53

Charles, his w. [ ], d. [ ] — A — 53

Charles Sedgwick, b. Apr. 7, 1842 — A — 53

Charlotte, of Canaan, m. Lewis B. **STURGIS**, of Sharon,

	Vol.	Page
HUMPHREY, (cont.)		
June 18, 1828, by Charles Prentice	A	86
Chauncey L., m. Ruthilda H. **PEAK**, b. of Canaan, [June 28, 1841], by Rev. Edward B. Emerson, of South Canaan	A	100
Cloe, d. Robert & Rebeckah, b. Feb. 3, 1759	A	5
Clarissa, m. Seymour **DEMING**, Jan. 8, 1828, by Charles Prentice	A	86
Cyrus, s. Russell & Lydia, b. Sept 25, 1769	A	23
Cyrus d., s. Salmon & Ruby, b. Aug. 28, 1787	A	47
David, s. Russell & Lydia, b. Apr. 22, 1767	A	23
Edward P., m. Carstine **BINGHAM**, b. of Canaan, Sept. 24, 1833, by Charles Prentice	A	91
Emeline, m. Reuben **HUNT**, Nov. 26, 1820, by Joshua Cornwall, J. P.	A	79
George Beebe, b. June 21, 1834	A	53
Hiram, s. Salmon & Ruby, b. May 28, 1795	A	47
Isaac, s. Russell & Lydia, b. Apr. 9, 1759	A	2
Lucy Caroline, b. Jan. 13, 1836	A	53
Lydia, d. Russell & Lydia, b. Feb. 18, 1772	A	23
Mary, of Canaan, m. Albert **SEDGWICK**, of Cornwall, Oct. 23, 1822, by Rev. Charles Prentice	A	81
Minervy, d. Salmon & Ruby, b. May 6, 1803	A	47
Phinehas, of Sharon, m. Charlotte **MILLS**, of Canaan, Jan. 6, 1830, by Pitkin Cowles	A	87
Poliy, d. Salmon & Ruby, b. Oct. 2, 1799	A	47
Polly, m. Amos B. **HOLOBIRD**, b. of Canaan, Oct. 30, 1822, by Rev. Charles Prentice	A	81
Reuben, s. Salmon & Ruby, b. Apr. 27, 1788	A	47
Reuben, m. Emeline **HUNT**, Nov. 26, 1820, by Joshua Cornwall, J. P.	A	79
Robert, of Canaan, m. Rebeckah **PECK**, d. Isaac, Dec. 26, 1753	LR2	238
Russell, s. Robert & Rebeckah, b. Mar. 11, 1756	A	5
Russell, m. Lydia **PECK**, May 3, 1758, by Rev. Mr. Farrand	A	2
Russell, s. Russell & Lydia, b. Oct. 11, 1762	A	5
Salmon, s. Russell & Lydia, b. Jan. 23, 1765	A	5
Salmon, s. Salmon & Ruby, b. Aug. 7, 1796	A	47
Samson Robert, s. Robert & Rebeckah, b. Feb. 23, 1761	A	5
Sarah, d. Robert & Rebeckah, b. June 11, 1763	A	5
HUNTINGTON, John, of Canaan, m. Julia M. **ADAMS**, of New Marlborough, Mass., Dec. 16, 1845, by Rev. D. D. Francis	A	106
Martha, m. Wilber C. **ROOD**, Aug. 21, 1845, by Lyman Lawrence, J. P.	A	104
Matilda, m. Salmon **PEASE**, June 14, 1803	A	51
HUNTLEY, Marcus, of Salisbury, m. Lucy **COLLINS**, of Canaan, July 2, 1837, by Aaron Rogers	A	96
HURD, Albert, of Goshen, m. Mary **DEAN**, of Canaan, Dec. 11,		

	Vol.	Page
HURD, (cont.)		
1831, by Charles Prentice	A	89
HURLBURT, HURLBUT, [see also **HOLABARD**], Anne, m.		
Elijah **KELLOGG**, Aug. 8, 1764	A	5
Bartholomew, s. Elisha & Elener, b. June 11, 1763	A	5
Catharine, d. Ira & Mabel, b. Aug. 12, 1807	A	52
Charlotte M., of Canaan, m. Uri **BRADFORD**, of Cornwall,		
Mar. 21, 1841, by Rev. Edward B. Emerson	A	100
Elisha, m. Elener **HUCKABOON**, Feb. 24, 1756	A	2
Elisha, s. Elisha & Elener, b. June 3, 1760	A	2
Elizabeth, d. Elisha & Elener, b. Jan. 27, 1758	A	2
Eunice, m. Samuel **WILLARD**, June 26, 1788	A	40
Ezra, s. Ira & Mabel, b. Dec. 21, 1809	A	52
Frederick W., s. Ira & Mabel, b. Oct. 13, 1805	A	52
Hannah, of Cornwall, m. Jacob **BROWN**, of Canaan, Mar. 5,		
1752	LR1	427
Jacob, m. Submit **GOODWIN**, Jan. 2, 1777	A	25
Jain, m. Asa **DEAN**, Feb. 27, 1783	A	38
Joseph, of Darien, m. Maria **BEEBE**, of Canaan, Nov. 26,		
1835, by Charles Prentice	A	94
Josiah, s. Elisha & Elener, b. Feb. 13, 1762	A	5
Lucinda, m. Julius **MANSFIELD**, b. of Canaan, Dec. 17,		
1828, by Charles Prentice	A	87
Lucy, d. Elisha & Elener, b. Dec. 11, 1756	A	2
Mabel, d. Ira & Diana, b. Dec. 31, 1814	A	52
Mary Ann, d. Ira & Diana, b. June 30, 1821	A	52
Melinda H., m. Porter **WHITE**, b. of Canaan, Mar. 21, 1841,		
by Rev. H. H. Woodbridge, of the 2nd Cong. Ch.	A	100
Yonake(?), d. Elisha & Elener, b. Feb. 20, 1759	A	2
HUXLEY, Asael, s. Jared, Jr. & Abigail, b. Mar. 15, 1770	A	13
Jared, Jr., m. Abigail **CAMFIELD**, Nov. 1, 1764	A	10
Lavina, d. Jared, Jr. & Abigail, b. June 26, 1767	A	10
Leah, m. Joseph **FELLOWS**, Mar. 7, 1754, by Rev. Mr.		
Farrand	A	4
Thankfull, d. Jared, Jr. & Abigail, b. Aug. 22, 1765	A	10
Thankfull, d. Jared, Jr. & Abigail, d. July 29, 1768	A	13
Thankfull, d. Jared, Jr. & Abigail, b. Oct. 30, 1768	A	13
INGRAHAM, [see also **INGRAM**], Asa, m. Charlotte **LANDON**,		
b. of Canaan, Oct. 8, 1828, by Charles Prentice	A	86
Harriet, m. Adam W. **MAINE**, b. of Canaan, June 2, 1833,		
by Charles Prentice. Int. Pub. May 31, 1833	A	91
INGRAM, [see also **INGRAHAM**], Hannah, Mrs. of Canaan, m.		
Lemuel **SPARKS**, of Sheffield, Mass., Sept. 1, 1844, by		
Rev. Stephen J. Stebbins	A	103
ISHAM, Sophia R., of Canaan, m. Sidney **STILLMAN**, of		
Henesdale, Pa., Sept. 25, 1839, by Rev. H. H.		
Woodbridge, of the 2nd Cong. Ch.	A	98
JACKSON, Charles, of Canaan, m. Eliza **FRANCIS**, of Salisbury,		

	Vol.	Page

JACKSON, (cont.)

July 18, 1824, by Pitkin Cowles — A 83

Mary, m. Edward B. **BENTON**, b. of Sheffield, Mass., Jan.
28, 1850, by Rev. D. D. Francis — A 108

JACKWAYS, [see under **JACQUES**]

JACOBS, JACOB, Ann, m. Jeremiah **BELDEN**, Jr., Feb. 11 , 1830,
by Charles Prentice — A 88

Himan, of Salisbury, m. Maria **DEAN**, of Canaan, May 1,
1822, by Rev. Charles Prentice — A 81

Jane, d. Himan & Lucretia, b. Oct. 29, 1792 — A 44

Sally, d. Himan & Lucretia, b. Nov. 29, 1797 — A 45

Samuel, s. Hyman & Aurelia, b. Oct. 14, 1790 — A 42

[JACQUES], JACKWAYS, JAKWAYS, JAQUA, JAKWAY,

Daniel, Jr., m. Lucy **DAY**, b. of Canaan, Jan. 21, 1822,
by P. Cowles — A 80

Elizabeth, m. Batchley T. **DAVIS**, b. of Canaan, May 6,
1827, by Pitkin Cowles — A 86

Mary J., of Canaan, m. Timothy P. **SKINNER**, of Winsted,
Mar. 22, 1840, by Rev. H. H. Woodbridge, of the 2nd
Cong. Ch. — A 99

Minerva Ann, of Canaan, m. William **BALDWIN**, of
Barkhamsted, Nov. 11, 1840, by Rev. H. H. Woodbridge,
of the 2nd Cong. Ch. Int. Pub. — A 99

Sarah, d. Ebenezer, m. John **BROWN**, May 19, 1785 — A 45

Stephen, m. Lucy **COBB**, b. of Canaan, Oct. 8, 1828, by
Pitkin Cowles — A 86

Tryphena, d. Ebenezer, m. Rufus **CLARK**, Aug. 4, 1785 — A 45

JAKWAY, [see under **JACQUES**]

JAMES, Joseph, m. Harriet M. **DEMING**, b. of Canaan, [Mar. 1,
1843], by Rev. Edward B. Emerson — A 103

JAQUA, [see under **JACQUES**]

JENCKS, JENCKES, Benjamin Welch, s. Nathan & Charlotte, b.
Sept. 30, 1809 — A 49

Betsey, d. Nathan & Charlotte, b. Aug. 9, 1813 — A 49

Charles, s. Nathan & Charlotte, b. Nov. 26, 1807 — A 49

Charlotte, d. Nathan & Charlotte, b. Jan. 17, 1801 — A 49

Elizabeth, d. Nathan & Charlotte, b. Nov. 22, 1798 — A 49

Jane Mariah, d. Nathan & Charlotte, b. Oct. 10, 1811 — A 49

Lucy Walter, d. Nathan & Charlotte, b. Sept. 27, 1805;
d. Feb. 26, 1807 — A 49

JEWEL, Oliver, m. Amy **STEVENS**, Feb. 23, 1777 — A 26

JOHNS, Lucretia, m. Benajah **DOUGLASS**, Nov. 28, 1822, by
Pitkin Cowles — A 82

JOHNSON, Albert, of Salisbury, m. Sarah D. **CATLIN**, of Canaan,
Apr. 17, 1834, by Rev. Aaron S. Hill — A 92

Alvina, of Canaan, m. Russell **PENDLETON**, of Goshen, Feb.
8, 1831, by Rev. Bradley Sillick — A 88

Asa, of Canaan, m. Thankfull **COWLES**, Apr. 28, 1757, by

	Vol.	Page
JOHNSON, (cont.)		
Rev. Daniel Farrand	LR2	227
Benjamin, s. Asa & Thankfull, b. Apr. 10, 1758	LR2	227
Ebenezer, s. Timothy & Mary, b. Aug. 9, 1754	LR2	233
Ebenezer, s. Timothy & Mary, d. Nov. 21, 1754	LR2	233
Edwin W., m. Sabina E. **SNYDER,** Feb. 9, 1851*, by Rev.		
Zephaniah D. Scobey *(Arnold Copy had "1857")	A	108
Elihu, m. Almira **HOSKINS,** b. of Canaan, Aug. 6, 1826,		
by Rev. Epaphras Goodman	A	85
Emma, b. Mar. 18, 1841, at Philadelphia, Pa.; m. Henry		
M. **DEAN,** June 28, 1866, at Philadelphia, Pa.	A	133
Hannah, d. Asa & Thankfull, b. Oct. 29, 1760	A	1
Hannah, m. Joseph **MOSELEY,** b. of Sheffield, June 18,		
1831, by Pitkin Cowles	A	89
Hiram, m. Laura **YALE,** Mar. 7, 1821, by Benjamin Sedgwick,		
J. P.	A	79
Lucy L., of Canaan, m. Harmon L. **STRONG,** of Salisbury,		
Aug. 23, 1840, by Rev. Henry H. Woodbridge, of the 2nd		
Cong. Ch. Int. Pub.	A	99
Margaret, m. William **HUGG,** July 14, 1756, by Rev. Mr.		
Farrand	LR2	233
Mary, d. Timothy & Mary, b. July 26, 1755	LR2	233
Mary, d. Timothy & Mary, d. Oct. 24, 1755	LR2	233
Mary Ann, m. George L. **PAGE,** b. of South Canaan, [Sept. 4,		
1842], by Rev. Edward B. Emerson	A	102
Rahamah, d. Elisha & Mary, b. July 16, 1763	A	5
Submit, m. Daniel **HARRIS,** Jr., Feb. 23, 1764, by Rev.		
Mr. Farrand	A	4
Thankfull, d. Timothy & Mary, b. July 22, 1756	LR2	233
Thankfull, d. Timothy & Mary, d. July 29, 1756	LR2	233
Timothy, of Canaan, m. Mary **PHELPS,** of Winsor, Dec. 5,		
1753	LR2	233
JONES, Ann, m. Daniel **RUSSELL,** Mar. 23, 1758	LR2	228
George, m. Mary **MO[O]RE,** b. of Canaan, Apr. 18, 1841,		
by Rev. H. H. Woodbridge	A	100
Rachel, m. John **DEAN,** 2nd, Mar. 1, 1759, by Rev. Mr.		
Farrand	LR2	227
JOSLIN, Milton, m. Lucy M. **ADAM,** Nov. 3, 1831	A	53
Milton, of Southbridge, Mass., m. Lucy M. **ADAM,** of Canaan,		
Nov. 3, 1831, by Pitkin Cowles	A	89
Richard E., of Pittsfield, N. Y., m. Sarah R. **FRENCH,**		
of Canaan, Nov. 16, 1846, by Rev. D. D. Francis	A	107
JUDD, Edwin, m. Samantha **HOWE,** b. of Canaan, Mar. 19, 1837,		
by Rev. H. H. Woodbridge, of the 2nd Cong. Ch.	A	96
Frederick, m. Charity **YALE,** b. of Canaan, Mar. 3, 1825,		
by Charles Prentice	A	84
Julia, m. Hiram W. **PECK,** May 3, 1831, by Daniel Coe	A	89
Maria, m. Harvey **MUNSON,** b. of Canaan, Sept. 24, 1822,		

	Vol.	Page
JUDD, (cont.)		
by Charles Prentice	A	81
KAIN, Naomi, of Canaan, m. Obed **FREEMAN,** of Cornwall, Apr. 6, 1826, by Rev. Elbert Osbom	A	85
KASSON, Salmon, of New Marlborough, Mass., m. Sarah **SMITH,** of Canaan, [ ], by Rev. Edward B. Emerson, Recorded Mar. 28, 1842	A	101
KEELIER, Matilda, of Walkill, Orange Co., N. Y., m. Henry S. **BRACKETT,** of Canaan, Mar. 31, 1840, by Rev. H. H. Woodbridge, of the 2nd Cong. Ch.	A	99
KELLEY, William H., of Durham, m. Mary A. **BOSTWICK,** of New Milford, Nov. 12, 1850, by Rev. Harley Goodwin	A	108
KELLOGG, Aaron, m. Tabitha **HANCOX,** Apr. 22, 1762, by Rev. Mr. Farrand	A	3
Albert B., of Sheffield, m. Rhoda **LAWRENCE,** of Canaan, Nov. 22, 1820, by Pitkin Cowles	A	79
Alma, m. William **DOOLITTLE,** b. of Canaan, Mar. 8, 1841, by Rev. H. H. Woodbridge	A	100
Amey E., m. Wesley **TRESCOTT,** b. of Canaan, July 12, 1842, by Rev. H. H. Woodbridge, of the 2nd Ch. Int. Pub.	A	101
Ann, m. Albert H. **WITHERELL,** b. of Canaan, Nov. 26, 1840, by Rev. H. H. Woodbridge, of the 2nd Cong. Ch.	A	99
Anna, m. James **MARSH,** June 20, 1765	A	6
Anne, d. Asahel & Naoma, b. Apr. 1, 1779	A	32
Asahel, m. Naoma **GAYLORD,** Sept. 10, 1778	A	32
Asahel, s. Asahel & Naoma, b. July 3, 1785	A	38
Asahel, m. Harriet Anna **BECKLEY,** b. of Canaan, Jan. 10, 1838, by H. H. Woodbridge	A	97
Asahel, m. Lucy A. **BECKLEY,** b. of Canaan, May 22, 1843, by Charles Kittridge	A	103
Benjamin, m. Comfort **THOMPSON,** of Wallingford, Nov. 20, 1754	A	2
Betsey Ann, m. Harvey **KELLOGG,** b. of Canaan, Oct. 20, 1835, by Charles Prentice	A	94
Charles, s. Joseph & Martha, b. Oct. 17, 1810	A	50
Charles, m. Adeline **PECK,** of Canaan, Jan. 16, 1839, by H. H. Woodbridge. Int. Pub.	A	98
Comfort, d. Benjamin & Comfort, b. Mar. 14, 1765	A	5
Ebenezer, s. Benjamin & Elizabeth, b. Oct. 25, 1750	LR1	425
Elijah, m. Anne **HURLBURT,** Aug. 8, 1764	A	5
Elizabeth, of Hartford, m. Joseph **HENSDIL,** Nov. 6, 1746	A	42
Elizabeth, d. Benjamin & Elizabeth, b. Mar. 15, 1753	LR2	239
Elizabeth, d. Joseph, Jr. & Prudence, b. Jan. 29, 1775	A	27
Elizabeth, d. Joseph, b. Jan. 29, 1775	A	46
Elizabeth, m. Jeremiah **BELDEN,** Feb. 18, 1796	A	46
Gerrit, m. Harriet E. **HOLOBIRD,** b. of Canaan, Dec. 10, 1828, by Charles Prentice	A	86

	Vol.	Page
KELLOGG, (cont.)		
Harvey, m. Betsey Ann **KELLOGG**, b. of Canaan, Oct. 20, 1835, by Charles Prentice	A	94
Henry, s. Joseph & Martha, b. Jan. 19, 1843	A	50
Isaac, s. Benjamin & Comfort, b. Sept. 21, 1755	A	2
Isaac, s. Joseph & Martha, b. Feb. 16, 1809	A	50
Isaac, m. Sarah Ann **BELDEN**, b. of Canaan, Feb. 6, 1833, by Charles Prentice	A	91
Joseph, Jr., m. Prudence **AUSTIN**, Mar. 10, 1774	A	27
Joseph, s. Joseph & Prudence, b. Sept. 18, 1778	A	31
Joseph Jr., m. Martha **BEEBE**, Oct. 13, 1803	A	47
Joseph E., s. Joseph, Jr. & Martha, b. Apr. 4, 1806	A	47
Martha, d. Joseph, Jr. & Martha, b. Oct. 14, 1804	A	47
Mary, d. Benjamin & Elizabeth, b. Jan. 17, 1748/9	LR1	425
Naoma, d. Ashbel & Naoma, b. Nov. 2, 1780	A	35
Nehemiah, s. Beniaman & Elizabeth, b. Mar. 4, 1747	LR1	425
Permela, d. Benjamin & Comfort, b. Oct. 19, 1762	A	5
Pheletus, s. Benjamin & Comfort, b. Apr. 22, 1760	A	2
Prudence, d. Joseph, Jr. & Prudence, b. Aug. 15, 1780	A	33
Rhoda, m. Samuel **SHAD**, Jan. 23, 1777	A	25
Ruth A., of Sandisfield, Co. of Berkshire, Mass., m. George M. **SEWARD**, of Canaan, Sept. 28, 1845, by Rev. D. D. Francis	A	106
Samuell, s. Benjamin & Comfort, b. Nov. 11, 1757	A	2
Samuel, s. Benjamin & Comfort, d. Dec. 19, 1759	A	2
Sarah, d. Elijah & Anne, b. Sept. 19, 1764	A	5
Sible, m. Jonathan **HANCOX**, Apr. 8, 1754, by Rev. Mr. Farrand	LR2	237
Tabitha, d. A[a]ron & Tabitha, b. Oct. 10, 1763	A	5
Tabitha, w. Aron, d. Oct. 30, 1763	A	5
Tabithy, m. Bartholomew **BELDING**, Jan. 11, 1780	A	38
Whiting Gaylord, s. Asahel & Naoma, b. May 23, 1783	A	38
KELSEY, David, m. Ruth **MILLER**, May [ ], 1823, by William Holobird, J. P.	A	82
KENT, Seth, m. Lois **BLOGIT**, Jan. 27, 1756	LR2	237
KETHAM, Anne, m. Luke **KNAP[P]**, July 18, 1764	A	32
KING, Orrin, of Sheffield, m. Elmira **CLARK**, of Jefferson, N. Y., Nov. 22, 1835, by Charles Prentice	A	94
KINGMAN, Betsey, d. Joseph & Sarah, b. Apr. 3, 1779	A	31
Betse Lawrence, d. Joseph & Sarah, b. Apr. 3, 1779	A	30
Eunice, m. Giles **HAMLIN**, May 20, 1762	A	9
Joseph, m. Sarah **LAWRENCE**, Sept. 15, 1774	A	26
William Henry, s. Joseph & Sarah, b. July 6, 1775	A	26
KINGSBURY, Abigail, d. Lemuel & Mary, b. Feb. 24, 1772	A	32
Abigail, [d. Lemuel & Mary], d. Aug. 12, 1776	A	32
Amy, d. Lemuel & Mary, b. Aug. 4, 1776	A	32
Charles William, s. William & Sally A., b. Aug. 25, 1816	A	52
Elizabeth, d. Andrew & Persilla, b. June 14, 1777	A	42

	Vol.	Page

KINGSBURY, (cont.)

Elizabeth, d. Stephen & Susanna, b. Feb. 3, 1787	A	41
Esther, d. Lemuel & Mary, b. Feb. 2, 1784; d. June 16, 1786	A	39
George, s. Lemuel & Mary, b. Jan. 23, 1770	A	32
Guy Marsh, s. William & Sally A., b. Aug. 18, 1809	A	48
Guy Marsh, s. William & Abigail, b. Aug. 18, 1809	A	49
John, s. Andrew & Persilla, b. Nov. 24, 1779	A	42
John Arthur, s. William & Abigail, b. Nov. 30, 1811	A	49
Joshua, s. Lemuel & Mary, b. Feb. 13, 1768	A	11
Joshua, s. Lemuel & Mary, b. Feb. 13, 1768	A	32
Lemuel, m. Mary WHITNEY, May 7, 1767	A	11
Lemuel, m. Mary WHITING*, May 7, 1767 *(Overwritten to read "WHITNEY")	A	32
Lucy, d. Lemuel & Mary, b. Dec. 4, 1778; d. June 23, 1786	A	32
Mary, d. Lemuel & Mary, b. Nov. 12, 1785; d. Sept [ ], 1786	A	39
Nancy, d. Stephen & Susanna, b. Aug. 11, 1789	A	41
Stephen, m. Susanna FELLOWS, Aug. 30, 1784	A	41
William, s. Lemuel & Mary, b. June 16, 1774	A	32
William, m. Sally Abigail MARSH, July 22, 1801	A	48
William, m. Abigail Sally MARSH, July 22, 1801	A	49

KNAPP, KNAP, Abigail J., m. George HOWES, Oct. 24, 1822, by

Pitkin Cowles	A	81
Anne, d. Luke & Anne, b. Apr. 15, 1776	A	33
Daniel, s. Luke & Anne, b. Aug. 14, 1765	A	32
Elihu Ketham, s. Luke & Anne, b. Jan. 10, 1768	A	32
Harriet, m. Charles LEWIS, b. of Canaan, Jan. 26, 1829, by Pitkin Cowles	A	87
Jacob, s. Luke & Anne, b. July 6, 1772	A	33
Luke, m. Anne KETHAM, July 18, 1764	A	32
Rachel, d. Luke & Anne, b. Apr. 25, 1770	A	32
Rachel, m. Samuel CLINTON, Oct. 27, 1822, by B. Knapp, J. P.	A	81
Sabra, d. Luke & Anna, b. Jan. 27, 1780	A	33
Zadock, s. Luke & Anne, b. Aug. 17, 1774	A	33

KNICKERBOCKER, Whiting H., of Canaan, m. Maria

HUBBELL, of Salisbury, Jan. 26, 1834, by Rev. Henry H. Woodbridge, of the 2nd Cong. Ch.	A	92

LADD, Cyrus, s. Eliphalet & Betsey, b. Nov. 29, 1795

	A	43
Eliphalet, m. Betsey FRINK, Jan. 29, 1794	A	43

LAKE, Lura, m. Elijah BULLARD, Nov. 5, 1822, by Bushnell

Knapp, J. P.	A	82

LANDON, Agatha, m. Henry HOWD, b. of Canaan, Nov. 26, 1825,

by Charles Prentice	A	85
Alice, m. Thomas BRENMAN, b. of Canaan, Jan. 3, 1836, by Charles Prentice. Int. Pub.	A	95
Charlotte, m. Asa INGRAHAM, b. of Canaan, Oct. 8, 1828, by Charles Prentice	A	86
Rachal, d. George & Ruth, b. Dec. 20, 1783	A	37

	Vol.	Page
LANE, LAIN, Ashbel, s. Ashbel & Prudence, b. July 24, 1765	A	7
Ashbel, m. Pircey **STILLMAN,** b. of Canaan, Sept. 20, 1820,		
by Pitkin Cowles	A	79
Isaac, s. Ashbel & Prudence, b. Dec. 28, 1754	LR2	233
Lidiah, d. Ashbel & Prudence, b. Jan. 27, 1760	A	2
Lydia, d. Ashbil & Purdence, b. June 27, 1760	A	7
Mary, d. Isaac & Sabra, b. Apr. 11, 1779	A	33
Matte, d. Ashbil & Prudence, b. Mar. 10, 1763	A	7
Mindwell, d. Arshbel & Purdence, b. Aug. 16, 1757	LR2	232
Narcissa, m. Darius N. **COWLES,** Mar. 7, 1822, by Pitkin		
Cowles	A	81
LATRIDGE (?)*, Nancy, d. James & Mahitabell, b. Jan. 5, 1781		
*("**PARTRIDGE**")	A	37
LAWREN, [see also **LAWRENCE**], Tryphena, of Littleton, m.		
Zenas **LAWRENCE,** Sept. 3, 1754	LR2	237
LAWRENCE, LARANCE, [see also **LAWREN**], Abel, s. Jonas &		
Tryphena, b. Sept. 22, 1763	A	4
Abel, m. Abigail **ROCKWELL,** Oct. 6, 1783	A	38
Abel & Abigail, had s. [ ], s. b. Aug. 21, 1784	A	38
Abel & Abigail, had s. [ ], s. b. Dec. 25, 1785	A	38
Abiah, d. Jonas & Tryphena, b. Nov. 30, 1760	A	1
Abiah, d. Josiah & Anna, b. Nov. 28, 1788	A	49
Abigail, d. Jonathan & Bettey, b. Apr. 28, 1776	A	25
Abigail, d. Josiah & Anna, b. Jan. 29, 1793	A	49
Abigail, m. Serena B. **GILLETT,** Dec. 30, 1812, by Rev.		
Pitkin Cowles	A	49
Abigail, m. Lawrence **GILLETT,** b. of Canaan, Jan. 2,		
1839, by H. H. Woodbridge. Int. Pub.	A	98
Abiram, s. Jonathan & Bette, b. Aug. 19, 1765	A	6
Adeline M., m. Daniel B. **LEWIS,** of New Hartford, Oct.		
21, 1835, by Rev. H. H. Woodbridge, of the 2nd Cong.		
Ch.	A	94
Albert, s. Nathaniel & Sarah, b. Dec. 23, 1797	A	49
Amy, m. Elijah **COBB,** Mar. 20, 1760	A	1
Amey, m. Thomas **TUBBS,** Nov. 10, 1779	A	32
Ame, m. Thomas **TUBBS,** Nov. 9, 1780	A	40
Ann Augusta, [d. Lyman & Betsey], b. Mar. 18, 1838	A	54
Anna, [w. Josiah], d. May 17, 1812	A	49
Anson, s. Nathaniel & Sarah, b. May 1, 1763	A	6
Apame, d. Isaac, Jr. & Mary, b. Dec. 7, 1772	A	17
Asa, s. Isaac & Lidia, d. July 24, 1750	LR1	426
Asa, s. Gideon & Jerusha, b. Oct. 7, 1750	LR1	423
Asa, s. Jonathan & Bette, b. Apr. 3, 1757	A	1
Asa, m. Lucy **MILLER,** Jan. 29, 1770	A	22
Azubah, of Canaan, m. Samuel **HIDE,** of Norwich, Oct. 25,		
1750	LR1	423
Benjamin, twin with Joseph, s. Jonathan & Bettey, b.		
May 25, 1774	A	21

	Vol.	Page
LAWRENCE, LARANCE, (cont.)		
Betsey, d. Nathan & Polly, b. Feb. 6, 1797	A	50
Betsey, d. Josiah & Anna, b. Feb. 21, 1799	A	49
Betsey, m. John **FRANKLIN**, b. of Canaan, Nov. 4, 1823,		
by Pitkin Cowles	A	82
Betsey Ann, m. Nathaniel **STEVENS**, b. of Canaan, Jan.		
22, 1827*, by H. H. Woodbridge *("1837"?)	A	96
Bette, d. Jonathan & Bette, b. Dec. 15, 1759	A	1
Betty, m. Roger **ROOD**, June 2, 1779	A	31
Betty, m. Roger **ROOD**, June 2, 1779	A	35
Bille, s. Jonas & Tryphena, b. Jan. 31, 1779	A	36
Charlotte, d. Jonas & Tryphena, b. Oct. 13, 1770	A	36
Charlotte, d. Capt. Nehemiah & Abigail, b. Jan. 11, 1788	A	40
Charlotte, d. Josiah & Anna, b. May 4, 1802	A	49
Charlotte, m. William **ADAM**, Sept. 15, 1824, by Pitkin Cowles	A	83
Charry, d. David & Sarah, b. Sept. 18, 1782	A	38
Consider, s. Jonas & Tryphena, b. Feb. 8, 1777	A	36
Daniel, s. Daniel, Jr. & Rachel, b. Aug. 30, 1748	LR1	423
Daniel, of Canaan, m. Jerusha **FELLOWS**, of Edgemont*,		
Jan. 4, 1827, by Pitkin Cowles *("Egremont"?)	A	86
David, m. Sarah **TUBBE**, Sept. 16, 1756	A	4
David, s. David & Sarah, b. Jan. 2, 1758	A	4
Eleanor, b. Jan. 23, 1762 (See under **VAN DUSEN**, for		
births of her children)	A	47
Elijah, s. Isaac & Mary, b. Oct. 17, 1763	A	4
Elisha, s. David & Sarah, b. Dec. 9, 1766	A	38
Elizabeth, w. Jeremiah, d. Mar. 31, 1772	A	20
Elizabeth, wid. Capt. Nehemiah, d. Mar. 5, 1786	A	38
Erastus, s. Isaac & Mary, b. Mar. 11, 1780	A	37
Esther, m. Samuel **RANSOM**, May 6, 1756, by David Whitney	A	3
Euluff*, s. Jonathan & Belle, b. Jan. 10, 1771		
*(Overwritten to read Ruluff"?)	A	14
Eunice, m. Willard **GREEN**, Mar. 1, 1759	A	6
Eunice, d. Asa & Lucy, b. Dec. 29, 1771	A	22
Experience, d. William Solomon & Esther, b. July 28, 1781	A	37
Frederic, s. William & Lotte, b. Aug. 15, 1813	A	51
George, s. Nathan & Polly, b. Sept. 8, 1791	A	50
Gideon, of Canaan, m. Jerusha **RICHARDS**, of Norfolk,		
Oct. 12, 1749	LR1	423
Hannah, d. Isaac & Lidiah, b. May 25, 1750	LR1	424
Harvey, s. Josiah & Anna, b. Mar. 19, 1791	A	49
Harvey, m. Betsey **DUNING**, Nov. 24, 1812, by Rev.		
Pitkin Cowles	A	49
Henry, s. Isaac, Jr. & Mary, b. Feb. [ ], 1778	A	31
Henry, s. Isaac & Mary, b. Feb. 25, 1778	A	32
Henry W., m. Abigail **DOOLITTLE**, b. of Canaan, Nov. 27,		
1845, by Rev. D. D. Francis	A	106
Isaac, m. Mary **BROWN**, of Stockbridge, Mar. 18, 1760	A	1

	Vol.	Page

LAWRENCE, LARANCE, (cont.)

	Vol.	Page
Isaac, s. Isaac, Jr. & Mary, b. Nov. 22, 1767	A	10
Jabez, s. Jeremiah & Elizabeth, b. Mar. 24, 1772	A	20
Jane, d. William & Lotte, b. July 29, 1808	A	51
Jane, m. Charles **FRANKLIN**, b. of Canaan, Nov. 27, 1833, by Rev. Henry H. Woodbridge, of the 2nd Cong. Ch.	A	92
Jedidiah, s. Asee & Lucy, b. Mar. 4, 1774	A	22
Jeremiah, s. Nehemiah & Elizabeth, b. June 15, 1760	A	39
Jeremiah, m. Elizabeth **SMITH**, June 23, 1772	A	16
Jeremiah, m. Elizabeth **HIGBE**, July 6, 1773	A	21
Jeremiah, m. Phebe **STEVENS**, Jan. 25, 1786	A	39
Jonas, s. William Solomon & Esther, b. Nov. 26, 1782	A	37
Jonathan, m. Bette **GREEN**, May 24, 1756	A	1
Jonathan, s. Jonathan & Bette, b. Feb. 20, 1762	A	5
Jonathan G., m. Julia M. **WATSON**, June 10, 1834, by Rev. Henry H. Woodbridge, of the 2nd Cong. Ch.	A	93
Joseph, s. David & Sarah, b. June 7, 1771	A	38
Joseph, twin with Benjamin, s. Jonathan & Bettey, b. May 25, 1774	A	21
Josiah, s. Jonas & Tryphena, b. Oct. 16, 1765	A	9
Josiah, b. Oct. 16, 1765; m. Anna **ROCKWELL**, Feb. 7, 1788	A	49
Julia, d. William & Lotte, b. Sept. 18, 1804	A	51
Julia, of Canaan, m. Frederick S. **PEASE**, of Albany, Sept 18, 1832, by Pitkin Cowles	A	90
Laura, d. William & Lotte, b. Nov. 5, 1802	A	51
Laura, m. Daniel **NORTON**, b. of Canaan, Oct. 13, 1825, by Pitkin Cowles	A	84
Leonard, s. Nathan & Polly, b. Aug. 4, 1802	A	50
Leonard, m. Chloe **COBB**, b. of Canaan, Oct. 6, 1824, by Pitkin Cowles	A	83
Leonard, m. Mary **DUNNING**, Oct. 26, 1835, by Rev. H. H. Woodbridge, of the 2nd Cong. Ch.	A	94
Lewis, s. Nathan & Polly, b. Feb. 21, 1793	A	50
Lewis C., of Canaan, m. Anna **POTTER**, of Hamden, Oct. 14, 1822, by Pitkin Cowles	A	81
Loes, d. Daniel, Jr. & Rachel, b. Apr. 12, 1743	LR1	423
Lois, m. Oliver **STRONG**, Apr. 10, 1760	LR2	227
Lucy, d. Nathan & Polly, b. June 14, 1799	A	50
Lucy, of Canaan, m. Almon **PAIN**, of Kent, Apr. 14, 1822, by Pitkin Cowles	A	81
Lidia, d. Isaac & Lidia, b. Dec. 2, 1747	LR1	424
Lidia, d. Isaac & Lidia, d. Aug. 4, 1750	LR1	426
Lidiah, d. Jonas & Tryphena, b. Oct. 22, 1756	LR2	228
Lidiah, d. Jonas & Tryphena, d. Jan. 5, 1757	LR2	228
Lidia, d. Isaac & Mary, b. Sept. 2, 1761	A	4
Lydia, d. Jonathan & Bette, b. Sept. 13, 1763	A	5
Lydia, w. Isaac, d. Nov. 14, 1767	A	10

	Vol.	Page

LAWRENCE, LARANCE, (cont.)

	Vol.	Page
Lyman, s. Nathaniel & Sarah, b. Sept. 25, 1801	A	49
Lyman, m. Betsey **WHITE**, Sept. 8, 1824, by Pitkin Cowles	A	83
Mariah, d. William & Lotte, b. Mar. 21, 1811	A	51
Maria, m. Charles **ADAM**, b. of Canaan, Sept. 21, 1846, by Rev. D. D. Francis	A	107
Martha, d. Nathaniel & Sarah, b. Jan. 11, 1761	A	6
Mary, d. Isaac, Jr., b. May 4, 1770	A	13
Mary, d. David & Sarah, b. Aug. 7, 1775	A	38
Mary Ann, m. John **WATSON**, 2nd, b. of Canaan, Jan. 27, 1831, by Pitkin Cowles	A	88
Mary Irene, [d. Lyman & Betsey], b. Sept. 26, 1833; d. Apr. 19, 1841	A	54
Nancy, m. Thompson **MOSES**, Apr. 2, 1843, by Charles Rittridge	A	103
Nathan, s. David & Sarah, b. Jan. 25, 1762	A	4
Nathan, m. Polly **WARD**, Jan. 27, 1787	A	50
Nathaniel, m. Sarah **STEVENS**, Feb. 11, 1796	A	49
Nehemiah, Capt., m. wid. Abigail **SUTTON**, Oct. 19, 17[ ]	A	39
Nehemiah, of Canaan, m. Sarah **BORDMAN**, of Sheffield, Nov. 28, 1749	LR1	426
Nehemiah, m. Elizabeth **ROBBARTS**, Apr. 12, 1753, by Daniel Farranad	LR2	239
Nehemiah, s. Nehemiah & Elizabeth, b. June 7, 1757	LR2	232
Olive, d. David & Sarah, b. Jan. 13, 1760	A	4
Olive, d. Jonathan & Betty, b. Aug. 20, 1767	A	11
Olive, w. Jeremiah, d. Apr. 17, 1772	A	16
Orrange, s. William Solomon & Esther, b. Feb. 23, 1796	A	45
Pamela, d. Isaac & Mary, b. May 17, 1782	A	37
Patience, s. Jeremiah & Elizabeth, b. Dec. 3, 1776	A	26
Pharlee, of Canaan, m. Asa **BIGELOW**, of Tyringham, Mass., Nov. 5, 1832, by Pitkin Cowles	A	90
Phebe, d. David & Sarah, b. July 9, 1773	A	38
Phebe, d. Nathaniel & Elizabeth, b. Aug. 8, 1780	A	43
Phebe, d. Nathaniel & Sarah, b. Sept. 20, 1810	A	49
Phebe, of Canaan, m. Lyman D. **GOODWIN**, of Deerfield, N. Y., May 26, 1842, by Rev. H. H. Woodbridge	A	101
Quincy, s. Jonathan & Bettey, b. Sept. 4, 1772	A	22
Rhoda, of Canaan, m. Albert B. **KELLOGG**, of Sheffield, Nov. 22, 1820, by Pitkin Cowles	A	79
Ruluff*, s. Jonathan & Belle, b. Jan. 10, 1771p1265 *(Arnold Copy has "Euluff")	A	14
Samuel, s. Isaac, Jr. & Mary, b. Nov. 19, 1765	A	10
Sarah, m. Thomas **FELLOWS**, b. of Canaan, May 3, 1750	LR1	424
Sarah, d. Nehemiah & Elizabeth, b. July 24, 1754	LR2	233
Sarah, d. Nathaniel & Sarah, b. Feb. 19 1759	A	6
Sarah, d. David & Sarah, b. Jan. 3, 1764	A	4
Sarah, w. Nathaniel, d. Mar. 9, 1765, in the 25th y. of her age	A	6

	Vol.	Page
LAWRENCE, LARANCE, (cont.)		
Sarah, d. David & Sarah, b. June 17, 1769	A	38
Sarah, m. Joseph KINGMAN, Sept. 15, 1774	A	26
Sarah E., of Canaan, m. Walter FERRIS, of Salisbury,		
Aug. 8, 1851, by Rev. Elisha Whittlesey	A	109
Sarah Elizabeth, d. Lyman & Betsey, b. Feb. 1, 1829	A	54
Silas, s. Nathaniel & Elizabeth, b. Sept. 26, 1774	A	43
Simon, s. David & Sarah, b. Jan. 22, 1768; d. Jan. 26, 1768	A	38
Solomon, s. Isaac & Lidia, d. July 21, 1750	LR1	424
Stephen, s. Daniel, Jr. & Rachel, b. Feb. 21, 1740/1	LR1	423
Thankfull, of Canaan, m. Daniel WHITE, of Norfolk, Mar.		
10, 1831, by Pitkin Cowles	A	89
Tryphena, d. Jonas & Tryphena, b. July 4, 1768	A	11
Villa, s. Nehemiah & Abigail, b. Dec. 6, 1789	A	41
Welthy, d. Nathan & Polly, b. July 29, 1801	A	50
Wealthy, m. Elijah B. PHELPS, of New Milford, Dec. 30,		
1821, by Pitkin Cowles	A	80
William, s. Isaac & Lidia, d. Jan. 5, 1750	LR1	424
William, s. Jeremiah & Elizabeth, b. Oct. 19, 1774	A	21
William, m. Lotte ROOD, Oct. 7, 1801	A	51
William, s. William & Lotte, b. July 22, 1806	A	51
William Solomon, s. Jonas & Tryphena, b. Oct. 31, 1758	LR2	228
William Solomon, m. Esther DUTTON, Oct. 12, 1780	A	37
Wolcott, s. Jeremiah & Phebe, b. Nov. 4, 1786	A	39
Zenas, m. Tryphena LAWREN, of Littleton, Sept. 3, 1754	LR2	237
LEAVENWORTH, Legranel, m. Rebecca MANSFIELD, b. of		
Canaan, May 12, 1834, by Charles Prentice	A	93
LEE, Electa, d. Samuell & Silance, b. Nov. 2, 1760	A	1
Sam[ue]ll, of Canaan, m. Silance FLETCHER, of Salisbury,		
Mar. 28, 1754, by David Whitney, J. P.	LR2	238
Samuell, s. Samuell & Silance, b. Nov. 19, 1754	LR2	238
Solomon, s. Samuell & Silance, b. June 21, 1756	LR2	233
William, s. Samuell & Silance, b. Mar. 13, 1763	A	4
LEFFINGWELL, Sarah Ann, m. Gilbert MARTIN, Feb. 9, 1836,		
by Rev. H. H. Woodbridge, of the 2nd Cong. Ch.	A	95
LEMERLY, Polly, m. Isaac FRENCH, b. of Canaan, Apr. 24, 1836,		
by Charles Prentice. Int. Pub.	A	95
LESTER, Eliza, of Canaan, m. Henry WELLS, of New Hartford,		
Dec. 1, 1837, by Rev. H. H. Woodbridge, of the 2nd		
Cong. Ch. Int. Pub.	A	96
LEWIS, Charles, s. Miles & Rhoda, b. Feb. 28, 1796	A	43
Charles, s. Miles & Rhoda, b. Feb. 28, 1796	A	44
Charles, s. Miles & Rhoda, b. May 26, 1800	A	45
Charles, m. Harriet KNAPP, b. of Canaan, Jan. 26, 1829,		
by Pitkin Cowles	A	87
Daniel B., of New Hartford, m. Adeline M. LAWRENCE, of		
[ ], Oct. 21, 1835, by Rev. H. H. Woodbridge, of the		
2nd Cong. Ch.	A	94

	Vol.	Page
LEWIS, (cont.)		
Elisha, Dea., d. Feb. 2, 1799	A	46
Eunice, m. Nathaniel **MARSH**, Nov. 27, 1770	A	12
Harriet, d. Miles & Rhoda, b. July 6, 1802	A	47
Harriet, d. Miles & Rhoda, d. Nov. 21, 1802, ae 4 m. 15 d.	A	48
Heman S., s. Miles & Rhoda, b. May 14, 1804	A	47
Heman Swift, d. Aug. 6, 1806, ae 2 y. 2 m. 22 d.	A	47
Mary, m. Sherman M. **ROSE**, b. of Canaan, Oct. 11, 1820,		
by Pitkin Cowles	A	79
Miles, m. Rhoda **SWIFT**, Oct. 5, 1794	A	44
Polly, d. Miles & Rhoda, b. Apr. 16, 1798	A	44
Polly, m. William **PARTRIDGE**, b. of Canaan, Sept. 23,		
1827, by Pitkin Cowles	A	86
Samuel Lyman, 6th child of Miles & Rhoda, b. Apr. 27, 1811	A	48
LIVINGSTONE, William D., of Sheffield, Mass., m. Hannah		
ROBINSON, of Canaan, Mar. 22, 1835, by Rev. H. H.		
Woodbridge, of the 2nd Cong. Ch.	A	94
LONG, Patrick, m. Mary **PIERCE**, Mar. 24, 1822, by Pitkin Cowles	A	81
LOOMIS, Henry, of Salisbury, m. Elizabeth **GRAVES**, of Canaan,		
Nov. 4, 1844, by Rev. Stephen J. Stebbins	A	104
LORANCE, [see under **LAWRENCE**]		
LOVELAND, Alice, of Canaan, m. Jacob **HINSDALE**, Jr., of		
Brewville, O., Oct. 18, 1837, by H. H. Woodbridge. Int.		
Pub.	A	96
LOWDEN, John L., s. James & Sarah, b. Nov. 10, 1810	A	48
LOWRY, LOWREY, Eleanor, m. George **HARRIS**, Apr. 23, 1829,		
by Charles Prentice	A	87
Frederick H., m. Charlotte Ann **HOSKINS**, b. of Canaan,		
Oct. 1, 1823, by Rev. Charles Prentice	A	82
Ira, s. Nathaniel & Jerusha, b. Nov. 11, 1771	A	21
Jerusha, d. Nathaniel & Jerusha, b. Feb. 21, 1774	A	21
Nathaniel, s. Nathaniel & Jerusha, b. Nov. 20, 1769	A	21
Sally, of Canaan, m. Horace **ROBERTS**, of Goshen, Oct. 17,		
1826, by Charles Prentice	A	85
LUCAS, LUCUS, John, s. David & Sarah, b. Apr. 28, 1779	A	36
Nathaniel, s. David & Sarah, b. Apr. 25, 1776	A	30
Oliver, s. David & Sarah, b. Jan. 6, 1770	A	17
Sarah, d. David & Sarah, b. Sept 29, 1772	A	17
McCOURT, Ann, m. John G. **BLACK**, b. of Canaan, Nov. 2, 1840,		
by Rev. H. H. Woodbridge, of the 2nd Cong. Ch.	A	99
McDANIELDS, Charles, of Salisbury, m. Jane **BOTSFORD**, of		
Salisbury, Apr. 27, 1845, by Rev. Stephen J. Stebbins	A	104
McHALE, Mary, m. Michael **CLARK**, b. of Salisbury, Jan. 23,		
1852, by Rev. John Smith	A	109
McINTIRE, Steven, of Salisbury, m. Jane A. **ROOD**, Nov. 11,		
1830, by Pitkin Cowles	A	88
McKEAN, Linus, m. Henriette **BULL**, b. of Canaan, Apr. 18, 1822,		
by Pitkin Cowles	A	81

	Vol.	Page

McKEAN, (cont.)

Lucy Ann, m. Lewis HOLCOMB, b. of Canaan, Nov. 8, 1830,
by Pitkin Cowles — A — 88

McMAHON, Thomas, of New Hartford, m. Sarah AUSTIN, of
Sheffield, Mass., Nov. 19, 1840, by Rev. H. H.
Woodbridge, of the 2nd Cong. Ch. — A — 99

MAINE, Adam W., m. Harriet INGRAHAM, b. of Canaan, June 2,
1833, by Charles Prentice. Int. Pub. May 31, 1833 — A — 91

MALTBIE, Seraph Elizabeth, d. Dr. Chareles B. & Elizabeth,
b. Mar. 18, 1852, m. Lee P. DEAN, May 27, 1874 — A — 133

MANLEY, Eleezer, m. Mary E. WICKHAM, b. of Canaan, May
12, 1830, by Charles Prentice — A — 88

Eleezer Butler, b. July 18, 1832; m. Ellen E. DEAN,
Nov. 1, 1857 — A — 133

Eluzer Butler, d. Feb. 9, 1862 — A — 133

Mary E., m. John B. REED, Sept. 24, 1838, by H. H.
Woodbridge — A — 97

Mary Ellen, d. Eluzer B. & Ellen E., b. Dec. 19, 1858,
at South Lee, Mass.; d. July 15, 1862, at Canaan — A — 133

MANSFIELD, Delia E., m Lee MARVIN, b. of Canaan, Nov. 15,
1846, by Rev. D. D. Francis — A — 107

Elisha D., m. Fanny MUNSON, b. of Canaan, June 25, 1834,
by Charles Prentice. Int. Pub. — A — 93

Julius, m. Lucinda HURLBURT, b. of Canaan, Dec. 17, 1828,
by Charles Prentice — A — 87

Lucy, m. John BEEBE, b. of Canaan, Nov. 18, 1838, by
Simeon Higley, J. P. — A — 98

Rachel, of Canaan, m. Ebenezer MILES, of Cornwall, Oct.
29, 1823, by Charles Prentice — A — 83

Rebecca, m. Legranel LEAVENWORTH, b. of Canaan, May
12, 1834, by Charles Prentice — A — 93

Sheldon, m. Olivia CATLIN b. of Canaan, Apr. 4, 1827, by [] — A — 86

MARKHAM, Eunice, m. Dudley HOLDRIDGE, May 5, 1768, by
Rev. Daniel Farrand — A — 15

MARSH, Abigail, d. Rufus & Sarah, b. Jan. 29, 1773;
d. July 13, 1773 — A — 17

Abigail Salle, d. Rufus & Sarah, b. Jan. 17, 1778 — A — 30

Abigail Sally, m. William KINGSBURY, July 22, 1801 — A — 49

Alice, d. Moses & Sibel, b. Sept. 3, 1769 — A — 13

Betsey, d. Nehemiah & Ruth, b. Dec. 3, 1785 — A — 45

Cyrus, s. Nathaniel, Jr. & Anice, b. Mar. 28, 1773 — A — 17

Cyrus, s. Nathaniel & Eunice, d. Sept. 10, 1782 — A — 36

Desire, w. Moses, d. July 25, 1765 — A — 13

Desire, d. William & Thankfull, b. Nov. 1, 1766 — A — 9

Elias, s. James & Anna, b. [ ], 1, 1768 — A — 3

Elizabeth, d. Moses & Desire, b. Jan. 9, 1752 — A — 13

Elizabeth, d. James & Anna, b. Mar. 14, 1766 — A — 13

Eunice, d. Moses & Sibel, b. Jan. 18, 1768 — A — 13

	Vol.	Page
MARSH, (cont.)		
Eunice, d. James & Anna, b. Mar. 6, 1770	A	13
Hannah, d. James & Mary, b. June 14, 1751	A	18
Hannah, d. William & Thankfull, b. July 9, 1762	A	7
Hannah, m. Noah HOLCOMB, Feb. 21, 1771	A	24
Irena, d. James & Anna, b. Mar. 16, 1772	A	16
James, m. Anna KELLOGG, June 20, 1765	A	6
Jonas, s. Moses & Desire, b. Dec. 21, 1758	LR2	227
Jonas, s. William, d. Apr. 11, 1770	A	22
Jonas, s. Nehemiah & Ruth, b. Aug. 31, 1783	A	45
Josiah Rosseter, s. Nehemiah & Ruth, b. Oct. 9, 1781	A	45
Lucy A., m. Renssalear W. RUSSELL, b. of Canaan, Oct. 8, 1839, by Rev. H. H. Woodbridge, of the 2nd Cong. Ch.	A	98
Mary, d. James & Marah, b. Nov. 22, 1756	A	18
Mary, d. William, d. Apr. 20, 1770	A	22
Mary, d. Nehemiah & Mary, b. Aug. 9, 1794	A	45
Mary, w. Nehemiah, d. Oct. 18, 1794	A	45
Moses, m. Desire STEVENS, Jan. 24, 1758, by Rev. Mr. Farrand	LR2	227
Moses, m. Sibel FITCH, Feb. 19, 1767	A	13
Moses, s. William & Thankfull, b. Jan. 24, 1773	A	22
Moses, m. Chloe ANDRUS, Dec. 5, 1780	A	38
Nathaniel, s. Jonas & Mary, b. Jan. 22, 1744	A	12
Nathaniel, s. William & Thankfull, b. July 22, 1770	A	12
Nathaniel, m. Eunice LEWIS, Nov. 27, 1770	A	12
Nathaniel, s. William, d. Apr. 17, 1771	A	22
Nathaniel, s. Nathaniel & Eunice, b. Nov. 21, 1771	A	15
Nehemiah, s. James & Mary, b. July 12, 1754	A	18
Nehemiah, m. Ruth ROSSETTER, of Killingsworth, Nov.16,1780	A	45
Nehemiah, m. Mary COLLOR, of New Marlborough, Nov. 17, 1791	A	45
Nehemiah, m. Ruth BELL, of Cornwall, June 10, 1795	A	45
Rufus, m. Sarah WAY, May 14, 1772	A	16
Ruth, w. Nehemiah, d. July 29, 1790	A	45
Sally Abigail, m. William KINGSBURY, July 22, 1801	A	48
Samuel, s. Moses & Chloe, b. Nov. 5, 1782* *(Arnold Copy has "1732")	A	38
Samuel, s. Nehemiah & Ruth, b. Jan. 21, 1799	A	45
Sarah d. Moses & Desire, b. Apr. 16, 1760	LR2	227
Sarah, d. Moses, d. Feb. 10, 1774	A	21
Sarah, d. Rufus & Sarah, b. Nov. 13, 1774	A	23
Sarah, d. Nathaniel & [E]unice, b. Mar. 18, 1775	A	24
Sarah, d. Rufus & Sarah, d. May 26, 1775	A	23
Sarah, wid. Rufus & d. John Way, of Wallingford, d. Feb. 11, 1793, in the 79th y. of her age	A	42
Susanna, d. William & Thankfull, b. Sept. 26, 1764	A	7
Sibbel, d. Moses & Sybbel, b. Mar. 14, 1772	A	17
Sybel, d. Moses & Sybel, b. Mar. 14, 1772	A	20

	Vol.	Page

MARSH, (cont.)

William, m. Thankfull **BAKER**, of Middletown, May 3, 1759,
by Rev. Mr. Farand — LR2 — 228

William, s. William & Thankfull, b. Oct. 3, 1760 — A — 1

William, s. William, d. Apr. 22, 1771 — A — 22

William, s. Nehemiah & Ruth, b. May 11, 1796 — A — 45

William S., of Winchester, m. Elizabeth S. **BREWSTER**, of
Canaan, June 15, 1836, by Charles Prentice — A — 95

MARTIN, Gilbert, m. Sarah Ann **LEFFINGWELL**, Feb. 9, 1836,
by Rev. H. H. Woodbridge, of the 2nd Cong. Ch. — A — 95

Peter, of Winsor, N. Y., m. Stella **WITHERELL**, Jan. 14,
1821, by Pitkin Cowles — A — 79

MARVIN, MARVEN, MERVIN, Asenath, m. Porter **ROSE,** b. of
Canaan, Sept. 29, 1831, by Pitkin Cowles — A — 89

Betsey, of Canaan, m. James **WARNER**, Jr., of Norfolk,
Dec. 16, 1835, by Rev. H. H. Woodbridge — A — 95

[E]unice, see Sarah **MERVIN** — A — 34

George, m. Phelomelia **GILBERT**, b. of Canaan, Oct. 16,
1845, by Rev. D. D. Francis — A — 106

Joseph L., of Goshen, m. Charlotte D. **GAINES**, of Canaan,
Mar. 20, 1834, by Charles Prentice. Int. Pub. — A — 92

Lebbeus Keep, s. Martin & [E]unice, b. July 18, 1777 — A — 26

Lee, m. Delia E. **MANSFIELD**, b. of Canaan, Nov. 15, 1846,
by Rev. D. D. Francis — A — 107

Lidiah, of Lime, m. Simeon **TUBBS**, Oct. 8, 1759 — LR2 — 227

Sarah, d. Martin & [E]unice, b. Sept. 24, 1779 — A — 33

Sarah, d. Martin & [E]unice, b. Sept. 24, 1779; had name
changed to [E]unice — A — 34

MATTHEWS, Daniel, of Plymouth, m. Cemantha **YALE**, of
Canaan, May 7, 1834, by Charles Prentice. Int. Pub. — A — 92

MEAD, Henry J., ae 24, of Canaan, m. Mary A. **TRESCOTT**, ae
22, of Canaan, Oct. 24, 1848, by Rev. C. H. Watrous — A — 105

William, of Ridgefield, m. Abiah L. **PARTRIDGE**, of Canaan,
Sept. 3, 1837, by Rev. Aaron Rogers — A — 96

MERRELLS, MERRALL, Abigail, of Hartford, m. Oliver
BELDING, May 8, 1755, by Rev. Mr. Colton — LR2 — 233

Anna, d. Elisha & Mary, b. Jan. 19, 1763 — A — 6

Chilion, s. David & Esther, b. Oct. 22, 1771 — A — 14

Elisha, m. Mary **FELLOWS**, Apr. 17, 1760 — A — 6

Lucy, d. Elisha & Mary, b. Mar. 18, 1765 — A — 6

Ruth, d. Elisha & Mary, b. Dec. 9, 1760 — A — 6

MERVIN, [see under **MARVIN**]

MILES, Ebenezer, of Cornwall, m. Rachel **MANSFIELD**, of
Canaan, Oct. 29, 1823, by Charles Prentice — A — 83

MILLER, L. B., of Great Barrington, Mass., m. Caroline **YALE**,
of South Canaan, May 30, 1842, by Rev. H. H.
Woodbridge. Int. Pub. — A — 101

Lucy, m. Asa **LAWRENCE**, Jan. 29, 1770 — A — 22

	Vol.	Page
MILLER, (cont.)		
Ruth, m. David **KELSEY**, May [ ], 1823, by William Holobird, J. P.	A	82
MILLS, Charlotte, of Canaan, m. Phinehas **HUNT**, of Sharon, Jan. 6, 1830, by Pitkin Cowles	A	87
Hiram, of Wis., m. Laura Ann **COLLINS**, of Canaan, May 7, 1846, by Rev. D. D. Francis	A	106
Samuel, of Watervliet (?), N. Y., m. Anna **FREEMAN**, of Canaan, Dec. 15, 1822, by Pitkin Cowles	A	82
MINOR, MINER, Clarrissa, m. William **BENNETT**, b. of Canaan, Mar. 4, 1833, by Charles Prentice, Int. Pub.	A	91
Edward Uriel, s. Uriel H., b. Dec. 31, 1846 (Date conflicts with birth of George Canfield **MINER**)	A	54
George Canfield, s. Uriel H., b. Sept. 11, 1846 (Date conflicts with birth of Edward Uriel **MINER**)	A	54
Miles, m. Harriet **BOARDMAN**, b. of Canaan, Mar. 29, 1832, by Charles Prentice	A	90
Nancy R., of Canaan, m. Rowland **NORTON**, of New Marlborough, Mass., Nov. 12, 1828, by Charles Prentice	A	86
Saliy, m. Theophilus **BUEL**, Nov. 27, 1834, by Charles Prentice	A	93
Whiting G., m. Ann M. **ROCKWELL**, b. of Canaan, Oct. 15, 1834, by Rev. H. H. Woodbridge, of North Canaan	A	93
MIX, Betsey Ann, of Canaan, m. John **SHORES**, of New Marlboro, Mass., Jan. 1, 1849, by Rev. D. D. Francis	A	107
Charles, s. Daniel & Union, b. July 31, 1806	A	48
John, s. Daniel & Union, b. Sept. 8, 1803	A	48
MOORE, MORE, Lucinda, m. Perry **SLATER**, Feb. 26, 1832, by James Fenn, J. P.	A	90
Mary, m. George **JONES**, b. of Canaan, Apr. 18, 1841, by Rev. H. H. Woodbridge	A	100
Ransom, m. Elizabeth **FELLOWS**, Feb. 5, 1832, by James Fenn, J. P.	A	90
MOREY, Calvin, m. Harriet **TOBY**, Mar. 10, 1822, by Bushnell Knapp, J. P.	A	81
MORGAN, MORGIN, MORGAIN, Almira, of Canaan, m. Archibald **AUSTIN**, of Goshen, Oct. 21, 1821, by Pitkin Cowles	A	80
Delia, of Goshen, m. Jacob **ROOD**, of Canaan, Sept. 30, 1822, by Pitkin Cowles	A	81
Ezra Spaulding, s. Joseph & Sarah, b. Aug. 30, 1770	A	13
Jacob, s. Joseph & Sarah, b. Jan. 1, 1775	A	22
Joseph, m. Sarah **SPAULDING**, Apr. 13, 1769	A	12
MORRIS, Julia, m. Horace **BEEBE**, Sept. 21, 1829, by Charles Prentice	A	87
Russell, m. Harriet **HOLCOMB**, b. of Canaan, [June] 27, 1820, by Rev. Charles Prentice, of South Canaan	A	79
MORSE, John, of Litchfield, m. Betsey **FENN**, of Canaan, Feb.		

	Vol.	Page
MORSE, (cont.)		
23, 1831, by Pitkin Cowles	A	88
MOSELEY, Joseph, m. Hannah **JOHNSON**, b. of Sheffield, June		
18, 1831, by Pitkin Cowles	A	89
MOSES, Jemima, of Canaan, m. John E. **BEECHER**, of Sheffield,		
Mass., Feb. 12, 1843, by Charles Rittridge, of N. Canaan	A	102
Kezia, d. Timothy & Thankfull, b. Feb. 7, 1768	A	10
Mary, d. Timothy & Thankfull, b. Apr. 19, 1761	A	2
Parnel, m. Benjamin **HARLEY**, b. of Canaan, Apr. 8, 1834,		
by Rev. Harmon Ellis, of Bap. Ch., Norfolk	A	92
Phidelia, m. Joshua N. **BENEDICT**, Nov. 30, 1843,		
by Thomas Benedict	A	103
Sarah, d. Timothy & Thankfull, b. July 27, 1757	A	2
Thankfull, d. Timothy & Thankfull, b. May 9, 1759	A	2
Thompson, m. Nancy **LAWRENCE**, Apr. 2, 1843, by Charles		
Rittridge	A	103
Timothy, s. Timothy & Thankfull, b. May 13, 1755	A	2
Zerviah, d. Timothy & Thankfull, b. Apr. 24, 1763	A	10
Zeruiah, m. Rufus **BABCOCK**, May 24, 1781	A	36
MOTT, Mary, d. Lent & Mary, b. July 11, 1764	A	8
MUDGE, Amasa, s. Joshua & Mary, b. Jan. 23, 1768	A	16
Ebenezer, s. Joshua & Mary, b. Dec. 29, 1769	A	17
Joshua, m. Mary **CORNISH**, Sept. 10, 1767	A	16
Mercy, d. Joshua & Mary, b. May 30, 1772	A	17
MULHALL, Julia, m. John **GRACE**, b. lately from Ireland, June		
27, 1852, by Rev. John Smith	A	109
MUNGER, Curtice, m. Mary A. **HENIS**, b. of Canaan, Dec. 9,		
1830, by Pitkin Cowles	A	88
MUNRO, Betsey, m. Daniel **BLAKESLEE**, Oct. 25, 1812	A	52
MUNS, Clarissa, of Sharon, m. Daniel **BAILEY**, of Kent, Mar.		
27, 1821, by Rev. Walter Smith, of Cornwall	A	80
MUNSON, MONSON, Aeneas, m. Elizabeth **HOLOBIRD**, b. of		
Canaan, May 30, 1838, by H. H. Woodbridge	A	97
Almira, d. Lyman & Comfort, b. July 27, 1810, at		
Hamden; m. Henry **DEAN**, s. Eli & Judeth, Mar. 23,		
1834	A	133
Almira, m. Henry **DEAN**, b. of Canaan, Mar. 23, 1834, by		
Charles Prentice. Int. Pub.	A	92
Cornelia, m. Henry **BELDEN**, b. of Canaan, Mar. 28, 1844,		
by Rev. Harley Goodwin	A	103
Eunice, m. Seth **STEVENS**, Apr. 22, 1824, by [ ]	A	83
Fanny, m. Elisha D. **MANSFIELD**, b. of Canaan, June 25,		
1834, by Charles Prentice. Int. Pub.	A	93
Forbes, s. Luther & Caroline, b. Feb. 17, 1827	A	53
Harvey, m. Maria **JUDD**, b. of Canaan, Sept. 24, 1822,		
by Charles Prentice	A	81
Luther, b. Mar. 11, 1798	A	53
Luther, m. Caroline **BECKLEY**, Sept. 9, 1824	A	53

	Vol.	Page

MUNSON, MONSON, (cont.(

Luther, m. Caroline **BECKLEY**, Sept. 9, 1824, by
Pitkin Cowles ... A ... 83

Rebecca, of Canaan, m. Augustus B. **SWIFT**, of Cornwall,
Sept. 20, 1820, by Rev. Charles Prentice ... A ... 79

Sarah D., m. John A. **BECKLEY**, May 4, 1836, by Charles
Prentice. Int. Pub. ... A ... 95

Urana, m. William **OULLEAN**, b. of Canaan, Dec. 24, 1821,
by Pitkin Cowles ... A ... 80

MURRAY, Rachel, m. James **DUNN**, b. from Ireland, now of
Norfolk, July 11, 1852, by Rev. John Smith, at Falls
Village ... A ... 109

MYRES, Caroline, of Clavarock, Columbia, Co., N. Y., m.
Peter **SNYDER**, of Canaan, Oct. 28, 1849, by Rev. D. D.
Francis ... A ... 108

NEWELL, Drewsilla, d. William & Mary, b. Apr. 26, 1776 ... A ... 45

Sarah, d. William & Mary, b. June 23, 1779 ... A ... 45

Sarah, m. Ephraim **BARTLETT**, Feb. 15, 1801 ... A ... 46

Susanna, m. Asee **NORTH**, Feb. 11, 1773 ... A ... 23

William, s. William & Mary, b. Dec. 13, 1788 ... A ... 45

NOBLE, NOBLES, Mary Ann, m. Fitch **FERRIS**, Aug. 22, 1838 ... A ... 53

Wealthy, m. Simeon **HIGLEY**, Jr., Feb. 20, 1822, by Rev.
Charles Prentice ... A ... 80

NORCOTT, Cyrus, of Stockbridge, Mass., m. Betsey **ROOT**, of
Canaan, Apr. 11, 1821, by Rev. Charles Prentice, of the
1st Ch. ... A ... 80

NORTH, Abiram, m. Abigail **HARRIS**, of Canaan, Nov. 20, 1826,
by Rev. Samuel Eighmy, of the M. E. Ch. ... A ... 85

Amy, d. John & Amy, b. Nov. 22, 1777 ... A ... 27

Asahel, s. Asa & Susannah, b. Mar. 6, 1786 ... A ... 40

Asee, m. Susanna **NEWELL**, Feb. 11, 1773 ... A ... 23

Charles, s. John & Amy, b. Aug. 14, 1773 ... A ... 27

Darius, s. Asa & Susanna, b. Aug. 18, 1775 ... A ... 24

John, s. John & Amey, b. Feb. 29, 1780 ... A ... 34

Jonathan, m. Abigail **HILL**, Nov. 5, 1778 ... A ... 31

Lucy Levina, d. Asa & Susannah, b. Dec. 10, 1782 ... A ... 37

Mary, w. Jonathan, d. May 22, 1778, in the 69th y. of her age ... A ... 29

Olive, d. Asee & Susannah, b. Nov. 14, 1713* *(Overwritten
to read "1773") ... A ... 23

Samuel, s. Asa & Susanna, b. May 2, 1778 ... A ... 29

NORTON, Alexander, Jr., of Goshen, m. Alice **HOWE**, of Canaan,
Jan. 30, 1827, by Charles Prentice ... A ... 86

Daniel, m. Laura **LAWRENCE**, b. of Canaan, Oct. 13, 1825,
by Pitkin Cowles ... A ... 84

Dorothy, [d. Thomas & Sarah], b. Jan. 23, 1769 ... A ... 36

Dorothy, m. Harmon **DEMING**, July 12, 1792 ... A ... 46

George, [s. Thomas & Sarah], b. July 16, 1772 ... A ... 36

Rowland, of New Marlborough, Mass., m. Nancy R. **MINOR,**

	Vol.	Page
NORTH, (cont.)		
of Canaan, Nov. 12, 1828, by Charles Prentice	A	86
Timothy, [s. Thomas & Sarah], b. May 31, 1779	A	36
OAKLEY, Almira, m. Ozias **ROOT**, b. of Canaan, Dec. 3, 1820,		
by William Holobird, J. P.	A	79
Lucinda Maretta, of Canaan, m. Sanford **WHITE**, of Sharon,		
Nov. 22, 1838, by Rev. Charles Stearns, of the M. E. Ch.	A	97
Stata, m. Reuben **ROOT**, b. of Canaan, Dec. 22, 1824,		
by Rev. Daniel Miller, of the M. E. Ch.	A	84
O'BRIAN, James, s. Patrick & Polly, b. Aug. 6, 1783	A	41
John, s. Patrick & Polly, b. Oct. 30, 1786	A	41
Martha, d. Patrick & Polly, b. Jan. 31, 1789	A	41
Nancy, d. Patrick & Polly, b. Feb. 5, 1785	A	41
William, s. Patrick & Polly, b. Mar. 12, 1788	A	41
ORMSBY, Almon, s. Amos & Lucy, b. Mar. 10, 1788	A	40
Amos, m. Lucy **FRANKLIN**, May 25, 1775	A	40
OULLEAN (?), William, m. Urana **MUNSON**, b. of Canaan, Dec.		
24, 1821, by Pitkin Cowles	A	80
PAGE, George L., m. Mary Ann **JOHNSON**, b. of South Canaan,		
[Sept. 4, 1842], by Rev. Edward B. Emerson	A	102
PAIN, Almon, of Kent, m. Lucy **LAWRENCE**, of Canaan, Apr. 14,		
1822, by Pitkin Cowles	A	81
John, m. Polly **SMITH**, b. of Canaan, June 10, 1822,		
by Charles Prentice	A	81
Lydia, m. Samuel **HOW**, Jr., June 30, 1768	A	18
PALMER, Andrew, of Goshen, m. Jane **RUSSELL**, of Canaan, Feb.		
7, 1837, by Charles Prentice	A	96
Anne, of Sheffield, m. Ephraim **FELLOWS**, Jr., May 11, 1749	LR1	423
Fanny, m. Joel **BUNNELL**, Jr., Mar. 2, 1834, by Rev.		
Walter Smith, of the North Cong. Ch.	A	92
Theodore H., of Otis, m. Lucinda **DEAN**, of Canaan, Sept.		
2, 1834, by Rev. Julius Field	A	93
William, s. Simeon & Marcy, b. Oct. 13, 1791	A	42
PARKER, John, of Essex, m. Jane E. **HUBBARD**, of Salisbury,		
Apr. 7, 1850, by Rev. D. D. Francis	A	108
PARNELY, Rhoda, of Salisbury, m. Symon J. **TAYLOR**, of		
Cornwall, Oct. 20, 1844, by Rev. Stephen J. Stebbins	A	104
PARTRIDGE, PATRIDGE, Abiah L., of Canaan, m. William		
MEAD, of Ridgefield, Sept. 3, 1837, by Rev. Aaron		
Rogers	A	96
Anna, m. Capt. David **WHITE**, b. of Canaan, May 21, 1826,		
by Pitkin Cowles	A	85
Calder, s. Stephen & Sarah, b. Dec. 21, 1782	A	43
Eliphal, d. Stephen & Sarah, b. Nov. 14, 1772	A	17
George, s. Stephen & Sarah, b. Oct. 19, 1790	A	43
Harvey, s. Stephen & Sarah, b. June 16, 1786	A	43
James, d. June 4, 1771	A	17
James, s. Stephen & Sarah, b. Aug. 3, 1774	A	43

	Vol.	Page

PARTRIDGE, PATRIDGE, (cont.)

Lucy, m. Moses **BENEDICT**, b. of Canaan, Jan. 25, 1825,
　by Pitkin Cowles — A — 84

Mary B., of Canaan, m. Joel C. **FORD**, of New Marlborough,
　Feb. 16, 1834, by Rev. Julius Field — A — 92

Nancy*, d. James & Mahitabell, b. Jan. 5, 1781　*(Arnold
　copy has "Nancy **LATRIDGE**") — A — 37

Rufus, s. Stephen & Sarah, b. Feb. 17, 1777 — A — 43

Sally, of Canaan, m. Henry **WOLF**, of New Marlborough,
　Feb. 5, 1822, by Pitkin Cowles — A — 80

Sally M., m. William W. **RICHARDSON**, b. of Canaan, Oct.
　18, 1821, by Pitkin Cowles — A — 80

Salome, d. Stephen & Sarah, b. Apr. 14, 1792 — A — 43

Sarah, d. Stephen & Sarah, b. Mar. 14, 1780 — A — 43

Sarah, d. Stephen & Sarah, d. Aug. 22, 1787 — A — 43

Stephen, m. Sarah **BROOKINS**, Feb. 6, 1772 — A — 17

Thankfull, m. Zebulon **STEVENS**, Oct. 14, 1773 — A — 43

William, m. Polly **LEWIS**, b. of Canaan, Sept. 23, 1827,
　by Pitkin Cowles — A — 86

PEAK, [see also **PECK & PEET**], Ruthilda H., m. Chauncey L.
　HUNT, b. of Canaan, [June 28, 1841], by Rev. Edward
　B. Emerson, of South Canaan — A — 100

PEASE, Erastus Huntington, s. Salmon & Matilda, b. Sept. 10, 1807 — A — 51

Frederick S., of Albany, m. Julia **LAWRENCE**, of Canaan,
　Sept. 18, 1832, by Pitkin Cowles — A — 90

Frederic Salmon, s. Salmon & Matilda, b. May 21, 1804 — A — 51

Haran Gaylord, s. Salmon & Matilda, b. Feb. 22, 1811 — A — 51

Salmon, m. Matilda **HUNTINGTON**, June 14, 1803 — A — 51

PECK, [see also **PEAK & PEET**], Adeline, m. Charles
　KELLOGG, b. of Canaan, Jan. 16, 1839, by H. H.
　Woodbridge. Int. Pub. — A — 98

Azubah, d. John & Mary, b. Jan. 4, 1755 — LR2 — 232

Eliza Mariah, m. Frederick William **ROCKWELL**, b. of
　Canaan, Jan. 29, 1832, by Pitkin Cowles — A — 90

Elizabeth, d. John, d. July 27, 1767 — A — 15

Forbes, s. John & Lucy, b. Nov. 4, 1775 — A — 25

Harmon, m. Sarah Ann **WELCH**, b. of Canaan, Apr. 13, 1824,
　by Rev. Stephen Beach, of the Epis. Ch. — A — 83

Harriet, of Wallingford, m. Myron **TUTTLE**, of Canaan, Dec.
　23, 1832, by Theodosius Clark — A — 91

Hiram W., m. Julia **JUDD**, May 3, 1831, by Daniel Coe — A — 89

Horatio, s. John, 2nd & Lucy, b. June 9, 1779 — A — 32

Jane, m. Hiram **BRIGGS**, b. of Canaan, Sept. 30, 1841,
　by Rev. H. H. Woodbridge, of the 2nd Cong. Ch. — A — 101

John, of Canaan, m. Mary **REED**, of Sharon, Jan. 24, 1754,
　by Mr. Williams — LR2 — 238

John, s. John, b. Sept. 23, 1768 — A — 15

John, s. John, 2nd & Lucy, b. Dec. 18, 1780 — A — 36

	Vol.	Page
PECK, (cont.)		
Joshua, s. John & Mary, b. Dec. 9, 1758	LR2	228
Julia, m. James F. **ADDAMS**, b. of Sheffield, May 13, 1838,		
by H. H. Woodbridge	A	97
Louisa, m. David **ROOT**, b. of Canaan, May 18, 1846, by		
Rev. D. D. Francis	A	106
Luck (?), d. John, 2nd & Lucy, b. May 9, 1777	A	26
Lydia, m. Russell **HUNT**, May 3, 1758, by Rev. Mr. Farrand	A	2
Mary, d. John & Mary, b. May 1, 1757	LR2	232
Mehetabel, m. Edmon **HUBBARD***, Jan. 1, 1776		
*(Overwritten to read **HOBART"**)	A	24
Mehitabel, m. Edmund **HOBART**, Jan. 1, 1776	A	43
Permelia, d. John, 2nd & Lucy, b. Nov. 21, 1782	A	37
Rebeckah, d. Isaac, m. Robert **HUNT**, Dec. 26, 1753	LR2	238
PEET, [ss also **PECK & PEAK**], Abijah, s. Abiram & Anna, b.		
Aug. 21, 1778	A	39
Abiram, Dr., d. Apr. 22, 1786	A	39
Abiram Lewis, s. Abiram & Anne, b. May 26, 1772	A	15
Anne, d. Abiram & Anne, b. Mar. 22, 1769	A	15
Anne, m. Frederick **PLUMB**, Jan. 5, 1785	A	38
Elihu, s. Abiram & Anna, b. May 6, 1781	A	39
Fanny, m. John R. **FULLER**, Nov. 27, 1844, at the house		
of Harmon Peet, by Rev. George Fash, of N. Canaan	A	104
Harriet, m. Frances S. **PELTON**, b. of Canaan, Aug. 20, 1823,		
by Pitkin Cowles	A	82
William, s. Abiram & Anna, b. Aug. 27, 1776	A	39
William, of Salisbury, m. Lucinda **CADY**, of Canaan, Jan.		
19, 1843, by Rev. Levi Warner	A	102
PELTON, Frances S., m. Harriet **PEET**, b. of Canaan, Aug. 20,		
1823, by Pitkin Cowles	A	82
PENDLETON, Russell, of Goshen, m. Alvina **JOHNSON**, of		
Canaan, Feb. 8, 1831, by Rev. Bradley Sillick	A	88
PERKINS, Allen, of Goshen, m. Asenath **COBB**, Feb. 10, 1830,		
by Pitkin Cowles	A	87
William, m. Cynthia **HUDSEL**, b. of Marlborough, Feb. 17,		
1833, by Theodosius Clark	A	91
PERRY, Henry D., m. Ann Jewett **WILLIAMS**, b. of Canaan, Apr.		
1, 1829, by Charles Prentice	A	87
Oren, m. Anna **BLAKE**, Oct. 18, 1826, by Charles Prentice	A	85
PHELPS, Austin, Capt. of Simsbury, m. Rhoda **YALE**, [Mar.] 7,		
1822, by Rev. Charles Prentice	A	81
Benjamin, Jr., m. Dorcas **CARPENTER**, Mar. 8, 1775, by		
Elisha Baker	A	22
Benjamin, s. Friend, b. Oct. 25, 1777	A	42
Bildad, d. Oct. 20, 1773	A	20
Elijah B., of New Milford, m. Wealthy **LAWRENCE**, Dec. 30,		
1821, by Pitkin Cowles	A	80
Friend, m. Rachel **PHELPS**, Jan. 2, 1777	A	25

	Vol.	Page

PHELPS, (cont.)

	Vol.	Page
Joel A., of Middletown, m. Louisa **GREEN**, of Sheffield, Jan. 10, 1832, by Pitkin Cowles	A	90
Laura, m. Charles **YALE**, b. of Canaan, Nov. 15, 1820, by Rev. Charles Prentice	A	79
Mary, of Winsor, m. Timothy **JOHNSON**, of Canaan, Dec. 5, 1753	LR2	233
Rachel, w. Benjamin, d. Aug. 30, 1776	A	25
Rachel, m. Friend **PHELPS**, Jan. 2, 1777	A	25
Rachal, d. Friend, b. Nov. 6, 1779	A	42
Riley, m. Polly **YALE**, b. of Canaan, Nov. 22, 1825, by Charles Prentice	A	85
Sarah, of Canaan, m. Solon E. **BETTIS**, of Sandisfield, July 26, 1825, by Charles Prentice	A	84
Susannah, m. Joel **COWLES**, Oct. 10, 1783	A	39
PHILLIPS, Edson M., m. Sarah Ann **ROOT**, b. of Canaan, Sept. 4, 1848, by Rev. K. W. Keeler	A	105
Lucinda, of Canaan, m. Rufus H. **GAMMONS**, of Salisbury, Apr. 27, 1836, by Charles Prentice	A	95
Nathan, m. Harriet **DEAN**, b. of Canaan, Apr. 17, 1823, by Rev. Charles Prentice	A	82
PIERCE, PEARCE, PEIRCE, Esther, d. Thomas & Olive, b. Oct. 16, 1766	A	9
Eunice, m. Silas **HILLAS**, June 15, 1834, by Reuben Hunt, J. P.	A	93
Harriet, of Canaan, m. Buel **GREEN**, of Sheffield, Jan. 21, 1822, by P. Cowles	A	80
John, s. Thomas & Olive, b. Apr. 20, 1764	A	5
Kezia, m. John **FRANKLIN**, Dec. 24, 1745	A	8
Mary, m. Patrick **LONG**, Mar. 24, 1822, by Pitkin Cowles	A	81
Mary, of Canaan, m. John A. **ELTON**, of Tyringham, Mass., Feb. 2, 1840, by Rev. H. H. Woodbridge, of the 2nd Cong. Ch.	A	99
Olive, d. Thomas & Olive, b. July 30, 1770	A	15
Ruth, d. Thomas & Olive, b. Oct. 8, 1759	A	3
Samuel, s. Thomas & Olive, b. Sept. 22, 1756	A	3
Sarah, d. Thomas & Olive, b. Nov. 20, 1761	A	3
Silas, s. Thomas & Olive, b. Feb. 24, 1772	A	15
Tryphena, d. Thomas & Olive, b. Jan. 22, 1758	A	3
William G., m. Jane E. A[D]AM (?), b. of Canaan, May 1, 1843, by Charles Kittridge	A	103
PIKE, Hiram, of New Marlborough, m. Alice **ROOD**, of Canaan, Dec. 1, 1825, by Pitkin Cowles	A	84
PLUMB, Frederic, m. Anne **PEET**, Jan. 5, 1785	A	38
Frederick, Dr., d. Apr. 12, 1812	A	51
POMEROY, Aurelia, d. Ebenezer & Sally, b. July 5, 1805	A	50
Eliza, d. Joel & Gratia, b. Dec. 9, 1796	A	51
Frederick, s. Joel & Betsey, b. Jan. 12, 1808	A	51

	Vol.	Page
POMEROY, (cont.)		
Gratia, d. Joel & Betsey, b. July 28, 1806	A	51
Jane, d. Joel & Betsey, b. Mar. 10, 1810	A	51
Joel, s. Joel & Betsey, b. July 9, 1812	A	51
Mary, d. Joel & Gratia, b. Feb. 1, 1795	A	51
Mary Ann, d. Ebenezer & Sally, b. Sept. 19, 1810	A	50
Sally, b. Sept. 8, 1801; m. Leman **CHURCH,** Mar. 18, 1819	A	53
Theodore, s. Joel & Gratia, b. Nov. 4, 1792	A	51
POPE, Caroline M., of Canaan, m. John A. **ENSIGN,** of Salisbury,		
Oct. 8, 1844, by Harley Goodwin	A	104
PORTER, Lucy, m. Matthew **WHITE,** Jr., June 8, 1815	A	52
Sarah, m. Hawley **DUNNING,** June 10, 1821, by Pitkin		
Cowles. Int. Pub.	A	80
POST, Henry, m. Hilpa **HOSKINS,** b. of Canaan, May 18, 1831,		
by Charles Prentice	A	89
Mary, of Canaan, m. Charles H. **SMITH,** of Cornwall, Aug.		
20, 1845, by Rev. Albert Nash	A	104
Melisa, of Canaan, m. Benjamin **BISSELL,** Jr., of Litchfield,		
Feb. 6, 1822, by Rev. Charles Prentice	A	80
POTTER, Anna, of Hamden, m. Lewis C. **LAWRENCE,** of		
Canaan, Oct. 14, 1822, by Pitkin Cowles	A	81
William J., of Salisbury, m. Laura **DABALL,** of Canaan,		
Sept. 9, 1841, by Rev. H. H. Woodbridge, of the 2nd		
Cong. Ch. Int. Pub	A	100
POWELL, Edward S., of New Marlborough, m. Mary **PRICE,** of		
Canaan, Mar. 20, 1839, by Samuel W. Smith	A	98
PRENTICE, Charles Theron, m. Harriet **ENSIGN,** Apr. 28, 1835,		
by Charles Prentice	A	94
Clarinda H., m. Sidney **ENSIGN,** Jan. 13, 1833, by		
Charles Prentice	A	91
Eliza A., m. Lucius S. **ADAMS,** Jan. 1, 1835, by Charles		
Prentice. Int. Pub.	A	94
Theodore, of Bridgeport, m. Sarah G. **HOSKINS,** of Canaan,		
[Oct. 31, 1841], by Rev. Edward B. Emerson, of the 1st		
Cong. Ch.	A	101
PRESTON, Cynthia, d. David & Cynthia, b. Feb. 1, 1798	A	44
David, m. Cynthia **SPRAGUE,** Oct. 28, 1781	A	36
David, s. David & Cynthia, b. Apr. 16, 1792	A	42
Harriet, m. Levi M. **GORHAM,** b. of Sheffield, Mass.,		
Mar. 7, 1841, by Rev. H. H. Woodbridge	A	100
John Sprague, s. David & Cynthia, b. Sept. 9, 1784	A	37
Lot, s. David & Cynthia, b. Sept. 27, 1794	A	44
Milo, s. David & Cynthia, b. Apr. 26, 1790	A	41
Milo, s. David & Cynthia, d. July 26, 1791	A	41
Samuel, s. David & C[y]nthia, b. Aug. 2, 1788	A	40
Sophia, d. David & Cynthia, b. Nov. 25, 1782	A	36
PRICE, Mary, of Canaan, m. Edward S. **POWELL,** of New		
Marlborough, Mar. 20, 1839, by Samuel W. Smith	A	98

	Vol.	Page
PRINDLE, Betsey, m. Thomas **BENEDICT**, on or about Feb. 15, 1824, by William Holobird, J. P.	A	83
Joanna, w. Samuell, d. Sept. 15, 1757	LR2	232
Moses, m. Christian **GRIMES**, of Goshen, Mar. 22, 1749	LR1	427
Philemon, Jr., m. Sybel **ROOT**, b. of Canaan, Jan. 4, 1826, by Charles Prentice	A	85
Samuel, s. Moses & Christian, b. Apr. 7, 1751	LR1	427
PRIOR, Amme, d. Clothiel & Anne, b. Mar. 17, 1778	A	30
Dimus, b. Dec. 6, 1768 (Perhaps child of "Clothiel **PRIOR**")	A	19
Jeremiah, s. Clothiel & Anne, b. Apr. 24, 1776	A	30
Rubah, d. Clothiel, b. Jan. 20, 1771	A	19
William, s. Clothiel, b. Feb. 12, 1774	A	19
PURCHAS, Han[n]ah, of Springfield, m. Samuel **TRESCOT**, of Canaan, July 23, 1747	LR1	425
Lydiah, m. Lemuel **ROBARTS**, Aug. 11, 1743	A	1
RACE, Melissa, m. Orlando **CLARK**, b. of Salisbury, Nov. 30, 1842, by Rev. Parmele Chamberlain. Witnesses: Miles Belden, Eliza Belden & Theo. S. Lodges	A	102
RAISONEW (?), Peter, of Great Barrington, Mass., m. Julia A. **BLACK**, of Canaan, Jan. 9, 1842, by Rev. Adam Reed	A	101
RANSOM, Samuel, m. Esther **LAWRENCE**, May 6, 1756, by David Whitney	A	3
Samuel, s. Samuell & Esther, b. Sept. 28, 1759	A	4
Sarah, d. Samuell & Esther, b. Aug. 23, 1757	A	4
[RATHBUN], **RATHBONE**, **RATHBURN**, Abigail, d. Job. & Abigail, b. Mar. 20, 1766	A	10
Job, m. Abigail **RUSSELL**, Dec. 7, 1758	LR2	227
Jobe, s. Job & Abigail, b. Apr. 11, 1770	A	16
John, s. Job & Abigail, b. Apr. 9, 1774	A	24
Josiah, s. Job & Abigail, b. Feb. 5, 1762	A	10
Martha, d. Job & Abigail, b. Mar. 4, 1760	LR2	227
Mehitable, d. Job & Abigail, b. July 25, 1784	A	40
Russell, s. Job & Abigail b. Mar. 18, 1772	A	16
Solomon, s. Job & Abigail, b. Mar. 3, 1764	A	10
Whitfield, s. Job & Abigail, b. Oct. 28, 1782	A	40
RAWLSON, Lyman, m. Sally **FERGUSON**, b. of Canaan, Dec. 10, 1826, by Pitkin Cowles	A	86
REED, Electa, of Canaan, m. Hiram **AUSTIN**, of Perrysbury, N. Y., Nov. 17, 1831, by Charles Prentice	A	89
Elias, m. Anna **FANNING**, b. of Canaan, Jan. 24, 1821, by Pitkin Cowles	A	79
John B., m. Julia **HOSKINS**, Feb. 20, 1828, by Charles Prentice	A	86
John B., m. Mary E. **MANLEY**, Sept. 24, 1838, by H. H. Woodbridge	A	97
Julia Ann, m. Herman **BLAKE**, b. of Canaan, Oct. 31, 1844, by Harley Goodwin	A	104
Mary, of Sharon, m. John **PECK**, of Canaan, Jan. 24, 1754,		

	Vol.	Page

REED, (cont.)

by Mr. Williams — LR2 238

Mary T., d. James & Rhoda, b. July 14, 1843; m. Myron
U. **DEAN,** Mar. 9, 1865 — A 133

Stephen, Dr., of Goshen, m. Emeline **BEEBE,** of Canaan,
May 20, 1829, by Charles Prentice — A 87

RHOADES, Kellogg, of New Marlborough, m. Maria **ANDRUS,** of
Canaan, July 4, 1837, by Rev. H. H. Woodbridge, of the
2nd Cong. Ch. — A 96

RICHARDS, Daniel, m. Hulda **FELLOWS,** Feb. 6, 1773 — A 17

Daniel, s. John & Rachel, b. July 22, 1774 — A 21

Electa, d. John & Abigail, b. Sept. 30, 1765 — A 12

Jerusha, of Norfolk, m. Gideon **LAWRENCE,** of Canaan,
Oct. 12, 1749 — LR1 423

John, m. Abigail **SACKET,** Nov. 30, 1764 — A 12

John, s. John & Abigail, b. June 4, 1773 — A 18

Jonathan, s. Daniel & Hulda, b. Feb. 8, 1773 (Date
conflicts with marriage of parents.) — A 17

Lovise, s. John & Abigail, b. Nov. 25, 1767 — A 12

Mary, of Norfolk, m. Jonathan **FELLOWS,** Sept. 13, 1752,
by David Whitney — LR2 238

Mary, m. Henry **DOOLITTLE,** Dec. 29, 1812 — A 49

Samuell, s. Samuell & Lidiah, b. Sept. 18, 175[ ] — LR2 239

Sarah, of Norfolk, m. William **FELLOWS,** of Canaan,
Feb. 26, 1746/7 — LR1 424

Sarah, m. Solomon **DRAKE,** June 22, 1834, by Reuben Hunt,
J. P. — A 93

RICHARDSON, Gillitt, m. Caroline **DIBBLE,** Dec. 2, 1830, by
James Fenn, J. P. — A 88

Huldah M., of Canaan, m. Henry **HART,** of Sheffield, Mass.,
Dec. 13, 1840, by Rev. H. H. Woodbridge, of the 2nd
Cong. Ch. — A 99

Polly, m. William M. **SMITH,** Dec. 19, 1830, by Pitkin
Cowles — A 88

William, m. Aurelia **BARNES,** b. of Canaan, Nov. 6, 1836,
by Rev. H. H. Woodbridge, of the 2nd Cong. Ch. — A 95

William W., m. Sally M. **PARTRIDGE,** b. of Canaan, Oct.,
18, 1821, by Pitkin Cowles — A 80

RISEING, Abigail, w. Ebenezer, d. Jan. 23, 1753 — LR2 239

Ebenezer, s. Ebenezer & Abigail, d. Jan. 15, 1753 — LR2 239

ROBBINS, ROBBIN, Abigail, m. Timothy **HOLCOMB,** May 20,
1766 — A 16

Amanda, of Canaan, m. Shaler **TROWBRIDGE,** of Sheffield,
Mass., Nov. 1, 1843, by Charles Kettridge — A 103

Elizabeth, d. Zebulon & Sarah, b. June 4, 1750 — LR1 424

Esther, d. Samuel & Salome, b. Jan. 29,. 1777 — A 31

Lucy, m. Harry **WAKEMAN,** June 6, 1833, by William
Holobird, J. P. — A 91

	Vol.	Page

ROBBINS, ROBBIN, (cont.)

Lucy, of Canaan, m. Martin **ROCKWELL,** of Colebrook, Oct. 14, 1834, by Charles Prentice. Int. Pub. — A — 93

Maria, of Canaan, m. Horace **TUCKER,** of Salisbury, July 6, 1840, by H. H. Woodbridge. Int. Pub. — A — 99

Salome, d. Samuel & Salome, b. Jan. 27, 1773 — A — 31

Salome, wid., m. Nathan **HALE,** Apr. 26, 1778 — A — 30

Samuel, s. Samuel & Salome, b. Dec. 17, 1774 — A — 31

ROBERTS, ROBARDS, ROBBERTS, ROBBARTS, ROBART, ROBARTS, Achsah, d. Lemuel, & Lidiah, b. Oct. 30, 1744 — A — 1

Albert, of West Stockbridge, Mass., m. Elizbeth **FAXON,** of Canaan, Nov. 13, 1829, by Pitkin Cowles — A — 87

Cediah*, d. Lemuel & Lidea, b. Sept. 21, 1753 *(Lydia"?) — LR2 — 239

Cornelius, s. Lemuel & Lydiah, b. Feb. 2, 1758 — A — 1

David, s. Lemuel & Lydiah, b. Nov. 30, 1760 — A — 1

Elizabeth, m. Nehemiah **LAWRENCE,** Apr. 12, 1753, by Daniel Farrand — LR2 — 239

Ezekiel, s. Lemuel & Lydiah, b. Dec. 22, 1746 — A — 1

Ezekiel, s. Limuel & Lydia, b. Dec. 22, 1746 — LR1 — 425

Horace, of Goshen, m. Sally **LOWRY,** of Canaan, Oct. 17, 1826, by Charles Prentice — A — 85

Lemuel, m. Lydiah **PURCHAS,** Aug. 11, 1743 — A — 1

Lemuel, s. Lemuel & Lydiah, b. May 3, 1752 — A — 1

Lemuel, s. Lemuel & Lidia, b. May 8, 1752 — LR2 — 239

Lydia (?)*, d. Lemuel & Lidea, b. Sept. 21, 1753 *(Arnold Copy has "Cediah") — LR2 — 239

Lydiah, d. Lemuel & Lydiah, b. Dec. 27, 1753 — A — 1

Mary, d. Lemuel & Lydiah, b. Feb. 20, 1756 — A — 1

Sarah, m. Solomon **WHITNEY,** Nov. 27, 1755, by Rev. Daniel Farrand — LR2 — 237

Stephen, of Goshen, m. Laura **CADY,** of Canaan, July 17, 1842, by Rev. H. H. Woodbridge, of the 2nd Cong. Ch. Int. Pub. — A — 102

William, d. May 28, 1747 — LR1 — 424

William, s. Lemuel & Lydiah, b. Feb. 21, 1749 — A — 1

ROBINSON, Hannah, of Canaan, m. William D. **LIVINGSTONE,** of Sheffield, Mass., Mar. 22, 1835, by Rev. H. H. Woodbridge, of the 2nd Cong. Ch. — A — 94

ROCKWELL, Abigail, m. Abel **LAWRENCE,** Oct. 6, 1783 — A — 38

Altha A., m. Erastus P. **ALLYN,** May 21, 1832, by Pitkin Cowles — A — 90

Ann M., m. Whiting G. **MINOR,** b. of Canaan, Oct. 15, 1834, by Rev. H. H. Woodbridge, of North Canaan — A — 93

Anna, b. May 4, 1762; m. Josiah **LAWRENCE,** Feb. 7, 1788 — A — 49

Betsey, of Canaan, m. Elias **CRANDALL,** of Goshen, Feb. 14, 1831, by Pitkin Cowles — A — 88

Edward, m. Martha Mariah **BUEL,** b. of Canaan, Sept. 13, 1835, by Rev. Thomas Sparkes — A — 94

	Vol.	Page

ROCKWELL, (cont.)

Emma E., of Canaan, m. William J. **SHOOK**, of Norfolk,
July 12, 1849, by Rev. J. W. Robinson — A — 105

Frederick William, m. Eliza Mariah **PECK**, b. of Canaan,
Jan. 29, 1832, by Pitkin Cowles — A — 90

Harmon, m. Sophronia **BALL**, Sept. 11, 1827, by
Pitkin Cowles — A — 86

Joel L., ae 45, of North Canaan, m. Dorothy S. **CHAPEL**,
ae 32, of Colebrook, Sept. 10, 1848, by Rev. Charles W.
Waterous — A — 105

Martin, of Colebrook, m. Lucy **ROBBINS**, of Canaan, Oct. 14,
1834, by Charles Prentice. Int. Pub. — A — 93

Mary, m. Reuben **GRISWOLD**, Feb. 26, 1776 — A — 24

Matilda, of Canaan, m. Charles **WALTER**, of Norfolk, June 3,
1822, by Pitkin Cowles — A — 81

Milo, of Canaan, m. Amanda **TUTTLE**, of Sheffield, Nov. 26,
1823, by Pitkin Cowles — A — 82

ROE, Elizabeth, m. Abiel **FELLOWS**, Jan. 19, 1758, by Col.
David Whitney — A — 11

ROOD, ROODS, RUDE, [see also **ROOT**], Abner, s. Marriner &
Mary, b. Oct. 23, 1785 — A — 40

Alice, of Canaan, m. Hiram **PIKE**, of New Marlborough,
Mass., Dec. 1, 1825, by Pitkin Cowles — A — 84

Asahel, twin with Isaac, s. Roger & Bette, b. Mar. 10, 1782 — A — 36

Daniel, d. David & Lucretia, b. Nov. 22, 1781 — A — 36

Darius, s. David & Lucretia, b. Jan. 25, 1788 — A — 40

David, m. Leucretia **STOW**, June 3, 1779 — A — 35

David, m. Lucretia **STOW**, June 31, 1779 — A — 31

Dorrance, m. Eliza **COLTON**, b. of Canaan, Nov. 29, 1820,
by Pitkin Cowles — A — 79

Elijah, s. Marriner & Mary, b. Sept. 9, 1748 — LR1 — 425

Elijah, m. Martha **STEPHENS**, Nov. 22, 1770 — A — 13

Elijah, s. Elijah & Martha, b. June 20, 1775 — A — 24

Esther, d. Robert & Mary, b. Aug. 9, 1771 — A — 14

[E]unice, d. Jabiz & Luice, b. Nov. 6, 1747 — LR1 — 423

Hannah, d. Marriner, Jr. & Mary, b. July 18, 1775 — A — 24

Ira, s. Elijah & Martha, b. Apr. 18, 1781 — A — 35

Isaac, twin with Asahel, s. Roger & Bette, b. Mar. 10, 1782 — A — 36

Jacob, of Canaan, m. Delia **MORGAN**, of Goshen, Sept. 30,
1822, by Pitkin Cowles — A — 81

James, s. James Rood & Martha Tuttle, b. Dec. 5, 1769 — A — 12

James, s. Marriner, Jr. & Mary, b. Sept. 4, 1773 — A — 24

Jane A., m. Steven **McINTIRE**, of Salisbury, Nov. 11, 1830,
by Pitkin Cowles — A — 88

John, s. Marriner, Jr. & Mary, b. Sept. 9, 1769 — A — 12

Jonathan, s. Roger & Elizabeth, b. Oct. 10, 1784 — A — 40

Laura, d. David & Lucretia, b. Apr. 24, 1786 — A — 40

Lotte, d. David & Lucretia, b. Nov. 30, 1783 — A — 40

	Vol.	Page

ROOD, ROODS, RUDE, (cont.)

Lotte, m. William **LAWRENCE**, Oct. 7, 1801	A	51
Lucy, d. David & Lucretia, b. Apr. 16, 1780	A	35
Lydiah, d. Marriner, b. Aug. 30, 1752	LR2	239
Lidea, d. Marriner, b. Aug. 30, 1752	LR2	239
Marriner, Jr., s. Marriner & Mary, b. Apr. 5, 17[ ]	A	37
Marriner, Jr., m. Mary **HENRY**, Nov. 30, 1768	A	12
Martha, of Canaan, m. Mark **CALENDER**, of Sheffield, Oct. 15, 1829, by Pitkin Cowles	A	87
Mary, d. Marriner & Mary, b. Mar. 11, 1747	LR1	425
Miranda, of Camden, m. Comfort **WHITE**, of Cornwall, May 31, 1837, by H. H. Woodbridge	A	96
Roger, s. Marriner & Mary, b. Apr. 30, 1755	LR2	237
Roger, m. Betty **LAWRENCE**, June 2, 1779	A	31
Roger, m. Betty **LAWRENCE**, June 2, 1779	A	35
Roswell, s. Marriner & Mary, b. Sept. 2, 1789	A	41
Rufus, m. Jerusha H. **STEVENS**, b. of Canaan, Sept. 10, 1838, by Rev. H. H. Woodbridge, of the 2nd Cong. Ch. Int. Pub.	A	97
Ruluff, s. Roger & Betty, b. June 3, 1780	A	35
Samuel, s. Marriner & Mary, b. Dec. 12, 1782	A	36
Sarah, m. Amos S. **HING**, Jan. 13, 1833, by Pitkin Cowles	A	91
Thankfull, d. Elijah & Martha, b. June 22, 1778	A	35
Wilber C., m. Martha **HUNTINGTON**, Aug. 21, 1845, by Lyman Lawrence, J. P.	A	104
William, s. Marriner, Jr. & Mary, b. Dec. 8, 1770	A	13
William, Jr., of Canaan, m. Julia Anna **CLARK**, of New Marlborough, Jan. 20, 1825, by Pitkin Cowles	A	84
ROOT, [see also **ROOD**], Abigail, d. Phinehas & Rebeckah, b. Apr. 18, 1780	A	34
Amelia M., m. Cryus **BAILY**, b. of Canaan, Sept. 4, 1848, by Rev. K. W. Keeler	A	105
Anna, m. Horace A. **BARNES**, Nov. 28, 1824, by Charles Prentice	A	84
Asa, of Canaan, m. Mary **SHAW**, of New Milbury, Jan. 30, 1755	LR2	238
Asa, s. Asa & Mary, b. Jan. 21, 1764	A	23
Betsey, m. Jonathan **FELLOWS**, Nov. 3, 1785	A	45
Betsey, of Canaan, m. Cyrus **NORCOTT**, of Stockbridge, Mass., Apr. 11, 1821, by Rev. Charles Prentice, of the 1st. Ch.	LR2 A	80
Candace, d. Simeon & Mehitabel, b. Aug. 23, 1763	A	40
Clarissa A., of Sheffield, Mass., m. Silas **TROWBRIDGE**, of Kalamazoo, Mich., Oct. 15, 1839, by Rev. H. H. Woodbridge, of the 2nd Cong. Ch.	A	98
Cyrus, s. Asa & Mary, b. June 28, 1774	A	23
David, s. Simeon & Mehitabel, b. Nov. 30, 1755	A	2
David, m. Louisa **PECK**, b. of Canaan, May 18, 1846,		

	Vol.	Page
ROOT, (cont.)		
Rachel, d. Joshua & Easter, b. May 3, 1757	LR2	232
Rachel, d. Phinehas & Rebeckah, b. Feb. 21, 1771	A	21
Rebeckah, d. Phinehas & Rebeckah, b. Apr. 9, 1772	A	21
Remmeline, of Canaan, m. Daniel **WHITE**, of Sharon,		
May 19, 1842, by Rev. H. H. Woodbridge	A	101
R[e]ubin, s. Joshua & Easther, b. Nov. 7, 1750	LR1	427
Reuben, m. Stata **OAKLEY**, b. of Canaan, Dec. 22, 1824,		
by Rev. Daniel Miller, of the Meth. E. Ch.	A	84
Rhoda, d. Asa & Mary, b. [ ] 3, 1756	A	3
Sarah, d. Asa & Mary, b. Apr. 9, 1771	A	23
Sarah, m. Samuel **BECKLEY**, May 28, 1771	A	16
Sarah Ann, m. Edson M. **PHILLIPS**, b. of Canaan, Sept. 4,		
1848, by Rev. K. W. Keeler	A	105
Cybel*, d. Samuel & Anna, b. Jan. 25, 1803 *("Sybel")	A	47
Sybel, m. Philemon **PRINDLE**, Jr., b. of Canaan, Jan. 4,		
1826, by Charles Prentice	A	85
Thirza, d. William & Elizabeth, b. Dec. 22, 1773	A	20
William, s. William & Elizabeth, b. July 29, 1770	A	20
Zuriah, d. Phinehas, b. Jan. 23, 1777	A	34
ROSE, Alban, m. Huldah **WOODRUFF**, of Harwinton, Dec. 23,		
1794, by Rev. Joshua Knapp	A	48
Alban, m. Anna **HASKEL**, Dec. 12, 1801, by Elizur Wright	A	48
Alban & Anna, had s. [ ], b. Sept. 12, 1810	A	48
Alban & Anna, had s. [ ], d. Sept 17, 1810, ae 5 d.	A	48
Herman, s. Alban & Anna, b. Mar. 29, 1807	A	48
Herman, s. Alban & Anna, d. May 15, 1807, ae 6 w. 5 d.	A	48
Huldah, w. Alban, d. June 1, 1800, ae 32 y.	A	48
Huldah, d. Alban & Anna, b. Mar. 10, 1808	A	48
Lucy Ann, d. Alban & Anna, b. Sept. 5, 1802	A	48
Norman, s. Alban & Huldah, d. Feb. 12, 1810, ae 11 y. 12 d.	A	48
Norman Woodruff, s. Alban & Huldah, b. Feb. 1, 1799	A	48
Porter, m. Asenath **MARVIN**, b. of Canaan, Sept. 29, 1831,		
by Pitkin Cowles	A	89
Rachel, d. Alban & Anna, b. Aug. 4, 1805	A	48
Sherman M., m. Mary **LEWIS**, b. of Canaan, Oct. 11, 1820,		
by Pitkin Cowles	A	79
ROSS, ROS, Almira, of Canaan, m. William B. **HINMAN**, of		
Shelffield, Mass., Aug. 19, 1840, by Rev. Henry H.		
Woodbridge, of the 2nd Cong. Ch.	A	99
Dorothy, m. Benjamin **HEWITT**, Oct. 30, 1765	A	6
ROSSITER, ROSSETTER, Ruth, of Killingsworth, m. Nehemiah		
MARSH, Nov. 16, 1780	A	45
Stephen, of Salisbury, m. Charlot **VICTORY**, of Canaan,		
Sept. 4, 1841, by Levi Warner	A	101
ROWLSTON, Esther, m. Benjamin **STEVENS**, 2nd, Nov. 4, 1781	A	38
Harriet, m. Benjamin **BUEL**, b. of Canaan, Nov. 24, 1831,		
by Pitkin Cowles	A	89

	Vol.	Page
RUDE, [see under ROOD]		
RUSSELL, RUSSEL, Abigail, m. Job **RATHBURN**, Dec. 7, 1758	LR2	227
Ann, d. Daniel & Ann, b. Aug. 26, 1758	LR1	228
Charlotte M., of Salisbury, m. Henry W. **WHITE**, of Canaan, Sept. 6, 1838, by Rev. H. H. Woodbridge, of the 2nd Cong. Ch. Int. Pub.	A	97
Daniel, m. Ann **JONES**, Mar. 23, 1758	LR2	228
Daniel & Ann, had d. [ ], b. Sept. 7, 1760	A	2
Horace, m. Martha Ann **CURREY**, b. of Canaan, July 15, 1838, by Adam Reed	A	97
Jane, of Canaan, m. Andrew **PALMER**, of Goshen, Feb. 7, 1837, by Charles Prentice	A	96
John, Jr., of Salisbury, m. Maria **ALLING**, of Canaan, Dec. 10, 1826, by Joshua Cornwall, J. P.	A	85
John G., of Great Barrington, Mass., m. Jennet E. **WILCOX**, of Canaan, Nov. 26, 1829, by Charles Prentice	A	87
Martha, m. David **WRIGHT**, Jr., June 11, [1753?], by Rev. Daniel Farrand	LR2	239
Rensselear W., m. Lucy A. **MARSH**, b. of Canaan, Oct. 8, 1839, by Rev. H. H. Woodbridge, of the 2nd Cong. Ch.	A	98
Sarah, d. Jonathan & Mehetabel, b. May 18, 1758	LR2	228
Solomon, s. Jonathan & Mehitabel, b. Sept. 26, 1752	LR2	239
William R. Jr., m. Mercy R. **BENEDICT**, Apr. 26, 1829, by Rufus Babcock, of Colebrook	A	87
SACKET[T], Abigail, m. John **RICHARDS**, Nov. 30, 1764	A	12
SAGE, Abigail, m. Salmon H. **ELTON**, b. of Canaan, Dec. 16, 1832, by Pitkin Cowles	A	90
ST. JOHN, Siles A., of Ontario, N. Y., m. Emeline H. **BUCKLEY**, of Canaan, July 5, 1832, by Charles Prentice	A	90
SAWYER, Maritta, m. Luther B. **BUCKLEY**, b. of Canaan, Aug. 16, 1825, by Charles Prentice	A	84
SEARS, Benjamin, of Sharon, m. Emeline **COUCH**, of Canaan, Sept. 11, 1844, by Harley Goodwin	A	103
SEDGWICK, Albert, of Cornwall, m. Mary **HUNT**, of Canaan, Oct. 23, 1822, by Rev. Charles Prentice	A	81
Benjamin, d. June 12, 1778	A	29
Benjamin, s. James & Louis, b. Nov. 25, 1803	A	50
Betsey Louisa, d. James & Louis, b. Nov. 5, 1812	A	50
Catharine Mary, d. Theodore & Abigail, b. Dec. 29, 1806, in New Marlborough	A	50
Elizabeth, d. Benjamin & Mary, b. Nov. 31, 1771	A	29
Frances Permela, d. James & Louis, b. Dec. 3, 1808	A	50
Jane, d. Theodore & Abigail, b. June 29, 1814	A	51
Julia Eliza, d. James & Louis, b. Apr. 22, 1806	A	50
Lois, d. Benjamin & Mary, b. May 7, 1775	A	29
Louisa, d. Theodore & Abigail, b. Nov. 29, 1808	A	50
Olive, d. Benjamin & Mary, b. Apr. 26, 1777	A	29
Thankfull, d. Benjamin & Mary, b. Apr. 26, 1773	A	29

	Vol.	Page

SEDGWICK, (cont.)

Theodore Russell, s. Theodore & Abigail, b. July 1, 1812 — A — 50

SEWARD, George M., of Canaan, m. Ruth A. **KELLOGG,**. of
Sandisfield, Co. of Berkshire, Mass., Sept. 28, 1845, by
Rev. D. D. Francis — A — 106

SHAD, Samuel, m. Rhoda **KELLOGG,** Jan. 23, 1777 — A — 25

SHAW, Mary, of New Milbury, m. Asa **ROOT,** of Canaan, Jan. 30,
1755 — LR2 — 238

SHEFFIELD, Micah, m. Rhoda **CURTISS,** Dec. 26, 1776 — A — 25

SHOOK, William J., of Norfolk, m. Emma E. **ROCKWELL,** of
Canaan, July 12, 1849, by Rev. J. W. Robinson — A — 105

SHORES, John, of New Marlboro, Mass., m. Betsey Ann **MIX,** of
Canaan, Jan. 1, 1849, by Rev. D. D. Francis — A — 107

SILL, John, Dea. of Bethany, Genessee Co. N. Y., m. Electa **DEAN,**
of Canaan, Oct. 21, 1836, by Charles Prentice — A — 95

SKINNER, Timothy P., of Winsted, m. Mary J. **JACKWAY,** of
Canaan, Mar. 22, 1840, by Rev. H. H. Woodbridge, of the
2nd Cong. Ch. — A — 99

SLATER, Perry, m. Lucinda **MOORE,** Feb. 26, 1832, by James
Fenn, J. P. — A — 90

SLOAN, Sarah, d. Samuel & Hannah, b. May 8, 1764 — A — 5

SMITH, Avery, of Norfolk, m. Lucinda **FOSTER,** of Canaan, Jan.
18, 1821, by Pitkin Cowles — A — 79

Azanah, m. Betsey **DEAN,** Apr. 6, 1828, by Charles Prentice — A — 86

Charles H., of Cornwall, m. Mary **POST,** of Canaan, Aug.
20, 1845, by Rev. Albert Nash — A — 104

Ebenezer, m. Lucy **STEVENS,** Oct. 15, 1781 — A — 43

Edward, of Salisbury, m. Sarah M. **GILLETT,** of Canaan,
Nov. 7, 1849, by Rev. D. D. Francis — A — 108

Elizabeth, m. Jeremiah **LAWRENCE,** June 23, 1772 — A — 16

George C., of Norfolk, m. Betsey **BARBER,** of Canaan, June
5, 1822, by Pitkin Cowles — A — 81

Horatio N., of Sharon, m. Mary **HOLCOMB,** of Canaan, June
26, 1828, by Rev. Silas Ambler — A — 86

Ithamer H., Dr., of Sheffield, m. Jane **DUNHAM,** of Canaan,
Jan. 17, 1832, by Pitkin Cowles — A — 90

J. Edmund, Dr. of West Cornwall, m. Mary F. **BABCOCK,** of
Hudson, N. Y., Oct. 5, 1847, by Rev. D. D. Francis — A — 107

Lucy Phebe, d. Ebenezer & Lucy, b. May 20, 1782 — A — 43

Polly, m. John **PAIN,** b. of Canaan, June 10, 1822, by
Charles Prentice — A — 81

Sarah, of Canaan, m. Salmon **KASSON,** of New Marlborough,
Mass., [ ], by Rev. Edward B. Emerson. Recorded Mar.
28, 1842 — A — 101

Sherman, m. Lydia **FELLOWS,** b. of Canaan, June 12, 1831,
by Harmon Ellis, of Bap. Ch., of Norfolk — A — 89

Wheeler M., m. Melinda **FELLOWS,** b. of Canaan, May 9,
1821, by Pitkin Cowles — A — 80

	Vol.	Page

SMITH, (cont.)

William M., m. Polly **RICHARDSON**, Dec. 19, 1830, by
Pitkin Cowles | A | 88

SNYDER, Peter, of Canaan, m. Caroline **MYRES**, of Clavarock,
Columbia Co., N. Y., Oct. 28, 1849, by Rev. D. D.
Francis | A | 108

Sabina E., m. Edwin W. **JOHNSON**, Feb. 9, 1851*, by Rev.
Zephaniah D. Scobey *(Arnold Copy has "1857") | A | 108

SOUTHWORTH, Constant, of Salisbury, m. Julia Mariah **YALE**,
of Canaan, Sept. 6, 1824, by Pitkin Cowles | A | 83

SPARKS, Lemuel, of Sheffield, Mass., m. Mrs. Hannah **INGRAM**,
of Canaan, Sept. 1, 1844, by Rev. Stephen J. Stebbins | A | 103

SPAULDING, Ariel, s. John & Sarah, b. Oct. 24, 1764 | A | 14

Emily, of Canaan, m. Joel **HINES**, of Norfolk, Feb. 24, 1844,
by Rev. Harley Goodwin | A | 103

Ezra, d. Apr. 29, 1767 | A | 11

Hannah, d. John & Sarah, b. Mar. 8, 1768 | A | 14

John, twin with Sarah, s. John & Sarah, b. Feb. 26, 1774 | A | 19

Juiia, m. James H. **HATCH**, b. of Canaan, Dec. 27, 1829,
by Rev. Noah Bigelow. Int. Pub. | A | 87

Linne, m. Reuben **DARLEY**, Oct. 27, 1779 | A | 34

Luranah, d. John & Sarah, b. Sept. 11, 1766 | A | 14

Mary, m. George W. **STEVENS**, Sept. 17, 1839, by Rev. A.
Bushnell, Jr. | A | 98

Rebeckah, d. John & Sarah, b. Sept. 25, 1771 | A | 14

Sarah, m. Joseph **MORGAN**, Apr. 13, 1769 | A | 12

Sarah, twin with John, d. John & Sarah, b. Feb. 26, 1774 | A | 19

SPERRY, Augustus Wooden,[s. Wooden & Anne], b. Aug. 30, 1780 | A | 36

Charlotte, [s. Wooden & Anne], b. Sept. 5, 1782 | A | 36

Clary, d. Wooden & Anne, b. June 13, 1774/5 | A | 36

Miles, s. [Wooden & Anne], b. Oct. 10, 1778 | A | 36

Polly, [d. Wooden & Anne], b. Sept. 13, 1776 | A | 36

SPRAGUE, Asenath, d. John & Sarah, b. Nov. 21, 1758 | A | 1

Scynthia, d. John, Jr. & Sarah, b. Jan. 1, 1756 | LR2 | 237

Cynthia, m. David **PRESTON**, Oct. 28, 1781 | A | 36

Samuel, s. John & Sarah, b. Oct. 7, 1760 | A | 1

Sarah, m. Ithamer **BLAKESLEE**, June 9, 1773 | A | 18

SQUIRE, Ame, d. Odel & Sarah, b. Mar. 4, 1757 | LR2 | 228

Jonathan, s. Odel & Sarah, b. Mar. 28, 1755 | LR2 | 228

Sarah, d. Odel & Sarah, b. May 11, 1759 | LR2 | 227

STEVENS, STEPHENS, Abigail, d. Benjamin & Elizabeth, b. Apr.
11, 1756 | A | 8

Abigail, d. Jesse & Sarah, b. Nov. 27, 1757 | A | 17

Adela, d. Benjamin & Esther, b. May 27, 1795 | A | 43

Ame, d. Andrew & Esther, b. May 17, 1747 | LR1 | 423

Amy, m. Oliver **JEWEL**, Feb. 23, 1777 | A | 26

Andrew, s. Andrew & Esther, b. July 20, 1749 | LR1 | 423

Annar, d. Samuel & Joanna, b. Aug. 30, 1769 | A | 23

	Vol.	Page

STEVENS, STEPHENS, (cont.)

	Vol.	Page
Anne, d. Jedediah & Mary, b. Mar. 17, 1753	LR2	239
Anne, m. Jeremiah BAKER, Mar. 4, 1773 *(Arnold Copy has "Linne")	A	24
Arthur, s. Benjamin & Esther, b. Nov. 26, 1791	A	41
Azubah, d. Reuben & Hannah, b. Aug. 7, 1773	A	22
Benjamin, s. Zebulon & Merriam, b. June 25, 1754	A	6
Benjamin, 2nd, m. Esther ROWLSTON, Nov. 4, 1781	A	38
Bridget, d. [Abel & Bridget], b. Aug. 8, 1777	A	40
Cloe, m. Elisha, FREEMAN, May 5, 1771	A	18
Clerresse, d. Joshua & Christian, b. Aug. 7, 1768	A	12
Cynthia, d. Jedediah & Mary, b. Sept. 26, 1768	A	29
Cyrus, s. Reuben & Hannah, b. Apr, 2, 1765	A	7
Daphne, d. Benjamin & Esther, b. Nov. 22, 1782	A	38
Desire, m. Moses MARSH, Jan. 24, 1758, by Rev. Mr. Farrand	LR2	227
Dorothy, d. John & Phebe, b. Oct. 19., 1769* *("1759"? written below)	A	7
Drusilla, d. Benjamin & Elizabeth, b. June 24, 1759	A	8
Dulana, d. Benjamin & Esther, b. Mar. 7, 1788	A	41
Dulana, d. Benjamin & Esther, d. Jan. 13, 1791	A	41
Elias, s. Henry & Sarah, b. June 6, 1755	A	9
Elizabeth, d. Benjamin & Elizabeth, b. Nov. 4, 1746	A	8
Elizabeth, d. Jesse & Sarah, b. Sept. 27, 1763	A	18
Elizabeth, d. [Abel & Bridget], b. Apr. 23, 1783	A	40
Ephraim, s. Zebulon & Merriam, b. Oct. 12, 1757; d. Aug. 26, 1760	A	6
Esther, d. Andrew & Esther, b. Apr. 26, 1745	LR1	423
Esther, d. John & Phebe, b. June 20, 1763	A	7
Esther, d. Richard P. & Sally, b. July 10, 1819	A	52
Esther, w. Benjamin, d. Dec. 10, 1835, ae 79 y. 1 m.	A	53
Eunice, d. Jedediah & Mary, b. June 12, 1757* * (Date conflicts with birth of Jedediah)	A	7
Eunice, d. Reuben & Hannah, b. Feb. 6, 1763	A	7
Eunice, d. [Abel & Bridget], b. June 28, 1785	A	40
Ezra, s. Henry & Anne, b. May 20, 1782	A	36
George W., m. Mary SPAULDING, Sept. 17, 1839, by Rev. A. Bushnell, Jr.	A	98
Guy, s. Benjamin & Esther, b. Jan. 14, 1790	A	41
Guy, s. Benjamin & Esther, d. Aug. 10, 1793	A	42
Hannah, d. Reuben & Hannah, b. Nov. 23, 1770	A	16
Huldah, d. James & Phebe, b. May 12, 1772	A	15
Huldah, d. James & Phebe, b. May 12, 1772	A	22
Ira, s. Jedidiah & Mary, b. July 18, 1759	A	7
James, m. Phebe GEUTAN (?), Jan. 19, 1768	A	12
Jane, d. Benjamin & Esther, b. May 28, 1786	A	39
Jedediah, s. Jedediah & Mary, b. May 11, 1757 (Date conflicts with birth of Eunice)	A	7
Jerusha H., m. Rufus ROOD, b. of Canaan, Sept. 10, 1838,		

	Vol.	Page
STEVENS, STEPHENS, (cont.)		
by Rev. H. H. Woodbridge, of the 2nd Cong. Ch.		
Int. Pub.	A	97
Jesse, d. Jan. 27, 1772	A	18
John, s. Andrew & Esther, b. Oct. 19, 1737	LR1	423
John, m. Phebe **HOW**, Jan. 2, 1759	LR2	228
Jonathan, s. Zebulon & Merriam, b. Mar. 7, 1767	A	12
Joshua, m. Christian **DUTCHER**, Oct. 27, 1767	A	11
Leander, s. Joshua & Christian, b. May 2, 1771	A	13
Linne *, m. Jeremiah **BAKER**, Mar. 4, 1773 *(Overwritten		
to read "Anne")	A	24
Lois, d. Reuben & Hannah, b. Feb. 14, 1761	A	7
Lois, m. David **FELLOWS**, Dec. 22, 1763, by Col. Whitney	A	4
Lucy, d. Henry, Jr., b. Sept. 4, 1752	LR2	239
Lucy, m. Ebenezer **SMITH**, Oct. 15, 1781	A	43
Lydia, d. Abel & Bridget, b. June 28, 1775	A	40
Marcy, d. Andrew & Esther, b. Aug. 20, 1740	LR1	423
Martha, d. John & Phebe, b. May 12, 1761	A	7
Martha, m. Elijah **ROOD**, Nov. 22, 1770	A	13
Mary, d. Benjamin & Elizabeth, b. Oct. 11, 1750	A	8
Mary, m. Thomas **WILLIAMS**, Nov. 15, 1753	LR2	237
Mary, m. Ezekiel **HAMILTON**, Aug. 1, 1771	A	16
Nathan, s. Jedidiah & Mary, b. Aug. 24, 1766	A	10
Nathaniel, m. Betsey Ann **LAWRENCE**, b. of Canaan, Jan.		
22, 1827* by H. H. Woodbridge *("1837"?)	A	96
Nehemiah S., m. Elisa F. **DAY**, b. of Canaan, Jan. 1,		
1846, by Rev. D. D. Francis	A	106
Phebe, d. John & Phebe, b. Feb. 21, 1766	A	39
Phebe, m. Jeremiah **LAWRENCE**, Jan. 25, 1786	A	39
Prissylla, d. [Abel & Bridget], b. Oct. 29, 1780	A	40
Reuben, m. Hannah **BROOKINS**, Jan. 14, 1760	A	7
Reuben, s. Reuben & Hannah, b. Aug. 24, 1768	A	12
Richard Price, s. Benjamin & Esther, b. Sept. 12, 1793	A	42
Richard Price, m. Sally **FOSTER**, Mar. 27, 1818	A	52
Rufus, s. Jedediah & Mary, b. May 2, 1762	A	7
Ruluff, s. Joshua & Christian, b. Oct. 18, 1773	A	17
Safford, s. Andrew & Esther, b. May 13, 1743	LR1	423
Sarah, d. Jesse & Sarah b. July [ ], 1760	A	18
Sarah, d. Benjamin & Elizabeth, b. Jan. 27, 1763	A	8
Sarah, d. James & Rhoda*, b. Nov. 15, 1774 *("Phebe"?)	A	20
Sarah, m. Nathaniel **LAWRENCE**, Feb. 11, 1796	A	49
Seth, m. Eunice **MUNSON**, Apr. 22, 1824, by [ ]	A	83
Stephen, s. Andrew & Esther, b. [ ], 19, 1751	LR1	423
Sylvia, d. Jedediah & Mary, b. June 14, 1764	A	7
Thomas, s. Zebulon & Merriam, b. May 5, 1760	A	6
Truman, s. James & Phebe, b. July 21, 1770	A	13
Tryphena, d. [Abel & Bridget], b. Mar, 12, 1789	A	40
Wealthy Ann, of Canaan, m. Martin F. **GLEASON**,		

	Vol.	Page
STEVENS, STEPHENS, (cont.)		
of Austerlitz, N. Y., Jan. 18, 1849, by Rev. D. D. Francis	A	108
William Fellows, s. Samuel & Joanna, b. June 7, 1771	A	23
Zebulon, m. Thankfull **PARTRIDGE**, Oct. 14, 1773	A	43
Zebulon, Jr., m., Sarah **HERRICK**, Mar. 28, 1779	A	31
STEWART, [see under **STUART**]		
STILLMAN, Sidney, of Henesdale, Pa., m. Sophia R. **ISHAM**, of		
Canaan, Sept. 25, 1839, by Rev. H. H. Woodbridge, of		
the 2nd Cong. Ch.	A	98
Pircey, m. Ashbel **LANE**, b. of Canaan, Sept. 20, 1820, by		
Pitkin Cowles	A	79
STODDARD, Esther, m. Erastus **BROWN**, Sept. 27, 1800	A	46
STOW, Hannah, d. Samuel & Lucretia, b. Dec. 10, 1769	A	31
Henry, s. Samuel & Lucretia, b. June 10, 1775	A	31
Leucretia, m. David **ROOD**, June 3, 1779	A	35
Lucretia, m. David **ROOD**, June 31, 1779	A	31
Margaret, d. Mar. 19, 1777	A	31
Samuel, s. Samuel & Lucretia, b. July 3, 1772	A	31
STRONG, Avial, s. Oliver & Lois, b. Feb. 21, 1763	A	3
Darius, s. Oliver & Lois, b. Apr. 27, 1761	A	3
Harmon L., of Salisbury, m. Lucy L. **JOHNSON**, of Canaan,		
Aug. 23, 1840, by Rev., Henry H. Woodbridge, of the		
2nd Cong. ch. Int. Pub.	A	99
Oliver, m. Lois **LAWRENCE**, Apr. 10, 1760	LR2	227
Rachel, d. Oliver & Lois, b. July 30, 1765	A	5
Sarah, m. William **HENSDELL**, June 14, 1781	A	35
STUART, STEWART, Duncan L., m. Catharine L. **DUTCHER**,		
Dec. 30, 1849, by Rev. William Atwell, of Christ Ch.	A	106
William T., of Milan, N. Y., m. Maria **TANNER**, of Canaan,		
Feb. 8, 1830, by Pitkin Cowles	A	87
STURGIS, Lewis B., of Sharon, m. Charlotte **HUNT**, of Canaan,		
June 18, 1828, by Charles Prentice	A	86
SUIDAM, Adoniram, of Salisbury, m. Alma C. **BLAKE**, of Canaan,		
Feb. 26, 1824, by Charles Prentice	A	83
SUTTON, Abigail, wid., m. Capt. Nehemiah **LAWRENCE**,		
Oct. 19, 17[ ]	A	39
Abigail, d. Edward & Abigail, b. Nov. 2, 1771	A	25
Charles Burrall, s. Edward & Abigail, b. Apr. 14, 1773	A	25
Edward, s. Edward & Abigail, b. Mar. 12, 1775	A	25
Edward, d. Sept, 6, 1776	A	25
[SUYDAM], [see under **SUIDAM**]		
SWEET, Franklin, of Cornwall, m. Emeline **HANCHET**, of Canaan,		
June 17, 1838, by H. H. Woodbridge	A	97
SWIFT, Augustus B., of Cornwall, m. Rebecca **MUNSON**, of		
Canaan, Sept. 20, 1820, by Rev. Charles Prentice	A	79
Rhoda, m. Miles **LEWIS**, Oct. 5, 1794	A	44
TANNER, Maria, of Canaan, m. William T. **STUART**, of Milan, N.		
Y., Feb. 8, 1830, by Pitkin Cowles	A	87

	Vol.	Page
TAYLOR, Anna, d. Lemuel & Berthsheba, b. June 14, 1752	LR2	237
Daniel, s. Lemuel & Berthsheba, b. Sept. 22, 1754	LR2	237
Hannah, m. Ebenezer **FULLER**, Apr. 17, 1775, by Elisha Baker	A	22
Lemuel, s. Lemuel & Barshebeth, b. May 2, 1762	A	3
Olive, d. Lemuel & Berthsheba, b. Nov. 18, 1756	LR2	237
Symon J., of Cornwall, m. Rhoda **PARNELY**, of Salisbury, Oct. 20, 1844, by Rev. Stephen J. Stebbins	A	104
[TEN EYECKE], TEN IKE, John, of Canaan, m. Eliza **ARMSTRONG**, of Pine Plains, N. Y., Oct. 10, 1830, by Pitkin Cowles	A	88
THATCHER, Desire, m. John **ASHLEY**, Apr. 24, 1765	A	7
THOMAS, James, s. Ephraim & Abigail, b. Apr. 1, 1742	A	4
John, s. Ephraim & Abigail, b. Mar. 17, 1744	A	4
Sarah, d. Ephraim & Abigail, b. Dec. 4, 1746	A	4
THOMPSON, THOMSON, Amos, Rev. had negro James, s. Jupeter & Fan, b. Mar. 23, 1790, & Laura, d. Jepeter & Fan, b. Dec. 1, 1791	A	41
Amos. Rev. had negro Betsey, d. Jupiter & Fan, b. May 3, 1794	A	42
Comfort, of Wallingford, m. Benjamin **KELLOGG**, Nov. 20, 1754	A	2
Egbert Newton, s. Samuel & Submit, b. Sept. 15, 1809	A	48
George, m. Sarah M. **CROFOOT**, b. of Canaan, July 22, 1845, by Rev. D. D. Francis	A	106
Giles, s. Levi & May, b. June 10, 1780	A	37
Isaac Orren, s. Samuel & Submit, b. Dec. 14, 1805	A	48
Prudence, d. Samuel & Submit, b. Oct. 14, 1807	A	48
TOBEY, Benjamin Franklin, m. Annah Minerva **COOPER**, b. of Canaan, Oct. 31, 1832, by Rev. Harmon Ellis, of the 1st Bap. Ch., Norfolk	A	90
Harriet, m. Calvin **MOREY**, Mar. 10, 1822, by Bushnell Knapp, J. P.	A	81
Henry A., of New Bedford, Mass., m. L. Sophia **HANCHET**, of Canaan, Oct. 22, 1849, by Rev. D. D. Francis	A	108
TOLLMADE, Milo, of Lee, Mass., m. Sarah Ann **HOWE**, of Canaan, Dec. 23, 1829, by Charles Prentice	A	87
TOOLEY, Abigail, d. Peter & Abigail, b. Jan. 17, 1776	A	39
Anna, d. Peter & Abigail, b. June 6, 1774	A	39
Caty, d. Peter & Abigail, b. Jan. 30, 1780	A	39
Jeremiah, s. Peter & Abigail, b. June 10, 1770	A	39
Olive, d. Peter & Abigail, b. June 26, 1772	A	39
TREADWAY, Marvin, of Torrington, m. Mrs. Mary **HERD**, of South Canaan, Feb. 21, 1841, by Rev. Erastus Doty, of Colebrook	A	100
TRESCOTT, TRESCOT, TRESCOTE, TRISCOT, Bridget, d. Samuell & Hannah, b. Aug. 16, 1756	LR2	233
Ebenezer, s. Samuell & Hannah, b. Jan. 2, 1751/2	LR1	426

	Vol.	Page
TRESCOTT, TRESCOT, TRESCOTE, TRISCOT, (cont.)		
Hannah, d. Samuell & Hannah, b. Dec. 18, 1754	LR2	237
Hannah, d. Samuell & Hannah, d. Nov. 15, 1756	LR2	233
Mary A., ae 22, of Canaan, m. Henry J. **MEAD**, ae 24, of		
Canaan, Oct. 24, 1848, by Rev. C. H. Watrous	A	105
Samuel, of Canaan, m. Hanah **PURCHAS**, of Springfield,		
July 23, 1747	LR1	425
Samuell, s. Samuell & Hannah, b. Mar. 13, 1749	LR1	426
Seth, s. Sam[ue]ll & Hannah, b. Mar. 24, 1753	LR2	238
Solon, s. Samuel & Hannah, b. June 15, 1750	LR1	426
Thomas, s. Samuel & Hanna, b. Jan. 1, 1758	LR2	228
Wesley, m. Amey E. **KELLOGG**, b. of Canaan, July 12, 1842,		
by Rev. H. H. Woodbridge, of the 2nd Cong. Ch. Int.		
Pub.	A	101
TROWBRIDGE, Shaler, of Sheffield, Mass., m. Amanda		
ROBBINS, of Canaan, Nov. 1, 1843, by Charles		
Kettridge	A	103
Silas, of Kalamazoo, Mich., m. Clarissa A. **ROOT**, of		
Sheffield, Mass., Oct. 15, 1839, by Rev. H. H.		
Woodbridge, of the 2nd Cong. Ch.	A	98
TUBBS, TUBB, Betsey, d. Simon & Lydia, b. Sept. 14, 1765	A	7
Betsey, m. David **WOODARD**, Oct. 3, 1785	A	42
John, [s. Thomas & Ame], b. Feb. 15, 1785; d. July 6, 1786	A	40
Lidiah, d. Simeon & Lidiah, b. Aug. 21, 1760	A	2
Mary, [d. Thomas & Ame], b. July 1, 1787	A	40
Phebe, [d. Thomas & Ame], b. Feb. 17, 1781	A	40
Sarah, m. David **LAWRENCE**, Sept. 16, 1756	A	4
Simeon, m. Lidiah **MARVEN**, of Lime, Oct. 8, 1759	LR2	227
Simon, s. Simon & Sarah, b. Jan. 16, 1756	LR2	228
Thomas, m. Amey **LAWRENCE**, Nov. 10, 1779	A	32
Thomas, m. Ame **LAWRENCE**, Nov. 9, 1780	A	40
Wealthy, [d. Thomas & Ame], b. July 19, 1782	A	40
TUCKER, Diana Anna, d. Isaac & Elizabeth, b. Feb. 15, 1786	A	39
Hannah, d. Isaac & Elizabeth, b. Mar. 16, 1784	A	37
Horace, of Salisbury, m. Maria **ROBBINS**, of Canaan,		
July 6, 1840, by H. H. Woodbridge. Int. Pub.	A	99
Isaac, m. Elizabeth **HORSFORD**, May 9, 1782	A	37
TURNER, Mary, m. Samuel **HOW**, Jr., Sept. 29, 1763	A	5
TUTTLE, Amanda, of Sheffield, m. Milo **ROCKWELL**, of Canaan,		
Nov. 26, 1823, by Pitkin Cowles	A	82
John W., m. Julia Ann **CONE**, Apr. 29, 1829, by Charles		
Prentice	A	87
Martha, had s. James **ROOD**, b. Dec. 5, 1769, f. James **ROOD**	A	12
Myron, of Canaan, m. Harriet **PECK**, of Wallingford, Dec.		
23, 1832, by Theodosius Clark	A	91
TYLER, Abigail, d. Nathaniel & Lydia, b. Aug. 15, 1761	A	9
Harriet, of Richmond, Mass., m. Benjamin L. **WOOD**, of		
Cornwall, Sept. 29, 1825, by Charles Prentice	A	84

	Vol.	Page
TYLER, (cont.)		
James, s. Nathaniel & Lydia, b. Dec. 27, 1763	A	9
UNDERWOOD, Jay A., m. Jane C. **DAY**, Oct. 28, 1850, by Rev.		
Isaac H. Scott, of M. E. Ch.	A	108
Louisa A., of Canaan, m. John R. **BALDWIN**, of Stamford,		
N. Y., Oct. 25, 1847, by Rev. D. D. Francis	A	107
UPSON, Lucy, m. Andrew **BACON**, Dec. 29, 1788	A	41
VAN BUREN, John, of Schadoe, N. Y., m. Julia E. **FENN**, of		
Canaan, Dec. 24, 1832, by Teodosius Clark	A	91
VAN DUSEN, VAN DUSON, Eleanor, had s. [ ], b. Apr. 8, 1792;		
d. same year	A	47
Harriet, [d. Eleanor], b. Mar. 27, 1801	A	47
Joseph, [s. Eleanor], b. June 8, 1796; d. Nov. [ ], 1799	A	47
Luther, [s. Eleanor], b. May 28, 1799	A	47
Margaret, [d. Eleanor], b. Mar. 17, 1785	A	47
Peter, of Sheffield, Mass., m. Harriet Louisa **FOSTER**,		
of Canaan, Dec. 31, 1840, by Rev. H. H. Woodbridge, of		
the 2nd Cong. Ch.	A	100
Phylles, [child of Eleanor], b. Dec. 25, 1787	A	47
Polly, [d. Eleanor], b. Jan. 3, 1794	A	47
Thomas, [s. Eleanor], b. Jan. 22, 1790	A	47
VAN NESS, Isaac, of Lenox, Mass., m. Hariet **HECTOR**, of		
Salisbury, Sept. 5, 1842, by Rev. H. H. Woodbridge	A	102
VICTORY, Charlot, of Canaan, m. Stephen **ROSSITER**, of		
Salisubry, Sept. 4, 1841, by Levi Warner	A	101
WADSWORTH, Recompence, of Wolcott, N. Y., m. Margaret		
DEAN, of [ ], Apr. 18, 1821, by Rev. Charles Prentice,		
of the 1st Ch.	A	80
WAKEMAN, Harry, m. Lucy **ROBBIN**, June 6, 1833, by William		
Holobird, J. P.	A	91
WALLER, Abraham B., of Washington City, m. Frances A. **WEBB**,		
of Canaan, July 21, 1826, by C. Prentice	A	85
WALLING, Jane, m. Mehitabel **BARNS**, Jan. 11, 1813	A	51
Lucinda, d. John & Mehitabel, b. Nov. 24, 1814	A	51
Ransom, s. John & Sarah Ann, b. Apr. 28, 1808	A	48
Sarah Ann, d. John & Sarah Ann, b. Feb. 25, 1806	A	48
WALLOW, Sarah, m. Harmon **HECTOR**, b. of Salisbury, Feb. 22,		
1841, by Rev. H. H. Woodbridge, of the 2nd Cong. Ch.	A	100
WALTER, Charles, of Norfolk, m. Matilda **ROCKWELL**, of		
Canaan, June 3, 1822, by Pitkin Cowles	A	81
WARD, Polly, m. Nathan **LAWRENCE**, Jan. 27, 1787	A	50
WARNER, Anna, m. Calvin S. **BARNES**, b. of Canaan, Dec. 19,		
1837, by Charles Prentice	A	96
Eleanor, of Suffield, m. Nathaniel **HOW**, Jr., Nov. 10, 1768	A	11
Elisa A., m. Luther A. **BRIGGS**, of Great Barrington, Mass.,		
Dec. 31, 1851, by Rev. Elisha Whittlesey	A	109
Henry D., of Austerlitz, N. Y., m. Betsey M. **BARBER**, of		
Canaan, Oct. 27, 1825, by Pitkin Cowles	A	84

	Vol.	Page

WARNER, (cont.)

James, Jr., of Norfolk, m. Betsey **MARVIN**, of Canaan,
Dec. 16, 1835, by Rev. H. H. Woodbridge — A — 95

Moses B., s. [Harvey D.], b. Feb. 21, 1829 — A — 53

Nancy A., d. Harvey D., b. May 18, 1827 — A — 53

----, of Canaan, m. Caroline **FOX**, of New Marlborough,
Mass., Jan. 1, 1839, by Rev. Charles Stearnes — A — 97

WATKINS, Malissa, m. Ormel K. **BRINTON**, Jan. 11, 1837, by
Charles Prentice — A — 96

WATSON, George, of Torrington, m. Jane **BELDEN**, of Canaan,
Sept. 11, 1833, by Charles Prentice — A — 91

Hezekiah, m. Abigail **FELLOWS**, May 10, 1779 — A — 31

John, Capt., d. Oct. 5, 1795 — A — 43

John, 2nd, m. Mary Ann **LAWRENCE**, b. of Canaan, Jan. 27,
1831, by Pitkin Cowles — A — 88

Julia M., m. Jonathan G. **LAWRENCE**, June 10, 1834, by
Rev. Henry H. Woodbridge, of the 2nd Cong. Ch. — A — 93

Wealthy, m. William **FAXON**, Mar. 23, 1794 — A — 44

WAY, Lucy, of Mereden, m. Gideon **BARNES**, Jr., Nov. 16, 1757,
by Rev. Mr. Hall — LR2 — 228

Febe, of Wallingford, m. Jerediah **BROWN**, Aug. 9, 1753,
by Rev. Mr. Farrand — LR2 — 239

Sarah, m. Rufus **MARSH**, May 14, 1772 — A — 16

Sarah, see Sarah **MARSH** — A — 42

WEBB, Frances A., of Canaan, m. Abraham B. **WALLER**, of
Washington City, July 21, 1826, by C. Prentice — A — 85

WEBSTER, Newman, of Kingsville, O., m. Eliza **HALL**, of
Canaan, Aug. 22, 1824, by Pitkin Cowles — A — 83

WEED, Horace, of Sharon, m. Abby **GILLETT**, Mar. 24, 1852, by
Rev. Elisha Whittlesey — A — 109

WELCH, Sarah Ann, m. Harmon **PECK**, b. of Canaan, Apr. 13,
1824, by Rev. Stephen Beach, of the Epis. Ch. — A — 83

WELLS, Hannah, m. Elijah **HOLCOMB**, Jr., Jan. 1, 1795 — A — 46

Henry, of New Hartford, m. Eliza **LESTER**, of Canaan, Dec.
1, 1837, by Rev. H. H. Woodbridge, of the 2nd Cong. Ch.
Int. Pub. — A — 96

Lucy, m. Ovid **BURRALL**, Oct. 12, 1783 — A — 39

Susanna, m. Edward **BROWNEL**, Jan. 27, 1774, by Rev.
Asahel Hart — A — 23

WELTON, David, s. David & Anna, b. Jan. 7, 1781 — A — 39

WENTER, Simon, m. Sarah **DOUGLASS**, May 8, 1754 — LR2 — 237

Steven, s. Simon & Sarah, b. Sept. 26, 1755 — LR2 — 237

WETHERELL, Horatio N., m. Mary **DIMING**, b. of Canaan, Dec.
24, 1825, by Charles Prentice — A — 85

WHEELER, Abi, twin with Anne, d. John & Mary, b. Sept. 11,
1769 — A — 13

Anne, twin with Abi, d. John & Mary, b. Sept. 11, 1769 — A — 13

Gribeon G., m. Helen M. **FANNING**, b. of Barrington, Mass.,

	Vol.	Page
WHEELER, (cont.)		
Sept. 11, 1842], by Rev. Edward B. Emerson	A	102
Mary, w. John, d. Dec. 21, 1770	A	13
Mary, see Polly **WHEELER**	A	13
Polly, d. John & Mary, b. July 18, 1767	A	10
Polly, d. John & Mary, is changed to "Mary" by the desire of her father	A	13
WHITE, Augustus, s. Oliver & Anna, b. Nov. 15, 1790	A	42
Betsey, m. Lyman **LAWRENCE**, Sept. 8, 1824, by Pitkin Cowles	A	83
Comfort, of Cornwall, m. Miranda **ROOD**, of Camden, May 31, 1837, by H. H. Woodbridge	A	96
Daniel, of Norfolk, m. Thankfull **LAWRENCE**, of Canaan, Mar. 10, 1831, by Pitkin Cowles	A	89
Daniel, of Sharon, m. Remmeline **ROOT**, of Canaan, May 19, 1842, by Rev. H. H. Woodbridge	A	101
David, Capt., m. Anna **PARTRIDGE**, b. of Canaan, May 21, 1826, by Pitkin Cowles	A	85
Dolly, of Canaan, m. Ezekiel **FULLER**, of Salisbury, Jan. 23, 1834, by Charles Prentice	A	92
Henry W., of Canaan, m. Charlotte M. **RUSSELL**, of Salisbury, Sept. 6, 1838, by Rev. H. H. Woodbridge, of the 2nd Cong. Ch. Int. Pub.	A	97
Isaac, m. Sarah **BUCKLEY**, b. of Canaan, Jan. 1, 1828, by C. Prentice	A	86
Mathew, Jr., m. Lucy **PORTER**, June 8, 1815	A	52
Porter, s. Matthew, Jr. & Lucy, b. Mar. 27, 1816	A	52
Porter, m. Melinda H. **HURLBURT**, b. of Canaan, Mar. 21, 1841, by Rev. H. H. Woodbridge, of the 2nd Cong. Ch.	A	100
Sanford, of Sharon, m. Lucinda Maretta, **OAKLEY**, of Canaan, Nov. 22, 1838, by Rev. Charles Stearns, of the M. E. Ch.	A	97
William, of Homer, N. Y., m. Sarah L. **COOPER**, of Canaan, May 10, 1845, by Rev. Stephen J. Stebbins	A	104
WHITERCER, Tabatha, d. Samuel & Esther, b. Sept. 23, 1762	A	25
WHITING, WHITEING, Ann, d. Gamaliel & Ann, b. Nov. 8, 1754	LR2	238
Elizabeth, d. Gamaliel & Ann, b. May 13, 1753	LR2	239
Gamaleil, of Canaan, m. Ann **GILLIT**, of Canaan, June 18, 1752	LR1	427
Gamaliel Bradford, s. Gamaliel & Ann, b. Feb. 7, 1764	A	4
Mary, d. Gamaliel & Ann, b. Dec. 11, 1758	LR2	228
Mary*, m. Lemuel **KINGSBURY**, May 7, 1767 *(Overwritten to read "Mary WHITNEY")	A	32
Sarah, d. Gamaliel & Anna, b. Apr. 26, 1762	A	3
Sarah, m. Jabez **CORNISH**, Jan. 30, 1770	A	12
William, s. Gamaliel & Ann, b. Feb. 11, 1757	LR2	232
WHITNEY, Anne*, d. Joshua & Anne*, b. July 6, 1774 *(Arnold Copy has "Linne")	A	20
David, Jr., m. Mary **GUN[N]**, Sept. 23, 1739	LR2	238

	Vol.	Page
WHITNEY (cont.)		
Elijah, m. Cloe **BECKLEY**, Sept. 24, 1772	A	16
Elijah, s. Elijah & Cloe, b. Feb. 25, 1773	A	20
Elisha, s. Elijah & Cloe, b. Aug. 10, 1774	A	20
Elizabeth, d. David, Jr. & Mary, b. Feb. 26, 1746	LR2	238
Easther, d. David & Mary, b. Mar. 5, 1743	LR2	238
Huldah, d. Joshua & Anne, b. Sept. 8, 1779	A	35
Jacob, s. David & Mary, b. Apr. 13, 1750	LR2	238
Joseph, s. Elijah & Cloe, b. July 21, 1776	A	25
Joshua, s. Joshua & Anne, b. Jan. 6, 1777	A	25
Kezia, d. David & Mary, b. Feb. 21, 1752	LR2	238
Linne*, d. Joshua & Linne*, b. July 6, 1774		
*(Overwritten to read "Anne")	A	20
Lydia, m. Moses **HINMAN**, June 6, 1799	A	50
Mary, d. David, Jr. & Mary, b. July 16, 1740	LR2	238
Mary, m. Lemuel **KINGSBURY**, May 7, 1767	A	11
Samuel, s. Solomon & Sarah, b. June 6, 1759	LR2	227
Sarah, d. David & Mary, b. Apr. 30, 1748	LR2	238
Sarah, d. Solomon & Sarah, b. Jan. 18, 1757	LR2	233
Sarah, m. Joel **HOLCOMB**, Jr., Mar. 4, 1773	A	17
Sarah, m. Elijah William **COBB**, Feb. 27, 178[ ]	A	39
Solomon, m. Sarah **ROBERTS**, Nov. 27, 1755, by Rev. Daniel Farrand	LR2	237
Solomon, s. Solomon & Sarah, b. Nov. 11, 1766	A	9
Solomon, d. July 29, 1772	A	16
Tarball, s. Solomon & Sarah, b. June 30, 1763	A	4
WHITTLESEY, Elisha, Rev., m. Almira **CURTISS**, Sept. 16, 1851, by Rev. Daniel Smith	A	109
WICKHAM, Albert, s. David & Hannah, b. Feb. 6, 1801	A	47
David, m. Hannah **WOOD**, Dec. 3, 1795	A	43
Esther M., m. Julius C. **HOSFORD**, b. of Canaan, Aug. 22, 1831, by Charles Prentice	A	89
Luman, s. David & Hannah, b. Mar. 20, 1797	A	43
Lyman, s. David & Hannah, b. Feb. 5, 1799	A	44
Lyman, m. Delana **ROOT**, b. of Canaan, Feb. 13, 1828, by Rev. P. Willson, of the Bap. Ch.	A	86
Mary E., m. Eluzer **MANLEY**, b. of Canaan, May 12, 1830, by Charles Prentice	A	88
WICKWIRE, Clarrissa T., of South Canaan, m. Lucius H. **FOOT**, of Wolcottville, July 10, 1836, by Charles Prentice. Int. Pub.	A	95
David, b. Oct. 25, 1842	A	54
Imogene, b. June 16, 1846	A	54
Joseph, b. May 26, 1845	A	54
Lee, b. Nov. 8, 1840	A	54
Ransom, of Cornwall, m. Abigail **DEAN**, of Canaan, Oct. 23, 1836, by Charles Prentice	A	95
----, infant, b. Mar. 31, 1847	A	54

	Vol.	Page
WILCOX, WILLCOX, Edmund, m. Phebe **BENEDICT**, Jan. 1, 1824, by Rufus Babcock, of Colebrook	A	83
Jennet E., of Canaan, m. John G. **RUSSELL**, of Great Barrington, Mass., Nov. 26, 1829, by Charles Prentice	A	87
Lucius, of Cornwall, m. Belinda S. **DEMING**, of Canaan, July 24, 1834, by Charles Prentice. Int. Pub.	A	93
Rodman, of Goshen, m. Rachel **GREEN**, of Canaan, June 12, 1832, by Charles Prentice	A	90
WILLARD, Samuel, m. Eunice **HURLBURT**, June 26, 1788	A	40
WILLEY, Alva, m. Delia **CHADWICK**, b. of Canaan, July 23, 1826, by Pitkin Cowles	A	85
Lucy, m. Bennet H. **HINES**, Apr. 9, 1843, by Charles Kettridge	A	103
Melissa, of Canaan, m. Moses **BORDEN**, of Norfolk, Feb. 16, 1846, by Rev. D. D. Francis	A	106
WILLIAMS, Ann Jewett, m. Henry D. **PERRY**, b. of Canaan, Apr. 1, 1829, by Charles Prentice	A	87
Ebenezer, s. Thomas & Mary, b. Sept. 2, 1754	LR2	237
Elizabeth, d. Jacob Williams & Thankfull, b. Aug. 19, 1770	A	12
Easther, of Weathersfield, m. Elizur **WRIGHT**, of Canaan, May 10, 1750, by Daniel Russel	LR1	423
George, of Great Barrington, m. Almira **DUNHAM**, of Canaan, Dec. 14, 1824, by Pitkin Cowles	A	84
Jacob, m. Thankfull **DEAN**, Feb. 23, 1769	A	13
James, s. Jacob & Thankfull, b. Feb. 23, 1765	A	5
Joseph, s. Thomas & Mary, b. Sept. 27, 1756	LR2	237
Rachel, d. Jacob & Thankfull, b. June 23, 1768	A	12
Ruth, d. Jacob & Thankfull, b. Nov. 27, 1776	A	26
Sarah, d. Jacob & Thankfull, b. Oct. 27, 1773	A	17
Sarah, m. Joseph **ELLIOTT**, July 7, 1833, by Reuben Hunt	A	91
Thomas, m. Mary **STEVENS**, Nov. 15, 1753	LR2	237
William, m. Mary **WRIGHT**, b. of Canaan, Sept. 20, 1846, by Harley Goodwin	A	104
WINCHELL, Ebenezer, of Torringford, m. Maria **YALE**, of Canaan, Jan. 26, 1829, by Charles Prentice	A	87
WING, Rebeckah, m. Phinehas **ROOT**, Dec. 29, 1757, by Rev. Mr. Farrand	LR2	232
Rebeckah, m. Phinehas **ROOT**, Dec. 29, 1758	A	21
WITHERELL, Albert H., m. Ann **KELLOGG**, b. of Canaan, Nov. 26, 1840, by Rev. H. H. Woodbridge, of the 2nd Cong. Ch.	A	99
John, of Canaan, m. Matilda **BUTLER**, of Norfolk, Oct. 24, 1848, by Rev. D. D. Francis	A	107
Mary, of Canaan, m. George **CARD**, of Anthram, N. Y., Sept. 12, 1824, by Pitkin Cowles	A	83
Stella, m. Peter **MARTIN**, of Winson, N. Y., Jan. 14, 1821, by Pitkin Cowles	A	79
WOLF, Henry, of New Marlborough, m. Sally **PARTRIDGE**, of		

	Vol.	Page
WOLF, (cont.)		
Canaan, Feb. 5, 1822, by Pitkin Cowles	A	80
WOOD, Benjamin L., of Cornwall, m. Harriet **TYLER**, of		
Richmond, Mass., Sept. 29, 1825, by Charles Prentice	A	84
Hannah, m. David **WICKHAM**, Dec. 3, 1795	A	43
WOODARD, [see under **WOODWARD**]		
WOODRUFF, Huldah, of Harwinton, m. Alban **ROSE**, Dec. 23,		
1794, by Rev. Joshua Knapp	A	48
WOODWARD, WOODARD, Abraham, d. Apr. 8, 1798, in the 36th		
y. of his age	A	45
Abraham, s. Abraham & Abigail, b. June 16, 1798	A	45
Daniel, s. David & Betsey, b. May 31, 1788	A	42
David, m. Betsey **TUBBS**, Oct. 3, 1785	A	42
Polly, d. David & Betsey, b. Aug. 7, 1786	A	42
Rhoda, d. David & Betsey, b. Jan. 8, 1792; d. Dec. 23, 179[ ]	A	42
Sophia, d. Abraham & Abigail, b. May 6, 1796, at Guilford	A	45
WOODWORTH, James, of Litchfield, m. Orie **HOUD**, of Canaan,		
Nov. 13, 1821, by Rev. Charles Prentice	A	80
WORTHINGTON, Olive, d. Samuel & Esther, b. Apr. 20, 1779	A	31
WRIGHT, Albert A., m. Frances A. **COWLES**, b. of Canaan, May		
17, 1831, by Pitkin Cowles	A	89
Amelia, d. Elizur & Rhoda, b. Feb. 2, 1797	A	46
Asa, s. Solomon & Sible, b. Nov. 2, 1759	A	1
David, Jr., m. Martha **RUSSEL**, June 11, [1753?], by Rev.		
Daniel Farrand	LR2	239
Elizur, of Canaan, m. Easther **WILLIAMS**, of Weathersfield,		
May 10, 1750, by Daniel Russel	LR1	423
Elezur, s. Elezur & Hanah, b. July 30, 1762	A	3
Elizur, Jr., m. Rhoda **HANMER**, Oct. 28, 1784	A	38
Elizur, Dea., d. Dec. 3, 1787	A	40
Easther, w. Elizur, d. Oct. 13, 1757	LR2	232
Francis Hanmer, s. Elizur, Jr. & Rhoda, b. July 29, 1787	A	39
Francis Hanmer, s. Elizur & Rhoda, d. Dec. 20, 1789	A	46
Francis Hanmer, s. Elizur & Rhoda, b. Apr. 16, 1795	A	46
Harriet, d. Elizur & Rhoda, b. Oct. 7, 1792	A	46
Isaac, s. David, Jr. & Martha, b. May 20, 1759	LR2	228
Mary, d. Solomon & Sarah, b. Jan. 29, 1754	LR2	238
Mary, m. William **WILLIAMS**, b. of Canaan, Sept. 20, 1846,		
by Harley Goodwin	A	104
Mehetabel, d. David, Jr. & Martha, b. Oct. 1, 1754	LR2	238
Philo, s. Elizur & Rhoda, b. Feb. 3, 1790	A	46
Polly, d. Elizur, Jr. & Rhoda, b. July 26, 1785	A	38
Rebeckah, m. Asahel **BEEBE**, Dec. 31, 1752	LR2	239
Rhoda, w. Elizur, d. Apr. 27, 1798	A	46
Samuell, s. David, Jr. & Martha, b. Dec. 19, 1756	LR2	237
Sarah, d. Solomon & Sarah, b. Dec. 7, 1757; d. Dec. 7, 1757	LR2	228
Sarah, w. Solomon, d. Dec. 9, 1757	LR2	228
Sarah, [twin with Solomon], d. Solomon & Sarah, b. Jan.	A	5

	Vol.	Page

WRIGHT, (cont.)

10, 1757; d. Jan. 17, 1757	LR2	228
Sibel, d. Solomon & Sible, b. July 10, 1764	A	5
Solomon, m. Sarah DAY, Dec. 13, 1752	LR2	239
Solomon, [twin with Sarah], s. Solomon & Sarah, b. Jan. 10, 1757; d. Jan. 13, 1757	LR2	228
Solomon, m. Sibel HANCOX, Jan. 23, 1759	A	1

YALE, Caroline, of South Canaan, m. L. B. **MILLER**, of Great Barrington, Mass., May 30, 1842, by Rev. H. H. Woodbridge. Int. Pub.

	A	101
Charity, m. Frederick **JUDD**, b. of Canaan, Mar. 3, 1825, by Charles Prentice	A	84
Charles, m. Laura **PHELPS**, b. of Canaan, Nov. 15, 1820, by Rev. Charles Prentice	A	79
Eber, m. Abigail **GILLETT**, b. of Canaan, Feb. 10, 1839, by Reuben Hunt, J. P.	A	98
Jane E., m. Solomon M. **HOWE**, b. of Canaan, Nov. 3, 1840, by Rev. H. H. Woodbridge, of the 2nd Cong. Ch. Int. Pub.	A	99
Julia Mariah, of Canaan, m. Constant **SOUTHWORTH**, of Salisbury, Sept. 6, 1824, by Pitkin Cowles	A	83
Laura, m. Hiram **JOHNSON**, Mar. 7, 1821, by Benjamin Sedgwick, J. P.	A	79
Maria, of Canaan, m. Ebenezer **WINCHELL**, of Torrington, Jan. 26, 1829, by Charles Prentice	A	87
Orril, d. Elisha & Rebeckah, b. Nov. 7, 1771	A	17
Polly, m. Riley **PHELPS**, b. of Canaan, Nov. 22, 1825, by Charles Prentice	A	85
Rhoda, m. Capt. Austin **PHELPS**, of Simsbury, [Mar.] 7, 1822, by Rev. Charles Prentice	A	81
Roderick, m. Ann **HOSKINS**, Nov. 13, 1826, by Charles Prentice	A	85
Cemantha*, of Canaan, m. Daniel **MATTHEWS**, of Plymouth, May 7, 1834, by Charles Prentice. Int. Pub.		
*("Samantha")	A	92

CANTERBURY VITAL RECORDS
1703 - 1850

	Vol.	Page
AAMA, [see under **AMA**]		
ABBOTT, Louisa, of Windham, m. Samuel **PRESTON**, Sept. 1, 1785	1	193
ADAMS, Aaron, s. Joseph & Mirriam, b. Apr. 14, 1741	1	55
Abel, s. David & Dorcas, b. Jan. 5, 1730/31	1	55
Abigail, m. Paul **DAVENPORT**, July 28, 1709	1	120
Abigail, d. Samuel & Mary, b. Nov. 12, 1712	1	54
Abigail, d. Thomas & Abigail, b. Mar. 23, 1725/6	1	54
Abigail, w. Thomas, d. June 3, 1733	1	66
Abigail, m. Ebenezer **PIKE**, Jan. 24, 1737/8	1	192
Abigail, m. Jeremiah **DURKE**, Mar. 25, 1747	1	120
Abigail, d. John & Abigail, d. Sept. 18, 1749	1	66
Abigail, d. Samuel & Abigail, b. Apr. 12, 1750	1	57
Abigail, d. Joseph & Dorotha, b. July 31, 1750	1	56
Abigail, d. Samuel & Abigail, b. Apr. 12, 1751	1	55
Abigail, d. John & Abigail, b. June 13, 1751	1	56
Abigail, [twin with Olive], d. Solomon & Abigail, b. May 20, 1752; d. June 7, 1752	1	56
Abigail, d. Solomon & Sarah, b. Feb. 10, 1766	1	58
Abigail, m. Elijah **WILLIAMS**, Nov. 19, 1768	1	236
Abigail, m. John **CLEVELAND**, Jr., Feb. 2, 1773	1	101
Abigail, d. Bradford, & Sarah, b. Mar. 20, 1781	1	60
Abigail, d. John & Mary, b. Oct. 31, 1781	1	61
Abigail, wid. Solomon, d. Sept. 17, 1784	1	67
Abigail, m. Reuben **BISHOP**, of Lisbon, Nov. 27,. 1808	1	73
Abigail, m. Reuben **HERRICK**, b. of Canterbury, Oct. 29, 1815	2	40
Abigail Allen, wid. John, d. Dec. 15, 1782 (?)	1	67
Abigail Whitney, d. [Fitch & Amey], b. May 5, 1811	1	64
Abijah, s. Jesse & Zerviah, b. Oct. 3, 1781	1	60
Adeline L., d. [Chauncey & Sarah], b. Nov. 15, 1832	2	202
Ahaziah, s. Henry & Sarah, b. July 22, 1715	1	54
Albert Mason, s. Joseph & Mary, b. Mar. 30, 180[ ]	1	63
Albert Mason, s. [Albert M. & Almira N.], b. Apr. 8, 1836	2	202
Alden, s. Timothy* & Susannah, b. Sept. 9, 1766 *(Perhaps Thomas?)	1	58
Alden, m. Mary **WILCOX**, Jan. [ ]	1	52
Alice, d. Solomon & Abigail, b. May 15, 1737	1	55
Alice, d. Isaac & Zerviah, b. July 12, 1745	1	56
Alice, d. Samuel & Abigail, b. July 1, 1756	1	57
Elles (Alice), m. Phinehas **DOWNING**, Oct. 18, 1756	1	120

	Vol.	Page
ADAMS, (cont.)		
Amos, s. Joseph, Jr. & Mary, b. June 27, 1790(?)	1	62
Amey, d. Samuel & Mary, b. Mar. 3, 1715	1	65
Amy, m. Tho[ma]s **NOWLDING**, May 30, 1734	1	189
Anna, d. Samuel & Mary, b. July 24, 1717	1	54
Anna, d. Samuel & Sarah, b. May 19, 1734	1	57
Anna, m. Asa **ASPENWALL**, Apr. 9, 1761	1	51
Anna, d. John & Mary, b. Jan. 7, 1784	1	61
Anna, d. Cornelius & Esther, b. Oct. 7, 1785	1	61
Anne, d. Solomon & Abigail, b. Aug. 29, 1745	1	55
Anson, s. Roswell & Eunice, b. Apr. 20, 1788	1	61
Anson, s. Joseph, Jr. & Phebe, b. Oct. 19, 179[ ]	1	62
Arethusa, d. [Joseph, 3rd, & Mary], b. June 9, 17[ ]	1	63
Arunah, s. Sam[ue]l & Phebe, b. May 15, 1768	1	59
Asa, s. Eliphalet & Mary, b. Sept. 25, 175[ ]	1	57
Asa, s. Samuel & Phebe, b. Nov. 17, 1766	1	58
Asa, s. Eliphalet & Mary, d. Oct. 14, [ ]	1	67
Asa[he]l, s. Timothy* & Susannah, b. Oct. 7, 1764 (*Perhaps		
Thomas?)	1	58
Asahel, s. [Levi & Margaret], b. June 20, 1766	1	59
Asa[h]el, s. [Asa[h]el & Olive], b. July 9, [ ]	1	63
Asenath, d. Levi & Margaret, b. Mar. 11, 1769	1	59
Asher, s. Parker & Freelove, b. Apr. 6, 1755	1	57
Asher, s. Parker & Freelove, d. Jan. 29, 1777	1	67
Asher, s. Eliashib & Mary, b. Aug. 17, 1777	1	60
Ashur, s. [Joseph, Jr. & Phebe], b. Nov. 11, 179 [ ]	1	62
Augustus, s. Sam[ue]l & Phebe, b. Oct. 10, 1784	1	61
Aurelia, d. John & Mary, b. Mar. 10, 179[ ]	1	62
Aurelia, m. Elijah **WOODWARD**, Dec. 25, 1814	1	237
Barnabus, s. Ebenezer & Elizabeth, b. Mar. 12, 1749	1	56
Barnabus, s. Jared & Anna, b. Dec. 5, 1783 (Perhaps		
Barnabus **ALLEN**)	1	61
Betsey, d. Elishab & Elizabeth, b. July 2, 1765	1	58
Betsey, d. Cornelius & Esther, b. June 16, 1790	1	62
Betsey, m. Samuel L. **HOUGH**, Dec. 2, 1810	1	156
Betsey, d. Asa[h]el & Olive, b. Dec. [ ]	1	63
Bradford, s. Joseph & Sarah, b. June 11, 1750	1	56
Bradford, m. Sarah **DAVENPORT**, Apr. 6, 1780	1	52
Calissa, d. Joseph, 3rd, & Mary, b. Sept. 10, 17[ ]	1	53
Catharine, m. David **ADAMS**, June 17, 1718	1	51
Cecelia Ann, of Canterbury, m. William Pitts **NOYES**, of		
Stonington, Dec. 26, 1833, by Rev. Otis C. Whiton	2	57
Chapman, s. Gordon & Sally, b. Dec. 15, 18[ ]	1	63
Charles, s. Thomas & Abigail, b. Jan. 2, 1715/16	1	54
Charles, m. Judah **HIDE**, Sept. 14, 1743 (?)	1	51
Charles, s. Eliphalet & Mary, b. July 29, 1761	1	57
Charles, s. John & Mary, b. June 11, 1793	1	62
Charles, s. John & Mary, b. June 11, 17[ ]	1	53

	Vol.	Page

ADAMS, (cont.)

Charles, m. Lucinda **BALDWIN**, May 1, 1837	1	53
Charles, m. Serinda **BALDWIN**, b. of Canterbury, May 1, 1837, by Rev. Tubal Wakefield	2	3
Charles Henry, s. [Chauncey & Tabitha G.], b. Mar 31, 1846	2	202
Chauncey, twin with Nancy, s. Jos[eph] & Lydia, b. Sept. 17, 179[ ]	1	62
Chauncey, m. Sally alias Sarah **ADAMS**, Jan. 1, 1822	1	53
Chaunc[e]y, m. Solly alias Sally **ADAMS**, b. of Canterbury, Jan. 1, 1822, by John Francis, J. P.	2	1
Chauncey, m. Tabitha **ROBINSON**, Jan. 6, 1841, by Rev. Asa King	2	4
Chauncey, d. Dec. 8, 1850	2	301
Chester, s. Eliashib & Mary, b. May 13, 1768	1	58
Chester, s. Eliashib & Mary, b. Jan. 22, 1780	1	60
Chester, s. Eliashib & Mary, d. Dec. 6, [ ]	1	67
Chloe, d. Eliashib & Mary, b. Aug. 12, 1770	1	58
Chloe Felch, d. Marvin & Almira, b. July 12, 1826	1	64
Constance, m. Robert **RE[Y]NOLDS**, Jan. 28, 1748	1	209
Cornelius, s. John & Abigail, b. Mar. 21, 1748	1	56
Cornelius, m. Esther **STEADMAN**, Apr. 14, 1774	1	52
Cornelius, s. Cornelius & Esther, b. Nov. 9, 1777	1	60
Cynthia, d. Eliashib & Elizabeth, b. Aug. 2, 1760	1	57
Cyrus, s. Timo[thy] & Susanna, b. Jan. 21, 1772	1	59
Cyrus, m. Fanny **ADAMS**, Oct. 28, 1827	1	53
Cyrus, m. Fanny **ADAMS**, b. of Canterbury, Oct. 28, 1827, by Rev. I. G. Rose, of Westminster	2	1
Cyrus, s. Timothy, Jr. & Patty, b. May 8, [ ]	1	63
D. Augustus, s. [Asa[h]el & Olive], b. Feb. 10, [ ]	1	63
Daniel, s. Elihu & Jerusha, b. Oct. 7, 175[ ]	1	57
Daniel, s. Cornelius & Esther, b. Mar. 6, 1783	1	61
Daniel, s. [Joseph, Jr. & Mary], b. Oct. 17, 1791	1	62
Davenport, s. Thomas & Abigail, b. Mar. 23, 1720	1	54
Davenport, s. [John B. & Sarah], b. July 19, 179[ ]	1	62
David, m. Catharine **ADAMS**, June 17, 1718	1	51
David, m. Dorcas **PAINE**, Aug. 27, 1723	1	51
David, s. David & Katharine, b. May 23, 1731	1	59
David, Jr., m. Sarah* **JACKSON**, Sept. 30, 1746 (*"Saml" in the Arnold Copy. See Probate Files for possible correction)	1	66
David, d. Aug. 29, 1753	1	66
David, s. [Levi & Margaret], b. Mar. 22, 1756	1	58
David, s. Jonathan & Hannah, b. Mar. 7, 1757	1	56
David, d. May 21, 1759	1	67
David, s. Samuel & Phebe, b. Aug. 24, 1772	1	59
David, m. Abigail **CARVER**, May [ ], 1777 (?)	1	52
David, s. Eleazer, d. Sept. 8, 1784	1	67
David, m. Sarah **PROCTOR**, Nov. 5, 17[ ]	1	51

	Vol.	Page
ADAMS, (cont.)		
David Fitch, m. Abby K. **CARY,** Apr. 4, 1832	1	53
David Fitch, m. Abby K, **CARY,** b. of Canterbury, Apr. 4,		
1832, by Rev. Demis Platt	2	2
David Titus, s. [Titus & Elizabeth], b. Apr. 17, 1821	2	201
Deborah, d. Solomon & Abigail, b. Mar. 7, 1733/4	1	55
Deborah, d. Ahaziah & Ellenor, b. May 15, 1747	1	56
Deborah, m. Benj[ami]n **BACON,** Dec. 14, 1749	1	69
Deborah, m. Jonathan **DOWNING,** Apr. 11, 1751	1	120
Deborah, wid., d. Mar. 27, 1767 (?)	1	67
Deborah, d. William & Sarah, b. Apr. 17, 1771, in Windham	1	59
Deborah, m. Elihu **PETTIS,** Jan. 27, 1805	1	194
Delight, d. Parker & Freelove, b. Nov. 14, 1750;		
d. Dec. 13, 1751	1	57
Deliverance, s. David & Catharine, b. Dec. 11, 1726	1	54
Deliverance, s. James & Sarah, b. Oct. 20, 1751	1	54
Deluand (?)*, s. Joseph & Mary, b. Jan. 18, 1789		
(*Deliverance?)	1	61
Desire, w. Jonathan, d. May 19, 1755	1	66
Desire, d. Jed[edia]h & Rosanna, d. Jan. 5, [ ]	1	67
Dolly, d. John & Submitt, b. Sept. 29, 1766	1	58
Dorcas, d. David & Dorcas, b. June 5, 1735	1	55
Dorcas, w. David, Jr., d. Mar. 3, 1745/6	1	66
Dorotha, d. Joseph & Dorotha, b. Oct. 18, 1746	1	56
Ebenezer (?), m. Elizabeth **SEARY,** Oct. 11, 1744	1	51
Eben[eze]r, s. Eben[eze]r & Elizabeth, b. Aug. 4, 1746	1	55
Ebenezer, s. John & Abigail, b. Oct. 6, 1749	1	56
Eben[eze]r, m. Mary **MORSE,** Apr. 8, 1779	1	52
Ebenezer, s. Ebenezer & Mary, b. Sept. 8, 1784	1	61
Ebenezer, m. Molly **MERRETT,** Mar. 13, 179[ ]	1	52
Ede, d. Jonathan & Desire, b. June 27, 1746	1	56
Edith, d. Jonathan & Desire, b. June 27, 1746	1	55
Edna, d. James, Jr. & Alice, b. Jan. 9, 17[ ], at Pomfret	1	63
Edwin Chapman, s. [Perrin & Susan], b. Apr. 23, 1829	2	201
Edwin Hubbard, s. [Albert M. & Sarah Ann], b. Jan. 31,		
1843* (*1845?)	2	102
Ele[a]ner, d. Ahaziah & Ele[a]ner, b. Sept. 22, 1739	1	55
Elinor, w. Ahaziah, d. June 19, 1748	1	66
Eleanor, m. Tho[ma]s **AUSTIN,** Dec. 30, 176[ ]	1	52
Eleazer, s. Solomon & Abigail, b. July 23, 1748	1	56
Eleaz[e]r, s. Eleaz[e]r & Prudence, b. Dec. 11, 1772	1	59
Eleaz[e]r, m. Prudence **BENNET,** June 15, 177[ ]	1	52
Eleazer, s. Eleazer & Prudence, d. Sept. 29, 1784	1	67
Eliashib, m. Mary **ANABLE,** Aug. 20, 1767	1	51
Eliashib, s. Eliashib & Mary, b. June 5, 1773	1	59
Elihu, s. Joseph & Susannah, b. June 11, 1731	1	54
Elihu, m. Jerusha **ADAMS,** Mar. 6, 1753	1	51
Elihu, s. Elihu & Jerusha, b. Sept. 28, 1759	1	57

	Vol.	Page
ADAMS, (cont.)		
Elihu, s. Elihu & Jerusha, d. Jan. 3, 1777	1	67
Elijah, s. Samuel & Bettey, b. Dec. 17, 1783	1	61
Eliphalet, s. Thomas, & Abigail, b. Feb. 28, 1723/4	1	54
Eliphalet, m. Mary **FROST**, June 5, 1753 (?)	1	51
Eliphalet, s. Eliphalet & Mary, b. May 24, 1759	1	57
Eliphalet, s. Thomas & Mary, b. Mar. 4, 1782	1	61
Eliphalet, d. Dec. 25, 17[ ]	1	67
Elisha, s. David & Dorcas, b. July 5, 1733	1	55
Elisha, s. Joseph & Sarah, d. Jan. 12, 1753 (?)	1	66
Elisha, [twin with Jesse], s. Joseph & Sarah, b. Dec. 7, 175[ ]	1	55
Elisha, s. Eleaz[e]r & Prudence, b. May 27, 1778	1	60
Elisha, s. Sam[ue]l & Bettey, b. Nov. 11, 1780	1	60
Elisha, s. [James & Jerusha], b. June 1, 1782	1	61
Elisha, Capt., of Groton, m. Caroline **DAVENPORT**, June 1, 1828	1	53
Elisha, Capt., of Groton, m. Caroline **DAVENPORT**, of Canterbury, June 1, 1828, by Rev. J. R. Murdock	2	2
Elizabeth, d. Richard & Mary, b. July 25, 1705	1	54
Elizabeth, d. James & Sarah, b. May 25, 1757	1	57
Elizabeth, d. Jo[hn], Jr. & Elizabeth, b. Sept. 18, 1774	1	60
Elizabeth, w. Eliashib, d. Mar. 9, 17[ ]	1	67
Elizabeth, m. Hart **WILLIAMS**, Dec. 24, 1845, by Rev. Daniel D. Lyon, of Packersville	2	88
Elizabeth C., m. John D. **BUTTS**, b. of Canterbury, Dec. 11, 1831, by Rev. Orrin Catlin	2	9
Ellen Miranda, d. [Marvin & Almira], b. May 2, 1839	1	65
Ellen Victoria, d. Amos J. **BEERS** & Harriet E. C. **ADAMS**, b. May 13, 1842	2	202
Elles, see under Alice		
Emeline, d. Joseph B. & Laurelia, b. Oct. 3, 1812	2	201
Emeline Adeline, d. [Cyrus & Fanny], b. Sept. 12, 1831	2	201
Ephraim, s. Jonathan & Desire, b. Apr. 8, 1748	1	56
Erastus, s. Thomas & Susannah, b. Aug. 10, 1767	1	58
Erastus, m. Polly **BROWN**, Apr. 28, 1790	1	52
Esther, d. Eleaz[e]r & Prudence, b. Aug. 21, 1775	1	59
Esther, d. Cornelius & Esther, b. June 24, 1788	1	61
Eugene Haskell, s. Perrin & Susan, b. Apr. 7, 1827	2	201
Eunice, d. Joseph & Eunice, b. July 25, 1713	1	54
Eunice, w. Capt. Joseph, d. Apr. 5, 1726	1	66
Eunice, m. Thomas **BRADFORD**, May 2, 1733	1	69
Eunice, d. Samuel & Abigail, b. June 17, 1746	1	55
Eunice, m. John **STARK**, Apr. 16, 1764	1	214
Eunice, d. Sam[ue]l, Jr. & Eunice, b. Nov. 23, 1770	1	59
Eunice, d. [Sam[ue]l & Phebe], b. June 3, 1786	1	61
Eveline, d. Jos[eph] & Mary, b. Feb. 12, 18[ ]	1	63
Eveline, m. James **SAFFORD**, b. of Canterbury, Aug. 29, 1830, by Rev. Dennis Platt	2	72

	Vol.	Page

ADAMS, (cont.)

	Vol.	Page
Experience, m. Abraham **HIDE**, Jan. 24, 1737/8	1	155
Experience, d. James & Sarah, b. Feb. 2, 1765	1	58
Ezra, s. Levi & Hannah, b. Nov. 22, 1772	1	60
Fanny, m. Cyrus **ADAMS**, Oct. 28, 1827	1	53
Fanny, m. Cyrus **ADAMS**, b. of Canterbury, Oct. 28, 1827, by Rev. I. G. Rose, of Westminster	2	1
Fanny, d. Olive & William, b. Aug. [ ]	1	63
Festus, s. Jesse & Zerviah, b. May 31, 1784	1	61
Fitch, m. Amy **BACON**, Jan. 16, 1800	1	53
Francis Fanny, d. [Titus & Elizabeth], b. July 23, 1818	2	201
Frances M., m. Timothy A. **LEWIS**, Nov. 24, 1840, by Rev. Asa King, Westminster	2	52
Frances Mary, of Canterbury, m. Simon **TRACY**, of Norwich, Mar. 13, 1832, by Rev. Dennis Platt	2	79
Frances Melissa, d. Will[ia]m & Olive, b. Apr. 4, 1821	1	201
Frederick, m. Lydia **FELCH**, June 21, [ ] (Should be Frederick **ANDREWS**. Corrected by L. B. B.)	1	52
Gamaliel Ripley, s. John, Jr. & Elizabeth, b. July 2, [ ]	1	63
George L., of New York City, m. Elizabeth G. **PELLET**, Apr. 20, 1836	1	53
George L., of New York City, m. Elizabeth G. **PELLET**, of Canterbury, Apr. 20, 1836, by Rev. Otis C. Whiton	2	3
George Leonard, s. Fitch & Amey, b. Aug. 29, 1808	1	64
George Martin, s. [Marvin & Almira], b. July 23, 1830	1	65
Gideon, s. Samuel & Abigail, b. May 2, 1743	1	55
Gideon, m. Mary **LEACH**, Jan. 5, [ ]	1	51
Gordon, s. Joseph, Jr. & Elizabeth, b. June 11, 1776	1	60
Gordon, m. Sally **SAFFORD**, Sept. 27, 18[ ]	1	52
Guy F., m. Susan **DAVENPORT**, Aug. 6, 1820	1	53
Guy F., m. Susan **DAVENPORT**, Aug. 6, 1820, by Asa Meech	2	1
Hannah, m. Jonathan **HIDE**, Apr. 15, 1736	1	155
Hannah, d. Solomon & Abigail, b. Aug. 31, 1742	1	55
Hannah, m. Daniel **DOWNING**, Oct. 1, 1760	1	120
Hanna[h], d. Samuel & Phebe, b. Mar. 4, 1764	1	58
Hannah, d. Samuel & Phebe, d. Mar. 7, 176[ ]	1	67
Hannah, of Gilsune, N. H., m. Eliphalet **FARNAM**, Oct. 16, 1786, at Keene	1	138
Hannah B., of Canterbury, m. Frances **BURT**, of Long Meadow, Mass., Dec. 25, 1840, by Rev. Samuel Rockwell, of Plainfield	2	12
Hannah Maria, d. Albert M. & Almira N., b. Apr. 11, 1833	2	202
Harriet, d. Jabez & Lucy, b. Aug. 23, 179[ ]	1	62
Harriet Brewer, d. Hub[b]ard, b. May 28, 1834	2	203
Harriet Elizabeth **CHAPMAN**, d. Orrin & Amy, b. Apr. 20, 1822	2	201
Harry, s. Jabez & Lucy, b. Mar. 30, 1790 (?)	1	62
Henry (?), m. Sarah **ADAMS**, Dec. 19, 1706	1	51

	Vol.	Page
ADAMS, (cont.)		
Henry, Sr., d. June 28, 1749	1	66
Henry, s. Solomon, Jr. & Sarah, b. Nov. 26, 1772	1	59
Henry d. May 30, [ ]	1	67
Henry, s. Solomon, Jr. & Sarah, d. Sept. 6, [ ]	1	67
Hezekiah, s. Sam[ue]l & Phebe, b. June 16, 1776	1	60
Hubbard, m. Sabina **ADAMS**, Mar. 25, 1830	1	53
Hubbard, m. Sabina **ADAMS**, Mar. 25, 1830, by Walter Williams, J. P.	2	2
Isaac, m. Gerviah* **BROWN**, Feb. 17, 1728/9 (*Zerviah?)	1	51
Isaac, s. Timo[thy] & Susanna, b. Dec. 12, 1769	1	59
Isabella, of Canterbury, m. William T. **DEMING**, of Windham, Sept 15, 1822, by Erastus Learned	2	21
Jabez, m. Deborah **HYDE**, Sept. 25, 1839	1	53
Jabez, m. Deborah **HYDE**, Sept. 25, 1839, by Rev. C. J. Warren	2	3
James, [s.] David & Catharine, b. May 3, 1721/2	1	54
James, twin with Sarah, s. Joseph & Sarah, b. June 7, 1748	1	56
James, m. Sarah **RICH**, Feb. 3, 1750/51	1	51
James, m. Jeresha **KNIGHT**, Feb. 16, 1772	1	52
James, s. James & Jerusha, b. Nov. 5, 1775	1	59
James, d. June 28, 1805	1	68
James, m. Delight **CARVER**, Oct. 15, 1837, by Peter Spicer, J. P.	2	3
James, m. Delight **CARVER**, Oct. 18, 1837	1	53
James, Jr., m. Alice **BRADFORD**, Jan. 31, [ ]	1	52
Jane Amelia, d. John & Harriet E. C., b. Mar. 11, 1847	2	202
Jarvis, s. William & Olive, b. Apr. 28, 1804	1	63
Jay, s. [Asa[h]el & Olive], b. June 30, 17[ ]	1	63
Jedediah, s. Jonathan & Desire, b. Apr. 16, 1753	1	56
Jedediah, s. Solomon & Sarah, b. Jan. 1, 1762	1	57
Jeremiah, s. Isaac & Zerviah, b. Mar. 1, 1732/3	1	55
Jerusha, m. Elihu **ADAMS**, Mar. 6, 1753	1	51
Jerusha, d. Elihu & Jerusha, b. Sept. 12, 1762	1	58
Jesse, s. Joseph & Sarah, b. Feb. 6, 1757	1	56
Jesse, [twin with Elisha], s. Joseph & Sarah, b. Dec. 7, 175[ ]	1	55
Jesse, m. Zerviah **CADY**, Nov. 30, 178[ ]	1	52
Joanna, d. [Levi & Margaret], b. Aug. 4, 1764	1	58
Johannah, d. John & Esther, b. Apr. 25, 1712	1	54
Johannah had s. Ebenezer **BALDWIN**, b. Apr. 6, 1745	1	78
John (?), m. Esther Cady, Mar. 27, 1711	1	51
John, s. John & Esther, b. Oct. 1, 1713	1	54
John, d. Feb. 16, 1724/5	1	66
John, s. Joseph & Sarah, b. Feb. 17, 1743	1	55
John, s. John & Abigail, b. Feb. 12, 1744	1	56
John, s. [Levi & Margaret], b. Dec. 15, 1762	1	58
John, m. Submitt **BUTT**, Dec. 2, 1765	1	51
John, Jr., m. Mary **PARKER**, Oct. 5, 1769	1	51

	Vol.	Page
ADAMS, (cont.)		
John, s. John, Jr. & Mary, b. Sept. 18, 1772	1	59
John, s. John & Submit, b. June 2, 1774	1	59
John, s. John & Submit, b. Jan. 20, 1776	1	60
John, Jr., m. Elizabeth **RIPLEY**, May 8, 179[ ]	1	52
John, s. John & Submitt, d. Dec. 27, [ ]	1	67
John Baldwin, s. Perrin & Susan, b. Sept. 23, 1831	2	201
John Chauncey, s. Chauncey & Tabitha, G., b. Oct. 8, 1841	2	202
John Cleveland, s. Eben[eze]r & Mary, b. Jan. 12, 1782	1	61
John F., m. Lydia **BRADFORD**, Mar. 22, 1835, by Rev. Asa King, Westminster	2	3
John F., m. Lydia **BRADFORD**, Apr. 6, 1835	1	53
John Frances, m. Mary Ann **LYON**, Oct. 13, 1824	1	53
John Frances, m. Mary Ann **LYON**, b. of Canterbury, Oct. 13, 1824, by Andrew Lee, Clerk	2	1
John Q., s. [Marvin & Almira], b. Mar. 13, 1844	1	65
Jonathan, s. David & Dorcas, b. May 25, 1724	1	54
Jonathan, s. David & Katharine, b. Nov. 4, 1732	1	56
Jonathan, m. Desire **ASHCRAFT**, Dec. 27, 1745	1	51
Jonathan, m. Hannah **TEARNAM***, Mar. 11, 1755 (*Should be **YEAMAN**. See **ADAMS GENEALOGY**)	1	51
Joseph (?), m. Eunice **SPAULDING**, July 23, 1708	1	51
Joseph, s. Joseph & Eunice, b. June 10, 1709; d. Sept. 7, 1709	1	54
Joseph, s. Joseph & Eunice, b. Dec. 6, 1715	1	54
Joseph, Capt., m. Susannah **ADAMS**, Apr. 4, 1728	1	51
Joseph, Capt., d. Mar. 3, 1739 (?)	1	66
Joseph, m. Dorothy **HIDES**, Apr. 12, 1742	1	51
Joseph, s. Joseph & Sarah, b. Feb. 21, 1745/6	1	56
Joseph, Sr., d. Dec. 9, 1748	1	66
Joseph, s. Joseph & Dorotha, b. Mar. 8, 1749	1	56
Joseph, s. Joseph & Dorothy, d. Sept. 4, 1749	1	66
Joseph, s. Joseph & Dorotha, b. Nov. 7, 1755	1	56
Joseph, s. Samuel & Abigail, b. Dec. 19, 1758	1	57
Joseph, s. Joseph & Dorothy, d. June 10, 1759 (?)	1	67
Joseph, s. Elihu & Jerusha, b. Nov. 9, 1767	1	58
Joseph, Jr., m. Elizabeth **CHAPMAN**, Nov. 26, 177[ ]	1	52
Joseph, d. Dec. 6, 1780	1	67
Joseph, m. Lydia **CHAPMAN**, June 19, 178[ ]	1	52
Joseph, Jr., m. Phebe **ROBINSON**, Mar. 22, 179[ ]	1	52
Joseph, Jr., m. Mary **HERRICK**, Jan. 3, 17[ ]	1	52
Joseph, d. Sept. 23, 1824	2	310
Joseph B., m. Lauralia **HEATH**, Dec. 20, 1811	1	53
Joseph B., m. Lauralia **MEACH**, Dec. 20, 1811	2	3
Joseph Bradford, s. [John B. & Sarah], b. Feb. 22, 1787 (?)	1	62
Joseph Merret, [twin with Mary Morse], s. Ebenezer & Molly, b. June 29, 1800	1	64
Joshua, s. Isaac & Zerviah, b. Jan. 2, 1731	1	56
Joshua, s. Jno. Jr. & Mary, b. Dec. 4, 1774	1	59

	Vol.	Page
ADAMS, (cont.)		
Josiah, s. Cornelius & Esther, b. Dec. 10, 1780	1	61
Judeth Leach, d. Gideon & Mary, b. Apr. 17, 1764	1	58
Katharine, w. David, d. Aug. 2, 1733	1	66
Kezia, m. Jesse **PARK**, Jan. 1, 1784	1	193
Larenza, d. James & Jerusha, b. June 30, 1780	1	61
Laura, m. Edwin **PHINNEY**, Mar. 16, 1848, by Rev. Asa King, Westminster	2	65
Leah, d. David & Dorcas, b. Aug. 18, 1738	1	55
Levi, m. Margaret **PERKINS**, Dec. 26, 1751	1	51
Levi, s. Levi & Margaret, b. Feb. 17, 1754	1	58
Levi, Jr., m. Hannah **PETTINGALL**, Aug. 9, 177[ ]	1	52
Lois, [d.] John & Abigail, b. Nov. 7, 1741	1	55
Lois, d. Eleazer & Prudence, b. Feb. 3, 1785	1	61
Luala, m. Harry **ALLEN**, Sept. 21, 1813	1	53
Lucretia Douglass, s. Albert M. & Sarah Ann, b. Feb. 22, 1843	2	202
Lucretia Maria, d. [Joseph B. & Laurelia], b. June 28, 1817	2	201
Lucy, d. Richard & Mary, b. July 12, 1731	1	56
Lucy, d. Levi & Margaret, b. Mar. 23, 1752	1	56
Lucy, d. Solomon & Sarah, b. June 4, 1764	1	58
Lucy, m. Jordon **DODGE**, Oct. 22, 1769	1	120
Lucy, d. [Levi & Hannah], b. May 23, 1775	1	60
Lucy, d. Jesse & Zerviah, b. Jan. 8, 1783	1	61
Lucy, d. James & Jerusha, d. Dec. 1, 1784	1	67
Lucy, [twin with Luther], d. James & Jerusha, b. Feb. 25, 1784; d. Dec. 5, 1784	1	61
Lucy, [twin with Sarah], d. Jesse & Zerviah, b. Sept. 13, 1787	1	61
Lucy, d. Jesse & Zerviah, d. July 14, 178[ ]	1	67
Lucy, d. [John B. & Sarah], b. Dec. 9, 178[ ]	1	62
Lucy, m. Fanning **TRACY**, Sept. 26, 1802	1	229
Lucy Ann, d. [Joseph B. & Laurelia], b. Dec. 15, 1830	2	201
Lucy Ann, d. [Chauncey & Sarah], b. Oct. 1, 1834	2	202
Luseba, d. John & Mary, b. Mar. 20, 1789	1	62
Luther, [twin with Lucy], s. James & Jerusha, b. Feb. 25, 1784	1	61
Luther, s. Samuel & Bettey, b. Feb. 22, 1785	1	61
Lydia, d. Solomon & Abigail, b. Jan. 7, 1730/1	1	54
Lydia, d. John & Abigail, b. June 12, 1746	1	56
Lydia, m. Parego **DOWNING**, Nov. 25, 1747	1	120
Lydia, m. Samuel **ADAMS**, 3rd, Apr. 1, 1756	1	51
Lydia, d. Samuel & Lydia, b. Apr. 28, 1760	1	58
Lydia, w. Samuel, 3rd, d. May 10, 1760	1	67
Lydia, m. John **WHEELER**, Nov. 15, 1764	1	236
Lydia, m. Robert **STEPHENS**, Dec. 4, 1781	1	214
Margaret, d. David & Catharine, b. May 6, 1724	1	54
Margaret, d. Jonathan & Desire, b. Jan. 16, 1750/51	1	56
Margaret, d. [Levi & Margaret]. b. Dec. 20, 1758	1	58
Margaret, 2d, d. [Levi & Margaret], b. Jan. 17, 1760	1	58
Marg[a]ret, d. Gideon & Mary, b. Mar. 11, 1767	1	58

	Vol.	Page

ADAMS, (cont.)

	Vol.	Page
Margaret, d. Levi & Margaret, d. Mar. 14, [ ]	1	67
Margaret, wid. Sam[ue]l, d. [ ]	1	66
Mariann L., d. Chauncey & Sarah, b. Jan. 15, 1827	2	202
Martha, d. Thomas & Susanna, b. Jan. 23, 1760	1	57
Marvin, s. Samuel Calvin & Susanna (**WALDEN**), b. Feb. 23, 1795	1	64
Marvin, m. Almira **BALDWIN**, d. John & Lucinda (**ENSWORTH**) **BALDWIN**, Apr. 20, 1820	1	53
Marvin, d. May 17, 1878, in Centreville, R. I.	1	68
Mary, d. Henry & Sarah, b. Sept. 9, 1707	1	54
Mary, w. Samuel, d. Mar. 28, 1718	1	66
Mary, d. David & Catharine, b. June 27, 1719	1	54
Mary, m. John **BALDWIN**, Feb. 22, 1720/21	1	69
Mary, m. Stephen **FROST**, Oct. 29, 1724	1	138
Mary, d. Samuel & Mary, d. Mar. 3, 1724/5	1	66
Mary, w. Samuel, Jr., d. Feb. 11, 1725/6	1	66
Mary, d. Mar. 7, 1732/3	1	66
Mary, m. Sam[ue]l **BUTT**, Jr., Jan. 8, 1735/6	1	69
Mary, d. Joseph & Dorothy, b. May 1, 1743	1	55
Mary, d. John & Abigail, b. June 23, 1743	1	55
Mary, d. John & Abigail, b. June 23, 1743	1	56
Mary, d. Joseph & Mary, d. May 30, 1746	1	66
Mary, d. Joseph & Sarah, b. Dec. 5, 1755	1	56
Mary, m. Eliphalet **FARNHAM**, Feb. 1, 1757	1	138
Mary, m. Bethuel **FROST**, June 20, 1765	1	138
Mary, d. Gideon & Mary, b. Apr. 17, 1769	1	59
Mary, d. James & Jerusha, b. Mar. 26, 1778	1	60
Mary, m. John **SIM[M]S**, Apr. 29, 1784	1	214
Mary, w. Joseph, Jr., d. Oct. 17, 1791	1	68
Mary, w. Ebenezer, d. Sept. 17, 1792	1	67
Mary, w. John, d. Oct. 11, 1798	1	68
Mary, d. John & Elizabeth, b. Apr. 7, 17[ ]	1	63
Mary, m. Reuben **SAFFORD**, b. of Canterbury, May 23, 1830, by Rev. Israel G. Rose, of Westminster	2	72
Mary B., m. James B. **CARY**, b. of Canterbury, Sept. 17, 1834, by Rev. Otis C. Whiton	2	17
Mary Elizabeth, d. Hub[b]ard, b. June 5, 1831	2	203
Mary Esther, d. Titus & Elizabeth, b. Nov. 27, 1815	2	201
Mary Esther, d. [Joseph B. & Laurelia], b. Oct. 18, 1824	2	201
Mary F., m. Charles **HYDE**, Apr. 31, 1850, by Rev. R. S. Hazen, of Westminster	2	100
Mary J., m. Samuel F. **FOWLER**, b. of Canterbury, June 25, 1848, by Rev. Nehemiah B. Hyde	2	33
Mary Juliaette, d. Moses B. & Clarrissa, b. May 25, 1828	2	201
Mary Morse, [twin with Joseph Merret, d. Ebenezer & Molly], b. June 29, 1800	1	64
Mason, s. [Asa[h]el & Olive], b. Mar. 24, 17[ ]	1	63

	Vol.	Page
ADAMS, (cont.)		
Mehetabell, d. Samuel & Mary, b. Aug. 28, 1721	1	54
Mehetable, m. John **SMITH**, Feb. 26, 1740/41	1	214
Mehetable, m. Phinehas **TRACY**, May 9, 1745	1	229
Mehetable, d. Eli[a]shib & Elizabeth, b. Feb. 11, 1763	1	58
Mehetable, d. Eliashib & Elizabeth, d. Sept. 13, 176[ ]	1	67
Mehetabel, d. Nathan & Phebe, b. June 16, 1772	1	59
Mehetable, d. Nathan & Phebe, d. Aug. 11, 1787	1	67
Mehetable, d. [John B. & Sarah], b. July 7, 178[ ]	1	62
Mehetable, m. Orin **PALMER**, Nov. 15, 1818	1	194
Mehetable, of Canterbury, m. Henry **SMITH**, of New York, Dec. 21, 1831, by Rev. Dennis Platt	2	72
Mikael, wid., d. Apr. 4, 1752	1	66
Milete, d. William & Olive, b. Mar. 1, 180[ ]	1	63
Molly, d. Ebenezer & Molly, b. Sept. 29, 179[ ]	1	62
Moses, s. John & Mary, b. Sept. 28, 1786	1	61
Moses B., m. Clarissa **CUTLER**, Mar. 20, 1828	1	53
Moses B., m. Clarissa **CUTLER**, b. of Canterbury, Mar. 20, 1828, by Rev. Israel G. Rose	2	2
Moses Bradford, s. James, Jr. & Alice, b. June 28, [ ]	1	63
Nancy, twin with Chauncey, d. Jos[eph] & Lydia, b. Sept. 17, 179[ ]	1	62
Nancy, m. Jeremiah **YOUNG**, b. of Canterbury, Nov. 20, 1831, by Rufus Johnson, J. P.	2	91
Nathan, s. Samuel & Abigail, b. Dec. 13, 1748(?)	1	57
Nathan, s. Samuel & Abigail, b. Dec. 22, 1748	1	55
Nathan, m. Phebe **ENSWORTH**, Apr. 4, 177[ ]	1	52
Nelson, s. Joseph, Jr. & Phebe, b. Nov. 29, [ ]	1	63
Olive, [twin with Abigail], d. Solomon & Abigail, b. May 20, 1752; d. June 7, 1752	1	56
Olive, d. [Asa[h]el & Olive], b. Apr. 5, 17[ ]	1	63
Orrin, of Canterbury, m. Ann S. **HOLT**, of Ledyard, Mar. 26, 1834, by R. S. Hazen	2	5
Parker, s. Joseph & Eunice, b. Apr. 18, 1722	1	55
Parker, m. Freelove **FANNING**, May 9, 1745	1	51
Parker, s. John, Jr. & Mary, b. May 6, 1779	1	60
Patty Lusina, d. Cyrus & Fanny, b. Sept. 24, 1828	2	201
Patty Susannah, d. Erastus & Mary, b. May 28, 1805	1	63
Paul D., m. Mary **LEWIS**, Feb. 3, 1822	1	53
Paul D., m. Mary **LEWIS**, Feb. 3, 1822, by Asa Meech	2	1
Perren, s. Joseph & Lydia, b. Dec. 31, 179[ ]	1	62
Perren, m. Susan **BALDWIN**, Mar. 29, 1824	1	53
Perrin, m. Susan **BALDWIN**, b. of Canterbury, Mar. 29, 1824, by Rev. Tho[ma]s J. Murdock	2	1
Phebe, d. Joseph & Dorothy, b. July 31, 1752	1	55
Phebe, d. Sam[ue]l & Phebe, b. Sept. 6, 1780	1	60
Phebe P., d. June [ ], 1820	1	68
Philetus B., s. [Joseph B. & Laurelia], b. Dec. 16, 1814	2	201

	Vol.	Page
ADAMS, (cont.)		
Phinehas, s. Isaac & Zerviah, b. Apr. 7, 1729	1	54
Polly, d. John, Jr. & Mary, b. May 27, 1777	1	60
Priscilla, d. James & Sarah, b. Oct. 6, 1757 (?)	1	57
Pre[s]cilla, of Canterbury, m. Henry **BENNET**, of Griswold, Apr. 11, 1822, by John Francis, J. P.	2	7
Prosper, s. Jesse & Zerviah, b. Nov. 27, 1785	1	61
Prudence, d. Eleaz[[e]r & Prudence, b. May 18, 1771	1	59
Prudence, d. Eleazer, d. Sept. 8, 1784	1	67
Rebeckah, d. Henry & Sarah, b. May 31, 1709	1	54
Rebeckah, d. Samuel & Mary, d. July 5, 1709	1	66
Rebeckah, d. David & Dorcas, b. Aug. 6, 1742	1	55
Rebeckah, d. [Timo[thy] & Susanna], b. June 20, 1774	1	59
Relefe, d. Thomas & Abigail, b. Feb. 12, 1721/2	1	54
R[e]uben, s. Thomas & Susannah, b. Oct. 22, 1761	1	57
Reuben, m. Abigail **LOVET[T]**, of Norwich, Dec. 4, 1783	1	52
Richard m. Mary **CADY**, July 21, 1709	1	5
Richard, s. Richard & Mary, b. July 28, 1712	1	54
Richard, m. Mary **CLEVELAND**, Mar. 30, 1730	1	51
Richard, d. Apr. 17, 1733	1	66
Roswell, s. Elihu & Jerusha, b. June 13, 1753	1	56
Roswell, m. Eunice, **DAVENPORT**, Nov. 23, 17[ ]	1	52
Roxa, d. Thomas & Susanna, b. Apr. 13, 1773	1	59
Roxa, d. Tho[ma]s & Susanna, d. Jan. 5, 1774 (?)	1	67
Roxanna, d. Thomas & Susanna, b. Oct. 14, 1765	1	58
Roxanna, d. Thomas & Susannah, d. May 17, 1766 (?)	1	67
Ruby, d. John B. & Sarah, b. Oct. 31, 1782 (?) (1783?)	1	62
Rufus, s. Nathan & Phebe, b. May 6, 1774	1	60
Russell, s. Erastus & Mary, b. Oct. 23, 179[ ]	1	62
Ruth, m. Abraham **PAINE**, Dec. 19, 1717	1	192
Ruth, m. Will[ia]m **COOPER**, Mar. 22, 1751	1	100
Ruth, d. John & Abigail, b. Mar. 12, 1757	1	57
Saberah, d. Parker & Freelove, b. Sept. 16, 1752	1	57
Sabina, m. Hubbard **ADAMS**, Mar. 25, 1830	1	53
Sabina, m. Hubbard **ADAMS**, Mar. 25, 1830, by Walter Williams, J. P.	2	2
Sabrina, d. [Joseph, 3rd, & Mary], b. Nov. 25, 17[ ]	1	63
Sally alias Sarah, m. Chauncey **ADAMS**, Jan. 1, 1822	1	53
Sally, see also Solly		
Sally E., m. Egbert **BINGHAM**, May 23, 1836, by Rev. Asa King, Westminster	2	10
Sally M., m. Daniel H. **BURDICK**, Oct. 3, 1836, by Walter Williams, J. P.	2	10
Salome, d. James, Jr. & Alice, b. June 14, 1804 (?)	1	63
Samuel (?), m. Mary **CADY**, July 21, 1709	1	51
Samuel, s. Joseph & Eunice, b. Sept. 4, 1710	1	54
Samuel, s. Samuel & Mary, b. Oct. 5, 1719	1	54
Samuel, s. Samuel & Mary, d. Feb. 23, 1724/5	1	66

	Vol.	Page
ADAMS, (cont.)		
Samuel, d. Nov. 26, 1727	1	66
Samuel, s. David & Catharine, b. June 11, 1728	1	54
Samuel, s. Samuel & Sarah, b. June 13, 1731 or 1737	1	57
Samuel, s. Joseph & Sarah, b. Mar. 30, 1742	1	55
Samuel, d. Apr. 24, 1742	1	66
Samuel, s. Joseph & Dorothy, b. Sept. 28, 1744	1	55
Samuel, s. John & Abigail, b. May 16, 1753	1	57
Samuel, 3rd, m. Lydia ADAMS, Apr. 1, 1756	1	51
Sam[ue]l, Jr., m. Eunice COOK, Feb. 8, 1770	1	52
Sam[ue]l, s. Sam[ue]l, 4th, & Bettey, b. Feb. 8, 1778	1	60
Sam[ue], 4th, m. Bettey LITTLEFIELD, May 11, 177[ ]	1	52
Samuel, d. Jan. 25, 1798	1	68
Samuel, s. John B. & Sarah, b. May 31, 17[ ]	1	63
Samuel, m. Phebe PELLET, Nov. 3, 17[ ]	1	51
Samuel, Capt. d. Dec. 29, 17[ ]	1	67
Samuel Calvin, s. Samuel & Phebe, b. Feb. 20, 1765	1	58
Sarah, m. Henry (?) ADAMS, Dec. 19, 1706	1	51
Sarah, d. Richard & Mary, b. July 30, 1710	1	54
Sarah, w. Samuel, Jr., d. Jan. 7, 1736	1	66
Sarah, d. Thomas & S. Deborah, b. Apr. 15, 1737	1	57
Sarie, d. Ahaziah & Elliger*, b. Dec. 31, 1737 *(Eleanor?)	1	55
Sarah, twin with James, d. Joseph & Sarah, b. June 7, 1748	1	56
Sarah, w. Henry, d. Apr. 16, 1751	1	66
Sarah, d. Samuel & Abigail, b. Nov. 1, 1753	1	57
Sarah, d. James & Sarah, b. Apr. 13, 1754	1	56
Sarah, d. Joseph & Dorothy, b. Apr. 30, 1758	1	57
Sarah, m. Asa STEVENS, Oct. 1, 1761	1	214
Sarah, m. John FELCH, Oct. 29, 1761	1	138
Sarah, wid., d. Oct. 26, 1767	1	67
Sarah, m. David HIDE, Feb. 23, 1769	1	155
Sarah, d. [Solomon, Jr. & Sarah], b. Aug. 3, 1774	1	59
Sarah, [twin with Lucy], d. Jesse & Zerviah, b. Sept. 13, 1787	1	61
Sarah, d. [John B. & Sarah], b. Nov. 14, 17[ ]	1	63
Sarah Bradford, d. James & Jerusha, b. Apr. 2, 1774	1	59
Sarah Davenport, d. [Joseph B. & Laurelia], b. Jan. 30, 1820	2	201
Sarah L., d. [Chauncey & Sarah], b. Sept. 13, 1829	2	202
Sarah L., of Canterbury, m. Douglass F. WATROUS, of Lisbon, Apr. 9, 1849, by Rev. Thomas Tallman	2	89
Sarah M., of Canterbury, m. William C. OSGOOD, of Norwich, Oct. 5, 1847, by Rev. Robert C. Learned	2	59
Sebera, d. Parker & Freelove, d. June 20, [ ]		
Sebera, see also Saberah		
Septy, s. [John B. & Sarah], b. Nov. 7, 17[ ]	1	63
Seth, s. Samuel & Mary, b. Feb. 3, 1725/6	1	54
Seth, s. Samuel & Mary, d. Mar. 30, 1726	1	66
Silvester, s. Jos[eph], Jr. & Elizabeth, b. Aug. 29, 1778	1	60
Solly alias Sally, m. Chaunc[e]y ADAMS, b. of Canterbury,		

	Vol.	Page
ADAMS, (cont.)		
Jan. 1, 1822, by John Francis, J. P.	2	1
Solly, see also Sally		
Solomon, s. Solomon, Jr. & Sarah, b. Dec. 8, 1767	1	59
Solomon, m. Sarah ME[A]CHAM, Apr. 8, 176[ ]	1	51
Solomon, d. Nov. 20, 1773 (?)	1	67
Statera, m. Charles CUTLER, Jan. 24, 1836, by Charles		
Adams, J. P.	2	17
Steadman, s. Cornelius & Esther, b. Sept. 25, 1778	1	61
Submit, d. Jno. & Submitt, b. Mar. 6, 1771	1	59
Suckey, d. [Asa[h]el & Olive], b. Sept. 5, 17[ ]	1	63
Susan Zerviah, d. Perrin & Susan, b. Feb. 3, 1834	2	201
Susannah, m. Capt. Joseph ADAMS, Apr. 4, 1728	1	51
Susannah, d. Joseph & Susannah, b. June 19, 1728/9	1	54
Susannah, d. Ahaziah & Ele[a]ner, b. Apr. 20, 1742	1	55
Susannah, d. Elihu & Jerusha, b. Apr. 16, 1765	1	58
Susannah, d. Timothy & Susannah, b. Nov. 2, 1776	1	60
Susannah, w. Tho[ma]s, d. Feb. 13, 1780	1	67
Susanna, d. Reuben & Abigail, b. Aug. 16, 1784	1	61
Susanna, m. Paul DAVENPORT, Jr., Apr. 4, 1790	1	121
Susannah, m. Peleg LEWIS, Oct. 6, 1801	1	176
Susannah, d. Joseph & Susannah, d. Oct. 2, [ ]	1	66
Synthia, see under Cynthia		
Thomas, s. Henry & Sarah, b. Jan. 14, 1711/12	1	54
Thomas, m. Abigail DAVENPORT, Feb. 23, 1714/15	1	51
Thomas, s. Joseph & Susannah, b. July 31, 1734	1	55
Thomas, s. Ahaziah & Ele[a]ner, b. May 20, 1745	1	55
Thomas, d. Apr. 4, 1752 (?)	1	66
Thomas, s. Eliphalet & Mary, b. Apr. 24, 1757	1	57
Thomas, m. Susanna PECK, Mar. 7, 176[ ]	1	51
Thomas, s. Cornelius & Esther, b. Mar. 21, 1775	1	59
Thomas, Capt., d. Apr. 22, 1815	1	68
Thomas, m. Mary MUDGE, Jan. 4, [ ]	1	52
Thomas Dwight, s. Hub[b]ard, b. Feb. 10, 1827	2	203
Timothy, s. Timothy & Susanna, b. Mar. 1, 1779	1	61
Thyphena, d. Joseph & Sarah, b. July 17, 1760	1	57
Tripheney, d. John & Submit, b. June 21, 1778	1	60
Ursuley, s. [Asa[h]el & Olive], b. July 9, [ ]	1	63
Waitstill, d. Thomas & Abigail, b. Oct. 5, 1717	1	54
Watestill, m. Solomon RAINSFORD, July [ ], 1735	1	209
Welcom[e] Kelley, s. [Titus & Elizabeth], b. Jan. 5, 1820	2	201
William, s. Will[ai]m & Susannah, d. Jan. 16, 173[ ]	1	66
Will[ia]m, s. Joseph & Sarah, b. Mar. 4, 1740	1	55
W[illia]m, s. John & Submitt, b. Dec. 5, 1768	1	59
Williams, m. Sarah KNIGHT, June 12, 1770 (?)	1	51
William, s. William & Sarah, b. Mar. 7, 1773, in Windham	1	59
William, s. Levi & Margaret, b. Feb. 8, 1774	1	60
William, s. W[illia]m & Sarah, b. July 10, 1780	1	60

	Vol.	Page
ADAMS, (cont.)		
William, m. Phyllys **ENSWORTH**, Dec. 18, 177[ ]	1	52
William, s. Joseph & Sarah, d. July 5, 17[ ]	1	67
William, m. Olive **BALDWIN**, Nov. 7, 17[ ]	1	52
William, s. W[illia]m & Sarah, d. Sept. 29, [ ]	1	67
William N., m. Mary **FAULKNER**, Mar. 25, 1837, by Rev. Asa King	2	3
William N., m. Mary **FAULKNER**, Mar. 26, 1837	1	53
William Nelson, s. William & Olive, b. Feb. 19, 1815	1	64
Wright, s. Nehemiah & Mary, b. Mar. 27, 1773	1	59
Zadoc, s. Eben[eze]r & Mary, b. Feb. 15, 1780	1	60
Zerviah, d. Parker & Freelove, b. May 6, 1748	1	57
Zerviah, m. Eliashid **TRACY**, Feb. 19, 1769	1	229
--apman, s. Joseph & Elizabeth, b. Apr. 6, 178[ ] (Probably Chapman)	1	62
--ary, d. Joseph & Eunice, b. Aug. 1, 1719	1	54
--attira, d. Joseph & Elizabeth, b. Feb. 11, 1789	1	62
--bberds, Erastus & Mary, b. May 10, 179[ ]	1	62
--eline, d. W[illia]m & Olive, d. Nov. 15, 1813 (Probably Emeline)	1	68
--my, d. July 16, 1716 (Perhaps Amy)	1	66
--roug, s. Joseph & Elizabeth, b. Mar. 15, 1783	1	62
--shua, s. Samuel & Mary, d. Feb. 23, 1724/5	1	66
--ter, d. July 19, 1820	1	68
----ty, s. John B. & Sarah, d. Feb. 21, 1797	1	68
----ty, w. Timothy, Jr., d. Jan. 29, 1804	1	68
-----y, d. [John B. & Sarah], d. Sept. 13, 1798	1	68
-----, d. Solomon & Abigail, b. Nov. 9, 1726	1	54
-----, wid, [of] Mikael, d. Apr. 4, 1752	1	66
-----, s. Joseph & Elizabeth, b. Apr. 5, 1781	1	62
-----, d. Erastus & Mary, b. Feb. 14, 17[ ]	1	62
-----, infant, d. [Chauncey & Sarah], b. Aug. 15, 1831	2	202
ALLEN, ALLEIN, [see also **ALLYN**], Abigail, relict of John **ADAMS**, d. Dec. 15, 1782 (?)	1	67
Adaline, d. [Barnabus & Elizabeth], b. July 18, 1822	2	202
Adaline, of Canterbury, m. John M. **HYDE**, of Greenville, Nov. 15, 1846, by Rev. Asa King, Westminster	2	42
Alexander, s. Pratt & Rhoda, b. Aug. 20, 1814	1	64
Anna, d. Barnabus & Elizabeth, b. Feb. 11, 1764	1	58
Anne, m. Augustus **WOOD**, Nov. 22, 1786	1	236
Asa, s. George W. & Mary, b. Feb. 12, 1836	2	201
Asahel, [twin with Desire], s. Asahel & Desire, b. Mar. 19, 1774	1	59
Barnabus, s. Jared & Anna, b. Dec. 5, 1783 (Arnold Copy has "Barnabus **ADAMS**". Corrected by L. B. B.)	1	61
Barnabus, Jr., m. Eliza **WALTON**, Feb. 18, 1808	1	52
Betty, m. Benjamin **MORSE**, Jan. 16, 1760	1	181
Charles, s. [Nathan & Nancy], b. May 25, 1820	1	64

	Vol.	Page
ALLEN, ALLEIN, (cont.)		
David W., s. Barnabus & Elizabeth, b. Mar. 8, 1815	2	202
Desire, [twin with Asahel], d. Asahel & Desire, b. Mar. 19, 1774	1	59
Desire, d. Pratt & Rhoda, b. Dec. 26, 179[ ]	1	62
Ebenezer, s. Pratt & Rhoda, b. Nov. 22, 179[ ]	1	62
Edwin, s. Roswell & Susannah, b. Sept. 5, 1810	1	64
Elizabeth (?), d. Tryphenia **DURFEE**, b. July 3, 1782	1	61
Elizabeth, d. Jared & Anna, b. May 21, 178[ ]	1	62
Elizabeth, m. Jed[edia]h **BAKER**, June 17, 1825, by Walter Williams, J. P.	2	7
Eunice, of Canterbury, m. Thomas **WHIPPLE**, of Hampton, Apr. 2, 1823, by Erastus Learned	2	85
George W., m. Mary **RUSSELL**, of Hartford, May 3, 1832	1	53
George W., of Canterbury, m. Mary **RUSSELL**, of Hartford, May 3, 1832, by Ebenezer Allen, J. P.	2	2
George Washington, s. Pratt & Rhoda, b. Jan. 19, 18[ ]	1	63
Hannah, d. Nathan & Nancy, b. June 22, 1818	1	64
Hannah, m. Samuel H. **SMITH**, Jan. 2, 1843, by Rev. Asa King, Westminster	2	74
Harriet, m. Mer[r]it B. **WILLIAMS**, Oct. 25, 1836, by Walter Williams, J. P.	2	86
Harriet E., d. Roswell & Susannah, b. Oct. 3, 1814	1	64
Harry, m. Luala **ADAMS**, Sept. 21, 1813	1	53
Harvey, s. Pratt & Rhoda, b. Sept. 28, 1789	1	62
Horace, s. [Roswell & Susanna], b. July 30, 1810	1	64
Jacob Marsh, s. Jared & Anna, b. Mar. 20, 1786	1	61
Jacob Marsh, s. [Barnabus & Elizabeth], b. Feb. 7, 1817	2	202
James E., of Woonsocket, R. I., m. Susan M. **NEFF**, of Canterbury, Oct. 17, 1832, by Rev. Thomas O. Rice, of West Killingly	2	4
Jared, s. Barnabus & Elizabeth, b. June 3, 1759	1	57
Jared, m. Anna **NEWEL**, of Saratoga, N. Y., Feb. 10, 1783	1	52
Jared, s. [Barnabus & Elizabeth], b. Feb. 19, 1825	2	202
Jedediah, s. Silas & Mary, b. Sept. 25, 1781	1	61
Jemima, m. Nathan[ie]l **CLARK**, Sept. 26, 1768	1	101
John Newell, s. Barnabus, Jr., b. Sept. 25, 1810	1	64
Julia, d. Roswell & Susanna, b. May 31, 1808	1	64
Lemuel, s. Silas & Mary, b. Mar. 11, 1777	1	60
Loesy, d. Barnabus & Elizabeth, b. May 12, 1766	1	58
Lois, d. Nathan & Nanny, b. Jan. 23, 1815	1	64
Lois, d. Roswell & Susannah, b. Feb. 5, 1817	1	64
Lois, m. Nathan **OLDS**, Sept. 30, 1838, by Rev. Asa King	2	17
Lois, d. Pratt & Rhoda, b. Oct. 19, 18[ ]	1	63
Louisa Caroline, d. Alexander & Caroline M., b. Feb. 18, 1844	2	202
Lucetta, d. [Barnabus & Elizabeth], b. Nov. 16, 1819	2	202
Lucretia, d. Pratt & Rhoda, b. May 29, 17[ ]	1	63
Lydia, d. Jared & Anna, b. Mar. 27, 178[ ]	1	62

	Vol.	Page

ALLEN, ALLEIN, (cont.)

	Vol.	Page
Lydia Eliza, d. Pratt & Rhoda, b. Mar. 24, 1809	1	64
Marrilla, of Smithfield, m. Daniel H. **PARKS**, of Canterbury, Apr. 21, 1843, by Rev. W. Clarke	2	64
Marvin Witter, s. Pratt & Rhoda, b. Apr. 17, 1811	1	64
Mary Eliza, d. George W. & Mary, b. Mar. 16, 1840	2	202
Mary Jane, m. Patrick **McSORLEY**, Sept. 15, 1851, by Peter Spicer, J. P.	2	95
Merrett, m. Lydia Ann **PERRY**, b. of Canterbury, Sept. 2, 1850, by Rev. E. W. Robinson, of Hanover Society, Lisbon	2	4
Merril[l], s. Roswell & Susanna, b. Feb. 2, 1824	2	201
Milton, m. Lucetta **MEECH**, Feb. 3, 1833	1	53
Milton, m. Lucetta **MEECH**, Feb. 3, 1833, by Rev. Asa King, Westminster	2	3
Nabby, d. David & Lydia, b. Oct. 4, 1777	1	60
Nancy, d. Nathan & Nancy, b. Jan. 28, 1829	2	201
Nancy, m. Albert **DEWEING**, May 21, 1848, by Rev. Asa King, Westminster	2	22
Nathan, s. [Nathan & Nancy], b. Nov. 29, 1824	2	201
Nathan, m. Nancy **HINKLEY**, Dec. 17, 18[ ]	1	52
Parker, s. Nathan & Ollive, b. Dec. 25, 1762	1	58
Parker, s. Nathan & Nancy, b. Jan. 5, 1822	2	201
Parker, s. Nathan & Nancy, d. July 23, 1823	2	301
Parker, d. Nov. 27, 1823	2	301
Priscilla, d. Barnabus, Jr. & Elizabeth, b. Oct. 25, 1812	1	64
Priscella, m. William **BAKER**, Sept. 6, 1837, by Rev. Asa King	2	11
Rebecca, d. Barnabus & Elizabeth, b. Aug. 26, 1761	1	57
Rebecca, m. Asa **CLARK**, June 2, 1779	1	101
Rebecca, d. [Jared & Anna], b. Apr. 26, 179[ ]	1	62
Rhoda, d. Pratt & Rhoda, b. Sept. 21, [ ]	1	63
Ruby, of Windham, m. Benjamin **BRADFORD**, Oct. 1, 1797	1	72
Sabrina, d. Barnabus & Eliza, b. Dec. 17, 1808	1	63
Sabrina, m. John M. **FRANCIS**, Oct. 11, 1835, by Rev. Jesse Fisher	2	31
Samuel, s. Barnabus & Elizabeth, b. Apr. 1, 1756	1	56
Samuel, s. Nathan & Nancy, b. June 10, 1827	2	201
Sarah, d. George W. & Mary, b. Mar. 8, 1833	2	201
Sarah M., of Cumberliand, R. I., m. Henry S. **ARNOLD**, Jan. 29, 1834, by R. S. Hazen	2	5
Silas, s. Barnabus & Elizabeth, b. Feb. 9, 1754	1	56
Silas, s. Barnabus & Elizabeth, b. Feb. 9, 1754	1	57
Silas, m. Mary **CLEVELAND**, May 16, 1776	1	52
Sophia, d. Roswell & Susannah, b. Sept. 29, 1819	1	64
Sophia, of Canterbury, m. Levi J. **BRANCH**, of Lisbon, Sept. 26, 1842, by Comfort D. Fillmore, Dea.	2	13
Theodore Burton, s. Jonathan & Aurelia, b. Nov. 14, 1826	2	201

	Vol.	Page
ALLEN, ALLEIN, (cont.)		
Waitey, d. Nathan & Nancy, b. June 25, 1831	2	201
Whiting, s. Silas & Mary, b. Apr. 16, 1779	1	60
--arinda, d. [Jared & Anna], b. Sept. 27, 179[ ]	1	62
---ther, s. Azor & Anna, b. June 7, 1791	1	62
-----, s. Azor & Anna, b. Sept. 13, 1788	1	62
ALLERTON, Anna, d. Isaac & Lucy, b. Apr. 20, 1757	1	57
Anne, m. David **RANSOM,** Apr. 20, 1777	1	209
David, s. Isaac & Lucy, b. Feb. 3, 1751	1	55
Jonathan, s. Isaac & Lucy, b. Sept. 15, 1746, at Plainfield	1	55
Reubin, s. Isaac & Lucy, b. Dec. 21, 1752	1	55
ALLYN, [see also **ALLEN**], Addison Williams, s. Jonathan &		
Aurelia, b. July 10, 1814	1	64
Hannah, m. Nathan[ie]l **COGSWELL,** Jan. 2, 1766	1	101
Isham Thomas, s. [Jonathan & Aurelia], b. Feb. 11, 1821	1	64
Jonathan Billings, s. [Jonathan & Aurelia], b. Aug. 5, 1818	1	64
Olive Brown, d. [Jonathan & Aurelia], b. July 3, 1816	1	64
AMA, AAMA, Betsey, d. Zacheus & Nancy, b. May 17, 1798		
[negroes]	1	249
Christopher, d. Jan. 26, 1802 [negro]	1	249
Ebenezer, s. Zacheus & Nancy, b. Jan. 22, 180[ ] [negroes]	1	249
Hardin, s. Zacheus & Nancy, b. May 4, 1794 [negroes]	1	249
Lote, d. Zacheus & Nancy, b. Jan. 17, 1800 [negroes]	1	249
Obadiah, s. Zacheus & Nancy, b. Nov. 16, 1792 [negroes]	1	249
Zacheus, s. Christ & Nancy, b. Jan. 25, 1765 [negroes]	1	249
AMASEL, Alice, d. Job & Sylvia, b. Aug. 27, 1794 (?) [negroes]	1	249
Christopher, s. Job & Sylvia, b. Jan. 22, 1793 [negroes]	1	249
Cyrus, s. Job & Sylvia, b. Aug. [ ], 1782 [negroes]	1	249
Joseph, s. Job & Sylvia, b. Jan. 26, 1790 [negroes]	1	249
Katy, d. Job & Sylvia, b. Oct. 4, 1778 [negroes]	1	249
Lucinda, d. Job & Sylvia, b. June 17, 1786 [negroes]	1	249
Primus, s. Job & Sylvia, b. Mar. 23, 1783 [negroes]	1	249
Rodman, s. Job & Sylvia, b. Nov. 19, 1791 [negroes]	1	249
Sylvia, d. Job & Sylvia, b. Nov. 30, 1784 [negroes]	1	249
AMES, ----, m. Irenah **WATE,** Jan. 2, 1755	1	51
AMY, Hardin, m. Mary Jane **BAILEY,** of Providence, R. I.,		
Dec. 7, 1828	1	53
Harding, of Canterbury, m. Mary Jane **BAILEY,** of Providence,		
R. I., Dec. 7, 1828, by Samuel L. Hough, J. P.	2	2
ANDERSON, William, of New London, m. Selinda **HARRIS,** of		
Canterbury, May 20, 1834, by Rev. Asa King	2	3
ANDRAS, [see under **ANDREWS**]		
ANDREE, ANDRA, [see also **ANDREWS**], George R., of		
Plainfield, m. Olive **BENNET[T],** Oct. 20, 1822	1	53
George R., of Plainfield, m. Olive **BENNET[T],** of Canterbury,		
Oct. 20, 1822, by Jonathan Gallup, J. P.	2	1
ANDREWS, ANDRAS, ANDRESS, [see also **ANDREE**],		
Augustus, s. [Frederick & Lydia], b. Dec. 7, 1788	1	61

	Vol.	Page
ANDREWS, ANDRAS, ANDRESS, (cont.)		
Chester, s. Frederic & Lydia, b. Sept. 17, 1781	1	61
Frederic, s. Frederic & Lydia, b. May 12, 179[ ]	1	62
Frederick, m. Lydia **FELCH**, June 21, [ ]	1	52
John, s. Frederick & Lydia, b. Mar. 1, 1786	1	61
Weeden, m. Abigail **AVERY**, b. of Canterbury, Aug. 12, 1832,		
by Rev. Demis Platt	2	2
Wheaton, m. Abigail **AVERY**, Aug. 12, 1832	1	53
William, of New London, m. Salinda **HARRIS**, ---y 20, 1834	1	53
William Felch, s. [Frederic & Lydia], b. Nov. 30, 179[ ]	1	62
ANGELL, Emily, m. John **HYDE**, b. of Canterbury, Sept. 27, 1847,		
by H. Slade	2	42
Emily, m. John **HYDE**, b. of Canterbury, Sept. 27, 1847,		
by H. Slade	2	48
ANNABLE, ANABLE, Barnabus, s. Nath[anie]l & Elizabeth, b.		
Mar. 3, [ ]	1	63
Betsey, d. Nathaniel & Elizabeth, b. Nov. 17, 1783	1	61
Chester, s. [Nath[anie]l & Elizabeth], b. Oct. 9, [ ]	1	63
Laura, [twin with Lury], d. Nath[anie]l & Eliz[abet]h, b.		
Apr. 11, 1786	1	61
Lury, [twin with Laura], d. Nath[anie]l & Eliz[abet]h,		
b. Apr. 11, 1786	1	61
Mary, m. Eliashib **ADAMS**, Aug. 20, 1767	1	51
Mary, d. Nath[anie]l & Elizabeth, b. Aug. 29, 1781	1	61
Nath[anie]l, m. Elizabeth **BARSTOW**, Dec. 2, [ ]	1	52
Polly, d. [Nath[anie]l & Elizabeth], b. Apr. 15, [ ]	1	63
APPLEY, APPLY, Festus, m. Mary **LAMPHERE**, Sept. 21, 1818	1	52
Lydia, m. Asa **PHINNEY**, May 28, 1795	1	194
Orrila F., of Canterbury, m. Charles W. **POTTER**, of Norwich,		
May 2, 1841, by Rev. Tubal Wakefield	2	63
Susanna Anna, d. Festus & Mary, b. Apr. 30, 1815	1	65
ARCHAR, Barah, m. John **LOMBARD**, June 21, 1733	1	176
ARMSTRONG, Althea, of Norwich, m. Peter **WOODARD**, Dec.		
24, 1755	1	236
Anne, m. Noah **WOODARD**, Nov. 25, 1741	1	236
Irena, of Norwich, m. Joseph **BUTT**, Apr. 12, 1759	1	70
ARNOLD, George, d. July 23, 1759 (an Indian)	1	67
Henry S., m. Sarah M. **ALLEN**, of Cumberland, R. I., Jan.		
29., 1834, by R. S. Hazen	2	5
ASHCRAFT, ASHCROFT, Abigail, d. Jedediah & Sarah, b. Dec.		
27, 1752	1	57
Desire, m. Jonathan **ADAMS**, Dec. 27, 1745	1	51
Jedediah or Zeddiah, m. Saranna **RHOW**, Feb. 28, 1744 (?)	1	51
Jedediah, s. Jedediah & Sarah, b. June 15, 1746	1	57
John, s. Jedediah & Sarah, b. May 15, 1748	1	56
John, s. Hannah **DEAN**, b. June 15, 1769	1	127
John, s. Hannah **DEAN**, single woman, d. Sept. 12, 1769	1	131
Sarah, d. Jedediah & Sarah, b. June 18, 17[ ]	1	55

	Vol.	Page

ASHCRAFT, ASHCROFT, (cont.)

William, s. Jedediah & Sarah, b. Dec. 15, 1750 — 1 — 57

Zeddiah, see under Jedediah

ASPENWALL, Abigail, d. Nathan[ie]l & Mary, d. Nov. 11, 175[ ] — 1 — 66

Almira, d. [William, Jr. & Olive], b. Dec. 2, 1806 — 1 — 64

Almira, of Canterbury, m. Thomas CLEVELAND, of
Plainfield, Apr. 2, 1826, by Rev. Tho[ma]s J. Murdock — 2 — 15

Anne, w. Asa, d. July 21, 1768 (?) — 1 — 67

Anne, d. Asa & Hannah, b. Jan. 5, 1774 — 1 — 60

Asa, m. Anna ADAMS, Apr. 9, 1761 — 1 — 51

Asa, m. Hannah BENNET[T], Jan. 21, 177[ ] — 1 — 52

Betsey, d. [William & Mary], b. July 9, 178[ ] — 1 — 62

Charles Johnson, s. James & Harriet, b. Jan. 18, 1824 — 2 — 201

Charles William, s. William, Jr. & Olive, b. Feb. 25, 1811 — 1 — 64

Charles William, s. [Will[ia]m], d. Apr. 6, 1821 — 2 — 301

Elizabeth, d. Nathan & Mary, b. Apr. 13, 1747, at Killingly — 1 — 56

Elizabeth, d. Asa & Hannah, b. Dec. 32, 1776 — 1 — 60

Emeret, d. [William, Jr. & Olive], b. May 6, 1809 — 1 — 64

Emerette, of Canterbury, m. George A. WILLIARD, of
Worcester, Mass., Dec. 25, [1838], by Rev. C. J. Warren — 2 — 87

Emily, d. William, Jr. & Olive, b. June 13, 1804 — 1 — 64

Emily, d. Will[ia]m, d. Oct. 24, 1820 — 2 — 301

Frederick, s. [Will[ia]m & Olive], b. June 28, 1820 — 2 — 201

Frederick, s. [Will[ia]m, d. July 2, 1821 — 2 — 301

George, s. [Will[ia]m & Olive], b. Nov. 2, 1818 — 2 — 201

Harriet, w. James, d. Mar. 29, 1824 — 2 — 301

James, m. Harriet JOHNSON, Dec. 22, 1822 — 1 — 53

James, m. Harriet JOHNSON, b. of Canterbury, Dec. 22,
1822, by Thomas J. Murdock — 2 — 1

Jane, d. Will[ia]m & Olive, b. Apr. 23, 1815 — 2 — 201

Jane, m. Silas MASON, b. of Canterbury, Feb. 2, 1836, by
Rev. Otis C. Whiton — 2 — 56

John, s. Asa & Hannah, b. Jan. 11, 1775 — 1 — 60

John, s. W[illia]m & Mary, b. Mar. 21, 1781 — 1 — 60

Loiza, d. Dolly CLEVELAND, single woman, b. Feb. 16, 1806 — 1 — 115

Mary, d. Nathaniel & Mary, d. Nov. 12, 1751;
d. Nov. 25, 175[ ] — 1 — 66

Mary, d. Asa & Anna, b. Oct. 7, 1763 — 1 — 58

Mary, d. W[illia]m & Mary, b. Apr. 21, 1779 — 1 — 60

Nathaniel, d. Oct. 12, 1777 — 1 — 67

Nathaniel, s. Asa & Hannah, b. Sept. 15, 1778 — 1 — 60

Olive Leach, d. William, Jr. & Olive, b. Sept. 17, 1812 — 1 — 64

Prescilla, d. Natha[nie]l & Mary, b. Aug. 6, 1751 — 1 — 56

Prescilla, m. Samuel BACON, Apr. 17, 1777 — 1 — 71

Samuel, s. Asa & Anna, b. Sept. 30, 1766 — 1 — 58

Sarah, d. W[illia]m & Mary, b. Nov. 19, 1777 — 1 — 60

Will[ia]m, s. Nathan & Mary, b. June 10, 1749 — 1 — 56

William, s. William & Mary, b. Oct. 8, 1775 — 1 — 60

	Vol.	Page
ASPENWALL, (cont.)		
William, m. Mary **SHAW**, Jan. 5, 177[ ]	1	52
William, m. Olive **LEACH**, Apr. 3, 18[ ]	1	52
----, s. William & Mary, b. June 19, 178[ ]	1	62
AUSTIN, Elles (Alice), m. Daniel **BAKER**, Apr. 25, 1758	1	70
Benjamin, s. Caleb & Hepsibath, b. July 26, 1762	1	58
Benjamin, s. Edmund & Esther, b. Mar. 6, 1775	1	60
Caleb, m. Hepsibath **JONES**, Apr. 15, 1761	1	51
Caleb, s. Caleb & Hepzibath, b. Feb. 9, 1764	1	58
David, [twin with Deborah, s. Peris & Lois], b. July 16, 1802	1	64
David, m. Eliza C. **GITCHELL**, Apr. 13, 1823	1	53
David, m. Eliza G. **MITCHELL**, b. of Canterbury, Apr. 13, 1823, by Andrew T. Judson, J. P.	2	1
Deborah, d. [Tho[ma]s & Eleanor], b. Dec. 12, 1768	1	59
Deborah, [twin with David, d. Peris & Lois], b. July 15, 1802	1	64
Dileverance, s. [George & Rachel], b. May 3, 1773	1	59
Ebenezer, s. George & Rachel, b. Oct. 13, 1758(?)	1	57
Edmund, m. Esther **RUSS**, Dec. 24, 1772	1	52
Elizabeth, d. Edw[ar]d & Elizabeth, b. Apr. 25, 174[ ]	1	55
Elizabeth D., of Canterbury, m. Martin A. **RICE**, of Plainfield, Mar. 8, 1840, by Rev. Tubal Wakefield	2	68
Elles, see under Alice		
Emala, d. [Peris & Lois], b. Sept. 27, 1811	1	64
Emily G., m. David C. **COMIES**, b. of Canterbury, Mar. 11, 1832, by Rev. Demis Platt	2	16
Erastus, s. George & Rachel, b. Apr. 10, 1776	1	60
George, m. Rebecca **CLEVELAND**, Jan. 18, 1758	1	51
Hannah, d. Edmund & Esther, b. July 5, 1773	1	59
Jerusha, d. [Peris & Lois], b. July 7, 1804	1	64
Jerusha, of Canterbury, m. Walter **EATON**, of Windham, Mar. 31, 1828, by Andrew T. Judson, J. P.	2	27
Jesse, s. [Peris & Lois], b. Mar. 10, 1800	1	64
John, s. [Peris & Lois], b. Dec. 10, 1808	1	64
John, m. Semiantha **RICHARDS**, Nov. 28, 1827	1	53
John, m. Semianthe **RICHARDS**, b. of Canterbury, Nov. 28, 1827, by Rev. James R. Wheelock	2	1
Joseph (?), m. Abigail **MORSE**, Sept. 12, 1758	1	51
Joseph, m. Abigail **MORSE**, Apr 15, 1761	1	51
Luther, s. Jos[eph] & Abigail, b. Dec. 17, 1771	1	59
Mary, d. [Peris & Lois], b. Sept. 6, 1806	1	64
Molley, d. Joseph & Abigail, b. Aug. 15, 1761	1	57
Nichols, of Jamestown, R. I., m. Elizabeth S. **EANSWORTH**, Nov. 28, 1830	1	53
Nichols, of Jamestown, R. I., m. Elizabeth S. **EANSWORTH**, of Canterbury, Nov. 28, 1830, by Rev. Demis Platt	2	2
Orra, d. Peris & Lois, b. June 21, 1798	1	64
Robert, d. July 30, 1756	1	66
Robert, s. [Caleb & Hephzibah], b. Aug. 23, 1768	1	58

	Vol.	Page
AUSTIN, (cont.)		
Ruth, m. Will[ia]m **BALDWIN**, Jan. 11, 1757	1	70
Ruth, d. Caleb & Hephzibah, b. June 16, 1766	1	58
Sarah, d. Tho[ma]s & Eleanor, b. Apr. 8, 1765	1	59
Sarah, d. George & Rachel, b. Mar. 29, 1770	1	59
Sarah, d. George, Jr. & Rachel, b. Mar. 29, 1770	1	59
Shuba[e]l, s. George & Rachel, b. Dec. 21, 1763	1	58
Thomas, s. Edward & Elizabeth, b. July 10, 1733 (?)	1	55
Tho[ma]s, m. Eleanor **ADAMS**, Dec. 30, 176[ ]	1	52
William, s. George & Rachal, b. July 10, 1766	1	58
AVERY, Abigail, m. Wheaton **ANDREWS**, Aug. 12, 1832	1	53
Abigail, m. Weeden **ANDREWS**, b. of Canterbury, Aug. 12, 1832, by Rev. Demis Platt	2	2
Joseph C., of Sacrarmento, Cal., m. Mary Susan **ELDREDGE**, of Canterbury, Feb. 22, 1853, by Rev. Robert C. Learned	2	4
BABCOCK, Mary, had illeg. child, John Henry, b. Apr. 10, 1828. Father John O. **BURLEY**	2	207
BACKUS, Anne Tracy, d. [Eliashib T. & Jerusha], b. Dec. 19, 1811	1	93
Bethiah, d. [Nathan & Bethiah], b. Mar. 4, 1787	1	90
Betsey Fosset, d. Elisha & Betsey, b. Aug. 4, 1780	1	86
Charles F., of Franklin, m. Mary **BUTTS**, of Canterbury, Apr. 8, 1832, by Rev. Orrin Catlin	2	9
Ebenezer, s. John & Johannah, b. Jan. 30, 1749/50	1	75
Eliashib I., m. Jerusha **ENSWORTH**, Oct. 8, 1809 (Perhaps Eliashib T.)	1	73
Eliashib Tracy, s. [Timothy, Jr. & Ruby], b. July 18, 1787	1	88
Elijah, s. Timothy & Mary, b. May 28, 1750	1	80
Elijah, s. Timothy & Mary, d. June 2, 1751	1	96
Elijah, s. John & Johannah, b. June 18, 1756	1	80
Elisha, s. Timothy & Mary, b. May 3, 1752	1	77
Elisha, m. Bette **JOHNSON**, Feb. 12, 1777	1	71
Elisha, s. Elisha & Betsey, b. Nov. 17, 1782	1	88
Elizabeth, m. Nathaniel **BOND**, Mar. 17, 1713/14	1	69
Eunice, d. Timothy & Sarah, b. [ ] 9, 1722	1	75
Eunice, m. David **CLEVELAND**, June 25, 1744	1	100
Eunice, d. Jno. & Johannah, b. Sept. 2, 1754	1	80
Eunice Elizabeth, d. Stephen & Eunice, b. Aug. 25, 1802	1	92
Isaac, m. Esther **SHEPERD**, Sept. 21, 1786	1	72
Isaac, s. Isaac & Esther, b. Nov. 27, 1789	1	89
Jeremiah, s. Timothy & Mary, b. May 7, 1760	1	81
Joanna, d. John & Joanna, b. Aug. 15, 1763	1	82
John, s. Timothy & Sarah, b. May 5, 1720	1	74
John, m. Johanna **DOWNING**, June 26, 1747	1	69
John, s. John & Johannah, b. Aug. 25, 1747	1	78
Joseph, s. John & Johannah, b. Sept. 18, 1748	1	78
Lucy, d. Timo[thy], Jr. & Ruby, b. Jan. 28, 1777	1	85
Lucy, m. James **ENSWORTH**, Mar. 2, 1797	1	133
Mary, d. Timothy & Sarah, b. Jan. 31, 1713/14	1	74

	Vol.	Page
BACKUS, (cont.)		
Mary, d. Timothy & Mary, b. Sept. 15, 1744	1	78
Mary, m. Samuel **FELCH**, Aug. 25, 1765	1	138
Mason, s. Isaac & Esther, b. Aug. 27, 1792	1	89
Olive, d. Nathan & Bethiah, b. Aug. 9, 1785	1	90
Patty, d. Timothy, Jr. & Ruby, b. Sept. 14, 1782	1	88
Polly, d. Timothy, Jr. & Reube, b. Sept. 14, 1782	1	94
Polly, d. [Nathan & Bethiah], b. Nov. 2, 1791	1	90
Polly, m. John **ENSWORTH**, Feb. 17, 1800, by Moses		
Cleveland. Recorded Apr. 4, 1835	2	27
Rebeckah, m. William **BAKER**, June 13, 1706	1	69
Rebeckah, d. John, [ ]	1	96
Ruby, d. Timo[thy], Jr. & Ruby, b. Aug. 17, 1779	1	87
Ruby, w. Timothy, Jr., d. July 18, 1787	1	98
Rufus, s. Timothy & Mary, b. Sept. 19, 1762	1	81
Samuel, s. Isaac & Esther, b. Sept. 16, 1787	1	88
Sarah, d. Timothy & Sarah, b. Apr. 5, 1711	1	74
Sarah, m. John **PIKE**, July 9, 1729	1	192
Sarah, d. John & Joanna, b. May 9, 1758	1	82
Sarah, w. Dea., d. Feb. 24, 1760	1	96
Sarah, d. [Timothy, Jr. & Ruby], b. Feb. 3, 1785	1	88
Sibel, d. [Nathan & Bethiah], b. Jan. 30, 1789	1	90
Solomon, s. John & Johannah, b. Dec. 11, 1752, n. s.	1	75
Stephen, d. Apr. 1, 1707	1	95
Stephen, s. Timothy & Sarah, b. Nov. 10, 1709	1	74
Stephen, s. Timothy & Mary, b. Aug. 27, 1747	1	78
Stephen, m. Abigail **BROWN**, Oct. 11, 1750	1	69
Stephen, d. Sept. 28, 1751	1	96
Stephen, m. Susannah **BALDWIN**, Apr. 21, 1773	1	71
Susan, d. Eliashib T. & Jerusha, b. Mar. 14, 1810	1	93
Susannah, w. Stephen, d. Nov. 10, 1796	1	98
Sybil, see under Sibel		
Timothy, m. Sarah **POST**, Jan. 26, 1708/9	1	69
Timothy, s. Timothy & Sarah, b. Nov. 18, 1717	1	74
Timothy, Jr., m. Mary **BACON**, Nov. 14, 1739	1	69
Timothy, s. Timothy & Mary, d. June 23, 1749	1	95
Timothy, s. John & Johannah, b. June 11, 1751	1	75
Timothy, s. Timothy & Mary, b. June 9, 1754	1	78
Timothy, Dea., d. Feb. 28, 1762	1	96
Timothy, Jr., m. Ruby **TRACY**, Feb. 14, 1776	1	71
Timothy, Jr., m. Jerusha **TRACY**, of Franklin, July 6, 1788	1	72
Timothy, s. Eliashib T. & Jerusha, b. May 1, 1815	1	93
BACON, Abigail, d. Asa & Abigail, b. Dec. 30, 1772	1	84
Abigail, d. Asa & Abigail, d. Dec. 2, 1781	1	98
Abigail, d. Asa & Abigail, b. Sept. 20, 1782	1	87
Abner, m. Abigail **ENSWORTH**, Jan. 26, 1764	1	70
Elles (Alice), d. Benjamin & Deborah, b. Dec. 4, 1760	1	82
Alice, d. Dan[ie]ll & Olive, b. July 12, 1778	1	85

	Vol.	Page
BACON, (cont.)		
Alice, m. Lasee **HIDE**, Nov. 16, 1785	1	156
Alvin, s. Daniel & Olive, b. Sept. 12, 1779	1	86
Ama, d. Asa & Abigail, b. Oct. 13, 1779	1	86
Amy, m. Fitch **ADAMS**, Jan. 16, 1800	1	53
Asa, s. John & Ruth, b. Nov. 21, 1735	1	76
Asa, m. Edith **BRADFORD**, May 16, 1765	1	70
Asa, m. Abigail **WHITNEY**, June 2, 1768	1	70
Asa, s. Asa & Abigail, b. Feb. 8, 1771	1	84
Asa[h]el, s. Benjamin & Deborah, b. Nov. 22, 1764	1	82
Asa[h]el, m. Alice **FULLER**, Aug. 19, 1795	1	72
Benjamin, s. John & Hannah, b. Dec. 17, 1726	1	75
Benjamin, s. John & Ruth, d. July 14, 1749	1	95
Benj[ami]n, m. Deborah **ADAMS**, Dec. 14, 1749	1	69
Benjamin, s. Benjamin & Deborah, b. June 17, 1757	1	82
Benjamin, s. Asa & Edith, b. Jan. 18, 1766	1	83
Benjamin, s. Asa & Edeth, d. Jan. 27, 1766	1	97
Benjamin, m. Irene **FARNHAM**, Jan. 29, 1783	1	72
Benjamin, s. Benjamin, Jr. & Irene, b. May 11, 1798	1	91
Betsey, d. Benj[ami]n, Jr. & Irene, b. Jan. 27, 1785	1	88
Cha[u]ncey, s. [Benj[ami]n, Jr. & Irene], b. Oct. 21, 1791	1	89
Daniel, d. [sic] Eben[eze]r & Margory, b. June 5, 1748	1	78
Daniel, m. Olive **DARBE**, Apr. 27, 1777	1	71
David, m. Elizabeth **ENSWORTH**, Dec. 10, 1767	1	70
David, s. Asa & Abigail, b. July 2, 1785	1	88
Deborah, d. Eben[eze]r & Margorie, b. Jan. 27, 1739/49	1	77
Deborah, d. Benj[ami]n & Deborah, b. Oct. 17, 1751	1	77
Ebenezer, m. Margery **MARKHAM**, July 21, 1737	1	69
Ebenezer, d. [sic] Eben[eze]r & Margory, b. Apr. 6, 1746	1	78
Eben[eze]r, s. Eben[eze]r & Marjorie, d. Sept. 11, 1749	1	95
Edeth, w. Asa, d. Mar. 2, 1766	1	97
Edeth, w. Asa, d. Mar. 3, 1766	1	97
Edmund, s. [Asa[h]el & Alice], b. May 30, 1806	2	207
Edwin, s. Jacob & Sarah, b. Oct. 11, 1789	1	89
Elizabeth, d. John & Hannah, b. Nov. 8, 1728	1	75
Elizabeth, d John & Hannah, d. Nov. 2, 1736	1	95
Elizabeth, d. John & Ruth, b. May 31, 1740	1	76
Elizabeth, d. John & Ruth, d. June 28, 1749	1	95
Elizabeth, d. Asa & Abigail, d. Feb. 27, 1770	1	97
Elles, see under Alice		
Emeline L., of Canterbury, m. Seth S. **SAFFORD**, of		
Windham, Oct. 21, 1832, by Rev. Dennis Platt	2	73
Emeline Lodema, d. [Asa[h]el & Alice], b. Mar. 23, 1809	2	207
Francis, s. Asa[h]el & Alice, b. Nov. 13, 1799	1	93
Hannah, m. Jabez **HIDE**, Feb. 27, 1740	1	155
Hannah, d. Eben[eze]r & Margory, b. Feb. 7, 1744	1	78
Hannah, d. Eben[eze]r & Marjorie, d. Aug. 6, 1749	1	95
Harriet Webb, d. Asa[h]el & Alice, b. May 16, 1801	2	207

	Vol.	Page
BACON, (cont.)		
Israel, s. Israel & Deliverance, b. Sept. 2, 1750	1	79
Jacob, s. Benj[ami]n & Deborah, b. Nov. 17, 1753	1	79
Jacob, m. Sarah JOHNSON, June 6, 1782	1	71
Jacob, m. Martha CLARK, Jan. 1, 1793	1	73
James Newton, s. [Asa[h]el & Alice], b. Oct. 24, 1814	2	207
John, m. Ruth SPAULDING, Sept. 24, 1734	1	71
John, s. John & Ruth, b. Apr. 9, 1738	1	76
John, Dea., d. Feb. 19, 1740	1	95
John, s. Asa & Abigail, b. Nov. 24, 1774	1	84
John, d. Oct. 2, 1790	1	98
John Fuller, s. Asa[h]el & Alice, b. Nov. 26, 1796	1	90
Jos[eph], m. Mary FITCH, b. of Canterbury, Oct. 16, 1745, at Groton, by Andrew Croswell	1	69
Joseph, m. Patience PARKS, Nov. 2, 1752	1	70
Jos[eph], s. Joseph & Patience, b. June 2, 1755	1	80
Julia, m. William SAFFORD, b. of Canterbury, Nov. 24, 1824, by Rev. Tho[ma]s J. Murdock	2	71
Julyett Maria, d. [Asa[h]el & Alice], b. May 20, 1803	2	207
Lucius, s. [Samuel & Prescilla], b. May 6, 1787	1	91
Lucy, d. John & Hannah, b. Dec. 27, 1723	1	75
Lucy, d. Eben[eze]r & Margory, b. Feb. 27, 1742	1	78
Lydia M., of Canterbury, m. Henry T. HOUGH, of Chaplin, Sept. 20, 1848, by Rev. Robert C. Learned	2	42
Lydia Mathewson, d. Chauncey & Rhoba, b. Jan. 1, 1821	2	207
Maria S., of Canterbury, m. Mason A. WOOD, of Plainfield, Sept. 13, 1849, by Rev. Robert C. Learned	2	89
Mariah Spaulding, d. Chauncey & Rhoba, b. May 25, 1828	2	207
Mary, d. John & Hannah, b. Jan. 30, 1720/21	1	74
Mary, m. Timothy BACKUS, Jr., Nov. 14, 1739	1	69
Mary, d. John & Ruth, b. Aug. 19, 1749	1	78
Mary, d. Joseph & Mary, b. May 29, 1750	1	80
Mary, w. Joseph, d. Mar. 21, 1752	1	96
Mary, m. Solomon PAINE, June 8, 1756	1	192
Mary, m. Thomas BUSWELL, Jr., June 10, 1772	1	70
Mary, m. Nathaniel FISH, Jr., June 28, 1775	1	138
Mary, m. Asa NOALEN, Oct. 20, 1785	1	189
Mary, m. William Pitt CLEVELAND, Feb. 2, 1796	1	102
Nancy, d. [Benj[ami]n, Jr. & Irene], b. July 4, 1789	1	89
Olive, d. John & Ruth, b. June 6, 1753	1	77
Olive, d. John & Ruth, d. Sept. 26, 1754	1	95
Olive, m. Joseph FISH, Jan. 14, 1781	1	138
Phebe, m. William BLANCHER, Nov. 8, 1750	1	70
Phelena Ann, of Canterbury, m. Elisha J. MORGAN, of Plainfield, Mar. 26, 1834, by Rev. Otis C. Whiton	2	55
Philura, d. Sam[ue]l & Priscilla, b. Mar. 15, 1783	1	87
Philura Ann, d. Lucius & Anna, b. May 15, 1809	1	92
Phinehas, s. Ebenezer & Margarie, b. Apr. 24, 1738	1	76

	Vol.	Page

BACON, (cont.)

Phenehas, s. [Eben[eze]r & Margorie], d. Sept. 27, 1740	1	77
Polly, d. Sam[ue]l & Prescilla, b. Mar. 20, 1778	1	86
Prescilla, w. John *, d. Oct. 19, 1826 (*Samuel)	2	307
Rebecca, d. Israel & Deliver[an]ce, b. Apr. 21, 1749	1	79
Roba, of Canterbury, m. Isaac **KNIGHT**, of Plainfield, Mar. 14, 1838, by Rev. Charles J. Warren	2	47
Ruby, d. Benj[ami]n, Jr. & Irene, b. Dec. 21, 1787	1	89
Rufus, s. Sam[ue]l & Prescilla, b. Sept. 23, 1780	1	86
Rufus, s. Samuel & Priscilla, d. Sept. 10, 1802, a 22 y.	1	98
Samuel, s. Joseph & Mary, b. Dec. 1, 1747	1	78
Samuel, m. Prescilla **ASPENWALL**, Apr. 17, 1777	1	71
Samuel, d. Dec. 12, 1822	2	307
Sarah, m. Eleazer **BROWN**, Nov. 13, 1749	1	69
Sarah A., of Canterbury, m. Leonard **HENDEE**, of Heebron, Aug. 19, 1829, by Andrew T. Judson, J. P.	2	39
Sarah Almira, d. Jacob & Martha, b. Sept. 15, 1796	1	93
Sophia, d. Samuel & Priscilla, b. Mar. 31, 1785	1	91
Sophia, m. Rev. Erastus **LEARNERD**, May 14, 1816	1	176
William, m. Jerush **ENSWORTH**, Mar. 7, 1765	1	70
----, child of Joseph & Mary, d. Mar. 21, 1752	1	96
BADGER, Sally, m. Rufus **PARISH**, Sept. 26, 1799	1	194
BADLOCK, [see under **BIDLAKE**]		
BAILEY, Mary Jane, of Providence, R. I., m. Hardin **AMY**, Dec. 7, 1828	1	53
Mary Jane, of Providence, R. I., m. Harding **AMY**, of Canterbury, Dec. 7, 1828, by Samuel L. Hough, J. P.	2	2
BAKER, Abiel, d. Benjamin & Jerusha, b. Nov. 17, 1746	1	77
Abiel, m. Solomon **CLEVELAND**, Oct. 3, 1748	1	100
Abigail, d. Tryal & Elizabeth, b. Nov. 26, 1735	1	76
Abigail, m. Gideon **BINGHAM**, Nov. 12,1761	1	70
Ellis (Alice), d. Daniel & Ellis (Alice), b. Jan. 21, 1759	1	81
Benjamin, m. Jerusha **PARRISH**, June 12, 1744	1	69
Benj[ami]n, s. Benj[ami]n & Jerusha, [b.] Apr. 25, 1745	1	77
Constance, m. Joshua **PAINE**, Jan. 6, 1736/7	1	192
Daniel, s. William & Rebeckah, b. June 21, 1713	1	74
Daniel, m. Elles (Alice) **AUSTIN**, Apr. 25, 1758	1	70
Deliverance, d. Israel & Deliverance, b. June 8, 1756	1	83
Elijah, m. Lois **ROOD**, Jan. 29, 1750/51	1	69
Elizabeth, d. William & Rebeccah, b. Mar. 28, 1707	1	74
Elizabeth, d. Tryall & Elizabeth, b. Oct. 4, 1721	1	75
Elizabeth, d. Israel & Deliver[an]ce, b. July 25, 1758	1	80
Elizabeth, d. Daniel & Ellis, b. Oct. 16, 1761	1	81
Ellis, see under Alice		
Esther, Tryal & Elizabeth, b. Aug. 31, 1738	1	76
Esther, d. Feb. 24, 1760	1	96
Hezekiah M., Capt., m. Anna **SMITH**, Mar. 30, 1830, by Walter Williams, J. P.	2	8

	Vol.	Page
BAKER, (cont.)		
Israel, m. Deliverance **CLEVELAND**, Sept. 16, 1747	1	69
Jed[edia]h, m. Elizabeth **ALLEN**, June 17, 1825, by Walter Williams, J. P.	2	7
Jerusha, d. Benj[ami]n & Jerusha, b. May 6, 1750	1	79
Mary, d. Tryall & Elizabeth, b. Sept. 5, 1724	1	75
Mary, d. Tryal & Elizabeth, d. Dec. 26, 1750, ae 26 y.	1	96
Mary, m. Rozel **BENNET[T]**, Dec. 15, 1777	1	71
Mehetable, m. Moses **BUSWELL**, Jan. 30, 1732/3	1	69
Reuben, Jr., of Plainfield, m. Lucy Ann **PERKINS**, of Canterbury, July 21, 1839, by Rev. Charles J. Warren	2	11
Sarah, m. Simeon **WOODARD**, Nov. 23, 1732	1	236
Solomon, s. Benj[ami]n & Jerusha, b. Jan. 7, 1755	1	79
Tryall, m. Elizabeth **TIBBETTS**, Dec. 24, 1718	1	69
Tryal, d. Oct. 12, 1776	1	97
William, m. Rebeckah **BACKUS**, June 13, 1706	1	69
William, s. William & Rebeckah, b. Feb. 2, 1708/9	1	74
Will[ia]m, Jr., d. Aug. 20, 1735	1	96
Will[ia]m, d. Aug. 2, 1750	1	96
William, s. Israel & Deliverance, b. June 3, 1754	1	83
William, m. Priscella **ALLEN**, Sept. 6, 1837, by Rev. Asa King	2	11
BALDING, [see also **BALDWIN**, Ebenezer, m. Hannah **RHEADE**, Nov. 22, 1744	1	69
John L., of Windham, m. Minerva **HERRICK**, of Canterbury, Mar. 28, 1830, by Rev. Israel G. Rose, of Westminster	2	8
Marcy, w. Henry, d. Oct. 25, 1760	1	96
Suzannah, d. Timothy & Suzannah, b. Mar. 19, 1749/50	1	79
BALDWIN, [see also **BALDING**], Aaron, s. Eben[ezer] & Hannah, b. Apr. 22, 1746	1	77
Aaron, m. Mehetable **LEONARD**, of Preston, Apr. 11, 1771	1	70
Abigail, m. John **HOUGH**, Nov. 11, 1753	1	155
Abigail, d. Benjamin & Lydia, b. Mar. 12, 1785	1	92
Alice, d. Elisha & Welthy, b. July 17, 1784	1	88
Alice S., of Canterbury, m. Louis **WALDO**, of Windham, Feb. 26, 1834, by Rev. Otis C. Whiton	2	86
Alice Susannah, d. Timothy & Mary, b. May 13, 1812	1	93
Almira, d. John & Lucinda, b. Nov. 30, 1802	1	92
Almira, d. John & Lucinda (**ENSWORTH**) **BALDWIN**, m. Marvin **ADAMS**, Apr. 20, 1820	1	53
Amy, d. Elijah & Hannah, b. Oct. 21, 1816	1	93
Amey, d. Elijah & Hannah, d. Mar. 3, 1842, in the 26th y. of her age	2	307
Anna, m. Nathan **GREEN**, July 17, 1775	1	149
Benjamin, d. Dec. 11, 1759	1	96
Benj[ami]n, m. Lydia **PIKE**, Dec. 4, 1775	1	71
Benjamin, s. [Benjamin & Lydia], b. Sept. 22, 1787	1	92
Billy, s. [Rufus & Hannah], b. Oct. 17, 1790	1	91

	Vol.	Page
BALDWIN, (cont.)		
Daniel, s. Benjamin & Hannah, b.May 26, 1705	1	74
Daniel, m. Hannah **PARTRIDGE**, Nov. 16, 1730	1	69
David, s. Timo[thy] & Susanna, b. May 8, 1742	1	76
David, s. Timothy & Susanna, b. May 9, 1742	1	81
David, m. Esther **PUFFER**, May 29, 1774	1	71
David, d. May 2, 1826, ae 84	2	307
David Clark, s. David & Esther, b. Sept. 9, 1784	1	88
David Clark, s. David & Esther, d. Oct. 15, 1788	1	98
David Clark, s. Timothy & Mary, b. Apr. 23, 1810	1	92
Dwight R., s. Rufus A. & Maria A., b. Aug. 1, 1846	2	208
Ebenezer, s. Benjamin & Hannah, b. Sept. 4, 1707	1	74
Ebenezer, d. Nov. 3, 1717	1	95
Ebenezer, s. John & Mary, b. Oct. 14, 1721	1	75
Ebenezer, s. Johannah **ADAMS**, Apr. 6, 1745	1	78
Edith, d. John & Mary, b. Feb. 27, 1726/7	1	75
Edith, d. John & Mary, d. Apr. 18, 1733	1	95
Elijah, s. David & Esther, b. Jan. 17, 1783	1	86
Elijah, s. Elijah & Hannah, b. Oct. 26, 1820	1	93
Elisha, s. James & Thankful, b. Mar. 13, 1759	1	81
Eliza T., of Plainfield, m. John H. **ENSWORTH**, of Canterbury, Sept. 14, 1846, by Rev. Hiram Dyer	2	28
Esther, d. Dr. Elijah & Hannah, b. Sept. 26, 1814	1	93
Esther, w. David, d. Feb. 13, 1825, ae 78	2	307
Esther, d. Elijah & Hannah, d. Aug. 31, 1844, in the 30th y. of her age	2	307
Eunice, m. John **FELCH**, Jr., Apr. 12, 1796	1	138
Festus, s. David & Esther, b. Nov. 24, 1777	1	85
George, m. Achsah Ann **SMITH**, b. of Canterbury, Nov. 30, 1837, by Rev. Joseph Ayer, of Lisbon	2	11
Hannah, d. Aaron & Mehet[ab]le, b. Oct. 24, 1773	1	84
Hannah, d. Oct. 2, 1778	1	97
Hannah, d. [Rufus & Hannah], b. Apr. 16, 1788	1	91
Hannah B., of Canterbury, m. Thomas **BISHOP**, of Lisbon, Nov. 5, 1833, by Rev. Levi Nelson	2	9
Hannah Burnham, d. Dr. Elijah & Hannah, b. June 1, 1812	1	93
Hannah Melissa, d. Isaac & Philura, b. Dec. 9, 1821	2	207
Harriet Atwood, d. Timo[th]y & Mary, b. Nov. 1, 1816	1	93
Henry, s. Benjamin & Hannah, b. Feb. 15, 1713/14	1	74
Horace, of Lenox, Penn., m. Olive P. **CLARK**, of Canterbury, June 19, 1825, by Rev. Tho[ma]s J. Murdock	2	7
Isaac, s. John & Mary, b. June 1, 1730	1	75
Isaac, m. Thankful **TRAP[P]**, Apr 4, 1751	1	70
Isaac, s. [Rufus & Hannah], b. Mar. 22, 1799	1	91
Isaac, m. Phelura **CAMPBELL**, Oct. 16, 1820	1	73
Jacob, s. Timothy & Susanna, b. Mar. 27, 1736	1	76
Jacob, m. Mary **LATHROP**, of Lisbon, May 7, 1788	1	72
Jacob, d. Sept. 12, 1795	1	98

	Vol.	Page
BALDWIN, (cont.)		
James, m. Thankful **CLARK**, Sept. 13, 1758	1	70
James, d. Nov. 9, 1761	1	96
James, s. Ebenezer & Hannah, b. Oct. 28, 1762	1	82
James, s. [Rufus & Hannah], b. Apr. 20, 1784	1	91
Jeanis, s. John & Mary, b. May 24, 1735	1	75
Jedediah, s. Eben[eze]r & Hannah, b. Nov. 23, 1749	1	76
Jedediah, s. Eben[eze]r & Hannah, d. Nov. [ ], 1754	1	96
Jerusha, d. [Rufus & Hannah], b. May 22, 1780	1	91
Jerusha, m. William **MORSE**, Sept. 28, 1800	1	181
John, m. Mary **ADAMS**, Feb. 22, 1720/21	1	69
John, s. Ebenezer & Hannah, b. Jan. 1, 1748	1	76
John, d. July 6, 1759	1	96
John, s. Rufus & Hannah, b. June 28, 1778, in Wyoming Valley	1	91
John, m. Lucinda **ENSWORTH**, Nov. 5, 1801	1	72
Jonathan, s. [Rufus & Hannah], b. Mar. 9, 1786	1	91
Joseph, s. Timothy & Susannah, b. July 24, 1734	1	75
Joseph, m. Thankful **BALDWIN**, June 1, 1763	1	70
Lois, d. Benj[ami]n & Lydia, b. Nov. 30, 1776	1	85
Lois, m. Jesse **SWEET**, Sept. 25, 1796	1	215
Lucinda, d. John & Lucinda, [b.] June 21, 1807	1	92
Lucinda, m. Charles **ADAMS**, May 1, 1837	1	53
Lucy, d. Ebenezer & Hannah, b. Nov. 11, 1755	1	80
Lucy, m. Andrew **EVANS**, Jan. 8, 1775	1	133
Lydia, d. Henry, d. Nov. 23, 1760	1	96
Lydia, d. Aaron & Mehetable, b. Jan. 26, 1772	1	84
Mary, d. John & Mary, b. Sept. 6, 1724	1	74
Mary, d. Joseph & Thankful, b. May 29, 1764	1	82
Mary, wid., d. Feb. 16, 1767	1	97
Mary, [twin with Samuel Leonard], d. [Aaron & Mehetable], b. May 17, 1783	1	88
Mary, m. Samuel **CARTER**, May 4, 1786	1	102
Mary Esther, d. Timothy & Mary, b. Aug. 7, 1808	1	92
Mehetable, d. Aaron & Mehetable, b. Dec. 7, 1780	1	88
Nancy, d. [Rufus & Hannah], b. July 20, 1797	1	91
Nancy Fitch, d. Timothy & Mary, b. Sept. 20, 1814	1	93
Olive, d. Aaron & Mehet[ab]le, b. Sept. 2, 1778	1	86
Olive, d. Benj[ami]n & Lydia, b. Sept. 2, 1779	1	86
Olive, m. William **ADAMS**, Nov. 7, 17[ ]	1	52
Patience, d. Benjamin & Hannah, b. Jan. 4, 1711/12	1	74
Phebe, m. Capt. Joseph **BUTTS**, Apr. 27, 1809	1	73
Polly, d. [Rufus & Hannah], b. Jan. 1, 1793	1	91
Polly, m. Luther **ENSWORTH**, Sept. 30, 1813	1	133
Ruby, d. Benj[amin] & Lydia, b. Mar. 4, 1778	1	86
Ruby, m. Nathan **FISH**, Jr., Oct. 22, 1801	1	138
Rufus, s. [Rufus & Hannah], b. May 12, 1795	1	91
Sabra, d. Aaron & Mehitable, b. Mar. 2, 1776	1	85

	Vol.	Page

BALDWIN, (cont.)

Samuel Leonard, [twin with Mary], s. [Aaron & Mehetable],
  b. May 17, 1783 — 1 — 88

Sarah, d. Ebenezer & Hannah, b. Oct. 2, 1759 — 1 — 82

Serinda, m. Charles **ADAMS**, b. of Canterbury, May 1, 1837,
  by Rev. Tubal Wakefield — 2 — 3

Sibbel, see under Sybel

Simeon Lathrop, s. Timothy & Mary, b. Apr. 4, 1821 — 1 — 93

Stephen, s. Timothy & Susannah, b. Apr. 1, 1746 — 1 — 77

Stephen, s. Timothy & Suzanna, d. Jan. 9, 1746/7 — 1 — 95

Susan, m. Perren **ADAMS**, Mar. 29, 1824 — 1 — 53

Susan, m. Perrin **ADAMS**, b. of Canterbury, Mar. 29, 1824,
  by Rev. Tho[ma]s J. Murdock — 2 — 1

Susanna, m. Stephen **BACKUS**, Apr. 21, 1773 — 1 — 71

Susanna, d. David & Esther, b. Aug. 28, 1780 — 1 — 86

Susanna, wid. Timothy, d. Oct. 30, 1795, ae 84 y. — 1 — 98

Sibbel, d. [Rufus & Hannah], b. Mar. 24, 1782 — 1 — 91

Sybel, m. Joseph **FARNHAM**, Oct. 20, 1803 — 1 — 139

Thankful, d. Ebenezer & Hannah, b. Oct. 14, 1753 — 1 — 78

Thankful, m. Joseph **BALDWIN**, June 1, 1763 — 1 — 70

Timothy, s. Benjamin & Hannah, b. Oct. 11, 1709 — 1 — 74

Timothy, s. Timothy & Susanna, b. July 22, 1752 — 1 — 75

Timothy, d. Nov. 22, 1772 — 1 — 97

Timothy, s. David & Esther, b. Apr. 15, 1775 — 1 — 85

Timothy, m. Mary **LATHROP**, of Lisbon, Nov. 14, 1805 — 1 — 73

William, s. John & Mary, b. Feb. 18, 1732/3 — 1 — 75

Will[ia]m, m. Ruth **AUSTIN**, Jan. 11, 1757 — 1 — 70

Zipporah, d. Timo[thy] & Susannah, b. July 22, 1738 — 1 — 76

Zip[p]orah, m. Charles **MORSE**, May 3, 1758 — 1 — 181

BALIS, John, m. Ehester (Esther) **HERRINGTON**, Sept. 6, 1761 — 1 — 70

BARBER, Barradel Jackson, d. Oliver & Sarah, b. Aug. 24, 1784 — 1 — 89

Laura E., of Canterbury, m. Charles **HICKS**, of Plainfield,
  Jan. 1, 1849, by Rev. Robert C. Learned — 2 — 42

Pamela, d. [Oliver & Sarah], b. Sept. 11, 1787 — 1 — 89

Sophia, m. Calvin **HERRICK**, Mar. 25, 1804 — 1 — 156

BARNET, Naomi, m. Alden **PEABODY**, b. of Providence, Sept. 14,
  1826, by Rev. Tho[ma]s J. Murdock — 2 — 61

BARON, Frederick A., of U. S. Navy, m. Sarah A. **HARRIS**, of
  Canterbury, Sept. 7, 1837, by Rev. Charles J. Warren — 2 — 11

BARRET, Samuel, m. Suffronia **FISKE**, of Thompson, Conn., Oct.
  4, 1842, by Rev. H. Slade — 2 — 13

BARSTOW, BASTOW, Adaline, d. [Calvin & Orvilla], b. Dec. 14,
  1826 — 2 — 207

Anne, d. John & Elizabeth, b. July 31, 1759 — 1 — 81

Anne, d. [Hezekiah & Olive], b. Nov. 20, 1793 — 1 — 90

Apheas, m. Constant **CARTER**, June 10, 1773 — 1 — 71

Benjamin Fitch, s. Sam[ue]l & Amey, b. Jan. 10, 1792 — 1 — 90

Bethiah, d. John, Jr. & Susanna, b. Mar. 25, 1780 — 1 — 86

	Vol.	Page
BARSTOW, BASTOW, (cont.)		
Calvin, s. John, Jr. & Susannah, b. May 25, 1786	1	88
Calvin, m. Orra **HERRICK**, Oct. 22, 1810	1	73
Catharine, d. Curtis & Elizabeth, b. June 12, 1812	1	93
Catharine, d. Mar. 19, 1814	1	99
Curtis, s. Samuel & Hannah, b. Sept. 5, 1782	1	87
Curtiss, m. Elizabeth **PARKE**, Aug. 27, 1809	1	73
Dwight, s. Hez[ekia]h, Jr. & Rebecca, b. Aug. 8, 1820	1	93
Ebenezer, s. John & Elizabeth, b. Sept. 7, 1756	1	80
Ebenezer, s. John & Susannah, b. Sept. 12, 1788	1	89
Ebenezer, m. Lucy **LEARNED**, Sept. 12, 1811	1	73
Elisha Paine, s. [Sam[ue]l & Amey], b. Aug. 15, 1793	1	90
Elizabeth, d. Hez[ekiah] J. & Rebecca, b. Apr. 7, 1822	2	207
Elizabeth, m. Nath[anie]l **ANABLE**, Dec. 2, [ ]	1	52
Emma, d. Calvin & Orra, b. Apr. 5, 1811	1	93
Eunice Park, d. Curtis & Elizabeth, b. July 8, 1814	1	93
Fidelia, d. Ebenezer & Lucy, b. Dec. 17, 1812	1	93
Frederic, s. Job & Luranah, b. June 19, 1785	1	88
George, s. [Curtis & Elizabeth], b. Aug. 13, 1816	1	93
Hannah, w. Samuel, d. Mar. 9, 1788	1	98
Hannah Spaulding, d. Curtiss & Elizabeth, b. Feb. 24, 1810	1	92
Harriet, w. John, 2d, d. Sept. 27, 1822	2	307
Harriet, d. Calvin & Orvilla, b. Mar. 23, 1824	2	207
Hezekiah, s. John & Elizabeth, b. Feb. 28, 1755	1	79
Hezekiah, m. Olive **BRADFORD**, May 23, 1776	1	72
Hezekiah, s. Hezekiah & Olive, d. Aug. 12, 1787	1	98
Hezekiah, s. [Hezekiah & Olive], b. Nov. 14, 1791	1	90
Hezekiah, Jr., m. Rebecca **GAGER**, Jan 28, 1818	1	73
Jerusha, d. John & Elizabeth, b. Mar. 22, 1767	1	83
Jerusha, m. Nathan **PALMER**, of Wilkesbarre, Penn., Sept. 9, 1794	1	193
Jerusha Bradford, d. Hez[ekiah] & Olive, b. Nov. 23, 1787	1	89
Job, s. John & Elizabeth, b. Mar. 5, 1761	1	81
Job, m. Lurana **CURTIS**, Dec. 9, 1783	1	71
John, s. John & Elizabeth, b. Oct. 2, 1751	1	79
John, s. John & Elizabeth, d. Jan. 19, 1752	1	95
John, s. Jno. & Elizabeth, b. Dec. 21, 1752	1	76
John, Jr., m. Susanna **SMITH**, May 19, 1779	1	71
John, s. [Sam[ue]l & Amey], b. Nov. 2, 1795	1	90
John, s. Calvin & Orra, b. Dec. 10, 1812	1	93
John, Dea., m. Elizabeth **MARSH**, b. of Canterbury, Mar. 28, 1830, by Rev. Israel G. Rose, of Westminster	2	8
Josiah Park, s. John, 2d, d. July 8, 1822	2	307
Luther, s. John, Jr. & Susanna, b. Feb. 3, 1784	1	87
Luther, s. [Calvin & Orra], b. Oct. 7, 1817	1	93
Luther, m. Mary **KINGSLEY**, Dec. 21, 1845, by Rev. Daniel Lyon, of Packerville	2	14
Martha, d. [Curtis & Elizabeth], b. Nov. 22, 1818	1	93

	Vol.	Page

BARSTOW, BASTOW, (cont.)

	Vol.	Page
Olive, d. Calvin & Orra, b. May 6, 1815	1	93
Orra, d. Samuel & Hannah, b. Mar. 24, 1786	1	88
Orra, m. Gad **BULKLEY**, Sept. 15, 1805	1	72
Orra, d. [Curtis & Elizabeth], b. May 7, 1821	1	94
Rebeckah Elizabeth, d. John & Elizabeth, b. June 11, 1763	1	82
Samuel, m. Amey **FITCH**, of Lisbon, Apr. 16, 1789	1	72
Samuel, d. July 18, 1822	2	307
Septimeus, s. John, Jr. & Susanna, b. Dec. 17, 1781	1	86
Simeon, s. Sam[ue]l & Hannah, b. Apr. 12, 1784	1	88
Sophia, d. Hezekiah & Olive, b. Oct. 24, 1789	1	90
Sophia, m. Russel[l] **PARK**, Nov. 21, 1810	1	194
Spaulding, s. Sam[ue]l & Hannah, b. Feb. 27, 1788	1	89
Susan B., m. Arthur F. **DRINKWATER**, of Blue Hills, Me., Aug. 30, 1847, by Rev. Asa King, Westminster	2	22
Susannah, d. [Sam[ue]l & Amey], b. Oct. 5, 1797	1	90
William Augustus, s. John & Elizabeth, b. Feb. 21, 1765	1	82
Zedediah, s. John & Susanna, b. Oct. 4, 1790	1	89

BARTLETT, John C., m. Ann Eliza **GREEN**, Jan. 17, 1847, by Rev. Asa King, Westminster — 2, 14

BASS, Eunice, m. Ebenezer **WITTER**, Sept. 12, 1799 — 1, 237

BATCHELLOR, Frederic A. P., m. Almyra J. **MATHEWSON**, Apr. 14, 1842, by Henry R. Dyar, J. P. — 2, 12

BATES, [see also **BUTTS**], Abigail, d. John & Sarah, b. May 11, 1752 — 1, 77

	Vol.	Page
Abigail, m. Benjamin **JEWETT**, Jan. 19, 1773	1	167
Alice, d. Jona & Eliza, b. Jan. 23, 1774	1	85
Daniel, s. John & Esther, b. Feb. 3, 1771	1	83
David, s. John & Sarah, b. July 28, 1747	1	77
Dolly, d. John & Ehester (Esther), b. Mar. 25, 1765	1	82
Dorkis, of Windham, m. Caleb **ORMSBY**, Jan. 12, 1761	1	250
Easther had s. Robert **RUNNOLDS**, b. Feb. 21, 1748	1	210
Esther, d. John & Sarah, b. Mar. 30, 1760	1	81
Esther, s. Gershom **MOTT**, Jr., Apr. 13, 1773	1	181
John, m. Sarah **BUTT**, June 15, 1747	1	69
John, s. John & Esther, b. Sept. 4, 1774	1	84
Jona, m. Elizabeth **JUSTIN**, Jan. 18, 1774	1	71
Jonathan, s. John & Sarah, b. Apr. 15, 1755	1	80
Lydia, m. Thomas **COTTON**, Apr. 11, 1771	1	101
Margaret, m. Henry **DEANS**, Apr. 18, 1744	1	120
Mary, d. John & Esther, b. Aug. 13, 1772	1	84
Phinehas, s. John & Esther, b. June 9, 1763	1	82
Roxa, m. John **LILLEE**, Apr. 8, 1779	1	176
Roxeyuencey, d. John & Sarah, b. Oct. 15, 1757	1	81
Sarah, w. John, d. May 8, 1761 [Arnold has "BUTTS")	1	97
Sarah, d. John & Esther, b. Aug. 9, 1768	1	83
Sibbel, d. John & Esther, b. Oct. 9, 1766	1	83

BAULDING, [see under **BALDING**]

	Vol.	Page
BEDLACK, [see under **BIDLAKE**]		
BEERS, Amos J., see under Ellen Victoria **ADAMS**		
BENJAMIN, Bathiah, see under Bethia		
Bela, s. Simeon & Abigail, b. June 24, 1771	1	84
Bathiah, d. Jabez & Rhoda, b. Aug. 8, 1743	1	79
Bethiah, d. Jabez & Rhoda, d. Mar. 10, 1749/50	1	96
Bathiah, d. Jabez & Rhoda, b. Mar. 8, 1754	1	79
Daniel, s. Jedediah & Patience, b. May 29, 1747;		
d. Oct. [ ], 1749	1	77
Daniel, s. Jabez & Rhoda, b. May 19, 1752	1	79
Doritha, d. Jedediah & Patience, b. Apr. 22, 1752	1	77
Eben, [twin with Sarah], s. Jabez & Rhoda, b. Feb. 4, 1746/7	1	79
Elizabeth, d. Jedediah & Patience, b. Oct. 12, 1749	1	77
Hannah, m. Benj[ami]n **BROWN**, Feb. 25, 1755	1	70
Hulda[h], d. Jedediah & Patience, b. Apr. 6, 1754	1	80
Jedediah, s. Jedediah & Patience, b. Aug. 28, 1741;		
d. Nov. [ ], 1745	1	77
Jedediah, s. [Simeon & Abigail], b. July 15, 1772	1	84
Jedediah, m. Mary **MAIN**, Dec. 6, 1778	1	71
Joannah, d. Jedediah & Patience, b. July 10, 1749	1	77
Mercy, d. Jabez & Rhoda, b. Jan. 22, 1740/41, in Preston	1	79
Patience, m. Hopestill **CLEVELAND**, May 9, 1754	1	100
Phillip, s. Jabez & Rhoda, b. Sept. 18, 1750	1	79
Phinehas, m. Zipporah **SPAULDING**, Nov. 14, 1759	1	70
Phinehas, s. Phinehas & Zipporah, b. Feb. 7, 1761	1	81
Rebecca, d. Simeon & Abigail, b. July 29, 1775	1	85
Sam[ue]ll, s. Jabez & Rhoda, b. Feb. 27, 1738/9, in Preston	1	79
Sarah, [twin with Eben], d. Jabez & Rhoda, b. Feb. 4, 1746/7	1	79
Sarah, d. Barzillai & Molly, b. Feb. 20, 1782	1	88
Simeon, s. Jedediah & Patience, b. Oct. 28, 1744	1	77
Simeon, m. Abigail **FOSTER**, Mar. 29, 1770	1	70
Zipporah, d. Phinehas & Zipporah, b. Apr. 20, 1763	1	82
Zipporah, w. Phinehas, d. Jan. 14, 1764	1	96
BENNETT, BENNET, Alice, m. Joseph **DAVENPORT**, Dec. 25,		
1783	1	121
Ebenezer S., m. Hannah **JONES**, b. of Canterbury, Mar. 12,		
1843, by Rev. John F. Blanchard	2	13
Elias, m. Alamantha M. **HEDGE**, b. of Canterbury, Mar. 14,		
1853, by Rev. Nehemiah B. Hyde	2	105
Elijah, d. Dec. 2, 1812	1	99
Elisha, m. Sarah H. **BENNETT**, Nov. 13, 1853, by R. S.		
Hazen	2	105
Elizabeth, m. Comfort **PIDGE**, Dec. 31, 1826, by Rev.		
George S. White	2	61
Elizabeth, m. George **RAY**, June 6, 1842, by Rev. W. Clarke	2	68
Elizabeth F., m. Samuel **CARPENTER**, of Stafford, Nov. 27,		
1845, by Rev. Asa King, Westminster	2	18
Ephraim, of Plainfield, m. Artimissa **MORGAN**, of Canterbury,	2	

	Vol.	Page
BENNETT, BENNET, (cont.)		
July 14, 1822, by Andrew J. Judson, J. P.	2	7
Eunice, m. Anthony **GLASS**, June 19, 1740	1	149
Ezra, m. Charlotte **BURNHAM**, July 3, 1843, by Rev. Asa		
King, Westminster	2	13
Hannah, m. Asa **ASPENWALL**, Jan. 21, 177[ ]	1	52
Henry, of Griswold, m. Pre[s]cilla **ADAMS**, of Canterbury,		
Apr. 11, 1822, by John Francis, J. P.	2	7
Hiram, of Canterbury, m. Susan **HOUSE**, of East Windsor,		
Oct. 8, 1850, by Rev. R. S. Hazen, of Westminster	2	14
James, s. James & Anna, b. May 22, 1748	1	78
Jarvis, s. Waterman & Abigail, b. May 27, 1800	1	91
Levy Stevens, s. [Rufus & Anna], b. Feb. 17, 1819	1	93
Lucinda, d. Waterman & Abigail, b. Dec. 10, 1798	1	90
Lydia, m. Eli **RAYNSFORD**, b. of Canterbury, July 23, 1815,		
by Daniel Frost, J. P.	2	68
Martha, m. William **HEBBARD**, Jr., Aug. 15, 1776	1	155
Mary, m. Enos **WOODARD**, Dec. 26, 1750	1	236
Mary, d. Ebenezer & Grace, b. Nov. 20, 1782	1	88
Mary L., of Canterbury, m. Micah L. **TAYLOR**, of Pomfret,		
Aug. 21, 1843, by Daniel Bennett, J. P.	2	79
Molly, m. Timo[thy] **WINTER**, Jr., Feb. 2, 1775	1	236
Nancy Henkal, d. [Rufus & Anna], b. Jan. 25, 1818	1	93
Nelson, s. Rufus & Anna, b. Mar. 6, 1816	1	93
Olive, m. George R. **ANDRA**, of Plainfield, Oct. 20, 1822	1	53
Olive, of Canterbury, m. George R. **ANDREE**, of Plainfield,		
Oct. 20, 1822, by Jonathan Gallup, J. P.	2	1
Oliver, s. Rozel & Mary, b. May 3, 1777	1	85
Pardon, of Brooklyn, m. Elizabeth **CARVER**, Mar. 12, 1843,		
by Rev. Asa King, Westminster	2	13
Penelope, d. July 11, 1814	1	99
Polly, m. Luther **BROWN**, Nov. 15, 1804	1	72
Prudence, m. Eleaz[e]r **ADAMS**, June 15, 177[ ]	1	52
Roger, s. John & Mary, b. May 3, 1753	1	77
Rozel, m. Mary **BAKER**, Dec. 15, 1777	1	71
Rufus, s. Ebenezer & Grace, b. Jan. 8, 1787	1	88
Rufus, m. Anna **STEPHENS**, Apr. 4, 1817	1	73
Samuel F., of Hampton, m. Lydia **ENSWORTH**, of		
Canterbury, Nov. 22, 1852, by R. S. Hazen	2	105
Sarah, d. Eben[eze]r & Grace, b. Nov. 4, 1788	1	89
Sarah H., m. Elisha **BENNETT**, Nov. 13, 1853, by R. S.		
Hazen	2	105
Sophronia, d. [Rufus & Anna], b. Oct. 30, 1820	1	93
Waterman, m. Abigail **MUNRO**, Feb. 1, 1798	1	72
BENTLEY, Hannah, of Franklin, m. Jonathan **HIDE**, [ ]	1	156
BESTOW, [see under **BARSTOW**]		
BETTEY, Lucy Ann, of Brooklyn, m. Luther **SANGER**, of		
Plainfield, Apr. 1, 1845, by Z. Baker	2	75

	Vol.	Page
BIDLAKE, BEDLACK, BADLOCK, BEDLOCK, [see also		
BABCOCK, Benj[ami]n, s. John & Mary, b. Oct. 10, 1751	1	79
Benjamin, s. James & Mehetable, b. Jan. 6, 1762	1	82
Hannah, of Windham, m. Benjamin **JEWETT**, Feb. 10, 1762	1	167
James, m. Mehetable **DURKE**, Feb. 14, 1749	1	69
James, s. Jeames & Mehetabel, b. Nov. 26, 1750	1	79
James, Jr., m. Abigail **FULLER**, Apr. 30, 1772	1	70
John, s. John & Mary, b. June 1, 1758	1	81
John, s. [James & Mehetable], b. Apr. 22, 1771	1	84
Mandurell, d. John & Mary, b. Aug. 29, 1756	1	81
Martha, d. James & Mehetable, b. Mar. 24, 1764	1	82
Mary, m. Silas **WOODARD**, Feb. 28, 1749/50	1	236
Mehetable, d. James & Mehetable, b. Dec. 25, 1758	1	80
Mehetable, d. John * & Mehetable, d. Nov. 22, 1759		
(*Perhaps James ?)	1	96
Mehetable, d. John * & Mehetable, b. Jan. 21, 1760		
(*Perhaps James?)	1	81
Mehetable, 2d, d. John * & Mehetable, d. Dec. 10, 1760		
(*Perhaps James?)	1	96
Phileman, s. James & Mehetable, b. July 20, 1769	1	84
Sarah, d. James & Mehitable, b. Apr. 30, 1756	1	80
Shubael, s. James & Mehitable, b. Aug. 24, 1752, o. s.	1	80
Stephen, s. James, Jr. & Abigail, b. Jan. 5, 1773	1	84
William, s. James & Mehitable, b. Aug. 8, 1754	1	80
BILLINGS, Sarah, of Killingly, m. Thomas **WILCOX**, of Griswold,		
Nov. 2, 1851, by Ephraim Browning, J.P., at Packersville	2	90
BINDICE, Parmelia, m. Joseph **HIBBARD**, b. of Canterbury, Sept.		
14, [ ], by Rev. James R. Wheelock	2	39
BINGHAM, Alice, d. [Gideon & Abigail], b. July 22, 1767	1	84
Alice, m. Richard **CADY**, Nov. 15, 1787	1	102
Alice, m. Roger **SMITH**, Apr. 29, 1792	1	215
Anne, m. Charles **MORSE**, Jr., Apr. 10, 1783	1	181
Aurelia, d. W[illia]m & Mary, b. Feb. 19, 1769	1	83
Delucina Lathrop, s. William & Mary, b. Sept. 19, 1764	1	82
Delucena Lathrop, d. William & Mary, b. Sept. 19, 1764	1	97
Ebgert, m. Sally E. **ADAMS**, May 23, 1836, by Rev. Asa		
King, Westminster	2	10
Elisha, s. Gideon & Abigail, b. Jan. 31, 1778	1	86
Elisha, m. Tryphena **OLNEY**, Nov. 9, 1806	1	73
Eunice Maria, d. [Zephaniah & Clarrissa], b. Nov. 2, 1835	2	207
Frances E., of Canterbury, m. Noah **SAUNDERS**, of		
Glastonbury, Nov. 25, 1852, by R. S. Hazen	2	76
George Washington, s. William & Ruby, b. July 29, 1794	1	89
Gideon, m. Abigail **BAKER**, Nov. 12, 1761	1	70
Gurdin, s. William & Mary, b. Aug. 16, 1762	1	81
Henry Derben, s. Jeremiah & Lois, b. Mar. 23, 1815	1	93
John, s. Mary **WINTER**, single woman, Mar. 12, 1780	1	86
John, s. Elisha & Tryphenia, b. Feb. 26, 1812	1	93

	Vol.	Page
BINGHAM, (cont.)		
Johnson, s. [Gideon & Abigail], b. Mar. 22, 1765	1	84
Joseph, s. [Gideon & Abigail], b. Nov. 1, 1771	1	84
Joseph, s. Elisha & Tryphenia, b. July 4, 1807	1	92
Julia, d. Luther & Abigail, b. May 3, 1787	1	89
Lorilla, d. Gurdon & Lucy, b. Sept. 1, 1793	1	89
Louisa, d. Elisha & Tryphenia, b. Oct. 10, 1809	1	93
Lucy, d. William & Mary, b. Nov. 27, 1766	1	83
Lucy, d. William, d. Feb. 5, 1774	1	97
Luther, s. William & Mary, b. May 10, 1760	1	81
Luther, m. Abigail **JOHNSON**, May 10, 1786	1	72
Mary, d. Gideon & Mary, b. Sept. 24, 1746	1	77
Ruth, m. David **DOWNING**, Nov. 2, 1795	1	121
Sam[ue]l, s. Gideon & Abigail, b. Sept. 11, 1762	1	84
Sophronia, m. Enoch E. **WALDO**, Oct. 6, 1831, by Rev.		
Israel G. Rose, of Westminster	2	86
Uriah Newton, s. Zephaniah & Clarrissa, b. May 11, 1832	2	207
*William, s. Will[ia]m & Mary, b. Mar. 18, 1759		
*"**BRIGHAM**" hand written in the margin of orginal		
manuscript	1	80
William, s. William & Mary, d. Aug. 8, 1759	1	96
William, s. William & Mary, b. July 27, 1772	1	84
William, m. Ruby **JOHNSON**, Oct. 20, 1793	1	72
Zepheniah, m. Clarrissa **WOODARD**, b. of Canterbury,		
Aug. 31, 1830, by Rev. I. G. Rose, of Westminster	2	8
BISHOP, Hannah, of Lisbon, m. Solomon **PAYNE**, Jr., Mar. 17,		
1818	1	194
Hannah B., w. Thomas, d. Jan. 18, 1834	2	307
Reuben, of Lisbon, m. Abigail **ADAMS**, Nov. 27, 1808	1	73
Sally, m. Daniel **HERRINGTON**, Jr., Sept. 3, 1820, by John		
Francis, J. P.	2	39
Selah, s. John & Sarah, b. Mar. 31, 1794	1	89
Thomas, of Lisbon, m. Hannah B. **BALDWIN**, of Canterbury,		
Nov. 5, 1833, by Rev. Levi Nelson	2	9
BLAKELEY, Daniel, m. Sally **THOMPSON**, Nov. 26, 1835, by		
Wi[llia]m Hutchins, J. P.	2	10
Daniel, m. Maryetta **GRIGGS**, b. of Hampton, June 23,		
1850, by Charles Adams, J. P.	2	14
BLANCHER, Amasa, s. William & Pheeby, b. June 30, 1753	1	81
Lucy, d. William & Pheeby, b. Oct. 10, 1755	1	81
Sebel, d. William & Pheeby, b. June 13, 1759	1	81
William, m. Phebe **BACON**, Nov. 8, 1750	1	70
William, s. William & Pheby, b. May 10, 1751	1	81
BLISS, Abby H., of Canterbury, m. William **HARVEY**, of Hartford,		
Dec. 1, 1839, by Rev. Charles J. Warren	2	41
Francis, b. May 6, 1807, in Canterbury	2	208
Francis, b. Mar. 3, 1852, in Brooklyn	2	208
Frank, s. Septemius & Abigail, b. May 6, 1806	1	92

	Vol.	Page
BLISS, (cont.)		
Frederick Wheeler, b. Apr. 2, 1838	2	208
Lydia E., m. Prentice **LEWIS**, b. of Canterbury, Oct. 31, 1847, by Rev. B. Cook, of Jewett City	2	53
Lydia Matilda, b. Apr. 12, 1810, in Washington, R. I.	2	208
Septemius, m. Abigail **PHINNEY**, Sept. 26, 1805	1	73
[BOARDMAN], [see under **BORDMAN**]		
BOLLES, Elisha T., of Ashford, m. Adeline **SMITH**, of Canterbury, Nov. 5, 1849, by Rev. R. S. Hazen, Westminster	2	14
BOMAN, [see under **BOWMAN**]		
BOND, Abigail, w. Jonas, d. June 3, 1764	1	97
Abigail, d. William & Sarah, b. Dec. 27, 1764	1	82
Alice, d. Jonas & Abigail, b. July 20, 1753	1	77
Bethiah, d. Jonas & Abigail, b. Feb. 29, 1760	1	82
Bethiah, m. John **BRADFORD**, Jr., Oct. 5, 1780	1	71
Bethuel, s. Nathaniel & Elizabeth, b. Apr. 24, 1728	1	75
Bethuel, m. Lidia **HIDES**, Sept. 20, 1753	1	70
Bethuel, m. Ruth **HERRICK**, Apr. 22, 1794	1	72
Cecelia Esther, d. [Joseph & Esther], b. Oct. 20, 1826	2	208
Charles James, [s. Daniel Herrick & Deborah], b. June 6, 1843	2	208
Daniel Herrick, s. Bethuel & Ruth, b. June 20, 1804	1	92
Daniel Herrick, m. Deborah **WHITE**, July 5, 1835, by Rev. George S. White	2	11
Daniel Webster, [s. Daniel Herrick & Deborah], b. Apr. 29, 1838	2	208
Deborah, d. Jonas & Abigail, b. July 18, 1757	1	81
Dorothy, d. Bethuel & Ruth, b. May 11, 1800	1	91
Elijah, s. Bethuel & Ruth, b. Apr. 23, 1796	1	90
Elizabeth, d. Nathaniel & Elizabeth, b. Sept. 17, 1717	1	74
Elizabeth, m. Daniel **FROST**, May 7, 1739	1	138
Elizabeth, wid. Nathaniel, d. Feb. 13, 1748/9	1	95
Elizabeth, d. Jonas & Abigail, b. Jan. 9, 1755	1	81
Eliza[beth], m. John **BRADFORD**, Apr. 22, 1773	1	71
Elizabeth Sargent, [d. Daniel Herrick & Deborah], b. July 21, 1841	2	208
Emmons Peleg, s. Joseph & Esther, b. Sept. 6, 1824	2	208
George White, twin with Mary White, s. [Daniel Herrick & Deborah], b. May 21, 1836	2	208
Hannah, d. Bethual & Lydia, b. Apr. 24, 1757	1	80
Hannah, d. William & Sarah, b. June 11, 1763	1	82
Hannah, d. Aug. 30, 1789	1	98
Isaac, s. Will[ia]m & Sarah, b. Oct. 2, 1755	1	80
Isaac, s. Will[ia]m & Sarah, d. July 13, 1759	1	96
Isaac, s. Bethuel & Ruth, b. July 26, 1798	1	90
Jonas, s. Nathaniel & Elizabeth, b. Aug. 5, 1720	1	74
Jonas, m. Abigail **DEWEY**, of Lebanon, Sept. 3, 1752	1	70
Jonas, s. Jonas & Abigail, b. Oct. 1, 1762	1	82
Jonas, m. Esther **[W]RIGHT**, of Lebanon, July 26, 1765	1	70

	Vol.	Page
BOND, (cont.)		
Jonas, Dea., m. Mary **WOOD**, of Norwich, May 19, 1784	1	72
Jonas, Dea., m. Sarah **MUNROW**, Mar. 28, 1793	1	72
Jonas, Dea., m. Mary **PARRISH**, Nov. 10, 1796	1	72
Jonas, m. Elizabeth **STORY**, b. of Canterbury, Nov, 28, 1822, by Erastus Larned	2	7
Joseph, s. Bethuel & Lydia, b. Feb. 15, 1754	1	77
Joseph, s. Bethuel & Ruth, b. Nov. 1, 1794	1	89
Joseph, m. Esther **FORD**, 2d, b. of Canterbury, Sept. 7, 1823, by Erastus Larned	2	7
Joseph, s. [Joseph & Esther], b. Dec. 16, 1830	2	208
Julius, s. [Joseph & Esther], b. Nov. 21, 1828	2	208
Lucy, d. Bethuel & Lydia, b. Mar. 2, 1759	1	81
Lucy, m. Charles **JUSTIN**, Apr. 23, 1789	1	167
Lydia, d. W[illia]m & Sarah, b. June 14, 1773	1	84
Marah, w. Dea. Jonas, d. Aug. 18, 1791	1	98
Mary, d. Nathaniel & Elizabeth, b. June 12, 1730	1	75
Mary, m. William **CAREW**, Oct. 4, 1764	1	101
Mary White, twin with George White, [d. Daniel Herrick & Deborah], b. May 21, 1836	2	208
Nathaniel, m. Elizabeth **BACKUS**, Mar. 17, 1713/14	1	69
Nathaniel, s. Nathaniel & Elizabeth, b. Jan. 12, 1715/16	1	74
Olive, d. Will[ia]m & Sarah, b. Dec. 30, 1758	1	80
Rebeckah, d. Nathaniel & Elizabeth, b. Aug. 30, 1726	1	75
Sarah, d. William & Sarah, b. May 18, 1761	1	81
Sarah, w. Dea. Jonas, d. Feb. 13, 1794	1	98
Stephen, s. Nathan[ie]ll & Elizabeth, b. Apr. 8, 1719	1	74
Susanna, d. Bethuel & Lydia, b. Jan. 5, 1761	1	81
Susanna, m. John **MUNRO**, Oct. 30, 1782	1	181
Vienna, d. William & Sarah, b. July 10, 1757	1	80
Vienna, m. Samuel **WRIGHT**, Feb. 16, 1775	1	236
Will[ia]m, m. Sarah **WOODARD**, Sept. 25, 1754	1	70
William, d. May 19, 1799	1	98
William, s. Bethuel & Ruth, b. Dec. 12, 1808	1	92
William Cowper, [s. Daniel Herrick & Deborah], b. Oct. 24, 1839	2	208
BORDMAN, Ja[me]s Roath, s. Jona & Prescilla, b. Aug. 17, 1771	1	84
Sarah, d. Jona & Priscilla, b. May 31, 1775	1	85
BOSWELL, [see under **BUSWELL**]		
BOWMAN, BOMAN, Abbilene, d. Ezra & Mary, b. Jan. 24, 1752	1	79
Betsey, d. Walter & Anne, b. Mar. 26, 1777	1	87
Elisha, m. Elizabeth **KIMBALL**, June 29, 1780	1	71
Erastus, s. Walter & Anne, b. Oct. 16, 1781	1	86
Hannah, d. Ezra & Mary, b. July 7, 1750	1	79
Hulda[h], d. Ezra & Mary, b. Dec. 2, 1755	1	81
John, s. Walter & Anne, b. Oct. 1, 1779	1·	87
Mary, w. Ezra, d. Jan. 28, 1760	1	96
Mary, m. Daniel **CUSHMAN**, Dec. 31, 1777	1	101

	Vol.	Page
BOWMAN, BOMAN, (cont.)		
Nathan, s. Elisha & Elizabeth, b. Mar. 15, 1782	1	87
Samuel W., m. Eunice S. **LONG,** Nov. 27, 1839, by Rev. Asa		
King, Westminster	2	12
Sarah, d. Ezra & Mary, b. Nov. 7, 1757	1	81
Sarah, d. Walter & Anne, b. July 29, 1775	1	87
Walter, m. Anne **LITCHFIELD,** Feb. 22, 1775	1	71
Zerviah, d. Ezra & Mary, b. Mar. 20, 1754	1	77
BRADFORD, Abigail, d. Will[ia]m & Mary, b. Sept. 2, 1753	1	77
Abigail, d. [Luther & Clarrissa], b. Oct. 10, 1824	2	207
Alice, d. John & Elizabeth, b. Mar. 8, 1777	1	85
Alice, m. James **ADAMS,** Jr., Jan. 31, [ ]	1	52
Ann, m. Nathan **NEFF,** b. of Canterbury, [ ], by Rev.		
I. G. Rose, of Westminster	2	57
Ann Sevar, d. [W[illia]m & Mehetable], b. Mar. 3, 1808	1	92
Anna, d. John & Bethiah, b. Mar. 10, 1781	1	87
Anne, m. Eleazer **CLEVELAND,** Apr. 25, 1750	1	100
Anne, twin with Mary, d. Joshua & Anne, b. Dec. 1, 1775	1	85
Annis, d. [Samuel & Lydia], b. Nov. 22, 1780	1	87
Araunah, m. Mary **DELAP,** Mar. 10, 1802	1	72
Archibald, s. [Thomas & Philenia], b. Jan. 12, 1792	1	92
Archibald, m. Emeline **HYDE,** Nov. 9, 1841, by Rev. Asa		
King	2	12
Augustus, s. John & Bethiah, b. Jan. 15, 1787	1	88
Benjamin, s. W[illia]m & Martha, b. Mar. 29, 1768	1	84
Benjamin, m. Ruby **ALLEN,** of Windham, Oct. 1, 1797	1	72
Benjamin Palmer, s. David & Rhoda, b. Mar. 28, 1781	1	87
Bethiah, d. John & Bethiah, b. Oct. 10, 1785	1	88
Bethiah, w. John, Jr., d. Jan. 8, 1788	1	98
B[e]ulah, d. William & Mary, b. Sept. 3, 1763	1	82
Beulah, d. [Josiah & Elizabeth], b. Apr. 5, 1791	1	90
Caroline, d. W[illia]m & Mehetable, b. July 13, 1806	1	92
David, s. Will[ia]m & Mary, b. May 8, 1748	1	77
David, m. Rhoda **PALMER,** July 1, 1770	1	71
Ebenezer, s. Will[ia]m & Mary, b. May 29, 1746	1	77
Ebenezer, s. [David & Rhoda], b. Aug. 18, 1773	1	86
Eben[eze]r, s. John & Elizabeth, b. Mar. 10, 1775	1	85
Ebenezer, s. John & Elizabeth, d. Mar. 31, 1776	1	97
Edith, d. Tho[ma]s & Eunice, b. Oct. 23, 1741	1	78
Edith, m. Asa **BACON,** May 16, 1765	1	70
Edith, d. Thomas & Philenia, b. Aug. 20, 1794	1	92
Elizabeth, d. [Josiah & Elizabeth], b. June 7, 1788	1	90
Elizabeth, w. John, d. Mar. 18, 1822	2	307
Elizabeth, d. [Archibald & Emeline], b. Mar. 31, 1847	2	208
Emily, of Canterbury, m. Robert **WATERMAN,** of Sheffield,		
Me., Nov. 11, 1828, by Chester Lyon, J. P.	2	86
Emmilla, d. Benj[ami]n & Ruby, b. July 6, 1801	1	91
Eunice, d. Tho[ma]s & Eunice, b. Apr. 6, 1739	1	76

	Vol.	Page
BRADFORD, (cont.)		
Eunice, d. Tho[ma]s & Eunice, b. Apr. 6, 1739	1	78
Eunice, d. Tho[ma]s & Eunice, d. Mar. 3, 1749/50	1	96
Eunice, d. John & Bethiah, b. Feb. 23, 1783	1	88
Eunice, m. Araunah **BUTT**, Mar. 6, 1802	1	72
Frances Elizabeth, d. James & Maria, b. May 18, 1822	2	207
Giles, m. Lydia **MORSE**, Jan. 17, 1853, by R. S. Hazen	2	105
Harriet, d. Archibald & Emeline, b. Dec. 14, 1844	2	208
James, s. Tho[ma]s & Eunice, b. Jan. 4, 1746	1	78
James, s. Thomas & Eunice, d. Sept. 27, 1749	1	95
James, s. Will[ia]m & Mary, b. Feb. 1, 1755	1	78
James, d. Mar. 26, 1762	1	96
James, s. W[illia]m & Mary, d. Sept. 17, 1775	1	97
James, s. Joshua & Anna, b. Oct. 27, 1777	1	85
James, s. [Josiah & Elizabeth], b. Jan. 25, 1793	1	90
James, m. Maria **MORSE**, May 27, 1821, by Peter Morse, J. P.	2	7
Jerusha, d. James, & Edith, b. June 27, 1716	1	74
Jerusha, m. Jonathan **PELLET**, Feb. 20, 1733	1	192
John, s. James & Ede, b. Jan. 30, 1714/15	1	74
John, s. Thomas & Eunice, b. July 1, 1735	1	75
John, s. Thomas & Eunice, b. July 12, 1735	1	77
John, s. Tho[ma]s & Eunice, d. May 18, 1750	1	96
John, s. Will[ia]m & Mary, b. July 27, 1750	1	77
John, s. Tho[ma]s & Eunice, b. Aug. 12, 1754	1	78
John, m. Eliza[beth] **BOND**, Apr. 22, 1773	1	71
John, Jr., m. Bethiah **BOND**, Oct. 5, 1780	1	71
John, Jr., m. Sarah **WILLIAMSON**, Sept. 4, 1788	1	72
John, s. Luther & Clarrissa, b. Aug. 18, 1820	2	207
John, m. Hannah **LYON**, b. of Canterbury, Jan. 15, 1823, by Erastus Larned	2	7
John, d. Oct. 9, 1827	2	307
Jonas, s. John & Eliza, b. Mar. 1, 1774	1	84
Jonas, s. Jonas* & Elizabeth, d. Sept. 28, 1775 (*Probably John)	1	97
Joseph, s. William & Martha, b. Jan. 22, 1767	1	83
Joseph, s. W[illia]m & Martha, d. Sept. 23, 1775	1	97
Joshua, s. Will[ia]m & Mary, b. Oct. 17, 1751	1	77
Joshua, m. Anne **CLEVELAND**, Feb. 9, 1775	1	71
Joshua, s. Joshua & Anna, b. Apr. 12, 1779	1	86
Josiah, s. Will[ia]m & Mary, b. Nov. 25, 1757	1	84
Josiah, m. Elizabeth **MERRET**, May 17, 1785	1	72
Josiah, d. Mar. 10, 1796	1	98
Keziah, d. [W[illia]m & Marhta], b. June 11, 1770	1	84
Kezia[h], [triplet with Zerviah & Martha], d. [W[illia]m & Martha], b. June 12, 1770	1	85
Keziah, d. W[illia]m & Martha, d. June 20, 1770	1	97
Keziah, d. W[illia]m & Martha, d. Sept. 23, 1775	1	97
Kezia[h], d. Benjamin & Ruby, b. Mar. 29, 1805	1	92

	Vol.	Page
BRADFORD, (cont.)		
Luther, s. John & Elizabeth, b. July 17, 1786	1	88
Lydia, d. Tho[ma]s & Eunice, b. Mar. 6, 1744	1	78
Lydia, d. Tho[ma]s & Eunice, d. May 24, 1750	1	96
Lydea, d. William & Mary, b. July 2, 1760	1	81
Lydia, d. John & Eliza, b. Apr. 9, 1779	1	87
Lydia, m. John F. **ADAMS**, Mar. 22, 1835, by Rev. Asa King, Westminster	2	3
Lydia, m. John F. **ADAMS**, Apr. 6, 1835	1	53
Maria, d. Benjamin & Ruby, b. Aug. 24, 1798	1	90
Maria, d. Benjamin & Ruby, d. Jan. 20, 1799	1	98
Martha, [triplet with Zerviah & Jezia], d. [William & Matilda], b. June 12, 1770	1	85
Martha, w. William, d. Sept. 8, 1775	1	97
Martha, d. W[illia]m & Martha, d. Sept. 23, 1775	1	97
Mary, d. Will[ia]m & Mary, b. Mar. 1, 1744	1	77
Mary, m. Joseph **WOODARD**, May 31, 1748	1	236
Mary, w. William, d. Aug. 6, 1765	1	97
Mary, d. David & Rhoda, b. July 10, 1771	1	86
Mary, twin with Anne, d. Joshua & Anne, b. Dec. 1, 1775	1	85
Mary Cleveland, d. [Josiah & Elizabeth], b. Sept. 2, 1789	1	90
Mehitable, w. William, d. Mar. 5, 1810	1	99
Merret, s. Josiah & Elizabeth, b. Mar. 2, 1786	1	90
Moses, s. William & Mary, b. Aug. 6, 1765	1	82
Moses, s. John & Elizabeth, b. June 11, 1781	1	87
Moses, s. Araunah & Mary, b. Mar. 30, 1803	1	92
Olive, d. Will[ia]m & Mary, b. July 13, 1756	1	80
Olive, m. Hezekiah **BARSTOW**, May 23, 1776	1	72
Pamela, d. [Samuel & Lydia], b. Apr. 30, 1788	1	88
Pamela, m. Calvin **WOODARD**, Nov. 22, 1821, by Asa Meech	2	85
Polly, d. Thomas & Philenia, b. Mar. 18, 1790	1	92
Rhoda, d. David & Rhoda, b. Apr. 7, 1783	1	87
Samuel, s. Thomas & Eunice, b. July 27, 1748	1	78
Samuel, m. Lydia **DEAN**, Jan. 19, 1778	1	71
Samuel, s. Samuel & Lydia, b. Jan. 18, 1783	1	88
Samuel Warren, s. [Wi[illia]m & Martha], b. Nov. 5, 1772. The 20th child	1	85
Sam[ue]l Warren, s. W[illia]m & Martha, d. Sept. 13, 1775	1	97
Sarah, d. James & Edith, b. Aug. 27, 1720	1	74
Sarah, d. Samuel & Lydia, b. Nov. 16, 1778	1	87
Sarah, d. Samuel & Lydia, d. Dec . 22, 1783	1	98
Sarah, d. Samuel & Lydia, b. Dec. 3, 1784	1	88
Simeon, s. Samuel & Lydia, b. Sept. 20, 1794	1	90
Simeon, m. Henrietta **HYDE**, b. of Canterbury, June 10, 1828, by Rev. J. R. Wheelock	2	8
Sophrenia, d. Benj[ami]n, b. Apr. 11, 1807	1	92
Submit, d. Thomas & Eunice, b. Feb. 21, 1749/50	1	79
Submit, m. Joseph **PELLET**, Apr. 29, 1782	1	193

	Vol.	Page
BRADFORD, (cont.)		
Susannah, d. Thomas & Eunice, b. Feb. 12, 1736/7	1	76
Susanna, d. Thomas & Eunice, b. Feb. 12, 1737	1	77
Susannah, w. James, d. Mar. 17, 1752	1	66
Susannah, w. Lieut. James, d. Mar. 17, 1752	1	96
Susannah, m. Ebenezer **BROWN**, Jan. 8, 1760	1	70
Sussanna, d. [Thomas & Philenia], b. Dec. 30, 1797	1	92
Sussannah, d. Thomas & Philenia, d. Dec. 29, 1798	1	98
Thomas, s. James & Ede, b. Nov. 14, 1712	1	74
Thomas, m. Eunice **ADAMS**, May 2, 1733	1	69
Thomas, s. Thomas & Eunice, b. Mar. 23, 1734	1	77
Thomas, s. Thomas & Eunice, d. Feb. 12, 1735/6	1	95
Thomas, s. Thomas & Eunice, d. Feb. 22, 1736	1	95
Thomas, s. Thomas & Eunice, b. Jan. 29, 1751/2	1	79
Thomas, m. Philenia **DAVISON**, Nov. 29, 1788	1	73
Thomas, d. June 8, 1807	1	98
Thomas, s. [Archibald & Emeline], b. Feb. 21, 1849	2	208
Triphena, d. [David & Rhoda], b. Dec. 18, 1778	1	86
Will[ia]m, s. James & Edith, b. July 1, 1718	1	74
Will[ia]m, m. Zerviah **LATHROP**, Dec. 13, 1739	1	69
William, m. Mary **CLEVELAND**, Apr. 6, 1743	1	69
Will[ia]m, s. Will[ia]m & Mary, b. Mar. 4, 1745	1	77
William, m. Martha **WARRAIN**, Mar. 24, 1766	1	70
William, s. John & Elizabeth, b. Sept. 28, 1783	1	88
William, m. Mehetable **PARISH**, Dec. 13, 1804	1	73
William Josiah, s. [Josiah & Elizabeth], b. Mar. 10, 1795	1	90
Zerviah, d. Will[ia]m & Zerviah, b. Sept. 6, 1740	1	76
Zerviah, w. Will[ia]m, d. Oct. 22, 1740	1	95
Zerviah, [triplet with Kezia & Martha], d. [W[illia]m & Martha], b. June 12, 1770	1	85
Zerviah, d. W[illia]m & Martha, d. Sept. 23, 1775	1	97
----, d. W[illia]m & Mary, b. Apr. [ ], 1759, s. b.	1	84
BRAMAN, Mary, of Canterbury, m. Ebenezer **HALL**, of Plainfield, Jan. 3, 1826, by Rev. Tho[ma]s J. Murdock	2	39
BRANCH, Levi J., of Lisbon, m. Sophia **ALLEN**, of Canterbury, Sept. 26, 1842, by Comfort D. Fillmore, Dea.	2	13
BRAYTON, Pardon P., of Griswold, m. Freelove **LATHROP**, of Canterbury, May 31, 1832, by Rev. Demis Platt	2	9
BREWSTER, Amos, m. Jerusha **KNIGHT**, Mar. 19, 1761	1	70
Anne, of Killingly, m. Rufus **PARISH**, Nov. 22, 1789	1	193
Anson, s. Jedediah & Prudence, b. Aug. 28, 1780	1	86
Asa, s. Will[ia]m & Damares, b. Oct. 11, 1739	1	76
Asenath, d. Jedediah & Asenath, b. Jan. 21, 1800	1	91
Damaris, d. Will[ia]m & Damaris, b. Nov. 24, 1743	1	76
Dameris, w. Will[ia]m, d. Sept. 7, 1751	1	96
Drusilla, d. Will[ia]m & Damaris, b. Nov. 3, 1745	1	77
Elizabeth, d. Will[ia]m & Damaris, b. Oct. 30, 1741	1	76
Florina, d. Jedediah & Prudence, b. May 6, 1777	1	86

	Vol.	Page

BREWSTER, (cont.)

	Vol.	Page
Grace, d. [Amos & Jerusha], b. Apr. 8, 1766	1	83
Harriet, m. Charles R. LYON, Nov. 2, 1845, by Rev. Z. Baker	2	53
Jedediah, m. Prudence ROBINSON, May 19, 1773	1	71
Jedediah, m. Asenath BUSHNELL, of Lisbon, Apr. 10, 1799	1	72
Jerusha, d. Will[ia]m & Damaris, b. Oct. 18, 1747	1	78
Johanna, m. Josiah CLEVELAND, June 5, 1755	1	100
Joseph, s. Jedediah & Prudence, d. Feb. 21, 1799	1	98
Ledah, of Preston, m. Ebenezer JOHNSON, Dec. 12, 1765	1	167
Lovisa, d. Amos & Jerusha, b. June 22, 1762	1	83
Lusena, m. Peter MORSE, Oct. 4, 1792	1	181
Peleg, d. Apr. 2, 1801, ae 84	1	98
Prudence, w. Jedediah, d. Jan. 17, 1799	1	98
Samuel, s. [Amos & Jerusha], b. May 21, 1764	1	83
Sarah, m. Johosaphat HOLMES, Jan. 10, 1745	1	155
Silas, s. Jedediah & Prudence, b. Nov. 2, 1775	1	86
W[illia]m, m. Ecater SABIN, of Norwich, Jan. 16, 1752	1	69
BRIGGS, George W., m. Eliza HILL, b. of Canterbury, Mar. 20, 1836, by Rev. Tubal Wakefield	2	10
James Lawton, s. James & Penelope, b. Jan. 27, 1821	2	207
Janes, of Sterling, m. Almira JUSTIN, of Canterbury, July 15, 1830, by Rev. I. J. Rose, of Westminster	2	8
BRIGHAM, (see also BINGHAM), Gideon, m. Abigail BAKER, Nov. 12, 1761 BINGHAM handwritten in original manuscript	1	70
Will[ia]m, m. Mary NAVINS, Nov. 9, 1758	1	70
BROOKS, Anne, m. Richard PELLETT, Apr. 2, 1703	1	192
Patience, m. Peter LEVENS, Dec. 27, 1704	1	176
BROWN, Abby, d. Luther & Polly, b. Aug. 9, 1811	1	94
Abigail, d. Deliver[an]ce & Abigail, b. Apr. 11, 1720	1	75
Abigail, d. John & Abigail, b. Mar. 31, 1726	1	75
Abigail, m. Hezekiah PELLET, Mar. 5, 1738/9	1	192
Abigail, w. Jabez, d. Nov. 17, 1749	1	96
Abigail, m. Stephen BACKUS, Oct. 11, 1750	1	69
Abigail, d. Abijah & Elizabeth, b. Oct. 13, 1754	1	78
Abigail, w. Dea. Deliverance, d. Sept. 25, 1763	1	96
Abigail, d. John & Triphena, b. Oct. 8, 1778	1	86
Abijah, s. Deliver[an]ce & Abigail, b. Mar. 22, 1718	1	75
Abijah, m. Elizabeth RICHARDS, Dec. 11, 1744	1	69
Abijah, d. Mar. 9, 1770	1	97
Alpheas, s. John & Lucy, b. Aug. 25, 1762	1	82
Anna, d. Benjamin & Hannah, b. Oct. 29, 1761	1	81
Araune (?), s. Benjamin & Hannah, b. Apr. 21, 1766	1	82
Asa[h]el, s. Ele[a]zer & Lydea, b. Jan. 4, 1762	1	81
Asahel, s. Eleazer & Lydia, b. Jan. 4, 1762	1	83
Aurelia, d. Benj[ami]n & Hannah, b. Aug. 11, 1778	1	85
Aurelia, d. [Luther & Polly], b. Apr. 7, 1817	1	94
Azariah, d. Apr. 12, 1711	1	95

	Vol.	Page

BROWN, (cont.)

	Vol.	Page
Azariah, s. Deliver[an]ce & Abigail, b. Jan. 15, 1733	1	75
Azariah, s. Deliverance, & Abigail, d. Mar. 20, 1736/7	1	95
Azariah, s. Phinehas & Abigail, b. Feb. 20, 1745	1	79
Benjamin, d. Feb. 12, 1710/11	1	95
Benjamin, s. Thomas & Rachel, b. Sept. 1, 1713	1	74
Benjamin, m. Mary SHIRTLEY, Mar. 24, 1735	1	69
Benj[ami]n, m. Hannah BENJAMIN, Feb. 25, 1755	1	70
Benj[ami]n, s. Benj[ami]n & Hannah, b. Jan. 1, 1756	1	80
Benj[ami]n, Jr., m. Esther STAPLES, Dec. 17, 1779	1	71
Betsey, d. [Deliverance & Mary], b. Sept. 7, 1793	1	89
Bial, s. [Benjamin & Hannah], b. Apr. 30, 1770	1	84
Billesent, d. Benjamin & Hannah, b. Sept. 13, 1764	1	82
Bridget, m. E[b]enezer FITCH, Sept. 18, 1712	1	138
Bridget, d. Thomas & Rachel, b. Aug. 16, 1719	1	74
Cancey, s. Waldo & Abigail, b. Mar. 14, 1802	1	91
Charlotte W., of Canterbury, m. Nathaniel WEST, of Providence, R. I., Nov. 26, 1848, by Rev. Robert O. Learned	2	89
Clarrisa Harlow, d. Benj[ami]n, Jr. & Esther, b. Aug. 30, 1780	1	86
Daniel, s. Benjamin & Hannah, b. Apr. 10, 1763	1	82
Daniel, s. [Eleazer & Lydia], b. Jan. 27, 1767	1	83
Daniel, m. Eunice SHAW, Aug. 29, 1769	1	71
Daniel, s. Daniel & Eunice, b. Dec. 13, 1769	1	86
Daniel, m. Roxalena SILSBURY, Sept. 9, 1794	1	72
Daniel, s. [Daniel & Roxalene], b. Apr. 3, 1797	1	91
Deliverance, m. Abigail WALDO, Oct. 28, 1717	1	69
Deliverance, s. Eben[eze]r & Susanna, b. Apr. 2, 1765	1	83
Deliverance, Dea. d. Jan. 14, 1768	1	97
Deliverance, m. Mary HIDE, Oct. 23, 1791	1	72
Dinah, d. Thomas & Rachel, b. Oct. 14, 1706	1	72
Dinah, d. Thomas & Rachel, d. Nov. 1, 1706	1	95
Dinah, wid. Eleazer, d. Mar. 11, 1706/7	1	95
Dinah, d. Thomas & Rachel, b. Aug. 7, 1715	1	74
Dinah, d. Thomas & Rachel, d. Jan. 10, 1718/19	1	95
Dinah, d. Deliver[an]ce & Abigail, b. Jan. 15, 1721/2	1	75
Dinah, d. Abijah & Elisabeth, b. Dec. 5, 1750	1	79
Dinah, m. Stephen SPAULDING, Oct. 24, 1771	1	214
Ebenezer, s. Deliverance & Abigail, b. June 15, 1737 (?)	1	75
Ebenezer, m. Susannah BRADFORD, Jan. 8, 1760	1	70
Ebenezer, s. Ebenezer & Susanna, b. Sept. 9, 1763	1	94
Eben[eze]r, s. Benjamin & Hannah, b. Feb. 7, 1773	1	84
Ebenezer, d. Jan. 1, 1798	1	98
Edith, d. [Eben[eze]r & Susanna], b. Sept. 17, 1767	1	83
Edith, m. Albe HIDE, Nov. 1, 1795	1	156
Eleazer, Dea., d. Jan. 22, 1719/20	1	95
Eleazer, s. Deliver[an]ce & Abigail, b. Oct. 11, 1724	1	75
Eleazer, m. Sarah BACON, Nov. 13, 1749	1	69

	Vol.	Page
BROWN, (cont.)		
Eleazer, m. Lydia **PUTNAM**, June 21, 1759	1	70
Eliza Mary, d. Luther & Polly, b. Aug. 29, 1807	1	92
Elisabeth, w. Abijah, d. Nov. 8, 1765	1	97
Emilia, d. Jeremiah & Polly, b. Dec. 23, 1798	1	91
Emilla, d. Jeremiah & Polly, b. Dec. 23, 1798	1	145
Emmilla, d. Jeremiah & Polly, b. Dec. 23, 1798	1	91
Esther, d. Tristam & Abigail b. May 28, 1748	1	79
Eunice, d. Tristam & Abigail, b. July 16, 1744	1	79
Eunice, d. Ebenezer & Susanna, b. June 18, 1760	1	81
Febe, see under Phebe		
Frederick O. H., m. Julia S. **SWEET**, Feb. 15, 1852, by		
Comfort S. Hyde, J. P.	2	105
Frederic Stanley, s. Luther & Polly, b. Dec. 11, 1805	1	92
Gerviah*, m. Isaac **ADAMS**, Feb. 17, 1728/9 (*Probably		
Zerviah)	1	51
Gerviah, see also Zerviah		
Hannah, d. Tristam & Abigail, b. July 24, 1735	1	76
Hannah, d. Benj[ami]n & Hannah, b. Nov. 5, 1767	1	83
Hannah, d. [Daniel & Eunice], b. Nov. 22, 1775	1	86
Harriet, d. Deliverance & Polly, b. Feb. 7, 1797	1	90
Hervey Benjamin, s. [Daniel & Lydia], b. Nov. 21, 1786	1	88
Hezekiah, s. Tristam & Abigail, b. July 5, 1741	1	79
Hucheson, s. Benjamin & Hannah, b. Jan. 16, 1760	1	81
Hutchinson, s. [Benjamin & Hannah], d. Sept. 7, 1778	1	97
Isaac, s. [Deliverance & Mary], b. Jan. 23, 1795	1	89
Jabez, s. John & Abigail, b. May 9, 1722	1	74
Jacob, m. Patty **CLARK**, Jan. 1, 1792	1	72
James, s. Eben[eze]r & Susannah, b. Oct. 24, 1769	1	83
James, s. Ebenezer & Susannah, d. June 12, 1795	1	98
Jedediah, s. Benj[ami]n & Hannah, b. Mar. 30, 1757	1	80
Jedediah, s. Jedediah & Lucy, b. Oct. 18, 1785	1	88
Jedediah, m. Wid. Lydia **JOHNSON**, Sept. 20, 1789	1	72
Jeremiah, s. Deliverance & Abigail, b. Mar. 12, 173[ ];		
d. Mar. 15, 173[ ]	1	75
Jeremiah, s. Abijah & Elizabeth, b. Dec. 30, 1745	1	78
Jeremiah, s. Abijah & Elizabeth, d. Aug. 11, 1749	1	95
Jeremiah, s. Eben[eze]r & Susanna, b. May 8, 1772	1	85
Jeremiah, m. Polly **MORSE**, of Pomfret, May 13, 1798	1	72
Jesse, s. Abijah & Elizabeth, b. Nov. 21, 1752	1	75
Jesse, s. Abijah & Eliza, b. Nov. 22, 1752	1	85
Joanna, d. Mary **HARRINGTON**, single woman, b. Nov. 16,		
1771	1	84
John, s. John & Abigail, b. Nov. 25, 1723	1	75
John, s. Deliver[an]ce & Abigail, b. May 5, 1727	1	75
John, s. Jabez & Abigail, b. June 12, 1749	1	79
John, m. Lucy **UNDERWOOD**, Mar. 13, 1750/51	1	70
John, s. John & Lucy, b. Mar. 9, 1757	1	80

	Vol.	Page
BROWN, (cont.)		
John, s. Benj[ami]n & Hannah, b. Aug. 27, 1758	1	80
John, Jr., m. Triphena **LITCHFIELD**, Feb. 4, 1773	1	71
John, s. Eben[eze]r & Susanna, b. May 30, 1774	1	85
John, m. Lucy **MAIN**, Oct. 1, 1780	1	71
Juliana, m. Daniel **HARRINGTON**, [ ], by Rev. Demis Platt	2	40
Lois, d. [Daniel & Roxalene], b. Mar. 14, 1799	1	91
Lucius, s. Deliverance & Mary, b. Dec. 9, 1791	1	89
Lucretia, d. Eleazer & Sarah, b. Feb. 7, 1749/50	1	78
Lucy, d. John & Lucy, b. Apr. 28, 1755	1	79
Lucy, d. John & Lucy, b. Apr. 28, 1755	1	80
Lucy, w. Capt. John, d. June 22, 1773	1	97
Lucy, d. John & Lucy, b. June 11, 1781	1	86
Lucy, d. Waldo & Abigail, b. Dec. 1, 1800	1	91
Luther, s. Benjamin & Hannah, b. Nov. 29, 1782	1	87
Luther, s. [Waldo & Abigail], b. May 21, 1796	1	89
Luther, m. Polly **BENNET**, Nov. 15, 1804	1	72
Lydia, d. Thomas & Rachel, b. Mar. 15, 1722	1	75
Lydia, d. [Eleazer & Lydia], b. Mar. 2, 1763	1	83
Lydia, d. Daniel & Roxalene, b. Apr. 22, 1795	1	91
Mansur, s. Betty **GREEN**, single woman, b. Aug. 18, 1793	1	89
Mary, d. Jabez & Abigail, b. Mar. 19, 1746/7	1	79
Mary Eliza, of Canterbury, m. Benjamin **CRANDALL**, of Canterbury, Sept. 23, 1827, by Luther Paine, J. P.	2	15
Mehetable, d. Thomas & Rachel, b. Nov. 15, 1725	1	74
Molly, d. [John & Triphena], b. May 29, 1780	1	86
Nabby Hide, d. Aruna[h] & Olive, b. Nov. 19, 1799	1	91
Naomy, d. Abijah & Elizabeth, b. Mar. 6, 1759	1	80
Naomi, m. Adams **STEVENS**, Mar. 9, 1800	1	215
Nathan, s. [Eleazer & Lydia], b. Aug. 13, 1764	1	83
Nehemiah, s. Waldo & Abigail, b. June 11, 1791	1	89
Obadiah, s. Phinehas & Abigail, b. Apr. 19, 1730	1	78
Obadiah, s. John & Lucy, b. Aug. 9, 1753	1	80
Olive, d. Abijah & Elizabeth, b. Jan. 20, 1757	1	80
Olive, d. John & Lucy, b. Aug. 4, 1766	1	83
Olive, d. Jno. Jr. & Tryphena, b. Mar. 5, 1774	1	85
Patience, d. Benjamin & Hannah, d. June 11, 1776	1	97
Peter, s. Thomas & Rachel, b. June 30, 1717	1	74
Peter, s. Phinehas & Abigail, b. Feb. 20, 1741	1	79
Peter, s. Abijah & Elizabeth, b. Oct. 10, 1747	1	78
Peter, s. Abijah & Elizabeth, d. Aug. 14, 1749	1	95
Phebe, d. Benjamin & Mary, b. Jan. 12, 1735/6	1	76
Febe, m. Joseph **BUTT**, Dec. 6, 1748	1	69
Phebe, m. Samuel **BUTT**, Dec. 24, 1765	1	70
Phinehas, s. Thomas & Rachel, b. Jan. 10, 1707/8	1	74
Phinehas, m. Abigail **JOHNSON**, June 19, 1729	1	69
Phinehas, s. Phinehas & Abigail, b. July 19, 1732	1	78
Polly, m. Erastus **ADAMS**, Apr. 28, 1790	1	52

	Vol.	Page
BROWN, (cont.)		
Prudence, d. Tristam & Abigail, b. Mar. 7, 1739	1	79
Rachel, wid. Dea. Tho[ma]s, d. May 22, 1755	1	95
Rebecca, d. Deliverance, & Abigail, b. Oct. 22, 172[ ]	1	75
Rebecca, d. Phinehas & Abigail, b. Mar. 30, 1738	1	78
Rebeccah, w. Dea. Eleazer, d. Sept. 17, 1727	1	95
Rebeckah, d. Deliverance & Abigail, d. Mar. 24, 1736/7	1	95
Rebeckah, d. John & Lucy, b. Mar. 11, 1761	1	81
Reuben, s. Phinehas & Abigail, b. June 30, 1747	1	79
Roswel[l], s. Moses & Abigail, b. Aug. 21, 1768	1	83
Rufus, s. Phinehas & Abigail, b. Jan. 19, 1734	1	78
Rufus, s. Benjamin & Hannah, b. Aug. 5, 1771	1	84
Sam[ue]l, s. Tristam & Abigail, b. Oct. 5, 1736	1	79
Samuel, s. Tristam & Abigail, b. Oct. 10, 1737	1	76
Samuel, s. Ebenezer & Susanna, b. Mar. 24, 1762	1	82
Samuel, s. Ebenezer & Susannah, d. July 25, 1781, in England	1	98
Sarah, w. Eleazer, d. Mar. 18, 1752	1	96
Sarah, d. Ele[a]zer & Lydia, b. Apr. 2, 1760	1	81
Sheperd, s. [Luther & Polly], b. Apr. 11, 1819	1	94
Shubael, s. [Abijah & Eliza], b. Mar. 12, 1761	1	85
Susannah, w. Ebenezer, d. Aug. 20, 1797	1	98
Sibbel, d. Abijah & Elizabeth, b. May 31, 1749	1	78
Sibbel, d. Abijah & Elizabeth, d. Feb. 21, 1749/50	1	96
Sibbel, d. John & Lucy, b. July 23, 1751	1	80
Sib[b]el, m. James **WOODARD**, Apr. 16, 1772	1	236
Thomas, m. Rachel **LEVENS**, Jan. 30, 1705/6	1	69
Thomas, s. Tristam & Abigail, b. Mar. 26, 1731	1	76
Thomas, Dea., d. Apr. 14, 1738	1	95
Tristam, s. Tristam & Abigail, b. Apr. 10, 1733	1	76
Waldo, s. John & Lucy, b. Apr. 25, 1759	1	80
Waldo, m. Abigail **FISH**, May 6, 1790	1	72
Waldo, s. Waldo & Abigail, b. July 5, 1793	1	89
Waterman, s. Luther & Polly, b. June 29, 1809	1	92
Waterman, of Plainfield, m. Mary P. **SPICER**, of Canterbury, Oct. 23, 1836, by Andrew T. Judson, J. P.	2	11
William, s. Daniel & Lydia, b. Feb. 18, 1785	1	88
Zadoc, s. [Eleazer & Lydia], b. Mar. 4, 1766	1	83
Zadok, s. Eleazer & Lydia, d. Mar. 25, 1766	1	97
Zerviah, d. Thomas & Rachel, b. Aug. 1, 1711	1	74
Zerviah, see also Gerviah		
BROWNING, Isaac, Dr., of Montville, m. Patty B. **HOW**, of Canterbury, Jan. 8 , 1840, by Rev. Tubal Wakefield	2	12
Thomas James, of Woodstock, m. Emily **BURNHAM**, of Canterbury, Dec. 6, 1830, by Rev. Demis Platt	2	9
BRUCE, Thaddeus, s. Esther **COLLINS**, single woman, b. Feb. 28, 1793	1	114
BRYAN, Patric[k], m. Catharine **WEAVER**, of Plainfield, Oct. 22, 1837, by Rev. C. J. Warren	2	11

	Vol.	Page
BUCKLEY, [see under BULKELEY]		
BUCKLIN, Nancy, m. Gideon ENSWORTH, Dec. 9, 1778	1	133
BUGBEE, Chester L., m. Lavina TUCKER, Oct. 26, 1845, by Rev.		
Zeph[ani]a Baker	2	13
Chester Leander, s. Chester & Pheby, b. July 2, 1818	1	93
Mary Malissa, d. Chester & Phebe, b. Aug. 18, 1820	2	207
BULKELEY, BUCKLEY, BULKLEY, Adeline, d. Gad & Orra, b.		
Nov. 27, 1807	1	92
Gad, m. Orra BARSTOW, Sept. 15, 1805	1	72
Samuel Barstow, s. Gad & Orra, b. Jan. 21, 1813	1	93
BULLARD, Elijah, s. John & Lucy, b. June 1, 1819	1	93
Jane Grey, d. John & Lucy, b. Aug. 13, 1822	2	207
John, m. Eunice S. CLARK, b. of Canterbury, June 21,		
1828, by Rev. J. R. Wheelock	2	8
BUNDAY, Deborah, m. John CARTER, Apr. 13, 1731	1	100
BURDICK, Amos, m. Debby PHILLIPS, Nov. 6, 1826, by Andrew		
T. Judson, J. P.	2	8
Barton D., of Westerly, R. I., m. Sarviah W. SUNDERLAND,		
of Groton, Feb. 18, 1827, by Rev. Asher Miner	2	8
Cranston L., m. Lucy Ann CRANDALL, b. of Canterbury,		
Feb. 11, 1832, by Rev. Demis Platt	2	9
Daniel H., m. Sally M. ADAMS, Oct. 3, 1836, by Walter		
Williams, J. P.	2	10
BURGESS, BURGES, Almira, m. Hezekiah CRANDALL, b. of		
Canterbury, Sept. 4, 1839,. by Rev. Charles J. Warren	2	17
Anna, d. [Asa & Sarah], b. Mar. 17, 1786	1	89
Anson, s. [Asa & Sarah], b. Apr. 6, 1796	1	90
Archibald, s. [Asa & Sarah], b. Feb. 2, 1790	1	89
Asa, m. Sarah MILES, July 2, 1780	1	71
Benjamin Sheperd, s. [Joseph & Mehetable], b. June 2, 1779	1	86
Chauncey, s. Asa & Sarah, b. Feb. 19, 1794	1	90
Elizabeth, d. Joseph & Mehetable, b. Apr. 2, 1765	1	86
Jason, s. Asa & Sarah, b. Apr. 16, 1781	1	87
John, s [Joseph & Mehetable], b. July 18, 1767	1	86
Joseph, s. [Joseph & Mehetable], b. Apr. 24, 1776	1	86
Lucinda, d. [Joseph & Mehetable, b. Sept. 24, 1769	1	86
Luther, s. [Asa & Sarah], b. Mar. 5, 1792	1	89
Maria, m. William LESTER, June 29, 1845, by Rev. Asa		
King, Westminster	2	53
Mary, d. [Asa & Sarah], b. Mar. 4, 1788	1	89
Mary, d. Asa & Sarah, d. Apr. 14, 1790	1	98
Mary, d. [Asa & Sarah], b. July 27, 1798	1	90
Mehetable, d. [Joseph & Mehetable], b. May 27, 1772	1	86
Philetus Mills, s. Luther & Almira, b. Aug. 25, 1824	2	207
Reuben, s. [Asa & sarah], b. July 25, 1782	1	87
Sarah, d. Asa & Sarah, b. Apr. 14, 1784	1	89
BURLEY, John Henry, illeg. child of John O. BURLEY, & Mary		
BABCOCK, b. Apr. 10, 1828	2	207

	Vol.	Page
BURLINGAME, Samuel, Jr., m. Judith **HYDE**, b. of Canterbury,		
Mar. 24, 1851, by Rev. Robert C. Learned	2	105
Samuel, d. Aug. 28, 1865	2	307
BURNAM, [see under **BURNHAM**]		
BURNAP, Elizabeth, m. Joseph **SMITH**, Apr. 25, 1716/17	1	214
BURNETT, Phebe, of Canterbury, m. J. Augustus **HALL**, of		
Perrysburg, O., Apr. 22, 1848, by Rev. Asa King,		
Westminster	2	42
BURNHAM, BURNAM, Bathiah, m. Theophiles **CLARK**, Jr., Jan.		
13, 1756	1	100
Charlotte, m. Ezra **BENNETT**, July 3, 1843, by Rev. Asa		
King, Westminster	2	13
Edmund, of Windham, m. Fanny **WEBB**, of Canterbury, Sept.		
10, 1834, by Rev. Samuel J. May, Brooklyn	2	10
Elizabeth Lorenda, d. Lucius & Lorenda, b. Mar. 20, 1829	2	207
Emily, of Canterbury, m. Thomas James **BROWNING**, of		
Woodstock, Dec. 6, 1830, by Rev. Demis Platt	2	9
Joshua P., of Hartford, m. Emily **JOHNSON**, of Canterbury,		
Sept. 25, 1825, by Rev. Tho[ma]s J. Murdock	2	7
Martha Amelia, d. Lucius & Lorenda, b. Nov. 11, 1830	2	207
Sarah Ann, m. Elisha **JONES**, Mar. 22, 1836, by Rev. Asa		
King, Westminster	2	43
Thomas D., m. Lucretia **LONG**, Jan. 17, 1836, by Rev. Asa		
King, Westminster	2	10
BURNS, Catharine, m. Daniel **PARKS**, Aug. 5, 1776	1	193
Dorcas, d. [James & Catharine], b. Apr. 28, 1773, at		
East Greenwich, R. I.	1	86
George, s. James & Catharine, b. May 22, 1769, at Dover,		
N. Y.	1	86
BURT, Frances, of Long Meadow, Mass., m. Hannah B. **ADAMS**,		
of Canterbury, Dec. 25, 1840, by Rev. Samuel Rockwell,		
of Plainfield	2	12
Sarah, m. Jedediah **CARTER**, July 10, 1768	1	101
BUSHNELL, Asenath, of Lisbon, m. Jedediah **BREWSTER**, Apr.		
10, 1799	1	72
BUSSEL, [see also **BUSWELL**], Abigail, d. Moses & Mehetable,		
b. Dec. 8, 1733	1	76
Lemual, s. [Moses & Mehetable], b. Aug. 22, 1735	1	76
Samuel, s. [Moses & Mehetable], b. Oct. 6, 1737	1	76
BUSSY, James, [twin with Nancy], s. James & Mary, b. Jan. 15,		
1822	2	207
Nancy, [twin with James], d. James & Mary, b. Jan. 15, 1822	2	207
BUSWELL, BOSWELL, BUSWEL, BUSSWELL, BUZWELL,		
[see also **BUSSEL**], Charles Thomas, s. Thomas &		
Thankful, b. Jan. 9, 1798	1	91
Hannah, w. Robert, d. Nov. 6, 1717	1	95
Hannah, m. Uriah **CADY**, Jan. 2, 1723/4	1	100
Hannah, d. Thomas & Prudence, b. Oct. 4, 1730	1	76

	Vol.	Page

BUSWELL, BOSWELL, BUSWEL, BUSSWELL, BUZWELL, (cont.)

	Vol.	Page
Hannah, m. Ichabod **PAINE**, Jan. 16, 1748	1	192
Hezekiah, s. Thomas & Prudence, b. Oct. 19, 1733	1	76
Hez[ekiah], d. Nov. 5, 1755, in camp near Lake George (soldier)	1	96
Jabe, s. [Thomas & Thankful], b. Nov. 23, 1789	1	89
John, s. [Thomas & Thankful], b. Aug. 3, 1791	1	89
Lydia, d. Thomas & Prudence, b. May 20, 1740	1	78
Mary, wid. Robert, d. July 20, 1743	1	95
Mehetable, d. June 16, 1766	1	97
Mercy, d. Thomas & Prudence, b. Sept. 2, 1737	1	78
Mercy, m. John **PIKE**, Jan. 22, 1761	1	192
Moses, s. Robert & Hannah, b. Nov. 8, 1708	1	74
Moses, m. Mehetabel **BAKER**, Jan. 30, 1732/3	1	69
Polly, d. Thomas & Thankful, b. June 23, 1787	1	89
Prudence, d. Thomas & Prudence, b. Jan. 7, 1731	1	76
Prudence, m. Paine **CLEVELAND**, Jan. 18, 1757	1	100
Robert, m. Mary **CLEVELAND**, Jan. 22, 1721/2	1	69
Sarah, m. Samuel **CLEVELAND**, Dec. 10, 1719	1	100
Thomas, s. Thomas & Prudence, b. Sept. 19, 1742	1	78
Thomas, Jr., m. Mary **BACON**, June 10, 1772	1	70
Thomas, m. Thankful **FOX**, Mar. 26, 1786	1	72

BUTT, [see under **BUTTS**]

BUTTERFIELD, Deborah, m. Joseph **CLEVELAND**, May 19,

	Vol.	Page
1718	1	100
Joanna, of N. H., m. Zackariah **WALDO**, Jr., Jan. 1, 1800	1	237

BUTTON, Abigail, d. [Raysford & Eleanor], b. Dec. 20, 1810

	Vol.	Page
	1	94
Anna, of Voluntown, m. Simon **PARK**, July 15, 1755, at Stonington	1	192
Asa, s. Matthais & Elizabeth, b. Jan. 17, 1765	1	82
Benjamin, s. Mat[t]hais & Phebe, b. Dec. 31, 1758	1	82
Charlotte, d. Matthais & Phebe, b. Mar. 26, 1762	1	82
Charlotte, d. Matthais, d. Dec. 29, 1766	1	97
Charlotte, d. Jos[eph] & Sarah, b. Aug. 6, 1773	1	84
Edward, s. [Raysford & Eleanor], b. Dec. 7, 1818	1	94
Elisabeth, d, Matthais & Elisabeth, b. Oct. 4, 1766	1	83
Elizabeth, m. Amos **MAINARD**, Apr. 20, 1769	1	181
Jesse, m. Abigail **RANSOM**, Dec. 7, 1780	1	71
Jesse, s. Ransford & Eleanor, b. July 27, 1806	1	92
Jonas, s. Matthais & Eliza, b. Mar. 10, 1769	1	83
Jonas, s. Capt. Mattais & Elizabeth, d. June 1, 1775	1	97
Joseph, s. Matthais & Phebe, b. Jan. 16, 1753	1	82
Joseph, s. Matthais & Phebe, b. Jan. 16, 1754	1	77
Joseph, m. Sarah **GLASS**, May 2, 1773	1	71
Mary, d. Peter & Hannah, b. July 30, 1768	1	83
Mary, m. Joseph **BUTTS**, Jan. 31, 1796, at Wells, Rutland Co. Vt.	1	72

	Vol.	Page
BUTTON, (cont.)		
Matthais, m. Phebe **BUTT**, May 16, 1753	1	70
Matthais, s. Matthais & Phebe, b. June 23, 1760	1	82
Matthais, m. Elizabeth **BUTT**, July 10, 1764	1	70
Molly, d. Matthais & Phebe, b. July 7, 1755	1	80
Molly, d. Jos[eph] & Sarah, b. Jan. 30, 1778	1	86
Molly, d. Joseph & Sarah, b. Jan. 30, 1778	1	211
Nathan, s. Matthais & Phebe, b. Apr. 21, 1757	1	80
Nathan, s. Matthais & Phebe, d. Sept. 29, 1759	1	96
Nathan, s. [Matthias & Eliza], b. Mar. 30, 1773	1	84
Peter, of Hopkinton, m. Hannah **RUSS**, June 15, 1768	1	70
Peter Parks, s. [Raysford & Eleanor], b. Nov. 7, 1816	1	94
Phebe, w. Matthais, d. Mar. 3, 1764	1	97
Ransford, m. Eleanor **PARKE**, Nov. 3, 1805	1	73
Richard, s. Raysford & Eleanor, b. Aug. 26, 1817	1	94
Robert, s. Jesse & Abigail, b. Mar. 28, 1782	1	87
Rosia, d. [Raysford & Eleanor], b. Feb. 16, 1820	1	94
Rufus, s. Jos[eph] & Sarah, b. Nov. 6, 1775	1	85
Sabastian, s. [Raysford & Eleanor], b. Apr. 18, 1809	1	94
Sebastian, m. Maria E. **JOHNSON**, b. of Canterbury, Oct. 24, 1841, by Samuel L. Hough, J.P.	2	12
Shubael, s. Mattias & Eliza, b. Apr. 30, 1771	1	84
BUTTS, BUTT, [see also **BATES**], Abadiah H., m. Elizabeth A. **KING**, Sept. 6, 1836, by Asa King, Westminster	2	10
Abigail, d. May 20, 1753	1	95
Abigail, d,. Nathan & Sarah, d. Mar. 18, 1758	1	96
Abigail, d. John & Abigail, b. Oct. 23, 1772	1	84
Abigail, w. James, d. July 4, 1774	1	97
Abigail, d. Jos[eph] & Irene, b. Aug. 16, 1774	1	85
Abigail, w. John, d. May 4, 1782	1	98
Adeline, d. Martin & Sophia, b. Dec. 6, 1812	1	93
Elles (Alice), d. Josiah & Elizabeth, b. Dec. 18, 1738	1	76
Ellis (Alice), m. Henry **FROST**, Feb. 28, 1765	1	138
Alice, d. Eben[eze]r & Prudence, b. Feb. 22, 1777	1	85
Alvin, s. Joseph & Mary, b. Sept. 8, 1803	1	92
Alvin, m. Nancy **YOUNG**, b. of Canterbury, Dec. 18, 1831, by Rev. Orrin Catlin	2	9
Amanda, d. John & Susanna, b. Nov. 4, 1790	1	91
Andrew, s. John & Susannah, b. Mar. 13, 1785	1	88
Avia or Anna, d. Samuel, Jr. & Eunice, b. Feb. 24, 1764	1	82
Anna, m. Daniel* **STORER**, Feb. 24, 1811 (*David)	2	74
Anne, d. Asa & Anne, b. Dec. 22, 1791	1	90
Anne, w. Asa, d. Sept. 4, 1805	1	98
Arunah, s. Sherebiah & Deborah, b. Apr. 19, 1777	1	85
Araunah, m. Eunice **BRADFORD**, Mar. 6, 1802	1	72
Araunah, m. Betsey **MORGAN**, Jan. 19, 1809	1	73
Asa, s. Sherebiah & Deborah, b. June 5, 1762	1	81
Asa, m. Anne **DIMMOCK**, Feb. 17, 1791	1	72

	Vol.	Page

BUTTS, BUTT, (cont.)

	Vol.	Page
Asa, s. Asa & Anne, b. Oct. 8, 1797	1	81
Asa, m. Cynthia **STANLEY**, Jan. 16, 1810	1	73
Asa, Jr., s. Asa, d. Mar. 10, 1824	2	307
Asa, d. June 14, 1827, ae 65	2	307
Asa King, s. Obadiah H. & Elizabeth Ann, b. Aug. 12, 1837	2	208
Asaph, s. Sherebiah, Jr. & Lydia, b. May 26, 1787	1	89
Avia, see under Anna		
Bethiah, d. [Asa & Anne], b. Jan. 26, 1796	1	90
Bethiah, d. Asa & Anna, d. Dec. 21, 1821	1	99
Betsey, d. Sam[ue]l, 3rd, & Eunice, b. June 6, 1778	1	85
Betsey, d. [Asa & Anne], b. Nov. 22, 1793	1	90
Byrissa Batista, d. Lorin & Harriet, b. Mar. 31, 1820	1	94
Catharine, d. Asa & Anne, b. Mar. 12, 1801	1	92
Catharine, d. Obadiah H. & Elizabeth A., b. Feb. 16, 1842	2	208
Cena, d. Eben[eze]r & Prudence, b. Sept. 5, 1771	1	83
Charlotte, d. Joseph & Mary, b. Feb. 3, 1799	1	91
Charlotte, m. Lyman **BUTTS**, b. of Canterbury, Nov. 14, 1820, by Erastus Larned	2	7
Chester Frost, s. David & Lucret[i]a, b. Sept. 28, 1790	1	89
Cynthia, d. Stephen & Lucy, b. Mar. 6, 1773	1	84
Cynthia, m. Phinehas **CARTER**, Nov. 3, 1794	1	102
Daniel, s. Gideon & Amy, b. Mar. 12, 1782	1	86
David, s. Sherebiah & Deborah, b. Dec. 14, 1767	1	83
David, m. Lucretia **FROST**, Jan. 24, 1793	1	72
David, m. Lucret[i]a **FROST**, Jan. 24, 1793	1	121
David, m. Nancy **DYAR**, Jan. 28, 1796	1	72
David, s. [David & Anne], b. June 6, 1805	1	92
David, m. Lucy **LEACH**, Oct. 12, 1834, by Rev. Anson S. Atwood	2	10
Deacon, s. Ebenezer & Prudence, b. Dec. 2, 1789	1	89
Deborah, w. Sherebiah, d. June 12, 1824	2	307
Delia Elizabeth, d. Obadiah Hudson & Elizabeth Ann, b. Jan. 31, 1839	2	208
Delia Elizabeth, d. Obadiah Hudson & Elizabeth Ann, b. Jan. 31, 1839	2	227
Delight, d. Nathaniel & Sarah, b. Nov. 5, 1749	1	78
Delilah, m. Peter **WOODWARD**, Aug. 19, 1785	1	236
Deliver[an]ce, d. Nath[anie]l & Sarah, b. Aug. 18, 1743	1	76
Deliver[an]ce, d. Josiah & Elizabeth, b. Aug. 1, 1749	1	80
Dyar Johnson, s. Josiah & Eunice, b. Oct. 1, 1790	1	90
Eben[eze]r, s. Nathan[ie]l & Sarah, b. June 10, 1742	1	76
Ebenezer, s. Nathaniel & Sarah, d. Oct. 8, 1743	1	95
Ebenezer, s. Josiah & Elizabeth, b. Sept. 13, 1747	1	80
Eben[eze]r, m. Prudence **GLASS**, Jan. 4, 1769	1	70
Elias, s. [Sherebiah, Jr. & Lydia], b. Nov. 25, 1796	1	90
Elihu, s. Gideon & Anna, b. Dec. 16, 1783	1	87
Elijah, s. James & Abigail, b. Apr. 9, 1771	1	84

	Vol.	Page
BUTTS, BUTT, (cont.)		
Elijah, s. James & Abigail, d. Nov. 7, 1774	1	97
Elijah, s. Sherebiah & Deborah, b. Dec. 26, 1774	1	85
Elijah, s. James & Elizabeth, b. Nov. 23, 1778	1	86
Elizabeth, d. Josiah & Elizabeth, b. Feb. 17, 1735	1	76
Elizabeth, m. Matthais BUTTON, July 10, 1764	1	70
Elizabeth, d. [Sam[ue]l & Phebe], b. July 18, 1770	1	86
Elles, see under Alice		
Erastus, s. Sherebiah & Deborah, b. Apr. 29, 1771	1	83
Erastus, s. Araunnah & Eunice, b. May 23, 1805	1	92
Esias, s. Joseph & Erena, b. June 4, 1766	1	83
Eunice, d. Eben & Prudence, b. Nov. 22, 1769	1	86
Eunice, d. Sam[ue]l, 3rd, & Eunice, b. Mar. 2, 1770	1	83
Eunice, w. Araunah, d. Aug. 15, 1807	1	99
Festus, s. Eben[eze]r & Prudence, b. Mar. 24, 1779	1	87
George Washington, s. Jos[eph] & Sarah, b. Jan. 28, 1777	1	85
Gideon, s. Josiah & Elizabeth, b. Aug. 8, 1758	1	82
Gideon, m. Anna KNIGHT, Oct. 28, 1779	1	71
Hannah, d. Samuel & Sarah, b. Aug. 14, 1722	1	75
Hannah, d. Samuel & Mary, b. Aug. 8, 1750	1	79
Hannah, d. Sherebiah & Deborah, b. June 17, 1765	1	82
Hannah, m. Jona PIKE, June 11, 1772	1	193
Hannah, d. Sherebiah & Deborah, d. June 28, 1776	1	97
Hannah, d. [Sam[ue]l & Phebe], b. Sept. 21, 1778	1	86
Hannah, d. Samuel & Hannah*, b. June 22, 1783		
(*Probably "Eunice")	1	87
Hannah, d. Sherebiah & Lydia, b. Sept. 27, 1784	1	88
Harriet Hyde, d. Lorin & Harriet, b. May 4, 1822	2	207
Harry, of Brooklyn, m. Lydia RICHARD, of Hampton, Dec.		
12, 1822, by Thomas J. Murdock	2	7
Henry H., s. Obadiah H. & Eliza, d. Oct. 14, 1847, ae 14 m.	2	307
Henry Hudsaon, s. Obadiah Hudson & Elizabeth Ann, b.		
Aug. 7, 1846	2	208
Hiram, s. David & Nancy, b. Oct. 26, 1796	1	90
Hiram, s. David & Anna, d. Aug. 29, 1797	1	98
Hutchens, s. Josiah, Jr. & Eunice, b. June 12, 1781	1	87
Irene, d. Jos[eph] & Irene, b. May 2, 1768	1	83
Irene, w. Joseph, d. Dec. 25, 1775	1	97
Jabez, s. Nath[anie]l & Mary, b. Feb. 21, 1776	1	85
Jacob, s. Sam[ue]l, 3rd, & Eunice, b. Feb. 26, 1768	1	83
James, s. Samuel & Mary, b. June 14, 1748	1	78
James, m. Abigail UTLEY, Feb. 15, 1770	1	71
James, m. Elizabeth HEBBARD, Sept. 8, 1776	1	71
James, s. James & Elizabeth, b. Sept. 21, 1777	1	86
John, s. Sam[ue]l & Sarah, b. Sept. 9, 1718	1	74
John, d. May 20, 1743	1	95
John, s. Samuel & Mary, b. Mar. 1, 1745	1	78
John, s. Josiah & Elisabeth, b. June 13, 1745	1	80

	Vol.	Page
BUTTS, BUTT, (cont.)		
John, m. Abigail **LILLEE**, Apr. 15, 1772	1	71
John, m. Susannah **KNIGHT**, of Norwich, June 24, 1784	1	72
John D., m. Elizabeth C. **ADAMS**, b. of Canterbury, Dec. 11, 1831, by Rev. Orrin Catlin	2	9
John Dyar, s. [David & Anne], b. July 9, 1807	1	92
John Turner, s. John & Abigail b. Spet. 6, 1774	1	85
John Turner, s. John & Abigail, d. Mar. 12, 1776	1	97
Joseph, s. Samuel & Sarah, b. Mar. 18, 1711	1	74
Joseph, s. Josiah & Elizabeth, b. June 16, 1731	1	76
Joseph, m. Febe **BROWN**, Dec. 6, 1748	1	69
Joseph, d. May 25, 1752	1	96
Joseph, m. Irena **ARMSTRONG**, of Norwich, Apr. 12, 1759	1	70
Joseph, s. Jos[eph] & Irena, b. Apr. 7, 1770	1	83
Joseph, s. Stephen & Lucy, b. May 14, 1770	1	83
Joseph, m. Sarah **CLEVELAND**, Apr. 11, 1776	1	71
Joseph, m. Mary **BUTTON**, Jan. 31, 1796, at Wells, Rutland Co. Vt.	1	72
Joseph, Capt., m. Phebe **BALDWIN**, Apr. 27, 1809	1	73
Joshua, s. [Sam[ue]l & Phebe], b. June 18, 1774	1	86
Josiah, m. Elizabeth **WILLIAMS**, Oct. 25, 1729	1	69
Josiah, s. Josiah & Elizabeth, b. Sept. 18, 1753	1	80
Josiah, s. Joseph & Irenah, b. Oct. 3, 1761	1	81
Josiah, m. Eunice **KNIGHT**, of Norwich, May 28, 1778	1	71
Josiah, d. Feb. 13, 1787	1	98
Josiah, d. May 5, 1814	1	99
Josiah Henry, s. Martin & Sophia, b. Aug. 10, 1814	1	93
Julia A., m. Nathan **NEFF**, Sept. 13, 1836, by Rev. Asa King, Westminster	2	57
Juliann, d. Araunnah & Betsey, b. Aug. 12, 1810	1	92
Lorin, s. Josiah & Eunice, b. Oct. 28, 1796	1	90
Lorin, m. Harriet **HIDE**, May 5, 1819	1	73
Lotilla, d. [Eben[eze]r & Prudence], b. Jan. 24, 1774/5	1	85
Lucretia, w. David, d. Nov. 19, 1794	1	98
Lucy, d. Sam[ue]l, 3rd, & Eunice, b. July 6, 1776	1	85
Lucy, d. John & Susannah, b. July 5, 1787	1	88
Lucy, of Brooklyn, m. William **DOWNING**, Apr. 24, 1796	1	72
Lucy, w. Stephen, d. Jan. 24, 1804, ae 52 y.	1	98
Lucy, d. Joseph & Phebe, b. May 20, 1811	1	93
Lucy, of Canterbury, m. Carr **NORTH[R]UP**, of Granville, N. Y., June 8, 1830, by Rev. Israel G. Rose, of Westminster	2	57
Luther, s. Samuel & Eunice, b. Jan. 25, 1781	1	86
Lydia, d. Nathaniel & Sarah, b. Apr. 7, 1752	1	75
Lyman, m. Charlotte **BUTTS**, b. of Canterbury, Nov. 14, 1820, by Erastus Larned	2	7
Marian, d. David & Anne, b. Mar. 15, 1803	1	92
Martin, s. Josiah & Eunice, b. Apr. 3, 1784	1	88

	Vol.	Page
BUTTS, BUTT, (cont.)		
Martin, m. Sophia **SMITH**, of Lisbon, Jan. 26, 1812	1	73
Mary, d. Samuel & Sarah, b. May 12, 1751 (1721)	1	75
Mary, d. Samuel & Mary, b. Apr. 28, 1739	1	76
Mary, d. Nathaniel & Sarah, b. Feb. 28, 1744/5	1	77
Mary, d. Josiah & Elizabeth, b. July 31, 1751	1	80
Mary, of Norwich, m. Samuel **NOWLING**, Jan. 14, 1761	1	189
Mary, d. Samuel & Eunice, b. Apr. 19, 1766	1	82
Mary, w. Sam[ue]l, d. Dec. 16, 1767, ae 61 y.	1	97
Mary, m. John **HERRICK**, 3rd, Mar. 28, 1771	1	155
Mary, d. Joseph & Mary, b. Mar. 31, 1808	1	93
Mary, w. Capt. Joseph, d. Apr. 27, 1808	1	99
Mary, of Canterbury, m. Charles F. **BACKUS**, of Franklin,		
Apr. 8, 1832, by Rev. Orrin Catlin	2	9
Mason, s. Nath[anie]l & Mary, b. Mar. 2, 1778	1	85
Mehetabel, [d. Joseph & Irenah], b. Dec. 25, 1758	1	81
Moses B., s. Araunah, d. Nov. 6, 1804	1	99
Moses Bradford, s. Araunah & Eunice, b. Aug. 7, 1803	1	92
Nathan, s. Eben[eze]r & Prudence, b. Mar. 1, 1781	1	87
Nathaniel, s. Samuel & Sarah, b. Feb. 17, 1714/15	1	74
Nathaniel, s. Joseph & Phebe, b. June 21, 1751	1	79
Nathaniel, s. [Sam[ue]l & Phebe], b. July 5, 1772	1	86
Nath[anie]l, m. Mary **MASON**, Apr. 12, 1775	1	71
Nelson, s. Joseph & Mary, b. Dec. 12, 1805	1	92
Obadiah, see also Abadiah		
Obadiah Hudson, s. Asa & Anna, b. Aug. 2, 1805	1	92
Orilla, d. [Sherebiah, Jr. & Lydia], b. July 15, 1794	1	90
Orra, d. John & Abigail, b. May 8, 1776	1	85
Orra, d. John & Abigail, d. Mar. 20, 1783	1	98
Orra, d. [Asa & Anne], b. Sept. 1, 1799	1	91
Phebe, m. Matthais **BUTTON**, May 16, 1753	1	70
Phebe, d. Samuel & Phebe, b. July 24, 1766	1	83
Phebe, d. Joseph & Mary, b. Apr. 24, 1801	1	91
Phebe, of Canterbury, m. Daniel **SPICER**, of Preston,		
Dec. 18, 1827, by Rev. Israel G. Rose, of Westminster	2	71
Philena, d. Josiah, Jr. & Eunice, b. May 16, 1779	1	86
Philura, m. Jared **PETTET**, Feb. 14, 1802	1	194
Rachel, d. [Sam[ue]l & Phebe], b. May 15, 1776	1	86
Ruby, d. Gideon & Amy, b. Oct. 23, 1780	1	86
Ruby, m. Silas **WHITMAN**, Feb. 4, 1796	1	237
Rufus, s. Nathan[ie]l & Sarah, b. Aug. 4, 1754	1	78
Rufus, s. Eben[eze]r & Prudence, b. July 26, 1783	1	88
Rufus, s. Joseph & Mary, b. Nov. 28, 1796	1	90
Sally, d. James & Abigail, b. Nov. 7, 1772	1	84
Sally, d. Ebenezer & Prudence, b. Feb. 18, 1791	1	89
Sally, d. David & Anne, b. Mar. 31, 1801	1	91
Sally, of Canterbury, m. Sam[ue]l **CHAPIN**, of Wilbraham,		
Mass., Feb. 16, 1825, by Rev. Tho[ma]s J. Murdock	2	15

	Vol.	Page
BUTTS, BUTT, (cont.)		
Samuel, s. Samuel & Sarah, b. Nov. 30, 1707	1	74
Sam[ue]l, Jr., m. Mary **ADAMS**, Jan. 8, 1735/6	1	69
Sam[ue]l, s. Josiah & Elizabeth, b. Feb. 23, 1741	1	79
Sam[ue]ll, s. Sam[ue]ll & Mary, b. Dec. 20, 1742	1	76
Samuel, d. May 20, 1747	1	95
Samuel, m. Phebe **BROWN**, Dec. 24, 1765	1	70
Samuel, s. Sam[ue]l & Phebe, b. Sept. 21, 1768	1	86
Samuel, m. Sarah **MILES**, May 21, 1772	1	71
Sarah, w. Samuel, d. Aug. 27, 1727	1	95
Sarah, d. Josiah & Elizabeth, b. May 31, 1730	1	75
Sarah, m. John **BATES**, June 15, 1747	1	69
Sarah, d. Nathan[ie]l & Sarah, b. July 7, 1747	1	77
Sarah, w. John, d. May 8, 1761 (Corrected to "Sarah **BATES**" by L. B. B.)	1	97
Sarah, d. James* & Irene, b. Apr. 24, 1764 (*Probably "Joseph")	1	82
Sarah, d. Sam[ue]l, 3d, & Eunice, b. May 11, 1774	1	84
Sarah A., m. Charles **PARK**, Feb. 11, 1842, by Rev. Asa King, Westminster	2	63
Sarah Ann, d. Lyman & Charlotte, b. Dec. 4, 1821	2	207
Seth, s. Sherebiah, Jr. & Lydia, b. Dec. 27, 1789	1	90
Sheldon, s. James & Elizabeth, b. June 15, 1780	1	86
Sherebiah, s. Josiah & Elizabeth, b. Feb. 11, 1733	1	76
Sherebiah, m. Deborah **[K]NIGHT**, Jan. 3, 1759	1	70
Sherebiah, s. Sherebiah & Deborah, b. Mar. 25, 1760	1	81
Sherebiah, Jr., m. Lydia **PETTINGILL**, of Norwich, Dec. 4, 1783	1	72
Sherebiah, d. Nov. 27, 1807	1	98
Sibbel, see under Sybil		
Simeon, s. Sam[ue]l & Eunice, b. May 2, 1772	1	84
Simeon, s. [Sherebiah, Jr. & Lydia], b. Mar. 2, 1792	1	90
Sophia, twin with Sophronia, d. [Asa & Anne], b. Apr. 29, 1803	1	92
Sophia, m. James **LAMSON**, of Woodstock, Mar. 28, 1849, by Rev. Asa King, Westminster	2	53
Sophronia, d. Asa & Anna, d. Mar. 8, 1805	1	98
Stephen, s. Stephen* & Phebe, b. June 15, 1749 (*Probably "Joseph". Corrected by L. B. B.	1	79
Stephen, m. Lucy **HEBBARD**, Oct. 8, 1769	1	70
Stephen, m. Lucy **PARKE**, Jan. 23, 1806	1	72
Stephen, d. Apr. 15, 1823, ae 73 y.	2	307
Submit, d. Josiah & Elizabeth, b. May 16, 1743	1	79
Submitt, m. John **ADAMS**, Dec. 2, 1765	1	51
Susannah, d. Josiah & Elizabeth, b. Feb. 9, 1737	1	76
Sibbel, d. Eben[eze]r & Prudence, b. Sept. 29, 1773	1	85
Thirza, d. Jos[eph] & Irene, b. Aug. 11, 1772	1	84
Thomas, s. Elizabeth, b. Apr. 1, 1759	1	82

	Vol.	Page
BUTTS, BUTT, (cont.)		
Whiting, s. Josiah & Eunice, b. Feb. 26, 1786	1	88
----, child of David & Anne, b. Apr. 22, 1798	1	91
CADY, Aaron, s. Aaron & Mercy, b. Dec. 7, 1718	1	103
Abigail, d. Richard & Alice, b. Feb. 22, 1789	1	115
Abijah, s. Jonathan & Hannah, b. Sept. 3, 1729	1	104
Alice, d. [Richard & Alice], b. Apr. 17, 1793	1	115
Almira A., m. Chester **PELLET**, b. of Canterbury, Dec. 8, 1822, by Tho[ma]s J. Murdock	2	61
Anne, d. Abijah & Lucy, b. Jan. 30, 1774	1	112
Bridget, m. David **KENDALL**, Mar. 5, 1767	1	173
Caphter, s. Abijah & Lucy, b. July 24, 1764	1	110
Daniel, d. Apr. 4, 1736	1	117
Daniel, s. Uriah & Hannah, b. Mar. 30, 1738	1	107
Daniel, m. Mary **SPAULDING**, Oct. 6, 1762	1	101
Darias, s. Ezra & Johanna, b. Dec. 18, 1732	1	108
Ebenezer, s. John & Elizabeth, b. Apr. 19, 1714	1	103
Edith, d. Abijah & Lucy, b. Sept. 20, 1768	1	111
Edith, d. Abijah & Lucy, b. Sept. 19, 1776	1	112
Eleazer, s. John & Elizabeth, b. Mar. 5, 1708	1	103
Elizabeth, d. John & Elizabeth, b. Mar. 5, 1701, in Old Groton	1	103
Elizabeth, s. [d.] Simeon & Ruth, b. Mar. 22, 1747	1	108
Elizabeth, m. Samuel **HARRIS**, Mar. 4, 1779	1	155
Esther, m. John (?) **ADAMS**, Mar. 27, 1711	1	51
Eunice, d. Uriah & Joanna, b. Jan. 28, 1763	1	109
Ezra, m. Johan[n]a **LEACH**, Apr. 8, 1721	1	100
Ezra, s. Ezra, d. Oct. 8, 1754	1	117
Ezra, d. May 30, 1758	1	118
Ezra, s. Ezra & Johanna, d. [ ]	1	118
Gideon, s. Ezra & Johanna, b. July 7, 1728	1	108
Hannah, d. Nathan & Rachel, b. Jan. 11, 1743	1	107
Henry, s. Jonathan & Hannah, b. Apr. 22, 1723	1	104
Johanna, [twin with Mary], d. Jonathan & Hannah, b. Oct. 14, 1718	1	103
John, s. John & Elizabeth, b. Aug. 9, 1699, in Old Groton	1	103
John, s. Jonathan & Hannah, b. Apr. 20, 1728	1	104
Johnson, s. [Richard & Alice], b. Mar. 28, 1791	1	115
Joshua, s. [Abijah & Lucy], b. July 2, 1771	1	111
Lemuel, s. Ezra & Johanna, d. Jan. 24, 1749/50	1	118
Leonard, s. Jonathan & Hannah, b. Jan. 5, 1725/6	1	104
Lucius, s. [Richard & Alice], b. Apr. 28, 1796	1	115
Lucy, m. John **LITCHFIELD**, July 17, 1750	1	176
Lucy, d. Abijah & Lucy, b. Dec. 24, 1753	1	106
Lucy, m. Elisha **LEACH**, Jan. 9, 1777	1	176
Lucy, d. [Richard & Alice], b. Oct. 30, 1798	1	115
Mary, m. Samuel (?) **ADAMS**, July 21, 1709	1	51
Mary, [twin with Johanna], d. Jonathan & Hannah, b. Oct. 14, 1718	1	103

	Vol.	Page
CADY, (cont.)		
Mary, w. Daniel, d. Apr. 11, 1736	1	117
Mary, d. Abijah & Lucy, b. Aug. 2, 1759	1	109
Nathaniel, s. Aaron & Anne, b. Dec. 7, 1746	1	107
Olive, d. Ezra & Johanna, b. Dec. 6, 1724	1	108
Olive had d. Trypheny **LITCHFIELD**, b. Dec. 18, 1751	1	177
Palmer, s. Aaron & Anne, b. July 4, 1748	1	107
Phebe, d. Ezra & Johanna, b. Nov. 30, 1722	1	108
Prudence, d. Uriah & Hannah, d. Dec. 23, 1744	1	118
Prudence, d. Uriah & Hannah, b. Sept. 2, 1745	1	107
Rachel, d. Uriah & Hannah, b. July 23, 1725	1	103
Rachel, d. Uriah & Hannah, b. July 23, 1745	1	107
Richard, s. Abijah & Lucy, b. Apr. 13, 1762	1	109
Richard, m. Alice **BINGHAM**, Nov. 15, 1787	1	102
Richard Bingham, s. [Richard & Alice], b. Dec. 15, 1807	1	115
Rosemond, d. Simeon & Ruth, b. July 11, 1751	1	108
Ruhama, m. Daniel **MEACH**, Feb. 16, 1809	1	181
Ruth, d. Simeon & Ruth, b. July 23, 1749	1	108
Ruth, w. Simeon, d. May 25, 1752	1	118
Sarah, d. Uriah & Hannah, b. May 18, 1740	1	107
Sibbel, see under Sybel		
Simeon, s. Ezra & Johanna, b. Aug. 30, 1721	1	108
Simeon, s. Jonathan & Hannah, b. Nov. 11, 1721	1	104
Simeon, m. Ruth **HARRIS**, Feb. 26, 1745	1	100
Simeon, s. Simeon & Ruth, b. Jan. 24, 1746	1	108
Simeon, d. Jan. 14, 1754	1	117
Susannah, d. Jonathan & Hannah, b. Aug. 5, 1716	1	103
Sibbel, d. Abijah & Lucy, b. Sept. 25, 1755	1	108
Sibbel, d. [Richard & Alice], b. June 27, 1801	1	115
Sybel, of Canterbury, m. Charles M. **CUMMINGS**, of		
Hampton, Jan. 21, 1824, by Rev. Thomas J. Murdock	2	15
Thankful, m. Horatio **PETTENGILL**, Sept. 24, 1802	1	194
Uriah, m. Hannah **BUZWELL**, Jan. 2, 1723/4	1	100
Uriah, s. Uriah & Hannah, b. Sept. 30, 1735	1	105
Uriah, s. Uriah & Hannah, b. Sept. 30, 1735	1	107
Uriah, m. Joanna **HUEIT**, Apr. 28, 1762	1	101
William, s. John & Elizabeth, b. Aug. 22, 1704	1	103
Zerviah, d. Abijah & Lucy, b. June 24, 1757	1	108
Zerviah, m. Jesse **ADAMS**, Nov. 30, 178[ ]	1	52
CALLEY, CALLY, John, s. John, d. June 12, 1704	1	117
Thomas, s. John, b. May 8, 1704	1	103
CAMPBELL, CAMBELL, CAMMELL, Clarissa, m. Jesse		
HAHES, of Brooklyn, Jan. 21, 1816	1	156
Mary, so-called d. of Elizabeth **DIXON**, so called,		
b. Dec. 30, 1753	1	150
Phelura, m. Isaac **BALDWIN**, Oct. 16, 1820	1	73
CANADA, CANNADA, Chloe, d. Dan[ie]l & Ruhamah, b. Sept. 19,		
1766	1	110

	Vol.	Page
CARTER, (cont.)		
Asa, s. Curtiss & Patience, b. Aug. 20, 1807	1	115
Benjamin, s. Joseph & Patience, b. May 23, 1764	1	110
Bethiah, d. John & Mary, b. Feb. 9, 1706/7	1	103
Bathiah, d. John & Deborah, b. Mar. 24, 1742/3	1	106
Bethiah, d. John & Deborah, d. Apr. 8, 1742	1	118
Carter, s. [Samuel & Mary], b. Mar. 3, 1791	1	114
Cedocius, s. Phinehas & Cynthia, b. Oct. 1, 1810	1	116
Sedosius, s. Phin[eha]s & Cynthia, d. Mar. 4, 1811	1	119
Clarinda, d. Jos[eph] & Patience, b. June 20, 1771	1	111
Constant, m. Apheas **BARSTOW**, June 10, 1773	1	71
Content, d. John & Deborah, b. Oct. 19, 1751	1	108
Curtis, s. John & Mary, b. Oct. 15, 1762	1	109
Curtiss, m. Lydia **KIMBALL**, Mar. 9, 1786	1	102
Curtiss, m. Patience **CARTER**, Nov. 29, 1800	1	102
Curtiss Murdock, s. Adin & Maria, b. Sept. 7, 1815	1	116
Cynthia, d. Phinehas & Cynthia, b. June 7, 1808	1	115
Cynthia, w. Phin[eha]s, d. Mar. 19, 1814	1	119
Cynthia, d. Phi[eha]s & Cynthia, d. July 14, 1823	2	315
Cynthia, d. Lucius & Lucy, b. Dec. 15, 1833	2	215
Deborah, d. John & Deborah, b. Aug. 24, 1734	1	105
Deborah, d. John & Deborah, d. Feb. 23, 1736/7	1	118
Deborah, d. John & Deborah, b. Nov. 8, 1753	1	108
Deborah, d. John & Deborah, d. May 22, 1754	1	117
Deborah, w. John, d. Mar. 9, 1755	1	117
Deborah, d. Reuben & Sibbel, b. Feb. 16, 1776	1	112
Eben[eze]r, s. John & Deborah, b. Aug. 8, 1745	1	106
Elias, s. Curtiss & Patience, b. Feb. 20, 1805	1	115
Eunice, d. [Curtiss & Lydia], b. July 6, 1794	1	115
Hiram, s. Samuel & Mary, b. Nov. 29, 1800	1	115
Increase, s. John & Deborah, b. Mar. 24, 1741	1	106
Increase, d. Nov. 24, 1759	1	118
Jedediah, s. John & Deborah, b. Jan. 26, 1742/3	1	106
Jedediah, m. Sarah **BURT**, July 10, 1768	1	101
Jedediah, s. Jedediah & Sarah, b. Jan. 28, 1772	1	111
John, s. John & Mary, b. Feb. 24, 1709	1	103
John, s. John & Deborah, b. Mar. 6, 1731	1	105
John, m. Deborah **BUNDAY**, Apr. 13, 1731	1	100
John, Jr., m. Mary **SMITH**, Oct. 31, 1753	1	100
John, m. Abigail **HAGGIT**, Mar. 2, 1756	1	100
John, d. Aug. 26, 1776, ae 68 y.	1	119
John, d. Sept. 26, 1781, ae 50 y.	1	119
John, s. Samuel & Mary, b. Oct. 17, 1786	1	114
Joseph, s. John & Deborah, b. July 18, 1736	1	105
Joeph, m. Patience (?) **PELLET**, Oct. 3, 1762	1	101
Lina, d. Jed[edia]h & Sarah, d. b. Jan. 29, 1776	1	112
Lucius, s. Phinehas & Cynthia, b. Aug. 10, 1799	1	114
Lucy, d. John & Mary, b. Mar. 22, 1766	1	110

	Vol.	Page
CARTER, (cont.)		
Lucy, d. Curtiss & Lydia, b. Feb. 25, 1787	1	115
Lucy, d. Phinehas & Cynthia, b. June 22, 1795	1	114
Lucy, m. Samuel **SPAULDING**, 2d, Jan. 19, 1829, by		
Rev. Israel G. Rose, of Westminster	2	72
Luther, s. [Samuel & Mary], b. Nov. 28, 1788	1	114
Lydia, d. Reuben & Sibbel, b. Aug. 22, 1774	1	112
Lydia, d. Curtiss & Patience, b. Mar. 9, 1801	1	115
Mary, w. John, Jr., d. Aug. 11, 1769	1	118
Mary, d. Jos[eph] & Patience, b. July 18, 1774	1	112
Mary Anne, d. [Lucius & Lucy], b. Sept. 22, 1835	2	215
Olive, d. [Samuel & Mary], b. June 11, 1798	1	114
Pamela, d. [Phinehas & Cynthia], b. May 20, 1797	1	114
Pamelia, d. Phin[eha]s, m. Benjamin **SPAULDING**, Mar. 28,		
1825, by Rev. Israel G. Rose	2	71
Patience, m. Curtiss **CARTER**, Nov. 29, 1800	1	102
Phinehas, s. John & Abigail, b. Apr. 21, 1757	1	108
Phinehas, s. John & Abigail, d. Nov. 16, 1760	1	118
Phinehas, s. Joseph & Patience, b. Nov. 23, 1766	1	110
Phinehas, m. Cynthia **BUTTS**, Nov. 3, 1794	1	102
Phinehas, d. Nov. 8, 1840, ae 73	2	315
Pliney, s. Phinehas & Cynthia, b. Apr. 7, 1806	1	115
Polly, d. [Samuel & Mary], b. Apr. 7, 1793	1	114
Polly, d. Phinehas & Cynthia, b. Nov. 24, 1801	1	115
Pulaski(?), s. [Phinehas & Cynthia], b. June 23, 1813	1	116
Reuben, s. John & Deborah, b. Dec. 20, 1749	1	107
Reuben, s. John & Deborah, b. Dec. 20, 1749	1	108
Reuben, m. Sibbel **SMITH**, June 22, 1769	1	101
Sam[ue]l, s. John & Mary, b. Oct. 30, 1755	1	108
Samuel, s. Joseph & Patience, b. May 3, 1769	1	110
Samuel, m. Mary **BALDWIN**, May 4, 1786	1	102
Samuel, s. [Samuel & Mary], b. Feb. 28, 1796	1	114
Sarah, d. Jedediah & Sarah, b. Oct. 22, 1773	1	112
Sarah E., m. John E. **DORRANCE**, July 7, 1844, by Rev.		
Asa King, Westminster	2	22
Sedocius, see under Cedocius		
Sibbel, see under Sybil		
Stephen, s. Phinehas & Cynthia, b. Mar. 4, 1804	1	115
Stephen, s. Phin[eha]s & Cynthia, d. Sept. 6, 1835, at		
Norwalk, Huron Co., Ohio	1	119
Sibbel, d. Reuben & Sibbel, b. Mar. 28, 1772	1	111
Will[ia]m, s. John & Deborah, b. Oct. 29, 1738	1	105
William, m. Anna **STANTON**, June 6, 1758	1	100
CARVER, Abigail, d. Jonathan & Abigail, b. May 29, 1748	1	107
Abigail, d. David & Susannah, b. May 21, 1754	1	109
Abigail, m. David **ADAMS**, May [ ], 1777(?)	1	52
Abigail, d. [Gideon & Abigail], b. Nov. 12, 1786	1	114
Almira, d. Waterman & Chloe, b. Oct. 16, 1817	1	116

	Vol.	Page
CARVER, (cont.)		
Benjamin, s. David & Sarah, b. Dec. 10, 1722	1	104
Caroline, d. [Waterman & Chloe], b. Feb. 19, 1811	1	116
Celecia, d. Waterman & Chloe, b. June 1, 1804	1	116
Dan[ie]l, s. Dan[ie]l & Abigail, b. Sept. 26, 1755	1	108
Daniel, s. [David, Jr. & Mary], b. Feb. 5, 1773	1	113
David, Ensign, d. Sept. 14, 1727	1	117
David, s. David & Susanna, b. May 2, 1745	1	106
David, Jr., m. Mary **PECK**, Jr., Jan. 26, 1769	1	101
David, d. May 29, 1793, ae 80	1	119
Delight, m. James **ADAMS**, Oct. 15, 1837, by Peter		
Spicer, J. P.	2	3
Delight, m. James **ADAMS**, Oct. 18, 1837	1	53
Dyer, s. [David, Jr. & Mary], b. Apr. 16, 1771	1	113
Dyer, s. David, Jr. & Mary, d. Sept. 2, 1776	1	119
Dyar, s. Gideon & Abigail, b. Nov. 9, 1777	1	113
Dyer, s. [David, Jr. & Mary], b. Sept. 4, 1778	1	113
Elihu, s. [David, Jr. & Mary], b. Jan. 6, 1777	1	113
Elizabeth, d. [David, Jr. & Mary], b. Nov. 18, 1774	1	113
Elizabeth, d. David, Jr. & Mary, d. Aug. 15, 1776	1	119
Elizabeth, m. Pardon **BENNETT**, of Brooklyn, Mar. 12, 1843,		
by Rev. Asa King, Westminster	2	13
Emaline, d. [Waterman & Chloe], b. June 20, 1814	1	116
Ezra, s. David, Jr. & Mary, b. Oct. 26, 1769	1	113
Frank, s. [Waterman & Chloe], b. June 3, 1812	1	116
Gideon, m. Abigail **HOVEY**, Dec. 15, 1774	1	101
Gideon, s. [Gideon & Abigail], b. Aug. 9, 1789	1	114
Hannah, d. David & Susanna, b. Mar. 24, 1740/41	1	106
Hannah, d. [Gideon & Abigail], b. Apr. 29, 1784	1	114
John, s. Samuel & Esther, b. May 17, 1734	1	105
John, s. [Gideon & Abigail], b. Dec. 25, 1791	1	114
Jonathan, m. Abigail **ROB[B]INS**, Oct. 20, 1746	1	100
Laura, d. [Waterman & Chloe], b. Apr. 1, 1809	1	116
Lucinda, d. Nathan & Martha, b. Dec. 25, 1771	1	111
Lydia, d. David & Susannah, b. Aug. 31, 1748	1	107
Mary, d. Jonathan & Abigail, b. Apr. 8, 1747	1	107
Millescent, d. David & Susannah, b. Nov. 11, 1757	1	109
Millescent, m. Samuel **STODDARD**, June 11, 1781	1	214
Nathan, s. David & Susannah, b. Mar. 5, 1742/3	1	106
Nathan, m. Martha **CHAPMAN**, Apr. 15, 1770	1	101
Nathan[ie]ll, s. David & Susanna, b. Aug. 8, 1752	1	106
Olive, d. Gideon & Abigail, b. July 8, 1796	1	114
Samuel, s. Samuel & Esther, b. June 5, 1732	1	105
Sarah, m. Solomon **PAINE**, Mar. 2, 1720/21	1	192
Sarah, d. Gideon & Abigail, b. Dec. 14, 1775	1	113
Sarah, m. Jesse **PECK**, Mar. 31, 1795	1	194
Susannah, d. David & Susannah, b. Mar. 31, 1756	1	109
Susannah, s. [d.] Gideon & Abigail, b. Apr. 19, 1782	1	114

	Vol.	Page
CARVER, (cont.)		
Susanna, m. Ebenezer **HIBBARD**, Feb. 13, 1783	1	155
Waterman, s. Gideon & Abigail, b. Aug. 10, 1779	1	113
Waterman, m. Chloe **WILLIAMS**, Feb. 27, 1803	1	102
CARY, [see under **CAREY**]		
CASE, Deborah, m. Willard **STEVENS**, Jan. 22, 1755	1	214
CHAFFEE, Ebenezer, m. Alice **FASSET**, Apr. 18, 1776	1	101
Ethan, s. Eben[eze]r & Alice, b. Oct. 29, 1780	1	113
Lydia, d. Ebenez[er] & Alice, b. Oct. 8, 1776	1	112
Olive, d. Eben[eze]r & Alice, b. Dec. 19, 1782	1	113
CHAMBERLAIN, Chauncey C., of Killingly, m. Harriet E.		
LeVALLEY, of Canterbury, Feb. 18, 1850, by Robert C.		
Learned	2	19
Elizabeth, of Woodstock, m. Dr. John **SPAULDING**, Jan. 8,		
1771	1	214
CHAMPION, Esther, of Colchester, m. Moses **CLEVELAND**, Mar.		
21, 1794	1	102
CHAMPLAIN, Sarah, of Killingly, m. Joshua **PICKET**, of		
Plainfield, [July] 3, 1842, by Martin Byrne	2	63
CHANDLER, Henrietta, m. Albe **HIDE**, Jan. 24, 1804	1	156
Thomas K., m. Betsey M. **DEWING**, Sept. 5, 1838, by		
Rev. Asa King, Westminster	2	17
CHAPIN, Alonzo B., of Wallingford, m. Hannah B. **WALDO**, of		
Canterbury, [Sept.] 24, 1832, by Rev. Samuel J. May	2	16
Sam[ue]l, of Wilbraham, Mass., m. Sally **BUTTS**, of		
Canterbury, Feb. 16, 1825, by Rev. Tho[ma]s J. Murdock	2	15
CHAPMAN, Elizabeth, m. Joseph **ADAMS**, Jr., Nov. 26, 177[ ]	1	52
Joseph, then of Pomfret, m. Hannah **FREEMAN**, of		
Martlake, May 16, 1751	1	100
Joseph, s. Joseph & Hannah, b. Aug. 2, 1752	1	103
Lydia, m. Joseph **ADAMS**, June 19, 178[ ]	1	52
Martha, m. Nathan **CARVER**, Apr. 15, 1770	1	101
CHESTER, Lemuel, of Windham, m. Esther **HEBBARD**, of		
Canterbury, Apr. 19, 1829, by Peter Morse, J. P.	2	15
CHURCH, Samuel A., of Hartford, m. Julia Eveline **SAFFORD**, of		
Canterbury, Dec. 26, 1852, by Rev. Robert C. Learned	2	19
Sarah, m. John **PAINE**, Feb. 12, 1729/30	1	192
Sarah, m. Paine **CLEVELAND**, Apr. 16, 1767	1	101
CINSON, Ralph W. R., m. Mary E. **WILLIAMS**, Aug. 17, 1834, by		
Rev. Jesse Fisher	2	16
CLARK, CLARKE, CLEARK, Adam, s. Theophilus & Martha, b.		
Mar. 5, 1734/5	1	105
Adam, m. Mehetable **GATES**, of Preston, Dec. 5, 1759	1	101
Ellis (Alice), d. Adam & Mehetable, b. Apr. 18, 1764	1	109
Allen Gates, s. [Asa & Rebeckah], b. Sept. 20, 1783	1	113
Almira, m. Chauncey **HERRICK**, Aug. 27, 1837, by Rev. Asa		
King, Westminster	2	40
Asa, m. Rebecca **ALLEN**, June 2, 1779	1	101

	Vol.	Page

CLARK, CLARKE, CLEARK, (cont.)

	Vol.	Page
Barnabus, s. Asa & Rebeckah, b. May 22, 1780	1	113
Barnabas, s. [Asa & Rebecca], d. Nov. 26, 1782	1	119
Benj[ami]n, s. Theophilus & Martha, b. May 16, 1738	1	107
Bethia Delia, d. [Seth & Olive], b. Apr. 19, 1797	1	114
Calvin, s. Jos[eph] & Abigail, b. Apr. 23, 1762, at Plainfield	1	112
Charles Pinkerey, s. [Seth & Olive], b. Dec. 10, 1806	1	116
Chester, s. Jos[eph] & Abigail, b. Sept. 19, 1769	1	112
Cyrus, s. Nathan & Abigail, b. Sept. 12, 1756	1	108
Cyrus, s. Adam & Mehitable, b. Aug. 1, 1766	1	110
Diah, s. [Jos[eph] & Abigail], b. Apr. 22, 1772	1	112
Elihu Palmer, s. [Seth & Olive], b. Aug. 22, 1812	1	116
Elizabeth, d. Seth, Jr. & Nabby, b. Mar. 22, 1815	1	116
Ellis, see under Alice		
Enos, [twin with Theophilus], s. Jonas & Abias, b. July 5, 1764	1	110
Erastus, of Ashford, m. Mary **FELCH**, of Canterbury, Aug. 10, 1824, by Rev. Tho[ma]s J. Murdock	2	15
Eunice S., m. John **BULLARD**, b. of Canterbury, June 21, 1828, by Rev. J. R. Wheelock	2	8
Eunice Smith, d. Seth & Olive, b. May 21, 1800	1	115
Ezra, s. Nathaniel & Thankful, b. May 27, 1766	1	110
Faunella, d. Jonas & Avis, b. Aug. 17, 1767	1	111
George W., of Norwich, m. Mary Ann **WILLOUGHBY**, of Canterbury, Sept. 9, 1822, by Erastus Larned	2	15
Guy Carlton, s. Seth & Olive, b. June 24, 1790	1	114
Henry, s. [Seth & Olive], b. Nov. 12, 1810	1	116
Isaac, s. Isaac & Susan, b. June 30, 1833	2	215
Jane C., of Canterbury, m. Samuel **COVERLY**, Jr., of Boston, Mass., Aug. 10, 1828, by Rev. James R. Wheelock	2	15
Jasper, s. Stephen & Elizabeth, b. Nov. 14, 1770	1	111
Jemima, Jr., m. Ephraim **STORY**, of Norwich, Mar. 7, 1792	1	215
John Milton, s. Seth & Olive, b. June 30, 1788	1	114
Johnson, s. Jos[eph] & Abigail, b. Feb. 8, 1767	1	112
Jonas, s. Theo[philu]s & Martha, b. Sept. 9, 1741	1	107
Jonas, m. Abias(?) **PAGE**, of Groton, Oct. 17, 1763	1	101
Jonas, s. Jonas & Avis, b. Dec. 30, 1774	1	114
Joseph, m. Abigail **JOHNSON**, Apr. 23, 1761	1	101
Louisa, m. Daniel **FROST**, Jr., Feb. 3, 1811	1	139
Louisa R., of Canterbury, m. Lucius L. **CLARKE**, of Pomfret, June 13, 1831, by Rev. Demis Platt	2	16
Lucius L., of Pomfret, m. Louisa R. **CLARK**, of Canterbury, June 13, 1831, by Rev. Demis Platt	2	16
Lucy, d. Theophilus & Bethiah, b. May 6, 1759	1	109
Luther, s. Seth & Olive, b. May 30, 1792	1	114
Maria, d. Seth, Jr. & Nabby b. Apr. 25, 1825 (handwritten in margin of original manuscript.)	1	112
Maria, of Canterbury, m. Caleb W. **TARBOX**, of East Greenwich, R. I., Dec. 8, 1844, by Rev. Daniel D. Lyon,		

	Vol.	Page
CLARK, CLARKE CLEARK, (cont.)		
of Packersville	2	80
Martha, d. Theophilus & Bathiah, b. Aug. 6, 1757	1	109
Martha, d. Theophilus & Bethiah, d. Dec. 11, 1759	1	118
Martha, d. Jonas & Avis, b. Oct. 6, 1772	1	114
Martha, wid. Dr. Theophilus, d. Mar. 4, 1789	1	119
Martha, m. Jacob BACON, Jan. 1, 1793	1	73
Mary, d. [Seth, Jr. & Nabby], b. July 30, 1818	1	116
Mehetable, d. Adam & Mehetable, b. May 25, 1769	1	111
Nathaniel, s. Theophilus & Martha, b. Mar. 29, 1730	1	105
Nathaniel, m. Thankful GATES, Apr. 30, 1751	1	101
Nathan[ie]l, m. Jemima ALLEN, Sept. 26, 1768	1	101
Nathan[ie]l, s. Nathan[ie]l & Jemima, b. June 1, 1773	1	112
Nathaniel, Jr., m. Rachel PARKE, Mar. 15, 1797	1	102
Olive, d. Jos[eph] & Abigail, b. July 4, 1764	1	112
Olive, d. [Seth, Jr. & Nabby], b. Oct. 19, 1821	1	116
Olive P., of Canterbury, m. Horace BALDWIN, of Lenox,		
Penn., June 19, 1825, by Rev. Tho[ma]s J. Murdock	2	7
Olive Palmer, d. Seth & Olive, b. May 4, 1794	1	114
Patty, m. Jacob BROWN, Jan. 1, 1792	1	72
Peter Morse, s. [Seth & Olive], b. July 4, 1802	1	115
Prudence, d. Adam & Mehetable, b. Apr. 2, 1762	1	109
Rachel, d. Jonas & Avis, b. Nov. 13, 1769	1	111
Rebecca, w. Asa, d. Sept. 1, 1784	1	119
Reuben, s. Theo[philu]s & Martha, b. July 4, 1747	1	107
Reubey, d. [Asa & Rebeckah], b. Mar. 10, 1782	1	113
Reuby, d. Asa & Rebecca, d. Oct. 29, 1782	1	119
Rosel, s. Nathaniel & Thankful, b. May 19, 1764	1	110
Ruby, see under Reuby		
Rufus, s. Nathaniel & Thankful, b. May 15, 1762	1	110
Seth, s. Theophilus & Bithiah, b. Sept. 11, 1762	1	109
Seth, m. Olive PALMER, Jan. 22, 1786	1	102
Seth, s. Seth & Olive, b. June 12, 1786	1	113
Sophia Hastins, d. Isaac & Susan, b. Jan. 18, 1827	2	215
Stephen, s. Theophilus & Martha, b. Feb. 1, 1744/5	1	107
Stephen, m. Elizabeth HOVEY, May 9, 1770	1	101
Susan Tracy, d. [Isaac & Susan], b. Jan. 15, 1829	2	215
Thankful, m. James BALDWIN, Sept. 13, 1758	1	70
Thankful, d. Nathaniel & Thankful, b. May 7, 1761	1	110
Thankful, w. Nathan[ie]l, d. May 16, 1768	1	118
Theophilus, s. Theophilus & Martha, b. Mar. 30, 1732	1	105
Theophiles, Jr., m. Bathiah BURNAM, Jan. 13, 1756	1	100
Theophilus, Dr., d. May 15, 1760	1	118
Theophilus, [twin with Enos], s. Jonas & Abias, b. July 5, 1764	1	110
Thomas Adams, s. Seth & Olive, b. Sept. 7, 1804	1	115
Willis, s. [Jos[eph] & Abigail], b. Nov. 9, 1775	1	112
CLEVELAND, Aaron, s. Josiah & Abigail, b. Nov. 27, 1727	1	104
Aaron, s. Benjamin & Anne, b. June 3, 1730	1	104

	Vol.	Page
CLEVELAND, (cont.)		
Aaron, m. Thankful **PAINE**, June 7, 1748	1	100
Aaron, s. Aaron & Thankful, b. June 18, 1750	1	106
Aaron, s. Aaron & Thankful, b. June 18, 1750	1	107
Aaron, Jr., m. Jemima **ROBINSON**, June 12, 1777	1	101
Abiel, d. Josiah & Mary, b. Oct. 9, 1709	1	103
Abigail, d. Samuel & Margaret, b. Apr. 23, 1700	1	103
Abigail, d. Josiah & Abigail, b. June 3, 1715	1	103
Abigail, d. Samuel & Margaret, d. Feb. 23, 1717/18	1	117
Abigail, w. Joseph, d. Dec. 16, 1724	1	117
Abigail, d. Timo[thy] & Abigail*, b. Mar. 27, 1728		
(*Probably Deborah. Corrected by L. B. B.)	1	104
Abigail, d. Benj[ami]n & Rachel, b. Aug. 13, 1746	1	106
Abigail, m. Will[ia]m **DARBE**, Nov. 9, 1749	1	120
Abigail, d. Sam[ue]l & Ruth, b. Aug. 6, 1758	1	108
Abigail, d. Samuel & Ruth, b. Aug. 6, 1758	1	109
Abigail, d. Aaron & Thankful, b. Aug. 5, 1759	1	109
Abigail, d. Josiah & Johanna, b. Feb. 10, 1762	1	109
Abigail, d. John & Betty, b. May 18, 1766	1	110
Abigail, m. John **HEBBARD**, Jr., Mar. 17, 1777	1	155
Abigail, d. Eliphas & Anna, b. Nov. 22, 1784	1	113
Abijah, s. Capt. Joseph, d. Nov. 3, 1736	1	117
Alice, d. Eleaz[e]r & Anne, b. Dec. 16, 1767	1	111
Alice, d. Will[ia]m & Rachel, b. July 21, 17[ ]	1	106
Ann, d. Aaron & Thankful, b. Aug. 29, 1756	1	108
Ann, d. Aaron & Thankful, d. Mar. 11, 1759	1	118
Anna, d. Enoch & Deborah, b. Oct. 15, 1756	1	108
Anna, d. Eliphaz & Anna, b. Oct. 20, 1797	1	114
Anne, d. Isaac & Elizabeth, b. June 6, 1703	1	103
Anne, d. Moses & Mary, b. Aug. 15, 1725	1	104
Anne, d. Benjamin & Anne, b. Mar. 23, 1731/2	1	105
Anne, d. Eleazer & Anne, b. Nov. 3, 1750	1	107
Anne, d. Sam[ue]l & Ruth, d. Aug. 17, 1773	1	119
Anne, m. Joshua **BRADFORD**, Feb. 9, 1775	1	71
Anne, d. Aaron, Jr. & Jemima, b. July 18, 1778	1	112
Anson, s. John & Bettey, b. Aug. 4, 1772	1	111
Arubah*, d. Tracy & Phebe, b. Dec. 25, 1775 (*Azubah?)	1	113
Arunah, d. Ezra & Jerusha, b. May 16, 1763	1	109
Arunah, d. Sam[ue]l & Ruth, b. Mar. 21, 1768	1	110
Asa, s. Josiah & Sarah, b. Aug. 1, 1736	1	105
Augustus, s. Moses & Zube, b. Mar. 29, 1778	1	113
Aury, d. David & Rebecca, b. Jan. 14, 1753	1	105
Azuba, see under Arubah		
Benjamin, s. Joseph & Abigail, b. May 20, 1714	1	103
Benj[ami]n, s. Benj[ami]n & Rachel, d. Nov. 25, 1749	1	118
Bethabra, s. Timothy & Esther, b. Oct. 31, 1763	1	109
Bethebra, m. Margery **PELLET**, Dec. 31, 1794	1	102
Betsey Anna, d. Perez & Betsey, b. June 12, 1805	1	116

	Vol.	Page
CLEVELAND, (cont.)		
Betty, d. Isaac & Susannah, b. June 11, 1733	1	105
Bradford, s. Eleazer & Anna, b. Sept. 9, 1764	1	110
Bridget, d. Joseph & Mary, b. Aug. 12, 1728	1	105
Caleb, s. John & Bettey, b. Feb. 9, 1770	1	111
Calvin, s. Moses & Azuba, b. Feb. 3, 1769	1	111
Cambden, s. Aaron & Thankful, b. Apr. 8, 1778	1	113
Caroline, d. W[illia]m Pitt & Mary, b. Aug. 18, 1799	1	114
Caroline, d. Will[ia]m P.& Mary, d. Feb. 28, 1800	1	119
Chester, s. Samuel & Ruth, b. Mar. 28, 1771	1	111
Clarissa, d. Silas & Eliz[abeth], b. June 4, 1765	1	111
Curtis, s. Isaac & Elizabeth, b. Jan. 23, 1701	1	103
Cyrus, s. Timo[thy] & Dorothy, b. Oct. 2, 1743	1	106
Cyrus, s. Timothy & Dorothy*, d. Feb. 23, 1748/9 (*Deborah. Corrected by L. B. B.)	1	118
Cyrus, s. Timothy & Esther, b. May 12, 1766	1	110
Daniel, s. [Silas & Eliz[abeth], b. July 6, 1767	1	111
David, s. Samuel & Sarah, b. June 1, 1724	1	104
David, m. Eunice BAC[K]US, June 25, 1744	1	100
David, m. Rebecca TRACY, of Preston, Aug. 15, 1750	1	100
David, s. Hopestill & Patience, b. July 9, 1765	1	110
David, s. Tracy & Phebe, b. Dec. 16, 1775	1	112
Deborah, w. Joseph, Jr., d. Nov. 14, 1724	1	117
Deborah, d. Joseph & Mary, b. Aug. 11, 1726	1	105
Deborah*, w. Capt. Timo[thy], d. Aug. 19, 1769 (*Arnold Copy has "Dorothy")	1	118
Deliverence, s. Joseph* & Mary, b. July 13, 1707 (*Probably Josiah. Corrected by L. B. B.)	1	103
Deliverance, w. Edward, d. June 7, 1717	1	117
Deliverance, s. Edward & Rebeckah, b. Mar. 10, 1723/4	1	104
Deliverence, d. Isaac & Susannah, b. Apr. 2, 1729	1	104
Diliver[an]ce, m. Keziah EATON, Jan. 20, 1731/2	1	100
Deliver[an]ce, m. Rebecca PAINE, July 4, 1744	1	100
Deliverance, m. Israel BAKER, Sept. 16, 1747	1	69
Deliverance, d. Paine & Sarah, b. May 30, 1772	1	112
Dolly, single woman, had d. Loiza ASPENWALL, b. Feb. 16, 1806	1	115
Dorcas, d. Moses & Mary, b. May 9, 1721	1	104
Dorothy, d. Joseph & Abigail, b. Mar. 31, 1716	1	103
Dorothy, d. Benj[ami]n & Rachel, b. June 10, 1744	1	106
Dorothy, d. Benj[ami]n, d. Nov. 12, 1749	1	118
Dorothy, d. Ezra & Jerusha, b. Sept. 14, 1767	1	110
Dorothy*, w. Capt. Timo[thy], d. Aug. 19, 1769 (*Deborah. Corrected by L. B. B.)	1	118
Dorothy, d. Timo[thy], Jr. & Esther, b. May 30, 1772	1	111
Dorothy, d. Timo[thy], Jr. & Esther, b. Oct. 12, 1779	1	113
Downer, s. [John & Betty], b. Feb. 10, 1768	1	110
Dyar, s. Josiah, Jr. & Alice, b. Mar. 3, 1780	1	113

	Vol.	Page
CLEVELAND,(cont.)		
Ebenezer, s. Josiah & Abigail, b. Dec. 25, 1725	1	103
Eben[eze]r, of Canterbury, m. Abigail **STEVENS,** of Canterbury, Oct. 16, 1745, at Groton, by Andrew Croswell	1	69
Edward, Jr., m. Rebeckah **PAINE,** Apr. 17, 1717, at Kingston, R. I., by John Eldred, Asst.	1	100
Edward, s. Paine & Susannah, b. Nov. 19, 1761	1	109
Edward, d. Nov. 3, 1771	1	119
Eleazer, s. Samuel & Sarah, b. Mar. 26, 1722	1	104
Eleazer, m. Anne **BRADFORD,** Apr. 25, 1750	1	100
Elijah, s. Joseph & Abigail, b. Jan. 5, 1720/21	1	104
Elijah, s. Josiah & Alice, b. Jan. 28, 1788	1	114
Eliphas, m. Anne **PELLET,** Sept. 1, 1784	1	102
Elisha, s. Josiah & Abigail, b. Jan. 7, 1716/17	1	103
Elizabeth, m. John **ENSWORTH,** Apr. 2, 1717	1	133
Elizabeth, m. Elihu **PAINE,** Nov. 24, 1748	1	192
Elizabeth, m. Nathan **KIMBALL,** Aug. 28, 1755	1	173
Elizabeth, d. Silas & Elizabeth, b. Apr. 30, 1758	1	108
Elkanah, s. Timo[thy] & Esther, b. June 9, 1782	1	113
Elkanah, s. Timo[thy] & Esther, d. June 21, 1782	1	119
Emmaline, d. Bethabra & Margary, b. Sept. 25, 1809	1	115
Ephraim, s. Joseph & Abigail, b. Feb. 3, 1711/12	1	103
Ephraim, d. Mar. 13, 1711	1	117
Ephraim, s. Timo[thy] & Dorothy, b. Aug. 20, 1740	1	106
Ephraim, m. Mary **GRIFFING,** of Windham, Mar. 6, 1766	1	101
Esther, d. Benjamin & Anne, b. Nov. 5, 1727	1	104
Esther, d. Hopestill & Patience, b. June 30, 1767	1	110
Esther, w. Timothy, d. Nov. 3, 1803	1	119
Eunice, w. David, d. Oct. 1, 1749	1	118
Experience, d. Edward & Rebeckah, b. Sept. 5, 1728	1	105
Experience, m. Jabez **HOLMES,** May 2, 1749	1	155
Ezra, s. Ezra & Jerusha, b. June 22, 1748	1	107
Francis Moses, s. Moses & Esther, b. Sept. 25, 1797	1	114
Hannah, d. Moses* & Sarah, b. May 5, 1721 (*Samuel?)	1	104
Hannah, d. Joseph & Mary, b. Nov. 2, 1732	1	105
Hannah, d. Capt. Jos[eph], b. Nov. 5, 1736	1	117
Hiram, s. Bethabra & Margery, b. Jan. 8, 1798	1	114
Hopestill, s. Samuel & Sarah, b. Apr. 17, 1726	1	104
Hopestill, m. Patience **BENJAMIN,** May 9, 1754	1	100
Isaac, m. Elizabeth **CURTIS,** July 17, 1699	1	100
Isaac, s. Isaac & Susanna, b. May 13, 1735	1	105
Jabez, s. Henry & Lucy, d. Nov. 13, 1736	1	117
Jabez, s. Henry & Lucy, b. Nov. 4, 1737	1	105
Jacob, s. Timothy & Esther, b. Mar. 6, 1761	1	109
Jacob, d. July 26, 1826	2	315
James, s. Sam[ue]l & Mary, b. July 3, 1730	1	105
James H., of Brooklyn, m. Julia A. **PARK,** of Canterbury,		

	Vol.	Page
CLEVELAND, (cont.)		
May 20, 1850, by Rev. Isaac H. Cole	2	19
Jedediah, s. Sam[ue]l & Ruth, b. May 8, 1756	1	108
Jeptha, s. Timo[thy], Jr. & Esther, b. Oct. 17, 1768	1	111
Jerusha, d. Ezra & Jerusha, b. Aug. 31, 1758	1	109
Jesse, s. Joseph & Mary, b. Oct. 20, 1739	1	106
Joann, m. Jedediah **ENSWORTH**, Nov. 15, 1819	1	133
Johannah, d. Edward & Rebeckah, b. July 22, 1717	1	103
John, s. Josiah & Mary, d. July 11, 1718	1	117
John, s. Joseph & Deborah, b. Dec. 31, 1721	1	104
John, s. Josiah & Abigail, b. Apr. 12, 1722	1	104
John, s. Abigail, b. Feb. 27, 1734/5	1	105
John, s. Capt. Jos[eph], d. Mar. 1, 1754	1	117
John, s. Eleazer & Anna, b. June 29, 1758	1	109
John, s. Aaron & Thankful, b. June 20, 1762	1	109
John, m. Betty **DOWNER**, of Windham, Nov. 17, 1762	1	101
John, s. John & Bettey, b. Aug. 13, 1764	1	110
John, Jr., m. Abigail **ADAMS**, Feb. 2, 1773	1	101
Johnson, s. Isaac & Susannah, b. Oct. 29, 1722	1	104
Jonas, s. Joseph & Deborah, b. Oct. 16, 1718	1	103
Jonathan, s. Joseph & Abigail, b. May 9, 1713	1	103
Jonathan, d. July 15, 1713	1	117
Jonathan, s. Capt. Joseph & Mary, b. Nov. 24, 1737	1	105
Jonathan, s. Joseph & Mary, b. Nov. 24, 1737	1	106
Jonathan, s. Capt. Joseph & Mary, d. Mar. 19, 1754	1	117
Joseph, m. Abigail **HIDE**, Feb. 7, 1710/11	1	100
Joseph, m. Deborah **BUTTERFIELD**, May 19, 1718	1	100
Joseph, m. Sarah **ENSWORTH**, Mar. 31, 1725	1	100
Joseph, m. Mary **WOODWARD**, June 24, 1725	1	100
Joseph, s. Joseph & Mary, b. Jan. 19, 1730	1	105
Joseph, s. Benj[ami]n & Rachel, b. May 14, 1737	1	105
Joseph, s. Benj[ami]n & Rachel, d. Nov. 17, 1749	1	118
Joseph, s. Sam[ue]ll & Ruth, b. Feb. 7, 1751/2	1	106
Joseph, s. Sam[ue]l & Ruth, b. Feb. 7, 1751/2	1	108
Joseph, Capt., d. May 12, 1752	1	118
Joseph, d. Mar. 11, 1766	1	118
Josiah, Sr., d. Apr. 26, 1709	1	117
Josiah, m. Abigail **PAINE**, Aug. 7, 1710	1	100
Josiah, s. Josiah & Abigail, b. Apr. 4, 1713	1	103
Josiah, Jr., m. Sarah **LAWRENCE**, Oct. 15, 1735	1	100
Josiah, d. Feb. 9, 1751/2	1	118
Josiah, s. Josiah & Sarah, b. Dec. 3, 1753	1	106
Josiah, m. Johanna **BREWSTER**, June 5, 1755	1	100
Josiah, Jr., m. Alice **DYAR**, June 3, 1778	1	101
Josiah, s. Josiah, Jr. & Alice, b. Jan. 10, 1782	1	113
Julian, s. Eliphaz & Anna, b. Oct. 21, 1793	1	114
Julius M., s. Moses & Esther, d. Sept. 30, 1822	1	315
Julius Moses, s. Moses & Esther, b. May 21, 1805	1	115

	Vol.	Page
CLEVELAND, (cont.)		
Keziah, d. Josiah & Abigail, b. Nov. 26, 1711	1	103
Keziah, d. Deliverance & Keziah, b. Apr. 6, 1740	1	106
Keziah, w. Deliverance, d. Sept. 19, 1742	1	117
Kezia[h], d. Shubael & Eunice, b. Sept. 24, 1770	1	111
Kezia[h], m. Levi **DOWNING**, Nov. 21, 1771	1	120
Lemuel, s. Isaac & Susannah, b. Aug. 13, 1725	1	104
Lois, d. Josiah & Abigail, b. Dec. 11, 1718	1	103
Lois, d. Sept. 29, 1736	1	117
Loiza, d. Dorothy, b. Feb. 16, 1806	1	115
Lucius, s. Perez & Betsey, b. July 29, 1803	1	115
Lucretia, d. Tim[othy] & Dorothy, b. Feb. 2, 1736/7	1	105
Lucretia, m. Jedediah **DARBE**, Jan. 2, 1755	1	120
Lucy, d. Henry & Lucy, b. Mar. 2, 1724/5	1	104
Luranah, d. Silas & Elizabeth, b. May 15, 1761	1	109
Luther, s. Moses & Zuba, d. May 4, 1771	1	119
Luther, s. Moses & Zuba, b. July 22, 1771	1	111
Luther, s. Moses & Azuba, b. Jan. 14, 1774	1	112
Luther, s. Bethabra & Margaret, b. Oct. 25, 1806	1	115
Lydia, d. Josiah & Mary, b. Dec. 7, 1704	1	103
Lydia, m. Obadiah **JOHNSON**, Nov. 6, 1723	1	167
Lydia, d. Josiah & Abigail, b. Feb. 16, 1723/4	1	104
Lydia, d. Josiah & Abigail, d. Mar. 26, 1745	1	118
Lydia, d. Eben[eze]r & Abigail, b. Mar. 29, 1747	1	107
Lydia, d. Josiah & Sarah, b. May 25, 1751	1	108
Lydia, d. Josiah & Sarah, d. Sept. 30, 1754	1	117
Lydia, d. Josiah & Johanus, b. Feb. 13, 1757	1	108
Margaret, m. Samuel **WOODARD**, Jan. 18, 1751	1	236
Maria, d. Seth, Jr. & Nabby, b. Apr. 25, 1825	1	116
Martha, d. John & Bettey, b. May 17, 1763	1	110
Marvin, s. [Perez & Betsey], b. May 8, 1795	1	114
Mary, d. Samuel & Percis, b. June 14, 1696	1	103
Mary, m. Richard **SMITH**, Jan. 30, 1715/16	1	214
Mary, d. Josiah & Abigail, b. June 29, 1720	1	104
Mary, m. Robert **BUZWELL**, Jan. 22, 1721/2	1	69
Mary, m. Richard **ADAMS**, Mar. 30, 1730	1	51
Mary, d. Isaac & Susannah, b. Jan. 10, 1730/31	1	104
Mary, d. Joseph & Mary, b. Apr. 19, 1731	1	105
Mary, d. Capt. Jos[eph], d. Nov. 8, 1736	1	117
Mary, d. Joseph & Mary, b. Aug. 5, 1742	1	106
Mary, d. Joseph & Mary, d. Aug. 21, 1742	1	118
Mary, m. William **BRADFORD**, Apr. 6, 1743	1	69
Mary, d. Josiah & Sarah, b. Jan. 6, 1747/8	1	107
Mary, d. Silas & Elizabeth, b. Jan. 22, 1752	1	108
Mary, d. Sam[ue]l & Ruth, b. Feb. 12, 1754	1	106
Mary, d. Benj[ami]n & Rachel], b. Apr. 14, 1758	1	109
Mary, d. Benjamin & Rachel, d. Jan. 27, 1763	1	118
Mary, d. Aaron & Thankful, b. July 3, 1765	1	110

	Vol.	Page
CLEVELAND, (cont.)		
Mary, d. Timo[thy], Jr. & Esther, b. Nov. 6, 1774	1	112
Mary, m. Silas **ALLEN**, May 16, 1776	1	52
Mary, m. Joseph **ENSWORTH**, Oct. 5, 1779* (* 1719. L. B. B.)	1	133
Mary, d. Bethabra & Margery, b. Aug. 26, 1803	1	115
Mary E., m. Andrew **HARRIS**, Feb. 2, 1813	1	156
Mary Esther, d. Moses & Esther, b. May 14, 1795	1	114
Mehetable, d. Sam[ue]l & Sarah, b. Feb. 16, 1727/8	1	104
Mehetable, m. Faxon **DEAN**, Oct. 15, 1746	1	120
Mehetable, d. Eleaz[e]r & Anne, b. July 14, 1756	1	108
Miriam, d. Isaac & Elizabeth, b. July 4, 1705	1	103
Miriam, d. Moses & Mary, b. Jan. 30, 1718/19	1	103
Molly, d. Aaron & Thankful, d. Oct. 12, 1775	1	119
Moses, m. Mary **JOHNSON**, Oct. 19, 1717	1	100
Moses, s. Josiah & Abigail, b. Apr. 18, 1730	1	104
Moses, s. Josiah & Abigail, d. Jan. 1, 1741	1	117
Moses, s. Josiah & Sarah, b. June 26, 1744	1	107
Moses, s. Aaron & Thankful, b. Jan. 29, 1754	1	106
Moses, m. Azubah **KENDALL**, Mar. 24, 1768	1	101
Moses, m. Esther **CHAMPION**, of Colchester, Mar. 21, 1794	1	102
Moses, s. Perez & Betsey, b. June 10, 1800	1	115
Moses, Gen., d. Nov. 16, 1806	1	119
Moses, s. Perez & Betsey, [d.]	1	119
Nancy, d. Bethabra & Margaret, b. Sept. 4, 1795	1	114
Nehemiah, s. Henry & Lucy, b. July 30, 1721	1	104
Newcombe, s. Ezra & Jerusha, b. Nov. 6, 1756	1	108
Obadiah, s. Moses & Mary, b. Sept. 16, 1723	1	104
Olive, d. Eben[eze]r & Abigail, b. Feb. 17, 1749	1	107
Paine, s. Edward & Rebeckah, b. Aug. 30, 1731	1	105
Paine, m. Prudence **BUSWELL**, Jan. 18, 1757	1	100
Paine, m. Susanna **FALKNER**, Mar. 10, 1761	1	101
Paine, m. Sarah **CHURCH**, Apr. 16, 1767	1	101
Paine, s. Paine & Susannah, b. Feb. 10, 1768	1	110
Paine, s. Aaron & Thankful, b. Mar. 30, 1768	1	110
Paine, d. Nov. 25, 1773	1	119
Palmer, s. Silas & Elizabeth, b. Sept. 17, 1762	1	109
Patience, d. Hopestill & Patience, b. Jan. 12, 1757	1	108
Penelope, d. Deliver[an]ce & Kezia, b. May 7, 1733	1	105
Penelope, m. Ezekiel **PARK**, Nov. 7, 1753	1	192
Percis, see under Persis		
Perez, s. Eleazer & Anna, b. July 17, 1760	1	109
Perez Franklin, s. [Perez & Betsey], b. May 29, 1798	1	114
Percis, w. Samuel, [d.] Feb. 22, 1698	1	117
Persis, d. Benj[ami]n & Rachel, b. June 18, 1752	1	107
Phebe, d. Benj[ami]n & Rachel, b. June 25, 1758	1	109
Phinehas, s. Sam[ue]l & Mary, b. Oct. 19, 1727	1	105
Polley, d. Eleazer & Anna, b. Aug. 19, 1762	1	109

	Vol.	Page
CLEVELAND, (cont.)		
Prudence, w. Paine, d. June 30, 1758	1	118
Prudence, d. Paine & Sarah, b. Oct. 13, 1770	1	111
Rachel, d. Capt. Jos[eph] & Mary, b. Mar. 3, 1736	1	105
Rachel, d. Capt. Jos[eph], d. Nov. 4, 1736	1	117
Rachel, d. Deliverance & Keziah, b. Oct. 29, 1738	1	106
Rachel, d. Benj[ami]n & Rachel, b. May 18, 1750	1	107
Rebecca, d. Edward & Rebecca, b. Mar. 16, 1719	1	103
Rebeckah, d. Moses & Mary, b. June 28, 1730	1	104
Rebecca, d. Solomon & Abial, b. July 6, 1751	1	108
Rebeckah, w. David, d. Nov. 30, 1754	1	117
Rebecca, m. George **AUSTIN**, Jan. 18, 1758	1	51
Rebeckah, d. [Tracy & Phebe], b. July 18, 1780	1	113
Rebecca, wid., d. Feb. [ ], 1784	1	119
Rebecca, d. Perez & Betsey, b. Nov. 6, 1790	1	114
Rebecca, w. Jacob, d. Oct. 2, 1824	2	315
Rufus, s. Benj[ami]n & Rachel, b. June 14, 1754	1	107
Samuel, m. Margaret **FISH**, July 25, 1699	1	100
Samuel, m. Sarah **BUSWELL**, Dec. 10, 1719	1	100
Samuel, d. Oct. 1, 1727	1	117
Samuel, s. Joseph & Sarah, b. June 7, 1730	1	104
Samuel, d. Mar. 12, 1735/6	1	117
Samuel, s. Timothy & Dorothy, b. Feb. 23, 1738/9	1	105
Sam[ue]l, s. David & Eunice, b. Sept. 18, 1747	1	107
Sam[ue]l, s. David & Eunice, b. Sept. 18, 1747	1	108
Sam[ue]l, m. Ruth **DARBE**, May 7, 1751	1	100
Samuel, s. Samuel & Ruth, b. Aug. 7, 1763	1	109
Sarah, d. David & Eunice, b. Sept. 3, 1744	1	107
Sarah, d. Deliver[an]ce & Rebecca, b. June 15, 1745	1	107
Sarah, d. Ezra & Jerusha, b. Oct. 29, 1754	1	107
Sarah, w. Josiah, d. Feb. 6, 1755	1	117
Sarah, w. Joseph, d. June 21, 1761	1	118
Sarah, m. Peter **STANTON**, Sept. 21, 1763	1	214
Sarah, m. Samuel **ENSWORTH**, May 28, 1772	1	133
Sarah, d. Paine & Sarah, b. May 22, 1774	1	112
Sarah, m. Joseph **BUTT**, Apr. 11, 1776	1	71
Sarah, d. Capt. Josiah, d. Apr. 23, 1784	1	119
Sebill, see under Sybil		
Shubael, s. Deliver[an]ce & Kezia, b. Mar. 29, 1735	1	105
Shubael, m. Eunice, **LUCE**, Mar. 30, 1769	1	101
Silas, s. Edward & Rebeckah, b. May 28, 1726	1	104
Silas, m. Elizabeth **HIDE**, May 10, 1750	1	100
Silas, s. Silas & Elizabeth, b. Mar. 17, 1756	1	108
Solomon, s. Edward & Rebeckah, b. June 1, 1720	1	104
Solomon, m. Abial **BAKER**, Oct. 3, 1748	1	100
Solomon, d. Mar. 14, 1752	1	118
Solomon, s. Enoch & Deborah, b. Feb. 27, 1754	1	106
Solomon, s. Silas & Elizabeth, b. Apr. 21, 1754	1	106

	Vol.	Page
CLEVELAND, (cont.)		
Sophia, d. Perez & Betsey, b. Feb. 17, 1793	1	114
Squires, s. Eleazer & Anne, b. July 29, 1754	1	107
Stephen, s. Paine & Susannah, b. Oct. 9, 1764	1	110
Susannah, d. Eleazer & Anne, b. July 29, 1752	1	105
Susanna, d. Eleazer & Anne, b. July 29, 1752	1	106
Susannah, d. Paine & Susannah, b. Jan. 26, 1766	1	110
Susannah, w. Paine, d. Jan. 26, 1766	1	118
Sebill, d. Joseph & Deborah, b. Jan. 7, 1719	1	103
Tamer, s. Edward & Rebeckah, b. Jan. 19. 1721/2	1	104
Thankful, d. Josiah & Joanna, b. Dec. 30, 1759	1	109
Thankful, 9th child of Aaron & Thankful, b. Oct. 29, 1773	1	112
Thankful, m. Thaddeus **PALMER**, Jan. 13, 1782	1	193
Thomas, s. Ezra & Jerusha, b. Mar. 25, 1752	1	108
Thomas, s. Bethabra & Margery, b. Sept. 14, 1801	1	115
Thomas, of Plainfield, m. Almira **ASPENWALL**, of		
Canterbury, Apr. 2, 1826, by Rev. Tho[ma][s J. Murdock	2	15
Timothy, s. Samuel & Margaret, b. Aug. 25, 1702	1	103
Timothy, s. Timothy & Dorothy, b. Dec. 29, 1734	1	105
Timothy, m. Esther **FISH**, Jan. 30, 1760	1	101
Timothy, d. Jan. 19, 1784, ae 84 y.	1	119
Timothy, d. Oct. 27, 1803	1	119
Tracy, s. David & Rebecca, b. May 8, 1751	1	107
Tracy, m. Phebe **HIDE**, Apr. 25, 1773	1	101
Tyzhall, s. Ezra & Jerusha, b. Apr. 26, 1750	1	107
Vester, s. Sam[ue]l & Ruth, b. Aug. 22, 1778	1	113
Wealthy, d. Tracy & Phebe, b. Feb. 4, 1774	1	112
William, s. Henry & Lucy, b. July 7, 1719	1	103
William, 10th child & 5th s. Eleazer & Anne, b. Feb. 22, 1771	1	111
William Darbee, s. Samuel & Ruth, b. Feb. 8, 1766	1	110
William P., s. William P. & Mary, b. May 14, 1797	1	114
W[illia]m Pitt, s. Aaron & Thankful, b. Dec. 18, 1770	1	111
William Pitt, m. Mary **BACON**, Feb. 2, 1796	1	102
Zenas, s. Benj[ami]n & Rachel, b. Sept. 21, 1748	1	107
Zerviah, d. Samuel & Ruth, b. Feb. 19, 1761	1	109
Zerviah, d. Ezra & Jerusha, b. Mar. 6, 1765	1	110
Zeru[i]ah, d. Samuel & Ruth, d. Oct. 25, 1766	1	118
Zipperah, d. Timothy & Dorothy, b. Sept. 4, 1729	1	104
Zipporah, m. Frances **SIMONDS**, Nov. 19, 1750	1	214
-----, infant of Deliverance, b. Aug. 20, [1742];		
d. Sept. 21, 1742	1	118
----, infant of Paine & Prudence, d. June 30, 1758	1	118
----, s. Tracy & Phebe, b. Feb. 20, 1778	1	112
----, s. Tracy & Phebe, d. Feb. 24, 1778, ae 4 d.	1	119
COATS, Matilda, of Plainfield, m. Lemuel **SMITH**, of New York,		
Sept. 9, 1822, by Erastus Learned	2	71
COBB, COB, Abigail, d. Judah & Dorothy, b. Sept. 16, 1735	1	106
Abigail, d. Elkanah & Sarah, b. Aug. 21, 1751	1	108

	Vol.	Page

COBB, COB, (cont.)

	Vol.	Page
Abigail, d. Elkanah & Sarah, d. Oct. 30, 1754	1	117
Abigail, d. Gideon & Abigail, b. Sept. 7, 1756	1	108
Deborah, d. Judah & Dorothy, b. Sept. 29, 1739	1	106
Dorothy, w. Judah, d. Oct. 4, 1739	1	117
Dorothy, w. Capt. Elkanah, d. Mar. 5, 1802	1	119
Elijah, s. Judah & Dorothy, b. June 30, 1734	1	104
Elijah, s. Judah & Dorothy, b. June 30, 1734	1	106
Elkanah, m. Sarah ENSWORTH, Aug. 23, 1749	1	100
Gideon, m. Abigail DYAR, Nov. 5, 1739	1	100
Gideon, s. Gideon & Abigail, b. May 31, 1740	1	106
Gideon, Capt., d. Feb. 22, 1759	1	118
Gideon, Jr., d. Dec. 26, 1760	1	118
James, s. Judah & Dorothy, b. June 9, 1737	1	105
James, s. Judah & Dorothy, b. June 9, 1737	1	116
James, m. Mary ENSWORTH, May 15, 1763	1	101
Liman, s. James & Mary, b. July 5, 1766	1	110
Lois, d. Elkanah & Sarah, b. Nov. 27, 1749	1	108
Lucinda, d. James & Mary, b. Aug. 17, 1771	1	112
Lucinda, m. Obadiah JOHNSON, Aug. 10, 1789	1	167
Lyman, see under Liman		
Miner, s. James & Mary, b. May 22, 1764	1	110
Nehemiah, s. Elkanah & Sarah, b. Jan. 26, 1754	1	106
Nehemiah, s. Elkanah & Sarah, d. Oct. 28, 1754	1	117
Sarah, w. Elkanah, d. Nov. 2, 1754	1	117
Sarah, d. Gideon & Abigail, b. Jan. 12, 1759	1	109
Wealthean, d. Gideon, Jr. & Abigail, b. Oct. 2, 1753	1	106
Wealthy, m. Thomas LATHROP, Dec. 19, 1771	1	176

COBURN, COBARN, Anne, d. Nath[anie]l & Hannah, b. Aug. 29, 1768

	Vol.	Page
	1	110
Esther, d. Sam[ue]l & Juda, b. Apr. 21, 1759	1	109
Hannah, w. Robert, d. June 12, 1766	1	118
Perltheny, d. Nathaniel & Hannah, b. July 17, 1765	1	110

COGSWELL, Abigail, wid. Sam[ue]l, d. June 17, 1753

	Vol.	Page
	1	117
Abigail, d. [Nath[anie]l & Hannah], b. Jan. 10, 1773	1	113
Abigail, d. Nath[anie]l & Hannah, d. Jan. 15, 1773	1	119
Alice, d. James & Alice, b. Dec. 7, 1749	1	106
Daniel, s. [Nath[anie]l & Hannah], b. Aug. 3, 1780	1	113
Hannah, m. Will[ia]m ENSWORTH, Feb. 20, 1754	1	133
Hannah, d. Nath[anie]l & Hannah, b. Feb. 3, 1770	1	113
Huldah, d. [Nath[anie]l & Hannah], b. Jan. 31, 1769	1	111
James, m. Ellis (Alice) FITCH, Apr. 24, 1745	1	100
James, s. James & Alice, b. July 31, 1746	1	106
Mason Fitch, s. James & Alice, b. Sept. 28, 1760	1	109
Molly, d. Nath[anie]l & Hannah, b. Apr. 20, 1767	1	111
Nathan, s. [Nath[anie]l & Hannah], d. Dec. 28, 1778	1	119
Nathan[ie]l, m. Hannah ALLYN, Jan. 2, 1766	1	101
Nathaniel, s. [Nath[anie]l & Hannah], b. Nov. 21, 1778	1	113

	Vol.	Page
COGSWELL, (cont.)		
Sally, d. [Nath[anie]l & Hannah], b. Jan. 30, 1775	1	113
Sam[ue]l, d. Mar. 21, 1752	1	117
Sam[ue]l, s. James & Alice, b. May 23, 1754	1	106
William H., Dr., of Plainfield, m. Lucretia Ann **PAYNE**, of Canterbury, Jan. 6, 1830, by Rev. Levi Nelson, of Lisbon	2	16
COIT, Frances Adams, d. [Stephen & Betsey], b. Apr. 20, 1824	2	215
Sarah Knickerbocker, d. Stephen & Betsey, b. May 10, 1820	2	215
Thomas, d. July 13, 1832	2	315
COLBORN, Sarah, of Windham, m. Ezekiel **ORMESBY**, Nov. 27, 1756	1	250
COLGROVE, Elizabeth, of Canterbury, m. Capt. Isaac **TUCKENMEN**, of Sterling, Mar. 1, 1824, by George W. Appleton	2	79
COLLINS, Esther, single woman had s. Thaddeus **BRUCE**, b. Feb. 28, 1793	1	114
Service, m. Benjamin **MOTT**, Aug. 29, 1787, at Windham	1	181
COLTON, Sarah, d. Thomas & Lydia, b. Jan. 18, 1772	1	111
COMIES, David C., m. Emily G. **AUSTIN**, b. of Canterbury, Mar. 11, 1832, by Rev. Demis Platt	2	16
CONE, David P., of Chatham, m. Mary Ann **FOX**, of Columbia, Nov. 14, 1853, by Thomas K. Peck, J. P.	2	20
CONGDON, John, of R. I., m. Thankful **CONGDON**, of Canterbury, Mar. 4, 1827, by Israel G. Rose	2	15
Thankful, of Preston, m. Lebbeus **ENSWORTH**, Sept. 14, 1802	1	133
Thankful, of Canterbury, m. John **CONGDON**, of R. I., Mar. 4, 1827, by Israel G. Rose	2	15
COOK, Anne, m. Daniel **FITCH**, Mar. 5, 1718/19	1	138
Barzillai, s. Richard & Mary, b. Sept. 28, 1735	1	105
Eunice, m. Sam[ue]l **ADAMS**, Jr., Feb. 8, 1770	1	52
Mary, d. Richard & Mary, b. May 3, 1739	1	106
Massa, s. Richard & Mary, b. Apr. 17, 1737	1	105
Nathaniel, s. Nathaniel & Sabra, b. June 14, 1800	1	115
COOPER, Aaron G., m. Sophia A. **PELLET**, Mar. 27, 1842, by Rev. Asa King, Westminster	2	18
Eunice, d. Will[ia]m & Ruth, b. Apr. 17, 1752	1	108
Melara B., m. Phinehas F. **SMITH**, Nov. 4, 1841, by Rev. Asa King, Westminster	2	74
Will[ia]m, m. Ruth **ADAMS**, Mar. 22, 1751	1	100
COPELAND, COPLAND, COPELIN, Abner, s. William & Sarah, b. Nov. 16, 1765	1	110
Abner, s. William & Sarah, d. Nov. 16, 1765	1	118
Anne, d. W[illia]m & Sarah, b. May 21, 1775	1	112
Asa, s. William & Sarah, b. Feb. 22, 1763	1	109
David, s. W[illia]m & Sarah, b. Feb. 21, 1768	1	110
Dilano, s. W[illia]m & Sarah, b. July 12, 1770	1	111

	Vol.	Page
COPELAND, COPLAND, COPELIN, (cont.)		
Delano, s. W[illia]m & Sarah, d. Feb. 26, 1773	1	119
Smith, s. William & Sarah, b. Jan. 15, 1773	1	111
Thankful, d. William & Sarah, b. Apr. 17, 1760	1	109
CORNING, Levi C., of Lisbon, m. Fanny **SAFFORD**, of		
Canterbury, Mar. 25, 1832, by Rev. Demis Platt	2	16
CORY, [see also **CAREY**], Martin, Jr., of Plainfield, m. Lucy		
GREEN, of Canterbury, Aug. 4, 1844, by Solomon		
Payne, J. P.	2	18
COTTON, Ezra, s. Thomas & Lydia, b. July 14, 1776	1	112
Martha, d. Tho[ma]s & Lydia, b. Apr. 17, 1774	1	112
Thomas, m. Lydia **BATES**, Apr. 11, 1771	1	101
COVERLY, Samuel, Jr., of Boston, Mass., m. Jane C. **CLARK**, of		
Canterbury, Aug. 10, 1828, by Rev. James R. Wheelock	2	15
CRAIG, John H., s. William & Sophia, b. May 28, 1840	2	215
William, of Plainfield, m. Sophia **RAYNSFORD**, Apr. 1, 1838,		
by Rev. Asa King, Westminster	2	17
William, of Plainfield, m. Sophia **RAYNSFORD**, Apr. 1, 1838,		
by Rev. Asa King, Westminster	2	40
CRAINE, CRAIN, John, m. Abigail **FALKNER**, Oct. 24, 1799, at		
Brooklyn	1	102
John, s. John & Abigail, b. July 25, 1800	1	114
Lucius, s. John & Abigail, b. Nov. 22, 1801	1	115
Mary, d. John & Abigail, b. Nov. 28, 1805	1	115
CRANDALL, Benjamin, m. Mary Eliza **BROWN**, b. of Canterbury,		
Sept. 23, 1827, by Luther Paine, J. P.	2	15
Christopher, m. Julia **HERRICK**, Jan. 13, 1833, by Rev.		
Asa King, Westminster	2	16
Christopher, m. Ruby **HERRICK**, Nov. 24, 1844, by Walter		
Williams, J. P.	2	18
Hezekiah, m. Almira **BURGESS**, b. of Canterbury, Sept. 4,		
1839, by Rev. Charles J. Warren	2	17
Hezekiah, m. Patience **LeVALLEY**, Mar. 22, 1852, by Rev.		
Robert C. Learned	2	19
John, m. Betsey **FRINK**, b. of Canterbury, Jan. 15, 1846,		
by Samuel S. Hough, J. P.	2	18
Joseph B., m. Maria T. **HER[R]ICK**, Mar. 18, 1839, by Rev.		
Asa King	2	17
Lucy Ann, m. Cranston L. **BURDICK**, b. of Canterbury, Feb.		
11, 1832, by Rev. Demis Platt	2	9
Robert H., of Exeter, R. I., m. Harriet **WILLOUGHBY**, of		
Canterbury, Oct. 16, 1827, by Andrew T. Judson, J. P.	2	15
[CRANE], [see under **CRAINE**]		
CROSBY, John, m. Polly **LASSEL**, of Windham, Apr. 1, 1795	1	102
Polly, d. John & Polly, b. June 10, 1796	1	114
CROSS, Susan, m. Peter **PARK**, Jr., Feb. 17, 1814	1	194
CUMMINGS, CUMMINS, Benj[ami]n, s. Stephen & Mary, b. May		
1, 1747	1	107

	Vol.	Page
CUMMINGS, CUMMINS, (cont.)		
Charles M., of Hampton, m. Sybel **CADY,** of Canterbury,		
Jan. 21, 1824, by Rev. Thomas J. Murdock	2	15
CUNDALL, [see also **CANDALL** and **KENDALL**], William		
Sisson, s. Joseph, b. Sept. 10, 1816	1	116
CURIAN,, Minerva B., of Providence, R. I., m. Benjamin F.		
JONES, of Coventry, R. I., Oct. 19,. 1834, by Rev. Otis		
C. Whiton	2	43
CURTIS, CURTISS, Abigail, m. Jonathan **HIDE,** Jan. 28, 1723/4	1	192
Abigail, d. Jno, Jr. & Hannah, b. Nov. 17, 1753	1	112
Anne, d. [Jno, Jr. & Hannah], b. Dec. 24, 1767	1	112
Ebenezer, s. [Jno. Jr. & Hannah], b. Mar. 4, 1765	1	112
Elisha, s. [Jno. Jr. & Hannah], b. July 3, 1772	1	112
Elizabeth, m. Isaac **CLEVELAND,** July 17, 1699	1	100
Elizabeth, d. [Jno. Jr. & Hannah], b. Feb. 18, 1770	1	112
Eppaph[r]as, s. [Jno. Jr. & Hannah], b. Oct. 12, 1762	1	112
Filura, twin with Josiah, d. [Frederic & Lurana], b.		
July 17, 1769	1	111
Frederic, s. [Jno. Jr. & Hannah], b. July 3, 1760	1	112
Frederic, m. Luranah **HIDE,** Dec. 17, 1760	1	101
Hannah, d. [Frederic & Lurana], b. Feb. 28, 1766	1	111
Isaac, s. Frederic & Lurana, b. July 28, 1762	1	109
Isaac, s. Frederic & Luranah, d. Dec. [ ]	1	118
John, Jr., m. Hannah **MOSELEY,** May 29, 1753	1	101
John, s. [Jno. Jr. & Hannah], b. Sept. 11, 1755	1	112
John, Esq., d. June 22, 1774. "Suddenly in a fit"	1	119
Josiah, twin with Filura, s. [Frederic & Lurana], b.		
July 17, 1769	1	111
Lurana, d. Frederic & Lurana, b. Apr. 18, 1764	1	111
Lurana, m. Job **BARSTOW,** Dec. 9, 1783	1	71
Moseley, of Windham, m. Mary E. **ROBINSON,** of		
Canterbury, Aug. 27, 1834, by Rev. Robert C. Learned	2	20
Philura, [see under Filura]		
Samuel, s. [Jno. Jr. & Hannah], b. Aug. 22, 1757	1	112
CUSHMAN, Daniel, m. Mary **BOWMAN,** Dec. 31, 1777	1	101
Dan[ie]l Sheldon, s. Dan[ie]l & Molly, b. Jan. 22 , 1780	1	113
John Jamieson, s. Daniel & Molly, b. Mar. 23, 1784	1	113
Nancy, d. [Daniel & Molly], b. Feb. 26, 1786	1	113
Sarah, d. Dan[ie]l & Mary, b. Feb. 1, 1778	1	113
Seth, s. Isaac & Sarah, b. May 14, 1782	1	113
CUTLER, Beulah, m. Jeames **DARBE,** Jr., Dec. 29, 1745	1	120
Charles, m. Statera **ADAMS,** Jan. 24, 1836, by Charles		
Adams, J. P.	2	17
Clarissa, m. Moses B. **ADAMS,** Mar. 20, 1828	1	53
Clarissa, m. Moses B. **ADAMS,** b. of Canterbury, Mar. 20,		
1828, by Rev. Israel G. Rose	2	2
Dorcas, m. Dan[ie]l **HERRINGTON,** Jr., Sept. 14, 1769	1	155
Francis Marylla, d. Thomas & Sally, b. Sept. 14, 1805	1	115

	Vol.	Page
CUSHMAN, (cont.)		
Simon, of Plainfield, m. Loisa **GORDON**, of Canterbury,		
Oct. 7, 1832, by Rev. Demis Platt	2	16
Thomas, m. Sally **SIMMS**, Apr. 14, 1801(?)	1	102
William Carlos, s. Thomas & Sally, b. Mar. 19, 1809	1	115
DAINS, DEAINS, [see under **DEAN**]		
DARBEE, DARBE, DARBY, Abigail, d. [William & Abigail], b.		
Feb. 11, 1758	1	126
Abigail, d. [William & Abigail], d. May 18, 1760	1	131
Abigail, d. James, Jr. & Beulah, b. June 15, 1767	1	127
Alpheas, s. James & Beulah, b. May 13, 1759	1	126
Ellis (Alice), d. [William & Abigail], b. Dec. 6, 1764	1	126
Eleis (Alice), d. William & Abigail, d. Jan. 21, 1766	1	131
Anne, d. Rufus & Dorothy, b. July 28, 1791	1	129
Annis, d. W[illia]m & Abigail, b. Feb. 3, 1769	1	126
Asa, s. [William & Abigail], b. Oct. 15, 1762	1	126
Asael, s. [James & Beulah], b. Dec. 24, 1764	1	126
Benjamin, s. [Jesse & Lydia], b. Aug. 17, 1765	1	126
Betsey, d. Rufus & Dorothy, b. Mar. 1, 1782	1	128
Betsey, d. Rufus & Dorothy, b. Mar. 1, 1782	1	129
Blanchard, s. William & Elizabeth, b. July 27, 1734	1	122
Daniel, d. Reuben & Sibael, b. Sept. 3, 1746	1	123
Daniel, d. Reuben & Sibilah, d. Mar. 27, 1747	1	131
Daniel, s. [Jesse & Lydia], b. Oct. 25, 1774	1	128
David, s. [Jeames & Beulah], b. Jan. 15, 1754	1	123
David, s. James & Beulah, d. Sept. 23, 1755	1	131
Dorkis, d. Sam[ue]l & Susanna, b. June 12, 1760	1	125
Eleanor, d. Jeames & Beulah, b. Oct. 26, 1746	1	123
Eleanor, d. James & Sarah, b. July 17, 1766	1	128
Ele[a]nor, s. W[illia]m & Abigail, b. Dec. 6, 1766	1	126
Eleazer, s. James & Eleanor, b. July 6, 1731	1	122
Eleis, see under Alice		
Eli, s. [Jesse & Lydia], b. July 8, 1772	1	128
Elizabeth, d. William & Elizabeth, b. Apr. 26, 1719	1	122
Elizabeth, m. Capt. Jabez **FITCH**, Jan. 14, 1754	1	138
Ellis, see under Alice		
Ervin, s. W[illia]m & Abigail, b. July 2, 1774	1	127
Ervin, s. William & Abigail, d. Nov. 3, 1776	1	132
Hannah, d. Jesse & Lydia, b. Dec. 17, 1763	1	126
James, s. James & Eleanor, b. May 26, 1724	1	122
Jeames, Jr., m. Beulah **CUTLER**, Dec. 29, 1745	1	120
Jedediah, s. William & Elizabeth, b. Aug. 25, 1730	1	122
Jedediah, m. Lucretia **CLEVELAND**, Jan. 2, 1755	1	120
Jerusha, d. Sam[ue]l & Susannah, b. Nov. 12, 1757	1	124
Jesse, s. James & Eleanor, b. Jan. 14, 1737/8	1	123
Jesse, s. [James & Beulah], b. Jan. 15, 1762	1	126
John, s. William & Elizabeth, b. Feb. 6, 1723	1	122
John, s. Sam[ue]l & Susanna, b. July 7, 1751	1	124

	Vol.	Page

DARBEE, DARBE, DARBY, (cont.)

Levinnah, d. Robert & Mehetable, b. [ ]. 1760 (Arnold
Copy had "Levinnah **DURGY**". Corrected by L. B. B. 1 125

Lucy, d. Robert & Mehitable, b. Oct. 16, 1758 (Arnold
Copy has "Lucy **DURGY**". Corrected by L. B. B. 1 124

Lydia, d. Jesse & Lydia, b. July 22, 1767 1 128
Martha, d. William & Elizabeth, b. Feb. 6, 1725 1 122
Martha, m. Joseph **DYAR**, Feb. 1, 1748/9 1 120
Mary, d. Will[ia]m & Elizabeth, b. Mar. 16, 1721 1 122
Mary, d. [William & Abigail], b. Oct. 30, 1759 1 125
Mary, d. William & Abigail, d. Nov. 27, 1759 1 131
Mehetable, d. Robert & Mehitable, b. May 27, 1756 1 124
Molly, d. Sam[ue]l & Susanna, b. July 21, 1755 1 124
Olive, d. Will[ia]m & Abigail, b. Apr. 9, 1750 1 124
Olive, m. Daniel **BACON**, Apr. 27, 1777 1 71
Phinehas, s. Reuben & Sibelah, b. Apr. 19, 1748 1 123
Polly, d. [Rufus & Dorothy], b. Oct. 7, 1786 1 129
Reuben, s. Rufus & Dorothy, b. Sept. 20, 1788 1 129
Robert, m. Mehetable **PAINE**, June 3, 1755 1 120
Roger, s. William & Abigail, b. Oct. 16, 1760 1 125
Rufus, s. [Rufus & Dorothy], b. Feb. 2, 1784 1 129
Ruth, d. William & Elizabeth, b. Sept. 26, 1732 1 122
Ruth, m. Sam[ue]l **CLEVELAND**, May 7, 1751 1 100
Samuel, s. James & Eleanor, b. Oct. 27, 1727 1 122
Samuel, d. July 17, 1767. "Killed by thunder and lightning" 1 131
Samuel, s. [Jesse & Lydia], b. July 25, 1769 1 128
Sarah, d. James & Beulah, b. July 23, 1756 1 124
Sarah, d. John & Mary, b. Apr. 5, 1774 1 127
Semanthe, d. Jedediah & Lucretia, b. Mar. 23, 1755 1 124
Shadrack, s. Will[ia]m & Abigail, b. Mar. 25, 1752 1 122
Shedreck, s. William & Abigail, b. Mar. 25, 1752
1756* (*So written in the Arnold Copy) 1 126
Squire, s. [Jeames & Beulah], b. Aug. 2, 1751 1 123
Will[ia]m, s. Will[ia]m & Elizabeth, b. July 10, 1727 1 122
William, s. [Jeames & Beulah], b. Mar. 19, 1749 1 123
Will[ia]m, m. Abigail **CLEVELAND**, Nov. 9, 1749 1 120
William, s. Will[ia]m & Abigail, b. May 18, 1756 1 124

DARLING, Olive, of Canterbury, m. Thomas **LATHROP,** of
Griswold, Feb. 19, 1826, by Sam[ue]l L. Hough, J. P. 2 51

DAVENPORT, Abigail, d. Paul & Abigail, b. Feb. 2, 1710 1 122
Abigail, m. Thomas **ADAMS**, Feb. 23, 1714/15 1 51
Abigail, d. Thomas & Mary, b. Apr. 7, 1735 1 122
Abigail, w. Paul, d. Apr. 11, 1747 1 131
Abigail, d. Paul & Elizabeth, b. Nov. 27, 1750 1 124
Abigail, d. Paul & Elizabeth, d. Mar. 7, 1752 1 131
Benjamin, s. Paul & Elizabeth, b. Aug. 16, 1772 1 127
Betsey, d. Samuel & Elizabeth, b. Sept. 10, 1788 1 129
Caroline, d. [Paul & Susanna], b. Dec. 20, 1799 1 130

	Vol.	Page

DAVENPORT, (cont.)

	Vol.	Page
Caroline, m. Capt. Elisha **ADAMS**, of Groton, June 1, 1828	1	53
Caroline, of Canterbury, m. Capt. Elisha **ADAMS**, of Groton, June 1, 1828, by Rev. J. R. Murdock	2	2
Charity, d. Charles & Waitstill, b. Sept. 5, 1749	1	124
Charles, s. Paul & Abigail, b. July 2, 1717	1	122
Charles, d. Nov. 4, 1754	1	131
Charles, s. Paul & Elizabeth, b. Apr. 3, 1755	1	124
Charles, m. Mabel **WILSON**, Mar. 3, 1791, at Brooklyn	1	121
Charles, d. Sept. 1, 1798, at Saratoga	1	132
Deliver[an]ce, d. Thomas & Mary, b. May 30, 1731	1	122
Elijah, s. Charles & Waitstill, b. Apr. 27, 1748	1	123
Elijah, s. Joseph & Alice, b. Feb. 13, 1790	1	129
Eliphalet, s. Paul & Elizabeth, b. Aug. 13, 1764	1	125
Eliphalet, s. Paul & Elizabeth, d. Dec. 15, 1766	1	131
Eliza, d. July 20, 1775	1	132
Elizabeth, d. Paul & Elizabeth, b. May 1, 1757	1	124
Elizabeth, d. Dec. 6, 1799	1	132
Eunice, d. Thomas & Mary, b. Sept. 26, 1717	1	122
Eunice, d. Paul & Elizabeth, b. Feb. 17, 1767	1	126
Eunice, m. Roswell **ADAMS**, Nov. 23, 17[ ]	1	52
Gay, s. [Charles & Mabel], b. Sept. 16, 1797	1	129
Joseph, s. Paul & Elizabeth, b. Aug. 15, 1748	1	123
Joseph, m. Alice **BENNETT**, Dec. 25, 1783	1	121
Joseph, d. Oct. 26, 1798	1	132
Lucinda, twin with Orinda, d. Charles & Mabel, b. June 27, 1791	1	129
Lucretia, d. [Charles & Mabel], b. Mar. 2, 1795	1	129
Lucy, d. [Joseph & Alice], b. Jan. 9, 1797	1	130
Mary, d. Thomas & Mary, b. Dec. 25, 1715	1	122
Mary, d. Paul & Abigail, b. June 21, 1720	1	122
Mary, d. Paul & Abigail, d. Dec. 12, 1721	1	131
Mary, m. Sam[ue]l **WILSON**, Sept. 25, 1734	1	236
Mary, d. Charles & Waitstill, b. Sept. 14, 1751	1	124
Nabby, d. Sam[ue]l & Elizabeth, b. Dec. 22, 1790	1	129
Orinda, twin with Lucinda, d. Charles & Mabel, b. June 27, 1791	1	129
Orinda, m. Joseph **FARNHAM**, Dec. 5, 1837, by Rev. Charles J. Warren	2	32
Paul, m. Abigail **ADAMS**, July 28, 1709	1	120
Paul, s. Paul & Abigail, b. Nov. 16, 1724	1	122
Paul, m. Elizabeth **FROST**, July 1, 1747	1	120
Paul, d. Oct. 10, 1754	1	131
Paul, s. Paul & Elizabeth, b. Feb. 28, 1762	1	125
Paul, Jr., m. Susanna **ADAMS**, Apr. 4, 1790	1	121
Paul, d. Apr. 12, 1800	1	132
Phinehas, s. Paul & Eliza, b. Feb. 22, 1769	1	126
Phinehas, s. Joseph & Alice, b. Jan. 22, 1785	1	129

	Vol.	Page
DAVENPORT, (cont.)		
Polly, d. [Joseph & Alice], b. July 10, 1794	1	130
Rufus Wilson, s. Charles & Mabel, b. Feb. 24, 1793	1	129
Sally, d. [Joseph & Alice], b. May 4, 1787	1	129
Samuel, s. Paul & Abigail, b. Mar. 19, 1721/2	1	122
Samuel, s. Paul & Abigail, d. Jan. 21, 1724/5	1	131
Sam[ue]l, s. Charles & Waitstill, b. Jan. 15, 1746	1	123
Sam[ue]l, s. Charles & Waitstill, d. July 29, 1749	1	131
Samuel, s. Paul & Elizabeth, b. Dec. 10, 1752	1	122
Samuel, m. Elizabeth **WILLIAMS**, Dec. 20, 1787	1	121
Sarah, d. Paul & Elizabeth, b. Oct. 24, 1759	1	124
Sarah, m. Bradford **ADAMS**, Apr. 6, 1780	1	52
Submit, d. Thomas & Mary, b. Feb. 5, 1727	1	122
Susan, d. Paul & Susanna, b. June 26, 1794	1	130
Susan, m. Guy F. **ADAMS**, Aug. 6, 1820	1	53
Susan, m. Guy F. **ADAMS**, Aug. 6, 1820, by Asa Meech	2	1
Waitstill, d. [Charles & Waitstill], b. Dec. 8, 1753	1	123
Waitstill, d. Charles & Waitstill, d. Nov. 1, 1754	1	131
DAVIS, DAVICE, Abby, d. [Elisha & Susan], b. Oct. 28, 1826	2	221
Adaline, d. [Elisha & Susan], b. Sept. 18, 1824	2	221
Ann Mariah, of Boston, m. Charles F. **HARRIS**, Mar. 28, 1833, by Rev. Asa King, Westminster	2	40
Daniel, m. Elizabeth **LATHROP**, Sept. 16, 1732	1	120
Dan[ie]l, Dr., d. June 1, 1777	1	132
Elizabeth, d. Daniel & Elizabeth, b. Oct. 13, 1733	1	122
Elizabeth, d. Dr. Dan[ie]l, d. May 12, 1777	1	132
Elizabeth, wid, Dr. Daniel, d. July 25, 1777	1	132
Ephraim, s. Ephraim & Mary, d. Oct. 5, 1715	1	131
Ephraim, s. [Daniel & Elizabeth], b. Apr. 2, 1742	1	125
Esther, d. Jonathan & Mehitable, b. Oct. 5, 1765	1	126
Hannah, d. Ephraim & Mary, b. Feb. 27, 1710/11	1	122
Jonathan, s. Daniel & Elizabeth, b. Apr. 9, 1735	1	122
Jonathan, m. Mehetable **RICHARDS**, of Norwich, May 20, 1762	1	120
Jonathan, m. Sarah **DAVISON**, Dec. 5, 1776	1	120
Lucy, d. Jona & Mehetable, b. Mar. 6, 1768	1	126
Lucy, m. Elijah **WHITE**, May 19, 1791	1	236
Mary, w. Ephraim, d. Aug. 19, 1732	1	131
Mary, d. [Daniel & Elizabeth], b. Apr. 4, 1738	1	125
Mary, d. Jona & Mehetable, b. Oct. 13, 1770	1	127
Mehetable, d. Daniel & Elizabeth, b. May 14, 1737	1	125
Mehetable, d. Daniel & Elizabeth, d. May 15, 1737	1	131
Mehetable, w. Jona[than], d. May 25, 1774	1	132
Sarah, d. [Daniel & Elizabeth], b. July 3, 1740	1	125
Sarah, d. Jona & Sarah, b. Apr. 27, 1781	1	128
Sarah, m. John **MARTIN**, Mar. 22, 1807	1	181
William, s. Elisha & Susan, b. Aug. 26, 1822	2	221
Zerviah, d. Jonathan & Mehetable, b. Oct. 30, 1763	1	125

	Vol.	Page
DAVIS, DAVICE, (cont.)		
----, wid., d. Jan. 20, 1767	1	131
DAVISON, Beriah, s. [Peter & Abigail], b. July 12, 1780	1	128
Ebenezer, s. Peter & Abigail, b. Oct. 17, 1769	1	127
Ephraim, s. Peter & Abigail, b. Dec. 5, 1772	1	127
Huldah, d. Peter & Abigail, b. Apr. 9, 1778	1	128
Mary, m. Thomas **PELLET**, Oct. 6, 1764	1	193
Peter, m. Abigail **WOODARD**, Apr. 28, 1768	1	120
Peter, s. Peter & Abigail, b. June 23, 1775	1	128
Philenia, m. Thomas **BRADFORD**, Nov. 29, 1788	1	73
Sarah, m. Jonathan **DAVIS**, Dec. 5, 1776	1	120
DEAN, DEANS, DAINS, DEANS, DEANE, Allen, of Killingly, m.		
Olive **GREEN**, Jan. 31, 1794	1	121
Asa, s. Ebenezer & Mary, b. June 7, 1764	1	127
C[h]loe, d. [Ebenezer & Mary], b. Nov. 11, 1767	1	127
Coddington, m. Cynthia **WRIGHT**, b. of Canterbury, Jan. 23,		
1834, by Rev. Otis C. Whiton	2	21
Cynthia, of Canterbury, m. Daniel **TEFT**, of Killingly,		
now resident of Canterbury, June 18, 1837, by Rev. C. J.		
Warren	2	79
Deborah, m. Nathaniel **GATES**, Feb. 22, 173[ ]	1	149
Eben[eze]r, m. Deborah **MONROW**, Nov. 9, 1738	1	120
Ebenezer, m. Mary **DURFFEY**, Nov. 14, 1763	1	120
Eleanor, d. Josiah & Annar, b. July 18, 1768	1	126
Faxon, m. Mehetable **CLEVELAND**, Oct. 15, 1746	1	120
Hannah, d. Eben[eze]r & Mary, b. Sept. 28, 1748	1	123
Hannah, m. Jonathan **T[H]OMPSON**, Jan. 10, 1748/9	1	229
Hannah had s. John **ASHCRAFT**, b. June 15, 1769	1	127
Hannah, single woman, had s. John **ASHCRAFT**, who d.		
Sept. 12, 1769	1	131
Henry, m. Margaret **BATES**, Apr. 18, 1744	1	120
Henry, s. Henry & Margaret, b. May 19, 1746	1	123
Jared, s. Eben[eze]r, Jr. & Mary, b. June 19, 1785	1	129
John, s. Eben[eze]r, Jr. & Mary, b. July 5, 1779	1	128
Jonathan, s. Henry & Margaret, b. May 2, 1744	1	123
Joseph, s. [Faxon & Mehetable], b. Feb. 17, 1748/9	1	123
Joseph, s. Faxon & Mehitable, d. Feb. 11, 1750/1	1	131
Josiah, m. Anna **LUDINGTON**, Sept. 26, 1765	1	120
Josiah, s. Josiah & Anor, b. Mar. 30, 1767	1	127
Lavina, d. Eben[eze]r, Jr. & Mary, b. Mar. 5, 1777	1	128
Lucy, d. Eben[eze]r, Jr. & Mary, b. Oct. 15, 1775	1	127
Lurana, d. Josiah & Anner, b. Mar. 22, 1774	1	127
Luranah, d. Josiah & Anner, d. Sept. 13, 1775	1	132
Lydia, m. Samuel **BRADFORD**, Jan. 19, 1778	1	71
Lydia, d. Eben[eze]r, Jr. & Mary, b. July 22, 1782	1	128
Martha, d. Feb. 26, 1822	2	321
Mary, d. Faxon & Mehetable, b. Aug. 12, 1744	1	123
Mary, d. [Faxon & Mehitable, d. Mar. 6, 1750/1	1	131

	Vol.	Page
DEAN, DEANS, DAINS, DEAINS, DEANE, (cont.)		
Mary, m. Elijah **ROBBINS**, Apr. 2, 1827, by Andrew T.		
Judson, J. P.	2	67
Mercy, wid., d. May 1, 1773	1	132
Nathan, m. Lucy **SHARP**, Nov. 16, 1774	1	120
Samuel, s. Faxon & Mehitable, b. Apr. 28, 1751	1	124
Willard, s. Nathan & Lucy, b. Oct. 19, 1775	1	127
DELOP, DELAP, Benjamin, s. James & Mercy, b. Sept. 11, 1740	1	124
Benj[ami]n, d. Jan. 4, 1768	1	131
Benjamin, s. James & Susanna, b. July 9, 1786	1	129
James, m. Mary **TEBBETTS**, Feb. [ ], 1733	1	120
James, s. James & Mercy, b. May 13, 1736	1	122
James, m. Susanna **FROST**, Apr. 25, 1771	1	120
James, s. James & Susanna, b. May 7, 1778	1	128
James, s. James & Susanna, d. June 4, 1779	1	132
James, s. James & Susanna, b. May 13, 1783	1	129
James, Capt., d. Oct. 9, 1801	1	132
Joseph, d. Feb. 24, 1752	1	131
Mary, d. James & Susanna, b. July 24, 1780	1	128
Mary, m. Araunah **BRADFORD**, Mar. 10, 1802	1	72
Mercy, d. Benj[ami]n & Catharine, b. June 27, 1768	1	126
Mercy, d. James & Susanna, b. Jan. 29, 1774	1	127
Mercy, d. Benj[ami]n & Catharine, d. June 14, 1778	1	132
Susannah, d. James & Susanna, b. Dec. 4, 1771	1	127
Susanna, m. Jabez **SAFFORD**, Nov. 27, 1794	1	215
DEMING, Eunice J., of Canterbury, m. Horace L. **WILSON**, of		
Windham, July 8, 1850, by Rev. R. S. Hazen, of		
Westminster	2	89
William T., of Windham, m. Isabella **ADAMS**, of Canterbury,		
Sept. 15, 1822, by Erastus Learned	2	21
DENISON, William M., of Sterling, m. Mary **ROBBINS**, of		
Brooklyn, May 10, 1835, by Rev. O. C. Whiton	2	21
DEWEY, Abigail, of Lebanon, m. Jonas **BOND**, Sept. 3, 1752	1	70
Abigail, d. Josiah & Huldah, b. Apr. 6, 1771	1	127
Elizabeth, d. Josiah & Huldah, b. June 11, 1775	1	127
Huldah, d. Josiah & Huldah, b. Mar. 9, 1761	1	125
Joel, s. Josiah & Huldah, b. Aug. 30, 1777	1	128
Joseph, s. Josiah & Huldah, b. June 3, 1759	1	124
Josiah, m. Huldy **FROST**, Jan. 3, 1769	1	120
Josiah, s. Josiah & Huldah, b. Sept. 24, 1759	1	127
Mary, d. Josiah & Huldah, b. July 2, 1765	1	126
Mehetable, d. Josiah & Huldah, b. [ ] 22, 1763	1	125
DEWING, Abijah, m. Talitha **WOOD**, b. of Canterbury, Nov. 30,		
1842, by M. Byrne	2	22
Albert, s. [Abijah & Abigail], b. Aug. 29, 1819	2	221
Albert, m. Nancy **ALLEN**, May 21, 1848, by Rev. Asa King,		
Westminster	2	22
Betsey M., m. Thomas K. **CHANDLER**, Sept. 5, 1838, by		

	Vol.	Page
DEWING, (cont.)		
Rev. Asa King, Westminster	2	17
Hezekiah, s. [Abijah & Abigail], b. June 2, 1823	2	221
Mary M., m. John **WITTER**, Sept. 3, 1834, by Rev. Asa King	2	86
Mary Maria, d. Abijah & Abigail, b. Mar. 22, 1815	2	221
Nancy Ann, d. [Abijah & Abigail], b. Apr. 30, 1821	2	221
Oliver Morse, s. [Abijah & Abigail], b. Aug. 6, 1829	2	221
DIMMOCK, DIMMICK, DIMOCK, Anna, d. [Rufus & Clarissa],		
b. Apr. 18, 1809	1	130
Anna, m. Horace A. **KIES**, of Killingly, Mar. 31, 1840,		
by Rev. Asa King, Westminster	2	47
Anne, m. Asa **BUTT**, Feb. 17, 1791	1	72
Clarace, d. Thomas & Sibbel, b. Jan. 8, 1762	1	125
Clarissa, w. Rufus, d. Oct. 12, 1811	1	132
Daniel Meach, s. Rufus Leveret & Ruhama, b. Nov. 24, 1817	1	130
Esther, d. Thomas & Sibbel, b. May 10, 1767	1	127
John Paine, s. Tho[ma]s & Sibbel, b. Sept. 20, 1768	1	126
John Paine, s. Tho[ma]s & Sibbel, d. May 31, 1773	1	132
John Paine, s. Tho[ma]s & Sibbel, b. Oct. 12, 1773	1	127
Rufus, s. [Thomas & Sibbel], b. Jan. 4, 1763	1	125
Rufus L., m. Abby H. **MORGAN**, Nov. 22, 1836, by Rev. Asa		
King, Westminster	2	21
Rufus Leverett, s. Rufus & Anne, b. Aug. 1, 1785	1	129
Rufus Leveret, m. Clarrissa **LEDYARD**, Nov. 12, 1806	1	121
Rufus Leveret, m. Ruhama **MEACH**, Mar. 3, 1817	1	121
Rufus Leveret, s. [Rufus Leveret & Ruhama], b. Aug. 15, 1819	1	130
Thomas, m. Sibbel **PAINE**, Mar. 12, 1761	1	120
Thomas, s. Rufus & Clarissa, b. Apr. 1, 1807	1	130
DIXON, Elizabeth, so called, had d. Mary **GOSSON**, so called,		
b. June 4, 1743	1	150
Elizabeth, so called, had s. Edward **GOSSON**, so called,		
b. May 25, 1747	1	150
Elizabeth had d. Mary **GOSSON**, who d. July 3, 1749	1	154
Elizabeth, so called, had s. Ichabod **GIBSON**, so called,		
b. Feb. 21, 1752	1	150
Elizabeth, so called, had d. Mary **CAMMEL**, so called, b.		
Dec. 30, 1753	1	150
DODGE, Asa, s. Edward & Lois, b. June 2, 1767		126
Christefor, s. John & Lydia, b. July 6, 1765	1	126
Christofor, s. John & Lydia, d. Nov. 9, 1765	1	131
Edward, m. Louice **MORGAN**, Oct. 6, 1763	1	120
Elizabeth, d. [John & Lydia], b. Feb. 2, 1756	1	126
Elizabeth, d. John & Lydia, d. Aug. 23, 1772	1	132
Elizabeth, d. Josias Rogers & Zerviah, b. Apr. 1, 1784	1	129
Israel, s. [John & Lydia], b. Sept. 3, 1760	1	126
Jeriel, s. [John & Lydia], b. Aug. 1, 1768	1	126
Joel, d. Oct. 26, 1770	1	131
John, m. Lydia **ROGERS**, Oct. 23, 1748	1	120

	Vol.	Page
DODGE, (cont.)		
John, s. [John & Lydia], b. July 12, 1751	1	126
John, m. Elizabeth **WILLES**, Dec. 3, 1770	1	120
Jordan, s. John & Lydia, b. Aug. 6, 1749	1	126
Jordon, m. Lucy **ADAMS**, Oct. 22, 1769	1	120
Josiah Rogers, s. [John & Lydia], b. Sept. 28, 1762	1	126
Josias Rogers, m. Zerviah **WILLES**, of Windham, Sept. 24, 1783	1	121
Lydia, d. [John & Lydia], b. May 18, 1758	1	126
Lydia, w. John, d. Sept. 3, 1770	1	131
Nehemiah, s. John & Lydia, b. July 3, 1770	1	127
Nehemiah, s. John & Lydia, b. July 3, 1770	1	128
Peter, s. [John & Lydia], b. Nov. 17, 1753	1	126
Peter, s. John & Lydia, d. Dec. 18, 1759	1	131
Roger, s. Edward & Louisa, b. Jan. 27, 1766	1	126
Roger, s. Edward & Lois, d. June 10, 1766	1	131
Tallethy, d. Edward & Louice, b. Apr. 11, 1764	1	125
DORRANCE, Charles, of Brooklyn, m. Jennette **SHARP**, of Canterbury, Feb. 26, 1849, by Rev. Robert C. Learned	2	23
John E., m. Sarah E. **CARTER**, July 7, 1844, by Rev. Asa King, Westminster	2	22
Otis M., m. Emeline **MEECH**, Nov. 22, 1836, by Rev. Asa King, Westminster	2	21
DOSSET, [see under **DOWSET**]		
DOUGLAS, DOWGLAS, DUGLIS, Abiah, d. Benajah & Abigail, b. Dec. 23, 1735	1	122
Benajah, m. Abigail **SPAULDING**, Aug. 6, 1733	1	120
Lucy, d. Asa & Rebecca, b. Jan. 12, 1746/7	1	123
Mary, d. Benajah & Abigail, b. May 23, 1734	1	122
DOW, Frederick, of Coventry, m. Henrietta **SAFFORD**, Oct. 17, 1841, by Rev. Asa King, Westminster	2	22
DOWING, [see under **DEWING**]		
DOWNER, Betty, of Windham, m. John **CLEVELAND**, Nov. 17, 1762	1	101
DOWNING, Abigail, d. [Ichabod & Abigail], b. June 5, 1735	1	123
Abigail, d. [Peregow & Lydia], b. Jan. 25, 1753	1	124
Abigail, d. [Stephen & Abigail], b. Jan. 29, 1767	1	126
Allis, see under Ellis		
Andrew, s. [Henry & Mary], b. July 1, 1788	1	129
Anna, d. [Daniel & Hannah], b. Oct. 13, 1763	1	125
Artemissa, d. [David & Ruth], b. Mar. 21, 1803	1	130
Asahel, s. [Jona, Jr. & Deborah], b. Sept. 12, 1771	1	127
Benj[ami]n, s. [Ichabod & Abigail], b. June 25, 1739; d. Dec. 3, 1742, in Windham	1	123
Benjamin, s. [Peregow & Lydia], b. May 2, 1756	1	124
Benjamin, m. Rachel **PERKINS**, May 15, 1777	1	121
Betsey, d. David & Ruth, b. July 21, 1796, in Windham	1	130
Cornelius, s. [Jonathan & Elizabeth], b. May 6, 1741	1	123

	Vol.	Page
DOWNING, (cont.)		
Cornelius, s. [Jona, Jr. & Deborah], b. Nov. 3, 1768	1	127
Daniel, s. [Jonathan & Elizabeth], b. May 28, 1733	1	123
Daniel, s. Jonathan & Elizabeth, d. June 25, 1738	1	131
Daniel, s. [Jonathan & Elizabeth], b. May 26, 1739	1	123
Daniel, s. Jonathan & Deborah, b. July 11, 1759	1	125
Daniel, s. Jonathan & Deborah, d. Aug. 10, 1759	1	131
Daniel, m. Hannah **ADAMS**, Oct. 1, 1760	1	120
Daniel, s. [Jonathan & Deborah], b. Aug. 31, 1761	1	125
Daniel, s. [Daniel & Hannah], b. Mar. 24, 1762	1	125
Daniel, m. Elizabeth **DOWNING**, Sept. 26, 1783	1	121
David, s. Stephen & Abigail, b. Feb. 21, 1769	1	127
David, m. Ruth **BINGHAM**, Nov. 2, 1795	1	131
David, s. [David & Ruth], b. Sept. 4, 1797, in Windham	1	130
Deborah, d. Jonathan & Deborah, b. July 12, 1752	1	124
Deborah, m. Richard **WOODARD**, Apr. 30, 1772	1	236
Deidamia, d. [Stephen & Abigail], b. Sept. 3, 1778	1	128
Diedamia, d. [Stephen & Abigail], d. Apr. 12, 1782	1	132
Deidamia, d. [Daniel & Elizabeth], b. May 19, 1793	1	130
Eleazer, s. [Stephen & Abigail], d. Dec. 12, 1786	1	132
Eleazer B., s. [Daniel & Elizabeth], b. Dec. 15, 1787	1	130
Elizabeth, d. [Jonathan & Elizabeth], b. Aug. 6, 1731	1	123
Elizabeth, m. Benjamin **DURFFEY**, Sept. 27, 1756	1	120
Elizabeth, d. Stephen & Abigail, b. Sept. 23, 1764	1	126
Elizabeth, m. Daniel **DOWNING**, Sept. 26, 1783	1	121
Ellis (Alice), d. Phinehas & Ellis, b. Aug. 11, 1757	1	124
Emma, d. [David & Ruth], b. June 5, 1806	1	130
Erastus, s. Levi & Kezia, b. Sept. 1, 1774	1	127
Erastus, s. Levi & Kezia, d. Aug. 8, 1776	1	132
Esther, d. [Dan[ie]l & Hannah], b. June 22, 1773	1	127
Eunice, d. [Phinehas & Elles], b. July 20, 1760	1	125
Fanny, d. Jona & Huldah, b. Nov. 19, 1781	1	128
George L., s. [Daniel & Elizabeth], b. Feb. 28, 1806	1	130
Hannah, d. Daniel & Hannah, b. Mar. 16, 1761	1	125
Harvey, s. [Daniel & Elizabeth], b. Apr. 16, 1791	1	130
Henry, s. [Peregow & Lydia], b. Mar. 5, 1751	1	124
Henry, m. Beulah **KIMBALL**, Feb. 11, 1791	1	121
Ichabod, s. Peregow & Lydia, b. July 28, 1748	1	124
Jairus, s. Jona, Jr. & Deborah, b. Sept. 6, 1766	1	127
James, s. Henry & Mary, b. June 30, 1781	1	128
Jemima, d. Stephen & Abigail, b. June 5, 1771	1	128
Jerusha, d. [Daniel & Elizabeth], b. Feb. 22, 1795	1	130
Joel, s. [Dan[ie]l & Hannah], b. June 3, 1771	1	127
Johanna, m. John **BACKUS**, June 26, 1747	1	69
John, s. Daniel & Hannah, b. Sept. 5, 1766	1	126
Jonathan, s. Jonathan & Elizabeth, b Nov. 28, 1729	1	123
Jonathan, m. Deborah **ADAMS**, Apr. 11, 1751	1	120
Jonathan, s. [Jonathan & Deborah], b. Mar. 10, 1754	1	124

DOWNING, (cont.)

	Vol.	Page
Jonathan, 3rd, m. Huldah **PERKINS**, Jan. 25, 1781	1	121
Jonathan, d. Sept. 24, 1786, ae 83 y.	1	132
Joseph, s. [Ichabod & Abigail], b. Aug. 3, 1737;		
d. Dec. 6, 1742, in Windham	1	123
Joseph, s. [Stephen & Abigail], d. Nov. 9, 1798	1	132
Kezia, d. [Stephen & Abigail], b. Sept. 11, 1773	1	128
Keziah, d. Stephen & Abigail, d. Dec. 31, 1781	1	132
Keziah, d. [Daniel & Elizabeth], b. Aug. 1, 1797	1	130
Levy, s. [Jonathan & Elizabeth], b. Oct. 1, 1746	1	123
Levi, m. Kezia **CLEVELAND**, Nov. 21, 1771	1	120
Levi, s. Levi & Kezia, b. Apr. 20, 1781	1	128
Levi, s. Levi & Keziah, d. Oct. 2, 1781	1	132
Levi, s. Levi & Kezia[h], b. Sept. 23, 1782	1	128
Lois, d. [Henry & Mary], b. Oct. 30, 1784	1	129
Lucretia, d. William & Lucy, b. Dec. 4, 1796	1	129
Lydia, d. Phinehas & Elias*, b. Feb. 17, 1764		
(*Probably Alice)	1	126
Lydia, d. [Henry & Mary], b. June 21, 1786	1	129
Mary, d. Ichabod & Abigail, b. June 4, 1733	1	123
Mary, d. [Dan[ie]l & Hannah], b. July 27, 1769	1	127
Mary, w. Henry, d. Apr. 2, 1791	1	132
Mehetable, d. [Henry & Mary], b. Feb. 11, 1792	1	129
Minor Walden, s. Minor Walden & Abigail, b. [ ] 16, 1789	1	245
Miriam, d. Uriah & Johannah, b. Jan. 18, 1739	1	122
Nancy, d. Cyrus & Zerviah, b. May 8, 1787	1	129
Nancy, d. Nov. 4, 1805	1	132
Nelly, d. Levi & Kezia, b. June 10, 1778	1	128
Olive, d. Dan[ie]l & Hannah, b. Apr. 10, 1768	1	127
Patty, d. [Daniel & Elizabeth], b. Sept. 2, 1800	1	130
Perigo, s. Jonathan & Elizabeth, b. Jan. 9, 1726, at Norwich	1	123
Parego, m. Lydia **ADAMS**, Nov. 25, 1747	1	120
Phinehas, s. [Jonathan & Elizabeth], b. Oct. 11, 1735	1	123
Phinehas, m. Elles (Alice) **ADAMS**, Oct. 18, 1756	1	120
Phinehas, s. Phinehas & Elles, b. Apr. 22, 1759	1	125
Reuben, s. [Jonathan & Elizabeth], b. June 10, 1744	1	123
R[e]uben, s. [Daniel & Hannah], b. Feb. 19, 1765	1	126
Roswell, s. [Daniel & Elizabeth], b. Mar. 23, 1789	1	130
Rufus, s. [Jonathan & Deborah], b. June 24, 1756	1	124
Rufus, s. Benjamin & Rachel, b. Jan. 6, 1778	1	128
Rufus, s. Daniel & Elizabeth, b. July 26, 1784	1	130
Saloma, d. [David & Ruth], b. Sept. 30, 1800	1	130
Sarah, d. Uriah & Johanna, b. Feb. 9, 1740	1	123
Sarah, d. Uriah & Johanna, d. Dec. 6, 1754	1	131
Sarah, d. Ph[i]n[eha]s & Alice, b. May 13, 1770	1	127
Sarah, d. Phin[eha]s & Alice, d. Mar. 27, 1772	1	131
Sarah, d. Phinehas & Alice, b. May 21, 1772	1	127
Sarah, d. Henry & Mary, b. May 25, 1783	1	129

	Vol.	Page
DOWNING, (cont.)		
Siras, s. Jonathan & Deborah, b. Jan. 16, 1765	1	126
Stephen, s. [Jonathan & Elizabeth], b. July 3, 1737	1	123
Stephen, s. [Phinehas & Elles], b. Feb. 20, 1762	1	125
Stephen, s. [Stephen & Abigail], b. Jan. 15, 1776	1	128
Susanna, d. Jonathan & Elizabeth, b. Sept. 14, 1727, at Norwich	1	123
Susannah, m. Sam[ue]l **PARRISH,** Apr. 11, 1751	1	192
Thomas Mervin, s. [David & Ruth], b. Nov. 14, 1807	1	130
William, s. Phin[eha]s & Alice, b. June 8, 1775	1	127
William, m. Lucy **BUTT,** of Brooklyn, Apr. 24, 1796	1	72
Zerviah, w. Cyrus, d. Aug. 19, 1787	1	132
DOWSET, DOSSET, Bettey, d. Joseph & Hannah, b. Dec. 2, 1784	1	129
Bylly, s. Joseph & Hannah, b. July 5, 1790	1	129
Nattila, d. [Joseph & Hannah], b. Mar. 24, 1787	1	129
DRINKWATER, Arthur F., of Blue Hills, Me., m. Susan B. **BARSTOW,** Aug. 30, 1847, by Rev. Asa King, Westminster	2	22
DURFEE, DURFEY, DURFY, DURFFEY, DURFY, Allethea, d. Benj[ami]n & Anna, b. Feb. 18, 1780	1	128
Anna, d. [Benj[ami]n & Anna], b. Sept. 10, 1773	1	128
Asa, s. [Benjamin & Elizabeth], b. Dec. 27, 1761	1	125
Benjamin, m. Elizabeth **DOWNING,** Sept. 27, 1756	1	120
Benj[ami]n, s. [Benjamin & Elizabeth], b. May 22, 1765	1	128
Benjamin, m. Marah **STEVENS,** b. of Lisbon, Feb. 22, 1791	1	121
Daniel, s. [James & Mary], b. Feb. 14, 1759	1	124
Ebenezer, s. Joseph & Abigail, b. Dec. 24, 1761	1	125
Elijah, s. Benjamin & Elizabeth, b. May 26, 1763	1	128
Elisha, s. [Benj[ami]n & Anna], b. Sept. 20, 1771	1	128
Elizabeth, d. [Benjamin & Elizabeth], b. July 26, 1758	1	125
Elizabeth, w. Benjamin, d. Aug. 8, 1768	1	131
Elizabeth, single woman, had s. Jedediah, b. Oct. 22, 1778	1	128
Israel, s. James & Mary, b. Sept. 3, 1754	1	124
James, s. [James & Mary], b. Aug. 9, 1769	1	128
Jedediah, s. Joseph & Abigail, b. June 27, 1758	1	125
Jedediah, s. Elizabeth, single woman, b. Oct. 22, 1778	1	128
John, d. Jan. 11, 1772	1	131
Lovisa, d. James & Mary, b. Sept. 2, 1762	1	128
Lydia, d. Benjamin & Elizabeth, b. Jan. 27, 1757	1	125
Martha, d. [James & Mary], b. Feb. 3, 1757	1	124
Martha, d. James & Mary, d. May 9, 1777	1	132
Mary, m. Ebenezer **DAINS,** Nov. 14, 1763	1	120
Mary, d. [James & Mary], b. Apr. 9, 1766	1	128
Nathan, s. Benj[ami]n & Anna, b. Nov. 21, 1769	1	128
Rufus, s. [Benj[ami]n & Anna], b. Sept. 21, 1776	1	128
Trypheney, d. [Benjamin & Elizabeth], b. Feb. 17, 1760	1	125
Tryphenia had d. Elizabeth (?) **ALLEN,** b. July 3, 1782	1	61
DURKEE, DURKE, Electa, m. Samuel **FELCH,** Jr., Nov. 10, 1793	1	138

	Vol.	Page
DURKEE, DURKE, (cont.)		
Jeremiah, m. Abigail **ADAMS**, Mar. 25, 1747	1	120
Mehetable, m. James **BEDLAKE**, Feb. 14, 1749	1	69
DYAR, DYER, Abigail, d. John & Abigail, b. Apr. 10, 1718	1	122
Abigail, m. Gideon **COBB**, Nov. 5, 1739	1	100
Abigail, w. Col., d. May 19, 1759	1	131
Abigail, d. James & Anna, b. May 10, 1761	1	125
Abigail, d. Sam[ue]l & Rachel, b. Sept. 10, 1800	1	130
Alice, d. Elijah & Elizabeth, b. Feb. 28, 1754	1	123
Alice, m. Josiah **CLEVELAND**, Jr., June 3, 1778	1	101
Anna, d. James & Anna, b. May 19, 1766	1	126
Anna, w. John, Jr., d. Oct. 15, 1776	1	132
Annas, s. Joseph & Martha, b. Mar. 7, 1766	1	126
Bille, s. Elijah & Elizabeth, b. Sept. 26, 1758	1	125
Billy, s. [Elijah & Elizabeth], d. Jan. 14, 1777	1	132
Billa, s. [Ebenezer & Mehetable], b. Aug. 23, 1786	1	129
Calista, d. Jareb* & Susannah, b. July 23, 1785 (*Jared?)	1	129
C[h[loe, d. Joseph & Martha, b. Aug. 16, 1750	1	124
Dillis, s. Ebenezer & Mehetable, b. Nov. 5, 1795	1	129
E. Porter, of Stow, Mass., m. Esther Ann **HOUGH**, of		
Canterbury, Dec. 2, 1838, by Rev. Charles J. Warren	2	21
E. Porter, of Stow, Mass., m. Esther Ann **HOUGH**, of		
Canterbury, Dec. 2, 1838, by Rev. Charles J. Warren	2	62
Ebenezer, s. John & Abigail, b. Sept. 19, 1729	1	122
Ebenezer, s. Elijah & Elizabeth, b. Aug. 26, 1756	1	124
Ebenezer, m. Mehetable **ENSWORTH**, June 24, 1784	1	121
Elijah, s. John & Abigail, b. Sept. 10, 1716	1	122
Elijah, m. Elizabeth **WILLIAMS**, of Plainfield, Nov. 16, 1752	1	120
Elijah, s. [Elijah & Elizabeth], b. Feb. 13, 1764	1	125
Elijah, Jr., of Norwich, m. Abigail C. **MORSE**, of Canterbury,		
Apr. 11, 1831, by Rev. Demis Platt	2	21
Elisha, s. John & Anna, b. Oct. 30, 1760	1	130
Eliza Mary, d. Samuel, b. Feb. 27, 1807	1	130
Elizabeth, m. William **JOHNSON**, Oct. 7, 1798	1	167
Eunice, d. Elijah & Elizabeth, b. Dec. 2, 1766	1	127
Eunice, m. Jedediah **JOHNSON**, Mar. 4, 1790	1	167
Harvey R., m. Sarah A. **WOOD**, b. of Canterbury, Sept. 2,		
1839, by Rev. Charles J. Warren	2	21
James, s. John & Abigail, b. Feb. 16, 1719/20	1	122
James, m. Anne **WHITING**, Dec. 8, 1753	1	120
James, s. James & Anna, b. Nov. 25, 1754* (*1759?)	1	124
James, s. James & Anna, d. Jan. 7, 1760	1	131
James, s. James & Anna, b. Feb. 10, 1764	1	125
James, m. Lydia **ENSWORTH**, May 27, 1790	1	121
Jared, m. Susannah **NEWELL**, of Roxbury, Nov. 6, 1784	1	121
Jarib*, s. Joseph & Martha, b. Oct. 3, 1754 (*Jared?)	1	124
Jedde, s. [Joseph & Martha], b. Oct. 17, 1752, with a		
notch in his left ear	1	124

	Vol.	Page

DYAR, DYER, (cont.)

Jedde, s. Capt. Jos[eph], d. Jan. 24, or 25, 1777, at

    York. Soldier ... 1 ... 132

John, m. Abigail **FITCH,** Oct. 22, 1713 ... 1 ... 120

John, s. John & Abigail, b. May 9, 1722 ... 1 ... 122

John, Col., had negro servant Shem, s. of Jenny, b.

    Apr. 11, 1751; Bristo, s. Jenny, b. July 26, 1764; Lettice,

    d. Jenny, b. Mar. 28, 1767; Rose, d. Jenny, b. Aug. 10,

    1771 ... 1 ... 249

John, m. Anna **PAISON,** Mar. 29, 1753 ... 1 ... 120

John, s. James & Anna, b. Mar. 24, 1757 ... 1 ... 124

John, Col., m. Johannah **LEFFINGWELL,** Oct. 4, 1759 ... 1 ... 120

John, s. John, Jr. & Anna, d. Sept. 17, 1776 ... 1 ... 132

John, s. James & Anna, d. Jan. 1, 1777, at Philadelphia ... 1 ... 132

John, s. James & Lydia, b. Jan. 6, 1795 ... 1 ... 244

John, s. James & Lydia, b. Jan. 27, 1795 ... 1 ... 129

Joseph, s. John & Abigail, b. Feb. 5, 1723/4 ... 1 ... 122

Joseph, m. Martha **DARBE,** Feb. 1, 1748/9 ... 1 ... 120

Joseph, s. Elijah & Elizabeth, b. June 19, 1772 ... 1 ... 127

Joseph, d. Dec. 8, 1781 ... 1 ... 132

Juda, s. [Jareb & Susanna], b. Apr. 21, 1789 ... 1 ... 129

Lotilla, d. Joseph & Martha, b. May 8, 1757 ... 1 ... 124

Lotilla, m. Jesse **ENSWORTH,** Apr. 17, 1777 ... 1 ... 133

Luther, s. Ebenezer & Mehetable, b. Feb. 23, 1785 ... 1 ... 129

Mansur, s. Ebenezer & Mehitable, b. July 22, 1791 ... 1 ... 129

Mansur, s. James & Lydia, b. June 23, 1801 ... 1 ... 130

Mansur Fitch, s. Joseph & Martha, b. Dec. 4, 1762 ... 1 ... 125

Mary, m. Nath[anie]l **ENSWORTH,** May 11, 1783 ... 1 ... 133

Mary E., of Canterbury, m. Kimball **KENNEY,** of Plainfield,

    Feb. 2, 1835, by Rev. Otis C. Whiton ... 2 ... 47

Mason, s. James & Lydia, b. June 3, 1797 or 1799 ... 1 ... 130

Mason, s. [James & Lydia], b. June 3, 1797(?) ... 1 ... 244

Mehetable, d. [Elijah & Elizabeth], b. Mar. 26, 1769 ... 1 ... 127

Mehetable, d. Elijah & Elizabeth, d. Oct. 15, 1776 ... 1 ... 132

Mehetable, d. Ebenezer & Mehetable, b. Aug. 13, 1788 ... 1 ... 129

Molly, d. John & Anna, b. May 11, 1754 ... 1 ... 123

Nancy, m. David **BUTT,** Jan. 28, 1796 ... 1 ... 72

Olive, d. John & Anna, b. Aug. 31, 1756 ... 1 ... 124

Orilla, d. Ebenezer & Mehetable, b. Apr. 30, 1798 ... 1 ... 129

Pamelia, d. [James & Anna], d. Dec. 27, 1789 ... 1 ... 132

Roger, s. John & Anna, b. Dec. 29, 1758 ... 1 ... 124

Samuel, s. James & Anne, b. Feb. 2, 1773 ... 1 ... 127

Samuel, m. Rachel **HERRICK,** Sept. 29, 1799 ... 1 ... 121

Sarah, d. John & Abigail, b. Nov. 14, 1727 ... 1 ... 122

Sarah, d. [James & Anna], d. Jan. 25, 1790 ... 1 ... 132

Sibbalath or Sibbel, d. John & Abigail, b. Oct. 26, 1714 ... 1 ... 122

Sibbel, d. [Elijah & Elizabeth], b. Dec. 29, 1761, at Norwich ... 1 ... 125

Sibbel, m. Luther **PAINE,** Jan. 9, 1783 ... 1 ... 193

	Vol.	Page
DYAR, DYER, (cont.)		
Will[ia]m, s. James & Anna, b. Jan. 29, 1755	1	123
Will[ia]m, s. James & Anna, d. July 22, 1756	1	131
Wyllys, s. [Joseph & Martha], b. Aug. 4, 1760	1	125
EATON, David, s. Ezekiel & Ruth, b. Feb. 10, 1782	1	135
David, s. Ezekiel & Ruth, d. Apr. 7, 1782	1	137
Ezekiel, m. Ruth **PIKE**, May 6, 1776	1	133
Frances, d. Walter & Jerusha, b. Oct. 18, 1829	2	227
Keziah, m. Diliver[an]ce **CLEVELAND**, Jan. 20, 1731/2	1	100
Phebe A., of Canterbury, m. Charles L. **RAY**, of Lisbon,		
Jan. 27, 1850, by Rev. Robert C. Learned	2	69
Ruth, w. Ezekiel, d. Apr. 17, 1786	1	137
Salla, d. Ezekiel & Ruth, b. May 25, 1777	1	135
Walter, of Windham, m. Jerusha **AUSTIN**, of Canterbury,		
Mar. 31, 1828, by Andrew T. Judson, J. P.	2	27
EDDY, Ira, of Pittstown, N. Y., m. Sally **LYON**, June 14, 1836,		
by Rev. Asa King, Westminster	2	27
EDMONDS, William, of Homer, m. Lydia **WOOD**, of Canterbury,		
Oct. 12, 1830, at Wid. Wood's, Canterbury, by Rev.		
William Palmer, Norwich	2	27
ELDREDGE, John C., m. Polly **FARNHAM**, b. of Canterbury,		
Dec. 5, 1824, by Rev. Tho[ma]s J. Murdock	2	27
John Damond, s. John C. & Polly, b. Dec. 20, 1825	2	227
Mary Susan, of Canterbury, m. Joseph C. **AVERY**, of		
Sacrarmento, Cal., Feb. 22, 1853, by Rev. Robert C.		
Learned	2	4
ELLIS, Thankful, of Stonington, m. Simon **FOBES**, of Preston,		
Mar. 24, 1748	1	138
ELLSWORTH, Tabathy Darkis, m. Ezekiel **PARKE**, Aug. 31, 1777	1	193
ENSWORTH, EANSWORTH, Abby Bacon, [d. Nehemiah &		
Polly], b. Apr. 21, 1821. Recorded June 7, 1851	2	227
Abigail, d. [Nehemiah & Abigail], b. May 23, 1740	1	134
Abigail, m. Abner **BACON**, Jan. 26, 1764	1	70
Abigail, d. Tyxhall & Jerusha, b. Apr. 22, 1768	1	135
Abigail, d. Sam[ue]l & Sarah, b. Mar. 17, 1773	1	135
Abigail, d. Sam[ue]l & Sarah, d. May 29, 1773	1	137
Alice, d. Tyxhall & Jerusha, b. July 21, 1752	1	134
Andrew Whitney, s. Roswell & Polly, b. Nov. 3, 1805	1	136
Ann, d. Nehemiah & Abigail, b. Apr. 21, 1753	1	134
Anna, d. Oct. 28, 1754	1	137
Anna, d. [John & Hannah], b. Aug. 7, 1756	1	135
Annis, d. [Roswell & Polly], b. Nov. 11, 1809	1	136
Azel, s. William & Hannah, b. Dec. 22, 1759	1	135
Backus, s. James & Lucy, b. Mar. 31, 1812	1	136
Charles Backus, s. [John & Polly], b. Dec. 19, 1806	2	227
Chloe, d. [Jesse & Lorilla], b. Aug. 9, 1779	1	135
C[h]loe, m. Martin **FELCH**, Feb. 15, 1810	1	138
Clarissa, d. Joseph & Betty, b. Oct. 19, 1763	1	135

	Vol.	Page
ENSWORTH, EANSWORTH, (cont.)		
Clarissa C., m. Marshal **SMITH**, Nov. 21, 1836, by Rev.		
Asa King, Westminster	2	73
Clarissa Congdon, d. Lebbeus & Thankful, b. Aug. 10,		
1809	1	136
Dolly, m. Abner **HIDE**, Oct. 18, 1801	1	156
Dorothy, d. Ezra & Elizabeth, b. Feb. 4, 1758	1	135
Dorothy, m. Stephen **JOHNSON**, Feb. 6, 1783	1	167
Ebenezer, s. John & Hannah, b. May 23, 1750	1	135
Ebenezer, s. John & Hannah, b. May 23, 1751	1	134
Elihu, s. Ezra & Elizabeth, b. Oct. 7, 1767	1	135
Elizabeth, d. [Nehemiah & Abigail], b. May 2, 1742	1	134
Elizabeth, d. [Tyxhal & Jerusha], b. June 26, 1750	1	134
Elizabeth, m. Amos **PIKE**, May 2, 1764	1	193
Elizabeth, m. David **BACON**, Dec. 10, 1767	1	70
Elizabeth, w. Ezra, d. June 18, 1788	1	137
Elizabeth S., m. Nichols **AUSTIN**, of Jamestown, R. I.,		
Nov. 28, 1830	1	53
Elizabeth S., of Canterbury, m. Nichols **AUSTIN**, of		
Jamestown, R. I., Nov. 28, 1830, by Rev. Demis Platt	2	2
Elizabeth Stuart, d. Libbeus & Thankful, b. Dec. 11, 1803,		
at R. I.	1	136
Ephraim, s. John & Elizabeth, b. Apr. 17, 1723	1	134
Ephraim, s. [Trxhall & Jerusha], b. Dec. 1, 1760	1	135
Eunice, d. [James & Anne], b. Sept. 14, 1782	1	136
Ezra, m. Elizabeth **PAINE**, Oct. 13, 1757	1	133
Ezra, s. Ezra & Elizabeth, b. Jan. 30, 1763	1	135
Fanny, d. [Nathaniel & Molly], b. Jan. 13, 1791	1	136
Fixhall, see under Tyxhall		
Frances C., d. Nehemiah, of Canterbury, m. Harrison G.		
WORK, of Providence, R. I., Apr. 5, 1854, by Rev.		
Robert C. Learned	2	90
Frances Cleveland, [d. Nehemiah & Polly], b. Sept. 13, 1825.		
Recorded June 7, 1851	2	227
George, s. [John & Polly], b. Sept. 21, 1818	2	227
Gideon, s. [Nehemiah & Abigail], b. June 24, 1744	1	134
Gideon, m. Nancy **BUCKLIN**, Dec. 9, 1778	1	133
Grace, d. [Will[ia]m & Grace], b. Feb. 9, 1747/8	1	134
Grace, w. Will[ia]m, d. Oct. 10, 1752, o. s.	1	137
Hannah, twin with John, d. [John & Hannah], b. May 22, 1758	1	135
Hannah, w. John, d. July 24, 1760	1	137
Hannah, d. Jos[eph], Jr. & Betty, b. July 2, 1768	1	135
Hannah, d. [W[illia]m & Hannah], b. Jan. 9, 1818	2	227
Henry, s. [John & Polly], b. Dec. 31, 1809	2	227
Henry Clay, s. Andrew W. & Charity, b. Aug. 13, 1834	2	227
Hezekiah, s. [Jos[eph], Jr. & Betty, b. Feb. 22, 1775	1	135
Horace, s. [John & Polly], b. Feb. 3, 1811	2	227
Hosmer, s. [John & Polly], b. Nov. 28, 1823	2	227

	Vol.	Page
ENSWORTH, EANSWORTH, (cont.)		
Hosmer, of Springfield, m. Elizabeth **HYDE**, of Canterbury,		
Dec. 29, 1851, by Rev. Robert C. Learned	2	28
Jabez, s. [Joseph & Mary], b. Apr. 12, 1723	1	134
Jabez, m. Mehetable **TRACY**, Nov. 17, 1748	1	133
James, s. [Will[ia]m & Grace], b. Dec. 17, 1746	1	134
James, m. Ann **TRACY**, of Norwich, Nov. 15, 1770	1	133
James, s. James & Anne, b. Mar. 25, 1773	1	136
James, m. Lucy **BACKUS**, Mar. 2, 1797	1	133
Jedediah, s. Trxhall & Jerusha, b. Sept. 1, 1758	1	135
Jedediah, s. Jesse & Lotilla, b. Sept. 23, 1796	1	136
Jedediah, m. Joann **CLEVELAND**, Nov. 15, 1819	1	133
Jerusha, d. Tyxhall & Jerusha, b. May 6, 1746	1	134
Jerusha, m. William **BACON**, Mar. 7, 1765	1	70
Jerusha, d. [James & Anne], b. Feb. 11, 1786	1	136
Jerusha, m. Eliashib I. **BACKUS***, Oct. 8, 1809 (*Should		
be Eliashib T. **BACKUS**)	1	73
Jesse, s. [Will[ia]m & Grace], b. Sept. 29, 1752, o. s.	1	134
Jesse, m. Lotilla **DYAR**, Apr. 17, 1777	1	133
John, m. Elizabeth **CLEVELAND**, Apr. 2, 1717	1	133
John, s. John & Elizabeth, b. Apr. 5, 1719	1	134
John, d. Aug. 25, 1723	1	137
John, twin with Hannah, s. [John & Hannah], b. May 22, 1758	1	135
John, m. Sarah **LUMMIS**, June 25, 1761	1	133
John, s. Gideon & Nancy, b. June 30, 1780	1	135
John, m. Polly **BACKUS**, Feb. 17, 1800, by Moses Cleveland.		
Recorded Apr. 4, 1835	2	27
John H., of Canterbury, m. Eliza T. **BALDWIN**, of Plainfield,		
Sept. 14, 1846, by Rev. Hiram Dyer	2	28
John Hascall, s. Luther & Polly, b. Dec. 17, 1824	2	227
Jos[eph], s. Tyxhall & Sarah, b. Aug. 21, 1694	1	135
Joseph, s. [Joseph & Mary], b. Nov. 23, 1725	1	134
Joseph, m. Betty **WASHBORN**, of Coventry, Jan. 25, 1763	1	133
Joseph, d. Sept. 30, 1770	1	137
Joseph, m. Mary **CLEVELAND**, Oct. 5, 1779* (*1719)	1	133
Joseph B., m. Lucy W. **SAFFORD**, Mar. 10, 1839, by Rev.		
Asa King, Westminster	2	27
Joseph Bucklin, s. Gideon & Nancy, b. Jan. 10, 1784	1	135
Joseph Bucklin, s. John & Polly, b. Oct. 21, 1802	2	227
Joseph Bucklin, s. John & Polly, d. May 2, 1814	2	325
Joseph Bucklin, s. [John & Polly], b. Aug. 13, 1815	2	227
Judah, d. John & Hannah, b. Apr. 28, 1749	1	134
Julia Ardell, d. Jedediah & Joanna, b. Oct. 24, 1820	1	136
Lebbeus, s. [Jos[eph], Jr. & Betty], b. May 11, 1771	1	135
Lebbeus, m. Thankful **CONGDON**, of Preston, Sept. 14, 1802	1	133
Lebbeus, s. [Libbeus & Thankful], b. May 11, 1805	1	136
Le[o]nard, s. Joseph & Betty, b. Mar. 13, 1766	1	135
Lotilla D., m. Harlow **WILLIAMS**, Apr. 17, 1844, by		

	Vol.	Page
ENSWORTH, EANSWORTH, (cont.)		
Ephraim Browning, J. P., at Packersville	2	88
Lotilla Dyer, d. Luther & Polly, b. Nov. 11, 1815	1	136
Lucinda, d. Jesse & Lorilla, b. Jan. 27, 1778	1	135
Lucinda, m. John **BALDWIN**, Nov. 5, 1801	1	72
Lucrese, d. Ezra & Elizabeth, b. Feb. 7, 1765	1	125
Lucretia, d. Ezra & Elizabeth, d. Mar. 7, 1788	1	137
Lucy, m. Joshua **PHINNIE**, June 10, 1764	1	193
Luther, s. [Sam[ue]l & Sarah], b. Apr. 9, 1776	1	135
Luther, s. Samuel & Sarah, d. Sept. 16, 1775	1	137
Luther, s. Jesse & Lotilla, b. Jan. 30, 1788	1	136
Luther, m. Polly **BALDWIN**, Sept. 30, 1813	1	133
Lydia, d. Joseph & Mary, b. Aug. 24, 1721	1	134
Lydia, d. [Joseph & Mary], b. June 16, 1734	1	134
Lydia, d. [Tyxhal & Jerusha], b. July 3, 1748	1	134
Lydia, m. Joseph **SAFFORD**, Apr. 25, 1753	1	214
Lydia, m. James **DYAR**, May 27, 1790	1	121
Lydia, d. W[illia]m & Hannah, b. Apr. 15, 1816	2	227
Lydia, of Canterbury, m. Samuel F. **BENNET**, of Hampton, Nov. 22, 1852, by R. S. Hazen	2	105
Mary, m. James **COBB**, May 15, 1763	1	101
Mary, w. Joseph, d. Mar. 11, 1766	1	137
Mary Elizabeth, [d. Nehemiah & Polly], b. Dec. 9, 1819. Recorded June 7, 1851	2	227
Mary H., of Canterbury, m. Amos **WITTER**, Jr., of Plainfield, Nov. 19, 1850, by Rev. J. B. Guild, at Packersville	2	89
Mehetable, w. Jabez, d. Mar. 22, 1757	1	137
Mehetable, d. Samuel & Sibel, b. Nov. 18, 1764	1	135
Mehetable, m. Ebenezer **DYAR**, June 24, 1784	1	121
Nancy, d. [Gideon & Nancy], b. Oct. 15, 1786	1	135
Nathan, s. [Nehemiah & Abigail], b. Feb. 9, 1750/51	1	134
Nathaniel, m. Rebeckah **KING**, Dec. 16, 1775	1	133
Nath[anie]l, m. Mary **DYAR**, May 11, 1783	1	133
Nathaniel, s. Nathaniel & Molly, b. Apr. 17, 1789	1	136
Nehemiah, s. Nehemiah & Abigail, b. Feb. 26, 1734/5	1	134
Nehemiah, Jr., d. Oct. 4, 1757	1	137
Nehemiah, s. [Sam[ue]l & Sarah], b. June 30, 1779	1	135
Olive, m. Nathan **FISH**, Dec. 23, 1757	1	138
Patience, d. [Will[ia]m & Grace], b. Nov. 20, 1749	1	134
Peris, s. Tyxhal & Jerusha, b. Nov. 26, 1754	1	134
Phebe, d. Jabez & Mehitable, b. Aug. 2, 1749	1	134
Phebe, m. Nathan **ADAMS**, Apr. 4, 177[ ]	1	52
Philis, d. Jabez & Mehitable, b. Apr. 26, 1753	1	134
Phyllys, m. William **ADAMS**, Dec. 18, 177[ ]	1	52
Polly, d. Nath[anie]l & Molly, b. Sept. 22, 1785	1	135
Rachel, d. [James & Anne], b. Jan. 13, 1778	1	136
Roswell, d. May 11, 1776	1	137
Roswell, s. Jesse & Lotilla, b. May 23, 1784	1	135

	Vol.	Page
ENSWORTH, EANSWORTH, (cont.)		
Roswell, m. Mary **KNIGHT**, of Plainfield, Aug. 12, 1804	1	133
Rosswell, Jr., m. Mary Ann **LEWIS**, Apr. 21, 1844, by Rev.		
Daniel D. Lyon, Packersville	2	27
Rozel, s. [Jabez & Mehitable], b. May 9, 1755	1	134
Ruby Tracy, d. James & Lucy, b. Aug. 31, 1798	1	136
Rufus, s. [Jabez & Mehitable], b. May 25, 1751	1	134
Rufus, s. Jabez & Mehetable, d. Feb. 2, 1756	1	137
Sally Bucklin, d. Gideon & Nancy, b. Aug. 22, 1781	1	135
Samuel, s. [Nehemiah & Abigail], b. Nov. 20, 1737	1	134
Samuel, m. Sibel **TRACY**, Nov. 17, 1763	1	133
Samuel, m. Sarah **CLEVELAND**, May 28, 1772	1	133
Samuel, s. [James & Anne], b. Nov. 12, 1775	1	136
Samuel, [s. Nehemiah & Polly], b. Feb. 27, 1812.		
Recorded June 7, 1851	2	227
Sarah, m. Joseph **CLEVELAND**, Mar. 31, 1725	1	100
Sarah, m. Elkanah **COBB**, Aug. 23, 1749	1	100
Sarah, d. [John & Hannah], b. Jan. 4, 1752	1	134
Sarah, d. [John & Hannah], b. Jan. 4, 1752	1	135
Sarah, d. Ezra & Elizabeth, b. Feb. 9, 1761	1	135
Sarah, [twin with Sibbal], d. Sam[ue]l & Sarah, b.		
Nov. 26, 1784	1	135
Sarah, w. Samuel, d. Nov. 26, 1784	1	137
Sarah Cleveland, [d. Nehemiah & Polly], b. Jan. 1, 1817.		
Recoreded June 7, 1851	2	227
Septa, s. Sam[ue]l & Sarah, b. Aug. 17, 1777	1	135
Sibbel, d. Nehemiah & Abigail, b. June 29, 1746	1	134
Sibbel, d. [Samuel & Sibel], b. Dec. 9, 1768	1	135
Sibbel, w. Sam[ue]l, d. Jan. 1, 1769	1	137
Sibbel, d. Sam[ue]l & Sibbel, d. Aug. 28, 1776	1	137
Sibbal, [twin with Sarah], d. Sam[ue]l & Sarah, b. Nov.		
26, 1784	1	135
Susan Geraldine, d. [Luther & Polly], b. June 22, 1821	1	136
Sybil, see under Sibbel		
Syrviah, d. [John & Hannah], b. Oct. 4, 1754	1	135
Thomas Boawall, s. Nehemiah & Polly, b. May 17, 1810.		
Recorded June 7, 1851	2	227
Tixwell, see under Tyxhall		
Tracy, m. Elizabeth **MUNROW**, Dec. 27, 1799	1	133
Tracy, s. [James & Anne], b. May 9, 1780	1	136
Tracy, s. Tracy & Elizabeth, b. Aug. 15, 1800	1	135
Tyxhall, d. June 24, 1712	1	137
Tyxhall, s. John & Elizabeth, b. Dec. 19, 1717	1	134
Fixhall, m. Jerusha **FITCH**, Dec. 6, 1742	1	133
Tyxhall, d. Jan. 6, 1776	1	137
Waite, d. Samuel & Sibel, b. Oct. 18, 1766	1	135
Waitstill, d. [Nehemiah & Abigail], b. Sept. 26, 1748	1	134
Waitstill, d. Nov. 8, 1752	1	137

	Vol.	Page
ENSWORTH, EANSWORTH, (cont.)		
Waterman, s. [Sam[ue]l & Sarah], b. May 24, 1774	1	135
Waterman, s. Sam[ue]l & Sarah, d. Aug. 21, 1776	1	137
William, s. Joseph & Mary, b. Feb. 24, 1719/20	1	134
William, m. Grace **GALE**, Mar. 26, 1745	1	133
Will[ia]m, s. Will[ia]m & Grace, b. Nov. 5, 1745	1	134
Will[ia]m, s. [Will[ia]m & Grace], b. Oct. 10, 1752	1	134
Will[ia]m, m. Hannah **COGSWELL**, Feb. 20, 1754	1	133
William, Jr., m. Catharine **YOUNG**, Oct. 11, 1768	1	133
Zerviah, see under Syrviah		
----, d. Jabez & Mehetable, b. Mar. 19, 1757, st. b.	1	137
ESTABROOK, ESTABROOKS, Hubbard, s. Samuel & Rebeckah,		
b. Dec. 17, 1716	1	134
Mary, d. [Samuel & Rebeckah], b. Sept. 4, 1718	1	134
Nehemiah, s. Samuel & Rebeckah, b. Apr. 1, 1715	1	134
Samuel, m. Rebeckah **HUBBERT**, Mar. 23, 1713/14	1	133
Samuel, Rev., d. June 26, 1727	1	137
EVANS, Andrew, m. Lucy **BALDWIN**, Jan. 8, 1775	1	133
FAGAN, Calista, m. Robert **HOVEY**, Nov. 30, 1828, by Asael		
Bacon, J. P.	2	39
FAIRBANKS, Rebeckah, m. Sam[ue]l **HUNTINGTON**, May 23,		
1751	1	155
FAIRWEATHER, George, of Kingston, R. I., m. Sarah Ann M.		
HARRIS, Nov. 28, 1833, by Rev. Asa King, Westminster	2	31
Prudence Crandall, d. George & Sarah Ann M., b. Sept.		
9, 1834	2	231
FALKNER, [see under **FAULKNER**]		
FANNING, Freelove, m. Parker **ADAMS**, May 9, 1745	1	51
FARNHAM, FARNUM, FARNAM, Abigail, d. [Joseph & Lydia],		
b. Nov. 5, 1738	1	141
Abigail, d. [William & Martha], b. Apr. 17, 1754	1	142
Alice, see under Ellice		
Amanda, d. Zabadiah & Mary, b. June 28, 1771	1	144
Amasa, s. William & Martha, b. Oct. 6, 1763	1	143
Anne, d. [Will[ia]m & Martha], b. Apr. 30, 1750	1	141
Benjamin, s. [Joseph & Lydia], b. Jan. 3, 1736	1	141
Benjamin, s. [Joseph & Lydia], b. June 20, 1775	1	145
Calvin, s. [Joseph & Sybel], b. Sept. 23, 1808	1	145
Calvin, m. Loisa **HYDE**, b. of Canterbury, Jan. 10, 1832,		
by Rev. Demis Platt	2	31
Edmund, s. [Joseph & Sybel], b. June 12, 1810	1	145
Edmund, m. Mary L. **FISH**, b. of Canterbury, Nov. 30, 1834,		
by John Francis, J. P.	2	31
Eliphalet, m. Mary **ROGERS**, Oct. 11, 1750	1	138
Eliphalet, s. Eliphalet & Mary, b. Sept. 14, 1751	1	141
Eliphalet, s. Eliphalet & Mary, d. Nov. 8, 1754	1	147
Eliphalet, m. Mary **ADAMS**, Feb. 1, 1757	1	138
Eliphalet, s. Eliphalet & Mary, b. Aug. 25, 1759	1	142

	Vol.	Page
FARNHAM, FARNUM, FARNAM, (cont.)		
Eliphalet, m. Hannah **ADAMS**, of Gilsune, N. H., Oct. 16,		
1786, at Keene	1	138
Ellice (Alice), d. [William & Martha], b. Sept. 27, 1756	1	142
Emeline, d. [Joseph & Sybel], b. Apr. 28, 1815	1	145
Eunice, d. [Joseph & Lydia], b. Aug. 4, 1748	1	141
Fanny, d. Joseph & Sybel, b. Sept. 21, 1804	1	145
George, s. [Joseph & Sybel], b. July 6, 1812	1	145
Hannah, d. [Joseph & Lydia], b. Mar. 10, 1740	1	141
Hannah, d. [Will[ia]m & Martha], b. May 13, 1746	1	141
Hannah, m. Eleazer **HIBBARD**, Apr. 20, 1762	1	155
Hannah, d. [Joseph & Lydia], b. Mar. 25, 1773	1	145
Irene, m. Benjamin **BACON**, Jan. 29, 1783	1	72
Jane J., of Canterbury, m. Charles L. **SLY**, of Addison,		
N. Y., Oct. 18, 1847, by Rev. Thomas Tallman	2	75
John, s. [William & Martha], b. Dec. 21, 1756	1	142
Joseph, s. [Joseph & Lydia], b. Dec. 2, 1732, in Windham	1	141
Joseph, m. Lydia **WHEELER**, of Plainfield, July 10, 1764	1	138
Joseph, s. [Joseph & Lydia], b. Dec. 25, 1778	1	145
Joseph, m. Sybel **BALDWIN**, Oct. 20, 1803	1	139
Joseph, s. [Joseph & Sybel], b. Mar. 22, 1821	1	146
Joseph, m. Orinda **DAVENPORT**, Dec. 5, 1837, by Rev.		
Charles J. Warren	2	32
Joseph, Jr., m. Tabitha Louisa **CARD**, b. of Canterbury,		
Dec. 2, 1845, by Rev. Daniel D. Lyon, of Packersville	2	32
Josiah, s. [William & Martha], b. June 17, 1758	1	142
Lucy, d. Joseph & Lydia, b. Feb. 1, 1744/5	1	141
Lucy, d. Joseph & Lydia, b. May 23, 1768	1	145
Lydia, d. Joseph & Lydia, b. Oct. 3, 1728, in Windham	1	141
Lydia, d. Henry & Sarah, b. Nov. 17, 1744	1	141
Lydia, d. [Joseph & Lydia], b. May 8, 1784	1	145
Martha, d. Will[ia]m & Martha, b. Nov. 11, 1743	1	141
Mary, d. [Joseph & Lydia], b. Jan. 28, 1730, in Windham	1	141
Mary, w. Eliphalet, d. May 1, 1753	1	147
Mary, d. Zeb[adia]h & Mary, b. Feb. 9, 1776	1	144
Mary, d. Eliphalet, Jr. & Hannah, b. Dec. 18, 1787	1	145
Olive, d. Joseph & Lydia, b. Nov. 19,. 1765	1	143
Orra, d. Zabadiah & Mary, b. May 6, 1774	1	144
Pamela, d. [Zebadiah & Mary], b. May 17, 1768	1	143
Phebe, d. Henry & Sarah, b. Mar. 7, 1746/7	1	141
Phebe, of Norwich, m. Dan[ie]l **FROST**, Dec. 16, 1773	1	138
Polly, d. [Joseph & Lydia], b. Nov. 27, 1770	1	145
Polly, d. [Joseph & Sybel], b. Nov. 1, 1806	1	145
Polly, m. John C. **ELDREDGE**, b. of Canterbury, Dec. 5,		
1824, by Rev. Tho[ma]s J. Murdock	2	27
Reuben, s. [Will[ia]m & Martha], b. May 9, 1748	1	141
Roger, s. Zabadiah & Mary, b. Nov. 2, 1772	1	144
Rufus, s. [Zebadiah & Mary], b. Mar. 9, 1766	1	143

	Vol.	Page
FARNHAM, FARNUM, FARNAM, (cont.)		
Sarah, d. [Joseph & Lydia], b. Nov. 28, 1734	1	141
Sibel, d. [Joseph & Sybel], b. Nov. 10, 1817	1	146
Stephen, s. [Joseph & Lydia], b. Oct. 16, 1741	1	141
Stephen, s. William & Martha, b. May 31, 1752	1	142
Stephen, s. [Joseph & Lydia], b. June 10, 1781	1	145
Sybil, see under Sibel		
Will[ia]m, s. [Will[ia]m & Martha], b. Feb. 9, 1745	1	141
Will[ia]m, s. [Joseph & Lydia], b. May 6, 1747	1	141
William, Jr., m. Sarah **HEBBARD**, May 8, 1766	1	138
Salinda, d. Zabadiah & Mary, b. May 29, 1770	1	144
Zebadiah, m. Mary **HEBBARD**, Nov. 10, 1763	1	138
Zebadiah, s. Zebadiah & Mary b. Feb. 1, 1765	1	143
FASSET, Adonijah, s. [Benjamin & Elizabeth], b. Sept. 23, 1720	1	140
Alice, d. Amos & Lydia, b. Mar. 30, 1753	1	141
Alice, m. Ebenezer **CHAFFEE**, Apr. 18, 1776	1	101
Amos, m. Lydia **JOHNSON**, Apr. 10, 1752	1	138
Amos, s. Amos & Lydia, b. May 26, 1755	1	141
Amos, s. Amos & Lydia, d. June 13, 1756	1	147
Amos, d. [ ], in Camp at Lake George (soldier)	1	147
Benjamin, s. Benjamin & Elizabeth, b. Feb. 6, 1716/17	1	140
Benjamin, s. [Benjamin & Elizabeth], b. Feb. 6, 1717	1	140
Betty, m. Will[ia]m **JOHNSON**, Nov. 29, 1750	1	167
Elizabeth, d. [Benjamin & Elizabeth], b. Mar. 4, 1715	1	140
John, s. Benjamin & Elizabeth, b. Mar. 16, 1719	1	140
John, s. John & Lydia, b. Nov. 9, 1756	1	142
Josiah, s. [Benjamin & Elizabeth], b. Mar. 2, 1725	1	140
Lydia, m. David **PAINE**, Apr. 5, 1759	1	192
Mary, m. Eben[eze]r **SPAULDING**, Feb. 24, 1742/3	1	214
Mary, d. John & Lydia, b. July 27, 1753	1	141
FAULKNER, FALKNER, Abigail, m. John **CRAINE**, Oct. 24,		
1799, at Brooklyn	1	102
Anna, d. Calob & Esther, b. Nov. 27, 1762	1	143
Caleb, m. Esther **MORSE**, Feb. 27, 1761	1	138
Caleb, s. Caleb & Esther, b. Mar. 28, 1763	1	143
Deborah, m. Comfort **HIDE**, May 8, 1779	1	155
Frederick, s. Caleb & Esther, b. Sept. 13, 1769	1	143
Joseph, s. Caleb & Esther, b. Jan. 8, 1765	1	143
Josiah Morse, s. Caleb & Esther, b. Mar. 14, 1773	1	144
Malissa, of Canterbury, m. David **SMITH**, of East Douglass,		
Mass., Nov. 6, 1853, by Rev. Robert C. Learned	2	76
Mary, d. Caleb & Esther, b. July 19, 1771	1	144
Mary, m. William N. **ADAMS**, Mar. 25, 1837, by Rev. Asa		
King	2	3
Mary, m. William N. **ADAMS**, Mar. 26, 1837	1	53
Samuel, s. [Caleb & Esther], b. Oct. 17, 1767	1	143
Susanna, m. Paine **CLEVELAND**, Mar. 10, 1761	1	101
Susanna, d. Caleb & Esther, b. Feb. 5, 1766	1	143

	Vol.	Page
FELCH, [see also FITCH], Ebenezer, s. [John & Sarah], b. Feb.		
18, 1750/51	1	141
Ebenezer, s. John & Sarah, d. Oct. 7, 1752	1	147
Eben[eze[r, s. John & Sarah, b. Mar. 19, 1754	1	141
Elizabeth, d. John & Elizabeth, b. Apr. 20, 1721	1	140
Elizabeth, d. John & Elizabeth, d. June 22, 1721	1	147
Elizabeth, w. John, d. July 14, 1735	1	147
Elizabeth, d. Jno. & Sarah, b. Jan. 16, 1737/8	1	140
Elizabeth, d. John & Sarah, d. Jan. 7, 1739/40	1	147
Hephzibah, d. John & Elizabeth, b. Feb. 20, 1715/16	1	140
Hephzibah, m. John PELLET, Nov. 12, 1741	1	192
John, m. Sarah GREEN, Mar. 7, 1737	1	138
John, s. [Jno. & Sarah], b. Oct. 5, 1739	1	140
John, m. Sarah ADAMS, Oct. 29, 1761	1	138
John, s. John & Sarah, b. July 24, 1770	1	144
John, Jr., m. Eunice BALDWIN, Apr. 12, 1796	1	138
Laura, d. Samuel, Jr. & Electa, b. Aug. 22, 1795	1	145
Lucretia Lord, d. Sam[ue]l, Jr. & Electa, b. Nov. 12, 1798	1	145
Lydia, d. John & Sarah, b. Sept. 1, 1764	1	143
Lydia, m. Frederick ANDREWS*, June 21, [ ] (*Arnold		
Copy has "ADAMS". Corrected by L. B. B.)	1	52
Martin, m. C[h]loe ENSWORTH, Feb. 15, 1810	1	138
Mary, d. [John & Elizabeth], b. Sept. 8, 1722	1	140
Mary, d. John & Sarah, b. Feb. 10, 1767	1	143
Mary, of Canterbury, m. Erastus CLARK, of Ashford, Aug.		
10, 1824, by Rev. Tho[ma]s J. Murdock	2	15
Poliy, d. John, Jr. & Eunice, b. Jan. 22, 1798	1	145
Samuel, s. John & Sarah, b. May 24, 1743, o. s.	1	143
Samuel, m. Mary BACKUS, Aug. 25, 1765	1	138
Samuel, s. Samuel & Mary, b. Sept. 9, 1766	1	143
Samuel, Jr., m. Electa DURKEE, Nov. 10, 1793	1	138
Sarah, d. John & Sarah, b. Nov. 19, 1745	1	141
Sarah, d. John & Sarah, d. Feb. 2, 1749/50	1	147
Sarah, d. Samuel & Mary, b. Jan. 17, 1769	1	143
Sarah, d. Sam[ue]l & Mary, d. Aug. 19, 1770	1	147
Sarah, wid., d. Apr. 17, 1776	1	148
Sophia, d. [Samuel, Jr. & Electa], b. Feb. 3, 1796	1	145
Will[ia]m, s. John & Elizabeth, b. Sept. 10, 1718	1	140
William, d. Mar. 21, 1752	1	147
William, s. John & Sarah, b. Sept. 16, 1762	1	143
FENNER, Cyrel, m. Phebe Ann PARK, Sept. 22, 1844, by Rev.		
Daniel D. Lyon, of Packersville	2	32
Sarah Ann, of Canterbury, m. Christopher Rhodes		
STAFFORD, of Providence, R. I., Mar. 16, 1824, by		
Rev. Tho[ma]s J. Murdock	2	71
FERWELL, Isaac, s. Isaac & Elizabeth, b. May 23, 1705	1	140
FILLIMORE, Charles L., of Lisbon, m. Emma Lane WILLIAMS,		
of Canterbury, Mar. 10, 1851, by Comfort D.		

	Vol.	Page
FILLIMORE, (cont.)		
Fillmore, Elder	2	33
Ralph H., of Lisbon, m. Ann E. **FITCH**, of Canterbury,		
Oct. 18, 1848, by Comfort D. Fillimore, Elder	2	33
FISH, Abigail, d. [Nathan & Olive], b. Dec. 23, 1767	1	143
Abigail, m. Waldo **BROWN**, May 6, 1790	1	72
Almira, d. [John & Alice], b. Mar. 27, 1799	1	145
Amanda, d. John & Alice, b. Aug. 17, 1794	1	145
Chloe, d. [Darius & Sarah], b. July 1, 1778	1	145
Clarissa, d. [David & Sibbel], b. Apr. 10, 1774	1	144
Derias, s. [John & Esther], b. Oct. 8, 1738	1	140
Derias, m. Sarah **HOWARD**, Feb. 7, 1765	1	138
Darius Augustus, s. Darius & Sarah, b. May 15, 1791	1	145
David, s. [John & Esther], b. Oct. 10, 1744	1	141
David, m. Sibbel **GENNINGS**, Oct. 28, 1769	1	138
Desire, d. [John & Esther], b. Oct. 30, 1729	1	140
Ele, d. [Darius & Sarah], b. Sept. 14, 1776	1	145
Elizabeth, d. [Darius & Sarah], b. Mar. 14, 1782	1	145
Esther, d. [John & Esther], b. Feb. 18, 1735/6	1	140
Esther, m. Timothy **CLEVELAND**, Jan. 30, 1760	1	101
Eunice, d. Nathan & Olive, b. Oct. 6, 1770	1	144
Jacob, s. John & Esther, b. Feb. 18, 1741/2	1	141
Jacob, s. John & Esther, d. Nov. 6, 1760	1	147
Jacob, s. [David & Sibbel], b. Feb. 26, 1772	1	144
John, s. John & Esther, b. [ ], 1727	1	140
John, s. John & Easter, d. July 12, 1752	1	147
John, s. Nathan & Olive, b. Apr. 21, 1761	1	142
John, s. Darius & Sarah, b. Dec. 30, 1769	1	143
John, s. [John & Alice], b. Oct. 17, 1796	1	145
Joseph, m. Olive **BACON**, Jan. 14, 1781	1	138
Lucy, d. Darius & Sarah, b. Jan. 6, 1788	1	145
Lydia, d. Darius & Sarah, b. Feb. 23, 1772	1	145
Margaret, m. Samuel **CLEVELAND**, July 25, 1699	1	100
Maria, d. Nathan, Jr. & Ruby, b. May 16, 1804	1	145
Mary, d. Darius & Sarah, b. Mar. 6, 1766	1	143
Mary, m. Eli **WASHBURN**, Mar. 9, 1786	1	236
Mary L., m. Edmund **FARNHAM**, b. of Canterbury, Nov. 30,		
1834, by John Francis, J. P.	2	31
Miranda, d. Nathan, Jr. & Ruby, b. Dec. 13, 1802	1	145
Nathan, m. Olive **ENSWORTH**, Dec. 23, 1757	1	138
Nathan, s. David & Sibbel, b. Feb. 20, 1770	1	144
Nathan, s. Nathan & Olive, b. Nov. 7, 1775	1	144
Nathan, Jr., m. Ruby **BALDWIN**, Oct. 22, 1801	1	138
Nathaniel, Jr., m. Mary **BACON**, June 28, 1775	1	138
Nehemiah, s. Nathan & Olive, b. Dec. 27, 1758	1	142
Olive, d. Nathan & Olive, b. Feb. 12, 1763	1	143
Permilla, [twin with Philury], d. [Darius & Sarah], b.		
Sept. 1, 1784	1	145

	Vol.	Page
FISH, (cont.)		
Phebe, of Canterbury, m. Perez **MINER**, of North Stonington, June 19, 1836, by Rev. Tubal Wakefield	2	56
Philury, [twin with Permilla], d. [Darius & Sarah], b. Sept. 1, 1784	1	145
Ruby, d. Nathan & Olive, b. Jan. 13, 1773	1	144
Sarah, d. Darius & Sarah, b. Nov. 23, 1767	1	143
Sarah, m. Erastus **HOUGH**, Apr. 8, 1790	1	156
Sibbel, d. Nathan & Olive, b. June 18, 1765	1	143
Thomas S., of Voluntown, m. Lucinda M. **PHILLIPS**, of Canterbury, Apr. 3, 1843, by Rev. W. Clarks	2	32
FISK, FISKE, Julia, of Canterbury, m. Timothy **PRINCE**, of Brooklyn, Mar. 20, 1844, by Rev. Holmes Slade	2	65
Suffronia, of Thompson, Conn., m. Samuel **BARRET**, Oct. 4, 1842, by Rev. H. Slade	2	13
FITCH, [see also **FELCH**], Abigail, m. John **DYAR**, Oct. 22, 1713	1	120
Abigail, d. [Will[ia]m & Mary], b. June 23, 1745	1	141
Abigail, d. Will[ia]m & Mary, b. June 23, 1745	1	142
Abigail, d. Capt. Jabez & Lydia, d. May 1, 1749	1	147
Abigail, d. Jabez & Lydia, b. July 24, 1762	1	142
Abigail, d. Jabez & Lydia, b. July 24, 1762	1	143
Abigail, d. Jabez & Lydia, d. Apr. 24, 1763	1	147
Alice, d. [Jabez & Lydia], b. Jan. 8, 1724/5	1	140
Alice, w. Major James, d. Mar. 15, 1745, ae 84 y.	1	148
Ellis, (Alice), m. James **COGSWELL**, Apr. 24, 1745	1	100
Alice, d. Jabez & Lydia, b. June 2, 1781	1	145
Amey, of Lisbon, m. Samuel **BARSTOW**, Apr. 16, 1789	1	72
Ann E., of Canterbury, m. Ralph H. **FILLIMORE**, of Lisbon, Oct. 18, 1848, by Comfort D. Fillimore, Elder	2	33
Anna, w. Daniel, d. July 27, 1735	1	147
Anna, d. Will[ia]m & Mary, b. July 1, 1742	1	141
Anna, m. Nathaniel **LATHROP**, Apr. 5, 1759	1	176
Anna, d. [Jabez, Jr. & Lydia], b. Feb. 3, 1768	1	143
Cha[u]ncey, s. Jebez, Jr. & Lydia, b. Jan. 17, 1771	1	144
Daniel, m. Anne **COOK**, Mar. 5, 1718/19	1	138
Daniel, s. [Daniel & Anne], b. Jan. 6, 1728/9	1	140
Daniel, s. Daniel & Anne, d. Mar. 8, 1739/40	1	147
Daniel, d. Aug. 3, 1752	1	147
E[b]enezer, m. Bridget **BROWN**, Sept. 18, 1712	1	138
Eben[eze]r, s. [Daniel & Anne], b. July 14, 1724	1	140
Ebenezer, s. Jabez & Lydia, b. Sept. 26, 1756, at Norwich	1	142
Elisha, s. [Will[ia]m & Mary], b. May 6, 1749	1	142
Elizabeth, d. Jedediah & Elizabeth, b. Sept. 30, 1703	1	140
Ellis, see under Alice		
Jabez, Capt., m. Elizabeth **DARBE**, Jan. 14, 1754	1	138
Jabez, Jr., m. Lydia **HUNTINGTON**, of Norwich, Aug. 22, 1754	1	138
Jabez Gaill, s. Jabez & Lydia, b. Mar. 20, 1764	1	143

	Vol.	Page
FITCH, (cont.)		
James, s. [Daniel & Anne], b. May 27, 1722	1	140
Jerusha, d. Jabez & Lydia, b. Jan. 30, 1722/3	1	140
Jerusha, m. Fixhall **ENSWORTH**, Dec. 6, 1742	1	133
John, m. Elizabeth **JOHNSON**, Oct. 18, 1714	1	138
John, s. [Daniel & Anne], b. Sept. 30, 1726	1	140
John, d. Apr. 22, 1754	1	147
Lucy, d. Jabez & Lydia, b. June 24, 1736	1	140
Lucy, d. Jabez, Jr. & Lydia, b. Mar. 24, 1777	1	144
Lidia, w. Capt., d. Aug. 22, 1753	1	147
Lydia, d. Jabez & Lydia, b. Oct. 9, 1758	1	142
Lydia, d. Jabez & Lydia, d. Aug. 2, 1759	1	147
Lydia, d. Jebez & Lydia, b. June 14, 1760	1	142
Lydia, m. Eliphaz **PERKINS**, Sept. 7, 1780	1	193
Mary, m. Jos[eph] **BACON**, b. of Canterbury, Oct. 16, 1745, at Groton, by Andrew Croswell	1	69
Mary, d. [Will[ia]m & Mary], b. Oct. 27, 1747	1	142
Mary, m. Jacob **PERKINS**, Jr., Oct. 9, 1766	1	193
Olive, [twin with Phebe], d. [Will[ia]m & Mary], b. Aug. 21, 1757	1	142
Peres, s. [Jabez & Lydia], b. Dec. [ ], 1726	1	140
Perez, s. Perez & Lydia, b. Sept 5, 1755; d. [Sept.] 26, [1755]	1	142
Peter, s. [Jedediah & Elizabeth], b. July 28, 1705	1	140
Phebe, [twin with Olive], d. [Will[ia]m & Mary], b. Aug. 21, 1757	1	142
Phebe, of Coventry, m. Joseph **SIMMS**, June 16, 1802	1	215
Priscilla, m. Solomon **PAINE**, May 31, 1732	1	192
Rufus, s. [Will[ia]m & Mary], b. July 26, 1755	1	142
Samuel, s. Jabez, Jr. & Lydia, b. Mar. 30, 1773	1	144
Sarah, d. Jabez, Jr. & Lydia, b. Apr. 28, 1766	1	143
Theophilus, s. [Daniel & Anne], b. July 14, 1731	1	140
Theophilus, m. Mary **HUNTINGTON**, Dec. 15, 1731	1	138
Theophilus, d. "awfully' July 20, 1751	1	147
Warren, of Tolland, m. Mary **SAFFORD**, of Canterbury, Nov. 16, 1820, by [ ]	2	31
William, s. Daniel & Anne, b. Aug. [ ], 1720	1	140
Will[ia]m, m. Mary **PAINE**, Jan. 27, 1740/41	1	138
Will[ia]m, s. Will[ia]m & Mary, b. Feb. 14, 1744/5	1	141
FOBES, Alice, see under Ellis		
Bethiah, d. Simon & Thankful, b. July 21, 1754	1	141
Ellis (Alice), d. Simon & Thankful, b. Nov. 19, 1760	1	142
Eunice, d. Simon & Thankful, b. July 12, 1763	1	143
Joshua, s. Simon & Thankful, b. Sept. 14, 1751	1	141
Joshua, s. Simon & Thankful, d. Jan. 4, 1755	1	147
Nathan, s. Simon & Thankful, b. July 24, 1758	1	142
Simon, of Preston, m. Thankful **ELLIS**, of Stonington, Mar. 24, 1748	1	138
Simon, s. Simon & Thankful, b. Apr. 5, 1756	1	142

	Vol.	Page

FOWLER, (cont.)

Deidama, m. Harvey **SPAULDING**, b. of Canterbury, July 20,
 1845, by Rev. Jacob Allen — 2 — 75

George Robert, s. [Robert D. & Mary E.], b. Oct. 22, 1840 — 2 — 231

Godfree Malbone, s. Charles & Sally, b. Sept. 17, 1815 — 1 — 145

Mary Elizabeth, d. Robert D. & Mary E., b. Sept. 19, 1836 — 2 — 231

Robert D., m. Mary E. **ROBINSON**, b. of Canterbury, Apr.
 8, 1835, by Rev. Otis C. Whiton — 2 — 31

Samuel F., m. Mary J. **ADAMS**, b. of Canterbury, June 25,
 1848, by Rev. Nehemiah B. Hyde — 2 — 33

FOX, Daniel, s. Eunice **FOX**, single woman, b. Jan. 13, 1780 — 1 — 144

Eunice, single woman, had s. Daniel **FOX**, b. Jan. 13, 1780 — 1 — 144

Mary Ann, of Columbia, m. David P. **CONE**, of Chatham,
 Nov. 14, 1853, by Thomas K, Peck, J. P. — 2 — 20

Thankful, m. Thomas **BUSWELL**, Mar. 26, 1786 — 1 — 72

FRANCIS, FRANCES, Fanny E., of Canterbury, m. Jesse H.
 TOURTELLOTT, of Thompson, Jan. 13, 1850, by Rev.
 Robert C. Learned — 2 — 80

Harriet, m. Luther **SANGER**, b. of Canterbury, June 7,
 1847, by Tho[ma]s L. Shipman, Jewett City — 2 — 76

Harriet N., m. Edward **HYDE**, b. of Canterbury, Nov. 19,
 1840, by Rev. Tubal Wakefield — 2 — 41

Jemima, of Canterbury, m. Norman **PARKS**, of Griswold,
 Nov. 10, 1839, by Rev. Charles J. Warren — 2 — 63

John, d. Jan. 24, 1826 — 2 — 329

John M., m. Sabrina **ALLEN**, Oct. 11, 1835, by Rev. Jesse
 Fisher — 2 — 31

Mary E., of Canterbury, m. Daniel P. **WHEELER**, of Norwich,
 Mar. 7, 1842, by Rev. Tubal Wakefield — 2 — 87

Sarah, of Canterbury, m. Erastus **KENNY**, of Plainfield,
 Aug. 13, 1850, by Rev. J. B. Guild, of Packersville — 2 — 48

FREEMAN, Abigail, d. Robert & Mary, b. Apr. 5, 1738 — 1 — 140

Hannah, of Martlake, m. Joseph **CHAPMAN**, then of Pomfret,
 May 16, 1751 — 1 — 100

Rebecca, m. Abraham **PAINE**, Mar. 8, 1743/4 — 1 — 192

FRENCH, Abner, s. John & Elizabeth, b. Mar. 3, 1757 — 1 — 142

Charity, m. Reuben **PECK**, Dec. 6, 1759 — 1 — 192

John, s. John & Elizabeth, b. Jan. 12, 1766 — 1 — 143

Nathan, s. Nathan* & Elizabeth, b. July 1, 1762
 (*Should be "John". Corrected by L. B. B.) — 1 — 142

Ruth, d. John & Elizabeth, b. Nov. 12, 1764 — 1 — 143

Ruth, d. John & Elizabeth, d. Apr. 18, 1766 — 1 — 147

Sarah, d. [John & Elizabeth], b. Apr. 27, 1760 — 1 — 142

FRINK, Betsey, m. John **CRANDALL**, b. of Canterbury, Jan. 15,
 1846, by Samuel S. Hough, J. P. — 2 — 18

FROST, Abigail, twin with Daniel, d. [Stephen & Elizabeth],
 b. May 1, 1715 — 1 — 140

Abigail, d. [Daniel & Elizabeth], b. Oct. 24, 1742 — 1 — 141

	Vol.	Page
FROST, (cont.)		
Abigail, single woman, d. May 18, 1768	1	147
Asa, s. Henry & Alice, b. Apr. 28, 1771	1	144
Asa, m. Mary **SMITH**, Mar. 8, 1795	1	138
Asher, s. Henry & Alice, b. Aug. 3, 1778	1	144
Bethuel, s. [Daniel & Elizabeth], b. Apr. 28, 1741	1	141
Bethuel, m. Mary **ADAMS**, June 20, 1765	1	138
Bethuel, d. Aug. 30, 1768	1	147
Daniel, twin with Abigail, s. [Stephen & Elizabeth],		
b. May 1, 1715	1	140
Daniel, m. Elizabeth **BOND**, May 7, 1739	1	138
Daniel, s. [Daniel & Elizabeth], b. July 6, 1748	1	142
Dan[ie]l, m. Phebe **FARNUM**, of Norwich, Dec. 16, 1773	1	138
Daniel, s. Daniel & Phebe, b. Apr. 17, 1787	1	144
Daniel, m. Hannah **STEVENS**, Dec. 21, 1809	1	138
Daniel, Jr., m. Louisa **CLARKE**, Feb. 3, 1811	1	139
Daniel Clarke, s. Daniel, Jr. & Louisa, b. June 14, 1812	1	145
Elizabeth, d. Stephen & Elizabeth, d. Feb. 10, 1722/3	1	147
Elizabeth, w. Stephen, d. Feb. 15, 1726/7	1	147
Elizabeth, d. [Stephen & Mary], b. Jan. 23, 1727	1	140
Elizabeth, m. Paul **DAVENPORT**, July 1, 1747	1	120
Elizabeth, d. [Daniel & Elizabeth], b. May 23, 1753	1	142
Elizabeth, m. Andrew **HEBBARD**, Dec. 3, 1782	1	155
Eunice, d. [Stephen & Mary], b. Apr. 8, 1747	1	142
Eunice, m. John **PARK**, July 12, 1764	1	193
Hannah, d. Stephen & Elizabeth, d. Mar. 13, 1724	1	147
Hannah, d. Daniel & Elizabeth, b. Mar. 19, 1740	1	141
Hannah, d. Sept. 21, 1761	1	147
Helen Louisa, d. [Daniel, Jr. & Louisa], b. May 17, 1821	1	145
Henry, s. Stephen & Mary, b. Oct. 1, 1735	1	140
Henry, m. Ellis (Alice) **BUTT**, Feb. 28, 1765	1	138
Hezekiah, s. Daniel & Elizabeth, b. Sept. 18, 1745	1	142
Hezekiah, s. Dan[ie]l & Phebe, b. Feb. 7, 1778	1	144
Huldah, d. Stephen & Elizabeth, b. Nov. 16, 1718	1	140
Huldah, d. Stephen & Mary, b. Mar. 15, 1737/8	1	140
Huldy, m. Josiah **DEWEY**, Jan. 3, 1759	1	120
Jonas, s. Stephen & Mary, b. Mar. 13, 1725	1	140
Joseph, s. [Stephen & Elizabeth], b. Oct. 25, 1712	1	140
Joseph, s. [Daniel & Elizabeth], b. Aug. 21, 1750	1	142
Jos[eph], d. Sept. 27, 1774	1	148
Lucretia, m. David **BUTT**, Jan. 24, 1793	1	72
Lucret[i]a, m. David **BUTTS**, Jan. 24, 1793	1	121
Lydia, d. [Daniel & Elizabeth], b. Apr. 28, 1755	1	142
Maria, d. Asa & Mary, b. Feb. 29, 1796	1	145
Mary, d. [Stephen & Mary], b. June 14, 1731	1	141
Mary, m. Eliphalet **ADAMS**, June 5, 1753(?)	1	51
Mary, w. Dea. Stephen, d. May 15, 1764	1	147
Mary, d. Henry & Ellis (Alice), b. Mar. 9, 1766	1	143

	Vol.	Page
FROST, (cont.)		
Mary, d. Henry & Ellis (Alice), d. Oct. 27, 1767	1	147
Mary, m. Peter **WOODARD**, Dec. 23, 1774	1	236
Phebe Elizabeth, d. [Daniel, Jr. & Louisa], b. Jan. 7, 1814	1	145
Phinehas, s. Stephen & Mary, b. June 27, 1741	1	142
Phinehas, s. Stephen & Mary, d. Oct. 10, 1760	1	147
Phinehas, s. Henry & Alice, b. Mar. 2, 1782	1	144
Sarah, d. [Stephen & Mary], b. Apr. 30, 1729	1	140
Sarah, d. Henry & Alice, b. Jan. 6, 1769	1	144
Sophronia, d. Asa & Mary, b. Jan. 10, 1798	1	145
Stephen, m. Mary **ADAMS**, Oct. 29, 1724	1	138
Stephen, d. Mar. 12, 1728	1	147
Stephen, s. [Stephen & Mary], b. Apr. 15, 1733	1	141
Stephen, m. Sarah **PIKE**, June 6, 1765	1	138
Susannah, d. Stephen & Elizabeth, b. May 13, 1711	1	140
Susanna, d. Stephen & Mary, b. Oct. 24, 1743	1	142
Susanna, m. James **DELAP**, Apr. 25, 1771	1	120
FULLER, Abigail, m. James **BEDLOCK**, Jr., Apr. 30, 1772	1	70
Alice, m. Asael **BACON**, Aug. 19, 1795	1	72
Benjamin, s. Jacob & Abigail, b. June 8, 1770	1	144
Edward J., Rev., of Chelsea, Mass., m. Anna C. **GREEN**, of Canterbury, May 23, 1832, by Rev. Demis Platt	2	31
Pearley B., of Lisbon, m. Esther **SMITH**, of Canterbury, June 3, 1835, by Rev. Levi Nelson	2	31
Penimah, m. Jacob **SMITH**, Jan. 23, 1758	1	214
GAGER, Rebecca, m. Hezekiah **BARSTOW**, Jr., Jan. 28, 1818	1	73
GALE, Abigail, d. [Richard & Sarah], b. Apr. 14, 1724	1	150
Grace, m. William **ENSWORTH**, Mar. 26, 1745	1	133
Hannah, d. Richard & Sarah, b. May 5, 1720	1	150
Jerusha, d. [Richard & Sarah], b. Sept. 2, 1722	1	150
Jonathan, s. [Richard & Sarah], b. Nov. 26, 1708	1	150
Lydia, d. [Richard & Sarah], b. Aug. 3, 1717	1	150
Mercy, d. [Richard & Sarah], b. Dec. 4, 1710	1	150
Sarah, d. Richard & Sarah, b. Aug. 14, 1706	1	150
Thankful, d. [Richard & Sarah], b. Feb. 14, 1714/15	1	150
GALLUP, David, m. Laura **HOW**, Oct. 11, 1827, by Chester Lyon, J. P.	2	35
Margaret, of Voluntown, m. Samuel **WALDO**, [ ]	1	237
Susannah W., m. Nathaniel S. **STANTON**, Sept. 17, 1843, by Rev. Asa King, Westminster	2	75
GARDINER, [see also **GARDNER**], John, m. Olive **NICHOLS**, Apr. 1, 1775	1	149
GARDNER, [see also **GARDINER**], Joseph, m. Orpha **REED**, Feb. 28, 1823, by Asael Bacon, J. P.	2	35
Rowland, of Plainfield, m. Martha M. **RICHARDS**, of Canterbury, Jan. 5, 1845, by Rev. Daniel D. Lyon, of Packerville	2	35
GATES, Abigail, twin with Benjamin, d. Silas & Mary, b. Nov. 4,		

	Vol.	Page
GATES, (cont.)		
1774	1	151
Alice, d. Nathaniel & Deborah, b. Nov. 15, 1783	1	152
Benjamin, twin with Abigail, s. Silas & Mary, b. Nov. 4, 1774	1	151
Bet[t]y, d. Nathaniel & Deborah, b. Jan. 13, 1765	1	151
Deborah, m. David **LILLIE**, Nov. 23, 1780 or 1785	1	176
Dorothy, of East Haddam, m. Sam[ue]l **HUNTINGTON**, May 25, 1757	1	155
John, s. Nath[anie]l & Deborah, b. Mar. 1, 1781	1	152
Mehetable, of Preston, m. Adam **CLARK**, Dec. 5, 1759	1	101
Mol[l]ey, d. Nathaniel & Deborah, b. Aug. 17, 1763	1	151
Nathaniel, m. Deborah **DEANS**, Feb. 22, 173[ ]	1	149
Nathaniel, s. Nathaniel & Deborah, b. Mar. 21, 1767	1	151
Seth, s. Silas & Mary, b. Aug. 20, 1772	1	151
Thankful, m. Nathaniel **CLARK**, Apr. 30, 1751	1	101
GAVIN, Sarah, m. Samuel **RANSOM**, Nov. 7, 1780	1	209
GEER, Asa, m. Rebeckah **MARTIN**, Nov. 13, 1764	1	149
Asa, d. Jan. [ ], 1781, in New York City. "Rev. Soldier"	1	154
David Martin, s. [Asa & Rebeckah], b. Aug. 11, 1780	1	152
Ebenezer Stowell, s. [Asa & Rebecca], b. June 16, 1768	1	151
Elizabeth, d. Asa & Rebeckah, b. May 2, 1778	1	152
Emeline, m. Henry **PARKIST**, b. of Canterbury, Apr. 18, 1829, by C. S. Hyde, J. P.	2	61
Fanny, d. Joseph & Hannah, b. Feb. 26, 1802	1	152
George, s. Asa & Rebecca, b. Dec. 3, 1765	1	151
John, s. [Asa & Rebecca], b. Feb. 21, 1773	1	151
Orra, d. [Joseph & Hannah], b. Feb. 1, 1804	1	152
Rebecca, m. Jonathan **PIKE**, Sept. 11, 1783	1	193
Samantha, d. Joseph & Hannah, b. Dec. 18, 1800	1	152
Sarah, d. [Asa & Rebecca], b. Mar. 15, 1775	1	151
Zillah, d. [Asa & Rebecca], b. Sept. 5, 1770	1	151
GENNINGS, Sibbel, m. David **FISH**, Oct. 28, 1769	1	138
GETCHELL, [see under **GITCHELL**]		
GIBBONS, [see also **GOSSON**], Sarah, d. Aug. 4, 1749	1	154
GIBBS, George J., m. Mary S. **MANNING**, b. of Canterbury, Jan. 1, 1852, by Rev. Robert C. Learned	2	36
GIBSON, Ephraim, d. Oct. 10, 1757	1	154
Ichabod, so called, s. of Elizabeth **DIXON**, so called, b. Feb. 21, 1752	1	150
Joanna, wid., m. Joseph **RAYNSFORD**, Feb. 4, 1752	1	209
Mary, m. Hezekiah **PELLET**, May 7, 1781	1	193
GILBERT, Elijah, s. Noah & Mary, b. May 18, 1743	1	150
Elizabeth, d. Noah & Sara[h], b. Feb. 25, 1735/6	1	150
Lucy, d. Noah & Sara[h], b. July 25, 1741	1	150
Mary, d. Noah & Sara[h], b. Mar. 11, 1728/9	1	150
Sara[h], d. Noah & Sara[h], b. Sept. 2, 1732	1	150
William, s. Noah & Sara[h], b. Feb. 5, 1733/4	1	150
GILDON, Eliza[beth], d. Rich[ar]d & Isabella, b. Dec. 13, 1773	1	150

	Vol.	Page
GITCHELL, Eliza C., m. David **AUSTIN**, Apr. 13, 1823	1	53
GLASS, Anthony, m. Eunice **BENNETT**, June 19, 1740	1	149
Eunice, d. Anthony & Eunice, b. Apr. 28, 1742	1	151
Eunice, d. Anthony & Eunice, d. Oct. 16, 1749	1	154
Eunice, d. Anthony & Eunice, b. Jan. 10, 1760	1	151
James, s. Anthony & Eunice, b. May 31, 1744	1	150
Lois, d. Anthony & Eunice, b. Jan. 1, 1743	1	151
Loes, m. Peter **STEVENS**, Nov. 1, 1759	1	214
Mary, d. Anthony & Eunice, b. June 15, 1753	1	151
Prudence, d. Anthony & Eunice, b. Mar. 8, 1748	1	151
Prudence, m. Eben[eze]r **BUTT**, Jan. 4, 1769	1	70
Rufus, s. Anthony & Eunice, b. Apr. 7, 1755	1	151
Samuel, s. Anthony & Eunice, b. Apr. 1, 1758	1	151
Sarah, d. Anthony & Eunice, b. Aug. 20, 1751	1	151
Sarah, m. Joseph **BUTTON**, May 2, 1773	1	71
Silas, s. Anthony & Eunice, b. Aug. 30, 1746	1	150
Stephen, s. Stephen & Bette, b. Oct. 18, 1742	1	150
GODFREY, Patience, m. Gershom **JUSTIN**, Mar. 7, 1780	1	167
GOFF, Calvin W., of East Haddam, m. Orrilla R. **SMITH**, of		
Canterbury, Mar. 31, 1851, by C. D. Fillimore, Elder	2	35
GOODALE, [see also **GOODELL**], Hannah, m. Benjamin		
SHEPARD, Nov. 24, 1748	1	214
GOODELL, [see also **GOODALE**], Allthea, d. Moses & Thankful,		
b. May 23, 1768	1	151
Ebenezer, d. May 20, 1772	1	154
Ebenezer, s. Moses & Thankful, b. June 4, 1776	1	152
Elias, s. [Moses & Thankful], b. Sept. 17, 1771	1	151
Moses, m. Thankful **FOBES**, Oct. 29, 1767	1	149
Simon, s. Moses & Thankful, b. July 16, 1782	1	152
GOODING, Pierce, m. Hannah **LUIS**, Dec. 7, 1761	1	149
GORDON, Alexander Milton, s. John & Lucy, b. Aug. 20, 1810	1	152
Archibald Wells, s. Archibald & Welthian, b. Apr. 10, 1781	1	152
Elizabeth, d. [Alexander & Margaret], b. Mar. [ ], 1778	1	152
Elliot, s. Alexander & Margaret, b. Jan. 11, 1772	1	152
Euretta Catharine, d. John & Lucy, b. Jan. 10, 1803	1	152
Harriet, d. Alexander & Hannah, b. Nov. 1, 1801	1	152
James, s. [Alexander & Margaret], b. Apr. 2, 1780	1	152
John, s. [Alexander & Margaret], b. June 9, 1776	1	152
John, m. Lucy **MOORE**, May 24, 1801	1	149
Loiza, d. John & Lucy, b. Jan. 31, 1807	1	152
Loisa, of Canterbury, m. Simon **CUTLER**, of Plainfield,		
Oct. 7, 1832, by Rev. Demis Platt	2	16
Maria, d. Alexan[de]r & Hannah, b. Sept. 7, 1799	1	152
Milton, s. [Alexander & Margaret], b. May 11, 1784	1	152
Samuel, s. [Alexander & Margaret], b. Mar. 26, 1774	1	152
Thomas, s. [Alexander & Margaret], b. Apr. 7, 1782	1	152
GORHAM, Ephraim, s. Nathan & Susanna, b. Mar. 31, 1753	1	152
George, s. Nathan & Susanna, b. July 19, 1759	1	151

GORHAM, (cont.)

Jabez, s. [Nathan & Susanna], b. May 19, 1765   1   151
John, s. Joseph & Hannah, b. Nov. 7, 1774   1   151
Joseph, s. Nathan & Susannah, b. Sept. 28, 1751   1   151
Jos[eph], m. Hannah **STAPLES**, Jan. 8, 1773   1   149
Nathan, s. Nathan & Suzannah, b. Sept. 10, 1757   1   151
Susannah, d. Jos[eph] & Hannah, b. May 8, 1777   1   152

GOSSON, [see also **GIBSON**], Edward, so called, s., Elizabeth
    DIXON, so called, b. May 25, 1747   1   150
Mary, so called d. of Elizabeth **DIXON**, so called, b.
    June 4, 1743   1   150
Mary, d. Elizabeth **DIXON**, d. July 3, 1749   1   154

GOULD, Benjamin, s. Edmund & Sarah, b. Apr. 19, 1792   1   152
Edmund, m. Sarah **MOTT**, Jan. 7, 1788   1   149
John, s. Edmund & Sarah, b. Nov. 28, 1789   1   152
Joseph, s. Edmund & Sarah, b. Sept. 1, 1788   1   152
Lydia, d. Edmund & Sarah, b. Jan. 9, 1791   1   152

GRAVES, Emily, d. Joseph & Eunice, b. Nov. 10, 1817   2   231
Joseph, illeg. child of Lucy **JEWETT**, b. Apr. 1, 1810   1   152

GREEN, GREENE, Abner, m. Abigail **JUSTIN**, Feb. 16, 1796, at
    Preston   1   149
Achsah, d. John & Abigail, b. Oct. 5, 1768   1   151
Alanson, s. Eunice **GREEN**, [single woman], b. June 12, 1784   1   152
Alford, s. John & Abigail, b. Aug. 18, 1764   1   151
Amason, s. Jabez & Sarah, d. Mar. 30, 1756   1   154
Amason, s. Jabez & Sarah, b. Dec. 4, 1761   1   151
Amos, s. Jabez & Hannah, b. June 1, 1751   1   151
Ame, d. Jabez & Sarah, b. June 30, 1758   1   151
Ann Eliza, m. John C. **BARTLETT**, Jan. 17, 1847, by Rev.
    Asa King, Westminster   2   14
Anna C., of Canterbury, m. Rev. Edward J. **FULLER**, of
    Chelsea, Mass., May 23, 1832, by Rev. Demis Platt   2   31
Anne, m. Festus **MORSE**, b. of Canterbury, Aug. 30, 1840,
    by Rev. Tubal Wakefield   2   56
Asahel, s. [John & Abigail], b. May 5, 1774   1   151
Benjamin, s. Robert & Ruth, b. Feb. 2, 1706/7   1   150
Benjamin, s. Benjamin & Elizabeth, b. Dec. 21, 1734   1   150
Betty, d. Benj[ami]n & Betty, b. June 24, 1738   1   150
Bet[t]ey, d. Olive, b. May 22, 1760   1   151
Betty, single woman, had s. Mansur **BROWN**, b. Aug. 18,
    1793   1   89
Calista, d. Bennet & Lucy, b. July 25, 1798   1   152
Charles, s. [Bennet & Lucy], b. Mar. 5, 1805   1   153
Dennison, m. Roxanna **GRIFFIN**, Sept. 1, 1828, by Rev.
    Israel G. Rose, of Westminster   2   35
Elijah, m. Louis Ann **HALL**, b. of Canterbury, Dec. 4, 1836,
    by John Francis, J. P.   2   35
Elizabeth had s. Jonathan Fairle **RUE**, b. Dec. 2, 1784   1   212

	Vol.	Page

GREEN, GREENE, (cont.)

Elizabeth, single woman, had d. Petifeel Pierpont **PHILLIPS**,
   b. Apr. 1, 1791 — 1 — 203

Eunice, d. Jabez & Hannah, b. Mar. 11, 1745 — 1 — 150

Eunice, [single woman], had s. Alanson, b. June 12, 1784 — 1 — 152

Eunice, single woman, had s. Ruley, b. Aug. 5, 1788 — 1 — 152

Grace, d. [Bennet & Lucy], b. Apr. 5, 1807 — 1 — 153

Harry, s. [Abner & Nabby], b. July 22, 1798 — 1 — 152

Hulda, d. Jabez & Sarah, b. Feb. 18, 1754 — 1 — 150

Jabez, Jr., m. Sarah **LAMBART**, May 1, 1754 — 1 — 149

Jane T., of Providence, R. I., m. Jerome B. D. **LeVALLEY**,
   of Warwick, R. I., Oct. 19, 1834, by Rev. Otis C. Whiton — 2 — 52

Jedediah, s. Jabez & Hannah, b. Jan. 29, 1754 — 1 — 151

Jedediah, m. Hannah **RUSS**, Feb. 22, 1774 — 1 — 149

Jedediah, s. Jedediah & Hannah, b. Feb. 18, 1777 — 1 — 152

John, of Veffer Co., N. Y., m. Abigail **RUDE**, of Norwich,
   Dec. 27, 1762 — 1 — 149

Lucretia, d. Jedediah & Hannah, b. Dec. 1, 1775 — 1 — 151

Lucy, of Canterbury, m. Martin **CORY**, Jr., of Plainfield,
   Aug. 4, 1844, by Solomon Payne, J. P. — 2 — 18

Luther, s. Abner & Nabby, b. Dec. 10, 1796 — 1 — 152

Lydia, d. Benj[ami]n & Betty, b. Feb. 24, 1745 — 1 — 151

Lydia M., m. Whitman **WILCOX**, Aug. 27, 1832, by Andrew
   T. Judson, J. P. — 2 — 86

Martin, s. Robert & Susanna, b. Mar. 30, 1751 — 1 — 150

Mary, d. Robert & Ruth, b. July 18, 1701 — 1 — 150

Mercy, d. Jabez & Hannah, b. Mar. 16, 1746/7 — 1 — 150

Nathan, m. Anna **BALDWIN**, July 17, 1775 — 1 — 149

Olive, d. Benj[ami]n & Betty, b. Nov. 1, 1737 — 1 — 150

Olive had d. Bet[t]ey, b. May 22, 1760 — 1 — 151

Olive, m. Allen **DEAN**, of Killingly, Jan. 31, 1794 — 1 — 121

Olive, d. [Bennet & Lucy], b. Jan. 9, 1801 — 1 — 152

Rebeckah, d. Robert & Ruth, b. Oct. [ ], 1703 — 1 — 150

Robert, s. Robert & Ruth, b. Jan. [ ], 1705/6 — 1 — 150

Robert, s. Benjamin & Elizabeth, b. Apr. 1, 1733 — 1 — 150

Robert, m. Susanna **WHITE**, Nov. 21, 1750 — 1 — 149

Robert, d. Apr. 9, 1752 — 1 — 154

Rosel, s. Jabez & Sarah, d. May 17, 1757 — 1 — 154

Roxanna, d. [Bennet & Lucy], b. Sept. 11, 1802 — 1 — 152

Rozel, s. Jabez & Sarah, b. Apr. 2, 1763 — 1 — 151

Ruley, s. Eunice **GREEN**, single woman, b. Aug. 5, 1788 — 1 — 152

Ruth, d. Robert & Ruth, b. [ ], 1711 — 1 — 150

Sabrah, d. [John & Abigail], b. Mar. 29, 1771 — 1 — 151

Sarah, d. Robert & Ruth, b. [ ], 1709 — 1 — 150

Sarah, m. John **FELCH**, Mar. 7, 1737 — 1 — 138

Sarah, d. Jabez & Hannah, b. May 6, 1749 — 1 — 150

Suzannah, d. Benj[ami]n & Betty, b. May 15, 1742 — 1 — 150

Will[ia]m, s. Benj[ami]n & Betty, b. Mar. 14, 1740 — 1 — 150

	Vol.	Page
GREENMAN, Sarah, m. Samuel **WARREN**, Dec. 30, 1798	1	237
GRIFFIN, GRIFFING, Mary, of Windham, m. Ephraim **CLEVELAND**, Mar. 6, 1766	1	101
Roxanna, m. Dennison **GREEN**, Sept. 1, 1828, by Rev. Israel G. Rose, of Westminster	2	35
GRIFFIS, Ruth, of Canterbury, m. Edwin **POLLOCK**, of Windham, Jan. 14, 1844, by Rev. John F. Blanchard. Witnesses: Eliza F. Bennett, Eben J. Bennett, Lucy Pollock	2	64
GRIGGS, Maryetta, m. Daniel **BLAKELEY**, b. of Hampton, June 23, 1850, by Charles Adams, J. P.	2	14
GROSVENOR, Elizabeth, m. Simens **PEIRCE**, May 4, 1779	1	193
GROW, John, s. John & Deborah, b. July 31, 1775	1	152
HAGGIT, Abigail, m. John **CARTER**, Mar. 2, 1756	1	100
HAHES*, Jesse, of Brooklyn, m. Clarissa **CAM[P]BELL**, Jan. 21, 1816 (*HAKES?)	1	156
HALL, Cornelius, of Hopkinton, R. I., m. Alice **MORSE**, of Lisbon, Apr. 10, 1803	1	156
Ebenezer, of Plainfield, m. Mary **BRAMAN**, of Canterbury, Jan. 3, 1826, by Rev. Tho[ma]s J. Murdock	2	39
Elizabeth, m. Solomon **CARPENTER**, Nov. 25, 1841, by Rev. Asa King, Westminster	2	18
J. Augustus, of Perrysburg, O., m. Phebe **BURNETT**, of Canterbury, Apr. 22, 1848, by Rev. Asa King, Westminster	2	42
Louis Ann, m. Elijah **GREEN**, b. of Canterbury, Dec. 4, 1836, by John Francis, J. P.	2	35
Lucretia, of Canterbury, m. Otis **HALL**, of Plainfield, Nov. 29, 1827, by Rev. Seth Bliss, of Griswold	2	39
Otis, of Plainfield, m. Lucretia **HALL**, of Canterbury, Nov. 29, 1827, by Rev. Seth Bliss, of Griswold	2	39
HAMBLIN, Elijah, s. Elijah & Mary, b. June 2, 1751	1	158
Elizabeth, d. Elijah & Mary, b. May 14, 1749	1	158
John, s. Elijah & Mary, b. May 12, 1753	1	158
HAMMOND, Abigail, m. Deleno **PEIRCE**, Nov. 1, 1770	1	193
Abigail, of Windham, m. Ebenezer **JEWETT**, Sept. 24, 1782	1	167
Alfred, of Hampton, m. Cynthia **STORER**, Apr. 28, 1841, by Rev. Asa King, Westminster	2	41
Elisha, s. Jason & Hannah, b. Feb. 7, 1769	1	161
Jason, m. Hannah **RANSOM**, Apr. 27, 1766	1	155
Jason, s. Jason & Hannah, b. May 8, 1767	1	161
HANDE, [see under HENDEE]		
HARRINGTON, Charity, d. Dan[ie]l & Anne, b. Aug. 30, 1772	1	161
Daniel, m. Juliana **BROWN**, [ ], by Rev. Demis Platt	2	40
Gershom, s. Daniel & Mary, d. Dec. 30, 1749	1	165
Lewis, of Killingly, m. Abey M. **ROBINSON**, of Canterbury, Oct. 20, 1849, by R. S. Hazen, of Westminster	2	42
Mary, single woman, had d. Joanna **BROWN**, b. Nov. 16, 1771	1	84
Paul, s. Benj[ami]n & Hannah, b. Nov. 10, 1740		159

	Vol.	Page
HARRIS, Abigail, m. James **WOODARD**, Jan. 14, 1762	1	236
Alma Maria, m. John **PENEY**, b. of Canterbury, July 18, 1830, by Rev. Dennis Platt	2	61
Andrew, m. Mary E. **CLEVELAND**, Feb. 2, 1813	1	156
Bethiah, d. [Reuben & Lydia], b. May 17, 1772	1	161
Celinda, see under Selinda		
Charles F., m. Ann Mariah **DAVIS**, of Boston, Mar. 28, 1833, by Rev. Asa King, Westminster	2	40
Daniel, s. Sam[ue]l & Elizabeth, b. Aug. 30, 1779	1	162
Ebenezer, s. Paul & Mary, b. July 16, 1771	1	162
Frances Eliza, d. And[rew] & Mary E., b. Nov. 4, 1815	1	164
Hannah, d. [Paul & Mary], b. Nov. 29, 1766	1	161
Henry, s. Silas & Mary, b. Sept. 27, 1759	1	160
John, m. Alethea **CARY**, Apr. 1, 1838, by Rev. Asa King	2	17
Jonathan, of Brooklyn, m. Emeline L. **KEESES**, of Lisbon, Sept. 27, 1829, by Peter Morse, J. P.	2	39
Joshua, m. Hannah **HOUGH**, Jan. 17, 1781	1	155
Leah, d. Silas & Mary, b. Sept. 2, 1755, at South Kingstown, R. I.	1	160
Lucy, d. Reuben & Lydia, b. Apr. 22, 1777* (*1771?)	1	161
Lucy, m. Roswell **PARISH**, Nov. 1, 1791	1	194
Maria Crandall, d. William & Sarah P., b. Dec. 9, 1836	2	239
Mary A., of Canterbury, m. Pullman M. **WILLIAMS**, of West Springfield, Mass., Apr. 13, 1845, by Erastus Dickinson	2	88
Mary E., m. David **YOUNG**, of Norwich, Aug. 29, 1842, by Rev. W. Clarke	2	91
Mary Esther, d. Andrew & Mary E., b. Mar. 21, 1814	1	164
Paul, m. Mary **HERRINGTON**, Sept. 22, 1749	1	155
Paul, s. Paul & Mary, b. June 3, 1753	1	158
Paul, d. Nov. 7, 1777, in the 53rd y. of his age	1	165
Phebe, d. Paul, & Mary, b. May 5, 1760	1	160
Reuben, m. Lydia **LANFAIR**, July 4, 1769	1	155
Reuben, s. Reuben & Lydia, b. Nov. 11, 1776	1	162
Ruth, m. Simeon **CADY**, Feb. 26, 1745	1	100
Ruth, d. Paul & Mary, b. Mar. 26, 1764	1	161
Sam[ue]l, s. Paul & Mary, b. Feb. 2, 1757	1	160
Samuel, m. Elizabeth **CADY**, Mar. 4, 1779	1	155
Sarah A., of Canterbury, m. Frederick A. **BARON**, of U. S. Navy, Sept. 7, 1837, by Rev. Charles J. Warren	2	11
Sarah Ann M., m. George **FAIRWEATHER**, of Kingston, R. I., Nov. 28, 1833, by Rev. Asa King, Westminster	2	31
Sarah Arnold, d. [Andrew & Mary E.], b. Nov. 30, 1817	1	164
Selinda, of Canterbury, m. William **ANDERSON**, of New London, May 20, 1834, by Rev. Asa King	2	3
Solinda, m. William **ANDREWS**, of New London, []y 20,1834	1	53
Silas, m. Mary **ORSBAND**, May 11, 1755	1	155
Silas Gapson, s. Silas & Mary, b. Aug. 20, 1762	1	160
Susanna, d. Reuben & Lydia, b. Sept. 5, 1774	1	162

	Vol.	Page
HARRIS, (cont.)		
William Lloyd Garrison, s. W[illia]m & Sarah, b. July 15, 1834	2	239
William Wilburforce, s. Charles F. & Ann Maria, b. Sept. 7, 1834	2	239
HARTSHORN, HARTSON, Asaph, s. Luther & Lucinda, b. Feb. 11, 1802	1	163
John, m. Mary Ann **WOODARD**, Nov. 17, 1829, by Rev. Israel G. Rose,. of Westminster	2	40
Luther, m. Lucinda **MORSE**, Apr. 5, 1801	1	156
Sally, of Griswold, m. Samuel **ROBBINS**, of Canterbury, Mar. 16, 1834, by Rev. Otis C. Whiton	2	67
Sarah, m. Tho[ma]s **MIGHEL**, Dec. 1, 1748	1	181
HARVEY, William, of Hartford, m. Abby H. **BLISS**, of Canterbury, Dec. 1, 1839, by Rev. Charles J. Warren	2	41
HASTINGS, Caroline, d. [Oliver & Philura], b. Dec. 17, 1802	1	163
George Truxton, s. [Oliver & Philura], b. Jan. 28, 1804	1	163
Juliana, d. [Oliver & Philura], b. Jan. 3, 1800	1	163
Oliver, m. Philura **PAINE**, Nov. 13, 1796	1	156
Paine or Perrine, s. Oliver & Philura, b. Nov. 13, 1797	1	163
HATCH, George W., s. George & Olive, b. Dec. 14, 1810	1	164
George W., m. Almira **HYDE**, b. of Canterbury, Mar. 23, 1835, by Rev. Otis C. Whiton	2	40
Henry Herbert, s. Henry Pond & Lucretia M., b. Aug. 4, 1841	2	240
Henry P., s. George & Olive, b. Nov. 22, 1813	1	164
Henry P., m. Lucretia M. **SAFFORD**, Sept. 13, 1840, by Rev. Asa King, Westminster	2	41
HAVENS, Phebe, wid., d. Mar. 31, 1789	1	166
HAXTON, Benj[ami]n, s. James & Hannah, b. June 15, 1741	1	157
Martha, d. James & Hannah, b. Aug. 7, 1743	1	157
HAYWOOD, Lydia Ann, m. William **HOUGHTON**, b. of Canterbury, Aug. 15, 1838, by Rev. Tubal Wakefield, at Packersville	2	40
HEATH, Lauralia, m. Joseph B. **ADAMS**, Dec. 20, 1811	1	53
HEBBARD, [see under HIBBARD]		
HEDGE, Alamantha M., m. Elias **BENNET**, b. of Canterbury, Mar. 14, 1853, by Rev. Nehemiah B. Hyde	2	105
HENDEE, HANDE, Leonard, of Heebron, m. Sarah A. **BACON**, of Canterbury, Aug. 19, 1829, by Andrew T. Judson, J. P.	2	39
Rachel, d. Jonathan & Rachel, b. Mar. 10, 1731	1	157
HERRICK, Albert A., s. [Dyer & Abby A.], b. Dec. 22, 1839	2	240
Amasa, s. John & Elizabeth, b. Sept. 3, 1758	1	160
Amasa, s. John & Elizabeth, d. Aug. 24, 1759	1	165
Amasa, s. Robert & Alice, b. May 23, 1784	1	162
Anna, d. [Calvin & Sophia], b. May 27, 1807	1	164
Anne, d. [John & Elizabeth], b. Apr. 28, 1765	1	161
Asael, s. John & Sarah, b. Sept. 15, 1761	1	160
Aurelia, d. Daniel & Olive, b. Oct. 29, 1789	1	163
Benjamin, s. Reuben & Abigail, b. Aug. 28, 1816	2	239

	Vol.	Page

HERRICK, (cont.)

	Vol.	Page
Betsey, d. Robert & Alice, b. Dec. 25, 1785	1	163
Calvin, s. John, 3rd, & Mary, b. Aug. 13, 1774	1	162
Calvin, m. Sophia **BARBER**, Mar. 25, 1804	1	156
Chauncey, s. Darius & Sarah, b. Mar. 12, 1802	1	164
Chauncey, m. Almira **CLARK**, Aug. 27, 1837, by Rev. Asa King, Westminster	2	40
Chester, s. Selah **HERRICK**, b. Apr. 24, 1797	1	163
Daniel, s. John & Elizabeth, b. Dec. 5, 1755	1	159
Daniel, d. Apr. 28, 1792	1	166
Daniel, s. Daniel & Olive, b. Aug. 10, 1792	1	163
Darius, m. Sally **MILLS**, Dec. 28, 1794	1	156
Darius Clark, s. Chauncey & Almira, b. May 3, 1844, at North Stonington	2	239
Dyer, s. [Reuben & Abigail], b. Apr. 12, 1818	2	239
Elijah, s. John & Elizabeth, b. Jan. 13, 1760	1	160
Elijah, s. John & Elizabeth, d. Mar. 18, 1761	1	165
Elijah, s. John & Elizabeth, b. July 10, 1761	1	160
Eliza, d. John, 3rd, & Mary, b. Oct. 9, 1771	1	161
Eliza, d. John, 3rd, & Mary, d. Apr. 12, 1773	1	165
Emily, d. [Reuben & Abigail], b. Feb. 10, 1820	2	239
George E., s. [Dyer & Abby A.], b. Feb. 22, 1845	2	240
Harriet, d. Darius & Sally, b. Feb. 18, 1800	1	163
Horace White, s. Rufus & Sally, b. May 10, 1807	1	245
John, m. Elizabeth **SMITH**, Sept. 27, 1753	1	155
John, m. Sarah **SMITH**, June 6, 1755	1	155
John, 3rd, m. Mary **BUTT**, Mar. 28, 1771	1	155
John, s. Calvin & Sophia, b. Jan. 21, 1814	1	164
John, d. Jan. 2, 1815, ae 63	1	166
John, m. Martha **CAREY**, Apr. 1, 1838, by Rev. Asa King, Westminster	2	40
Joseph, s. John & Elizabeth, b. June 27, 1763	1	161
Julia, d. Darius & Sally, b. Nov. 24, 1797	1	163
Julia, m. Christopher **CRANDALL**, Jan. 13, 1833, by Rev. Asa King, Westminster	2	16
Julia A., d. [Dyer & Abby A.], b. July 4, 1842	2	240
Lewis B., s. Dyer & Abby A., b. Feb. 16, 1838	2	240
Luther, s. Asael & Selah, b. Mar. 10, 1789	1	164
Marcy, d. John & Elizabeth, b. Apr. 18, 1757	1	159
Maria T., m. Joseph B. **CRANDALL**, Mar. 18, 1839, by Rev. Asa King	2	17
Mary, m. Joseph **ADAMS**, Jr., Jan. 3, 17[ ]	1	52
Mary, of Canterbury, m. Stephen **KINNE**, of Ward, Mass., June 17, 1822, by Erastus Learned	2	47
Mary Esther, d. Chauncey & Almira, b. Dec. 31, 1838	2	239
Mehetabel, d. John & Sarah, b. June 1, 1756	1	160
Minerva, d. Rufus & Sally, b. Feb. 9, 1809	1	164
Minerva, of Canterbury, m. John L. **BALDING**, of Windham,		

	Vol.	Page
HERRICK, (cont.)		
Mar. 28, 1830, by Rev. Israel G. Rose, of Westminster	2	8
Olive, d. David & Sarah, b. May 15, 1794	1	163
Orra, m. Calvin **BARSTOW**, Oct. 22, 1810	1	73
Pamelia, d. Calvin & Sophia, b. Dec. 1, 1810	1	164
Rachel, w. John, d. July 18, 1752	1	165
Rachel, d. John, 3rd, & Mary, b. Nov. 9, 1778	1	162
Rachel, m. Samuel **DYAR**, Sept. 29, 1799	1	121
Reuben, m. Abigail **ADAMS**, b. of Canterbury, Oct. 29, 1815	2	40
Reuben W., s. [Dyer & Abby A.], b. May 29, 1848	2	240
Robert, s. John & Elizabeth, b. Oct. 17, 1754	1	159
Ruby, m. Christopher **CRANDALL**, Nov. 24, 1844, by Walter Williams, J. P.	2	18
Ruth, d. [John & Elizabeth], b. July 12, 1767	1	161
Ruth, m. Bethuel **BOND**, Apr. 22, 1794	1	72
Sally, d. [David & Sarah], b. Oct. 28, 1798	1	163
Sarah, d. John & Sarah, b. Aug. 21, 1758	1	160
Selah had s. Chester, b. Apr. 24, 1797	1	163
Susanna, d. Calvin & Sophia, b. Jan. 19, 1805	1	164
Susannah, m. Welcome **TINKHAM**, of Glocester, R. I., Nov. 14, 1827, by Luther Paine, J. P.	2	79
HERRINGTON, [see also **HARRINGTON**], Anna, d. Daniel & Mary, b. Mar. 10, 1752	1	160
Benjamin, s. Daniel & Mary, b. Oct. 20, 1743	1	160
Benj[ami]n, s. Dan[ie]l, Jr. & Dorcas, b. June 10, 1770	1	161
Benjamin, s. Heber & Hannah, b. July 3, 1801	1	163
Daniel, s. Elizabeth **UTTER**, b. Mar. 19, 1729/30	1	157
Daniel, m. Mary **MOTT**, Jan. 8, 1741	1	155
Daniel, [twin with Mary], d. Daniel & Mary, b. Apr. 5, 1746	1	160
Dan[ie]l, Jr., m. Dorcas **CUTLER**, Sept. 14, 1769	1	155
Daniel, d. Apr. 22, 1776	1	165
Daniel, Jr., m. Sally **BISHOP**, Sept. 3, 1820, by John Francis, J. P.	2	39
Daniel, d. Sept. 7, 1822	2	333
Diana, d. Dan[ie]l, Jr. & Dorcas, b. Oct. 3, 1771	1	161
Elisha, m. Anna **WILLIAMS**, Oct. 11, 1764	1	155
Enoch, s. Dan[ie]l & Anna, b. Jan. 15, 1774	1	162
Enoch, m. Polly **JUSTIN**, Oct. 14, 1803	1	156
Esther, d. Daniel & Mary, b. Sept. 19, 1741	1	160
Ehester (Esther), m. John **BALIS**, Sept. 6, 1761	1	70
Ezekiel, s. Daniel & Mary, b. Sept. 29, 1757	1	160
Gershom, s. Daniel & Mary, b. Feb. 22, 1749	1	160
Hannah, d. Daniel & Mary, b. July 2, 1754	1	160
Harriet Amanda, d. Enoch & Polly, b. June 30, 1804	1	164
Heber, s. Dan[ie]l, Jr. & Dorcas, b. July 12, 1773	1	161
Heber, m. Hannah **WHITFORD**, May 12, 1793	1	156
Jane, d. [Heber & Hannah], b. May 9, 1803	1	164
Loadisa, d. Dan[ie]l & Dorcas, b. June 15, 1775	1	162

	Vol.	Page
HERRINGTON, (cont.)		
Loadisa, m. Lemuel **LAMPHIRE**, May 13, 1793	1	176
Lydia, m. James **NICHOLS**, Mar. 9, 1774	1	189
Lydia, d. [Heber & Hannah], b. Apr. 15, 1799	1	163
Mary, [twin with Daniel], d. Daniel & Mary, b. Apr. 5, 1746	1	160
Mary, m. Paul **HARRIS**, Sept. 22, 1749	1	155
Mary, w. Daniel, d. Dec. 10, 1769	1	165
Mary Ette, d. Enoch & Polly, b. Apr. 28, 1806	1	164
Sally, m. Charles W. **FOWLER**, Dec. 1, 1814	1	139
Sally, d. Aug. 2, 1822	2	333
Sophronia, d. Heber & Hannah, b. June 19, 1797	1	163
HEWITT, HEWET, HEWIT, HEWETT, HUIT, HUEIT, Amos,		
s. Henry & Johanna, d. May 17, 1753	1	165
Amos, s. [Increase & Betty], b. June 5, 1765	1	161
Angelba, of Canterbury, m. L[l]oyd **WILLIAMS**, of		
Brookline, July 12, 1846, by Rev. H. Slade, of Scotland	2	88
Anne, d. Henry & Johanna, b. July 1, 1754	1	159
Betsey, d. Increase & Eliza, b. June 3, 1776	1	162
Content, d. Henry & Johanna, b. May 1, 1748	1	159
Daniel, s. [Increase & Betty], b. Aug. 18, 1768	1	161
Hannah, d. Henry & Johanna, b. May 23, 1750	1	159
Henry, s. Increase & Elizabeth, b. May 25, 1782	1	162
Increase, s. Increase & Elizabeth, b. Dec. 11, 1772	1	161
Joanna, m. Uriah **CADY**, Apr. 28, 1762	1	101
Joseph Denison, s. Stephen & Alice, b. Aug. 14, 1782	1	162
Mehetable, d. Increase & Betty, b. May 3, 1764	1	161
Stephen, s. Henry & Johanna, b. July 10, 1752	1	158
Stephen, s. Henry & Johannah, b. June 7, 1757	1	160
Thomas, s. Increase & Eliza, b. Oct. 13, 1773	1	162
HIBBARD, HEBBARD, Abigail, d. Jno. & Elizabeth, b. May 8,		
1749	1	159
Abigail, m. Joshua **HUCHINS**, Aug. 22, 1769	1	155
Amanda, d. William & Martha, b. Aug. 2, 1792	1	163
Amanda, d. W[illia]m, Jr. & Martha, d. Dec. 16, 1808	1	166
Andrew, s. Will[ia]m & Dorothy, b. Oct. 30, 1754	1	159
Andrew, m. Elizabeth **FROST**, Dec. 3, 1782	1	155
Andrew, m. Ruth **LOOMISS**, of Hampton, Nov. 11, 1792	1	156
Ann, d. John & Martha, b. Aug. 13, 1734	1	158
Anne, d. John & Martha, d. Dec. 29, 1759	1	165
Araunah, s. W[illia]m & Dorothy, b. Jan. 13, 1770	1	161
Arunah, s. John, Jr. & Abigail, b. Dec. 28, 1777	1	162
Daniel, s. John & Martha, b. Sept. 29, 1738	1	158
Daniel Frost, s. Andrew & Elizabeth, b. Dec. 19, 1784	1	162
Dorothy, d. William & Dorothy, b. Oct. 11, 1766	1	161
Dorothy, m. Eleazer **PARK**, Oct. 7, 1783	1	193
Ebenezer, s. William & Dorothy, b. Sept. 16, 1761	1	160
Ebenezer, m. Susanna **CARVER**, Feb. 13, 1783	1	155
Edmund, s. W[illia]m, 3rd, d. Feb. 15, 1805	1	166

	Vol.	Page
HIBBARD, HEBBARD, (cont.)		
Edmund, s. W[illia]m, 3rd, & Lucy, b. Aug. 22, 1805	1	164
Eleazer, s. John & Martha, b. Aug. 20, 1732	1	158
Eleazer, m. Hannah **FARNAM**, Apr. 20, 1762	1	155
Elizabeth, d. John & Martha, b. Feb. 15, 1746; d. Aug. 31, 1748	1	158
Elizabeth, d. John & Martha, b. Mar. 8, 1748/9; d. Apr. 6, 1753	1	158
Elizabeth, d. John & Elizabeth, b. Oct. 25, 1751	1	159
Elizabeth, d. John & Elizabeth, d. Sept. 25, 1754	1	165
Elizabeth, m. James **BUTT**, Sept. 8, 1776	1	71
Elizabeth, d. Andrew & Elizabeth, b. Sept. 24, 1786	1	162
Elizabeth, w. Andrew, d. Dec. 20, 1788	1	166
Esther, of Canterbury, m. Lemuel **CHESTER**, of Windham, Apr. 19, 1829, by Peter Morse, J. P.	2	15
Esther Pamelia, d. [Joseph F. & Permilla], b. Aug. 4, 1833	2	239
Frances Caroline, d. Jeptha, & Polly, b. Dec. 19, 1808	1	164
Francis Edmund, s. W[illia]m, 3rd, & Lucy], b. Mar. 5, 1807	1	164
Harvey, s. Ebenezer & Susanna, b. Apr. 9, 1784	1	162
Harvey, s. Ebenezer & Susanna, d. Nov. 15, 1784	1	166
Harvey, s. Ebenezer & Susannah, b. Apr. 10, 1787	1	163
Heli, s. [William & Martha], b. May 9, 1789	1	163
Henry, s. [William & Martha], b. Feb. 16, 1784	1	163
Hosea, s. [William & Martha], b. Jan. 23, 1787	1	163
James, s. John & Elizabeth, b. June 30, 1753	1	158
James, m. Susanna **SHEPERD**, Aug. 15, 1773	1	155
Jedediah, s. John & Martha, b. Oct. 14, 1740	1	158
Jepthah, m. Mary **JOHNSON**, Apr. 22, 1806	1	156
Jerusha, d. [William & Martha], b. Aug. 13, 1781	1	163
John, s. John & Martha, b. Dec. 9, 1728	1	158
John, m. Elizabeth **PEARL**, Feb. 14, 1749	1	155
John, s. John & Elizabeth, b. Sept. 15, 1755	1	159
John, d. Mar. 23, 1762, ae 57 y. 5 m.	1	165
John, Jr., m. Abigail **CLEVELAND**, Mar. 17, 1777	1	155
John Fenton, s. Joseph F. & Permilla, b. Aug. 7, 1831	2	239
John Loouis, s. Andrew & Ruth, b. Aug. 20, 1791	1	163
Joseph, s. William & Dorothy, b. Sept. 26, 1763	1	150
Joseph, m. Parmelia **BINDICE**, b. of Canterbury, Sept. 14, [1827?], by Rev. James R. Wheelock	2	39
Joseph Baldwin, s. Joseph & Lydia, b. Mar. 14, 1792	1	163
Lemuel, s. John & Martha, b. Feb. 8, 1742/3	1	158
Lewis Burnham, s. Francis & Lydia, b. Dec. 31, 1835	2	239
Lovel, s. James & Susannah, b. Mar. 28, 1774	1	162
Lucy, d. Benj[ami]n & Susannah, b. Nov. 10, 1751	1	158
Lucy, d. William & Dorothy, b. Feb. 21, 1752	1	159
Lucy, m. Stephen **BUTT**, Oct. 8, 1769	1	70
Lucy, m. William **HEBBARD**, 3rd, Dec. 27, 1804	1	156
Lyman, s. [W[illia]m, 3rd, & Lucy], b. Mar. 28, 1809	1	164
Martha, d. Jno. & Martha, b. Dec. 21, 1726	1	158

	Vol.	Page

HIBBARD, HEBBARD, (cont.)

	Vol.	Page
Mary, d. John & Martha, b. Sept. 30, 1736	1	158
Mary, m. Zebadiah **FARNAM**, Nov. 10, 1763	1	138
Mary Ann, d. William & Lucy, b. Mar. 11, 1815	2	239
Millecent, d. Ebenezer & Susannah, b. Jan. 20, 1786	1	162
Moses, s. Benj[ami]n & Susannah, b. July 15, 1753	1	158
Nancy, d. W[illia]m, Jr. & Lucy, b. Aug. 8, 1812	1	164
Patte, d. William & Martha, b. July 19, 1779	1	163
Rufus, s. William & Dorothy, b. Jan. 4, 1758	1	160
Sally Mary, d. Jepthah & Polly, b. Mar. 23, 1807	1	164
Sarah, d. John & Martha, b. Feb. 2, 1744/5	1	158
Sarah, m. William **FARNUM**, Jr., May 8, 1766	1	138
Sarah, d. W[illia]m, Jr. & Martha, b. Nov. 1, 1796	1	164
Timothy, s. Jno. & Elizabeth, b. Sept. 5, 1750; d. Dec. 9, 1750	1	159
Timothy, s. John & Elizabeth, b. Dec. 31, 1757	1	160
Timothy, s. John & Elizabeth, d. Mar. 4, 1758	1	165
Timo[thy], s. John & Eliza, b. Jan. 4, 1759	1	162
Will[ia]m, s. John & Martha, b. Jan. 20, 1730/31	1	158
William, Jr., m. Martha **BENNETT**, Aug. 15, 1776	1	155
William, s. William, Jr. & Martha, b. May 28, 1777	1	162
William, 3rd, m. Lucy **HEBBARD**, Dec. 27, 1804	1	156
W[illia]m, Capt., d. Mar. 17, 1811, ae 81	1	166
William Handy, s. [William & Lucy], b. May 21, 1817	2	239
----, d. John & Martha, b. Nov. 26, 1751; d. same day	1	158
HICKS, Charles, of Plainfield, m. Laura E. **BARBER**, of Canterbury, Jan. 1, 1849, by Rev. Robert C. Learned	2	42
HIDE, [see under **HYDE**]		
HIGHSTED, Abigail, d. Edward & Anna, b. July 30, 1736	1	157
Elizabeth, d. Edward & Anna, b. July 3, 1734	1	157
Lucy, d. Edward & Anna, b. Oct. 6, 1732; d. Oct. 26, 1732	1	157
HILL, Edward E., of Plainfield, m. Julia B. **SHEPARD**, of Canterbury, May 13, 1851, by Rev. Joseph P. Brown, Plainfield	2	100
Eliza, m. George W. **BRIGGS**, b. of Canterbury, Mar. 20, 1836, by Rev. Tubal Wakefield	2	10
Mary Ann, of Canterbury, m. Stephen V. R. **PECKHAM**, of Plainfield, Jan. 1, 1837, by Rev. Tubal Wakefield, Packersville	2	62
HINKLEY, Nancy, m. Nathan **ALLEN**, Dec. 17, 18[ ]	1	52
HOLBROOK, George W., of Pomfret, m. Sarah **SAFFORD**, Nov. 28, 1833, by Rev. Asa King, Westminster	2	35
HOLDEN, Charles, s. [Prince & Violet], b. Dec. 16, 180[ ][negroes]	1	249
Henry, s. Prince & Violet, b. Sept. 11, 180[ ] [negroes]	1	249
HOLLIS, Mary, m. John **SWEET**, b. of Canterbury, Mar. 12, 1835, by John Francis, J. P.	2	73
HOLLOWAY, Weden, of Exeter, R. I., m. Lydia **SWEET**, of Canterbury, Nov. 9, 1828, by Chester Lyon, J. P.	2	39
HOLMES, HOMES, Anne, d. Jehosaphat & Sarah, b. Mar. 21,		

	Vol.	Page
HOLMES, HOMES, (cont.)		
1746/7	1	159
Asa, s. Nathan & Desire, b. Aug. 4, 1755	1	159
Desiah, d. Nathaniel & Desire, b. Apr. 4, 1750	1	158
Etehana, s. Nathaniel & Desire, b. Dec. 10, 1743 (Stephen?)	1	158
Experience, d. Jabez & Experience, b. Feb. 23, 1750/51	1	159
Jabez, m. Experience **CLEVELAND**, May 2, 1749	1	155
Johosaphat, m. Sarah **BREWSTER**, Jan. 10, 1745	1	155
Lucy, d. Nathaniel & Desire, b. Aug. 17, 1748	1	158
Mary, d. Nathaniel & Desire, b. Mar. 10, 1745/6	1	158
Nathaniel, s. Nathaniel & Desire, b. Nov. 18, 1752	1	158
Sarah, d. Jabez & Experience, b. Dec. 15, 1749	1	159
Sibbel, d. Nathan[ie]l & Desire, b. Sept. 2, 1757	1	159
HOLT, Ann S., of Ledyard, m. Orrin **ADAMS**, of Canterbury, Mar.		
26, 1834, by R. S. Hazen	2	5
Cynthia, m. Abel **STAPLES**, Dec. 3, 1777	1	214
Phebe, m. Israel **LITCHFIELD**, Jan. 14, 1766	1	176
Sarah, m. Capt. Benj[ami]n **PEIRCE**, Jan. 28, 1762	1	192
HORTON, Rosilla W., m. Reuben **ROUSE**, Jr., Nov. 17, 1837, by		
Rev. C. J. Warren	2	68
William, of Canterbury, m. Laura **STARKWEATHER**, of		
Plainfield, Oct. 5, 1828, by Rev. James R. Wheelock	2	39
William Sidney, s. William & Laura, b. Mar. 30, 1831	2	239
HOUGH, Derastus, s. John & Abigail, b. Oct. 27, 1760	1	160
Derastus, see also Erastus		
Eliza, d. [Samuel & Betsey], b. June 11, 1819	2	239
Erastus, m. Sarah **FISH**, Apr. 8, 1790	1	156
Erastus, see also Derastus		
Esther Ann, d. Samuel & Betsey, b. Oct. 25, 1815	2	239
Esther Ann, of Canterbury, m. E. Porter **DYER**, of Stow,		
Mass., Dec. 2, 1838, by Rev. Charles J. Warren	2	21
Esther Ann, of Canterbury, m. E. Porter **DYER**, of Stow,		
Mass., Dec. 2, 1838, by Rev. Charles J. Warren	2	62
Hannah, m. Joshua **HARRIS**, Jan. 17, 1781	1	155
Henry T., of Chaplin, m. Lydia M. **BACON**, of Canterbury,		
Sept. 20, 1848, by Rev. Robert C. Learned	2	42
John, m. Abigail **BALDWIN**, Nov. 11, 1753	1	155
John, s. John & Abigail, b. Feb. 16, 1767	1	161
John, s. John & Abigail, d. May 20, 1775	1	165
John, s. Erastus & Sarah, b. Apr. 29, 1799	1	163
John, s. Erastus & Sarah, d. Nov. 8, 1811	1	166
Nabby, d. Erastus, & Sarah, b. June 10, 1791	1	163
Pollidore Perkins, s. Erastus & Sarah, b. June 6, 1802	1	163
Samuel L., s. Olive **PELLETT**, single woman, b. July 27, 1808	1	164
Samuel L., m. Betsey **ADAMS**, Dec. 2, 1810	1	156
Samuel Lockwood, s. Walter & Martha, b. June 25, 1785	1	162
Sarah Ann, d. Erastus & Sarah, b. Feb. 19, 1805	1	164
Sarah Jones, d. [Samuel & Betsey], b. Apr. 7, 1821	2	239

	Vol.	Page
HOUGH, (cont.)		
Thomas, s. Erastus & Sarah, b. Apr. 20, 1794	1	163
Walter, s. John & Abigail, b. Dec. 15, 1753	1	159
HOUGHTON, William, m. Lydia Ann **HAYWOOD**, b. of		
Canterbury, Aug. 15, 1838, by Rev. Tubal Wakefield, at		
Packersville	2	40
HOUSE, Susan, of East Windsor, m. Hiram **BENNET**, of		
Canterbury, Oct. 8, 1850, by Rev. R. S. Hazen, of		
Westminster	2	14
HOVEY, Abiel, s. Samuel & Abigail, b. Oct. 31, 1776	1	162
Abigail, m. Gideon **CARVER**, Dec. 15, 1774	1	101
Abner, s. Samuel & Abigail, b. Nov. 5, 1766	1	161
Alvan, s. Sam[ue]l & Abigail, b. Mar. 3, 1779	1	162
Elizabeth, m. Stephen **CLARK**, May 9, 1770	1	101
Joseph, of Westerly, R. I., m. Nancy A. **JACKSON**, of		
Canterbury, (both colored), Dec. 7, 1851, by Rev. Robert		
C. Learned	2	100
Mary, d. [Samuel & Abigail], b. May 26, 1768	1	161
Rebecka, d. Sam[ue]l & Abigail, b. Sept. 6, 1772	1	162
Robert, m. Calista **FAGAN**, Nov. 30, 1828, by Asael Bacon,		
J. P.	2	39
Rufus, s. Sam[ue]l & Abigail, b. Aug. 29, 1770	1	162
Samuel, s. Samuel & Abigail, b. Oct. 20, 1774	1	162
HOW, [see under **HOWE**]		
HOWARD, Mary, of Windham, m. Obadiah **JOHNSON**, Apr. 29,		
1762	1	167
Phebe, m. James **CARY**, Jr., Oct. 25, 1804	1	102
Sarah, m. Derias **FISH**, Feb. 7, 1765	1	138
HOWE, HOW, Alice Williams, d. [John & Mary], b. May [ ], 1824	2	239
Amanda, d. Isaac & Lydia, b. Sept. 16, 1805	1	164
Frances P., m. Benjamin A. **JORDAN**, of Coventry, R. I.,		
Sept. 4, 1827, by Israel G. Rose	2	43
Frederick Spaulding, s. John & Mary, b. Apr. 2, 1821	2	239
Harry, s. Isaac & Lydia, b. Apr. 8, 1800, at Plainfield	1	164
Laura, d. [Isaac & Lydia], b. Feb. 27, 1800, at Plainfield	1	164
Laura, m. David **GALLUP**, Oct. 11, 1827, by Chester Lyon,		
J. P.	2	35
Lydia W., m. Gilbert B. **REYNOLDS**, Sept. 9, 1827, by		
Chester Lyon, J. P.	2	67
Patty B., of Canterbury, m. Dr. Isaac **BROWNING**, of		
Montville, Jan. 8, 1840, by Rev. Tubal Wakefield	2	12
Smith, s. Isaac & Lydia, b. Apr. 8, 1803	1	164
HOXIE, HOXSIE, Avery, m. Hannah **LILLIBRIDGE**, Dec. 26,		
1850, by Rev. J. B. Guild, at Packersville	2	101
Samuel, of Willimantic, m. Temperance E. **LEWIS**, of		
Canterbury, Jan. 20, 1839, by Rev. Tubal Wakefield, at		
Packersville	2	40
HUBBERT, Rebeckah, m. Samuel **ESTABROOKS**, Mar. 23,		

	Vol.	Page
HUBBERT, (cont.)		
1713/14	1	133
HUCHENS, [see under HUTCHINS]		
HUNTINGTON, Dorothy, d. Samuel & Dorothy, b. Mar. 29, 1762	1	160
Hannah, d. Sam[ue]l & Dorothy, b. Apr. 25, 1758	1	160
Hannah, d. Samuel & Dorothy, d. June 11, 1759	1	165
Jeremiah Gates, s. Samuel & Dorothy, b. Apr. 9, 1760	1	160
Lydia, of Norwich, m. Jabez FITCH, Jr., Aug. 22, 1754	1	138
Mary, m. Theophilus FITCH, Dec. 15, 1731	1	138
Rebeckah, d. Sam[ue]l & Rebecca, b. May 17, 1752	1	159
Rebeckah, w. Dea. Sam[ue]l, d. Sept. 15, 1754	1	165
Rebeckah, d. Samuel & Rebeckah, d. June 11, 1759	1	165
Sam[ue]l, m. Rebeckah FAIRBANKS, May 23, 1751	1	155
Sam[ue]l, m. Dorothy GATES, of East Haddam, May 25, 1757	1	155
Samuel, s. Samuel & Dorothy, b. June 4, 1764	1	161
HUTCHINS, HUCHENS, HUCHINS, Abigail. d. Joshua &		
Abig[ai]l, b. Nov. 1, 1744	1	162
Amy, d. [Joshua & Abigail], b. July 15, 1772	1	162
Elizabeth, d. Joshua & Abigail, b. Mar. 28, 1770	1	162
Joshua, m. Abigail HEBBARD, Aug. 22, 1769	1	155
Samuel, m. Lydia SHEPARD, of Plainfield, Feb. 12, 1811	1	156
Sarah, wid., d. Jan. 16, 1773, ae 88	1	165
HYDE, HIDE, HIDES, Abby W., of Canterbury, m. Jacob		
RUSSELL, of New York City, Nov. 5, 1849, by Rev.		
Isaac H. Coe	2	69
Abigail, m. Joseph CLEVELAND, Feb. 7, 1710/11	1	100
Abigail, d. Jonathan & Thankful, b. Dec. 28, 1739	1	157
Abigail, wid. Jonathan, d. May 29, 1751	1	165
Abigail, d. Jno. & Mary, b. Aug. 7, 1755	1	159
Abigail, d. Isaac, 3rd, & Betty, b. Oct. 6, 1772	1	161
Abigail, d. Comfort & Deborah, b. Dec. 23, 1779	1	162
Abigail, d. May 14, 1829, ae 97	2	333
Abigail, m. Nehemiah HIDE, [ ]	1	155
Abigail Waldo, d. David & Mary W., b. July 7, 1817	2	239
Abner, [twin with Sarah], s. Isaac & Sarah, b. July 8, 1779	1	162
Abner, m. Dolly ENSWORTH, Oct. 18, 1801	1	156
Abraham, s. James & Mary, b. Oct. 2, 1713	1	157
Abraham, m. Experience ADAMS, Jan. 24, 1737/8	1	155
Agate, d. Nathan & Abigail, b. Oct. 7, 1787	1	163
Albe, s. Isaac, Jr. & Sarah, b. June 1, 1769	1	161
Albe, m. Edith BROWN, Nov. 1, 1795	1	156
Albe, m. Henrietta CHANDLER, Jan. 24, 1804	1	156
Albert, s. [Nehemiah B. & Rebecca], b. Nov. 9, 1829	2	239
Alfred, s. [Comfort & Deborah], b. Sept. 10, 1789	1	163
Alfred, m. Sophia KUZAR, Mar. 15, 1811	1	156
Almira, m. George W. HATCH, b. of Canterbury, Mar. 23,		
1835, by Rev. Otis C. Whiton	2	40
Amasa, s. Abraham & Experience, b. Oct. 8, 1757	1	159

	Vol.	Page
HYDE, HIDE, HIDES, (cont.)		
Asahel, s. Abraham & Experience, b. June 3, 1755	1	159
Asahel, s. Abraham & Experience, d. Apr. 23, 1757	1	165
Benj[ami]n, s. Jonathan & Thankful, b. Nov. 23, 1736	1	157
Benjamin, s. Caleb & Lidia, b. Sept. 23, 1741	1	158
Benj[ami]n, s. Abraham & Experience, b. Feb. 16, 1742/3	1	157
Benjamin, m. Hannah **PELLET**, Oct. 5, 1772	1	155
Betty, m. Simon **NEWTON**, Nov. 5, 1783	1	189
Charles, s. [Nehemiah B. & Rebecca], b. Nov. 15, 1827	2	239
Charles, m. Mary F. **ADAMS**, Apr. 31, 1850, by Rev. R. S. Hazen, of Westminster	2	100
Charles L., of Canterbury, m. Sarah A. **LEWIS**, of Plainfield, July 4, 1845, by Rev. Zephaniah Baker	2	41
Clarinda, d. John & Mary, b. Feb. 24, 1769	1	161
Clarrissa A., d. [Nehemiah B. & Rebecca], b. Feb. 8, 1836	2	239
Comfort, s. Isaac & Elizabeth, b. Aug. 24, 1737	1	157
Comfort, m. Deborah **FAULKNER**, May 8, 1779	1	155
Comfort Star, s. [Comfort & Deborah], b. Aug. 8, 1784	1	162
David, s. Isaac & Elizabeth, b. Mar. 15, 1744/5	1	159
David, m. Sarah **ADAMS**, Feb. 23, 1769	1	155
David, s. Nathan & Abigail, b. Feb. 29, 1784	1	162
David, d. July 6, 1816	1	166
David, m. Mary W. **MANNING**, Oct. 10, 1816	1	156
David R., s. [David & Mary W.], b. Oct. 31, 1822	2	239
Deborah, m. Jabez **ADAMS**, Sept. 25, 1839	1	53
Deborah, m. Jabez **ADAMS**, Sept. 25, 1839, by Rev. C. J. Warren	2	3
Dorothy, m. Joseph **ADAMS**, Apr. 12, 1742	1	51
Dorothy, d. John & Mary, b. Jan. 4, 1760	1	161
Dorothy, m. Samuel **PHINNEY**, May 5, 1782	1	194
Ebenezer, s. James & Mary, b. Apr. 12, 1719	1	157
Eben[eze]r, m. Mercy **THATCHER**, Apr. 12, 1742	1	155
Eben[eze]r, s. Ebenezer & Marcy, b. Jan. 13, 1742/3	1	157
Eben[eze]r, s. Isaac & Elizabeth, d. Dec. 22, 1755, at New Marlboro	1	165
Eben[eze]r, s. Jonathan & Lucy, b. Oct. 3, 1757	1	159
Ebenezer, Dr., d. Nov. 24, 1801	1	166
Edith, d. Albe & Edith, b. Dec. 30, 1800	1	163
Edith, w. Albe, d. Jan. 14, 1801	1	166
Edward, m. Harriet N. **FRANCIS**, b. of Canterbury, Nov. 19, 1840, by Rev. Tubal Wakefield	2	41
Eliza, d. Dec. 26, 1771, ae 94	1	165
Elizabeth, d. Isaac & Elizabeth, b. Apr. 8, 1731	1	157
Elizabeth, d. Jonathan & Thankful, b. Mar. 27, 1743	1	158
Elizabeth, m. Silas **CLEVELAND**, May 10, 1750	1	100
Elizabeth, d. Abraham* & Lucy, b. Mar. 2, 1753 (*Jonathan)	1	157
Elizabeth, d. [Comfort & Deborah], b. Feb. 20, 1781	1	162
Elizabeth, d. Deborah & Comfort, d. Aug. 29, 1784	1	166

	Vol.	Page
HYDE, HIDE, HIDES, (cont.)		
Elizabeth, d. [Nehemiah B. & Rebecca], b. July 11, 1844	2	239
Elizabeth, of Canterbury, m. Hosmer **ENSWORTH**, of		
Springfield, Dec. 29, 1851, by Rev. Robert C. Learned	2	28
Emeline, m. Archibald **BRADFORD**, Nov. 9, 1841, by Rev.		
Asa King	2	12
Esther, d. Caleb & Lidia, b. Mar. 26, 1743	1	158
Esther, d. Caleb & Lydia, d. July 10, 1750	1	165
Esther, d. Benj[ami]n & Hannah, b. July 22, 1773	1	161
Eunice, d. Isaac & Sarah, b. Apr. 11, 1783	1	163
Festus, s. Elasa & Alice, b. May 14, 1788	1	163
Festus, m. Hannah **MOORE**, b. of Canterbury, Sept. 10, 1822,		
by Erastus Learned	2	39
George, s. [Albe & Henrietta], b. [ ], 1806	1	164
Hannah, m. James **PIKE**, May 25, 1741	1	192
Hannah, d. Caleb & Lydia, d. July 11, 1750	1	165
Hannah, m. Jonathan **RAYNSFORD**, May 17, 1759	1	209
Hannah, d. [Comfort & Deborah], b. Nov. 6, 1782	1	162
Hannah Adelaide, d. John L. & Mary Ann, b. June 6, 1852	2	240
Harriet, d. Abner & Sally, b. Oct. 14, 1802	1	164
Harriet, m. Lorin **BUTTS**, May 5, 1819	1	73
Harry, s. Albe & Edith, b. Oct. 2, 1796	1	163
Harvey, s. Isaac & Sarah, b. Mar. 17, 1776	1	162
Henrietta, d. Albe & Henrietta, b. Oct. 21, 1804	1	164
Henrietta, m. Simeon **BRADFORD**, b. of Canterbury, June 10,		
1828, by Rev. J. R. Wheelock	2	8
Henry, [twin with James], s. Jabez & Hannah, b. Jan. 10,		
1748, in Oblong, N. Y.	1	160
Ichabod, s. Abraham & Experience, b. Apr. 30, 1749	1	159
Isaac, s. Isaac & Elisabeth, b. Apr. 24, 1735	1	157
Isaac, s. Caleb & Lydia, b. Feb. 25, 1750	1	158
Isaac, Jr., m. Sarah **MARSHALL**, May 4, 1768	1	155
Isaac, s. Isaac, Jr. & Sarah, b. Dec. 2, 1771	1	161
Isaac, 3rd, m. Betty **TYLER**, Feb. 6, 1772	1	155
Isaac, Capt., d. Feb. 1, 1776	1	165
Jabez, s. James & Mary, b. May 22, 1716	1	157
Jabez, m. Hannah **BACON**, Feb. 27, 1740	1	155
Jabez, s. Jabez & Hannah, b. Dec. 13, 1741	1	157
Jabez, s. Jabez & Hannah, b. July 25, 1750, in Oblong, N. Y.	1	160
Jabez, d. Sept. 23, 1758, a soldier at Green Bush	1	165
Jacob, s. Josiah & Elizabeth, b. Jan. 24, 1738/9	1	157
James, s. James & Mary, b. Apr. 22, 1709	1	157
James, d. Dec. 5, 1732	1	165
James, s. James & Mary, b. Dec. 8, 1732	1	157
James, [twin with Henry], s. Jabez & Hannah, b. Jan. 10,		
1748, in Oblong, N. Y.	1	160
James, m. Miriam **WOODARD**, Dec. 3, 1754	1	155
James, d. Sept. 13, 1756, a soldier at Camp at Fort Edward	1	165

	Vol.	Page
HYDE, HIDE, HIDES, (cont.)		
James, s. James & Miriam, b. Oct. 9, 1756	1	159
James, s. Jabez & Hannah, d. July 4, 1764	1	165
Jarvis, s. Nehemiah B. & Rebecca, b. Dec. 21, 1831	2	239
Jedediah, [twin with Sarah], s. Abram & Experience, b.		
May 31, 1752	1	157
Jedediah, s. Benj[ami]n & Hannah, b. Aug. 14, 1777	1	162
John, s. Eben & Mercy, b. Aug. 28, 1747	1	158
John, m. Mary THOMPSON, Apr. 18, 1753	1	155
John, s. John & Mary, b. Aug. 27, 1757	1	161
John, s. Jonathan & Hannah, b. Aug. 8, 1807	1	164
John, s. Comfort S. & Abigail, b. Feb. 18, 1813	1	164
John, m. Emily ANGELL, b. of Canterbury, Sept. 27, 1847,		
by H. Slade	2	42
John, m. Emily ANGELL, b. of Canterbury, Sept. 27, 1847,		
by H. Slade	2	48
John L., m. Mary Ann OLIN, b. of Canterbury, Mar. 24,		
1851, by C. D. Fillmore, Elder	2	100
John Lewis, s. Nehemiah B. & Rebecca, b. June 12, 1826	2	239
John M., of Greenville, m. Adaline ALLEN, of Canterbury,		
Nov. 15, 1846, by Rev. Asa King, Westminster	2	42
Jona, s. Nehemiah & Abigail, b. Nov. 10, 1769	1	161
Jonathan, s. James & Mary, b. Mar. 9, 1711	1	157
Jonathan, m. Abigail CURTIS, Jan. 28, 1723/4	1	192
Jonathan, m. Hannah ADAMS, Apr. 15, 1736	1	155
Jonathan, d. Mar. 8, 1738/9	1	165
Jonathan, s. Abraham & Experience, b. Sept. 20, 1740	1	157
Jonathan, m. Lucy TRACY, Feb. 4, 1744/5	1	155
Jonathan, s. Jonathan & Thankful, b. Mar. 17, 1748	1	159
Jonathan, s. Jonathan & Lucy, b. Jan. 8, 1760	1	160
Jonathan, d. Mar. 2, 1803, ae 89	1	166
Jonathan, m. Hannah BENTLEY, of Franklin, [ ]	1	156
Josiah, s. [Josiah & Elizabeth], b. June 10, 1745	1	160
Josiah, m. Sophronia HYDE, b. of Canterbury, Oct. 13,		
[1851], by Rev. Robert C. Learned	2	100
Judah, m. Charles ADAMS, Sept. 14, 1743(?)	1	51
Judeth, d. John & Mary, b. Sept. 29, 1761	1	161
Judith, m. Samuel BURLINGAME, Jr., b. of Canterbury,		
Mar. 24, 1851, by Rev. Robert C. Learned	2	105
Lase, s. Jonathan & Lucy, b. May 17, 1755	1	159
Lasee, m. Alice BACON, Nov. 16, 1785	1	156
Loesaena, d. Nehemiah & Abigail, b. Oct. 19, 1766	1	161
Loesaena, see also Louisiana		
Loisa, m. Calvin FARNHAM, b. of Canterbury, Jan. 10,		
1832, by Rev. Demis Platt	2	31
Loretta, d. [Nehemiah B. & Rebecca], b. Oct. 2, 1838	2	239
Louisiana, d. Nehemiah & Abigail, d. Dec. 3, 1783	1	166
Louisiana, see also Loesaena		

	Vol.	Page
HYDE, HIDE, HIDES, (cont.)		
Lucy, d. Abraham & Experience, b. June 9, 1747, at Pomfret	1	159
Lucy. m. Phinehas TYLER, Nov. 19, 1766	1	229
Lucy, w. Jonathan, d. Jan. 21, 1799, ae 83	1	166
Luranah, d. Isaac & Elizabeth, b. Mar. 22, 1742	1	157
Luranah, m. Frederic CURTIS, Dec. 17, 1760	1	101
Lydia, d. Josiah & Elizabeth, b. July 24, 1734	1	157
Lidia, m. Bethuel BOND, Sept. 20, 1753	1	70
Lydia, d. Caleb & Lydia, b. Jan. 24, 1754	1	159
Mary, d. James & Mary, d. July 27, 1724	1	165
Mary, d. Isaac & Elizabeth, b. Feb. 1, 1732/3	1	157
Mary, d. Jonathan & Thankful, b. Nov. 11, 1735	1	157
Mary, m. Jacob SMITH, Dec. 27, 1742	1	214
Mary, d. Abraham & Experience, b. June 20, 1745	1	157
Mary, d. Jabez & Hannah, b. July 24, 1746, in Oblong, N. Y.	1	160
Mary, d. Caleb & Lidia, b. Mar. 22, 1748; d. June 28, 1750	1	158
Mary, d. Isaac & Elizabeth, d. June 6, 1751	1	165
Mary, d. James & Mary, b. Sept. 2, 1751* (*1721)	1	157
Mary, d. Isaac, Jr. & Sarah, b. Aug. 28, 1770	1	161
Mary, m. Deliverance BROWN, Oct. 23, 1791	1	72
Mary Matilda, d. [David & Mary W.], b. Feb. 9, 1819	2	239
Miriam, m. Peter MILLER, Sept. 30, 1766	1	181
Nathan, s. [Josiah & Elizabeth], b. June 10, 1747	1	160
Nathan, s. Josiah & Elizabeth, d. Sept. 29, 1749	1	165
Nathan, s. Capt. Isaac & Elizabeth, b. Sept. 23, 1751	1	159
Nathan, m. Abigail WALDO, May 16, 1782	1	155
Nathan, d. Apr. 21, 1829, ae 77	2	333
Nathan Manning, s. [David & Mary W.], b. Jan. 29, 1821	2	239
Nehemiah, s. Josiah & Elizabeth, b. July 4, 1736	1	160
Nehemiah, m. Abigail HIDE, [ ]	1	155
Nehemiah B., m. Rebecca LEWIS, Nov. 26, 1823, by Andrew T. Judson, J. P.	2	39
Nehemiah Bentley, s. Jonathan & Hannah, b. Sept. 8, 1801	1	163
Olive, d. Nehemiah & Abigail, b. Nov. 14, 1763	1	161
Olive, d. Nehe[mia]h B. & Rebecca, b. June 6, 1824	2	239
Percis, d. Jabez & Hannah, b. Oct. 13, 1752, at Killingly	1	160
Phebe, d. Jonathan & Lucy, b. Apr. 2, 1748	1	159
Phebe, d. James & Miriam, b. Mar. 18, 1755	1	159
Phebe, m. Tracy CLEVELAND, Apr. 25, 1773	1	101
Prescilla, d. Jabez & Hannah, b. Apr. 16, 1757	1	160
Ralph, m. Samuel STEAVENS, b. of Canterbury, Nov. 26, 1820, by Asa Meech (So written in Arnold Copy)	2	71
Rufus, s. Jonathan & Lucy, b. Sept. 4, 1750	1	159
Samuel, s. Abraham & Experience, b. Dec. 2, 1738	1	157
Sam[ue]l Wadsworth, s. Benjamin & Hannah, b. June 22, 1784	1	162
Sarah, m. John PIKE, May 23, 1706	1	192
Sarah, d. Josiah & Elizabeth, b. Sept. 12, 1732	1	160
Sarah, m. Josiah MUNROW, Apr. 12, 1752	1	181

	Vol.	Page
HYDE, HIDE, HIDES, (cont.)		
Sarah, [twin with Jedediah], d. Abram & Experience, b.		
May 31, 1752	1	157
Sarah, [twin with Abner], d. Isaac & Sarah, b. July 8, 1779	1	162
Sarah, d. Comfort & Deborah, b. May 4, 1786	1	163
Sarah P., d. [Nehemiah B. & Rebecca], b. Aug. 19, 1841	2	239
Seth, s. Jonathan & Hannah, b. Mar. 12, 1736/7	1	157
Seth, d. Oct. 25, 1760	1	165
Solomon, s. Jonathan & Lucy, b. June 2, 1746	1	159
Solomon, s. Jonathan & Lucy, d. Aug. 16, 1749	1	165
Sophronia, m. Josiah HYDE, b. of Canterbury, Oct. 13,		
[1851], by Rev. Robert C. Learned	2	100
Sophronia Tracy, d. [Elasa & Alice], b. Sept. 3, 1794	1	163
Star, s. Alfred & Sophia, b. Oct. 5, 1812	1	164
Susan, of Canterbury, m. Giles E. RIX, of Norwich, Feb.		
15, 1849, by Rev. Robert C. Learned	2	68
Susanna, d. Caleb & Lidia, b. Mar. 25, 1745	1	158
Susannah, d. [Nehemiah B. & Rebecca], b. Mar. 5, 1834	2	239
Temperance, d. Caleb & Lida, b. Feb. 8, 1738/9	1	157
Temperance, d. Caleb & Lidia, b. Feb. 8, 1748/9	1	158
Temperance, d. Caleb & Lydia, d. July 14, 1750	1	165
Thaddeus, s. Jonathan & Thankful, b. Apr. 25, 1742	1	157
Thankful, d. Jonathan & Thankful, b. Feb. 3, 1737	1	157
Theophilus, s. Jno. & Mary, b. Dec. 25, 1753	1	159
Timothy, s. Isaac & Elizabeth, b. Feb. 6, 1738/9	1	157
Timothy, s. Isaac & Elizabeth, d. Oct. 22, 1740	1	165
Timothy, s. Eben[eze]r & Mercy, b. Mar. 27, 1745	1	158
William, s. John & Mary, b. July 26, 1764	1	161
Wyllys, s. John & Mary, b. Jan. 13, 1767	1	161
INGRAHAM, John, s. Stephen & Katharine, b. Mar. 5, 1793	1	169
Reuben Gager, s. Stephen & Katharine, b. June 15, 1796	1	170
Stephen, m. Katherine McCARTEE, Oct. 23, 1791	1	167
JACKSON, Ebenezer, s. Joseph & Esther, b. July 23, 1736	1	168
Jeremiah, s. Joseph & Esther, b. Jan. 19, 1737/8	1	168
Joseph, s. Joseph & Esther, b. Sept. 20, 1733	1	168
Lorin, m. Mehetable F. SMITH, June 18, 1837, by Rev.		
Asa King	2	43
Michael, s. Joseph & Esther, b. Mar. 16, 1735	1	168
Nancy A., of Canterbury, m. Joseph HOVEY, of Westerly,		
R. I., (both colored), Dec. 7, 1851, by Rev. Robert C.		
Learned	2	100
Sam[ue]l*, m. David ADAMS, Jr., Sept. 30, 1746 (*Sarah?)	1	51
JACOBS, Jane Gray, d. Jeremiah & Mary, b. Oct. 5, 1835	2	243
JEFFERS, Deborah, m. Job LATHROP, Oct. 23, 1799 [negroes]	1	248
JENCKES, Zelotes, of Norwich, m. Charlotte WILLOUGHBY, of		
Canterbury, May 11, 1827, by Andrew T. Judson, J. P.	2	43
[JENNINGS], GENNINGS, Sibbel, m. David FISH, Oct. 28, 1769	1	138
[JEWELL], JUEL, Abigail, m. Deliver[an]ce WOODARD, Mar. 7,		

	Vol.	Page
[JEWELL], JUEL, (cont.)		
1737	1	236
JEWETT, Abigail, d. [Thomas & Prudence], b. Mar. 8, 1790, at		
Windham	1	169
Anna, d. Benj[ami]n, Jr. & Abigail, b. Jan. 5, 1781	1	169
Benjamin, m. Hannah **BEDLOCK**, of Windham, Feb. 10, 1762	1	167
Benjamin, m. Abigail **BATES**, Jan. 19, 1773	1	167
Clalissa, d. [Thomas & Prudence], b. July 9, 1800	1	170
David, s. [Benjamin, Jr. & Abigail], b. July 27, 1775	1	169
Ebenezer, m. Abigail **HAMMOND**, of Windham, Sept. 24,		
1782	1	167
Elijah, s. [Thomas & Prudence], b. Feb. 10, 1797	1	170
Hannah, w. Benjamin, d. July 19, 1769	1	172
Hannah, m. Jos[eph] **PIKE**, Nov. 14, 1775	1	193
Hannah, d. Benjamin, Jr. & Abigail, b. July 21, 1778	1	169
Josiah, s. Benjamin, Jr. & Abigail, b. Oct. 21, 1773	1	169
Lucy, d. Benj[ami]n, Jr. & Abigail, b. Jan. 17, 1783	1	169
Lucy had illeg. child Joseph **GRAVES**, b. Apr. 1, 1810	1	152
Luther, s. Thomas & Prudence, b. Feb. 1, 1792	1	169
Mary, of Norwich, m. John **SMITH**, Jan. 16, 1754	1	214
Mary, d. Thomas & Prudence, b. May 7, 1794	1	170
Olive, d. Benjamin & Hannah, b. July 26, 1767	1	169
Polly, d. Ebenezer & Abigail, b. Sept. 3, 1783	1	169
Prudence, d. Thomas & Prudence, b. Nov. 29, 1787	1	169
Ruhama, d. Benjamin & Hannah, b. Sept. 29, 1763	1	168
Samuel, s. [Benjamin, Jr. & Abigail], b. July 10, 1785	1	169
Sarah, d. Benjamin & Hannah, b. Aug. 4, 1765	1	168
JOHNSON, Abigail, d. William, b. Aug. 12, 1706	1	168
Abigail, d. Obadiah & Rebeckah, b. Sept. 29, 1710	1	168
Abigail, m. Phinehas **BROWN**, June 19, 1729	1	69
Abigail, d. Obadiah & Lydia, b. Nov. 7, 1742	1	168
Abigail, d. William & Bette, b. Oct. 20, 1759	1	168
Abigail, m. Joseph **CLEARK**, Apr. 23, 1761	1	101
Abigail, m. Luther **BINGHAM**, May 10, 1786	1	72
Alice, d. [W[illia]m & Betty], b. Sept. 22, 1769	1	169
Amos, s. William & Bette, b. June 11, 1763	1	168
Anna, d. Eben[eze]r & Lydia, b. Dec. 9, 1769	1	169
Betsey, w. W[illia]m, d. Apr. 1, 1779	1	172
Betsey, d. Jedediah & Eunice, b. June 10, 1797	1	170
Bette, d. Will[ia]m & Bette, b. Oct. 21, 1753	1	168
Bette, m. Elisha **BACKUS**, Feb. 12, 1777	1	71
Daniel, s. [Rufus & Hannah], b. Oct. 1, 1795	1	170
David, twin with Jonathan, s. John & Phyllys, b. Jan. 13, 1770	1	169
Eben[eze]r, s. Obadiah & Lydia, b. July 16, 1745	1	168
Ebenezer, m. Ledah **BREWSTER**, of Preston, Dec. 12, 1765	1	167
Eben[eze]r, s. [Eben[eze]r & Lydia], b. Aug. 16, 1774	1	169
Eben[eze]r, d. Oct. 8, 1774	1	172
Eleazer, s. Obadiah & Lucy, b. May 29, 1770	1	169

	Vol.	Page

JOHNSON, (cont.)

Eleaz[e]r, s. Obadiah & Lucy, d. Feb. 4, 1771	1	172
Elisha, s. Eben[eze]r & Lydia, b. Dec. 26, 1766	1	169
Elizabeth, m. John FITCH, Oct. 18, 1714	1	138
Elizabeth, w. Joseph, d. Dec. 11, 1724	1	172
Elizabeth, m. Joseph JONES, Sept. 29, 1726	1	167
Emily, of Canterbury, m. Joshua P. BURNHAM, of Hartford, Sept. 25, 1825, by Rev. Tho[ma]s J. Murdock	2	7
Emma, twin with Emmelia, d. Jedediah & Eunice, b. Nov. 29, 1792	1	170
Emmelia, twin with Emma, d. Jedediah & Eunice, b. Nov. 29, 1792	1	170
Esther, d. Obadiah & Rebeckah, b. Sept. 1, 1704	1	168
Frances, d. Dr. Rufus, b. Apr. 18, 1800	1	171
Francis B., s. Dr. Rufus, b. Jan. 22, 1798	1	170
Hannah, w. Dr. Rufus, d. Apr. 9, 1812	1	172
Harriet, d. Jedediah & Eunice, b. Jan. 23, 1791	1	169
Harriet, m. James ASPENWALL, Dec. 22, 1822	1	53
Harriet, m. James ASPENWALL, b. of Canterbury, Dec. 22, 1822, by Thomas J. Murdock	2	1
Henry Hubbard, s. Nathan & Mary, b. Feb. 15, 1801	1	170
Isaac, s. Joseph & Elizabeth, b. June 24, 1708	1	168
Jacob, s. Obadiah & Rebeckah, b. Mar. 16, 1699	1	168
Jacob, m. Mary SHEPERD, June 14, 1722	1	167
Jacob, s. Jacob & Mary, b. Dec. 3, 1731	1	168
Jacob, s. Obadiah & Lydia, b. Mar. 24, 1739/40	1	168
Jacob, m. Abigail WALDO, Apr. 7, 1763	1	167
James Louis, s. James H. & Almira, b. Dec. 30, 1840	2	243
Jedediah, s. Obadiah & Lydia, d. Oct. 27, 1732	1	172
Jedediah, s. John & Philus, b. Nov. 29, 1762	1	168
Jedediah, m. Eunice, DYAR, Mar. 4, 1790	1	167
John, s. Obadiah & Rebeckah, b. Oct. 6, 1707	1	168
John, s. Obadiah & Rebeckah, d. June 13, 1726	1	172
John, s. Jacob & Mary, b. Oct. 15, 1726	1	168
John, s. Obadiah & Lydia, b. Mar. 23, 1730/31	1	168
John, m. Felis PELLET, Mar. 11, 1756	1	167
John, s. John & Philus, b. Sept. 3, 1759	1	168
John, s. John & Phyllis, d. Feb. 3, 1763	1	172
John, s. John & Phyllis, b. Nov. 5, 1764	1	168
John, s. Obadiah & Lucy, b. Sept. 26, 1774	1	169
Jonathan, twin with David, s. John & Phyllys, b. Jan. 13, 1770	1	169
Joseph, s. Jacob & Mary, b. Aug. 12, 1730	1	168
Joseph, d. Mar. 16, 1755	1	172
Joseph, s. John & Phillys, b. May 20, 1767	1	169
Laura, m. Jeremiah PELLET, Jan. 2, 1793	1	193
Leedeoma, w. W[illia]m, d. Sept. 14, 1797	1	172
Lucinda, d. Obadiah & Lucinda, b. Jan. 5, 1790	1	170
Lucy, d. William & Betty, b. June 22, 1766	1	169

	Vol.	Page
JOHNSON, (cont.)		
Lydia, d. Obadiah & Lydia, b. Oct. 4, 1733	1	168
Lydia, m. Amos **FASSET**, Apr. 10, 1752	1	138
Lydia, d. Will[ia]m & Bette, b. Nov. 17, 1757	1	168
Lydia, d. [Eben[eze]r & Lydia], b. Apr. 17, 1772	1	169
Lydia, wid., m. Jedediah **BROWN**, Sept. 20, 1789	1	72
Maria E., m. Sebastian **BUTTON**, b. of Canterbury, Oct.		
24, 1841, by Samuel L. Hough, J. P.	2	12
Mary, d. Obadiah & Rebeckah, b. Oct. 10, 1697	1	168
Mary, m. Moses **CLEVELAND**, Oct. 19, 1717	1	100
Mary, m. Elisha **PAINE**, Nov. 24, 1720	1	192
Mary, w. Jacob, d. Mar. 5, 1731/2	1	172
Mary, w. Obadiah, Jr., d. Dec. 10, 1763	1	172
Mary, d. Nathan & Mary, b. Jan. 23, 1805	1	171
Mary, m. Jepthah **HEBBARD**, Apr. 22, 1806	1	156
Mason, s. W[illia]m, Jr. & Wealthy, b. June 8, 1799	1	170
Nathan, s. Obadiah & Lucy, b. Dec. 20, 1771	1	169
Obadiah, m. Rebeckah [ ], Sept. 7, 1696	1	167
Obadiah, s. Obadiah & Rebeckah, b. June 23, 1702	1	168
Obadiah, m. Lydia **CLEVELAND**, Nov. 6, 1723	1	167
Obadiah, s. Obadiah & Lydia, b. Feb. 18, 1735/6	1	168
Obadiah, m. Mary **HOWARD**, of Windham, Apr. 29, 1762	1	167
Obadiah, Capt., d. Apr. 10, 1765	1	172
Obadiah, m. Lucy **SPAULDING**, of Plainfield, July 6, 1765	1	167
Obadiah, s. Obadiah & Lucy, b. Feb. 21, 1766	1	169
Obadiah, m. Lucinda **COBB**, Aug. 10, 1789	1	167
Obadiah, s. Nathan & Mary, b. Dec. 8, 1802	1	170
Olive, d. Obadiah & Lydia, b. Aug. 23, 1726	1	168
Olive, d. Will[ia]m & Bette, b. Oct. 17, 1751	1	168
Olive, d. Obad[ia]h & Lucy, b. Oct. 23, 1767	1	169
Olive, m. Phinehas **KENDALL**, Dec. 27, 1772	1	173
Orra, d. John & Felis, b. Jan. 13, 1757	1	168
Ora, m. David **PELLET**, Sept. 17, 1778	1	193
Polly, d. Rufus & Hannah, b. Aug. 5, 1786	1	170
Polly, d. [Jedediah & Eunice], b. Mar. 17, 1800	1	170
Ralph, s. William & Wealthy, b. Apr. 3, 1804	1	170
Rebecca, d. Dec. 1, 1752	1	172
Ruby, d. W[illia]m & Betty, b. May 31, 1774	1	169
Ruby, m. William **BINGHAM**, Oct. 20, 1793	1	72
Ruby, d. William & Welthy, b. Dec. 24, 1794	1	170
Rufus, s. Obadiah & Mary, b. Nov. 24, 1763	1	168
Rufus, s. [Rufus & Hannah], b. Jan. 12, 1793	1	170
Rufus, Dr., m. Sarah **PERKINS**, Oct. 27, 1812	1	167
Sally, d. [Rufus & Hannah], b. Sept. 10, 1788	1	170
Sally, d. Rufus & Hannah, d. Dec. 2, 1789	1	172
Sally, d. [Rufus & Hannah], b. Dec. 28, 1790	1	170
Sally, d. Rufus & Hannah, d. Sept. 23, 1800	1	172
Salome, d. Samuel & Hannah, b. Sept. 30, 1792	1	170

	Vol.	Page

JOHNSON, (cont.)

	Vol.	Page
Samuel, s. Jacob & Mary, b. Sept. 3, 1723	1	168
Samuel, s. William & Bette, b. June 4, 1761	1	168
Sarah, d. Will[ia]m & Bette, b. Nov. 1, 1755	1	168
Sarah, m. Jacob **BACON**, June 6, 1782	1	71
Stephen, m. Dorothy **ENSWORTH**, Feb. 6, 1783	1	167
William, Ensign, d. Sept. 23, 1713	1	172
William, s. Obadiah & Lydia, b. Aug. 13, 1724	1	168
Will[ia]m, m. Betty **FASSET**, Nov. 29, 1750	1	167
William, s. William & Betty, b. Mar. 25, 1768	1	169
William, s. W[illia]m & Betty, b. Mar. 25, 1768	1	169
William, Jr., m. Wealthy **PELLET**, Mar. 29, 1795	1	167
William, m. Elizabeth **DYAR**, Oct. 7, 1798	1	167
----, wid. John, d. Dec. 2, 1717	1	172

JONES, Benjamin F., of Coventry, R. I., m. Minerva B. **CURIAN**,

	Vol.	Page
of Providence, R. I., Oct. 19, 1834, by Rev. Otis C. Whiton	2	43
Elisha, m. Sarah Ann **BURNHAM**, Mar. 22, 1836, by Rev. Asa King, Westminster	2	43
Hannah, m. Ebenezer S. **BENNETT**, b. of Canterbury, Mar. 12, 1843, by Rev. John F. Blanchard	2	13
Hepsibath, m. Caleb **AUSTIN**, Apr. 15, 1761	1	51
Joseph, m. Elizabeth **JOHNSON**, Sept. 29, 1726	1	167

JORDAN, Benjamin A., of Coventry, R. I., m. Frances P. **HOWE**,

	Vol.	Page
Sept. 4, 1827, by Israel G. Rose	2	43

JUEL, [see under JEWELL]

JUSTIN, Abigail, m. Abner **GREEN**, Feb. 16, 1796, at Preston

	Vol.	Page
	1	149
Almira, d. Charles & Lucy, b. Mar. 8, 1807	1	170
Almira, of Canterbury, m. Janes **BRIGGS**, of Sterling, July 15, 1830, by Rev. I. J. Rose, of Westminster	2	8
Amos, s. Miner & Meriam, b. Feb. 6, 1788	1	170
Andrew, s. Charles & Sarah, b. Mar. 3, 1788	1	170
Benajah, s. [W[illia]m & Patience], b. July 23, 1766	1	169
Bethany, d. W[illia]m & Mary, d. July 14, 1749	1	172
Canadilla, d. Minor & Miriam, b. Apr. 9, 1804	1	170
Charles, m. Sarah **WINCHESTER**, Nov. 3, 1784	1	167
Charles, m. Lucy **BOND**, Apr. 23, 1789	1	167
Charles, m. Mary **YOUNG**, Aug. 13, 1820, by Erastus Larned	2	43
David Augustus, s. [George & Lucy], b. July 29, 1794	1	171
Deborah, d. [W[illia]m & Patience], b. Aug. 5, 1762	1	169
Dillicene, s. Minor & Miriam, b. Feb. 9, 1802	1	170
Elizabeth, d. W[illia]m & Patience, b. May 15, 1750	1	169
Elizabeth, m. Jona **BATES**, Jan. 18, 1774	1	71
Elizabeth Morse, d. Minor & Mary, b. Jan. 27, 1815	1	171
Ephraim, s. [Miner & Meriam], b. Oct. 13, 1789	1	170
George King, s. [George & Lucy], b. Sept. 4, 1804	1	171
Gershom, s. [W[illia]m & Patience], b. Feb. 13, 1756	1	169
Gershom, m. Patience **GODFREY**, Mar. 7, 1780	1	167

	Vol.	Page
JUSTIN, (cont.)		
Hannah, d. Charles & Lucy, b. Apr. 17, 1792	1	169
Hannah, d. Charles & Lucy, b. Apr. 17, 1792	1	170
Harriet, d. [Minor & Miriam], b. Apr. 20, 1806	1	170
Ire, s. Charles & Sarah, b. Aug. 17, 1785	1	169
Jacob Galusha, s. [George & Lucy], b. Apr. 14, 1810	1	171
Lucy, d. [George & Lucy], b. Apr. 20, 1796	1	171
Lucy, d. [Charles & Lucy], b. Aug. 29, 1797	1	170
Lydia, d. [Charles & Lucy], b. Mar. 20, 1794	1	170
Mary, d. [Minor & Miriam], b. July 28, 1810	1	170
Merebah, d. [Charles & Lucy], b. May 28, 1799	1	170
Milla, d. [Miner & Meriam], b. Mar. 2, 1800	1	170
Miller, s. [Miner & Meriam], b. July 20, 1797	1	170
Miner, s. Miriam **MILLER**, Apr. 9, 1787	1	167
Patience, d. [W[illia]m & Patience], b. June 22, 1753	1	169
Philena, m. Elmer **WEAVER**, b. of Canterbury, [ ], by		
Rev. Tho[ma]s J. Murdock	2	85
Polly, m. Enoch **HERRINGTON**, Oct. 14, 1803	1	156
Rachel, d. [W[illia]m & Patience], b. July 2, 1760	1	169
Rebecca, d. George & Lucy, b. Jan. 16, 1787	1	171
Reuben, s. [George & Lucy], b. Dec. 19, 1792	1	171
Samuel, s. [Miner & Meriam], b. Oct. 24, 1795	1	170
Sophia, d. [George & Lucy], b. June 10, 1802	1	171
Sussy, d. [Charles & Lucy], b. Apr. 17, 1795	1	170
Wallcut, s. [W[illia]m & Patience], b. July 22, 1763	1	169
William, d. Sept. 18, 1775	1	172
W[illia]m Wheeler, s. [Minor & Miriam], b. Aug. 19, 1808	1	170
Zadock, s. [Miner & Meriam], b. Jan. 27, 1794	1	170
KASSON, Phebe, m. Jedediah **LEACH**, Nov. 4, 1779	1	176
KAZAR, Sophia, m. Alfred **HIDE**, Mar. 15, 1811	1	156
KEESES, Emeline L., of Lisbon, m. Jonathan **HARRIS**, of		
Brooklyn, Sept. 27, 1829, by Peter Morse, J. P.	2	39
KENDALL, [see also **CANDALL** and **CUNDALL**], Alice, d. John		
& Lois, b. Feb. 8, 1784	1	174
Azubah, m. Moses **CLEVELAND**, Mar. 24, 1768	1	101
Betsey, d. [Phinehas & Olive], b. Mar. 28, 1781	1	174
Betsey, w. Peter, d. Nov. 16, 1793, ae 39	1	175
Billy, s. Peter & Betsey, b. July 26, 1785	1	174
David, m. Bridget **CADY**, Mar. 5, 1767	1	173
George Timothy, s. [John & Sally], b. Oct. 30, 1821	1	174
Harry, s. [Peter & Betsey], b. June 18, 1791	1	174
Henry, m. Emeline H. **STEVENS**, b. of Canterbury, Mar. 19,		
1848, by Rev. Robert C. Learned	2	48
Hervey, s. Peter & Betsey, b. June 18, 1791	1	174
Jaen, w. David, d. Aug. 5, 1766	1	175
Jeduthan, s. Phinehas & Olive, b. Aug. 5, 1773	1	174
John, Jr., m. Sally **PARKIS**, Aug. 22, 1819	1	173
John W., m. Harriet A. N. **SHARP**, Feb. 26, 1843, by Rev. Asa		

	Vol.	Page
KENDALL, (cont.)		
Asa King	2	47
John Waldo, s. John & Sally, b. June 6, 1820	1	174
Johnson, s. [Phinehas & Olive], b. Feb. 16, 1779	1	174
Lois, d. John & Lois, b. Oct. 20, 1781	1	174
Lucy, d. Peter & Betsey, b. Sept. 4, 1777	1	174
Phinehas, m. Olive JOHNSON, Dec. 27, 1772	1	173
Sally, d. Peter & Betsey, b. Jan. 10, 1783	1	174
Sarah, d. Phinehas & Olive, b. Apr. 18, 1791	1	174
Septemius, s. [Phinehas & Olive], b. Mar. 16, 1777	1	174
William, s. David & Jaen, b. July 16, 1766	1	174
KENNEDY, Ruth, m. Jeremiah SMITH, May 19, 1818	1	215
KENNEY, KENNY, [see also **KINNE**], Erastus, of Plainfield, m.		
Sarah **FRANCIS**, of Canterbury, Aug. 13, 1850, by Rev.		
J. B. Guild, of Packersville	2	48
Kimball, of Plainfield, m. Mary E. **DYER**, of Canterbury,		
Feb. 2, 1835, by Rev. Otis C. Whiton	2	47
KIES, Horace A., of Killingly, m. Anna **DIMMICK**, Mar. 31, 1840,		
by Rev. Asa King, Westminster	2	47
KILLAIN, Abigail, d. Phinehas & Thankful, b. Mar. 6, 1748	1	174
Esther, d. Phinehas & Thankful, b. Jan. 29, 1749/50	1	174
Olive, d. Phinehas & Thankful, b. Sept. 3, 1740	1	174
Olive, d. Phinehas & Thankful, b. June 5, 1744	1	174
Sarah, d. Phinehas & Thankful, b. Apr. 20, 1742	1	174
Thankful, d. Phinehas & Thankful, b. Apr. 13, 1746	1•	174
KIMBALL, Abigail, m. Thomas **RATHBUN**, Nov. 15, 1755	1	209
Albert, of Scotland, m. Malissa **WOODARD**, of Westminster,		
Mar. 14, 1831, by Rev. I. G. Rose, of Westminster	2	47
Beulah, m. Henry **DOWNING**, Feb. 11, 1791	1	121
Elizabeth, w. Nathan, d. Jan. 17, 1758	1	175
Elizabeth, d. Nathan & Elizabeth, b. Sept. 12, 1760	1	174
Elizabeth, m. Elisha **BOWMAN**, June 29, 1780	1	71
Lydia, m. Curtiss **CARTER**, Mar. 9, 1786	1	102
Martha, m. Ezekiel **SPAULDING**, Nov. 24, 1737	1	214
Mary, w. Nathan, d. [ ]	1	175
Nathan, m. Elizabeth **CLEVELAND**, Aug. 28, 1755	1	173
Nathan, m. Elizabeth **MEACHAM**, Dec. 28, 1758	1	173
KING, Benj[ami]n, s. Tho[ma]s & Mehetable, b. June 14, 1770	1	174
Elizabeth, d. Sept. 25, 1842, ae 77	2	341
Elizabeth A., m. Abadiah H. **BUTTS**, Sept. 6, 1836, by Rev.		
Asa King, Westminster	2	10
Eunice, w. Rev. Asa, d. Apr. 4, 1843, ae 71	2	341
John Spencer, s. Elisha & Sabra, b. July 21, 1785	1	174
Polly, d. Elisha & Sabra, b. Nov. 7, 1790	1	174
Rebeckah, m. Nathaniel **ENSWORTH**, Dec. 16, 1775	1	133
Sally, d. Elisha & Sabra, b. Oct. 30, 1787	1	174
Samuel, s. Elisha & Sabra, b. Sept. 28, 1783	1	174
Tryphena, d. Tho[ma]s & Mehetable, b. Mar. 24, 1772	1	174

	Vol.	Page
KINGSLEY, Abby Ann, d. [Hez[ekiah], Jr. & Deborah Eliza],		
b. Sept. 2, 1831	2	247
Edward, s. Hez[ekiah], Jr. & Deborah Eliza, b. May 5, 1832	2	247
Elias, s. Eben[eze]r & Ruth, b. Aug. 30, 1770	1	174
Hannah S., d. Hezekiah, of Canterbury, m. J. A. **SPAULDING**,		
of Killingly, Jan. 2, 1854, by Rev. Robert C. Learned	2	76
Hannah Sharp, d. [Hez[ekiah], Jr. & Deborah Eliza], b.		
Mar. 7, 1834	2	247
Irena, wid., d. Dec. 17, 1822	2	341
John, m. Mary **RAYMOND**, b. of Canterbury, Aug. 22, 1822,		
by Erastus Learned	2	47
John Peck, s. John & Mary, b. Nov. [ ], 1823	2	247
Mary, m. Luther **BARSTOW**, Dec. 21, 1845, by Rev. Daniel		
Lyon, of Packerville	2	14
Polly, m. Joseph **SAFFORD**, Jan. 24, 1831, by Rev. Dennis		
Platt	2	72
Rhoda, of Canterbury, m. John P. **WEBB**, of Windham, Feb.		
20, 1850, by Rev. R. S. Hazen, of Westminster	2	89
Sarah Hyde, d. Hez[ekiah], Jr. & Deborah Eliza, b. June		
7, 1828	2	247
Susannah, of Lisbon, m. Joseph **LYON**, Mar. 6, 1797	1	176
KINNE, [see also **KENNEY**], Stephen, of Ward, Mass., m. Mary		
HERRICK, of Canterbury, June 17, 1822, by Erastus		
Learned	2	47
KINYON, Ele[a]nor, d. [Sheperd E. & Ele[a]nor], b. June 18, 1833	2	247
Isaac Lawton, s. [Sheperd E. & Ele[a]nor], b. Oct. 20, 1834	2	247
Mary Lawton, d. Sheperd E. & Ele[a]nor, b. Apr. 22, 1832	2	247
KNAPPING, KNAPING, George, s. Thomas & Phebe, b. Dec. 17,		
1754	1	174
Jeremiah, s. Thomas & Phebe, b. Sept. 23, 1756	1	174
John, s. Tho[ma]s & Phebe, d. Aug. 4, 1750	1	175
John, s. Tho[ma]s & Phebe, b. Sept. 14, 1750	1	174
Mehetable, d. Tho[ma]s & Phebe, b. Mar. 11, 1752	1	174
Mehetable, d. Tho[ma]s & Phebe, d. June 4, 1752	1	175
Sam[ue]l, s. Thomas & Phebe, b. May 14, 1744	1	174
Sara[h], d. Thomas & Phebe, b. Apr. 1, 1746	1	174
Tho[ma]s, s. Tho[ma]s & Phebe, b. Mar. 15, 1742	1	174
KNIGHT, NIGHT, Abigail, of Norwich, m. Isaiah **WILLIAMS**,		
May 5, 1744	1	236
Anna, m. Gideon **BUTTS**, Oct. 28, 1779	1	71
Deborah, m. Sherebiah **BUTT**, Jan. 3, 1759	1	70
Eunice, of Norwich, m. Josiah **BUTT**, May 28, 1778	1	71
Isaac, of Plainfield, m. Roba **BACON**, of Canterbury,		
Mar. 14, 1838, by Rev. Charles J. Warren	2	47
Jerusha, m. Amos **BREWSTER**, Mar. 19, 1761	1	70
Jeresha, m. James **ADAMS**, Feb. 16, 1772	1	52
Mary, of Plainfield, m. Roswell **ENSWORTH**, Aug. 12, 1804	1	133
Sarah, m. Williams **ADAMS**, June 12, 1770 (?)	1	51

	Vol.	Page

KNIGHT, NIGHT, (cont.)

Susannah, of Norwich, m. John **BUTT,** June 24, 1784 — 1 — 72

LAD[D], Jonathan, m. Elizabeth **STILES,** Apr. 26, 1759 — 1 — 176

LAMBART, Sarah, m. Jabez **GREEN,** Jr., May 1, 1754 — 1 — 149

LAMPHERE, LAMPHIRE, LANFAIR, Isaac, s. Lemuel &
  Loadisa, b. Jan. 5, 1796 — 1 — 178

Lemuel, m. Loadisa **HERRINGTON,** May 13, 1793 — 1 — 176

Lydia, m. Reuben **HARRIS,** July 4, 1769 — 1 — 155

Mary, m. Festus **APPLY,** Sept. 21, 1818 — 1 — 52

Roxana, d. Lemuel & Loadisa, b. Jan. 3, 1794 — 1 — 178

Theophilus, m. Elizabeth Sabeny **STEVENS,** Dec. 31, 1799 — 1 — 176

LAMSON, James, of Woodstock, m. Sophia **BUTTS,** Mar. 28,
  1849, by Rev. Asa King, Westminster — 2 — 53

LASSEL, Polly, of Windham, m. John **CROSBY,** Apr. 1, 1795 — 1 — 102

LATEMAN, Elizabeth, m. Gershom **MOTT,** Apr. 28, 1748 — 1 — 181

LATHROP, Benjamin, d. June 16, 1758 — 1 — 180

Benjamin, s. Nathaniel & Anna, b. Feb. 18, 1760 — 1 — 177

Benjamin Merrell, s. [Job & Deborah], b. June 9, 1808 [negros] — 1 — 248

Elizabeth, m. Daniel **DAVIS,** Sept. 16, 1732 — 1 — 120

Freelove, d. [Job & Deborah], b. July 30, 1810 [negroes] — 1 — 248

Freelove, of Canterbury, m. Pardon P. **BRAYTON,** of
  Griswold, May 31, 1832, by Rev. Demis Platt — 2 — 9

Freeman, s. [Job & Deborah], b. July 19, 1802 [negroes] — 1 — 248

George Lewis, s. Thomas & Annette, b. Feb. 7, 1847 — 2 — 251

Hannah, of Franklin, m. Joshua Waldo **RANSFORD,** Apr. 20,
  1800 — 1 — 209

Job, m. Deborah **JEFFERS,** Oct. 23, 1799 [negroes] — 1 — 248

John B., of Norwich, m. Harriet M. **LESTER,** of Canterbury,
  Nov. 27, 1823, by Tho[ma]s J. Murdock — 2 — 51

John Willard, s. [Thomas & Annette], b. Nov. 6, 1842 — 2 — 251

Joseph Edward, s. Thomas & Annette, b. Apr. 24, 1838 — 2 — 251

Leb[b]eus, s. Nathaniel & Anna, b. Oct. 23, 1761 — 1 — 177

Luke, s. [Job & Deborah], b. July 7, 1806 [negroes] — 1 — 248

Mary, m. David **NEVINS,** Oct. 14, 1746 — 1 — 189

Mary, of Lisbon, m. Jacob **BALDWIN,** May 7, 1788 — 1 — 72

Mary, d. Job & Deborah, b. Aug. 20, 1800 [negroes] — 1 — 248

Mary, of Lisbon, m. Timothy **BALDWIN,** Nov. 14, 1805 — 1 — 73

Mary, d. Thomas & Anette, b. Feb. 25, 1832 [negroes] — 1 — 248

Mary, m. George E. **WILLARD,** of Uxbridge, Mass., Apr. 5,
  1837, by Rev. Asa King, Westminster — 2 — 87

Mary Ann, d. [Thomas & Annette], b. Apr. 12, 1841 — 2 — 251

Nathaniel, m. Anna **FITCH,** Apr. 5, 1759 — 1 — 176

Thomas, m. Wealthy **COBB,** Dec. 19, 1771 — 1 — 176

Thomas, s. [Job & Deborah], b. May 28, 1804 [negroes] — 1 — 248

Thomas, of Griswold, m. Olive **DARLING,** of Canterbury,
  Feb. 19, 1826, by Sam[ue]l L. Hough, J. P. — 2 — 51

Thomas, m. Arnette **WILLIAMS,** b. of Norwich, Nov. 25,
  1830, by Alfred Mitchell, Norwich — 2 — 51

	Vol.	Page

LATHROP, (cont.)

Thomas Williams, s. [Thomas & Annette], b. Apr. 12, 1834	2	251
Thomas Williams, s. [Thomas & An[n]ette], b. Apr. 9, 1836 [negroes]	1	248
Zerviah, m. Will[ia]m **BRADFORD**, Dec. 13, 1739	1	69

LAWRENCE, LORRANCE, James, s. Isaac & Lydia, b. Dec. 1,

1728	1	177
Sarah, m. Josiah **CLEVELAND**, Jr., Oct. 15, 1735	1	100

LEACH, Elisha, s. Joseph & Mary, b. June 22, 1754 | 1 | 177

Elisha, m. Lucy **CADY**, Jan. 9, 1777	1	176
Eunice, m. Ephraim **LYON**, Dec. 31, 1766	1	176
Harvey, s. Jedediah & Phebe, b. Dec. 21, 1786	1	178
James, s. [Joseph & Mary], b. Apr. 5, 1759	1	177
Jedediah, m. Phebe **KASSON**, Nov. 4, 1779	1	176
Johan[n]a, m. Ezra **CADY**, Apr. 8, 1721	1	100
Joseph, d. Oct. 30, 1776, at Stamford, Conn.	1	180
Lucy, m. David **BUTTS**, Oct. 12, 1834, by Rev. Anson S. Atwood	2	10
Lury, d. Jedediah & Phebe, b. Dec. 7, 1780 (Lucy?)	1	178
Luther Dixson, s. Jedediah & Phebe, b. May 4, 1785	1	178
Mary, m. Gideon **ADAMS**, Jan. 5, [ ]	1	51
Olive, d. Jedediah & Phebe, b. Aug. 21, 1782	1	178
Olive, m. William **ASPENWALL**, Apr. 3, 18[ ]	1	52
Orra, d. Elisha & Lucy, b. Jan. 10, 1778	1	177
Phinehas, s. Joseph & Mary, b. May 24, 1742	1	177
Sarah, d. [Joseph & Mary], b. July 23, 1756	1	177
Sarah, m. Asa **SMITH**, Apr. 16, 1777	1	214
Susannah, m. Abel **LYON**, Oct. 2, 1765	1	176

LEADBETTER, Danville, of U. S. A., m. Elizabeth **WATERMAN**,

of Canterbury, Aug. 8, 1836, by Rev. Tubal Wakefield	2	52

LEARNED, [see also **LEONARD**], Dwight Whitney, s. Robert C. &

Sarah B., b. Oct. 12, 1848	2	251
Edward Whitney, s. Robert C. & Sarah B., b. Aug. 14, 1851	2	251
Edwin, s. Erastus & Freelove, b. May 24, 1806	1	179
Edwin, s. Rev. Erastus & Freelove, d. Mar. 5, 1817	1	180
Edwin Bacon, s. Rev. Erastus & Sophia, b. Dec. 2, 1818	1	179
Elizabeth, of Canterbury, m. George L. **LEAVENS**, of Dudley, Mass., Oct. 17, 1823, by Erastus Learned	2	51
Erastus, Rev., m. Sophia **BACON**, May 14, 1816	1	176
Erastus, Rev. d. June 30, 1824	2	343
Freelove, w. Rev. Erastus, d. Oct. 26, 1815	1	180
Grace Hallum, d. Robert C. & Sarah B., b. Mar. 14, 1854	2	251
Juliette, d. [Erastus & Freelove], b. Oct. 27, 1808	1	179
Lucy, m. Ebenezer **BARSTOW**, Sept. 12, 1811	1	73
Mary Bacon, d. Rev. Erastus & Sophia, b. Dec. 18, 1821	1	179
Melissa, m. James C. **MORSE**, b. of Canterbury, Sept. 11, 1823, by Erastus Learned	2	55
Paschal Paoli, s. Erastus & Freelove, b. July 15, 1813	1	179

	Vol.	Page
LEARNED, (cont.)		
Samuel Julius, s. Rev. Erastus & Sophia, b. Oct. 23, 1823	1	179
Selina, d. [Erastus & Freelove], b. Aug. 10, 1810	1	179
Sophia Ann, d. Rev. Erastus & Sophia, b. Dec. 2, 1818	1	179
Sophia B., d. Feb. 11, 1830	2	343
LEAVENS, LEVENS, George L., of Dudley, Mass., m. Elizabeth **LEARNED**, of Canterbury, Oct. 17, 1823, by Erastus Learned	2	51
Peter, m. Patience **BROOKS**, Dec. 27, 1704	1	176
Rachel, m. Thomas **BROWN**, Jan. 30, 1705/6	1	69
LEDYARD, Clarrissa, m. Rufus Leveret **DIMMOCK**, Nov. 12, 1806	1	121
LEFFINGWELL, Asa, m. Elizabeth **SMITH**, Nov. 12, 1771	1	176
Asa, d. June 28, 1788	1	180
Johannah, m. Col. John **DYAR**, Oct. 4, 1759	1	120
LEONARD, [see also **LEARNED**], Mehetable, of Preston, m. Aaron **BALDWIN**, Apr. 11, 1771	1	70
LESTER, Abigail, d. [Phinehas & Elizabeth], b. June 8, 1783	1	178
Andrew, s. [Phinehas & Elizabeth], b. May 27, 1779	1	178
David, m. Betsey **STEVENS**, b. of Canterbury, Nov. 16, 1826, by Rev. Tho[ma]s J. Murdock	2	51
Elisha, s. Andrew & Priscilla, b. June 23, 1758	1	177
Hannah M., d. David & Betsey, b. Apr. 25, 1828	2	251
Harriet M., of Canterbury, m. John B. **LATHROP**, of Norwich, Nov. 27, 1823, by Tho[ma]s J. Murdock	2	51
Hephzibah, d. [Phinehas & Elizabeth], b. Oct. 31, 1787	1	178
John, s. [Phinehas & Elizabeth], b. July 18, 1781	1	178
John, [of] Cumberland, R. I., m. Mary **WILBREW**, of Plainfield, July 16, 1832, by Rev. Dennis Platt	2	51
Joseph P., m. Sally **MARSH**, Feb. 24, 1840, by Rev. Asa King, Westminster	2	53
Lucinda, d. Phin[eha]s & Eliza, b. Feb. 16, 1773	1	177
Lucinda, d. Phinehas & Elizabeth, b. Feb. 16, 1773	1	178
Lucy, d. Andrew & Priscilla, b. Mar. 6, 1763	1	177
Lydia, m. Seth **PAINE**, Nov. 17, 1774	1	193
Mary, d. [Phin[eha]s & Eliza], b. Feb. 14, 1775	1	177
Mary, d. [Phinehas & Elizabeth], b. Feb. 14, 1775	1	178
Mary E., of Canterbury, m. Rev. Ebenezer **MEAD**, of Attica, N. Y., May 20, 1828, by Rev. James R. Wheelock	2	55
Mehetable, m. Luther **SAFFORD**, May 28, 1834, by Rev. Otis C. Whiton	2	73
Nathan, s. Andrew & Priscilla, b. June 15, 1760	1	177
Phinehas, m. Elizabeth **PELLET**, Dec. 1, 1771	1	176
Phinehas, m. Betty **PETTET**, Dec. 1, 1772	1	176
Priscilla, d. [Phinehas & Elizabeth], b. Apr. 3, 1775	1	178
William, s. [Phinehas & Elizabeth], b. June 4, 1785	1	178
William, m. Maria **BURGESS**, June 29, 1845, by Rev. Asa King, Westminster	2	53

	Vol.	Page
LeVALLEY, Harriet E., of Canterbury, m. Chauncey C.		
CHAMBERLAIN, of Killingly, Feb. 18, 1850, by Robert		
C. Learned	2	19
Jerome B. D., of Warwick, R. I., m. Jane T. **GREENE**, of		
Providence, R. I., Oct. 19, 1834, by Rev. Otis C. Whiton	2	52
Patience, m. Hezekiah **CRANDALL**, Mar. 22, 1852, by Rev.		
Robert C. Learned	2	19
LEVENS, [see under **LEAVENS**]		
LEWIS, LUIS, Clarissa, d. [Peleg & Susannah], b. Oct. 28, 1803	1	178
Clarissa, m. Jedediah S. **LEWIS**, b. of Canterbury, Nov.		
23, 1831, by Andrew T. Judson, J. P.	2	51
Emerilla, d. Peleg, b. Aug. 21, 1810	1	179
Francis C., of Canterbury, m. Marie M. **PRICE**, of Plainfield,		
Apr. 15, 1839, by Rev. Thomas L. Shipman	2	52
Frances Cordelia, d. Timothy A. & Frances M., b. Apr.		
20, 1842	2	251
Hannah, m. Pierce **GOODING**, Dec. 7, 1761	1	149
Jedediah S., m. Clarissa **LEWIS**, b. of Canterbury, Nov.		
23, 1831, by Andrew T. Judson, J. P.	2	51
Laura, d. [Peleg & Susannah], b. Nov. 13, 1805	1	179
Laura, d. Peleg & Susannah, d. Dec. 16, 1806	1	180
Laura, d. Peleg & Susanna, b. Jan. 28, 1808	1	179
Lucy Ann, m. Allen **SPENCER**, Nov. 6, 1825, by And[re]w		
T. Judson, J. P.	2	71
Mary, m. Paul D. **ADAMS**, Feb. 3, 1822	1	53
Mary, m. Paul D. **ADAMS**, Feb. 3, 1822, by Asa Meech	2	1
Mary Ann, m. Rosswell **ENSWORTH**, Jr., Apr. 21, 1844, by		
Rev. Daniel D. Lyon, Packersville	2	27
Peleg, m. Susannah **ADAMS**, Oct. 6, 1801	1	176
Perley W., s. Timothy A. & Frances M., b. Sept. 14, 1852	2	252
Prentice, m. Lydia E. **BLISS**, b. of Canterbury, Oct. 31,		
1847, by Rev. B. Cook, of Jewett City	2	53
Rebecca, d. Peleg & Susannah, b. Dec. 27, 1801	1	178
Rebecca, m. Nehemiah B. **HYDE**, Nov. 26, 1823, by Andrew		
T. Judson, J. P.	2	39
Rhoda, of Plainfield, m. Jared **MAIN**, Jr., of Canterbury,		
Jan. 22, 1826, by San[uel] L. Hough, J. P.	2	55
Samuel, of Plainfield, m. Sarah **SMITH**, of Canterbury,		
Oct. 2, 1842, by John Francis, J. P.	2	52
Sarah A., of Plainfield, m. Charles L. **HYDE**, of Canterbury,		
July 4, 1845, by Rev. Zephaniah Baker	2	41
Temperance E., of Canterbury, m. Samuel **HOXSIE**, of		
Willamantic, Jan. 20, 1839, by Rev. Tubal Wakefield, at		
Packersville	2	40
Timothy A., m. Frances M. **ADAMS**, Nov. 24, 1840, by Rev.		
Asa King, Westminster	2	52
Timothy Adams, s. Peleg & Susannah, b. Sept. 10, 1814	1	179
LILLIBRIDGE, Hannah, m. Avery **HOXIE**, Dec. 26, 1850, by Rev.		

	Vol.	Page
LILLIBRIDGE, (cont.)		
J. B. Guild, at Packersville	2	101
LILLIE, LILLEE, Abigail, m. John **BUTT**, Apr. 15, 1772	1	71
Benjamin, s. [David & Deborah], b. Jan. 15, 1793	1	178
Calvin, s. [David & Deborah], b. May 20, 1791	1	178
David, m. Deborah **GATES**, Nov. 23, 1780 or 1785	1	176
John, m. Roxa **BATES**, Apr. 8, 1779	1	176
Lemuel, s. David & Deborah, b. Sept. 11, 1787	1	178
Lemuel, s. David & Deborah, d. Feb. 14, 1788	1	180
Loomis, s. [David & Deborah], b. Apr. 30, 1795	1	178
Lucy, d. John & Roxa, b. June 8, 1782	1	178
Luther, s. [David & Deborah], b. Feb. 21, 1789	1	178
Luther, m. Aurelia **MORGAN**, Dec. 14, 1809	1	176
Lydia, d. John & Roxalena, b. June 9, 1788	1	178
Mary, d. John & Roza, b. Apr. 30, 1780	1	178
Prince or Prime, s. John & Roxalene, b. July 19, 1785	1	178
----, s. John & Roxa, b. July 2, 1784; d. July 2, 1784	1	178
LITCHFIELD, Ann, d. John & Lucy, b. Apr. 15, 1755	1	177
Anne, m. Walter **BOWMAN**, Feb. 22, 1775	1	71
Betty, d. Israel & Penelope, b. Mar. 15, 1755	1	177
Bettey, see under Bettey **LITTLEFIELD**		
Bridget, d. John & Lucy, b. July 13, 1763	1	177
Daniel, s. John & Lucy, b. Sept. 16, 1773	1	177
David, m. Kezia **MORSE**, Dec. 2, 1784	1	176
Diedama, d. [David & Kezia], b. Jan. 30, 1799	1	178
Eleazer, s. John & Lucy, b. Aug. 26, 1757	1	177
Elisha, s. David & Kezia, b. July 12, 1785	1	178
Festus, s. [David & Kezia], b. Sept. 14, 1796	1	178
Hitty Morse, d. [David & Kezia], b. Aug. 5, 1792	1	178
Israel, m. Phebe **HOLT**, Jan. 14, 1766	1	176
John, m. Lucy **CADY**, July 17, 1750	1	176
John, s. John & Lucy, b. Feb. 18, 1760	1	177
Kezia, d. David & Kezia, b. Aug. 8, 1787	1	178
Leonard, s. [Israel & Phebe], b. Jan. 26, 1772	1	177
Lucy, d. John & Lucy, b. Jan. 3, 1769	1	177
Lyman, s. [David & Kezia], b. June 30, 1790	1	178
Mark, s. Israel & Phebe, b. Mar. 14, 1768	1	177
Penelope, d. [Israel & Phebe], b. May 18, 1775	1	177
Roby, m. Eben[eze]r **PARKER**, Dec. 9, 1779	1	193
Sally, d. David & Kezia, b. May 6, 1794	1	178
Sarah, d. John & Lucy, b. Nov. 9, 1753	1	177
Susanna, d. John & Lucy, b. Dec. 9, 1750	1	177
Trypheny, d. Olive **CADY**, b. Dec. 18, 1751	1	177
Triphena, m. John **BROWN**, Jr., Feb. 4, 1773	1	71
Uriah, s. John & Lucy, b. May 10, 1766	1	177
LITTLEFIELD, Bettey, m. Sam[ue]l **ADAMS**, 4th, May 11, 177[ ]	1	52
Bettey, see also Bettey **LITCHFIELD**	1	177
LOMBARD, LAMBART, Amy, d. John & Sarah, b. Oct. 12, 1745	1	177

	Vol.	Page
LOMBARD, LAMBART, (cont.)		
Amy, d. John & Sarah, d. Sept. 8, 1749	1	180
Anna, d. John & Sara[h], b. Feb. 24, 1739/40	1	177
John, m. Sarah **ARCHAR**, June 21, 1733	1	176
John, d. Jan. 19, 1772	1	180
Mehetable, d. John & Sarah, b. Aug. 8, 1748	1	177
Olive, d. John & Sarah, b. Nov. 9, 1743	1	177
Olive, had s. John **McCARTER**, b. Sept. 24, 1767	1	110
Olive, single woman had s. John **McCARTEE**, b. Sept. 24, 1767	1	177
Olive, m. John **McCARTER**, Dec. 3, 1767	1	101
Olive, m. John **McCARTEE**, Dec. 3, 1767	1	181
Sara[h], d. John & Sara[h], b. June 7, 1735	1	177
Sarah had d. Lucy **WILKASON**, b. May 26, 1751	1	239
Sarah*, m. Jabez **GREEN**, Jr., May 1, 1754 (*Sarah **LAMBART**)	1	149
Sarah, w. John, d. Aug. 15, 1762	1	180
LONG, Eunice J., m. Leona L. **PLACE**, Jan. 30, [1843], by Rev. Asa King	2	64
Eunice S., m. Samuel W. **BOWMAN**, Nov. 27, 1839, by Rev. Asa King, Westminster	2	12
Lucretia, m. Thomas D. **BURNHAM**, Jan. 17, 1836, by Rev. Asa King, Westminster	2	10
LOOMIS, LOOMISS, Charles F., s. [Alvin & Ruhamah], b. May 6, 1831	2	251
Dwight Ripley, s. [Alvin & Ruhamah], b. June 24, 1826	2	251
Emma B., d. [Alvin & Ruhamah], b. Jan. 16, 1830	2	251
Laura W., d. [Alvin & Ruhamah], b. Nov. 15, 1835	2	251
Lydia, d. Alvin & Ruhamah, b. Nov. 12, 1824	2	251
Merrel, s. Alvin & Rhuamah, b. Dec. 25, 1827	2	251
Ruth, of Hampton, m. Andrew **HIBBARD**, Nov. 11, 1792	1	156
Sarah, m. John **ENSWORTH**, June 25, 1761	1	133
William P., s. [Alvin & Ruhamah], b. Oct. 29, 1832	2	251
LORD, Anne Hamlinton, d. William & Lydia, b. Mar. 4, 1799	1	178
Benjamin, s. William & Lydia, b. Jan. 21, 1791	1	178
LORRANCE, [see under **LAWRENCE**]		
LOVET, Abigail, of Norwich, m. Reuben **ADAMS**, Dec. 4, 1783	1	52
LUCE, Eunice, m. Shubael **CLEVELAND**, Mar. 30, 1769	1	101
Jerusha, m. Benj[ami]n **RAYNSFORD**, July 12, 1781	1	209
John Crandall, s. Nathaniel & Hannah, b. Jan. 27, 1823	2	251
Nathaniel, m. Lucy **MASON**, Apr. 8, 1821, by Asa Meech	2	51
Nath[anie]l, m. Hannah **CANDALL**, Apr. 18, 1822, by Asa Meech	2	51
LUD[D]INGTON, Anna, m. Josiah **DAINS**, Sept. 26, 1765	1	120
LUIS, [see under **LEWIS**]		
LUMMIS, [see under **LOOMIS**]		
LYON, Abel, m. Susannah **LEACH**, Oct. 2, 1765	1	176
Albertus, s. [Ephraim & Eunice], b. Aug. 2, 1768	1	177

	Vol.	Page
LYON, (cont.)		
Albertus, s. [Eph[rai]m & Eunice], d. Aug. 30, 1768	1	180
Alexander, s. Spencer & Sally, b. Aug. 16, 1812	1	179
Casper Lavather, [s. Chester], b. Oct. 31, 1815	2	251
Casper Lavater, s. Chester, d. Nov. 8, 1840	2	343
Charles R., m. Harriet **BREWSTER**, Nov. 2, 1845, by Rev.		
Z. Baker	2	53
Charles Robinson, [s. Chester], b. Mar. 18, 1820	2	251
Ebenezer, s. Abel & Susanna, b. Dec. 25, 1769	1	178
Eliza Barstow, [d. Chester], b. Apr. 10, 1827	2	251
Eliza Barstow, d. [Chester], d. Mar. 17, 1849	2	343
Ephraim, m. Eunice **LEACH**, Dec. 31, 1766	1	176
Ephraim Chester, [s. Chester], b. June 27, 1830	2	251
Ephraim Chester, s. [Chester], d. Jan. 12, 1851	2	343
Eunice, d. [Ephraim & Eunice], b. Oct. 2, 1770	1	177
Eunice, m. William Throop **SIMMS**, Nov. 16, 1788	1	215
Festus, s. Ephraim & Eunice, b. Feb. 2, 1773	1	177
Festus, s. Eph[rai]m & Eunice, d. June 23, 1777	1	180
Festus Pearl, [s. Chester], b. Apr. 17, 1824	2	251
George Washington, s. [Spencer & Sally], b. Jan. 12, 1819	1	179
Giles Prescott, [s. Chester], b. Mar. 26, 1822	2	251
Giles Prescott, s. [Chester], d. June 21, 1845	2	343
Hannah, m. John **BRADFORD**, b. of Canterbury, Jan. 15,		
1823, by Erastus Larned	2	7
Harriet, [d. Chester], b. Sept. 9, 1811	2	251
Henry D., m. Anna E. **MORSE**, b. of Canterbury, June 1,		
1845, by Rev. Zephaniah Baker	2	52
Henry Dwight, [s. Chester], b. Mar. 18, 1818	2	251
Joseph, m. Susannah **KINGSLEY**, of Lesbon, Mar. 6, 1797	1	176
Joseph Leach, s. [Abel & Susanna], b. June 13, 1775	1	178
Louisa, d. Ephraim & Eunice, b. Sept. 2, 1767	1	177
Lovisa, d. Eph[rai]m & Eunice, d. Nov. 2, 1767	1	180
Marcus, s. [Spencer & Sally], b. June 18, 1806	1	179
Mary Ann, m. John Frances **ADAMS**, Oct. 13, 1824	1	53
Mary Ann, m. John Frances **ADAMS**, b. of Canterbury, Oct.		
13, 1824, by Andrew Lee, Clerk	2	1
Morgan, d. [sic] [Spencer & Sally], b. Jan. 29, 1804	1	179
Nelson, s. Spencer & Sally, b. Mar. 30, 1802	1	179
Rebecca, of Pomfret, m. Josiah **MORSE**, Jan. 1, 1794	1	181
Rockwell Manning, [s. Chester], b. Oct. 20, 1812	2	251
Sally, [d. Chester], b. Nov. 11, 1816	2	251
Sally, m. Ira **EDDY**, of Pittstown, N. Y., June 14, 1836,		
by Rev. Asa King, Westminster	2	27
Sarah, d. Abel & Susanna, b. Jan. 4, 1768	1	177
Sarah, m. Benjamin **SMITH**, Jr., Sept. 22, 1785	1	215
Spencer, s. [Abel & Susanna], b. Mar. 30, 1778	1	178
Spencer, m. Sally **WILLIAMS**, Nov. 9, 1800	1	176
Susan, m. Walter **SMITH**, Mar. 18, 1835, by Rev. Asa King,		

	Vol.	Page
LYON, (cont.)		
Westminster	2	73
Susannah, d. [Spencer & Sally], b. Jan. 6, 1817	1	179
William Lawrence, s. [Spencer & Sally], b. Oct. 9, 1808	1	179
MAIN, Jared, Jr., of Canterbury, m. Rhoda **LEWIS**, of Plainfield, Jan. 22, 1826, by Sam[ue]l L. Hough, J. P.	2	55
John V., m. Sally **RIXFORD**, b. of Canterbury, June 8, 1828, by Rev. J. R. Wheelock	2	55
Lucy, m. John **BROWN**, Oct. 1, 1780	1	71
Mary, m. Jedediah **BENJAMIN**, Dec. 6, 1778	1	71
MAINARD, [see also **MUNARD**], Amos, m. Elizabeth **BUTTON**, Apr. 20, 1769	1	181
MANNING, Edward Kirk, s. [Mansur & Susannah], b. Sept. 29, 1831	2	255
John Young, s. [Mansur & Susannah], b. May 22, 1835	2	255
Lucretia Ensworth, d. [Mansur & Susannah], b. Nov. 10, 1823	2	255
Mary S., m. George J. **GIBBS**, b. of Canterbury, Jan. 1, 1852, by Rev. Robert C. Learned	2	36
Mary Safford, d. [Mansur & Susannah], b. May 13, 1826	2	255
Mary W., m. David **HIDE**, Oct. 10, 1816	1	156
Matthew Hale, s. [Mansur & Susannah], b. July 29, 1828	2	255
Pascal Rockwell, s. Mansur & Susannah, b. May 18, 1818	2	255
Pashall Rockwell, s. Mansur & Susannah, d. Mar. 29, 1837	2	345
Sarah, d. [Mansur & Susannah], b. Apr. 2, 1821	2	255
MARKHAM, Margery, m. Ebenezer **BACON**, July 21, 1737	1	69
MARSH, Elizabeth, m. Dea. John **BARSTOW**, b. of Canterbury, Mar. 28, 1830, by Rev. Israel G. Rose, of Westminster	2	8
Sally, m. Joseph P. **LESTER**, Feb. 24, 1840, by Rev. Asa King, Westminster	2	53
MARSHALL, Abigail, d. Joseph & Persilah, b. Sept. 28, 1763	1	183
Joseph, m. Priscilla **PALMER**, of Norwich, Apr. 17, 1760	1	181
Joseph, s. Jos[eph] & Priscilla, b. May 13, 1777	1	184
Ruby, d. Joseph & Prescilla, b. July 14, 1767	1	183
Samuel, s. Joseph & Priscilla, b. Apr. 16, 1761	1	183
Sarah, m. Isaac **HIDE**, Jr., May 4, 1768	1	155
MARTIN, John, m. Sarah **DAVIS**, Mar. 22, 1807	1	181
John Denison, s. John & Sarah, b. May 21, 1809	1	186
Orison, s. [John & Sarah], b. Jan. 8, 1811	1	186
Orison, s. John & Sarah, d. Mar. 15, 1811	1	187
Rebeckah, m. Asa **GEER**, Nov. 13, 1764	1	149
MASH, Mary, m. Samuel **WADSWORTH**, Mar. 21, 1744	1	236
MASON, Agnes L., d. Silas & Jane A., b. Oct. 29, 1840	2	255
Jane, of Canterbury, m. Anson **ROGERS**, of Lebanon, Nov. 28, 1822, by Walter Williams, J. P.	2	67
Lucy, m. Nathaniel **LUCE**, Apr. 8, 1821, by Asa Meech	2	51
Mary, m. Nath[anie]l **BUTT**, Apr. 12, 1775	1	71
Silas, m. Jane **ASPENWALL**, b. of Canterbury, Feb. 2, 1836, by Rev. Otis C. Whiton	2	56

238 BARBOUR COLLECTION

	Vol.	Page
MATHEWSON, Almyra J., m. Frederic A. P. BATCHELLOR, Apr. 14, 1842, by Henry R. Dyar, J. P.	2	12
Samuel G., of New Hartford, m. Beulah M. WHEELER, of Canterbury, June 22, 1834, by Rev. Asa King, Westminster	2	56
MAY, Thomas, of Woodstock, m. Ruth WITTER, of Canterbury, Feb. 2, 1836, by Rev. Asa King, Westminster	2	56
McCARTEE, McCARTER, Dan[ie]l, s. John & Olive, b. June 6, 1777	1	184
Daniel, s. John & Olive, b. June 8, 1777	1	113
Dan[ie]l, s. John & Olive, [ ]	1	187
James, s. [John & Olive], b. Jan. 8, 1779	1	113
James, s. John & Olive, b. Jan. 8, 1779	1	184
John, s. Olive LOMBARD, b. Sept. 24, 1767	1	110
John, s. Olive LOMBARD, single woman, b. Sept. 24, 1767	1	177
John, m. Olive LOMBARD, Dec. 3, 1767	1	101
John, m. Olive LOMBARD, Dec. 3, 1767	1	181
Katharine, d. John & Olive, b. Apr. 10, 1771	1	111
Katherine, m. Stephen INGRAHAM, Oct. 23, 1791	1	167
Molly, d. John & Olive, b. July 13, 1769	1	111
Sarah, d. John & Olive, b. Sept. 20, 1775	1	112
William, s. [John & Olive], b. Feb. 2, 1781	1	113
McDONALD, James, m. Henrietta SMITH, Feb. 1, 1827, by Sam[uel] L. Hough, J. P.	2	55
McLEAN, Dudley B., of Simsbury, m. Mary PAYNE, of Canterbury, Sept. 16, 1846, by Allen McLean	2	95
McSORLEY, Patrick, m. Mary Jane ALLEN, Sept. 15, 1851, by Peter Spicer, J. P.	2	95
MEACHAM, MECHAM, Elizabeth, m. Nathan KIMBALL, Dec. 28, 1758	1	173
Hannah, m. Amos WOODWARD, May 6, 1735	1	236
Sarah, m. Solomon ADAMS, Apr. 8, 176[ ]	1	51
MEAD, Ebenezer, Rev., of Attica, N. Y., m. Mary E. LESTER, of Canterbury, May 20, 1828, by Rev. James R. Wheelock	2	55
MECLOTHLIN, Daniel, d. Jan. 29, 1758	1	187
MEECH, MEACH, Ama, d. Daniel & Kathran, b. June 27, 1752	1	183
Ama, d. Amos & Esther, b. June 28, 1780	1	184
Amos, m. Esther PARKE, Apr. 27, 1762	1	181
Amos. s. Amos & Esther, b. June 17, 1766	1	183
Amos, d. Apr. 16, 1789	1	187
Amos, s. Amos & Esther, d. July 14, 1807	1	187
Daniel, m. Kathering STODDARD, Jan. 22, 1749/50	1	181
Daniel, s. Amos & Esther, b. Aug. 3, 1785	1	185
Daniel, m. Ruhama CADY, Feb. 16, 1809	1	181
Daniel, d. Mar. 21, 1814	1	188
Emeline, d. [Daniel & Ruhama], b. Dec. 2, 1811	1	186
Emeline, m. Otis M. DORRANCE, Nov. 22, 1836, by Rev.		

	Vol.	Page
MEECH, MEACH, (cont.)		
Asa King, Westminster	2	21
Esther, d. Amos & Esther, d. Sept. 28, 1764	1	183
Eunice, d. Daniel & Kathren, b. Sept. 1, 1753	1	183
Hezekiah, s. Amos & Hester, b. Mar. 4, 1763	1	183
Lauralia, m. Joseph B. **ADAMS,** Dec. 20, 1811	2	3
Lucetta, d. Daniel & Ruhama, b. Mar. 25, 1813	1	186
Lucetta, m. Milton **ALLEN,** Feb. 3, 1833	1	53
Lucetta, m. Milton **ALLEN,** Feb. 3, 1833, by Rev. Asa King, Westminister	2	3
Ruhama, m. Rufus Leveret **DIMMOCK,** Mar. 3, 1817	1	121
Sally, d. Daniel & Katharine, b. Nov. 12, 1750	1	181
Sally, d. Daniel & Ruhama, b. Apr. 21, 1810	1	186
Sally, d. Daniel & Ruhama, d. Apr. 13, 1811	1	188
Sarah, d. Amos & Esther, b. July 29, 1768	1	183
Sarah, d. Amos & Esther, d. Dec. 14, 1788	1	187
MERRET, MERRETT, Elizabeth, m. Josiah **BRADFORD,** May 17, 1785	1	72
Molly, m. Ebenezer **ADAMS,** Mar. 13, 179[ ]	1	52
Thomas, Jr., m. Zilpha **TYLER,** July 14, 1777	1	181
MIGHEL, Hartshorn, s. Tho[ma]s & Sarah, b. Nov. 26, 1749	1	181
Jesse, s. Thomas & Sarah, b. Sept. 6, 1756	1	181
Joseph, s. Tho[ma]s & Sarah, d. Mar. 18, 1754	1	187
Joshua, s. Tho[ma]s & Sarah, b. Apr. 2, 1754	1	181
Mary, w. Tho[ma]s. d. Dec. 9, 1747	1	187
Mary, d. Tho[ma]s & Mary, d. Apr. 2, 1749	1	187
Parker, s. Thomas & Sarah, b. Oct. 14, 1751	1	181
Parker, s. Tho[ma]s & Sarah, d. Oct. 9, 1754	1	187
Reuben, [twin with Sarah], s. Tho[ma]s & Sarah, b. May 23, 1759	1	181
Sarah, [twin with Reuben], d. Tho[ma]s & Sarah, b. May 23, 1759	1	181
Tho[ma]s, m. Sarah **HARTSHORN,** Dec. 1, 1748	1	181
MILES, Betsey, d. [Tho[ma]s & Jerusha], b. Jan. 27, 1772	1	184
John, s. [Tho[ma]s & Jerusha], b. Oct. 12, 1773	1	184
Joseph, s. [Tho[ma]s & Jerusha], b. Jan. 19, 1770	1	184
Orra, d. Tho[ma]s & Jerusha, b. Mar. 14, 1776	1	184
Roxana, d. Tho[ma]s & Jerusha, b. Feb. 13, 1768	1	184
Sarah, m. Samuel **BUTT,** May 21, 1772	1	71
Sarah, m. Asa **BURGESS,** July 2, 1780	1	71
Thomas, m. [ ], Sept. 11, 1766	1	181
MILLER, Lois, d. Peter & Meriam, b. Oct. 17, 1768	1	183
Miriam, d. Peter & Miriam, b. Mar. 4, 1767	1	183
Miriam, m. Miner **JUSTIN,** Apr. 9, 1787	1	167
Peter, m. Miriam **HIDE,** Sept. 30, 1766	1	181
MILLS, Sally, m. Darius **HERRICK,** Dec. 28, 1794	1	156
Sarah, m. Capt. Benj[ami]n **PEIRCE,** Aug. 31, 1758	1	192
MINARD, Zilpha, m. W[illia]m **WOODARD,** Dec. 10, 1772	1	236

	Vol.	Page
MINER, Perez, of North Stonington, m. Phebe **FISH**, of Canterbury,		
June 19, 1836, by Rev. Tubal Wakefield	2	56
MITCHELL, Eliza G., m. David **AUSTIN**, b. of Canterbury, Apr.		
13, 1823, by Andrew T. Judson, J. P.	2	1
[MONROE], MONROW, MUNROW, MUNRO, Abigail, d. David		
& Deborah, b. Jan. 10, 1710/11	1	182
Abigail, d. David & Mary, d. Jan. 16, 1750	1	187
Abigail, d. David & Mary, b. Feb. 18, 1773	1	184
Abigail, m. Waterman **BENNET**, Feb. 1, 1798	1	72
Amasa, s. [John & Susannah], b. Jan. 15, 1786	1	185
Bette, d. David & Deborah, b. May 25, 1718	1	182
David s. David & Deborah, b. Dec. 26, 1708	1	182
David, m. Mary **VALLET**, May 20, 1733	1	181
David, s. David & Mary, b. Nov. 7, 1737	1	181
David, d. June 19, 1755	1	187
David, d. July 15, 1762	1	187
David, s. Josiah & Sarah, b. Sept. 26, 1768	1	183
David, m. Mary **WOODARD**, Nov. 30, 1769	1	181
David, s. David & Mary, b. Sept. 10, 1770	1	183
Deborah, d. David & Deborah, b. Apr. 4, 1705	1	182
Deborah, d. David & Deborah, d. Sept. 16, 1705	1	187
Deborah, d. David & Deborah, b. Jan. 12, 1712/13	1	182
Deborah, m. Eben[eze]r **DEANS**, Nov. 9, 1738	1	120
Deborah, d. Sam[ue]l & Abigail, b. Nov. 5, 1747	1	181
Deborah, w. David, d. Sept. 1, 1748	1	187
Eleanor, d. David & Deborah, b. Sept. 27, 1715	1	182
Elijah, m. Sarah **SPAULDING**, Mar. 1, 1758	1	181
Elijah, s. Elijah & Sarah, b. Aug. 17, 1760	1	183
Elizabeth, d. Josiah & Sarah, b. Nov. 14, 1756	1	181
Elizabeth, d. David & Mary, b. Sept. 19, 1778	1	184
Elizabeth, m. Tracy **ENSWORTH**, Dec. 27, 1799	1	133
Hannah, d. John & Susannah, b. Dec. 19, 1788	1	185
Hannah, d. John & Susannah, d. July 9, 1789	1	188
Hannah, d. John & Susannah, b. [ ]	1	89
Jesse, s. Josiah & Sarah, b. Sept. 10, 1770	1	183
John, s. David & Mary, b. Apr. 9, 1743	1	181
John, s. David & Mary, d. June 9, 1750	1	187
John, s. Josiah & Sarah, b. Oct. 30, 1758	1	181
John, s. David & Mary, b. Sept. 25, 1774	1	184
John, m. Susanna **BOND**, Oct. 30, 1782	1	181
Joseph, s. John & Susannah, b. Oct. 3, 1783; d. Oct. 17, 1783	1	185
Josiah, s. David & Deborah, b. Sept. 11, 1728	1	181
Josiah, m. Sarah **HIDE**, Apr. 12, 1752	1	181
Josiah, s. Josiah & Sarah, b. Sept. 2, 1754	1	181
Josiah, s. Josiah & Sarah, d. Dec. 16, 1760	1	187
Josiah, s. Josiah & Sarah, b. Jan. 25, 1764	1	183
Lydia, d. Josiah & Sarah, b. Apr. 22, 1766	1	183
Mary, d. David & Deborah, b. Jan. 9, 1706/7	1	182

	Vol.	Page
[MONROE], MONROW, MUNROW, MUNRO, (cont.)		
Mary, d. David & Mary, b. Mar. 26, 1731* (*1734)	1	181
Mary, d. David & Mary, d. Mar. 27, 1737	1	187
Mary, d. David & Mary, b. Dec. 18, 1771	1	184
Nathan, s. Josiah & Sarah, b. Oct. 19, 1752, n. s.	1	181
Nehemiah, s. Elijah & Sarah, b. Aug. 13, 1759	1	181
Olive, d. Josiah & Sarah, b. Nov. 21, 1760	1	181
Olive, d. Josiah & Sarah, d. Feb. 7, 1761	1	187
Olive, d. Josiah & Sarah, b. Feb. 4, 1773	1	184
Olive, d. Josiah & Sarah, d. Mar. 3, 1773	1	187
Samuel, s. David & Deborah, b. Sept. 9, 1720	1	182
Sarah, d. David & Deborah, b. July 24, 1723	1	181
Sarah, d. Josiah & Sarah, b. Jan. 28, 1774	1	184
Sarah, m. Dea. Jonas **BOND**, Mar. 28, 1793	1	72
Vienna, d. David & Mary, b. July 12, 1776	1	184
William, s. David & Deborah, b. June 5, 1726	1	182
William, d. Nov. 6, 1760	1	187
William, s. Josiah & Sarah, b. Dec. 20, 1761	1	183
MOORE, Abigail, w. Joseph, d. Apr. 5, 1785	1	187
Abigail, d. Joseph & Hannah, b. Nov. 13, 1786	1	185
Charles Sheperd, s. Esther, b. Apr. 15, 1833	2	272
Ebenezer, s. [Joseph & Hannah], b. July 30, 1788	1	185
Ebenezer, s. Joseph, d. Oct. 21, 1788	1	187
Esther, d. [Joseph & Hannah], b. Oct. 31, 1796	1	185
Esther had s. Charles Sheperd **MOORE**, b. Apr. 15, 1833	2	272
Hannah, d. [Joseph & Hannah], b. Nov. 30, 1798	1	186
Hannah, m. Festus **HYDE**, b. of Canterbury, Sept. 10, 1822,		
by Erastus Learned	2	39
Hiram, s. [Joseph & Hannah], b. Feb. 28, 1790	1	185
Hiram, s. [Joseph], d. July 20, 1790	1	187
Joseph, s. Joseph & Abigail, b. Jan. 24, 1778	1	184
Joseph, m. Hannah **SHEPARD**, Nov. 2, 1785	1	181
Joseph, s. [Joseph], d. Nov. 11, 1803, in West Indies	1	187
Lucy, m. John **GORDON**, May 24, 1801	1	149
Polly, d. [Joseph & Hannah], b. Jan. 26, 1792	1	185
Polly, d. [Joseph], d. Dec. 12, 1796	1	187
Sally, d. [Joseph & Hannah], b. Dec. 15, 1793	1	185
MORGAN, Abby H., m. Rufus L. **DIMMICK**, Nov. 22, 1836, by		
Rev. Asa King, Westminster	2	21
Anna, d. Edward & Thede, b. Nov. 6, 1790	1	185
Artemesia, d. [Edward & Thede], b. Mar. 27, 1803	1	185
Artimissa, of Canterbury, m. Ephraim **BENNET**, of Plainfield,		
July 14, 1822, by Andrew J. Judson, J. P.	2	7
Asa Spaulding, s. Lot & Kezia, b. Mar. 21, 1799	1	185
Aurelia, m. Luther **LILLIE**, Dec. 14, 1809	1	176
Betsey, m. Araunah **BUTTS**, Jan. 19, 1809	1	73
Billy, s. [Edward & Thede], b. Oct. 7, 1796	1	185
Daniel, s. Isaac & Polly, b. Mar. 22, 1813	1	186

	Vol.	Page
MORGAN, (cont.)		
Dolly, m. Ephraim **SAFFORD**, Nov. 14, 1793	1	215
Edward, s. Edward & Thede, b. Sept. 5, 1801	1	185
Elisha J., of Plainfield, m. Phelena Ann **BACON**, of		
Canterbury, Mar. 26, 1834, by Rev. Otis C. Whiton	2	55
Henry A., of Canterbury, m. Alice A. **TYLER**, of Griswold,		
Jan. 13, 1828, by Rev. James R. Wheelock	2	55
Henry Augustus, s. [Isaac & Polly], b. May 13, 1805	1	186
Isaac Parker, s. [Isaac & Polly], b. Dec. 20, 1807	1	186
James, s. [Isaac & Polly], b. Dec. 17, 1817	1	186
James L., of Windham, m. Rachel **SAFFORD**, of Canterbury,		
Dec. 13, 1831, by Rufus Johnson, Jr., J. P.	2	55
Louice, m. Edward **DODGE**, Oct. 6, 1763	1	120
Mary, m. Joseph R. **WILLOUGHBY**, Aug. 26, 1797	1	237
Mary A., m. William C. B. **STANTON**, Mar. 2, 1838, by Rev.		
Asa King, Westminster	2	74
Mary Adams, d. [Isaac & Polly], b. May 19, 1815	1	186
Mary Hannah, d. Will[ia]m R. & Eunice, b. Aug. 11, 1827	2	255
Nancy, d. Lot & Kezia, b. June 25, 1795	1	185
Polly, d. [Edward & Thede], b. Oct. 7, 1793	1	185
Talitha, d. Edward & Theda, b. May 19, 1805	1	186
Thede, d. [Edward & Thede], b. Feb. 12, 1792	1	185
W[illia]m Rowland, s. Isaac & Polly, b. July 13, 1803	1	186
MORSE, Abigail, m. Joseph (?) **AUSTIN**, Sept. 12, 1758	1	51
Abigail, m. Joseph **AUSTIN**, Apr. 15, 1761	1	51
Abigail, d. Benjamin & Betty, b. July 30, 1766	1	183
Abigail, d. Apr. 26, 1778	1	187
Abigail C., of Canterbury, m. Elijah **DYER**, Jr., of Norwich,		
Apr. 11, 1831, by Rev. Demis Platt	2	21
Alice, of Lisbon, m. Cornelius **HALL**, of Hopkinton, R. I.,		
Apr. 10, 1803	1	156
Alpheas, s. [Charles & Zipporah], b. Sept. 12, 1767	1	183
Alpheas, m. Anne **ROUSE**, Jan. 6, 1791	1	181
Alpheas, s. [Alpheas & Anna], b. Aug. 20, 1799	1	186
Amos, s. Peter & Sarah, b. Oct. 26, 1763	1	183
Anna E., m. Henry D. **LYON**, b. of Canterbury, June 1,		
1845, by Rev. Zephaniah Baker	2	52
Anthony, m. Sarah **WARREN**, May 11, 1762	1	181
Asaph, s. Benjamin & Betty, b. Nov. 18, 1760	1	183
Benjamin, m. Betty **ALLEIN**, Jan. 16, 1760	1	181
Benj[ami]n, s. Charles & Zipporah, b. Feb. 12, 1766	1	183
Benjamin, s. Charles & Zipporah, d. Mar. 24, 1766	1	187
Benjamin, twin with Joseph, s. [Benj[ami]n, Jr. & Katharine],		
b. July 8, 1772	1	184
Benjamin, s. Benj[ami]n & Betty, b. Feb. 24, 1775	1	184
Benjamin, s. [Benjamin & Katharine], d. Aug. 11, 1776	1	187
Benjamin, s. Alpheas & Anna, b. June 16, 1805	1	186
Betty, d. Benj[ami]n & Betty, b. July 17, 1770	1	183

	Vol.	Page
MORSE, (cont.)		
Charles, m. Zip[p]orah **BALDWIN,** May 3, 1758	1	181
Charles, s. Charles & Siporah, b. Apr. 23, 1764	1	183
Charles, Jr., m. Anne **BINGHAM,** Apr. 10, 1783	1	181
Chauncey, s. Peter & Lusena, b. July 23, 1793	1	185
Chauncey, s. Charles Jr. & Anne, b. May 16, 1798	1	185
Synthia, d. Alpheas & Anna, b. Apr. 20, 1791	1	186
Deidama, d. Joseph & Keziah, b. Feb. 22, 1748	1	181
Deidama, d. [Anthony & Sarah], b. July 14, 1777	1	184
Dillis, s. [Alpheas & Anna], b. Jan. 27, 1795	1	186
Eleanor, d. Charles & Sip[p]orah, b. Aug. 30, 1760	1	183
Elizabeth, d. [Peter & Lusena], b. Dec. 25, 1794	1	185
Esther, m. Caleb **FAULKNER,** Feb. 27, 1761	1	138
Festus, s. Alpheas & Anna, b. July 26, 1802	1	186
Festus, m. Anne **GREENE,** b. of Canterbury, Aug. 30, 1840, by Rev. Tubal Wakefield	2	56
Frances, d. Benj[ami]n & Merah, b. Oct. 14, 173[ ]	1	181
Hannah, m. Benjamin **NICKELS,** May [ ], 1741	1	189
Hezekiah, s. [Charles & Zipporah], b. Aug. 15, 1769	1	183
Jacob, s. Charles & Zipporah, b. Jan. 14, 1772	1	184
James, s. Frances, b. Sept. 21, 1761	1	183
James C., m. Melissa **LEARNED,** b. of Canterbury, Sept. 11, 1823, by Erastus Learned	2	55
Jedediah, s. Anthony & Sarah, b. Nov. 6, 1762	1	183
Jedediah, s. Anthony & Sarah, b. Nov. 6, 1762	1	184
Jedediah, s. [Charles, Jr. & Anna], b. Mar. 5, 1789	1	185
Jedediah Waterman, s. Jedediah & Fanny, b. Sept. 8, 1793	1	185
John, s. [Anthony & Sarah], b. Oct. 7, 1764	1	184
Jos[eph], s. Jos[eph] & Ruth, b. Feb. 18, 1769	1	184
Joseph, twin with Benjamin, s. [Benj[ami]n, Jr. & Katharine], b. July 8, 1772	1	184
Joseph, s. Benjamin & Katharine, d. Oct. 11, 1772	1	187
Joseph, d. Mar. 1, 1777, ae 70	1	187
Josiah, m. Mehetable **TRISKETT,** Feb. 22, 1758	1	181
Josiah, s. Benjamin & Betty, b. Aug. 22, 1762	1	183
Josiah, m. Rebecca **LYON,** of Pomfret, Jan. 1, 1794	1	181
Kezia, w. Joseph, d. Sept. 4, 1758	1	187
Kezia,, d. [Anthony & Sarah], b. Aug. 14, 1766	1	184
Kezia, m. David **LITCHFIELD,** Dec. 2, 1784	1	176
Lavina, d. Benj[ami]n & Betty, b. July 24, 1768	1	183
Lemuel Bingham, s. Charles, Jr. & Anna, b. Nov. 11, 1783	1	185
Lucinda, d. Benj[ami]n & Betty, b. Oct. 20, 1772	1	184
Lucinda, m. Luther **HARTSON,** Apr. 5, 1801	1	156
Lucy, d. [Charles, Jr. & Anna], b. Aug. 23, 1785	1	185
Lura, of Canterbury, m. Elisha **SYDLEMAN,** of Pawtucket, May 6, 1827, by Israel G. Rose	2	71
Luther, s. [Alpheas & Anna], b. Apr. 4, 1810	1	186
Lydia, d. Benjamin & Betty, b. Aug. 9, 1764	1	183

	Vol.	Page
MORSE, (cont.)		
Lydia, d. [Anthony & Sarah], b. Oct. 13, 1779	1	185
Lydia, d. [Alpheas & Anna], b. Feb. 27, 1793	1	186
Lydia, d. [Jedediah & Fanny], b. Apr. 3, 1797	1	185
Lydia, m. Giles **BRADFORD**, Jan. 17, 1853, by R. S. Hazen	2	105
Maria, d. [Jedediah & Fanny], b. Oct. 30, 1795	1	185
Maria, m. James **BRADFORD**, May 27, 1821, by Peter Morse, J. P.	2	7
Martin, s. [Alpheas & Anna], b. June 27, 1803	1	186
Mary, d. Jos[eph] & Keziah, b. Mar. 9, 1752	1	181
Mary, d. Benj[ami]n, Jr. & Katharine, b. Dec. 20, 1768	1	184
Mary, d. [Anthony & Sarah], b. Oct. 12, 1770	1	184
Mary, m. Eben[eze]r **ADAMS**, Apr. 8, 1779	1	52
Mary A., of Canterbury, m. Charles R. **PRIOR**, of Plainfield, Sept. 3, 1850, by Rev. Robert C. Learned	2	65
Mason, m. Henrietta **SAFFORD**, Oct. 16, 1837, by Rev. Asa King, Westminster	2	56
Meribah, d. Solomon & Elizabeth, b. Mar. 10, 1766	1	183
Moses, s. Peter & Sarah, b. June 21, 1767	1	183
Nathan Brewster, s. [Peter & Lusena], b. Nov. 14, 1799	1	185
Peter, m. Sarah **RAYNSOM**, Nov. 19, 1762	1	181
Peter, s. [Anthony & Sarah], b. Sept. 18, 1768	1	184
Peter, m. Lusena **BREWSTER**, Oct. 4, 1792	1	181
Polly, of Pomfret, m. Jeremiah **BROWN**, May 13, 1798	1	72
Polly Bingham, d. [Charles, Jr. & Anna], b. Aug. 16, 1792	1	185
Priscilla, d. [Jos[eph] & Ruth], b. June 2, 1771	1	184
Rufus, s. Charles & Zip[p]orah, b. Nov. 5, 1758	1	181
Rufus, s. Peter & Sarah, b. July 5, 1765	1	183
Sarah, d. [Solomon & Elizabeth], b. Feb. 8, 1768	1	183
Sarah, d. Anthony & Sarah, b. Dec. 24, 1773	1	184
Saryan (Sarah Ann), d. [Alpheas & Anna], b. July 2, 1797	1	186
Solomon, m. Elizabeth **WENER**, of Norwich, Mar. 21, 1765	1	181
Susanna, m. Amos **PAINE**, Sept. 19, 1792	1	193
Susanna, d. [Alpheas & Anna], b. Sept. 2, 1807	1	186
Synthia, see under Cynthia		
William, s. Charles & Zipporah, b. Jan. 23, 1781	1	185
William, m. Jerusha **BALDWIN**, Sept. 28, 1800	1	181
Zerviah M., d. Anthony & Sarah, b. Feb. 28, 1783	1	185
MOSELEY, Hannah, m. John **CURTIS**, Jr., May 29, 1753	1	101
MOTT, MOOT, Anna, [triplet with Gershom & Margaret], d. Gershom & Anna, b. Sept. 6, 1724	1	181
Benjamin, s. John & Martha, b. July 25, 1758	1	181
Benjamin, m. Service **COLLINS**, Aug. 29, 1787, at Windham	1	181
Eliza, w. Gershom, Jr., d. Jan. 12, 1773	1	187
Elizabeth, d. John & Martha, b. Mar. 26, 1756	1	181
Gershom, [triplet with Anna & Margaret], s. Gershom & Anna, b. Sept. 6, 1724	1	181
Gershom, m. Elizabeth **LATEMAN**, Apr. 28, 1748	1	181

	Vol.	Page
MOTT, MOOT, (cont.)		
Gershom*, m. Esther **BATES**, Apr. 13, 1773 (*Jr.)	1	181
Gershom, d. Oct. 12, 1776	1	187
Jacob, s. Jeremiah, Jr. & Abigail, b. Dec. 12, 1779	1	184
Jacob, d. Aug. 9, 1780	1	187
Jareb, s. John & Martha, b. Jan. 5, 1761	1	183
Jeremiah, s. Gershom & Elizabeth, b. Aug. 25, 1731	1	181
Jeremiah, m. Patience **MOOT**, Aug. 10, 1752	1	181
John, s. Gershom & Elizabeth, b. Apr. 16, 1730	1	181
John, m. Martha **WENTWORTH**, May 8, 1753	1	181
John, s. John & Martha, b. Feb. 8, 1754	1	181
John, d. June 3, 1770	1	187
John, m. Eunice **THOMPSON**, Apr. 16, 1778	1	181
Margaret, [triplet with Gershom & Anna], d. Gershom & Anna, b. Sept. 6, 1724	1	181
Mary, m. Daniel **HERRINGTON**, Jan. 8, 1741	1	155
Mehetable, d. Jere[mia]h & Abigail, d. Sept. 15, 1776	1	187
Patience, d. Gershom & Elizabeth, b. Sept. 26, 1732	1	181
Patience, m. Jeremiah **MOOTS**, Aug. 10, 1752	1	181
Samuel, s. John & Eunice, b. Aug. 22, 1781	1	185
Sarah, d. John & Martha, b. Aug. 16, 1769	1	183
Sarah, d. Jere[mia]h, Jr. & Abigail b. Sept. 15, 1776	1	184
Sarah, m. Edmund **GOULD**, Jan. 7, 1788	1	149
William, s. John & Eunice, b. Apr. 27, 1779	1	184
MUDGE, Lydia, m. Walter **SMITH**, Mar. 4, 1802	1	215
Mary, m. Thomas **ADAMS**, Jan. 4, [ ]	1	52
MULKEN, Mary, wid., d. Aug. 15, 1760	1	187
MUNARD, [see also **MAINARD**], Eunice, d. Cyrus & Lucretia, b. Nov. 3, 1769, at Windham	1	184
Hannah, d. [Cyrus & Lucretia], b. Sept. 25, 1777	1	184
Shubael, s. [Cyrus & Lucretia], b. Mar. 1, 1775	1	184
MUNROW, [see under **MONROE**]		
MURDOCK, Lusia Kinsman, w. Rev. Tho[ma]s J., d. June 29, 1824	2	345
Lusia Thompson, d. Rev. Tho[ma]s J. & Lusia Hinsman, b. May 9, 1824	2	255
Maria, m. Adin **CARTER**, Dec. 1, 1814	1	102
MURPHY, MURPHEY, MURFEE, Chester, s. Leonard & Alice, b. Nov. 4, 1793	1	185
Leonard, s. Olive **NICHOLS**, single woman, b. Oct. 4, 1771	1	184
Leonard, m. Alice **STEPHENS**, July 18, 1793	1	181
Olive, d. [Leonard & Alice], b. Sept. 18, 1796	1	185
William, s. [Leonard & Alice], b. Oct. 4, 1794	1	185
NAVINS, [see under **NEVINS**]		
NEFF, Abby J., d. [Harvey], b. July 7, 1838	2	257
Aseph M., s. Harvey, b. May 21, 1828	2	257
Caroline E., d. [Harvey], b. Jan. 1, 1833	2	257
Emeline M., d. [Harvey], b. Aug. 20, 1836	2	257
Joseph H., s. [Harvey], b. Sept. 21, 1830	2	257

	Vol.	Page

MURPHY, MURPHEY, MURFEE, (cont.)

Nathan, m. Julia A. **BUTTS**, Sept. 13, 1836, by Rev. Asa
    King, Westminster — 2 — 57

Nathan, m. Ann **BRADFORD**, b. of Canterbury, [ ], by Rev.
    I. G. Rose, of Westminster — 2 — 57

Rena, m. Samuel **RANSOM**, June 23, 1785 — 1 — 209

Seymour, m. Rachel **PENRE**, b. of Canterbury, July 19,
    1829, by Rev. Israel G. Rose, Westminster — 2 — 57

Susan M., of Canterbury, m. James E. **ALLEN**, of
    Woonsocket, R. I., Oct. 17, 1832, by Rev. Thomas O.
    Rice, of West Killingly — 2 — 4

NEVINS, NAVINS, NEVENS, Cynthia, d. David & Mary, b. Apr 7,
    1757 — 1 — 190

Cynthia, d. David & Mary, d. Aug. 16, 1759 — 1 — 191

David, m. Mary **LATHROP**, Oct. 14, 1746 — 1 — 189

David, s. David & Mary, b. Sept. 12, 1747 — 1 — 190

David, d. Jan. 6, 1758 — 1 — 191

Elizabeth, d. David & Mary, b. Feb. 15, 1753 — 1 — 190

Martha, d. David & Mary, b. Sept. 8, 1755 — 1 — 190

Mary, d. David & Mary, b. Mar. 8, 1751 — 1 — 190

Mary, m. Will[ia]m **BINGHAM***, Nov. 9, 1758 *(Corrected
    in handwriting in margin of manuscript) — 1 — 70

Samuel, s. David & Mary, b. Mar. 4, 1748/9 — 1 — 190

NEWELL, NEWEL, Anna, of Saratoga, N. Y., m. Jared **ALLEN**,
    Feb. 10, 1783 — 1 — 52

Susannah, of Roxbury, m. Jared **DYER**, Nov. 6, 1784 — 1 — 121

NEWTON, Simon, m. Betty **HIDE**, Nov. 5, 1783 — 1 — 189

NICHOLS, NICKELS, Abigail, d. Benjamin & Hannah, b. June 18,
    1758 — 1 — 190

Benjamin, m. Hannah **MORS[E]**, May [ ], 1741 — 1 — 189

Hannah, d. Benjamin & Hannah, b. Jan. 23, 1765 — 1 — 190

Hannah, d. [James & Lydia], b. Mar. 18, 1778 — 1 — 190

James, s. Benjamin & Hannah, b. Sept. 30, 1755 — 1 — 190

James, m. Lydia **HERRINGTON**, Mar. 9, 1774 — 1 — 189

John, s. Benj[ami]n & Hannah, b. July 27, 1744 — 1 — 190

Joseph, s. Benj[ami]n & Hannah, b. Apr. 12, 1747 — 1 — 190

Joseph, m. Zerviah **WALTON**, Mar. 11, 1766 — 1 — 189

Margaret, d. Benj[ami]n & Hannah, b. June 12, 1752 — 1 — 190

Olive, d. Benj[ami]n & Hannah, b. Aug. 9, 1749 — 1 — 190

Olive, single woman, had s. Leonard **MURFEE**, b. Oct. 4,
    1771 — 1 — 184

Olive, m. John **GARDINER**, Apr. 1, 1775 — 1 — 149

Polly, d. James & Lydia, b. Feb. 26, 1776 — 1 — 190

Welthian, d. Joseph & Zerviah, b. Mar. 18, 1767 — 1 — 190

NIGHT, [see under **KNIGHT**]

NOALEN, [see under **NOWLEN**]

NORTH[R]UP, Carr, of Granville, N. Y., m. Lucy **BUTTS**, of
    Canterbury, June 8, 1830, by Rev. Israel G. Rose, of

	Vol.	Page
NORTH[R]UP, (cont.)		
Westminster	1	57
NORWOOD, Zerviah, d. Stephen & Zerviah, b. Feb. 26, 1739/40	1	190
Zerviah, m. Richard **RAYNSFORD,** Nov. 29, 1750	1	209
NOTT, Temperance, m. Samson **SPAULDING,** June 27, 1779	1	214
NOWLEN, NOWLING, NOALEN, NOWLDING, Amy, d. Nov. 29, 1785	1	191
Asa, m. Mary **BACON,** Oct. 20, 1785	1	189
Asa, s. Asa & Mary, b. Feb. 1, 1787	1	190
Dorinda, d. [Asa & Mary], b. July 20, 1790	1	190
Gurdon, s. [Asa & Mary], b. Sept. 22, 1793	1	190
Jasper, s. [Asa & Mary], b. Oct. 21, 1788	1	190
Joshua, s. Tho[ma]s & Amy, b. Apr. 15, 1736	1	190
Lucius, s. Asa & Mary, b. Apr. 3, 1797	1	190
Mary, d. Thomas & Amy, b. Aug. 14, 1734	1	190
Polly, d. [Asa & Mary], b. Feb. 1, 1792	1	190
Sam[ue]l, s. Tho[ma]s & Amy, b. Aug. 16, 1739	1	190
Sanuel, m. Mary **BUTT,** of Norwich, Jan. 14, 1761	1	189
Sophia, d. [Asa & Mary], b. July 16, 1795	1	190
Tho[ma]s, m. Amy **ADAMS,** May 30, 1734	1	189
NOYES, William Pitts, of Stonington, m. Cecelia Ann **ADAMS,** of Canterbury, Dec. 26, 1833, by Rev. Otis C. Whiton	2	57
OLDS, Betsey, m. Samuel **SKINNER,** Nov. 27, 1845, by Rev. Henry J. Coe	2	75
Edward Payson, s. Nathan & Lois A., b. June 12, 1841	2	259
Malissa, of Canterbury, m. George **TRACY,** of Windham, Apr. 14, 1833, by Rev. Alfred Burnham, at Archibald Olds	2	79
Nathan, m. Lois **ALLEN,** Sept. 30, 1838, by Rev. Asa King	2	17
Nathan, Jr., s. Nathan & Lois A., b. Aug. 16, 1839	2	259
OLIN, Mary Ann, m. John L. **HYDE,** b. of Canterbury, Mar. 24, 1851, by C. D. Fillmore, Elder	2	100
OLNEY, Tryphena, m. Elisha **BINGHAM,** Nov. 9, 1806	1	73
ORMSBY, ORMESBY, Abner Williams, s. Caleb & Dorkis, b. May 4, 1769 or 1770?	1	251
Caleb, m. Dorkis **BATES,** of Windham, Jan. 12, 1761	1	250
Elijah, s. John & Mehetable, b. July 13, 1745	1	251
Elijah, s. John & Mehetable, d. Sept. 4, 1749	1	252
Elijah, s. Ezekiel & Sarah, b. July 19, 1757	1	251
Elijah, s. Caleb & Dorcas, b. Feb. 26, 1761	1	251
Elisha, s. Ezekiel & Sarah, d. July 31, 1757	1	252
Ezekiel, m. Sarah **COLBORN,** of Windham, Nov. 27, 1756	1	250
Jeremiah, s. John & Mehetable, b. June 3, 1742	1	251
Jeremiah, s. John & Mehetable, d. Sept. 10, 1749	1	252
Jeremiah, s. Ezekiel & Sarah, b. July 19, 1757	1	251
John, s. Caleb & Dorkis, b. Apr. 18, 1765	1	251
John, d. Feb. 23, 1766	1	252
Levy, s. John & Mehetable, d. Sept. 21, 1749	1	252

	Vol.	Page
ORMSBY, ORMESBY,, (cont.)		
Lucy, d. John & Mehetable, b. Nov. 4, 1748	1	251
Lucy, d. John & Mehetable, d. Sept. 19*, 1749		
(*Perhaps Sept. 1)	1	252
Mary, d. John & Mehetable, b. Apr. 22, 1747	1	251
Mary, d. John & Mehetable, d. Sept. 6, 1749	1	252
Phebe, d. Caleb & Dorkis, b. Feb. 6, 1763	1	251
Rhoda, d. John & Mehetable, d. Sept. 14, 1749	1	252
ORSBAND, Mary, m. Silas **HARRIS,** May 11, 1755	1	155
OSGOOD, William C., of Norwich, m. Sarah M. **ADAMS,** of		
Canterbury, Oct. 5, 1847, by Rev. Robert C. Learned	2	59
PACKER, Mary H., of Canterbury (Packersville), m. Dr. Lewis		
PHINNEY, of North Yarmouth, Me., Sept. 11, 1839, by		
Rev. Tubal Wakefield	2	62
PAGE, Abias(?), of Groton, m. Jonas **CLARK,** Oct. 17, 1763	1	101
PAINE, PAYNE, Abigail, m. Josiah **CLEVELAND,** Aug. 7, 1710	1	100
Abigail, d. Abraham & Ruth, b. Dec. 27, 1720	1	195
Abigail, d. Elisha & Mary, b. Nov. 13, 1728	1	196
Abigail, d. Elijah* & Mary, d. Sept. 2, 1736 (*Elisha)	1	206
Abigail, d. Joshua & Constance, d. Aug. 1, 1749	1	206
Abigail had s. David, b. Apr. 5, 1753	1	197
Abigail, d. Elisha & Ann, b. Apr. 7, 1757	1	198
Abraham, m. Ruth **ADAMS,** Dec. 19, 1717	1	192
Abraham, s. Abraham & Ruth, b. May 2, 1722	1	195
Abraham, m. Rebecca **FREEMAN,** Mar. 8, 1743/4	1	192
Abraham, s. Lot, Jr. & Hannah, b. Nov. 14, 1818	1	205
Amos, m. Susanna **MORSE,** Sept. 19, 1792	1	193
Anna, w. Elisha, d. May 15, 1759	1	207
Anne, d. Elisha & Anne, b. Mar. 21, 1759	1	198
Benjamin, s. Abraham & Ruth, b. Mar. 29, 1726	1	195
Bethiah, d. Abraham & Ruth, b. Aug. 5, 1718	1	195
Bathiah, d. Abraham & Ruth, d. May 25, 1720	1	206
Betsey, d. Elisha & Anne, b. Dec. 27, 1787	1	203
Charles, s. Amos & Susanna, b. Dec. 28, 1793	1	203
Constance, d. Elisha & Rebecca, b. Feb. 17, 1704/5	1	195
Dan, s. Amos & Susanne, b. Oct. 25, 1797	1	204
David, s. Solomon & Sarah, b. [ ] 18, 1729	1	196
David, s. Abigail, b. Apr. 5, 1753	1	197
David, m. Lydia **FASSET,** Apr. 5, 1759	1	192
David, s. Luther & Sibbel, b. Aug. 7, 1795	1	203
Dorcas, m. David **ADAMS,** Aug. 27, 1723	1	192
Elihu, s. Solomon & Sarah, b. Aug. 5, 1725	1	195
Elihu, m. Elizabeth **CLEVELAND,** Nov. 24, 1748	1	192
Elihew, d. Feb. 27, 1752	1	206
Elijah, s. Seth & Lydia, b. July 27, 1782	1	202
Elijah Dyar, s. [Luther & Sibbel], b. Dec. 7, 1803	1	205
Elisha, m. Mary **JOHNSON,** Nov. 24, 1720	1	192
Elisha, s. Elisha & Mary, b. Mar. 7, 1730 /31	1	196

	Vol.	Page
PAINE, PAYNE (cont.)		
Elisha, d. Feb. 7, 1735/6	1	206
Elisha, s. Solomon & Prescilla, b. Nov. 16, 1736	1	196
Elisha, s. Abraham & Rebecca, b. Dec. 9, 1744	1	197
Elisha, m. Anne **WALDO**, Apr. 12, 1753	1	192
Elisha, s. Sol[omo]n & Prescilla, d. Nov. 27, 1755, at Albany, N. Y.	1	206
Elisha, s. Solomon & Mary, b. July 2, 1757	1	200
Elisha, s. Elisha & Elizabeth, b. Mar. 21, 1763	1	199
Elisha, s. Elisha & Anne, b. Nov. 11, 1796	1	203
Elisha, d. Jan. 21, 1803	1	208
Elizabeth, d. Elihu & Elizabeth, b. July 25, 1752	1	196
Elizabeth, m. Ezra **ENSWORTH**, Oct. 13, 1757	1	133
Ephraim, s. Joshua & Rebecca, b. Aug. 19, 1730	1	196
Frances Loisa, d. Amos & Susannah, b. July 15, 1806	1	205
Henry, s. Luther & Sibbel, b. Feb. 28, 1799	1	205
Horatio, s. Seth & Lydia, b. Oct. 20, 1777	1	201
Horatio, s. Seth & Lydia, d. Apr. 27, 1778	1	207
Ichabod, s. Solomon & Sarah, b. Sept. 7, 1727	1	195
Ichabod, m. Hannah **BUSWELL**, Jan. 16, 1748	1	192
Ichabod Sparro, s. Joshua & Rebecca, b. Sept. 10, 1736	1	196
James, s. Elisha & Mary, b. June 2, 1725	1	195
James, s. Elisha & Mary, b. June 2, 1725; d. June 5, 1729	1	196
James, s. Abraham & Ruth, b. Nov. 11, 1737	1	196
John, s. Elisha & Rebecca, b. July 12, 1707	1	195
John, m. Sarah **CHURCH**, Feb. 12, 1729/30	1	192
Joseph, s. Seth & Lydia, b. July 1, 1780	1	201
Joshua, m. Constance **BAKER**, Jan. 6, 1736/7	1	192
Laura, d. Luther & Sibbel, b. Jan. 30, 1788	1	203
Lucretia Ann, d. Elisha & Anne, b. Oct. 31, 1802	1	204
Lucretia Ann, of Canterbury, m. Dr. William H. **COGSWELL**, of Plainfield, Jan. 6, 1830, by Rev. Levi Nelson, of Lisbon	2	16
Luther, s. Davis & Lydia, b. Apr. 16, 1760	1	198
Luther, m. Sibbel **DYAR**, Jan. 9, 1783	1	193
Lydia, d. David & Lydia, b. July 25, 1762	1	199
Lydia, m. Rufus **SPAULDING**, Jan. 10, 1782	1	214
Maria, d. Luther & Sibbel, b. June 11, 1791	1	203
Mary, d. Elisha & Mary, b. Apr. 12, 1723	1	195
Mary, d. Elisha & Mary, b. Apr. 12, 1723	1	196
Mary, m. Will[ia]m **FITCH**, Jan. 27, 1740/1	1	138
Mary, d. Elisha & Anne, b. Jan. 12, 1755	1	198
Mary, d. Solomon & Mary, b. June 16, 1759	1	200
Mary, w. Sol[omo]n, d. Sept. 22, 1820	1	208
Mary, d. [Lot, Jr. & Hannah], b. Dec. 15, 1820	1	205
Mary, of Canterbury, m. Dudley B. **McLEAN**, of Simsbury, Sept. 16, 1846, by Allen McLean	2	95
Mehetable, m. Robert **DARBE**, June 3, 1755	1	120

	Vol.	Page
PAINE, PAYNE, (cont.)		
Mehet[abl]e, d. Seth & Lydia, b. Dec. 19, 1775	1	201
Mehetable, d. [Seth & Lydia], d. May 4, 1778	1	207
Mehetable, d. Seth & Lydia, b. Feb. 17, 1779	1	201
Mehetable, d. Seth & Lydia, d. Apr. 13, 1779	1	207
Molly, m. Ebenezer **SPAULDING**, May 29, 1783	1	215
Moses, s. Joshua & Constance, d. July 24, 1749	1	206
Nancy, d. Luther & Sibbel, b. May 9, 1786	1	202
Olive, d. David & Lydia, b. Oct. 30, 1764	1	199
Olive, d. [Elisha & Anna], b. July 24, 1792	1	203
Philura, d. Lydia & David, b. Aug. 1, 1772	1	201
Philura, m. Oliver **HASTINGS**, Nov. 13, 1796	1	156
Polly, d. Elisha, & Anna, b. July 19, 1790	1	203
Polly, d. Elisha & Anna, d. Mar. 1, 1796	1	207
Prescilla, d. Solomon & Prescilla, b. Aug. 20, 1734	1	196
Priscilla, wid. Solomon, d. May 6, 1782	1	207
Rebeckah, m. Edward **CLEVELAND**, Jr., Apr. 17, 1717, at		
Kingston, R. I., by John Eldred, Asst.	1	100
Rebeckah, d. Joshua & Rebeckah, b. June 18, 1732	1	196
Rebecca, w. Joshua, d. Sept. 15, 1736	1	206
Rebecca, m. Deliver[an]ce **CLEVELAND**, July 4, 1744	1	100
Rebecca, d. Dec. 19, 1758	1	207
Rufus, s. Elihu & Elizabeth, b. Apr. 8, 1750	1	197
Ruth, d. Solomon & Sarah, b. May 25, 1723	1	195
Ruth, d. Abraham & Ruth, b. Apr. 4, 1728	1	195
Samuel, s. Abraham & Ruth, b. Oct. 4, 1729	1	195
Sarah, d. John & Sarah, b. Nov. 6, 1730	1	195
Sarah, w. Solomon, d. Aug. 9, 1731	1	206
Sarah, d. David & Lydia, b. May 5, 1767	1	200
Sarah, m. Jairus **SMITH**, Aug. 2, 1787	1	215
Seth, m. Lydia **LESTER**, Nov. 17, 1774	1	193
Sibel, d. John & Sarah, b. Jan. 18, 1734/5	1	196
Sibbel, m. Thomas **DIMMOCK**, Mar. 12, 1761	1	120
Solomon, m. Sarah **CARVER**, Mar. 2, 1720/21	1	192
Solomon, s. Solomon & Sarah, b. May 29, 1722	1	195
Solomon, s. Solomon & Sarah, d. June 18, 1722	1	206
Solomon, s. Solomon & Sarah, b. Mar. 21, 1722/3	1	195
Solomon, m. Priscilla **FITCH**, May 31, 1732	1	192
Solomon, s. Solomon & Prescilla, b. Mar. 8, 1732/3	1	196
Solomon, d. Oct. 25, 1754	1	206
Solomon, m. Mary **BACON**, June 8, 1756	1	192
Solomon, s., Elisha & Anna, b. Jan. 6, 1786	1	202
Solomon, Jr., m. Hannah **BISHOP**, of Lisbon, Mar. 17, 1818	1	194
Solomon, d. Feb. 22, 1822	2	351
Susannah, d. Amos & Susannah, b. June 24, 1813	1	205
Sybel, see under Sibel		
Thankful, d. Elisha & Mary, b. Mar. 25, 1733	1	196
Thankful, m. Aaron **CLEVELAND**, June 7, 1748	1	100

	Vol.	Page
PAINE, PAYNE, (cont.)		
Thomas Luther, s. Luther & Sibbel, b. June 10, 1793	1	203
Uriah, s. Joshua & Constance, d. July 19, 1749	1	206
William, s. Amos & Susannah, b. June 28, 1804	1	204
PAISON, Anna, m. John **DYAR,** Mar. 29, 1753	1	120
PALMER, Charles M., of Windham, m. Amanda T. **PERRY,** of		
Canterbury, Nov. 30, 1848, by Rev. Joseph Ayer, Lisbon	2	65
Hannah, m. Jona **PELLET,** Jr., Jan. 29, 1777	1	193
Ira, s. Thaddeus & Thankful, b. Aug. 17, 1786	1	202
Joanna, d. Thaddeus & Thankful, b. July 21, 1796	1	203
Josiah C., m. Elvira A. **STEVENS,** b. of Canterbury, Nov.		
8, 1852, by Rev. Robert C. Learned	2	4
Josiah C., m. Elvira A. **STEVENS,** b. of Canterbury,		
[ ], by Rev. Robert C. Learned	2	65
Josiah Cleaveland, s. [Orin & Mehetable], b. Nov. 13, 1821	2	261
Lucy, d. Elihu & Lois, b. Aug. 24, 1771	1	200
Lucy, d. Thaddeus & Thankful, b. Aug. 6, 1794	1	203
Nathan, of Wilkesbarre, Penn., m. Jerusha **BARSTOW,** Sept.		
9, 1794	1	193
Olive, m. Seth **CLARK,** Jan. 22, 1786	1	102
Oren, s. Thaddeus & Thankful, b. July 14, 1784	1	203
Orin, m. Mehetable **ADAMS,** Nov. 15, 1818	1	194
Priscilla, of Norwich, m. Joseph **MARSHAL,** Apr. 17, 1760	1	181
Rhoda, d. Benj[ami]n & Rhoda, b. July 7, 1754	1	201
Rhoda, m. David **BRADFORD,** July 1, 1770	1	71
Samuel Adams, s. [Orin & Mehetable], b. Sept. 24, 1825	2	261
Sarah Maria, d. Orin & Mehetable, b. Oct. 7, 1819	2	261
Thaddeus, m. Thankful **CLEVELAND,** Jan. 13, 1782	1	193
Thaddeus, d. Sept. 17, 1797	1	208
Thaddeus, s. [Orin & Mehetable], b. Oct. 17, 1823	2	261
Thomas, m. Sarah M. **SPICER,** Mar. 20, 1843, by Rev. Asa		
King, Westminster	2	64
PARISH, [see under **PARRISH**]		
PARK, PARKE, PARKS, [see also **PARKIS**], Abiather, s.		
Ebenezer & Mary, b. Oct. 7, 1791	1	203
Abijah, s. Isaac & Lydia, b. Apr. 4, 1748	1	197
Albert, s. Russell & Sophia, b. Apr. 4, 1815	1	205
Alethea, d. Elijah & Anna, b. Nov. 23, 1780	1	202
Ama, d. Simeon & Anna, b. June 20, 1770	1	200
Amasa Rockwell, s. Reuben & Sarah, b. Apr. 7, 1780	1	202
Anna, d. Simeon & Anna, b. Oct. 13, 1760	1	200
Anna, m. Jesse **PELLET,** Oct. 17, 1786	1	193
Asa, s. Ezekiel & Penelope, b. Apr. 25, 1755	1	198
Asa, s. Eleazer & Dorothy, b. May 14, 1787	1	202
Betsey B., of Canterbury, m. Alden H. **WALKER,** of		
Southbridge, Mass., Sept. 4, 1836, by Rev. Tubal		
Wakefield	2	86
Charles, m. Sarah A. **BUTTS,** Feb. 11, 1842, by Rev. Asa		

	Vol.	Page
PARK, PARKE, PARKS, (cont.)		
King, Westminster	2	63
Charles Burnham, s. Asa & Elizabeth, b. Feb. 8, 1815	1	205
Curtis, s. Simeon & Elizabeth, b. Dec. 4, 1793	1	203
Cynthia, m. Zachariah **WALDO**, Nov. 18, 1806	1	237
Daniel, d. Dec. 11, 1763	1	207
Daniel, m. Catharine **BURNS**, Aug. 5, 1776	1	193
Daniel H., of Canterbury, m. Marrilla **ALLEN**, of Smithfield,		
Apr. 21, 1843, by Rev. W. Clarke	2	64
Ebenezer, s. Thomas & Patience, b. Mar. 2, 1750	1	197
Ebenezer, s. Simeon & Anna, b. Mar. 29, 1759	1	200
Ebenezer, m. Mary **PARK**, Apr. 17, 1783	1	193
Ebenezer, s. Ebenezer & Mary, b. Feb. 25, 1805	1	204
Eleanor, d. Jesse & Kezia, b. Oct. 15, 1784	1	203
Eleanor, m. Ransford **BUTTON**, Nov. 3, 1805	1	73
Eleazer, m. Dorothy **HIBBARD**, Oct. 7, 1783	1	193
Eleazer, s. Ebenezer & Mary, b. June 4, 1800	1	204
Eleazer Edmond, s. Asa & Elizabeth, b. Apr. 30, 1813	1	205
Elijah, s. Thomas & Patience, b. June 18, 1743/4	1	198
Elijah, s. Tho[ma]s & Patience, b. June 18, 1744	1	197
Elijah, s. Simeon & Anna, b. Apr. 25, 1756	1	199
Elijah, m. Anna **SMITH**, Mar. 16, 1780	1	193
Elijah, s. Ebenezer & Mary, b. May 15, 1788	1	203
Elijah, m. Hannah **PARTON**(?), Mar. 14, 1813	1	194
Elipha, m. Eleazer **SMITH**, Nov. 16, 1787	1	215
Elithel, d. Simeon & Anna, b. Nov. 28, 1766	1	200
Elizabeth, d. Simeon & Anna, b. Oct. 30, 1757	1	200
Elizabeth, m. Cornelius **WALDO**, Mar. 2, 1763	1	236
Elizabeth, d. John & Eunice, b. Aug. 12, 1785	1	202
Elizabeth, d. Simeon & Elizabeth, b. Sept. 12, 1791	1	203
Elizabeth, m. Curtiss **BARSTOW**, Aug. 27, 1809	1	73
Elizabeth, d. Russell & Sophia, b. Dec. 18, 1811	1	205
Esther, d. Daniel & Esther, b. Mar. 22, 1750, at Norwich	1	199
Esther, m. Amos **MEACH**, Apr. 27, 1762	1	181
Ezekiel, m. Penelope **CLEVELAND**, Nov. 7, 1753	1	192
Ezekiel, s. Daniel & Esther, b. Jan. 16, 1754, at Norwich	1	199
Ezekiel, m. Tabathy Darkis **ELLSWORTH**, Aug. 31, 1777	1	193
Harriet, d. Josiah & Sarah, b. Sept. 16, 1799	1	204
Harriet, d. Elijah & Hannah, b. Aug. 2, 1816	1	205
Henry William, s. Ebenezer & Phebe, b. Mar. 24, 1839	2	261
Isaac, s. Daniel & Esther, b. Mar. 20, 1752, at Norwich	1	199
Isaac, s. Ezekiel & Dorcas, b. Aug. 25, 1778	1	201
James, s. [Daniel & Catharine], b. Nov. 3, 1778	1	201
Jason, s. John, Jr. & Eunice, b. Oct. 9, 1779	1	201
Jemima, m. Sam[ue]l **TORRENCE**, Aug. 30, 1741	1	229
Jesse, s. Ez[ekie]l & Penelope, b. Apr. 20, 1769	1	200
Jesse, m. Kezia **ADAMS**, Jan. 1, 1784	1	193
John, m. Eunice **FROST**, July 12, 1764	1	193

	Vol.	Page
PARK, PARKE, PARKS, (cont.)		
Reuben, Jr., m. Maria **SAFFORD**, Dec. 8, 1796	1	193
Reuel, s. Eleazer & Dorothy, b. June 1, 1792	1	203
Rosalinda Amanda, d. Asa & Elizabeth, b. June 23, 1816	1	205
Russel[l], m. Sophia **BARSTOW**, Nov. 21, 1810	1	194
Sarah, m. John **POST**, Dec. 12, 1723	1	192
Sarah, d. John & Sarah, d. Jan. 22, 1767	1	207
Sarah, d. John, Jr. & Eunice, b. Apr. 5, 1777	1	201
Sarah, d. Daniel & Catharine, b. Apr. 30, 1777	1	201
Sarah, m. Elias **WILLIAMS**, b. of Canterbury, Mar. 5, 1828, by Rev. Israel Rose, of Westminster	2	85
Sibbel, m. Charles **SHELDING**, Dec. 13, 1774	1	214
Simeon, s. Simeon & Anna, b. Mar. 21, 1768	1	200
Simon, m. Anna **BUTTON**, of Voluntown, July 15, 1755, at Stonington	1	192
Thankful, d. Simeon & Anne, b. Aug. 24, 1773	1	201
Thomas, m. Patience **RUDD**, June 9, 1743	1	192
Thomas, d. Mar. 31, 1752	1	206
PARKER, Eben[eze]r, s. Joshua & Jemima, b. Apr. 30, 1756	1	198
Eben[eze]r, m. Roby **LITCHFIELD**, Dec. 9, 1779	1	193
Mary, m. John **ADAMS**, Jr., Oct. 5, 1769	1	51
Rachel, d. Joshua & Jemima, b. July 30, 1758	1	198
Rosel, s. Joshua & Jemima, b. Oct. 16, 1760	1	199
Samuel Davenport, s. Joshua & Jemima, b. Apr. 24, 1763	1	199
PARKHURST, PARKIST, [see also **PARK** and **PARKIS**],		
Harvey, of Plainfield, m. Lucretia **SAFFORD**, of Canterbury, May 29, 1832, by Rev. Dennis Platt	2	61
Henry, m. Emeline **GEER**, b. of Canterbury, Apr. 18, 1829, by C. S. Hyde, J. P.	2	61
Jabez, of Plainfield, m. Mehetable **ROBINSON**, of Canterbury, Oct. 13, 1842, by Rev. W. Clarke	2	64
PARKIS, [see also **PARK** and **PARKHURST**], Sally, m. John **KENDALL**, Aug. 22, 1819	1	173
PARRISH, PARISH, Abadiah, see under Obadiah		
Abigail, d. Nehemiah & Patience, b. Nov. 14, 1762	1	199
Anna, w. Rufus, d. Aug. 19, 1798	1	208
Ariel, s. [Elijah & Eunice], b. Nov. 29, 1764	1	200
Artemissa, d. Roswell & Lucy, b. Oct. 5, 1792	1	204
Benj[ami]n, m. Mercy **ROOD**, Jan. 29, 1735/6	1	192
Cynthia, d. Lemuel & Zerv[ia]h, b. Feb. 19, 1770	1	200
Cynthia, m. Ebenezer **WALDO**, May 31, 1798	1	237
Deborah, d. Sam[ue]l & Mary, b. June 19, 1746	1	197
Deborah, d. Sam[ue]l & Mary, d. Aug. 29, 1749	1	206
Eben[eze]r, m. Susannah **WILLIAMS**, Feb. 13, 1752	1	192
Ebene[z]er, s. Rufus & Sally, b. June 3, 1800	1	204
Elijah, s. Sam[ue]l & Mary, b. Feb. 7, 1739/40	1	196
Elijah, m. Eunice **FOSTER**, Feb. 11, 1762	1	193
Elijah, s. Elijah & Eunice, b. Nov. 6, 1762	1	200

	Vol.	Page
PARRISH, PARISH, (cont.)		
Elisha, s. Sam[ue]l & Mary, b. Jan. 3, 1742/3	1	197
Elisha, d. Nov. 18, 1766	1	207
Elisha, s. Samuel & Susannah, b. June 16, 1768	1	200
Ephraim Durfee, s. Levi & Elizabeth, b. Mar. 20, 1783	1	202
Erastus, s. Roswell & Mehetable, b. July 28, 1783	1	202
Even, m. Betsey **WALDO**, b. of Canterbury, Apr. 14, 1839, by Rev. Hezekiah Thatcher	2	62
Ezekiel, s. Joel & Rebecca, b. Oct. 5, 1742	1	197
Gurdon, s. [Rufus & Anne], b. Apr. 13, 1793	1	203
Gurdon, s. Rufus, Anne, d. Dec. 3, 1793	1	207
Horatio Nelson, s. Roswell & Lucy, b. Dec. 16, 1798	1	204
Horatio Nelson, s. Roswell & Lucy, d. Feb. 14, 1799	1	208
Jacob, s. Benj[ami]n & Mercy, b. Feb. 1, 1736/7	1	196
Jeremiah, s. Nehemiah & Patience, b. Feb. 17, 1765	1	199
Jeremiah, s. Lemuel & Zerviah, b. Oct. 17, 1775	1	201
Jerusha, m. Benjamin **BAKER**, June 12, 1744	1	69
Joel, s. Joel & Rebecca, b. Oct. 5, 1739	1	197
John, s. Joel & Rebecca, b. Jan. 16, 1734	1	197
John, s. Joel & Rebeckah, d. Mar. 9, 1734	1	206
John, s. Nehemiah & Patience, b. July 12, 1760	1	198
John, s. Lemuel & Zerviah, b. June 11, 1761	1	198
John Ryley, s. [Roswell & Mehetable], b. Oct. 6, 1786	1	202
Julia, d. [Roswell & Lucy], b. Mar. 28, 1797	1	204
Levi, s. Samuel, Jr. & Susannah, b. Mar. 2, 1758	1	198
Levi Harding, s. Levi & Elizabeth, b. Dec. 31, 1784	1	203
Lucy, d. Sam[ue]l & Susannah, b. Oct. 18, 1756	1	198
Lucy, d. [Roswell & Lucy], b. Jan. 7, 1801	1	204
Lucy, m. Jedediah **READ**, May 19, 1822, by Jedediah Morse, J. P.	2	67
Lydia, d. Nehemiah & Ruth, b. Sept. 26, 1739	1	198
Lydia had d. Patience, b. May 13, 1763	1	199
Mary, w. Sam[ue]l, d. May 8, 1755	1	206
Mary, m. Dea. Jonas **BOND**, Nov. 10, 1796	1	72
Mehitable, d. Lemuel & Zerviah, b. Jan. 22, 1773	1	201
Mehetable, d. [Roswell & Mehetable], b. Sept. 7, 1784	1	202
Mehetable, m. William **BRADFORD**, Dec. 13, 1804	1	73
Mehetable Melody, w. Roswell, d. Apr. 10, 1790	1	208
Nehemiah, m. Patience **SMITH**, May 24, 1758	1	192
Nehemiah, s. Nehemiah & Patience, b. Jan. 12, 1759	1	198
Obadiah, s. Lemuel & Zerviah, b. Sept. 22, 1764	1	199
Abadiah, s. Rufus & Anna, b. Nov. 14, 1794	1	204
Olive, d. Samuel & Susannah, b. Jan. 7, 1755	1	198
Patience, d. Lydia, b. May 13, 1763	1	199
Phebe, d. Nehemiah & Patience, b. Mar. 9, 1767	1	200
Phebe, d. Nehemiah & Patience, d. Jan. 4, 1776	1	207
Phelomela, d. [Elijah & Eunice], b. Dec. 4, 1767	1	200
Phinehas, s. Prescilla, single woman, b. June 16, 1781	1	202

	Vol.	Page
PARRISH, PARISH, (cont.)		
Polly, d. Rufus & Anne, b. Sept. 3, 1790	1	203
Priscilla, d. Nehemiah & Ruth, b. Apr. 17, 1744	1	198
Prescilla, single woman, had s. Phinehas, b. June 16, 1781	1	202
Reuben, s. Samuel & Susannah, b. Feb. 24, 1761	1	198
Roswell, m. Lucy **HARRIS**, Nov. 1, 1791	1	194
Roswell, s. [Roswell & Lucy], b. Apr. 1, 1795	1	204
Rozel, s. Samuel & Zerviah, b. Oct. 18, 1759	1	198
Rufus, s. Lemuel & Zerviah, b. Sept. 18, 1768	1	200
Rufus, m. Anne **BREWSTER**, of Killingly, Nov. 22, 1789	1	193
Rufus, m. Sally **BADGER**, Sept. 26, 1799	1	194
Ruth, d. Joel & Rebecca, b. May 15, 1733	1	197
Ruth, w. Nehemiah, d. Dec. 26, 1754	1	206
Sam[ue]l, m. Susannah **DOWNING**, Apr. 11, 1751	1	192
Samuel, m. Zerviah **SMITH**, May 4, 1758	1	192
Silva, d. Samuel & Susanna, b. Oct. 28, 1764	1	199
Susannah, d. Sam[ue]l & Susanna, b. Apr. 17, 1752	1	196
Zerviah, d. Roswell & Mehetable Melody, b. Feb. 16, 1788	1	204
PARSONS, Lucy, m. Erastus **ROBBINS**, Feb. 14, 1833, by Daniel		
G. Sprague	2	67
PARTON(?), Hannah, m. Elijah **PARK**, Mar. 14, 1813	1	194
PARTRIDGE, Hannah, m. Daniel **BALDWIN**, Nov. 16, 1730	1	69
PATTEN, PATEN, Anne, m. Amos **WOODARD**, Feb. 21, 1760	1	236
Sarah, d. Tho[ma]s & Sarah, d. Nov. 18, 1750	1	206
PAYSON, [see under **PAISON**]		
PEABODY, Alden, m. Naomi **BARNET**, b. of Providence, Sept. 14,		
1826, by Rev. Tho[ma]s J. Murdock	2	61
Joseph, of Norwich, m. Mary **WHITE**, of Canterbury, July		
9, 1836, by Rev. George S. White	2	62
Joseph, of Norwich, m. Mary **WHITE**, of Canterbury, Aug.		
9, 1836, by George S. White	2	11
PEARL, Elizabeth, m. John **HEBBARD**, Feb. 14, 1749	1	155
PECK, Benjamin, s. Reuben & Charity, b. Sept. 4, 1760	1	198
Benjamin, s. [Jesse & Sarah], b. Jan. 26, 1800	1	204
Dulucenia, m. Merit B. **WILLIAMS**, b. of Canterbury, Jan.		
27, 1846, by Walter Williams, J. P.	2	88
Harriet, d. Jesse & Sarah, b. Mar. 31, 1802	1	205
Jemima, d. Reuben & Charity, b. Sept. 18, 1770	1	201
Jesse, s. Reuben & Charity, b. Oct. 3, 1764	1	199
Jesse, m. Sarah **CARVER**, Mar. 31, 1795	1	194
John, s, [Reuben & Charity], b. Jan. 31, 1775	1	201
Joseph, s. Jesse & Sarah, b. May 14, 1807	1	205
Maria*, w. Reuben, Jr., d. Mar. 4, 1798 (*Probably		
"Maria **PARK**". Corrected by L. B. B.)	1	208
Mary, Jr., m. David **CARVER**, Jr., Jan. 26, 1769	1	101
Newton, s. Reuben & Charity, b. Mar. 3, 1777	1	201
Newton, s. Jesse & Sarah, b. Nov. 7, 1804	1	205
Newton Carver, s. Jesse & Sarah, b. Nov. 17, 1809	1	205

	Vol.	Page
PECK, (cont.)		
Reuben, m. Charity **FRENCH**, Dec. 6, 1759	1	192
Rhoda, d. Jesse & Sarah, b. June 11, 1813	1	205
Sarah, d. [Reuben & Charity], b. Feb. 27, 1773	1	201
Sophronia, m. Walter **PECK**, b. of Canterbury, Jan. 1,		
1823, by Walter Williams, J. P.	2	61
Susanna, m. Thomas **ADAMS**, Mar. 7, 176[ ]	1	51
Susannah, d. Jesse & Sarah, b. Apr. 14, 1796	1	204
Thomas, s. Reuben & Charity, b. Aug. 15, 1762	1	199
Walter, s. [Jesse & Sarah], b. Jan. 2, 1798(?)	1	204
Walter, m. Sophronia **PECK**, b. of Canterbury, Jan. 1,		
1823, by Walter Williams, J. P.	2	61
PECKHAM, Stephen V. R., of Plainfield, m. Mary Ann **HILL**, of		
Canterbury, Jan. 1, 1837, by Rev. Tubal Wakefield,		
Packersville	2	62
PEIRCE, [see under **PIERCE**]		
PELLET, PELLETT, Abigail, d. Hezekiah & Abigail, b. Mar. 20,		
1739/40	1	196
Abigail, d. Hez[ekiah] & Abigail, d. Nov. 5, 1756	1	207
Abigail, d. John & Hephzibah, b. Dec. 12, 1757	1	199
Abigail, d. Eph[rai]m & Hannah, b. Mar. 7, 1780	1	202
Abner, s. Ephraim & Hannah, b. Feb. 19, 1773	1	201
Alice, b. June 26, 1759	1	199
Alice, d. Samuel & Hannah, b. Aug. 24, 1759	1	207
Alice, d. [Jeremiah & Lucy], b. June 16, 1799	1	204
Alonzo D., s. Nelson B. & Harriet E., b. Feb. 7, 1838	2	261
Amasa, s. Jesse & Anna, b. Dec. 9, 1788	1	203
Amasa, d. Jan. 14, 1846	2	351
Anna, d. Ephraim & Hannah, b. Sept. 23, 1763	1	199
Anna, d. Eph[rai]m & Hannah, b. May 15, 1771	1	201
Anna, d. Jesse & Anne, b. June 28, 1787	1	202
Anne, [twin with Patience], d. Richard & Anne, b.		
Aug. 8, 1721	1	195
Anne, d. John & Hephzibah, b. Oct. 28, 1745	1	197
Anne, d. Hez[ekiah] & Abigail, b. July 7, 1756	1	198
Anne, w. Richard, d. Oct. 25, 1756	1	206
Anne, m. Eliphas **CLEVELAND**, Sept. 1, 1784	1	102
Archibald, s. Hez[ekia]h, Jr. & Mary, b. Nov. 30, 1783	1	202
Archibald S., [s. Chester & Almira], b. May 2, 1827	2	261
Asa, s. Hezekiah & Abigail, b. Nov. 11, 1751	1	197
Asa, s. Hezekiah & Abigail, d. Oct. 31, 1756	1	207
Betty, m. Phinehas **LESTER**, Dec. 1, 1772	1	176
Caroline E., m. Ahira **SMITH**, b. of Canterbury, Oct. 19,		
1828, by Rev. J. R. Wheelock	2	72
Caroline Eliza, d. Amasa & Lydia, b. Dec. 26, 1811	1	205
Charles Worthington, s. Luther & Mary Ann, b. Apr. 3, 1836	2	261
Chester, s. [Rufus & Drusilla], b. May 17, 1797	1	204
Chester, m. Almira A. **CADY**, b. of Canterbury, Dec.		

	Vol.	Page
PELLET, PELLETT, (cont.		
8, 1822, by Tho[ma[s J. Murdock	2	61
Chester Knight, s. Jared & Philura, b. Sept. 24, 1806	1	205
Daniel Huchens, s. Jared & Philena, b. Dec. 14, 1803	1	204
David, s. Jonathan & Jerusha, b. Feb. 21, 1750	1	198
David, m. Ora JOHNSON, Sept. 17, 1778	1	193
David, s. David & Orra, b. July 25, 1787	1	202
Delucena, s. [Jeremiah & Lucy], b. Nov. 1, 1796	1	204
Edee, d. [Hez[ekia]h, Jr. & Mary], b. Mar. 22, 1786	1	202
Edith, d. Jonathan & Jerusha, b. Mar. 25, 1735	1	198
Edwin Demast, s. [Amasa & Lydia], b. Apr. 9, 1817	1	205
Edwin F., s. [Nelson B. & Harriet E.], b. Nov. 9, 1843	2	261
Elijah Martin, s. Jared & Philena, b. Nov. 18, 1816	1	205
Elijah Palmer, s. [Chester & Almira], b. Apr. 13, 1825	2	261
Elisha, s. Joseph & Submit, b. Apr. 24, 1785	1	203
Elizabeth, d. John & Hephzibah, b. June 15, 1750	1	197
Elizabeth, m. Phinehas LESTER, Dec. 1, 1771	1	176
Elizabeth G., m. George L. ADAMS, of New York City, Apr. 20, 1836	1	53
Elizabeth G., of Canterbury, m. George L. ADAMS, of New York City, Apr. 20, 1836, by Rev. Otis C. Whiton	2	3
Elizabeth Wadsworth, d. Sam[ue]l & Margaret, b. Aug. 15, 1743	1	197
Elizabeth Wadsworth, d. Sam[ue]l & Margaret, d. Aug. 4, 1749	1	206
Ephraim, s. Richard & Anna, b. June 21, 1718	1	195
Ephraim, m. Hannah UNDERWOOD, Oct. 6, 1761	1	192
Ephraim, s. Ephraim & Hannah, b. Apr. 3, 1762	1	199
Ephraim, s. Ephraim & Hannah, d. May 13, 1763	1	207
Ephraim, s. Ephraim & Hannah, b. Apr. 13, 1769	1	200
Ernest, [s. Chester & Almira], b. Apr. 14, 1837	2	261
Esther, d. Rufus & Drusilla, b. Dec. 9, 1786	1	203
Eunice, d. Samuel & Hannah, b. Aug. 8, 1753	1	198
Eunice, d. Rufus & Drusilla, b. Oct. 26, 1784	1	202
Felis, m. John JOHNSON, Mar. 11, 1756	1	167
George G., [s. Chester & Almira], b. Feb. 2, 1833	2	261
George Washington, s. Jared & Nancy, b. Apr. 28, 1795	1	203
Hannah, d. Sam[ue]l & Margaret, b. Apr. 15, 1747	1	197
Hannah, m. Benjamin HIDE, Oct. 5, 1772	1	155
Hezekiah, s. Richard & Anne, b. Apr. 28, 1712	1	195
Hezekiah, m. Abigail BROWN, Mar. 5, 1738/9	1	192
Hezekiah, s. Hezekiah & Abigail, b. Dec. 22, 1746; d. Jan. 4, 1746/7	1	197
Hezekiah, s. Hezekiah & Abigail, b. Apr. 26, 1748	1	197
Hezekiah, s. Hezekiah & Abigail, d. Oct. 4, 1752	1	206
Hezekiah, s. Jonathan & Jerusha, b. Feb. 25, 1757	1	198
Hezekiah, m. Mary GIBSON, May 7, 1781	1	193
Hezekiah, s. Jesse & Anna, b. Oct. 21, 1796	1	203
James, s. Jonathan & Jerusha, b. Feb. 9, 1737	1	198

	Vol.	Page
PELLET, PELLETT, (cont.)		
James, d. May 13, 1766	1	207
James s. Tho[ma]s & Mâry, b. Sept. 21, 1767	1	200
James P., [s. Chester & Almira], b. Oct. 20, 1840	2	261
Jared, s. [Ephraim & Hannah], b. Aug. 31, 1767	1	200
Jared, m. Nancy **PIKE**, of Brooklyn, Jan. 10, 1788, at Pomfret	1	193
Jared, m. Philura **BUTT**, Feb. 14, 1802	1	194
Jedediah, s. Jared & Nancy, b. May 17, 1788	1	203
Jeremiah, s. Hez[ekiah] & Abigail, b. Mar. 3, 1754	1	197
Jeremiah, s. Hez[ekia]h & Abigail, d. Oct. 28, 1756	1	207
Jeremiah, s. Samuel & Hannah, b. Oct. 11, 1763	1	199
Jeremiah, m. Laura **JOHNSON**, Jan. 2, 1793	1	193
Jerusha, d. Jonathan & Jerusha, b. June 6, 1744	1	198
Jerusha, d. [Hez[ekia]h & Mary], b. Dec. 28, 1790, at		
Sc[h]enactade	1	203
Jesse, s. Hezekiah & Abigail, b. Aug. 26, 1760	1	198
Jesse, m. Anna **PARKS**, Oct. 17, 1786	1	193
Jesse, d. July 4, 1808, ae 47	1	208
John, m. Hephzibah **FELTCH**, Nov. 12, 1741	1	192
John, s. John & Hephzibah, b. Feb. 2, 1748	1	197
John, s. Rufus & Drusilla, b. Feb. 4, 1783	1	204
John, s. Hez[ekia]h & Mary, b. Nov. 15, 1788, at Sc[h]enactade	1	203
John, s. Richard & Anna, b. Apr. 4, [ ]	1	195
John Chester, s. Chester & Almira, b. Mar. 26, 1824	2	261
John Dennis, s. Amasa & Lydia, b. Dec. 30, 1832	2	261
John Nelson, s. [Rufus & Mindwell], b. Aug. 2, 1818	1	205
John Nelson, s. [Rufus & Mindwell], b. Aug. 2, 1818	1	208
Jonathan, s. Richard & Anna, b. Mar. 2, 1704	1	195
Jonathan, m. Jerusha **BRADFORD**, Feb. 20, 1733	1	192
Jonathan, s. Jonathan & Jerusha, b. June 20, 1733	1	198
Jonathan, s. Jonathan & Jerusha, d. Mar. 8, 1735/6	1	206
Jonathan, s. Jonathan & Jerusha, b. Oct. 19, 1739	1	198
Jonathan, s. Jonathan & Jerusha, b. July 12, 1753	1	198
Jona[than], Jr., m. Hannah **PALMER**, Jan. 29, 1777	1	193
Jonathan, d. Oct. 4, 1782	1	207
Jonathan, s. [Rufus & Drusilla], b. Aug. 18, 1792	1	204
Joseph, s. Sam[ue]l & Margaret, b. Mar. 6, 1745	1	197
Joseph, s. Jonathan & Jerusha, b. Mar. 18, 1748	1	198
Joseph, m. Submit **BRADFORD**, Apr. 29, 1782	1	193
Joseph, [s. Chester & Almira], b. Apr. 29, 1843	2	261
Josiah, s. [Ephraim & Hannah], b. Apr. 9, 1775	1	201
Julia S., d. [Nelson B. & Harriet E.] , b. Mar. 4, 1846	2	261
Lois, d. Jona[than], Jr. & Hannah, b. Sept. 8, 1778	1	201
Lora, d. Jeremiah & Lucy, b. Dec. 24, 1793	1	204
Lucinda, d. Amasa & Lydia, b. Nov. 12, 1819	1	205
Lucretia, b. May 18, 1755	1	199
Lucretia, d. [Amasa & Lydia], b. Aug. 14, 1825	2	261
Lucy, d. [Eph[rai]m & Hannah], b. Jan. 21, 1782	1	202

	Vol.	Page
PELLET, PELLETT, (cont.)		
Luis J., [s. Chester & Almira], b. May 25, 1835	2	261
Luther, s. Jona[than], Jr. & Hannah, b. Dec. 21, 1779	1	201
Luther, s. Jared & Philena, b. June 2, 1809	1	205
Lydia M., of Canterbury, m. Frances S. **YOUNG**, of Griswold, May 8, 1843, by Rev. W. Clarke	2	91
Lydia Maria, d. Amasa & Lydia, b. May 30, 1823	2	261
Margaret, w. Sam[ue]l, d. Feb. 28, 1748/9	1	206
Margaret, b. June 12, 1757	1	199
Margary, d. Tho[ma]s & Mary, b. June 2, 1770	1	200
Margery, m. Bethabra **CLEVELAND**, Dec. 31, 1794	1	102
Maria, d. Rufus & Drusilla, b. Apr. 22, 1800	1	204
Marian, d. Rufus & Drusilla, b. Mar. 25, 1803	1	205
Mary, d. Hez[ekia] & Abigail, b. June 24, 1744	1	197
Mary, d. John & Hephzibah, b. Apr. 5, 1755	1	199
Mary, d. Hez[ekia]h & Abigail, d. Nov. 1, 1756	1	207
Mary, d. Tho[ma]s & Mary, b. Mar. 30, 1773	1	201
Mary, d. [Ephraim & Hannah], b. Apr. 22, 1777	1	201
Miranda, d. Rufus & Mindwell, b. Jan. 23, 1816	1	205
Miranda, d. Rufus & Mindwell, b. Jan. 23, 1816 (Arnold note: "Died" crossed out)	1	208
Nancy, d. Jonathan & Hannah, b. June 5, 1785	1	202
Nancy, m. Nathan Landia **TIFFANY**, July 18, 1805	1	229
Nelson Bingham, s. [Amasa & Lydia], b. June 26, 1814	1	205
Olive, d. Samuel & Hannah, b. June 5, 1762	1	199
Olive, twin with Orra, d. David & Orra, b. Jan. 27, 1783	1	202
Olive, single woman, had s. Samuel L. **HOUGH**, b. July 27, 1808	1	164
Orra, twin with Olive, d. David & Orra, b. Jan. 27, 1783	1	202
Paschall, [s. Chester & Almira], b. July 24, 1831	2	261
Patience, [twin with Anne], d. Richard & Anne, b. Aug. 8, 1721	1	195
Patience, d. Sam[ue]l & Margaret, b. June 12, 1739	1	197
Patience(?), m. Joseph **CARTER**, Oct. 3, 1762	1	101
Patience, d. Ephraim & Hannah, b. Dec. 25, 1765	1	200
Phebe, m. Samuel **ADAMS**, Nov. 3, 17[ ]	1	51
Phebe, d. Hez[ekiah] & Abigail, b. June 28, 1742	1	196
Phyllys, d. David & Orra, b. Mar. 20, 1779	1	201
Richard, m. Anne **BROOKS**, Apr. 2, 1703	1	192
Richard, d. June 15, 1758	1	207
Rufus, s. Jonathan & Jerusha, b. May 25, 1760	1	199
Rufus, m. Drusilla **WHEELER**, Mar. 15, 1781	1	193
Rufus, s. Rufus & Drusilla, b. Nov. 4, 1781	1	202
Rufus, d. Sept. 16, 1806	1	208
Samuel, s. Richard & Anne, b. Mar. 7, 1709	1	195
Sam[ue]l, s. Sam[ue]l & Margaret, b. Apr. 4, 1741	1	197
Sam[ue]l, s. Sam[ue]l & Margaret, d. Aug. 3, 1749	1	206
Samuel, m. Hannah **UNDERWOOD**, July [ ], 1752	1	192

	Vol.	Page

PERKINS, (cont)

Samuel, s. Leonard & Grace, b. Sept. 10, 1786 — 1 — 204

Sarah, d. [Leonard & Grace], b. Nov. 21, 1791 — 1 — 204

Sarah, m. Dr. Rufus **JOHNSON**, Oct. 27, 1812 — 1 — 167

Warren, s. [Leonard & Grace], b. Mar. 19, 1789 — 1 — 204

William Fitch, s. [Jacob & Mary], b. Aug. 22, 1773 — 1 — 201

William Marderson, s. Leonard & Grace, b. Apr. 27, 1809 — 1 — 205

PERRY, Amanda T., of Canterbury, m. Charles M. **PALMER**, of

Windham, Nov. 30, 1848, by Rev. Joseph Ayer, Lisbon — 2 — 65

Lydia Ann, m. Merrett **ALLEN**, b. of Canterbury, Sept. 2,

1850, by Rev. E. W. Robinson, of Hanover Society,

Lisbon — 2 — 4

PETERSON, Andrew, s. John & Jemima, b. May 5, 1750 — 1 — 200

---, wid., d. Feb. 15, 1763 — 1 — 207

PETTINGILL, PETTINGALL, PETTENGILL, Hannah, m. Levi

ADAMS, Jr., Aug. 9, 177[ ] — 1 — 52

Horatio, m. Thankful **CADY**, Sept. 24, 1802 — 1 — 194

Horatio, s. Horatio & Thankfull, b. Sept. 2, 1804 — 1 — 205

Lydia, of Norwich, m. Sherebiah **BUTT**, Jr., Dec. 4, 1783 — 1 — 72

PETTIS, Elihu, m. Deborah **ADAMS**, Jan. 27, 1805 — 1 — 194

PHILLIPS, Charles E., m. Elizabeth **POTTER**, b. of Packersville,

Sept. 19, 1842, by M. Byrne — 2 — 63

Debby, m. Amos **BURDICK**, Nov. 6, 1826, by Andrew T.

Judson, J. P. — 2 — 8

Frederick F., of Griswold, m. Mehetable **WADE**, of

Canterbury, Aug. 4, 1822, by Erastus Learned — 2 — 61

Lucinda M., of Canterbury, m. Thomas S. **FISH**, of

Voluntown, Apr. 3, 1843, by Rev. W. Clarke — 2 — 32

Margaret, m. Alpheas **SPAULDING**, Dec. 9, 1771 — 1 — 214

Petifeel Pierpont, d. Elizabeth **GREEN**, single woman, b.

Apr. 1, 1791 — 1 — 203

PHINNEY, PHINNIE, PHINNE, Abigail, m. Septemius **BLISS**,

Sept. 26, 1805 — 1 — 73

Asa, m. Lydia **APPLEY**, May 28, 1795 — 1 — 194

Asa, s. Asa & Lydia, b. Aug. 16, 1803 — 1 — 204

Asa, d. Aug. 8, 1851 — 1 — 208

Asa, d. Aug. 8, 1852, ae 90 y. 7 m. — 2 — 351

Asael, s. Joshua & Lucy, b. May 22, 1761 — 1 — 199

Dorothy, d. Sam[ue]l & Dorothy, b. May 21, 1797 — 1 — 204

Edwin, m. Laura **ADAMS**, Mar. 16, 1848, by Rev. Asa King,

Westminster — 2 — 65

Edwin S., m. Betsey **SMITH**, Nov. 18, 1829, by Rev. Israel

G. Rose, of Westminster — 2 — 61

Edwin Safford, s. John & Henrietta, b. May 13, 1807 — 1 — 205

Elisha, s. Asa & Lydia, b. Mar. 20, 1809 — 1 — 205

Elisa, d. Asa & Lydia, b. Apr. 1, 1800 — 1 — 204

Frederic Elliott, s. William & Lydia Angeline **WHEELER**,

b. May 26, 1843 — 2 — 261

	Vol.	Page
PHINNEY, PHINNIE, PHINNE, (cont.)		
Frederic Eliot, s. William & Lydia A. W., d. July 17, 1845	2	351
John, s. Samuel & Dorothy, b. Feb. 2, 1783	1	202
John, m. Henrietta, **SAFFORD,** Apr. 10, 1806	1	194
Joshua, s. Joshua & Lucy, b. Apr. 4, 1755	1	142
Joshua, s. Joshua & Lucy, b. Apr. 4, 1755	1	198
Joshua, m. Lucy **ENSWORTH,** June 10, 1764	1	193
Joshua, d. Oct. 4, 1787	1	207
Joshua, s. Samuel & Dorothy, b. Feb. 14, 1801	1	204
Lewis, Dr., of North Yarmouth, Me., m. Mary H. **PACKER,** of Canterbury, [Packersville], Sept. 11, 1839, by Rev. Tubal Wakefield	2	62
Lucas Osiander, s. Asa & Lydia, b. Feb. 16, 1805	1	204
Lucy, d. June 6, 1811	1	208
Lydia, d. Asa & Lydia, b. Feb. 14, 1797	1	204
Lydia, w. Asa, d. May 15, 1815	1	208
Markus, s. [Asa & Lydia], b. May 6, 1811	1	205
Mary, d. Sam[ue]ll & Dorothy, b. Oct. 29, 1794	1	203
Nancy, d. [Asa & Lydia], b. Mar. 7, 1799	1	204
Samuel, s. [Joshua & Lucy], b. June 23, 1758	1	142
Samuel, s. Joshua & Lucy, b. June 23, 1758	1	198
Samuel, m. Dorothy **HIDE,** May 5, 1782	1	194
Samuel, s. Samuel & Dorothy, b. July 2, 1786	1	202
William, s. Samuel & Dorothy, b. May 12, 1791	1	203
William, s. [Asa & Lydia], b. May 5, 1815	1	205
PICKER, John, see Abigail **TUCKER**		
PICKET, Joshua, of Plainfield, m. Sarah **CHAMPLAIN,** of Killingly, [July] 3, 1842, by Martin Byrne	2	63
PIDGE, Comfort, m. Elizabeth **BENNET,** Dec. 31, 1826, by Rev. George S. White	2	61
PIERCE, PEIRCE, Abigail, d. [Deleno & Abigail], b. July 9, 1773	1	201
Benj[ami]n, m. Naomie **RICHARDS,** July 11, 1737	1	192
Benj[ami]n, Capt., m. Sarah **MILLS,** Aug. 31, 1758	1	192
Benj[ami]n, Capt., m. Sarah **HOLT,** Jan. 28, 1762	1	192
Benjamin, s. Nehemiah & Lydia, b. Sept. 4, 1762	1	199
Benjamin, Capt., d. Feb. 7, 1782, ae 72	1	207
Benjamin, s. Delano & Abigail, b. Sept. 1, 1783	1	202
Betsey, d. Deleno & Abigail, b. May 15, 1771	1	201
David, s. Nehemiah & Lydia, d. Apr. 22, 1769	1	207
Deidama, d. Benj[ami]n & Naomi, b. Apr. 14, 1756	1	198
Delano, s. Benjamin & Naomi, b. Nov. 19, 1748	1	197
Deleno, m. Abigail **HAMMOND,** Nov. 1, 1770	1	193
Elias, s. Delano & Abigail, b. Jan. 29, 1781	1	202
Erastus, s. Delano & Abigail, b. June 22, 1778	1	201
Ezra, s. John & Sarah, b. Jan. 14, 1767	1	200
Frederick, s Nehemiah & Lydia, b. July 22, 1768	1	200
Hannah, d. [Benj[ami]n & Hannah], b. Feb. 5, 1733	1	200
Hannah, w. Benjamin, d. Sept. 25, 1736	1	206

	Vol.	Page
PIERCE, PEIRCE, (cont.)		
Lyte, d. Benj[ami]n & Naomi, b. July 23, 1745	1	197
Naomi, w. Ensign **BENJAMIN**, d. July 20, 1757	1	207
Nehemiah, s. Benj[ami]n & Hannah, b. May 27, 1730	1	200
Nehemiah, s. Nehemiah & Lydia, b. May 11, 1771	1	200
Olive, d. Benj[ami]n & Naomi, b. Mar. 29, 1738	1	196
Olive, d. Delano & Abigail, b. Feb. 25, 1776	1	201
Oliver, s. Benjamin & Hannah, b. June 27, 1736	1	196
Payson Grosvenor, s. Timens & Elizabeth, b. Sept. 10, 1781	1	202
Rachel, d. Benj[ami]n & Naomi, b. Feb. 19, 1742/3	1	197
Rizpah, d. Timens & Elizabeth, b. July 19, 1783	1	202
Rufus, s. Benj[ami]n & Naomi, b. Sept. 27, 1740	1	196
Rufus, s. Benj[ami]n & Naomi, d. Dec. 28, 1741	1	206
Rufus, s. Benjamin & Naomi, b. Sept. 7, 1753	1	197
Rufus, s. Timens & Elizabeth, b. June 20, 1785	1	202
Rufus, s. Timeas & Elizabeth, d. Feb. 24, 1786	1	207
Sarah, w. Capt. Benj[ami]n, d. Sept. 7, 1759	1	207
Simens, m. Elizabeth **GROSVENOR**, May 4, 1779	1	193
Simens, see also Timens		
Sophia, d. Timens & Elizabeth, b. Feb. 13, 1780	1	201
Timens*, s. Benj[ami]n & Naomi, b. June 3, 1751		
(*Perhaps Simens?)	1	197
Timens, see also Simens		
PIKE, Abigail, d. Ebenezer & Abigail, b. Apr. 21, 1742	1	196
Amos, s. John & Sarah, b. Dec. 16, 1736	1	196
Amos, m. Elizabeth **ENSWORTH**, May 2, 1764	1	193
Amos, s. Amos & Elizabeth, b. Sept. 10, 1766	1	200
Anna, d. Amos & Elizabeth, b. Sept. 10, 1766	1	200
Asa, s. Ebenezer & Abigail, b. Nov. 18, 1738	1	196
David, s. John & Sarah, b. Jan. 9, 1719/20	1	195
David, d. July 2, 1758	1	207
Ebenezer, s. John & Sarah, b. Mar. 3, 1709	1	195
Ebenezer, m. Abigail **ADAMS**, Jan. 24, 1737/8	1	192
Elijah, s. John & Sarah, b. Nov. 9, 1717	1	195
Elijah, s. John & Sarah, d. Aug. 22, 1719	1	206
Elijah, s. John & Sarah, b. Dec. 4, 1733	1	196
Elijah, s. John & Sarah, d. Oct. 16, 1751	1	206
Elizabeth, d. John & Sarah, b. Mar. 25, 1711	1	195
Elizabeth, d. Oct. 20, 1778, ae 68	1	207
Eunice, d. John & Sarah, d. May 26, 1756	1	206
Hannah, d. James & Hannah, b. Aug. 3, 1744	1	197
Hannah, d. James & Hannah, d. Sept. 6, 1749	1	206
Hannah, w. Jonathan, d. Feb. 3, 1783	1	207
James, s. John & Sarah, b. Nov. 7, 1715	1	195
James, m. Hannah **HIDE**, May 25, 1741	1	192
Ja[me]s*, m. Hannah **JEWETT**, Nov. 14, 1775 (*Perhaps		
"Jos[eph]")	1	193
James, s. Jonathan & Rebecca, b. July 30, 1784	1	203

	Vol.	Page
PIKE, (cont.)		
James, of Sterling, m. Mary E. **SHEPERD**, of Canterbury,		
May 1, 1853, by Rev. Robert C. Learned	2	66
Jarvis, s. John & Sarah, b. June 14, 1714	1	195
Jesse, s. John & Sarah, b. Aug. 17, 1735	1	196
Jesse, s. John & Sarah, d. Nov. 23, 1755, in Camp at		
Lake George	1	206
John, m. Sarah **HIDE**, May 23, 1706	1	192
John, s. John & Sarah, b. July 23, 1707	1	195
John, m. Sarah **BACKUS**, July 9, 1729	1	192
John, d. Sept. 21, 1754	1	206
John, m. Mercy **BUSWELL**, Jan. 22, 1761	1	192
Jonathan, s. John & Sarah, b. Apr. 1, 1713	1	195
Jonathan, s. Ebenezer & Abigail, b. Dec. 27, 1740	1	196
Jonathan, s. Ebenezer & Abigail, d. June 1, 1741	1	196
Jonathan, s. James & Hannah, b. Mar. 5, 1741/2	1	196
Jona[than], m. Hannah **BUTT**, June 11, 1772	1	193
Jonathan, m. Rebecca **GEER**, Sept. 11, 1783	1	193
Joseph, s. Jeames & Hannah, b. Oct. 9, 1750	1	197
Jos[eph]*, m. Hannah **JEWETT**, Nov. 14, 1775 (*Probably		
"Ja[me]s")	1	193
Lydia, d. John & Sarah, b. Apr. 3, 1748	1	197
Lydia, d. John & Mercy, b. Feb. 17, 1765	1	199
Lydia, m. Benj[ami]n **BALDWIN**, Dec. 4, 1775	1	71
Mary, d. John & Sarah, b. Apr. 1, 1740	1	196
Mary, d. John & Sarah, d. Oct. 16, 1751	1	206
Mary, d. John & Mercy, b. June 28, 1763	1	199
Mary, m. Lemuel **STEVENS**, Feb. 21, 1782	1	214
Nancy, of Brooklyn, m. Jared **PELLET**, Jan. 10, 1788,		
at Pomfret	1	193
Nathan, s. John & Sarah, b. June 5, 1738	1	196
Ruth, d. James & Hannah, b. Apr. 2, 1747	1	197
Ruth, m. Ezekiel **EATON**, May 6, 1776	1	133
Sarah, d. John & Sarah, b. Feb. 14, 1724/5	1	195
Sarah, d. John & Sarah, b. Nov. 2, 1745	1	197
Sarah, d. John & Sarah, d. Oct. 11, 1751	1	206
Sarah, d. Amos & Elizabeth, b. Oct. 22, 1764	1	199
Sarah, m. Stephen **FROST**, June 6, 1765	1	138
Seth, s. Jona[than] & Hannah, b. July 15, 1773	1	201
Solomon, s. John & Sarah, d. June 17, 1723	1	206
Stephen, s. Jno. & Sarah, b. Feb. 27, 1743/4	1	197
Stephen, s. John & Sarah, d. Oct. 10, 1751	1	206
PLACE, Leona L., m. Eunice J. **LONG**, Jan. 30, (1843), by Rev.		
Asa King	2	64
PLIMPTON, Sarah, d. Jeremiah & Elizabeth, b. Oct. 17, 1709	1	195
Sibbilath, d. Jeremiah & Elizabeth, b. Aug. 20, 1712	1	195
POLLOCK, Edwin, of Windham, m. Ruth **GRIFFIS**, of Canterbury,		
Jan. 14, 1844, by Rev. John F. Blanchard. Witnesses:		

	Vol.	Page
POLLOCK, (cont.)		
Eliza F. Bennett, Eben J. Bennett, Lucy Pollock	2	64
POST, John, m. Sarah **PARKS,** Dec. 12, 1723	1	192
Sarah, m. Timothy **BACKUS,** Jan. 26, 1708/9	1	69
POTTER, Charles W., of Norwich, m. Orilla F. **APPLEY,** of		
Canterbury, May 2, 1841, by Rev. Tubal Wakefield	2	63
Elizabeth, m. Charles E. **PHILLIPS,** b. of Packersville,		
Sept. 19, 1842, by M. Byrne	2	63
PRENTICE, John Dow, s. Ephraim & Mary, b. Aug. 15, 1799	1	204
PRESTON, Asenath, m. Turner **STANTON,** of Lisbon, Jan. 30,		
1837, by Rev. Asa King	2	74
Harvey, s. Samuel & Louisa, b. Jan. 27, 1786	1	202
Henry, s. Joseph & Phebe, b. Feb. 12, 1736/7	1	196
Jacob, s. Jacob & Mary, b. Oct. 28, 1760	1	198
Ruhaunnah, m. Daniel **CANADA,** Nov. 17, 1763	1	101
Samuel, m. Louisa **ABBOTT,** of Windham, Sept. 1, 1785	1	193
PRICE, Marie M., of Plainfield, m. Francis C. **LEWIS,** of		
Canterbury, Apr. 15, 1839, by Rev. Thomas L. Shipman	2	52
PRIDMORE, Thomas, of Parma, N. Y., m. Jerusha **SMITH,** of		
Canterbury, [ ], by Comfort D. Fillmore, Dea.	2	63
PRINCE, Timothy, of Brooklyn, m. Julia **FISK,** of Canterbury,		
Mar. 20, 1844, by Rev. Holmes Slade	2	65
PRIOR, Charles R., of Plainfield, m. Mary A. **MORSE,** of		
Canterbury, Sept. 3, 1850, by Rev. Robert C. Learned	2	65
PROCTOR, Esther, d. John & Sarah, b. Nov. 16, 1734	1	196
Hannah, d. John & Sarah, b. Aug. 19, 1732	1	196
Hannah, d. Nov. 22, 1753	1	206
John, s. John & Sarah, b. Mar. 28, 1737	1	196
John, d. May 18, 1743	1	206
Sarah, m. David **ADAMS,** Nov. 5, 17[ ]	1	51
PUFFER, Esther, m. David **BALDWIN,** May 29, 1774	1	71
Esther, w. Timo[thy], d. Aug. 21, 1805, ae 90	1	208
Hannah, d. Timo[thy] & Esther, b. Apr. 22, 1749	1	200
Olive, d. [Timo[thy] & Esther], b. Dec. 1, 1751	1	200
Timothy, s. [Timo[thy] & Esther], b. June 6, 1756	1	200
-----, wid., d. Nov. 14, 1762	1	207
PUTNAM, Lydia, m. Eleazer **BROWN,** June 21, 1759	1	70
Rebecca, m. Ward **WOODARD,** Oct. 19, 1780	1	236
RANSOM, RAYNSOM, Abigail, m. Jesse **BUTTON,** Dec. 7, 1780	1	71
Betty, d. Robert & Hannah, b. Oct. 27, 1755	1	210
Betty, m. Claghorn **ROBINSON,** Jan. 29, 1777	1	209
Beulah, d. Jona[than] & Leah, b. Feb. 23, 1775	1	211
David, m. Anne **ALLERTON,** Apr. 20, 1777	1	209
Ebenezer, s. Robert & Hannah, b. Apr. 4, 1754	1	210
Ebenezer, s. Robert & Hannah, b. Aug. 17, 1760	1	211
Hannah, m. Jason **HAMMOND,** Apr. 27, 1766	1	155
James D., m. Abigail [ ], Dec. 11, 1843, Westminster		
(Arnold Note: Entry crossed out)	2	64

	Vol.	Page
RANSOM, RAYNSOM, (cont.)		
James D., m. Abigail **SPICER**, Dec. 11, 1843, by Rev. Asa		
King, Westminster	2	68
Jonathan, s. Robert & Hannah, b. Mar. 3, 1749/50	1	210
Jonathan, m. Leah **SPAULDING**, Nov. 24, 1773	1	209
Lois, d. Robert & Hannah, b. May 17, 1770	1	211
Mary, d. Robert & Hannah, b. Sept. 2, 1764	1	211
Olive, d. Robert & Hannah, b. Jan. 7, 1768	1	211
Reuben, s. Robert & Hannah, b. July 18, 1762	1	211
Reuben, s. David & Anne, b. Oct. 28, 1782	1	212
Robert, s. Robert & Hannah, b. Mar. 8, 1752	1	210
Robert, Jr., d. Apr. 13, 1775	1	213
Robert, s. Jona[than] & Leah, b. Sept. 22, 1776	1	211
Robert, s. Sam[ue]l & Rena, b. May 23, 1786	1	212
Rufus, s. Jona[than] & Leah, b. Mar. 16, 1778	1	211
Sally, d. [Sam[ue]l & Sarah], b. June 20, 1783	1	212
Sally, d. Sam[ue]l & Sarah, d. Sept. 2, 1784	1	213
Samuel, m. Sarah **GAVIN**, Nov. 7, 1780	1	209
Samuel, s. David & Anne, b. Jan. 15, 1781	1	212
Samuel, m. Rena **NEFF**, June 23, 1785	1	209
Samuel, s. [Sam[ue]l & Rena], b. Mar. 22, 1788	1	212
Sarah, m. Peter **MORSE**, Nov. 19, 1762	1	181
Sarah, d. Jonathan & Leah, b. Dec. 15, 1779	1	212
Sarah, w. Samuel, d. Dec. 16, 1784	1	213
Thankful, d. Robert & Hannah, b. June 26, 1758	1	211
William, s. Sam[ue]l & Sarah, b. Aug. 6, 1781	1	212
RATHBURN, RATHBOURNE, RATHUN, RATHBONE, Alice,		
d. Jos[eph] & Zilp[ha], b. Oct. 5, 1792	1	212
Asa, s. Tho[ma]s & Abigail, b. Sept. 19, 1756	1	211
Benjamin, s. Joseph & Zilpha, b. June 16, 1786	1	212
Benjamin, m. Naoma **STEVENS**, of Lisbon, Jan. 28, 1790	1	209
Dan[ie]l, s. Joseph & Zilpha, b. Feb. 1, 1780	1	212
Elizabeth, d. [Samuel & Elizabeth], b. Nov. 30, 1759	1	211
Eunice, d. Samuel & Elizabeth, b Feb. 21, 1761	1	211
Job, s. Job & Mary, b. Jan. 22, 1738/9	1	210
John, s. John & Content, b. Oct. 20, 1751	1	210
John, s. Benjamin & Naomi, b. Mar. 3, 1791	1	212
Joseph, s. [Samuel & Elizabeth], b. Dec. 8, 1751	1	211
Joseph, m. Zilpha **STEVENS**, May 2, 1777	1	209
Lois, d. Joseph & Zilpha, b. Sept. 3, 1782	1	212
Lydia, d. Tho[ma]s & Abigail, b. Oct. 3, 1754(?)	1	211
Mary, d. [Samuel & Elizabeth], b. Sept. 28, 1756	1	211
Patience, d. Samuel & Elizabeth, b. Oct. 13, 1749	1	211
Patience, m. Adam **STEVENS**, Oct. 21, 1773	1	214
Rebecca, d. Samuel & Elizabeth, b. Mar. 19, 1763	1	211
Samuel, m. Elizabeth **STEVENS**, Sept. 16, 1747	1	209
Sam[ue]l, s. Joseph & Zilpha, b. Dec. 3, 1777	1	211
Sebil, d. [Samuel & Elizabeth], b. Apr. 7, 1754	1	211

	Vol.	Page
RATHBURN, RATHBOURNE, RATHUN, RATHBONE, (cont.)		
Thomas, m. Abigail **KIMBALL**, Nov. 15, 1755	1	209
Zerviah, d. Tho[ma]s & Abigail, b. Feb. 18, 1759	1	211
Zilpha, d. [Jos[eph] & Zilp]ha], b. Dec. 7, 1793	1	212
RAY, Charles L., of Lisbon, m. Phebe A. **EATON**, of Canterbury,		
Jan. 27, 1850, by Rev. Robert C. Learned	2	69
George, m. Elizabeth **BENNET**, June 6, 1842, by Rev. W.		
Clarke	2	68
RAYMOND, Mary, m. John **KINGSLEY**, b. of Canterbury, Aug.		
22, 1822, by Erastus Learned	2	47
Sarah B., m. Kerby **SAFFORD**, June 8, 1835, by Rev. Asa		
King	2	73
RAYNSFORD, RANSFORD, RAYNESFORD, RAINSFORD,		
Abigail, d. Solomon & Watestill, b. Sept. 18, 1735	1	210
Abigail, d. Joseph & Joanna, b. Nov. 15, 1756	1	211
Abigail, w. Edward, d. May 12, 1763	1	213
Abigail, d. David & Hephzibah, b. May 17, 1780	1	211
Achsah, d. David & Hephzibah, b. Feb. 16, 1782	1	212
Anne, d. Nathan & Esther, b. Feb. 13, 1741	1	210
Anne, d. [Benjamin & Jerusha], b. July 29, 1784	1	212
Atoa, s. [Eli & Lydia], b. Oct. 15, 1834	2	267
Benj[ami]n, s. Ritchard & Zerviah, b. Aug. 23, 1751	1	210
Benj[ami]n, m. Jerusha **LUCE**, July 12, 1781	1	209
David, s. Joseph & Joannah, b. July 22, 1754	1	210
David, m. Hephzibah **FOSTER**, Mar. 17, 1778	1	209
David, s. David & Hephzibah, b. Mar. 3, 1787	1	212
Edward, d. Nathan & Esther, b. Aug. 17, 1738	1	210
Eli, s. Benjamin & Jerusha, b. Feb. 12, 1787	1	212
Eli, m. Lydia **BENNET**, b. of Canterbury, July 23, 1815,		
by Daniel Frost, J. P.	2	68
Elizabeth, d. David & Hephzibah, b. Mar. 17, 1779	1	211
Elizabeth, m. Elisha **WHEELER**, Feb. 9, 1797	1	237
Fanny, d. Benjamin & Jerusha, b. July 25, 1792	1	212
George, s. [Eli & Lydia], b. June 5, 1822	2	267
Hannah, d. Solomon & Watestill, b. Oct. 28, 1736/7	1	210
Harriet Eliza, d. Eli & Lydia, b. Feb. 9, 1817	2	267
Hephzibah Prentice, d. David & Hephzibah, b. Aug. 19, 1797	1	212
Jerusha, w. Benjamin, d. Feb. 20, 1822	2	355
John, s. David & Hannah, b. Jan. 2, 1723/4	1	210
Jonathan, s. David, d. Nov. 6, 1749	1	213
Jonathan, m. Hannah **HIDE**, May 17, 1759	1	209
Joseph, s. Edward & Abigail, b. June 24, 1725	1	210
Joseph, m. Wid. Joanna **GIBSON**, Feb. 4, 1752	1	209
Joseph, s. Joseph & Joanna, b. Nov. 13, 1752	1	210
Joseph, m. Anne **WALDO**, Aug. 3, 1777	1	209
Joshua Waldo, s. Jos[eph], Jr. & Anne, b. July 6, 1779	1	212
Joshua Waldo, m. Hannah **LATHROP**, of Franklin, Apr. 20,		
1800	1	209

	Vol.	Page
RAYNSFORD, RANSFORD, RAYNESFORD, RAINSFORD, (cont.)		
Marthaett, d. [Eli & Lydia], b. Nov. 15, 1831	2	267
Nathan, m. [Esther], July 12, 1737	1	210
Nathan, s. Jonathan & Hannah, b. Oct. 20, 1765	1	211
Polly, d. Joseph, Jr. & Ann, b. Aug. 29, 1781	1	212
Rebecca, d. David & Hephzibah, b. Feb. 14, 1790	1	212
Richard, m. Zerviah **NORWOOD**, Nov. 29, 1750	1	209
Richard, s. Richard & Zerviah, b. Apr. 13, 1755	1	210
Ruby, d. David & Hephzibah, b. Feb. 27, 1784	1	212
Russel[l], s. David & Hephzibah, b. Apr. 14, 1792	1	212
Sibbel, d. Richard & Zerviah, b. Mar. 14, 1753	1	210
Sibbel, d. Benj[ami]n & Jerusha, b. May 26, 1782	1	212
Solomon, m. Watestill **ADAMS**, July [ ], 1735	1	209
Sophia, d. [Eli & Lydia], b. Sept. 12, 1819	2	267
Sophia, m. William **CRAIG**, of Plainfield, Apr. 1, 1838, by Rev. Asa King, Westminster	2	17
Sophia, m. William **CRAIG**, of Plainfield, Apr. 1, 1838, by Rev. Asa King, Westminster	2	40
Sybil, see under Sibbel		
Thomas, s. Solomon & Watestill, b. Nov. 7, 1739	1	210
Waldo, s. [Eli & Lydia], b. Mar. 22, 1825	2	267
Watestill, d. Solomon & Watestill, b. Feb. 18, 1742	1	210
Zervia[h], w. Richard, d. June 2, 1756	1	213
READ, REED, Abijah, m. Anne **WHITE**, Sept. 7, 1773	1	209
Abijah, d. Jan, 20, 1777, at New York, a prisoner	1	213
Alfred, of Warwick, R. I., m. Annis **SMITH**, of Canterbury, May 29, 1831, by Rev. Dennis Platt	2	67
Ammitta, m. David **WELCH**, Mar. 4, 1740/41	1	236
Charity, m. Hezekiah **CAPRON**, May 14, 1761	1	101
Charles Dwight, s. [Jedediah & Lucy], b. Feb. 14, 1831	2	267
Deborah, m. Timothy **RUSS**, Mar. 23, 1769	1	209
Hannah, m. Ebenezer **BAULDING**, Nov. 22, 1744	1	69
Harriet, d. Bela & Betsey, b. June 27, 1799	1	212
Jedediah, m. Lucy **PARRISH**, May 19, 1822, by Jedediah Morse, J. P.	2	67
Martha White, d. Abijah & Anne, b. Mar. 13, 1775	1	211
Orpha, m. Joseph **GARDNER**, Feb. 28, 1823, by Asael Bacon, J. P.	2	35
Roswell Parish, s. Jedediah & Lucy, b. Feb. 18, 1827	2	267
REYNOLDS, RENOLDS, RUNNOLDS, Gilbert B., m. Lydia W. **HOW**, Sept. 9, 1827, by Chester Lyon, J. P.	2	67
Huldah, m. W[illia]m **ROBINSON**, Oct. 20, 1830, by Chester Lyon, J. P.	2	67
Lydia Ann, m. Ripley **WICKS**, b. of Canterbury, Jan. 11, 1846, by Rev. Thomas Tallman	2	41
Robert, m. Constance **ADAMS**, Jan. 28, 1748	1	209
Robert, s. Easther **BATES**, b. Feb. 21, 1748	1	210

	Vol.	Page
READ, REED, (cont.)		
Sarah, d. Robert & Constance, b. June 12, 1748	1	210
RHEADE, [see under **READ**]		
RHOW, [see also **ROE** and **RUE**], Saranna, m. Jedediah or Zeddiah ASHCROFT, Feb. 28, 1744(?)	1	51
RICE, Martin A., of Plainfield, m. Elizabeth D. **AUSTIN**, of Canterbury, Mar. 8, 1840, by Rev. Tubal Wakefield	2	68
RICH, Sarah, m. James **ADAMS**, Feb. 3, 1750/51	1	51
RICHARDS, Abigail, d. Zebulon & Lydia, b. Oct. 10, 1740	1	210
Elizabeth, m. Abijah **BROWN**, Dec. 11, 1744	1	69
John, s. Zebulon & Lydia, b. Sept. 23, 1748	1	210
Lydia, d. Zebulon & Lydia, b. Aug. 17, 1746	1	210
Lydia, of Hampton, m. Harry **BUTTS**, of Brooklyn, Dec. 12, 1822, by Thomas J. Murdock	2	7
Martha M., of Canterbury, m. Rowland **GARDNER**, of Plainfield, Jan. 5, 1845, by Rev. Daniel D. Lyon, of Packerville	2	35
Mehetable, of Norwich, m. Jonathan **DAUICE**, May 20, 1762	1	120
Naomie, m. Benj[ami]n **PEIRCE**, July 11, 1737	1	192
Prescilla, d. Zebulon & Lydia, b. Feb. 11, 1744	1	210
Semiantha, m. John **AUSTIN**, Nov. 28, 1827	1	53
Semianthe, m. John **AUSTIN**, b. of Canterbury, Nov. 28, 1827, by Rev. James R. Wheelock	2	1
Zerviah, d. Zebulon & Lydia, b. Sept. 11, 1742	1	210
RICHARDSON, Abigail, w. Samuel, d. Feb. 28, 1767	1	213
Eunice, m. Joseph **RUST**, May 2, 1759	1	209
Jeremiah, s. Sam[ue]l & Abigail, b. Feb. 1, 1757	1	211
Josiah Cooper, s. Sam[ue]l & Abigail, b. [ ]	1	210
Nathan, s. Sam[ue]l & Abigail, b. Mar. 26, 1759	1	211
Sarah, d. Sam[ue]l & Abigail, b. Dec. 10, 1754	1	210
RICHMOND, Apollos, m. Asenath **WALDO**, May 15, 1836, by Rev. Asa King, Westminster	2	68
RIGHT, [see under **WRIGHT**]		
RIPLEY, Elizabeth, m. John **ADAMS**, Jr., May 8, 179[ ]	1	52
Harriet, d. July 18, 1822	2	355
RIX, Giles E., of Norwich, m. Susan **HYDE**, of Canterbury, Feb. 15, 1849, by Rev. Robert C. Learned	2	68
RIXFORD, Sally, m. John V. **MAIN**, b. of Canterbury, June 8, 1828, by Rev. J. R. Wheelock	2	55
ROBARDSON, Mary, of Killingly, m. Benjamin **SHAW**, Nov. 14, 1763	1	214
ROBBINS, ROBINS, Abigail, m. Jonathan **CARVER**, Oct. 20, 1746	1	100
Annah, d. Nathaniel & Elizabeth, b. Dec. 10, 1716	1	210
Elijah, m. Mary **DEANS**, Apr. 2, 1827, by Andrew T. Judson, J. P.	2	67
Elizabeth, d. Nathaniel & Elizabeth, b. Feb. 19, 1712/13	1	210
Elizabeth, w. Nathaniel, d. Sept. 9, 1729	1	213

	Vol.	Page
ROBBINS, ROBINS, (cont.)		
Erastus, m. Lucy **PARSONS**, Feb. 14, 1833, by Daniel G. Sprague	2	67
Jehiel, s. Nathaniel & Elizabeth, b. Apr. 27, 1719	1	210
John, s. Nathaniel & Elizabeth, b. July 12, 1721	1	210
Mary, d. Nathaniel & Elizabeth, b. Nov. 22, 1714	1	210
Mary, of Brooklyn, m. William M. **DENISON**, of Sterling, May 10, 1835, by Rev. O. C. Whiton	2	21
Patience, m. Eben **SMITH**, Jan. 31, 1743	1	214
Samuel, of Canterbury, m. Sally **HARTSHORN**, of Griswold, Mar. 16, 1834, by Rev. Otis C. Whiton	2	67
ROBERTSON, [see under **ROBARDSON**]		
ROBINSON, Abey M., of Canterbury, m. Lewis **HARRINGTON**, of Killingly, Oct. 20, 1849, by Rev. R. S. Hazen, Westminster	2	42
Asenath, [d. Ralph W. & Mary E.], b. June 6, 1840	2	267
Claghorn, m. Betty **RANSOM**, Jan. 29, 1777	1	209
Elba Haskall, d. Samuel P. & Helen L. G., b. May 12, 1847	2	267
Jemima, m. Aaron **CLEVELAND**, Jr., June 12, 1777	1	101
Keron, [child of Ralph W. & Mary E.], b. May 1, 1844	2	267
Marvins, [s. Ralph W. & Mary E.], b. Dec. 25, 1834	2	267
Mary E., of Canterbury, m. Moseley **CURTIS**, of Windham, Aug. 27, 1834, by Rev. Robert C. Learned	2	20
Mary E., m. Robert D. **FOWLER**, b. of Canterbury, Apr. 8, 1835, by Rev. Otis C. Whiton	2	31
Mehetable, of Canterbury, m. Jabez **PARKHURST**, of Plainfield, Oct. 13, 1842, by Rev. W. Clarke	2	64
Phebe, m. Joseph **ADAMS**, Jr., Mar. 22, 179[ ]	1	52
Prudence, m Jedediah **BREWSTER**, May 19, 1773	1	71
Ralph W., m. Mary E. **WILLIAMS**, Aug. 17, 1834, by Rev. Jesse Fisher	2	67
Remus, [s. Ralph W. & Mary E.], b. June 13, 1837	2	267
Rienzi, [child of Ralph W. & Mary E.]. b. May 31, 1842	2	267
Samuel, d. Aug. 9, 1843	2	355
Tabitha, m. Chauncey **ADAMS**, Jan. 6, 1841, by Rev. Asa King	2	4
W[illia]m, m. Huldah **REYNOLDS**, Oct. 20, 1830, by Chester Lyon, J. P.	2	67
ROCKWELL, Sarah, of Preston, m. Reuben **PARK**, June 10, 1762	1	193
ROE, [see also **RHOW**, and **RUE**], William, d. Mar. 8, 1748/9	1	213
ROGERS, Anson, of Lebanon, m. Jane **MASON**, of Canterbury, Nov. 28, 1822, by Walter Williams, J. P.	2	67
Bixbee, [s. Jethro & Hannah], b. Nov. 9, 1758	1	211
Elizabeth, d. Josiah & Hannah, b. Apr. 8, 1751	1	210
Hannah, d. Jethro & Hannah, b. Dec. 19, 1752	1	211
Hannah, d. Josiah & Hannah, d. Feb. 6, 1753	1	213
Joseph [W]right, s. Jethro & Hannah, b. June 10, 1764	1	211
Josiah, s. Josiah & Hannah, b. May 17, 1753	1	210

	Vol.	Page

ROBERS, (cont.)

Josiah, s. Jethro & Hannah, b. Dec. 14, 1760 — 1 — 211

Lydia, m. John **DODGE**, Oct. 23, 1748 — 1 — 120

Mary, m. Eliphalet **FARNUM**, Oct. 11, 1750 — 1 — 138

Mary, d. Jethro & Hannah, b. Nov. 23, 1750 — 1 — 210

Sarah, d. Jethro & Hannah, b. Oct. 30, 1754 — 1 — 211

ROOD, [see under **RUDE**]

ROUSE, Anne, m. Alpheas **MORSE**, Jan. 6, 1791 — 1 — 181

Reuben, Jr., m. Rosilla W. **HORTON**, Nov. 17, 1837, by Rev. C. J. Warren — 2 — 68

RUDD, Patience, m. Thomas **PARK**, June 9, 1743 — 1 — 192

RUDE, ROOD, Abigail, of Norwich, m. John **GREEN**, of Veffer Co. N. Y., Dec. 27, 1762 — 1 — 149

Betsey Steadman, d. James & Hannah, b. Mar. 16, 1809 — 1 — 212

Lois, m. Elijah **BAKER**, Jan. 29, 1750/51 — 1 — 69

Mercy, m. Benj[ami]n **PARRISH**, Jan. 29, 1735/6 — 1 — 192

Robert, s. Oliver & Silence, b. Mar. 20, 1741/2 — 1 — 210

RUE, [see also **RHOW** and **ROE**], Jonathan Fairle, s. Elizabeth **GREEN**, b. Dec. 2, 1784 — 1 — 212

RUNNOLDS, [see under **REYNOLDS**]

RUSS, Ebenezer, s. Joseph & Eunice, b. Mar. 21, 1764 — 1 — 211

Esther, m. Edmund **AUSTIN**, Dec. 24, 1772 — 1 — 52

Hannah, m. Peter **BUTTON**, of Hopkinton, June 15, 1768 — 1 — 70

Hannah, m. Jedediah **GREEN**, Feb. 22, 1774 — 1 — 149

Jedediah, s. Timo[thy] & Deborah, b. June 22, 1769 — 1 — 211

Mary, d. Timothy & Deborah, b. Sept. 13, 1771 — 1 — 211

Timothy, m. Deborah **REED**, Mar. 23, 1769 — 1 — 209

----, infant child of Joseph & Eunice, d. Nov. 1, 1761 — 1 — 213

----, infant child [of Joseph & Eunice], d. Nov. 26, 1761 — 1 — 213

RUSSELL, RUSSEL, Jacob, of New York City, m. Abby W. **HYDE**, of Canterbury, Nov. 5, 1849, by Rev. Isaac H. Coe — 2 — 69

RUSSELL, Lydia M., m. William W. **WILLIAMS**, b. of Scituate, R. I., May 27, 1851, by Rev. Robert C. Learned — 2 — 90

Mary, of Hartford, m. George W. **ALLEN**, May 3, 1832 — 1 — 53

Mary, of Hartford, m. George W. **ALLEN**, of Canterbury, May 3, 1832, by Ebenezer Allen, J. P. — 2 — 2

Samuel, s. Samuel & Diana, b. June 29, 1797 — 1 — 212

RUST, Amasa, s. Joseph & Eunice, b. June 19, 1760 — 1 — 211

Joseph, m. Eunice **RICHARDSON**, May 2, 1759 — 1 — 209

----, 2d infant, d. Joseph & Eunice, b. Oct. 22, 1761 — 1 — 211

SABIN, Ecater, of Norwich m. W[illia]m **BREWSTER**, Jan. 16, 1752 — 1 — 69

SAFFORD, Abigail, d. [Josiah & Deborah], b. Sept. 15, 176[ ] — 1 — 221

Adaline, [d. Joseph], b. Feb. 18, 1822 — 2 — 272

Albert R., [s. Joseph], b. May 3, 1838 — 2 — 272

Benjamin Smith, s. Roswell & Esther, b. Sept. 18, 1798 — 1 — 224

David, s. Jos[eph] & Lydia, b. Nov. 21, 175[ ] — 1 — 221

	Vol.	Page
SAFFORD, (cont.)		
Dwight, [s. Joseph], b. Apr. 3, 1819	2	272
Epaphais, s. [Joseph & Lydia], b. May 1, 1771	1	222
Ephraim, s. [Joseph & Lydia], b. May 9, 1769	1	222
Ephraim, m. Dolly **MORGAN**, Nov. 14, 1793	1	215
Eph[rai]m Sprague, s. Josiah & Deborah, b. May 31, 176[ ]	1	221
Fanny, [d. Joseph], b. Jan. 18, 1811	2	272
Fanny, of Canterbury, m. Levi C. **CORNING**, of Lisbon, Mar. 25, 1832, by Rev. Demis Platt	2	16
George W., [s. Joseph], b. Dec. 28, 1823	2	272
Halsey, m. Mary E. **SAFFORD**, Feb. 19, 1837, by Rev. Asa King	2	74
Harriet, [d. Joseph], b. Jan. 2, 1810	2	272
Harriet, m. Charles A. **SCHOVEL**, Aug. [ ], 1829, by Rev. Geo[rge] S. White	2	72
Henrietta, d. Rufus & Mary, b. June 13, 1787	1	223
Henrietta, m. John **PHINNEY**, Apr. 10, 1806	1	194
Henrietta, [d. Joseph], b. Feb. 23, 1821	2	272
Henrietta, m. Mason **MORSE**, Oct. 16, 1837, by Rev. Asa King, Westminster	2	56
Henrietta, m. Frederick **DOW**, of Coventry, Oct. 17, 1841, by Rev. Asa King, Westminster	2	22
Jabez(?), s. [Joseph & Lydia], b. Nov. 7, 1766	1	222
Jabez, m. Susanna **DELAP**, Nov. 27, 1794	1	215
Jabez Ensworth, s. Jabez & Susanna, b. Jan. 21, 1798	1	224
James, s. Jabez & Susanna, b. Sept. 6, 1806	1	225
James, m. Eveline **ADAMS**, b. of Canterbury, Aug. 29, 1830, by Rev. Dennis Platt	2	72
Jason, s. Jabez & Susanna, b. Jan. 6, 1805	1	225
Jerusha Smith, d. Roswell & Esther, b. Aug. 6, 1802	1	225
John, s. Joseph & Lyd[i]ah, b. Aug. 27, 1762	1	220
John, s. [John & Rachel], b. Jan. 7, 1792	1	224
John, [s. Joseph], b. Oct. 25, 1827	2	272
Joseph, m. Lydia **ENSWORTH**, Apr. 25, 1753	1	214
Joseph, s. [Joseph & Lydia], b. Jan. 16, 1757	1	219
Joseph, m. Polly **KINGSLEY**, Jan. 24, 1831, by Rev. Dennis Platt	2	72
Julia Eveline, of Canterbury, m. Samuel A. **CHURCH**, of Hartford, Dec. 26, 1852, by Rev. Robert C. Learned	2	19
Laura, d. Reuben & Mary, b. Mar. 15, 1831	2	271
Lucretia, d. [John & Rachel], b. June 6, 1788	1	224
Lucretia, [d. Joseph], b. June 10, 1815	2	272
Lucretia, of Canterbury, m. Harvey **PARKHURST**, of Plainfield, May 29, 1832, by Rev. Dennis Platt	2	61
Lucretia M., m. Henry P. **HATCH**, Sept. 13, 1840, by Rev. Asa King, Westminster	2	41
Lucy, d. [Ephraim & Dolly], b. Jan. 7, 1798	1	224
Lucy W., m Joseph B. **ENSWORTH**, Mar. 10, 1839, by		

	Vol.	Page
SAFFORD, (cont.)		
Rev. Asa King, Westminster	2	27
Lury, d. Joseph & Tryphena, b. Nov. 4, 1791	1	225
Luther, m. Mehetable **LESTER**, May 28, 1834, by Rev. Otis		
C. Whiton	2	73
Lydia, d. Joseph & Lydia, b. Jan. 28, 1754	1	219
Lydia, d. Reuben & Mercy, b. Dec. 22, 1832	2	271
Lydia N., [d. Joseph], b. Dec. 6, 1832	2	272
Maria, m. Reuben **PARK**, Jr., Dec. 8, 1796	1	193
Maria, d. [Ephraim & Dolly], b. June 29, 1800	1	224
Mary, d. [Joseph & Lydia], b. Sept. 21, 1760	1	219
Mary, d. Rufus & Mary, b. Feb. 22, 1801	1	224
Mary, of Canterbury, m. Warren **FITCH**, of Tolland, Nov.		
16, 1820 by [ ]	2	31
Mary, d. Jabez, d. Aug. 6, 1825	2	357
Mary E., m. Halsey **SAFFORD**, Feb. 19, 1837, by Rev. Asa		
King	2	74
Morgan, s. Eph[rai]m & Dolly, b. Dec. 18, 1805	1	225
Nelson, [s. Joseph], b. Feb. 11, 1818	2	272
Oliver, s. Thomas & Ruth, b. July 25, 1808	1	226
Oliver, s. Thomas & Ruth, b. July 25, 1808	1	245
Rachel, of Canterbury, m. James L. **MORGAN**, of Windham,		
Dec. 13, 1831, by Rufus Johnson, Jr., J. P.	2	55
Reuben, s. Ephraim & Dolly, b. Feb. 21, 1796	1	224
Reuben, m. Mary **ADAMS**, b. of Canterbury, May 23, 1830,		
by Rev. Israel G. Rose, of Westminster	2	72
Roswell, s. [Joseph & Lydia], b. Aug. 22, 1775	1	222
Roswell, m. Esther **SMITH**, Oct. 12, 1797	1	215
Rufus, s. [Joseph & Lydia], b. Sept. 4, 1755	1	219
Rufus, s. Jabez & Susanna, b. June 1, 1800	1	224
Sally, [d. Joseph], b. July 8, 1816	2	272
Sally, m. Gordon **ADAMS**, Sept. 27, 18[ ]	1	52
Sarah, d. Jonathan & Susanna, b. Jan. 22, 1765	1	220
Sarah, d. [Joseph & Lydia], b. Sept. 17, 1773	1	222
Sarah, m. Josiah **PARK**, Apr. 9, 1795	1	193
Sarah, m. George W. **HOLBROOK**, of Pomfret, Nov. 28,		
1833, by Rev. Asa King, Westminster	2	35
Seth S., of Windham, m. Emeline L. **BACON**, of Canterbury,		
Oct. 21, 1832, by Rev. Dennis Platt	2	73
Susanna, d. Jonathan & Susanna, b. July 13, 1762	1	220
Susanna, d. Jabez & Susanna, b. May 15, 1796	1	223
Susannah, w. Jabez, d. Aug. 29, 1832	2	357
Thomas, s. John & Rachel, b. Feb. 8, 1785	1	224
Thomas, m. Ruth **WALDO**, [ ], 1806	1	237
Triphena, wid. Joseph, d. Feb. 4, 1826	2	357
Truman, s. Ephraim & Dolly, b. Aug. 22, 1803	1	225
William, s. Joseph & Lydia, b. Oct. 3, 1764	1	222
William, s. Joseph & Lydia, d. Aug. 29, 1778,		

	Vol.	Page
SAFFORD, (cont.)		
by a fall from a stack of straw which he had been making	1	228
William, s. Rufus & Mary, b. Jan. 13, 1784, in Bolton	1	223
William, s. Rufus & Mary, d. Sept. 1, 179[ ]	1	228
William, s. Roswell & Esther, b. Nov. 5, 1800	1	224
William, m. Julia **BACON**, b. of Canterbury, Nov. 24,		
1824, by Rev. Tho[ma]s J. Murdock	2	71
SALTER, John W., of Mansfield, m. Harriet L. **STEDMAN**, of		
Hampton, Sept. 25, 1825, by Rev. Tho[ma]s J. Murdock	2	71
SANFORD, Caleb, of Griswold, m. Loiza **WOODWARD**, Apr. 10,		
1842, by Rev. Asa King, Westminster	2	74
SANGER, Ebenezer Chaffee, s. Ebenezer & Olive, b. Apr. 11, 1816	2	271
George, s. Eben[eze]r & Eunice, b. May 13, 1825	2	271
Hannah, d. Eben[eze]r & Eunice, b. Dec. 12, 1829	2	271
Luther, s. Eben[eze]r & Olive, b. Apr. 21, 1818	2	271
Luther, of Plainfield, m. Lucy Ann **BETTEY**, of Brooklyn,		
Apr. 1, 1845, by Z. Baker	2	75
Luther, m. Harriet **FRANCES**, b. of Canterbury, June 7,		
1847, by Tho[ma]s L. Shipman, Jewett City	2	76
Marvin H., s. Eben[eze]r & Eunice, b. Apr. 12, 1827	2	271
Olive Chaffee, d. Eben[eze]r & Eunice, b. Aug. 17, 1832	2	271
William Wallace, s. Ira & Mary, b. Aug. 10, 1819	1	226
SANSAMON, Isaac, s. [Isaac & Elizabeh (Indians)], b. May 27,		
1751; d. Mar. 27, 1752	1	217
Isaac, d. June 27, 1752	1	217
Jonas, s. Isaac & Elizabeth (Indians), b. Apr. 20, 1744	1	217
Nathan[ie]l, s. [Isaac & Elizabeth (Indians)], b. Apr. 9, 1748	1	217
SATTERLEE, Noah, s. Nath[anie]l & Deborah, b. Jan. 16, 1773	1	221
Samuel, s. Nath[anie]l & Deborah, b. Apr. 5, 1771(?)	1	221
SAUNDERS, Edwin Clarke, m. Lydia **SHAW**, Mar. 2, 1767	1	214
Hannah, d. Edward Clark & Lydia, b. Feb. 25, 1771	1	221
Lydia, d. Edward Clark & Lydia, b. Jan. 27, 1773	1	221
Noah, of Glastonbury, m. Frances E. **BINGHAM**, of		
Canterbury, Nov. 25, 1852, by R. S. Hazen	2	76
SAWYER, Kezia, m. Daniel **FOSTER**, Apr. 1, 1765	1	138
SCHELLINGER, [see under **SKILLINGER**]		
SCHOVEL, Charles A., m. Harriet **SAFFORD**, Aug. [ ], 1829, by		
Rev. Geo[rge] S. White	2	72
SCOT[T], Elizabeth, d. Henry & Mary, b. Aug. 3, 1726	1	216
Elizabeth, d. Henry & Mary, b. Aug. 4, 1726	1	217
John, s. Henry & Mary, b. Aug. 21, 1728	1	217
[**SCOVILL**], [see under **SCHOVEL**]		
SEARL, **SEARLS**, John, d. Sept. 8, 1755, in battle at Lake		
George. Soldier	1	227
Tho[ma]s, s. John & Abigail, b. Oct. 14, 1754	1	218
SEARY, Elizabeth, m. Ebenezer (?) **ADAMS**, Oct. 11, 1744	1	51
SHARP, **SHARPE**, Abigail Hide, d. Willard, b. Apr. 10, 1812	1	225
Harriet A. N., m. John W. **KENDALL**, Feb. 26, 1843, by		

	Vol.	Page
SHARP, SHARPE, (cont.)		
Rev. Asa King	2	47
Huldah, m. Ithamer **WOODARD**, Nov. 23, 1773	1	236
Jennette, of Canterbury, m. Charles **DORRANCE**, of Brooklyn,		
Feb. 26, 1849, by Rev. Robert C. Learned	2	23
Lucy, m. Nathan **DEAN**, Nov. 16, 1774	1	120
Sarah Ann, m. Ebenezer **STORER**, May 10, 1835, by Rev.		
Asa King	2	73
SHAVAULEER, Abner, s. Elias & Mary, b. July 22, 1747	1	218
SHAW, Benjamin, m. Mary **ROBARDSON**, of Killingly, Nov. 14,		
1763	1	214
Benjamin, s. Benj[ami]n & Mary, b. Dec. 1, 177[ ]	1	221
Darius, s. [Jona[than] & Martha], b. Dec. 29, 17[ ]	1	221
Deidama, d. Benj[ami]n & Mary, b. Dec. 8, 17[ ]	1	220
Eben[eze]r, s. [Jona[than] & Martha], b. Dec. 25, 1765	1	221
Elias, s. Jonathan & Martha, b. May 21, 1762	1	220
Elizabeth, d. Jan. 21, 1782, ae 81	1	228
Eunice, m. Daniel **BROWN**, Aug. 29, 1769	1	71
John, s. Jonathan & Martha, b. July 15, 1760	1	220
Jonathan, m. Martha **WEEKS**, Dec. 4, 1759	1	214
Jona[than], s. Jona[than] & Martha, b. June 25, 1773	1	221
Joseph, s. William & Elizabeth, d. Jan. 12, 176[ ]	1	227
Joseph, s. [Benj[ami]n & Mary], b. Jan. 3, 1768	1	220
Lucy, d. Jona[than] & Martha, b. July 17, 17[ ]	1	221
Lydia, m. Edward Clarke **SAUNDERS**, Mar. 2, 1767	1	214
Martha, d. Jona[than] & Martha, b. Aug. 23, 1775	1	222
Mary, m. William **ASPENWALL**, Jan. 5, 177[ ]	1	52
Samuel, s. Benjamin & Mary, b. Feb. 9, 1775	1	222
Samuel, s. Benj[ami]n & Mary, b. Sept. 1, 1780	1	222
William, d. Aug. 23, 1763	1	227
---love, d. Jona[than] & Martha, b. Nov. 28, 1770	1	221
SHELDING, Charles, m. Sibbel **PARK**, Dec. 13, 1774	1	214
SHEPARD, SHEPERD, Benjamin, m. Hannah **GOODALE**, Nov.		
24, 1748	1	214
David, s. Benjamin & Martha, b. Mar. 19, 1761	1	219
David, s. Whitmore & Clarissa, b. Jan. 17, 1785	1	223
Dorcas, d. Benj[ami]n & Hannah, b. May 2, 1751	1	218
Elisha, s. Henry & Esther, b. Oct. 4, 1772	1	221
Esther, m. Isaac **BACKUS**, Sept. 21, 1786	1	72
Hannah, d. Benj[ami]n & Hannah, b. May 29, 1753	1	217
Hannah, d. Benjamin & Hannah, b. June 30, 1757	1	219
Hannah, w. Benj[amin], d. July 26, 1757	1	227
Hannah, m. Joseph **MOORE**, Nov. 2, 1785	1	181
Harriet, m. Rufus **WALDO**, b. of Canterbury, Mar. 20, 1823,		
by Thomas J. Murdock	2	85
Henry, s. Benj[ami]n & Hannah, b. Aug. 26, 1749	1	218
Julia B., of Canterbury, m. Edward E. **HILL**, of Plainfield,		
May 13, 1851, by Rev. Joseph P. Brown, Plainfield	2	100

	Vol.	Page
SHEPARD, SHEPERD, (cont.)		
Lucy, d. Nathan & Susanna, b. Aug. 14, 1753	1	216
Lucy, d. Benjamin & Martha, b. Oct. 10, 1758	1	219
Lydia, of Plainfield, m. Samuel **HUTCHINS**, Feb. 12, 1811	1	156
Mary, m. Jacob **JOHNSON**, June 14, 1722	1	167
Mary E., of Canterbury, m. James **PIKE**, of Sterling, May 1, 1853, by Rev. Robert C. Learned	2	66
Mary Hannah, d. Sylvanus & Esther, b. Nov. 6, 1838	2	272
Samuel, s. Squier & Sarah, b. Feb. 2, 1760	1	220
Samuel, m. Alice **WEAVER**, Mar. 20, 1826, by Asael Bacon, J. P.	2	71
Sarah, d. Squier & Sarah, b. May 4, 1762	1	220
Susanna, m. James **HEBBARD**, Aug. 15, 1773	1	155
Timothy, s. Squier & Sarah, b. June 18, 1764	1	220
Whitmore, s. Benjamin & Martha, b. Aug. 12, 1761	1	220
SHERMAN, Mary L., m. Edward **TYLER**, Oct. 13, 1850, by Rev. Robert C. Learned	2	80
SHIRTLEY, Mary, m. Benjamin **BROWN**, Mar. 24, 1735	1	69
SHIRTLOFF, Mehetable, m. Daniel **TYLOR**, Sept. 16, 1742	1	229
SHOLES, Emily F., of Canterbury, m. Samuel **WEEKS**, of Pomfret, Sept. 19, 1841, by Samuel S. Hough, J. P.	2	87
SILSBURY, [see also **SYLSBY**], Roxalena, m. Daniel **BROWN**, Sept. 9, 1794	1	72
SIMMS, SIMS, SYMES, Abigail, d. John & Mary, d. Sept. 11, 179[ ]	1	228
Benjamin, [twin with Joseph], s. Jno. & Mary, b. Sept. 3, 1773	1	221
Benjamin, m. Mehetable **WHITE**, June 22, 1797	1	215
Chester, s. William & Eunice, b. Oct. 13, 1790	1	223
Dan, s. John & Mary, b. Aug. 3, 1770	1	221
Dan, s. John & Mary, d. Feb. 10, 1785	1	228
Dan, s. William Throop & Eunice, b. Mar. 9, 1789	1	223
Derius, s. John & Mary, b. Mar. 26, 1763	1	220
Ephraim Fitch, s. Joseph & Phebe, b. Apr. 24, 1803	1	225
Hannah Morse, d. Benj[ami]n & Mehetable, b. Dec. 31, 1799	1	224
Jeptha, s. Joseph & Phebe, b. Jan. 1, 1808	1	225
John, m. Mary **STEVENS**, Apr. 12, 1762	1	214
John, s. John & Mary, b. Dec. 18, 1764	1	220
John, m. Mary **ADAMS**, Apr. 29, 1784	1	214
John White, s. Benjamin & Mehetable, b. Oct. 19, 1797	1	224
Joseph, [twin with Benjamin], s. Jno. & Mary, b. Sept. 3, 1773	1	221
Joseph, m. Phebe **FITCH**, of Coventry, June 16, 1802	1	215
Josiah, s. John & Mary, b. Oct. 7, 1780	1	222
Mary, d. John & Mary, d. June 3, 1784	1	228
Mary, d. Benjamin & Mehetable, b. Aug. 4, 1805	1	225
Polly, d. John & Mary, b. Sept. 17, 1784	1	223
Ralph, s. Benjamin & Mehetable, b. Sept. 9, 1802	1	225
Ruth, d. Joseph & Ruth, b. Oct. 4, 1800	1	224
Ruth, d. Joseph & Ruth, d. Oct. 8, 180[ ]	1	228

	Vol.	Page
SIMMS, SIMS, SYMES, (cont.)		
Ruth, w. Joseph, d. Oct. 10, 1800	1	228
Ruth Cutler, d. [Joseph & Phebe], b. Aug. 27, 1804	1	225
Salla, d. John & Mary, b. Sept. 7, 1785	1	223
Sally, m. Thomas **CUTLER**, Apr. 14, 1801(?)	1	102
Troop, s. John & Mary, b. Nov. 18, 176[ ]	1	221
Troop, s. John & Mary, d. Sept. 6, 1767(?). Drowned	1	227
Viscount Nelson, twin child, s. Benjamin & Mehetable,		
b. Jan. 22, 1808 (See also Jeptha)	1	225
William Troop, s. [John & Mary], b. July 6, 176[ ]	1	221
William Throop, m. Eunice **LYON**, Nov. 16, 1788	1	215
William Throop, d. Oct. 30, 179[ ]	1	228
----ail, d. John & Mary, b. May 21, 1776	1	222
-----, s. John & Mary, b. June 24, 1778	1	222
SIMONDS, SIMONS, Abel, s. Francis & Zipporah, b. Oct. 16,		
1752	1	217
Amos, s. Frances & Zipporah, b. Apr. 7, 1761	1	219
Ebenezer, s. Francis & Zipporah, b. Nov. 29, 1754	1	218
Frances, m. Zipporah **CLEVELAND**, Nov. 19, 1750	1	214
Lydia, d. Francis & Zipporah, b. Feb. 4, 1750/51	1	218
Lidia, d. Frances & Zipporah, d. Aug. 9, 1755	1	227
Lydeah, d. Francis & Zipporah, b. Oct. 20, 1763	1	220
Lydiah, d. Francis & Zip[po]rah, b. Oct. 20, 1763	1	143
Molly, d. Francis & Zipporah, b. Sept. 20, 1756	1	219
Reuben, s. Francis & Zipporah, b. Mar. 1, 1759	1	219
SKILLINGER, SCHELLINGER, Daniel, s. Daniel & Lois, b. Mar.		
12, 1757	1	219
Elisha Paine, s. Daniel & Lois, b. Apr. 22, 1759	1	219
SKINNER, Mercy, wid. Jos[eph], d. Sept. 22, 1787(?)	1	228
Samuel, m. Betsey **OLDS**, Nov. 27, 1845, by Rev. Henry J.		
Coe	2	75
SLY, Charles L., of Addison, N. Y., m. Jane J. **FARNHAM**, of		
Canterbury, Oct. 18, 1847, by Rev. Thomas Tallman	2	75
SMITH, Aaron, s. Jedediah & Abiel, b. Sept. 4, 1747	1	217
Abigail, d. Henry & Hannah, b. Oct. 15, 1722	1	216
Abigail, d. Tho[ma]s & Abigail, d. Nov. 16, 174[ ].		
(Shoud be "Abigail **SPAULDING**". Corrected by L. B.		
B.)	1	227
Abigail, had s. Rufus **CARPENTER**, b. May 22, 1746	1	107
Abigail, d. Jacob & Mary, b. Mar. 2, 1749/50	1	218
Abigail, [twin with Zerviah], d. John & Mary, b. June 13, 1753	1	219
Abigail, d. John & Mary, d. June 27, 17[ ]	1	227
Abraham, s. Jere[mia]h & Martha, b. May 11, 1825	2	271
Abram, s. Jeremiah B. & Martha, b. May 11, 1825	2	272
Actisah, d. [Ichabod & Actisah], b. June 25, 1816	1	226
Achsah Ann, m. George **BALDWIN**, b. of Canterbury, Nov.		
30, 1837, by Rev. Joseph Ayer, of Lisbon	2	11
Adeline, d. [Asher & Lucinda], b. Feb. 5, 1826	2	271

	Vol.	Page
SMITH, (cont.)		
Adeline, of Canterbury, m. Elisha T. **BOLLES,** of Ashford,		
Nov. 5, 1849, by Rev. R. S. Hazen, Westminster	2	14
Ahirah, s. [Ichabod & Actisah], b. June 20, 1807	1	226
Ahira, m. Caroline E. **PELLET,** b. of Canterbury, Oct. 19,		
1828, by Rev. J. R. Wheelock	2	72
Albert, s. Roger & Alice, b. July 17, 1798	1	224
Alice, d. Jedediah & Abiel, b. Feb. 6, 1745	1	217
Alice, d. Ebenezer & Patience, b. May 16, 1753	1	217
Alice, twin with Annis, d. [Roger & Alice], b. May 8, 1805	1	225
Almond Augustus, s. W[illia]m S. & Amelia, b. Sept. 21, 1816	1	225
Anna, w. Joseph, Jr., d. July 30, 1751	1	227
Anna, m. Elijah **PARK,** Mar. 16, 1780	1	193
Anna, m. Capt. Hezekiah M. **BAKER,** Mar. 30, 1830, by		
Walter Williams, J. P.	2	8
Anne, d. Joseph & Anne, b. July 26, 1751	1	218
Annis, twin with Alice, d. [Roger & Alice], b. May 8, 1805	1	225
Annis, of Canterbury, m. Alfred **READ,** of Warwick, R. I.,		
May 29, 1831, by Rev. Dennis Platt	2	67
Asa, s. Ebenezer & Patience, b. Feb. 19, 1751	1	218
Asa, s. Moses & Mary, b. Nov. 13, 1757	1	219
Asa, s. Richard & Olive, b. Sept. 3, 1772	1	221
Asa, m. Sarah **LEACH,** Apr. 16, 1777	1	214
Asahel A., s. [Ichabod & Actisah], b. Oct. 20, 1809	1	226
Asher, s. [Nath[anie]l & Lucy], b. Oct. 19, 1787	1	225
Austin, [s. Jeremiah B. & Martha], b. Mar. 16, 1831	2	272
Benajah, s. James & Mary, b. Jan. 2, 1712	1	216
Benjamin, s. James & Mary, b. Mar. 8, 1709	1	216
Benjamin, s. James & Mary, b. Mar. 8, 1710	1	216
Benjamin, [twin with Joseph], s. Joseph & Elizabeth, b.		
Jan. 14, 1716/17	1	216
Benjamin, s. Jacob & Mary, b. Feb. 20, 1759	1	219
Benjamin, s. John & Mary, b. Dec. 31, 1761	1	220
Benjamin, Jr., m. Sarah **LYON,** Sept. 22, 1785	1	215
Betsey, d. Benjamin, Jr. & Sarah, b. Jan. 18, 1787	1	223
Betsey, d. Walter & Lydia, b. Oct. 26, 1806	1	225
Betsey, m. Benjamin **WILLIAMS,** Oct. 29, 1807	1	237
Betsey, m. Edwin S. **PHINNEY,** Nov. 18, 1829, by Rev.		
Israel G. Rose, of Westminster	2	61
Chester, of Rochester, Vt., m. Sarah M. **SMITH,** of		
Canterbury, Dec. 2, 1850, by Rev. R. S. Hazen, of		
Westminster	2	76
Dan, s. Joseph & Anne, b. Feb. 3, 1748/9	1	218
David, s. Joseph & Elizabeth, b. Apr. 8, 1721	1	216
David, s. Jacob & Penninah, b. May 23, 1758	1	219
David, of East Douglass, Mass., m. Malissa **FAULKNER,** of		
Canterbury, Nov. 6, 1853, by Rev. Robert C. Learned	2	76
David Augustus, s. Jairus & Sarah, b. Dec. 26, 1787	1	223

	Vol.	Page
SMITH, (cont.)		
Desire, d. [Ichabod & Actisah], b. Aug. 26, 1811	1	226
Eben, m. Patience **ROB[B]INS**, Jan. 31, 1743	1	214
Ebenezer, s. Richard & Mary, b. Feb. 17, 1723/4	1	216
Eben[eze]r, s. Eben[eze]r & Patience, b. Apr. 13, 1745	1	218
Ebenezer, s. Ebenezer & Patience, d. Oct. 4, 1749	1	227
Ebenezer, d. Sept. 8, 1755, in the Army at Lake George.		
Soldier	1	227
Ebenezer, s. John & Mary, b. July 17, 1758	1	219
Ebenezer, s. Asa & Sarah, b. Nov. 25, 1777	1	222
Ebenezer, m. Hephzibah **TOOLEY**, of Bozrah, Oct. 13, 1799	1	215
Edmund, s. [John & Emeline], b. Nov. 8, 1833	2	271
Eleazer, s. Elipha **PARK**, Nov. 16, 1787	1	215
Eleizer, s. Eleizer & Eliphah, b. Feb. 21, 1797	1	224
Eleazer, Jr., of Lisbon, m. Susan **SMITH**, of Canterbury,		
Dec. 26, 1826, by Israel G. Rose	2	71
Elizabeth, d. Moses & Mary, b. Apr. 18, 1751	1	217
Elizabeth, m. John **HERRICK**, Sept. 27, 1753	1	155
Elizabeth, d. Jacob & Mary, b. Sept. 24, 1754	1	218
Elizabeth, m. Asa **LEFFINGWELL**, Nov. 12, 1771	1	176
Elizabeth, wid. Joseph, d. June 11, 1778	1	228
Elkanah, s. Jacob & Penninah, b. Apr. 10, 1760	1	219
Erastus, of Hartford, m. Mary Anne **WOODARD**, of		
Canterbury, June 27, 1839, by Rev. Charles J. Warren	2	74
Esther, d. John & Mary, b. Dec. 5, 1777	1	222
Esther, m. Roswell **SAFFORD**, Oct. 12, 1797	1	215
Esther, d. [Roger & Alice], b. Nov. 16, 1802	1	225
Esther, d. Roger & Alice, d. Mar. 7, 1809	1	228
Esther, of Canterbury, m. Pearley B. **FULLER**, of Lisbon,		
June 3, 1835, by Rev. Levi Nelson	2	31
Easter Palmer, d. Roger & Alice, b. July 1, 1811	1	225
Eunice Bingham, d. Ahira & Caroline, b. Sept. 12, 1831	2	271
Ezra, s. Moses & Mary, b. Nov. 28, 1748	1	218
Fuller, s. Nath[anie]l & Lucy, b. Sept. 11, 1785	1	225
Hannah, d. Henry & Hannah, b. Oct. 5, 1712	1	216
Hannah, d. Jedediah & Abiel, b. July 13, 1729	1	217
Hannah, d. Jacob & Mary, b. May 22, 1748	1	218
Hannah, w. Henry, d. Dec. 11, 1763	1	227
Harriet Lucinda, d. [Asher & Lucinda], b. July 16, 1823	2	271
Harriet W., d. John & Emeline, b. July 15, 1831	2	271
Henrietta, m. James **McDONALD**, Feb. 1, 1827, by Sam[uel]		
L. Hough, J. P.	2	55
Henry, s. Jedediah & Abiel, b. Feb. 8, 1739	1	217
Henry, d. Jan. (?) 28, 1773	1.	227
Henry, s. Walter & Lydia, b. Nov. 9, 1802	1	225
Henry(?), s. Walter & Lydia, d. Aug. 12, 1813	1	228
Henry, of New York, m. Mehetable **ADAMS**, of Canterbury,		
Dec. 21, 1831, by Rev. Dennis Platt	2	72

	Vol.	Page
SMITH, (cont.)		
Hudson, [s. Jeremiah B. & Martha], b. Nov. 18, 1841	2	272
Jacob, m. Mary **HIDE**, Dec. 27, 1742	1	214
Jacob, m. Penimah **FULLER**, Jan. 23, 1758	1	214
Jacob, d. Apr. 27, 1765	1	227
Jacob, d. Feb. 26, 1782	1	228
Jairus, m. Sarah **PAINE**, Aug. 2, 1787	1	215
Jairus, s. Jairus & Sarah, b. Apr. 26, 1792	1	223
James, s. James & Mary, b. Dec. 17, 1704	1	216
James, s. Jacob & Mary, b. Dec. 20, 1756	1	219
Jason, s. Ishabod & Actisah, b. July 26, 1805	1	226
Jatham Graves, s. Asher & Lucinda, b. Nov. 23, 1814	1	225
Jedediah, s. Henry & Hannah, b. Dec. 24, 1706	1	216
Jedediah, s. Jedediah & Abiel, b. Aug. 2, 1734	1	217
Jedediah, s. Moses & Mary, b. Apr. 18, 1753	1	217
Jeremiah, s. John & Mehetable, b. June 21, 1748	1	218
Jeremiah, m. Ruth **KENNEDY**, May 19, 1818	1	215
Jeremiah Bingham, s. Roger & Alice, b. Aug. 30, 1793	1	223
Jerusha, d. John & Mary, b. Sept. 11, 1764	1	220
Jerusha(?), d. John & Mary, d. May 12, 179[ ]	1	228
Jerusha, d. [Ichabod & Actisah], b. Mar. 20, 1814	1	226
Jerusha, b. Canterbury, m. Thomas **PRIDMORE**, of Parma,		
N. Y., [ ], by Dea. Comfort D. Fillmore	2	63
Joanna, d. John & Mary, b. Sept. 13, 1754	1	219
Joanna, d. [Walter & Lydia], b. Aug. 12, 1808	1	225
Joanna, m. Samuel **SMITH**, b. of Canterbury, Mar. 27, 1833,		
by Walter Williams, J. P.	2	73
Joel, s. [John & Mary], b. Aug. 30, 177[ ]	1	221
John, s. Richard & Mary, b. May 20, 1719	1	216
John, s. Joseph & Elizabeth, b. Feb. 28, 1725/6	1	216
John, m. Mehetable **ADAMS**, Feb. 26, 1740/41	1	214
John, s. John & Mehetable, b. Jan. 14, 1743/4	1	218
John, s. Mary **SMITH**, Jan. 10, 1751	1	214
John, m. Mary **JEWETT**, of Norwich, Jan. 16, 1754	1	214
John, d. Nov. 3, 176[ ]	1	227
John, Jr., d. Nov. 27, 176[ ]	1	227
John, s. Roger & Alice, b. July 13, 1800	1	225
John, Capt., m. Emeline **WILLIAMS**, Dec. 10, 1829, by Rev.		
Israel G. Rose, of Westminster	2	72
John Cotton, s. Asher & Lucinda, b. Feb. 15, 1819	2	271
John Kennedy, s. [Jeremiah B. & Martha], b. May 15, 1829	2	272
John Owen, s. John & Emeline, b. Oct. 31, 1840	2	273
Jonathan, s. Joseph & Elizabeth, b. Jan. 31, 1718/19	1	216
Jonathan, s. Jacob & Mary, b. Jan. 21, 1752	1	218
Jonathan, s. Jacob & Mary, d. Mar. 28, 1758	1	227
Joseph, [twin with Benjamin], s. Joseph & Elizabeth, b.		
Jan. 14, 1716/17	1	216
Joseph, m. Elizabeth **BURNAP**, Apr. 25, 1716/17	1	214

	Vol.	Page
SMITH, (cont.)		
Joseph, s. Jacob & Peninah, b. Apr. 17, 1765	1	223
Joseph, d. Sept. 5, 1765	1	227
Lemuel, of New York, m. Matilda **COATS**, of Plainfield,		
Sept. 9, 1822, by Erastus Learned	2	71
Lucretia Elizabth, d. Ahira & Caroline, b. July 28, 1828	2	271
Lucy, d. Moses & Mary, b. Oct. 9, 1743	1	218
Lucy, twin with Nath[anie]l, [d. Nath[anie]l & Lucy],		
b. Feb. 5, 1789	1	225
Luther Paine, s. Jairus & Sarah, b. Jan. 4, 1790	1	223
Lydia, [twin with Samuel], d. Richard & Mary, b. Sept.		
26, 1728	1	216
Lydia, d. Eben & Patience, b. May 27, 1755	1	219
Lydia, d. [Walter & Lydia], b. June 2, 1813	1	226
Marshall, s. Roger & Alice, b. Aug. 13, 1808	1	225
Marshall, m. Clarissa C. **ENSWORTH**, Nov. 21, 1836, by		
Rev. Asa King, Westminster	2	73
Martin Wilson, [s. Jeremiah B. & Martha], b. Apr. 9, 1836	2	272
Mary, d. Henry & Hannah, b. Sept. 7, 1720	1	216
Mary, d. Joseph & Elizabeth, b. Dec. 8, 1723	1	216
Mary, d. Joseph, d. [ ] 20, 1725	1	227
Mary, d. Richard & Mary, b. Aug. 20, 1736	1	217
Mary, d. Jacob & Mary, d. Mar. 6, 1749/50	1	227
Mary, m. John **SMITH**, Jan. 10, 1751	1	214
Mary, m. John **CARTER**, Jr., Oct. 31, 1753	1	100
Mary, d. John & Mary, b. Apr. 17, 1756	1	219
Mary, w. John, d. May 9, 178[ ]	1	228
Mary, m. Asa **FROST**, Mar. 8, 1795	1	138
Mary, d. Roger & Alice, b. June 25, 1796	1	224
Mehetable, w. John, d. Mar. 16, 1749/50	1	227
Mehetable F., m. Lorin **JACKSON**, June 18, 1837, by Rev.		
Asa King	2	43
Moses, s. Henry & Hannah, b. Jan. 31, 1718/19	1	216
Moses, m. Mary **WHEELER**, Nov. 5, 1741	1	214
Nathan, s. Jedediah & Abiel, b. July 27, 1741	1	217
Nathaniel, s. Jacob & Penninah, b. Aug. 11, 1761	1	220
Nathaniel, m. Lucy **WILKINSON**, Sept. 8, 1784	1	215
Nath[anie]l, twin with Lucy, [s. Nath[anie]l & Lucy],		
b. Feb. 5, 1789	1	225
Nehemiah, s. Moses & Mary, b. Sept. 9, 1755	1	219
Norris, s. Ebenezer & Hephzibah, b. June 22, 1801	1	224
Olive, d. Phinehas & Rebeckah, of Pomfret, b. Aug. 17, 1736	1	217
Olive, d. Joseph & Anne, b. May 29, 1750	1	218
Olive, d. John & Mary, b. June 6, 1754	1	219
Oliver, s. James & Mary, b. Mar. 2, 1706/7	1	216
Orra, d. Richard & Olive, b. May 19, 1765	1	220
Orrilla R., of Canterbury, m. Calvin W. **GOFF**, of East		
Haddam, Mar. 31, 1851, by C. D. Fillimore, Elder	2	35

	Vol.	Page
SMITH, (cont.)		
Orrin, [s. Jeremiah B. & Martha], b. Feb. 20, 1838	2	272
Oswell, [s. Jeremiah B. & Martha], b. Dec. 18, 1826	2	272
Patience, m. Nehemiah **PARRISH**, May 24, 1758	1	192
Phinehas, m. Henry & Hannah, b. July 5, 1710	1	216
Phinehas F., m. Melara B. **COOPER**, Nov. 4, 1841, by Rev.		
Asa King, Westminster	2	74
Phinehas Frary, s. Asher & Lucinda, b. Nov. 18, 1816	1	226
Polly, d. [Nath[anie]l & Lucy], b. June 16, 1792	1	225
Rachel, d. Henry & Hannah, b. Dec. 22, 1714	1	216
Rachel, d. Jedediah & Abiel, b. Dec. 1, 1736	1	217
Rezinah, d. John & Mary, b. Aug. 13, 1751	1	219
Rhoda, wid. Jacob, d. June 7, 1778	1	228
Richard, m. Mary **CLEVELAND**, Jan. 30, 1715/16	1	214
Richard, s. Richard & Mary, b. Sept. 11, 1734; d. Oct. 23, 1734	1	216
Richard, d. Sept. 12, 1742	1	227
Richard, s. Eben[eze]r & Patience, b. Oct. 1, 1743	1	218
Richard, m. Olive **SPAULDING**, Jan. 15, 1765	1	214
Roger, m. Alice **BINGHAM**, Apr. 29, 1792	1	215
Roger, s. John & Mary, b. Oct. 16, 17[ ]	1	221
Ruth, w. Jeremiah B., d. Oct. 6, 1823	2	357
Ruth Kennedy, d. Jere[mia]h B. & Ruth, b. Jan. 27, 1823	2	271
Ruth Kennedy, d. Jeremiah B. & Ruth, b. Jan. 27, 1823	2	272
Sally Maria, d. [Asher & Lucinda], b. May 30, 1821	2	271
Salmon, s. Eleazer & Elipha, b. Feb. 8, 1788	1	223
Samuel, [twin with Lydia], s. Richard & Mary, b. Sept.		
26, 1728	1	216
Samuel, s. John & Mehetable, b. Jan. 28, 1745/6	1	218
Samuel, s. Joseph & Anne, b. Dec. 25, 1747	1	217
Samuel, d. Mar. 18, 1752	1	227
Samuel, s. Asa & Sarah, b. Nov. 5, 1780	1	222
Samuel, m. Joanna **SMITH**, b. of Canterbury, Mar. 27, 1833,		
by Walter Williams, J. P.	2	73
Samuel H., m. Hannah **ALLEN**, Jan. 2, 1843, by Rev. Asa		
King, Westminster	2	74
Sarah, d. Henry & Hannah, b. Sept. 21, 1728	1	216
Sarah, d. Phinehas & Rebeckah, of Pomfret, b. Dec. 12, 1734	1	216
Sarah, m. John **HERRICK**, June 6, 1755	1	155
Sarah, of Canterbury, m. Samuel **LEWIS**, of Plainfield,		
Oct. 2, 1842, by John Francis, J. P.	2	52
Sarah M., of Canterbury, m. Chester **SMITH**, of Rochester,		
Vt., Dec. 2, 1850, by Rev. R. S. Hazen, of Westminster	2	76
Sibbel, d. Jedediah & Abiel, b. June 6, 1732	1	217
Sibbel, s. [d.] Eben[eze]r & Patience, b. Nov. 21, 1748	1	218
Sibbel, d. John & Mary, b. July 17, 1760	1	211
Sibbel, d. John & Mary, b. July 17, 1760	1	219
Sibbel, m. Reuben **CARTER**, June 22, 1769	1	101
Sophia, of Lisbon, m. Martin **BUTTS**, Jan. 26, 1812	1	73

	Vol.	Page
SMITH, (cont.)		
Susan, of Canterbury, m. Eleazer **SMITH**, Jr., of Lisbon,		
Dec. 26, 1826, by Israel G. Rose	2	71
Susanna, d. [John & Mary], b. Oct. 30, 1756	1	219
Susanna, m. John **BARSTOW**, Jr., May 19, 1779	1	71
Susanna, d. Walter & Lydia, b. Jan. 13, 180[ ]	1	228
Susanna, d. Walter & Lydia, b. Jan. 13, 1805	1	225
Sybil, see under Sibbel		
Sydney, s. Jairus & Sarah, b. June 2, 1800	1	224
Talitha, d. Benjamin, Jr. & Sarah, b. Sept. 22, 1790	1	223
Thomas, s. Phinehas & Rebecca, of Pomfret, b. Jan. 23, 1738/9	1	217
Thomas, s. Henry & Hannah, b. Feb. 18, 1708	1	216
Walter, s. John & Mary, b. Sept. 4, 1773	1	222
Walter, m. Lydia **MUDGE**, Mar. 4, 1802	1	215
Walter, s. [Walter & Lydia], b. Feb. 12, 1811	1	226
Walter, m. Susan **LYON**, Mar. 18, 1835, by Rev. Asa King,		
Westminster	2	73
Washington, s. [Jeremiah B. & Martha], b. Jan. 10, 1833	2	272
Willard, s. Moses & Mary, b. Sept. 14, 1745	1	218
William, s. Richard & Olive, b. Aug. 7, 1777	1	223
Zedekiah, s. John & Mary, b. Feb. 23, 1759	1	219
Zedekiah, s. John & Mary, d. May 21, 1776	1	228
Zerviah, d. John & Mary, d. July 2, 1700	1	227
Zerviah, d. Richard & Mary, b. Jan. 28, 1716/17	1	216
Zerviah, d. John & Mehetable, b. Nov. 7, 1741	1	218
Zerviah, [twin with Abigail], d. John & Mary, b. June 13, 1753	1	219
Zerviah, m. Samuel **PARRISH**, May 4, 1758	1	192
----h, d. Asa & Sarah, b. Mar. 25, 1779	1	222
SNOW, Abigail, d. Abraham & Elizabeth, b. June 29, 1762	1	220
Chloe, d. Abraham & Elizabeth, b. June 23, 1775	1	222
Rufus, s. Abraham & Elizabeth, b. Mar. 4, 1769	1	222
Simeon, s. Abraham & Elizabeth, b. June 5, 1776	1	222
William, s. Abraham & Elizabeth, b. Jan. 5, 1772	1	222
SPAULDING, SPALDING, Abiah, d. Thomas & Abigail, b. Nov.		
12, 1745	1	218
Abigail, d. Edward & Mary, b. Mar. 10, 1713	1	216
Abigail, m. Benajah **DOUGLAS**, Aug. 6, 1733	1	120
Abigail, d. Tho[ma]s & Abigail, d. Nov. 16, 174[ ]		
(Arnold Copy has "Abigail **SMITH**". Corrected by		
L. B. B.	1	227
Abigail, d. Tho[ma]s & Abigail, b. Jan. 25, 1752	1	218
Alpheas, m. Margaret **PHILLIPS**, Dec. 9, 1771	1	214
Alpheas, d. Jan. 13, 1776	1	227
Asa, s. Ebenezer & Mary, b. May 20, 1757	1	219
Bela Payne, s. Ebenezer & Molly, b. Mar. 26, 1784	1	223
Benjamin, m. Pamelia **CARTER**, d. of Phin[eha]s, Mar. 28,		
1825, by Rev. Israel G. Rose	2	71
Bridget, d. Samuel & Mary, b. Feb. 13, 1712/13	1	216

	Vol.	Page
SPAULDING, SPALDING, (cont.)		
Caroline, of Canterbury, m. David P. **WALDING,** of		
Windham, June 12, 1825, by Geo[rge] S. White	2	85
Curtis, d. Jan. 26, 1777	1	228
Ebenezer, s. Edward & Mary, b. June 24, 1717	1	216
Eben[eze]r, m. Mary **FASSET,** Feb. 24, 1742/3	1	214
Ebenezer, s. Eben[eze]r & Mary, b. Nov. 15, 1745	1	217
Ebenezer, s. Ebenezer & Mary, d. July 13, 1746	1	227
Ebenezer, s. Ebenezer & Mary, b. July 13, 1751	1	218
Ebenezer, m. Molly **PAINE,** May 29, 1783	1	215
Edward, Lieut., d. Nov. 29, 1739	1	227
Elijah, s. Josiah & Hannah, b. Nov. 2, 1758	1	219
Elijah, s. Josiah & Hannah, d. Feb. 25, 1763	1	227
Elijah, s. Stephen & Dinah, b. Feb. 11, 1773	1	222
Elijah, s. Stephen & Dinah, d. Feb. 12, 1773	1	227
Elizabeth, d. Josiah & Hannah, b. Oct. 22, 1746	1	218
Elizabeth, d. Ezekiel & Martha, b. July 24, 1749	1	218
Elizabeth, d. [Stephen & Dinah], b. Feb. 9, 1774	1	222
Elizabeth, d. [Stephen & Dinah], d. Apr. 1, 1774	1	228
Eunice, m. Joseph(?) **ADAMS,** July 23, 1708	1	51
Ezekiel, m. Martha **KIMBALL,** Nov. 24, 1737	1	214
Ezekiel, [twin with ----], s. Ezekiel & Martha, b. Aug. 7, 1756	1	218
Ezekiel, s. Ezekiel & Martha, d. Jan. 29, 1758(?)	1	227
Hannah, d. Josiah & Hannah, b. July 26, 1750	1	218
Harvey, m. Deidama **FOWLER,** b. of Canterbury, July 20,		
1845, by Rev. Jacob Allen	2	75
J. A., of Killingly, m. Hannah S. **KINGSLEY,** d. of Hezekiah,		
of Canterbury, Jan. 2, 1854, by Rev. Robert C. Learned	2	76
Joel Dodge, s. Josiah & Hannah, b. Apr. 21, 1767	1	220
John, s. Edward & Mary, b. Dec. 1, 1721	1	216
John, Dr., m. Elizabeth **CHAMBERLAIN,** of Woodstock, Jan.		
8, 1771	1	214
John, s. John & Eliza, b. Jan. 6, 1772	1	221
Jonathan, s. Samuel & Mary, b. Aug. 16, 1707	1	216
Josiah, Jr., d. May 6, 1770	1	227
Josiah, s. [Stephen & Dinah], b. Feb. 15, 1775	1	222
Leah, d. Josiah & Hannah, b. May 28, 1752	1	216
Leah, m. Jonathan **RANSOM,** Nov. 24, 1773	1	209
Lucy, of Plainfield, m. Obadiah **JOHNSON,** July 6, 1765	1	167
Luther, s. Ebenezer & Mary, b. Mar. 22, 1762	1	220
Lydia, d. Ebenezer & Mary, b. Apr. 20, 1753	1	217
Lydia, d. Ezekiel & Martha, b. Jan. 3, 1759	1	219
Lydia, d. Stephen & Dinah, b. Apr. 17, 1777	1	222
Lydia, d. Ezekiel & Martha, d. July 31, [ ]	1	227
Lidia, d. Eben[eze]r & Mary, d. Sept. 11, 17[ ]	1	227
Margaret, wid. Alpheas, d. Dec. 29, 1777	1	228
Mary, d. Samuel & Mary, b. Mar. 2, 1710	1	216
Mary, d. Eben[eze]r & Mary, b. Dec. 6, 1743	1	217

	Vol.	Page
SPAULDING, SPALDING, (cont.)		
Mary, d. Thomas & Abigail, b. Feb. 13, 1749/50	1	218
Mary, wid. Lieut. Edward, d. Sept. 20, 1754	1	227
Mary, m. Daniel **CADY**, Oct. 6, 1762	1	101
Mehetable, d. Ezekiel & Martha, b. Aug. 26, 1738	1	217
Olive, d. Thomas & Abigail b. Jan. 2, 1747/8	1	218
Olive, m. Richard **SMITH**, Jan. 15, 1765	1	214
Polly, d. Ebenezer & Molly, b. Apr. 17, 1786	1	223
Prescilla, d. Eben[eze]r & Patience, b. June 8, 1749	1	218
Prescilla, d. Eben[ezer] & Mary, d. Dec. 18, [ ]	1	227
Rachel, d. Josiah & Hannah, b. May 3, 1756	1	218
Rufus, s. Ebenezer & Mary, b. Jan. 8, 1760	1	219
Rufus, m. Lydia **PAINE**, Jan. 10, 1782	1	214
Ruth, d. Edward & Mary, b. Sept. 28, 1710	1	216
Ruth, m. John **BACON**, Sept. 24, 1734	1	71
Ruth, d. Thomas & Abigail, b. June 2, 1763	1	220
Samson, s. Josiah & Hannah, b. Apr. 18, 1754	1	217
Samson, m. Temperance **NOTT**, June 27, 1779	1	214
Sam[ue]l, s. Eben[eze]r & Mary, d. Sept. 11, 17[ ]	1	227
Samuel, 2d, m. Lucy **CARTER**, Jan. 19, 1829, by Rev. Israel G. Rose, of Westminster	2	72
Sarah, d. Eben[eze]r & Mary, b. Mar. 15, 1755	1	218
Sarah, m. Elijah **MUNROW**, Mar. 1, 1758	1	181
Sarah, m. Standish **FOSTER**, Mar. 23, 1774	1	138
Sarah Frances, d. Cyrel & Lusee, b. May 11, 1845	2	273
Simeon, s. Josiah & Hannah, b. July 1, 1760	1	219
Stephen, s. Josiah & Hannah, b. July 23, 1748	1	218
Stephen, m. Dinah **BROWN**, Oct. 24, 1771	1	214
Temperance, d. Samson & Temperance, b. June 12, 1780	1	222
Thomas, s. Edward & Mary, b. Aug. 7, 1719	1	216
William, s. Tho[ma]s & Abigail, b. Feb. 1, 1754	1	218
Zipporah, m. Phinehas **BENJAMIN**, Nov. 14, 1759	1	70
----, twin with Ezekiel, d. Ezekiel & Martha, b. Aug. 7, 1756; d. Sept. 3, 1756	1	218-9
SPENCER, Allen, m. Lucy Ann **LEWIS**, Nov. 6, 1825, by And[re]w T. Judson, J. P.	2	71
John, s. John & Wealthy, b. Apr. 30, 1778	1	222
Wealthy, d. John & Wealthy, b. Apr. 8, 1781	1	223
SPICER, Abigail, m. James D. **RANSOM**, Dec. 11, 1843, by Rev. Asa King, Westminster	2	68
Daniel, of Preston, m. Phebe **BUTTS**, of Canterbury, Dec. 18, 1827, by Rev. Israel G. Rose, of Westminster	2	71
Mary P., of Canterbury, m. Waterman **BROWN**, of Plainfield, Oct. 23, 1836, by Andrew T. Judson, J. P.	2	11
Sarah M., m. Thomas **PALMER**, Mar. 20, 1843, by Rev. Asa King, Westminster	2	64
SQUIRE, Miriam, m. Phillip **WETHY**, Jan. 28, 1779	1	236
STAFFORD, Christopher Rhodes, of Providence, R. I., m. Sarah		

	Vol.	Page
STAFFORD, (cont.)		
Ann **FENNER**, of Canterbury, Mar. 16, 1824, by Rev.		
Tho[ma]s J. Murdock	2	71
STANLEY, Cynthia, m. Asa **BUTTS**, Jan. 16, 1810	1	73
STANTON, Abiah, d. Amey, single woman, b. Nov. 14, 175[ ]	1	221
Abigail, d. Thomas & Sarah, b. Sept. 24, 1747	1	219
Aman*, s. Amey, single woman, b. June 27, 17[ ] (*Amos?)	1	221
Amos, s. Joseph & Abigail, b. Mar. 12, 1742	1	217
Amey, single woman, had d. Abiah b. Nov. 14, 175[ ]	1	221
Amey, single woman, had s. Hosea b. May 9, 176[ ]	1	221
Amey, single woman, had s. Aman*, b. June 27, 17[ ](*Amos?)	1	221
Amey, single woman, had d. Content, b. July 12, 17[ ]	1	221
Amey, single woman, had s. Joel, b. Aug. 16, 17[ ]	1	221
Anna, m. William **CARTER**, June 6, 1758	1	100
Content, d. [Amey, single woman], b. July 12, 17[ ]	1	221
David, s. Peter & Sarah, b. Dec. 26, 1764	1	220
Hosea, s. [Amey, single woman], b. May 9, 176[ ]	1	221
Joel, s. [Amey, single woman], b. Aug. 16, 17[ ]	1	221
John, d. Aug. 10, 1755	1	227
Joseph, s. Joseph & Abigail, b. Aug. 27, 1746	1	217
Nathaniel S., m. Susannah W. **GALLUP**, Sept. 17, 1843, by		
Rev. Asa King, Westminster	2	75
Peter, s. Thomas & Sarah, b. May 18, 1743	1	219
Peter, m. Sarah **CLEVELAND**, Sept. 21, 1763	1	214
Rufus, s. Joseph & Abigail, b. Apr. 26, 1744	1	217
Ruth, d. Jacob & Jemima, b. Sept. 17, 1757	1	219
Samuel, s. Peter & Sarah, b. Feb. 13, 1767	1	220
Samuel, s. Peter & Sarah, d. May 23, 1767	1	227
Sarah, d. Peter & Sarah, b. Mar 4, 1784	1	223
Turner, of Lisbon, m. Asenath **PRESTON**, Jan. 30, 1837,		
by Rev. Asa King	2	74
William C. B., m. Mary A. **MORGAN**, Mar. 2, 1838, by Rev.		
Asa King, Westminster	2	74
STAPLES, Abel, m. Cynthia **HOLT**, Dec. 3, 1777	1	214
Amos, s. Abel & Cynthia, b. July 1, 1778	1	222
Anne, d. Abel & Cynthia, b. Oct. 9, 1782	1	223
Esther, m. Benj[ami]n **BROWN**, Jr., Dec. 17, 1779	1	71
Hannah, single woman, had d. Mary b. Jan. 12, 1771	1	221
Hannah, m. Jos[eph] **GORHAM**, Jan. 8, 1773	1	149
Job, s. [John & Susanna], b. Aug. 23, 1786	1	224
John, s. John & Susanna, b. Apr. 23, 1773	1	223
John, d. Feb. 27, 1776	1	228
Lucius, s. [John & Susanna], b. Mar. 12, 1794	1	224
Lucy, d. Abel & Cynthia, b. Jan. 20, 1785	1	223
Mary, d. Hannah, single woman, b. Jan. 12, 1771	1	221
Mat[t]hew, s. [John & Susanna], b. May 1, 1784	1	224
Mat[t]hew, s. [John & Susanna], b. [ ]	1	223
Nathaniel, s. Abel & Cynthia, b. June 30, 1780	1	222

	Vol.	Page
STAPLES, (cont.)		
Seth, s. [John & Susanna], b. Aug. 31, 1776	1	223
Sophia, d. [John & Susanna], b. Oct. 13, 1792	1	224
Sophas, s. [John & Susanna], b. Dec. 12, 1788	1	224
Susanna, d. [John & Susanna], b. Aug. 1, 1779	1	223
----nice, d. Jacob & Eunice, b. July 11, 1763	1	222
STARK, STARKE, STARTE, Eunice, d. John & Eunice, b. Apr. 9,		
1766	1	220
John, m. Eunice **ADAMS**, Apr. 16, 1764	1	214
Samuel, s. John & Eunice, b. July 19, 1764	1	220
STARKWEATHER, Laura, of Plainfield, m. William **HORTON**, of		
Canterbury, Oct. 5, 1828, by Rev. James R. Wheelock	2	39
Leonard, s. [Belcher & Mary], b. Sept. 16, 1791	1	223
Polly, d. Belcher & Mary, b. Oct. 5, 1789	1	223
STARTE, [see under **STARK**]		
STEDMAN, STEADMAN, Esther, m. Cornelius **ADAMS**, Apr. 14,		
1774	1	52
Harriet L., of Hampton, m. John W. **SALTER**, of Mansfield,		
Sept. 25, 1825, by Rev. Tho[ma]s J. Murdock	2	71
STEPHENS, [see also **STEVENS**], Alice, m. Leonard **MURPHY**,		
July 18, 1793	1	181
Anna, m. Rufus **BENNET**, Apr. 4, 1817	1	73
Robert, m. Lydia **ADAMS**, Dec. 4, 1781	1	214
STEVENS, STEAVENS, [see also **STEPHENS**], Abiathar, s. Moses		
& Susanna, b. Aug. 6, 1796	1	224
Abigail, m. Eben[eze]r **CLEVELAND**, b. of Canterbury,		
Oct. 16, 1745, at Groton, by Andrew Croswell	1	69
Abigail, d. Jonathan & Mary, b. Mar. 1, 1748	1	217
Abigail, w. Peter, d. Apr. 15, 179[ ], ae 85	1	228
Abner, s. [Peter, Jr. & Lois], b. Mar. 4, 1770	1	221
Adams, s. John & Ruth, b. Nov. 10, 1752, n. s.	1	216
Adam, m. Patience **RATHBURN**, Oct. 21, 1773	1	214
Adams, m. Naomi **BROWN**, Mar. 9, 1800	1	215
Alice, d. [Adams & Patience], b. Apr. 2, 1775	1	222
Alvira Ann, d. [Samuel & Edeth], b. Sept. 11, 1823	2	271
Asa, s. Peter & Louis, b. Sept. 21, 1760	1	220
Asa, m. Sarah **ADAMS**, Oct. 1, 1761	1	214
Asa, s. Asa & Sarah, b. Jan. 19, 176[ ]	1	221
Beriah, s. John & Ruth, b. Jan. 22, 1760	1	219
Betsey, m. David **LESTER**, b. of Canterbury, Nov. 16, 1826,		
by Rev. Tho[ma]s J. Murdock	2	51
Dan, s. Adams & Patience, b. Nov. 19, 1785	1	223
Darius, s. Robert & Lydia, b. Aug. 13, 1796	1	224
Darius, m. Edith **STEVENS**, b. of Canterbury, May 18, 1834,		
by Rev. Otis C. Whiton	2	73
Diah, s. Adams & Patience, b. Oct. 6, 1783	1	223
Ebenezer, s. Peter, Jr. & Lois, b. Feb. 14, 1768	1	221
Edith, m. Darius **STEVENS**, b. of Canterbury, May 18,		

	Vol.	Page
STEVENS, STEAVENS, (cont.)		
1834, by Rev. Otis C. Whiton	2	73
Elizabeth, m. Samuel **RATHBURN**, Sept. 16, 1747	1	209
Elizabeth Sabra, d. Adam & Patience, b. Oct. 6, 1777	1	222
Elizabeth Sabeny, m. Theophilus **LAMPHIRE**, Dec. 31, 1799	1	176
Elvira A., m. Josiah C. **PALMER**, b. of Canterbury, Nov. 8, 1852, by Rev. Robert C. Learned	2	4
Elvira A., m. Josiah C. **PALMER**, b. of Canterbury, [ ], by Rev. Robert C. Learned	2	65
Emeline H., m. Henry **KENDALL**, b. of Canterbury, Mar. 19, 1848, by Rev. Robert C. Learned	2	48
Eunice, d. Adam & Patience, b. July 3, 1779	1	222
Hannah, d. [Levi & Nancy], b. Mar. 22, 1793	1	224
Hannah, m. Daniel **FROST**, Dec. 21, 1809	1	138
Isaac, s. Adam & Patience, b. Oct. 6, 1791	1	224
James, s. Peter & Lois, b. Jan. 31, 1766	1	220
John, s. John & Thankful, b. Nov. 26, 1775	1	222
John Hathaway, s. Robert & Mary, b. Sept. 20, 1766	1	220
John Hathaway, s. Samuel & Edeth, b. Dec. 4, 1821	2	271
Jonathan, m. Mary **TRACY**, June 3, 1732	1	214
Jonathan, s. Asa & Sarah, b. July 16, 1764	1	220
Ledeah, d. Peter & Louis, b. May 30, 1762	1	220
Ledeah, see also Lydia		
Lemuel, m. Mary **PIKE**, Feb. 21, 1782	1	214
Luther, s. [Peter, Jr. & Lois], b. Mar. 18, 1772	1	221
Lydia, d. Adams & Naomi, b. Oct. 30, 1784	1	224
Lydia, d. [Robert & Lydia], b. July 19, 1789	1	223
Lydia, d. Levi & Nancy, b. Jan. 16, 1790	1	224
Lydia, see also Ledeah		
Marah, m. Benjamin **DURFEE**, b. of Lisbon, Feb. 22, 1791	1	121
Marian, d. Robert & Lydia, b. Aug. 8, 1800	1	224
Martha, d. John & Ruth, b. Aug. 9, 1763	1	220
Martha, d. Robert & Lydia, b. Apr. 2, 1787	1	223
Martin, s. Adams & Patience, b. Feb. 6, 1788	1	223
Mary, d. Jonathan & Mary, b. Jan. 27, 1743	1	217
Mary, d. John & Ruth, b. Dec. 15, 1761	1	220
Mary, m. John **SIM[M]S**, Apr. 12, 1762	1	214
Mary, d. [Willard & Deborah], b. Apr. 24, 176[ ]	1	221
Nancy, d. [Levi & Nancy], b. Sept. 16, 1791	1	224
Naomi, d. John & Ruth, b. Dec. 16, 176[ ]	1	220
Naoma, of Lisbon, m. Benjamin **RATHBOURNE**, Jan. 28, 1790	1	209
Nathan, s. Peter & Louis, b. Apr. 13, 1764	1	220
Patience, w. Adams, d. Dec. 28, 179[ ]	1	228
Peter, m. Loes **GLASS**, Nov. 1, 1759	1	214
Peter, d. Feb. 28, 178[ ], ae about 70	1	228
Phinehas, s. [Willard & Deborah], b. Jan. 13, 175[ ]	1	221
Robert, s. Robert & Lydia, b. Mar. 30, 1795	1	223

	Vol.	Page
STEVENS, STEAVENS, (cont.)		
Roger, s. Asa & Sarah, b. Mar, 21, 1763	1	220
Ruby, d. Adams & Patience, b. Jan. 18, 1774	1	222
Ruby, d. [Robert & Lydia], b. Nov. 25, 1801	1	224
Rufus, s. Peter, Jr. & Lois, b. Sept. 16, 1779	1	222
Samuel, s. [Robert & Lydia], b. Mar. 11, 1793	1	223
Samuel, m. Ralph **HYDE**, b., of Canterbury, Nov. 26, 1820,		
by Asa Meech (So in Arnold Copy)	2	71
Sarah, d. Jonathan & Mary, b. June 3, 1750	1	217
Sarah, d. Asa & Sarah, b. Jan. 19, 1766	1	220
Sarah, d. Robert & Lydia, b. July 19, 1784	1	223
Silve, d. Robert & Mary, b. Mar. 25, 1763	1	220
Simon, s. Jonathan & Mary, b. Nov. 25, 1736	1	217
Simon, s. [Willard & Deborah], b. Feb. 7, 176[ ]	1	221
Simons Aradatha, s. Moses & Susanna, b. May 29, 1803	1	185
Solomon, s. Jonathan & Mary, b. Mar. 10, 1754	1	217
Susanna, d. Adam & Naomi, b. Dec. 27, 1788	1	224
Thede, d. John & Ruth, b. June 18, 1769	1	221
T[h]eresa, d. Robert & Lydia, b. May 24, 1791	1	223
Tho[ma]s, d. [ ], in Camp at Lake George. Soldier	1	227
Wilder, s. Willard & Deborah, b. Nov. 3, 175[ ]	1	221
Willard, s. Jonathan & Mary, b. Oct. 26, 1732	1	217
Willard, m. Deborah **CASE**, Jan. 22, 1755	1	214
Willard, s. [Willard & Deborah], b. June 28, 176[ ]	1	221
Willard, of Plainfield, d. Dec. 27, 1780	1	228
Zilpha, m. Joseph **RATHBURN**, May 2, 1777	1	209
----, d. Peter & Lois, b. May 10, 1774	1	222
----, s. Peter & Lois, b. Aug. 10, 1776	1	222
STEWART, James, s. James & Easther, b. Sept. 27, 1747	1	217
STILES, Elizabeth, m. Jonathan **LAD[D]**, Apr. 26, 1759	1	176
STILLMAN, Charlotte A., m. Augustus J. **FOSTER**, June 2, 1846,		
by Samuel L. Hough, J. P.	2	32
STOCKWELL, Henry Hough, s. Marvin & Chloe, b. Oct. 25, 1807	1	225
STODDARD, Kathering, m. Daniel **MEACH**, Jan. 22, 1749/50	1	181
Samuel, m. Millescent **CARVER**, Jan. 11, 1781	1	214
STORER, Ann Hudson, d. [David & Anna], b. Apr. 7, 1817	2	271
Asa Butts, s. [David & Anna], b. Sept. 10, 1814	2	271
Cynthia, d. [David & Anna], b. Jan. 1, 1823	2	272
Cynthia, m. Alfred **HAMMOND**, of Hampton, Apr. 28, 1841,		
by Rev. Asa King, Westminster	2	41
Daniel*, m. Anna **BUTTS**, Feb. 24, 1811 (*David.		
Corrected by L. B. B.)	2	74
David, s. David & Anna, b. July 10, 1820	2	272
Ebenezer, s. David & Anna, b. July 5, 1812	2	271
Ebenezer, m. Sarah Ann **SHARPE**, May 10, 1835, by Rev.		
Asa King	2	73
Egbert, s. [David & Anna], b. Jan. 9, 1834	2	272
Elizabeth, d. [Jonathan & Lydia], b. Nov. 18, 1824	2	271

	Vol.	Page
STORER, (cont.)		
Emily, d. [Jonathan & Lydia], b. Nov. 7, 1827	2	271
Emma, d. [Jonathan & Lydia], b. Nov. 7, 1827	2	271
Jemime, d. [Jonathan & Lydia], b. Oct. 6, 1819	2	271
John, s. [Jonathan & Lydia], b. June 11, 1822	2	271
John, s. [David & Anna], b. Feb. 19, 1831	2	272
Lucinda, d. Jonathan & Lydia, b. Sept. 11, 1812	1	225
Mary, d. [Jonathan & Lydia], b. Oct. 20, 1817	2	271
Melita, d. Jonathan & Lydia, b. Oct. 10, 1814	2	271
Orra, d. [David & Anna], b. Dec. 23, 1825	2	272
Simon Brewster, s. [David & Anna], b. Apr. 23, 1828	2	272
STORY, Elizabeth, twin with Jemima, d. [Ephraim & Jemima],		
b. Sept. 23, 1797	1	224
Elizabeth, m. Jonas **BOND**, b. of Canterbury, Nov. 28,		
1822, by Erastus Larned	2	7
Ephraim, of Norwich, m. Jemima **CLARK**, Jr., Mar. 7, 1792	1	215
Ephraim, s. [Ephraim & Jemima], b. Apr. 3, 1800	1	224
Jemima, twin with Elizabeth, d. [Ephraim & Jemima], b.		
Sept. 23, 1797	1	224
John, s. [Ephraim & Jemima], b. Feb. 9, 1795	1	224
John, s. Ephraim & Jemima, d. Feb. 21, 179[ ]	1	228
Lydia, d. Ephraim & Jemima, b. Mar. 27, 1793	1	224
Mary S., m. Will[ia]m H. **WILLIAMS**, Nov. 11, 1827, by Rev.		
Israel G. Rose, of Westminster	2	85
Mary Sophronia, d. Ephraim & Jemima, b. June 25, 1804	1	225
Nathaniel Clark, s. Eph[rai]m & Jemima, b. Sept. 15, 1803	1	225
Peletiah Perit, s. [Eph[rai]m & Jemima], b. Aug. 13, 1806	1	225
SUNDERLAND, Sarviah W., of Groton, m. Barton D. **BURDICK**,		
of Westerly, R. I., Feb. 18, 1827, by Rev. Asher Miner	2	8
SWEET, Calvin, s. [Jesse & Lois], b. June 27, 1801	1	225
Jay, s. [Jesse & Lois], b. July 2, 1805	1	225
Jesse, m. Lois **BALDWIIN**, Sept. 25, 1796	1	215
John, m. Mary **HOLLIS**, b. of Canterbury, Mar. 12, 1835,		
by John Francis, J. P.	2	73
Julia S., m. Frederick O. H. **BROWN**, Feb. 15, 1852, by		
Comfort S. Hyde, J. P.	2	105
Lydia, d. [Jesse & Lois], b. Jan. 29, 1799	1	225
Lydia, of Canterbury, m. Weden **HOLLOWAY**, of Exeter,		
R. I., Nov. 9, 1828, by Chester Lyon, J. P.	2	39
Lyman, s. [Jesse & Lois], b. Mar. 2, 1803	1	225
William, s. Jesse & Lois, b. Mar. 20, 1797	1	225
SYDLEMAN, Elisha, of Pawtucket, m. Lura **MORSE**, of		
Canterbury, May 6, 1827, by Israel G. Rose	2	71
SYLSBY, [see also **SILSBURY**], Elizabeth, m. Joseph		
WOODWARD, June 24, 1714	1	236
SYLVESTER, Emily Whitfield, d. Elias J. & Mary D., b. June 26,		
1840, in Brooklyn, N. Y.	2	273
Mary, d. Elias J. & Mary D., b. Mar. 6, 1842	2	273

	Vol.	Page
SYLVESTER, (cont.)		
William Tompkins, s. Elias J. & Mary D., b. Jan. 16, 1839, in New York City	2	273
TARBOX, Caleb W., of East Greenwich, R. I., m. Maria **CLARK**, of Canterbury, Dec. 8, 1844, by Rev. Daniel D. Lyon, of Packersville	2	80
TAYLOR, Micah L., of Pomfret, m. Mary L. **BENNETT**, of Canterbury, Aug. 21, 1843, by Daniel Bennett, J. P.	2	79
TEFT, Daniel, of Killingly, now resident of Canterbury, m. Cynthia **DEAN**, of Canterbury, June 18, 1837, by Rev. C. J. Warren	2	79
THATCHER, Mercy, s. Eben[eze]r **HIDES**, Apr. 12, 1742	1	155
Rhoda Ann, d. [Hezekiah & Hannah], b. Sept. 19, 1819	1	231
Rufus Lathrop, s. Hezekiah & Hannah, b. Sept. 13, 1810	1	231
THOMPSON, Asa, s. William & Prudence, b. Aug. 11, 1751	1	231
Elizabeth, d. William & Prudence, b. Oct. 2, 1745	1	231
Eunice, d. Sam[ue]l & Eunice, b. Sept. 4, 1754	1	230
Eunice, m. John **MOTT**, Apr. 16, 1778	1	181
John, s. William & Prudence, b. Oct. 2, 1748	1	231
John, s. Jonathan & Hannah, b. Jan. 19, 1750/51	1	230
Jonathan, m. Hannah **DEAN**, Jan. 10, 1748/9	1	229
Mary, m. John **HIDE**, Apr. 18, 1753	1	155
Rachel, d. Sam[ue]l & Lucy, b. Nov. 23, 1758	1	231
Sally, m. Daniel **BLAKELEY**, Nov. 26, 1835, by W[illia]m Hutchins, J. P.	2	10
Samuel, s. Samuel & Lucy, b. June 18, 1760	1	231
TIBBETTS, TEBBETTS, Benjamin, d. Aug. 10, 1713	1	233
Elizabeth, m. Tryall **BAKER**, Dec. 24, 1718	1	69
Martha, m. Tho[ma]s **PELLET**, Mar. 8, 1729/30	1	192
Mary, m. James **DELAP**, Feb. [ ], 1733	1	120
TIFFANY, Albert Gallenten, s. [Daniel & Pamela], b. May 26, 1806	1	231
Emelas, s. Nathan & Nancy, b. Jan. 2, 1807	1	231
George Clinton, s. Daniel & Pamela, b. June 25, 1804	1	231
Loisa Maria, d. [Nathan & Nancy], b. Oct. [ ], 1810	1	231
Lyman, s. Nathan & Nancy, b. July 2, 1806	1	231
Nathan Landia, m. Nancy **PELLET**, July 18, 1805	1	229
TILLINGHAST, Lucretia, of East Greenwich, R. I., m. William **WHITFORD**, s. Dan[ie]l, of Canterbury, Sept. 6, 1824, by Thomas Manchester, Elder, East Greenwich	2	85
TICKHAM, Welcome, of Glocester, R. I., m. Susannah **HERRICK**, Nov. 14, 1827, by Luther Paine, J. P.	2	79
TOOLEY, Hephzibah, of Bozrah, m. Ebenezer **SMITH**, Oct. 13, 1799	1	215
TORRANCE, Agnes, d. Sam[ue]l & Jemima, b. Apr. 19, 1746	1	230
John, s. Sam[ue]l & Jemima, b. Jan. 18, 1741	1	230
Sam[ue]l, m. Jemima **PARK**, Aug. 30, 1741	1	229
Will[ia]m, s. Sam[ue]l & Jemima, b. Mar. 8, 1744	1	230
TOURTELLOTT, Jesse H., of Thompson, m. Fanny E. **FRANCIS**,		

	Vol.	Page
TOURTELLOTT, (cont.)		
of Canterbury, Jan. 13, 1850, by Rev. Robert C. Learned	2	80
TOWNSEND, Chauncey, m. Sophia WILSON, b. of Canterbury,		
Feb. 5, 1824, by Walter Williams, J. P.	2	79
TRACY, Abdiel, s. Joshua & Sarah, b. Sept. 26, 1771	1	231
Abigail, d. Solomon & Sarah, b. Aug. 14, 1726	1	230
Ann, of Norwich, m. James ENSWORTH, Nov. 15, 1770	1	133
Anne, d. Solomon & Sarah, b. May 1, 1719	1	230
Asa, s. Phinehas & Mehetable, b. Aug. 28, 1745	1	230
Asa, d. May 4, 1787	1	233
Charles, s. [Fanning & Lucy], b. June 5, 1807	1	231
Eliashib, m. Zerviah ADAMS, Feb. 19, 1769	1	229
Eliashib, d. Feb. 25, 1786	1	233
Eliashib, s. [Fanning & Lucy], b. Dec. 6, 1813	1	232
Elizabeth, s. [d.] Phinehas & Mehetable, b. Mar. 27, 1748	1	230
Fanning, s. [Eliashib & Zerviah], b. July 31, 1773	1	231
Fanning, m. Lucy ADAMS, Sept. 26, 1802	1	229
George, of Windham, m. Malissa OLDS, of Canterbury, Apr.		
14, 1833, by Rev. Alfred Burnham, at Archibald Olds'	2	79
Jabez Ensworth, s. [Fanning & Lucy], b. Feb. 21, 1817	1	232
Jerusha, of Franklin, m. Timothy BACKUS,Jr., July 6, 1788	1	72
Joseph, s. Oliver & Abigail, b. Jan. 5, 1781	1	231
Learned, s. David & Abiel, d. Apr. 29, 1759	1	233
Lucy, d. Solomon & Sarah, b. May 23, 1716	1	230
Lucy, m. Jonathan HIDE, Feb. 4, 1744/5	1	155
Lucy, w. Fanning, d. Mar. 12, 18[ ]	1	233
Lucy Adams, d. [Fanning & Lucy], b. Sept. 21, 1811	1	231
Mary, d. Solomon & Sarah, b. Jan. 10, 1711/12	1	230
Mary, m. Jonathan STEVENS, June 3, 1732	1	214
Mehetable, m. Jabez ENSWORTH, Nov. 17, 1748	1	133
Myriam, d. Solomon & Sarah, b. Mar. 22, 1723/4	1	230
Miriam, d. Phinehas & Mehetable, b. Oct. 12, 1750;		
d. Oct. 31, 1750	1	230
Miriam, d. Phinehas & Mehetable, b. Oct. 12, 1751	1	230
Phinehas, s. Solomon & Sarah, b. Nov. [ ], 1721	1	230
Phinehas, m. Mehetable ADAMS, May 9, 1745	1	229
Phinehas, d. Sept. 6, 1760	1	233
Phin[eha]s, s. Eliashib & Zerviah, b. May 22, 1769	1	231
Polly, d. Oliver & Abigail, b. Dec. 6, 1778	1	231
Rebecca, of Preston, m. David CLEVELAND, Aug. 15, 1750	1	100
Rubie, d. Phinehas & Mehetable, b. Feb. 24, 1755	1	230
Ruby, m. Timothy BACKUS, Jr., Feb. 14, 1776	1	71
Sarah, d. Solomon & Sarah, b. July 6, 1709	1	230
Sarah, wid., d. Dec. 1, 1765	1	233
Sibbel, d. Solomon & Mehetable, b. Feb. 18, 1744/5	1	230
Sibel, m. Samuel ENSWORTH, Nov. 17, 1763	1	133
Simon, of Norwich, m. Frances Mary ADAMS, of Canterbury,		
Mar. 13, 1832, by Rev. Dennis Platt	2	79

	Vol.	Page
TRACY, (cont.)		
Solomon, s. Solomon & Sarah, b. Mar. 11, 1713	1	230
Solomon, d. June 17, 1751	1	233
Solomon, s. David & Abiel, b. Oct. 7, 1758	1	231
Solomon, s. [Fanning & Lucy], b. Aug. 25, 1805	1	231
Sybil, see under Sibbel		
Thomas, s. [Fanning & Lucy], b. May 12, 1809	1	231
William, s. Fanning & Lucy, b. Nov. 18, 1803	1	231
W[illia]m Winslow, s. [Joshua & Sarah], b. Oct. 8, 1773	1	231
TRAP, Thankful, m. Isaac **BALDWIN,** Apr. 4, 1751	1	70
TRISKETT, Mehetable, m. Josiah **MORSE,** Feb. 22, 1758	1	181
TROWBRIDGE, Abigail, d. Thomas & Susannah, b. June 3, 1722	1	230
Susanna, d. Tho[ma]s & Susannah, b. Apr. 27, 1718	1	230
TUCKER, Abigail, d. John Picker & Abigail, b. Oct. 26, 1766	1	231
Lavina, m. Chester L. **BUGBEE,** Oct. 26, 1845, by Rev.		
Zeph[ani]a Baker	2	13
TUCKERMEN, Isaac, Capt., of Sterling, m. Elizabeth		
COLEGROVE, of Canterbury, Mar. 1, 1824, by George		
W. Appleton	2	79
TYLER, TYLOR, Alice A., of Griswold, m. Henry A. **MORGAN,**		
of Canterbury, Jan. 13, 1828, by Rev. James R. Wheelock	2	55
Almeran, s. Asa & Antis, b. Mar. 12, 1767	1	231
Amasa, s. [Phin[eha]s & Lucy], b. July 10, 1780	1	231
Amy, d. Daniel & Jane, b. Dec. 10, 1733	1	230
Asa, s. Daniel & Jane, b. Mar. 5, 1731	1	230
Asahel, s. Phinehas & Lucy, b. July 6, 1768	1	231
Betty, d. John & Elizabeth, b. Apr. 11, 1745	1	230
Betty, m. Isaac **HIDE,** 3rd, Feb. 6, 1772	1	155
Daniel, m. Mehetable **SHIRTLOFF,** Sept. 16, 1742	1	229
Daniel, s. Daniel & Mehetable, b. May 21, 1750	1	230
Edward, m. Mary L. **SHERMAN,** Oct. 13, 1850, by Rev.		
Robert C. Learned	2	80
Elijah, s. Daniel & Jane, b. Apr. 19, 1729	1	230
Elijah, s. Phin[eha]s & Lucy, b. Feb. 12, 1775	1	231
Elizabeth, d. Daniel & Mehetable, b. Dec. 15, 1744	1	230
Eunice, d. Dan[ie]l & Mary, b. May 25, 1771	1	231
Jeames, s. Daniel & Mehetable, b. July 25, 1743	1	230
John, s. John & Elizabeth, b. Apr. 30, 1748	1	230
John, s. John & Eliza, d. Jan. 20, 1770	1	233
John, s. Phinehas & Lucy, b. July 15, 1770	1	231
John Fenner, s. Reuben & Sally, b. July 21, 1809	1	231
Leah, d. Daniel & Mehetable, b. June 30, 1752	1	230
Lucy, d. Daniel & Jane, b. Nov. 13, 1735	1	230
Lucy, d. [Phin[eha]s & Lucy], b. Oct. 12, 1782	1	231
Mabel, d. Daniel & Jane, b. June 20, 1724, in Preston	1	230
Mary E., of Lisbon, m. Daniel B. **FOWLER,** of Canterbury,		
Nov. 25, 1849, by Rev. J. Lovejoy, Norwich	2	33
Molly, d. Phin[eha]s & Lucy, b. Sept. 4, 1772	1	231

	Vol.	Page
TYLER, TYLOR, (cont.)		
Oliver, s. Jno & Elizabeth, b. Mar. 2, 1740/41	1	230
Oliver, s. John & Elizabeth, d. June 4, 1750	1	233
Oliver, s. John & Elizabeth, b. Jan. 2, 1754	1	230
Oliver, m. Abigail **WARREN**, Jan. 4, 1775	1	229
Phinehas, s. John & Elizabeth, b. May 17, 1738	1	230
Phinehas, m. Lucy **HIDE**, Nov. 19, 1766	1	229
Polly, w. Rev. Royal, of Andover, d. Mar. 13, 1792	1	233
Prudence, d. John & Elizabeth, b. Feb. 16, 1742/3	1	230
Reuben, m. Sally **WIGGINS**, July 5, 1809	1	229
William, s. Daniel & Mehetable, b. Aug. 8, 1748	1	230
Zebulon, s. John & Elizabeth, b. Mar. 11, 1736	1	231
Zerviah, d. Oliver & Abigail, b. Mar. 16, 1776	1	231
Zilpha, d. Daniel & Mehetable, b. June 28, 1758	1	231
Zilpha, m. Thomas **MERRETT**, Jr., July 14, 1777	1	181
Zilpha, d. Phin[eha]s & Lucy, b. Sept. 2, 1777	1	231
UNDERWOOD, Hannah, m. Samuel **PELLET**, July [ ], 1752	1	192
Hannah, m. Ephraim **PELLET**, Oct. 6, 1761	1	192
Lucy, m. John **BROWN**, Mar. 13, 1750/51	1	70
UTLEY, Abigail, m. James **BUTT**, Feb. 15, 1770	1	71
UTTER, Elizabeth had s. Daniel **HERRINGTON**, b. Mar. 19,		
1729/30	1	157
Mary, w. Jabez, d. Feb. 13, 1729/30	1	234
VALLET, Mary, m. David **MUNROW**, May 20, 1733	1	181
VAWN, (**VAUGHAN**), Jemima, d. Richard & Ann, b. Mar. 27,		
1741	1	235
WADE, Mehetable, of Canterbury, m. Frederick F. **PHILLIPS**, of		
Griswold, Aug. 4, 1822, by Erastus Learned	2	61
Sarah, d. John & Sarah, b. Aug. 16, 1775	1	242
WADSWORTH, Abigail, d. John & Abigail, b. Apr. 18, 173[ ]	1	238
Abigail, d. John & Abigail, b. Apr. 18, 173[ ]	1	238
Elizabeth, d. John & Abigail, b. Oct. 18, 173[ ]	1	238
John, s. John & Abigail, b. July 31, 1731	1	238
Lucy, d. Jno. & Abigail, b. Feb. 4, 1742/3	1	238
Mary, d. John & Abigail, b. June 28, 1742	1	239
Ruth, d. John & Abigail, b. May 28, 1737	1	238
Samuel, m. Mary **MASH**, Mar. 21, 1744	1	236
Selah, d. Sam[ue]l & Mary, b. Mar. 26, 1745	1	239
WALBRIG, Theodah, d. Amos & Theodah, b. Aug. 8, 1733	1	238
WALDING, [see also **WALDO**], David P., of Windham, m.		
Caroline **SPAULDING**, of Canterbury, June 12, 1825, by		
Geo[rge] S. White	2	85
WALDO, [see also **WALDING**], Abigail, m. Delivereance		
BROWN, Oct. 28, 1717	1	69
Abigail, d. Edward & Abigail, b. July 15, 1744	1	239
Abigail, d. Cornelius & Abigail, d. Oct. 22, 1749	1	246
Abigail, d. Cornelius & Abigail, b. Mar. 31, 1753	1	239
Abigail, d. Cornelius & Abigail, d. Dec. 6, 1754	1	246

	Vol.	Page

WALDO, (cont.)

	Vol.	Page
Abigail, m. Jacob **JOHNSON**, Apr. 7, 1763	1	167
Abigail, m. Nathan **HIDE**, May 16, 1782	1	155
Alice, d. Nathan & Zerviah, b. Feb. 7, 1772	1	241
Alice, d. [Nathan & Zerviah], d. Apr. 27, 1772	1	246
Ann, d. Edward & Abigail, b. Sept. 5, 1735	1	239
Anna, d. Nathan & Zerv[ia]h, b. Oct. 3, 1769	1	241
Anna, d. John Elderkin & Beulah, b. Mar. 16, 1784	1	242
Anne, m. Elisha **PAINE**, Apr. 12, 1753	1	192
Anne, d. Zackariah & Elizabeth, b. Aug. 27, 1759	1	240
Anne, m. Joseph **RAYNSFORD**, Aug. 3, 1777	1	209
Asenath, m. Apollos **RICHMOND**, May 15, 1836, by Rev. Asa King, Westminster	2	68
Betsey, m. Even **PARISH**, b. of Canterbury, Apr. 14, 1839, by Rev. Hezekiah Thatcher	2	62
Clarrissa Sheperd, d. Rufus & Harriet, b. Feb. 13, 1836	2	285
Cornelius, m. Elizabeth **PARK**, Mar. 2, 1763	1	236
Eben[eze]r, s. Zachariah & Elizabeth, b. Apr. 6, 1771	1	241
Ebenezer, m. Cynthia **PARISH**, May 31, 1798	1	237
Edwin, s. Rufus & Harriet, b. Mar. 16, 1834	2	285
Elderkin, s. Rufus & Harriet, b. Feb. 16, 1824	2	285
Elizabeth, d. Zachariah & Elizabeth, b. Jan. 23, 1767	1	241
Elizabeth, w. Zackariah, d. Sept. 7, 1800	1	246
Elizabeth, d. Zachariah, Jr. & Joanna, b. May 21, 1802	1	244
Enoch E., m. Sophronia **BINGHAM**, Oct. 6, 1831, by Rev. Israel G. Rose, of Westminster	2	86
George, s. Rufus & Harriet S., b. Nov. 20, 1839	2	285
Hannah B., of Canterbury, m. Alonzo B. **CHAPIN**, of Wallingford, [Sept.] 24, 1832, by Rev. Samuel J. May	2	16
Harriet, d. Rufus & Harriet, b. Dec. 30, 1829	2	285
Hiram, s. Zachariah, Jr. & Joanna, b. Aug. 12, 1803	1	244
Isaac, s. Cornelius & Abigail, b. Sept. 28, 1748	1	239
Isaac, s. Cornelius & Abigail, d. Oct. 18, 1749	1	246
Isaac, s. Cornelius & Abigail, b. Apr. 8, 1751	1	239
Isaac, s. Cornelius & Abigail, d. Mar. 23, 1752	1	246
John, s. Rufus & Harriet, b. Mar. 25, 1826	2	285
John Elderkin, s. Zachariah & Elizabeth, b. Oct. 5, 1761	1	240
John Elderkin, m. Beulah **FOSTER**, May 22, 1783	1	236
Loren, s. Ebenezer & Cynthia, b. Feb. 2, 1802	1	244
Louis, of Windham, m. Alice S. **BALDWIN**, of Canterbury, Feb. 26, 1834, by Rev. Otis C. Whiton	2	86
Louisa, d. Nathan & Zerviah, b. June 3, 1764	1	240
Lovisa, d. Nathan & Zerviah, d. Oct. 25, 1764	1	246
Mary, d. John E. & Beulah, b. Oct. 25, 1785	1	243
Mary, d. Rufus & Harriet S. T., b. May 19, 1844	2	286
Mercy, d. Samuel & Margaret, b. Mar. 29, 1804	1	244
Moses, s. Zachariah & Joanna, b. Sept. 16, 180[ ]	1	244
Nathan, s. Edward & Abigail, b. June 23, 1743	1	239

	Vol.	Page
WALDO, (cont.		
Nathan, s. Nathan & Zerviah, b. Oct. 5, 1767	1	241
Obadiah, s. Ebenezer & Cynthia, b. June 8, 1800	1	244
Rufus, m. Harriet **SHEPARD**, b. of Canterbury, Mar. 20,		
1823, by Thomas J. Murdock	2	85
Ruth, m. Thomas **SAFFORD**, [ ], 1806	1	237
Samuel, s. Zachariah & Eliza, b. Mar. 3, 1779	1	242
Samuel, m. Margaret **GALLUP**, of Voluntown, [ ]	1	237
Sarah, d. Rufus & Harriet, b. Oct. 26, 1831	2	285
Simon Sheperd, s. Rufus & Harriet, b. Feb. 15, 1828	2	285
Susanna, d. Cornelius & Abigail, b. Aug. 10, 1749	1	239
Susanna, d. Samuel & Margaret, b. Dec. 8, 1802	1	244
Zachariah, s. Edward & Abigail, b. Feb. 1, 1734/5, at Windham	1	239
Zachariah, m. Elizabeth **WIGHT**, 3rd, of Windham, Nov. 21,		
1758	1	236
Zachariah, s. Zachariah & Elizabeth, b. May 8, 1764	1	240
Zachariah, Jr., m. Joanna **BUTTERFIELD**, of N. H., Jan.		
1, 1800	1	237
Zachariah, m. Cynthia **PARKE**, Nov. 18, 1806	1	237
Zerviah, d. Nathan & Zerviah, b. Aug. 19, 1765	1	241
WALKER, Alden H., of Southbridge, Mass., m. Betsey B. **PARK**,		
of Canterbury, Sept. 4, 1836, by Rev. Tubal Wakefield	2	86
WALTON, Eliza, m. Barnabus **ALLEN**, Jr., Feb. 18, 1808	1	52
Jasper, s. Oliver & Alice, b. Aug. 27, 1785	1	243
Larrance, s. Nathaniel & Jemima, b. Dec. 15, 1717	1	238
Zerviah, m. Joseph **NICKELS**, Mar. 11, 1766	1	189
WARREN, WARRAIN, Abigail, m. Oliver **TYLER**, Jan. 4, 1775	1	229
George, s. [Samuel & Sarah], b. Oct. 28, 1801	1	244
Jabez, s. Moses & Sarah, b. Aug. 11, 1781	1	242
Joseph, twin with Moses, s. [Moses & Sarah], b. Jan. 23, 1776	1	242
Laura, d. Samuel & Sarah, b. Nov. 2, 1799	1	244
Martha, m. William **BRADFORD**, Mar. 24, 1766	1	70
Moses, m. Sarah **WHEELER**, Mar. 8, 1773	1	236
Moses, twin with Joseph, s. [Moses & Sarah], b. Jan. 23, 1776	1	242
Samuel, s. Moses & Sarah, b. May 24, 1774	1	242
Samuel, m. Sarah **GREENMAN**, Dec. 30, 1798	1	237
Samuel N., s. [Samuel & Sarah], b. Aug. 15, 1803	1	244
Sarah, m. Anthony **MORSE**, May 11, 1762	1	181
WASHBURN, WASHBORN, Betty, of Coventry, m. Joseph		
ENSWORTH, Jan. 25, 1763	1	133
Eli, m. Mary **FISH**, Mar. 9, 1786	1	236
Eli, s. Eli & Mary, b. Dec. 8, 1796	1	243
John, s. Eli & Mary, b. Feb. 13, 1787	1	243
Mary, d. Eli & Mary, b. Oct. 24, 1789	1	243
WATE, Irenah, m. [ ] **AMES**, Jan. 2, 1755	1	51
WATERMAN, Anna Angell, d. Nathan & Anna, d. Feb. 26, 1843	2	362
Elizabeth, of Canterbury, m. Danville **LEADBETTER**, of U.		
S. A., Aug. 8, 1836, by Rev. Tubal Wakefield	2	52

	Vol.	Page

WATERMAN, (cont.)

    Joseph Wheaton, s. Nathan & Anna, d. Apr. 3, 1842 — 2 — 362

    Rebecca, of Canterbury, m. Charles Jarvis **WHITING**, of
        Ellesville, Me., June 24, 1841, by Rev. Tubal Wakefield — 2 — 87

    Robert, of Sheffield, Me., m. Emily **BRADFORD**, of
        Canterbury, Nov. 11, 1828, by Chester Lyon, J. P. — 2 — 86

WATKINS, William, s. of a single woman, b. Mar. 8, 1784, in
    Ashford — 1 — 245

WATROUS, Douglass F., of Lisbon, m. Sarah L. **ADAMS**, of
    Canterbury, Apr. 9, 1849, by Rev. Thomas Tallman — 2 — 89

WEAVER, Alice, m. Samuel **SHEPERD**, Mar. 20, 1826, by Asael
    Bacon, J. P. — 2 — 71

    Catharine, of Plainfield, m. Patric[k] **BRYAN**, Oct. 22,
        1837, by Rev. C. J. Warren — 2 — 11

    Elmer, s. [Remington & Molly], b. Feb. 5, 1801 — 1 — 245

    Elmer, m. Philena **JUSTIN**, b. of Canterbury, [   ], by
        Rev. Tho[ma]s J. Murdock — 2 — 85

    Nabby, d. [Remington & Molly], b. Jan. 26, 1795 — 1 — 245

    W[illia]m Jefferds, s. Remington & Molly, b. Sept. 28, 1792 — 1 — 245

WEBB, Elizabeth, m. John **WINTWORTH**, Nov. 25, 1773 — 1 — 236

    Fanny, of Canterbury, m. Edmund **BURNHAM**, of Windham,
        Sept. 10, 1834, by Rev. Samuel J. May, Brooklyn — 2 — 10

    John P., of Windham, m. Rhoda **KINGSLEY**, of Canterbury,
        Feb. 20, 1850, by Rev. R. S. Hazen, of Westminster — 2 — 89

WEDGE, WEEDG, Isaac, s. Isaac & Hannah, b. June 1, 1705 — 1 — 238

    Joseph Harlin, s. [Joseph & Emily], b. May 7, 1828 — 2 — 285

    Leander Alcidees, s. [Joseph & Emily], b. Dec. 2, 1825 — 2 — 285

    Palina Keziah, d. Joseph & Emily, b. Sept. 13, 1823 — 2 — 285

    Palina Keziah, d. Joseph, d. Aug. 15, 1825 — 2 — 362

    Philander Norton, s. [Joseph & Emily], b. Dec. 11, 1830 — 2 — 285

WEEKS, Martha, m. Jonathan **SHAW**, Dec. 4, 1759 — 1 — 214

    Samuel, of Pomfret, m. Emily F. **SHOLES**, of Canterbury,
        Sept. 19, 1841, by Samuel S. Hough, J. P. — 2 — 87

WELCH, David, m. Ammitta **READ**, Mar. 4, 1740/41 — 1 — 236

WELLES, WELLS, Benj[ami]n, of Tolland, m. Mary B. **FORD**, of
    Canterbury, Dec. 6, 1826, by Israel G. Rose — 2 — 85

    Gideon, s. Gideon & Wealthian, d. Feb. 27, 1787(?) — 1 — 246

    Harding Jones, s. Gideon & Wealthian, d. Apr. 21, 1790 — 1 — 246

    John Whiting, s. Gideon & Wealthian, d. Jan. 4, 1794 — 1 — 246

    Polly Tyler, d. Gideon & Wealthian, d. Mar. 13, 1792 — 1 — 246

    Welthian, w. Gideon, d. Dec. 5, 1793 — 1 — 246

WENER, Elizabeth, of Norwich, m. Solomon **MORSE**, Mar. 21,
    1765 — 1 — 181

WENTWORTH, WINTWORTH, Charles, s. [John & Elizabeth], b.
    May 18, 1775 — 1 — 242

    Elizabeth, d. John & Elizabeth, b. Sept. 7, 1775 — 1 — 242

    John, m. Elizabeth **WEBB**, Nov. 25, 1773 — 1 — 236

    John, s. John & Elizabeth, b. May 10, 1774 — 1 — 242

	Vol.	Page
WENTWORTH, WINTWORTH, (cont.)		
Martha, m. John **MOOT***, May 8, 1753 (***MOTT**)	1	181
Phebe, d. John & Elizabeth, b. Jan. 14, 1779	1	242
Sarah, m. John **PENRE**, Nov. 14, 1765	1	193
WEST, Nathaniel, of Providence, R. I., m. Charlotte W. **BROWN,**		
of Canterbury, Nov. 26, 1848, by Rev. Robert C. Learned	2	89
WETHY, Phillip, m. Miriam **SQUIRE**, Jan. 28, 1779	1	236
Sally, d. Phillip & Miriam, b. May 6, 1780	1	242
WHEAT, Elisha, s. Salmon & Marse (Mary), b. Nov. 7, 1742	1	238
Eunice, d. Salmon & Marse (Mary), b. Sept. 15, 1739	1	238
Eunice, d. Salmon & Marse (Mercy), b. Sept. 29, 1739	1	238
Jonathan, s. Salmon & Mary, b. Apr. 1, 1735	1	238
Lidia, d. Salmon & Mary, b. Mar. 22, 1732/3	1	238
WHEELER, Abigail, d. John & Lydia, b. Nov. 4, 1786	1	243
Ama, d. [Jonathan & Mary], b. Apr. 21, 1772	1	244
Ama Augusta, d. Elisha & Elizabeth, b. Jan. 12, 1805	1	245
Azubah, d. [Jonathan & Mary], b. Oct. 15, 1777	1	244
Azubah, d. [Jonathan & Mary], d. Mar. 15, 1794	1	246
Benjamin, [s.] Jonathan & Mary, b. Dec. 30, 1779	1	244
Benjamin, s. [Jonathan & Mary], d. Mar. 20, 1796	1	247
Betsey, d. [Jonathan & Mary], b. Nov. 25, 1773	1	244
Betsey, d. [Jonathan & Mary], d. Apr. 6, 1793	1	246
Beulah M., of Canterbury, m. Samuel G. **MATHEWSON,** of		
New Hartford, June 22, 1834, by Rev. Asa King,		
Westminster	2	56
Calvin, s. [Jonathan & Mary], b. Jan. 19, 1788	1	244
Caroline, of Canterbury, m. Augustus **WOODARD,** of		
Brooklyn, Sept. 17, 1829, by Peter Morse, J. P.	2	86
Cornelius, s. John & Lydia, b. Aug. 10, 1769	1	341
Daniel P., of Norwich, m. Mary E. **FRANCES**, of Canterbury,		
Mar. 7, 1842, by Rev. Tubal Wakefield	2	87
Drusilla, m. Rufus **PELLET**, Mar. 15, 1781	1	193
Eben[eze]r, s. John & Lydia, b. Mar. 20, 1771	1	241
Elisha, s. [Jonathan & Mary], b. Sept. 21, 1770	1	244
Elisha, m. Elizabeth **RANSFORD**, Feb. 9, 1797	1	237
Elizabeth, d. Elisha & Elizabeth, b. July 30, 1798	1	244
John, m. Lydia **ADAMS**, Nov. 15, 1764	1	236
John, s. John & Lydia, b. Nov. 13, 1772	1	241
John, m. Mary **WHEELER**, Oct. 20, 1797	1	237
Jonathan, s. [Jonathan & Mary], b. Sept. 21, 1775	1	244
Jonathan, d. July 4, 1796	1	247
Joseph, s. John & Lydia, b. Sept. 21, 1774	1	242
Lois, d. John & Lydia, b. Mar. 3, 1785	1	243
Lydia, of Plainfield, m. Joseph **FARNUM**, July 10, 1764	1	138
Lydia, d. John & Lydia, b. June 17, 1767	1	241
Lydia, w. John, d. Feb. 26, 1795	1	246
Mary, d. Jonathan & Grace, b. Jan. 26, 1739, at Preston	1	238
Mary, m. Moses **SMITH**, Nov. 5, 1741	1	214

	Vol.	Page
WHEELER, (cont.)		
Mary, m. John **WHEELER,** Oct. 20, 1797	1	237
Mary, d. [Elisha & Elizabeth], b. Oct. 4, 1800	1	244
Nathan, s. John & Lydia, b. Jan. 7, 1779	1	242
Polly, d. [Jonathan & Mary], b. Nov. 30, 1768	1	244
Sally, d. Jonathan & Mary, b. Jan. 16, 1767	1	244
Sally, d. Jonathan & Mary, d. Mar. 6, 1786	1	246
Samuel Adams, s. John & Lydia, b. Oct. 5, 1776	1	242
Sarah, m. Moses **WARREN,** Mar. 8, 1773	1	236
Sarah, d. [Jonathan & Mary], b. Mar. 9, 1790	1	244
Susanna, d. [Elisha & Elizabeth], b. Sept. 1, 1802	1	244
Warren, s. [Jonathan & Mary], b. Dec. 15, 1781	1	244
William, s. [Jonathan & Mary], b. Feb. 9, 1784	1	244
WHIPPLE, Thomas, of Hampton, m. Eunice **ALLEN,** of		
Canterbury, Apr. 2, 1823, by Erastus Learned	2	85
WHITE, Andrew Judson, s. Rev. George S. & Mary, b. May 19,		
1824	2	285
Anne, m. Abijah **REED,** Sept. 7, 1773	1	209
Deborah, m. Daniel Herrick **BOND,** July 5, 1835, by Rev.		
George S. White	2	11
Elijah, m. Lucy **DAVIS,** May 19, 1791	1	236
Elizabeth Sargent, [twin with Thomas Edward], d. Rev.		
George S. & Mary, b. Jan. 6, 1822	2	285
John Adams, s. George S. & Mary, b. Feb. 19, 1827	2	285
Lucy, d. [Elijah & Lucy], b. Apr. 29, 1797	1	243
Mary, of Canterbury, m. Joseph **PEABODY,** of Norwich, July		
9, 1836, by Rev. George S. White	2	62
Mary, of Canterbury, m. Joseph **PEABODY,** of Norwich, Aug.		
9, 1836, by George S. White	2	11
Mehetable, m. Benjamin **SIMMS,** June 22, 1797	1	215
Polly, d. Elijah & Lucy, b. Sept. 21, 1791	1	243
Susanna, m. Robert **GREEN,** Nov. 21, 1750	1	149
Susanna, d. Elijah & Lucy, b. Apr. 5, 1794	1	243
Thomas Edward, [twin with Elizabeth Sargent], s. Rev. George		
S. & Mary, b. Jan. 6, 1822	2	285
WHITFORD, Hannah, m. Heber **HERRINGTON,** May 12, 1793	1	156
Mary Eliza, d. William & Lucetta, b. June 30, 1825	2	285
William, s. Dan[ie]l, of Canterbury, m. Lucretia		
TILLINGHAST, of East Greenwich, R. I., Sept. 6, 1824,		
by Thomas Manchester, Elder, East Greenwich	2	85
WHITING, Anne, m. James **DYAR,** Dec. 8, 1753	1	120
Charles, s. John & Parnel, b. June 3, 1802	1	244
Charles Jarvis, of Ellesville, Mr., m. Rebecca **WATERMAN,**		
of Canterbury, June 24, 1841, by Rev. Tubal Wakefield	2	87
James, s. John & Parnel, b. Aug. 7, 1799	1	244
James, s. John & Parnel, b. Aug. 22, 179[ ]	1	244
WHITMAN, Joshua, s. Silas & Ruby, b. Aug. 19, 1797	1	243
Silas, m. Ruby **BUTTS,** Feb. 4, 1796	1	237

	Vol.	Page
WILLIAMS, (cont.)		
Chloe, m. Waterman **CARVER**, Feb. 27, 1803	1	102
Daniel, d. Mar. 4, 1764	1	246
Desire, d. Daniel & Jane, b. Feb. 5, 1747	1	239
Dorcas, d. Daniel & Jane, b. Jan. 20, 1738	1	239
Dwight, s. Benjamin & Betsey, b. Mar. 25, 1821	1	245
Dyar, s. James & Meriam, b. Sept. 9, 1760	1	241
Ebenezer, s. Daniel & Jane, b. Dec. 29, 1740	1	239
Elias, m. Sarah **PARK**, b. of Canterbury, Mar. 5, 1828,		
by Rev. Israel Rose, of Westminister	2	85
Elijah, s. Isaiah & Abigail, b. Aug. 22, 1747	1	240
Elijah, m. Abigail **ADAMS**, Nov. 19, 1768	1	236
Elijah, s. [Elijah & Abigail], b. Sept. 8, 1774	1	242
Elizabeth, m. Josiah **BUTT**, Oct. 25, 1729	1	69
Elizabeth, of Plainfield, m. Elijah **DYAR**, Nov. 16, 1752	1	120
Elizabeth, m. Samuel **DAVENPORT**, Dec. 20, 1787	1	121
Emeline, m. Capt. John **SMITH**, Dec. 10, 1829, by Rev.		
Israel G. Rose, of Westminster	2	72
Emma Lane, of Canterbury, m. Charles L. **FILLIMORE**, of		
Lisbon, Mar. 10, 1851, by Comfort D. Fillimore, Elder	2	33
Eunice, d. Isaiah & Abigail, b. Mar. 19, 1760	1	240
Fanny, d. Nathan & Hannah, b. July 3, 1782	1	243
Grace, d. Daniel & Jane, b. Mar. 3, 1745	1	239
Hannah, m. Ephraim **WOODARD**, Jan. 14, 1735	1	236
Harlow, m. Lotilla D. **ENSWORTH**, Apr. 17, 1844, by		
Ephraim Browning, J. P., at Packersville	2	88
Hart, m. Elizabeth **ADAMS**, Dec. 24, 1845, by Rev. Daniel		
D. Lyon, of Packersville	2	88
Isaiah, m. Abigail **KNIGHT**, of Norwich, May 5, 1744	1	236
Isaiah, s. Isaiah & Abigail, b. Mar. 19, 1754	1	240
Isaiah, s. [Benj[ami]n & Betsey], b. Mar. 6, 1813	1	245
James, s. Isaiah & Abigail, b. Sept. 19, 1751	1	240
Jane, w. Daniel, d. Apr. [ ], 1753	1	246
Jason Fitch, s. [Elijah, Jr. & Elizabeth], b. Mar. 19, 1803	1	245
Job, s. Nathan & Waitstill, b. Oct. 8, 1758	1	240
L[l]oyd, of Brookline, m. Angelba **HEWITT**, of Canterbury,		
July 12, 1846, by Rev. H. Slade, of Scotland	2	88
Lydea, d. Isaiah & Abigail, b. Aug. 19, 1749	1	240
Mary E., m. Ralph W. R. **CINSON**, Aug. 17, 1834, by Rev.		
Jesse Fisher	2	16
Mary E., m. Ralph W. **ROBINSON**, Aug. 17, 1834, by Rev.		
Jesse Fisher	2	67
Mary Ellsy, d. Benjamin & Betsey, b. July 27, 1808	1	245
Merret, s. Benj[ami]n & Betsey, b. Apr. 3, 1810	1	245
Mer[r]it B., m. Harriet **ALLEN**, Oct. 25, 1836, by Walter		
Williams, J. P.	2	86
Mer[r]it B., m. Dulucenia **PECK**, b. of Canterbury, Jan.		
27, 1846, by Walter Williams, J. P.	2	88

	Vol.	Page
WILLIAMS, (cont.)		
Nathan, s. Daniel & Jane, b. Dec. 6, 1749	1	239
Nathan, s. Nathan & Waitstill, b. Sept. 23, 1760	1	240
Olive, d. Nathan & Waitstill, b. May 5, 1756	1	240
Pullman M., of West Springfield, Mass., m. Mary A. HARRIS, of Canterbury, Apr. 13, 1845, by Eratus Dickinson	2	88
Roger Alden, s. [Elijah, Jr. & Elizabeth], b. Sept. 15, 1805	1	245
Roger Smith, s. Benjamin & Betsey, b. Mar. 27, 1817	1	245
Sally, m. Spencer **LYON**, Nov. 9, 1800	1	176
Samuel, s. Elijah & Abigail, b. Apr. 6, 1771	1	242
Sarah L., d. Merret B. & Harriet E., b. Aug. 17, 1837	2	285
Susannah, m. Eben[eze]r **PARRISH**, Feb. 13, 1752	1	192
Waitstill, d. [Nathan & Hannah], b. Mar. 30, 1788	1	243
Will[ia]m H., m. Mary S. **STORY**, Nov. 11, 1827, by Rev. Israel G. Rose, of Westminster	2	85
William Hubbard, s. Elijah, Jr. & Elizabeth, b. Jan. 22, 1801	1	245
William W., m. Lydia M. **RUSSELL**, b. of Scituate, R. I., May 27, 1851, by Rev. Robert C. Learned	2	90
Zadoo, s. Simeon & Prudence, b. Mar. 20, 1780	1	242
Zipporah, d. James & Meriam, b. Feb. 13, 1758	1	241
WILLIAMSON, Asenath, d. George & Mary, b. Oct. 10, 1781	1	242
Cornelius, d. Aug. 7, 1823	2	362
Ebenezer, s. Nathan & Polly, b. Nov. 10, 1791	1	243
George, m. Mary **FOSTER**, July 9, 1778	1	236
Lucy, single woman, had d. Sarah, b. Apr. 28, 1783	1	242
Sarah, d. Lucy, single woman, b. Apr. 28, 1783	1	242
Sarah, m. John **BRADFORD**, Jr., Sept. 4, 1788	1	72
W[illia]m Durkee, s. George & Mary, b. July 31, 1779	1	242
WILLOUGHBY, Charlotte, d. [Joseph R. & Mary], b. June 20, 1803	1	244
Charlotte, of Canterbury, m. Zelotes **JENCKES**, of Norwich, May 11, 1827, by Andrew T. Judson, J. P.	2	43
Harriet, of Canterbury, m. Robert H. **CRANDALL**, of Exeter, R. I., Oct. 16, 1827, by Andrew T. Judson, J. P.	2	15
Joseph R., m. Mary **MORGAN**, Aug. 26, 1797	1	237
Marian, d. Joseph R. & Mary, b. May 29, 1800	1	244
Mary Ann, of Canterbury, m. George W. **CLARK**, of Norwich, Sept. 9, 1822, by Erastus Larned	2	15
William F., m. Phebe H. **CAREY**, Oct. 15, 1827, by Rev. Israel G. Rose, of Westminster	2	85
William Frederic, s. [Joseph R. & Mary], b. Jan. 14, 1801	1	244
WILSON,, Horace L., of Windham, m. Eunice J. **DEMING**, of Canterbury, July 8, 1850, by Rev. R. S. Hazen, of Westminster	2	89
John, s. Sam[ue]l & Mary, b. July 3, 1735	1	238
Mabel, m. Charles **DAVENPORT**, Mar. 3, 1791, at Brooklyn	1	121
Sam[ue]l, m. Mary **DAVENPORT**, Sept. 25, 1734	1	236

	Vol.	Page
WILSON, (cont.)		
Sophia, m. Chauncey **TOWNSEND**, b. of Canterbury, Feb. 5, 1824, by Walter Williams, J. P.	2	79
WINCHESTER, Abel, s. [Joel & Mary], b. Aug. 15, 1809	1	245
Andrew, d. May 18, 1793	1	247
Asa, s. [Joel & Mary], b. Oct. 29, 1803	1	245
Eunice, d. Andrew & Lydia, b. Feb. 6, 1776	1	242
Hervey, s. Joel & Mary, b. Aug. 23, 1801	1	245
James, s. [Joel & Mary], b. Dec. 16, 1797	1	243
Joanna, d. Joel & Mary, b. Mar. 19, 1795	1	243
Joanna, d. May 12, 1808	1	247
John, s. [Joel & Mary], b. July 17, 1796	1	243
Lorain, s. [Joel & Mary], b. Oct. 16, 1799	1	243
Mary, d. [Joel & Mary], b. May 28, 1811	1	245
Sarah, m. Charles **JUSTIN**, Nov. 3, 1784	1	167
Susanna, d. [Joel & Mary], b. Dec. 16, 1805	1	245
WINTER, Abigail, d. Timothy & Elizabeth, b. Mar. 9, 1753	1	239
Abigail, d. Timothy & Elizabeth, b. Mar. 9, 1753	1	240
Elizabeth, d. Timothy & Elizabeth, b. Feb. 10, 1758	1	240
Jonathan Weeks, s. Timothy & Elizabeth, b. Sept. 7, 1763	1	240
Mary, d. Timothy & Elizabeth, b. Aug. 5, 1760	1	240
Mary, single woman, had s. John **BINGHAM**, b. Mar. 12, 1780	1	86
Timothy, s. Timothy & Elizabeth, b. Sept. 16, 1755	1	239
Timo[thy], Jr., m. Molly **BENNET**, Feb. 2, 1775	1	236
WITTER, Amos, Jr., of Plainfield, m. Mary H. **ENSWORTH**, of Canterbury, Nov. 19, 1850, by Rev. J. B. Guild, at Packersville	2	89
Asa, s. Ebenezer & Eunice, b. Oct. 4, 1800	1	245
Betsey, d. Ada & Joanna, b. May 25, 1773	1	241
Dorothy, d. Jos[eph] & Hannah, b. July 15, 1759	1	241
Ebenezer, s. Dea. Asa & Joanna, b. Mar. 13, 1778	1	242
Ebenezer, m. Eunice **BASS**, Sept. 12, 1799	1	237
Hannah, d. [Jos[eph] & Hannah], b. Mar. 9, 1765	1	241
Joanna, d. Asa & Joanna, b. July 2, 1792	1	243
Joanna, d. [Ebenezer & Eunice,], b. Apr. 8, 1816	1	245
John, s. [Ebenezer & Eunice], b. Sept. 27, 1812	1	245
John, m. Mary M. **DOWING**, Sept. 3, 1834, by Rev. Asa King	2	86
Joseph, s. Joseph & Hannah, b. Apr. 7, 1762	1	240
Joseph, s. [Jos[eph] & Hannah], b. Apr. 7, 1762	1	241
Lucinda, d. [Jos[eph] & Hannah], b. Jan. 25, 1768	1	241
Lyman, s. [Ebenezer & Eunice], b. Sept. 26, 1807	1	245
Maria Dewing, d. John & Maria, b. Dec. 16, 1835	2	285
Polly, d. Asa & Joanna, b. Apr. 9, 1788	1	243
Rhoda, d. Asa & Joanna, b. June 8, 1770	1.	241
Ruth, d. [Ebenezer & Eunice], b. Apr. 8, 1810	1	245
Ruth, of Canterbury, m. Thomas **MAY**, of Woodstock, Feb. 2, 1836, by Rev. Asa King, Westminster	2	56

	Vol.	Page
WITTER, (cont.)		
Sarah, d. Asa & Joanna, b. July 1, 1775	1	242
William, s. [Ebenezer & Eunice], b. May 1, 1804	1	245
WOOD, Augustus, m. Anne **ALLEN,** Nov. 22, 1786	1	236
Elvira, d. Augustus & Anna, b. Dec. 22, 1788	1	243
Eunice M., of Canterbury, m. Rev. Benjamin Smith **WILLIAMS,** of Smithville, Chenango Co., N. Y., Oct. 18, 1838, by Rev. Tubal Wakefield	2	87
Hepsibah, d. Augustus & Anne, b. Feb. 11, 1799	1	243
Lora, d. Augustus & Anne, b. Oct. 1, 1800	1	244
Lydia, d. Augustus & Anna, b. July 25, 1795	1	243
Lydia, of Canterbury, m. William **EDMONDS,** of Homer, Oct. 12, 1830, at Wid. Wood's, Canterbury, by Rev. William Palmer, Norwich	2	27
Mary, of Norwich, m. Dea. Jonas **BOND,** May 19, 1784	1	72
Mason A., of Plainfield, m. Maria S. **BACON,** of Canterbury, Sept. 13, 1849, by Rev. Robert C. Learned	2	89
Milton, s. [Augustus & Anna], b. Dec. 9, 1790	1	243
Orrin, s. Augustus & Anne, b. May 22, 1787	1	243
Polly, d. Augustus & Anna, b. Dec. 13, 1792	1	243
Rebecca Allen, d. Augustus & Anne, b. Oct. 2, 1802	1	244
Sarah A., m. Harvey R. **DYER,** b. of Canterbury, Sept. 2, 1839, by Rev. Charles J. Warren	2	21
Talitha, d. Augustus & Anne, b. Mar. 30, 1797	1	243
Talitha, m. Abijah **DEWING,** b. of Canterbury, Nov. 30, 1842, by M. Byrne	2	22
Victoria, d. Levi, Jr. & Sarah, b. Aug. 11, 1838	2	285
WOODWARD, WOODARD, Aaron, s. Ward & Rebecca, b. Sept. 20, 1781	1	242
Abby Luceba, d. Elijah & Aurelia, b. Oct. 14, 1828	2	285
Abigail, d. Deliver[an]ce & Abigail, b. Feb. 9, 1738	1	240
Abigail, d. Ephraim & Huldah, b. Mar. 24, 1742/3	1	240
Abigail, m. Peter **DAVISON,** Apr. 28, 1768	1	120
Abigail, d. [Sam[ue]l & Margaret], b. Feb. 28, 1772	1	241
Abisha, s. Enos & Mary, b. Jan. 10, 1768	1	241
Alithea, w. Peter, d. Mar. 16, 1774	1	246
Alpheas, s. Noah & Anne, b. Jan. 2, 1742/3	1	238
Amos, m. Hannah **MEACHAM,** May 6, 1735	1	236
Amos, s. Amos & Hannah, b. Aug. 19, 1735	1	238
Amos, d. Jan. 28, 1753	1	246
Amos, s. Silas & Mary, b. Aug. 14, 1753	1	239
Amos, m. Anna **PATEN,** Feb. 21, 1760	1	236
Anna Maria, d. Elijah & Amelia, b. Aug. 27, 1820	2	285
Anne, d. Noah & Anne, b. Aug. 3, 1746	1	239
Art, s. Sam[ue]l & Margaret, b. Feb. 21, 1761	1	241
Arunnah, s. Joseph & Mary, b. Dec. 27, 1753	1	239
Arunnah, s. James & Sibbel, b. Apr. 20, 1774	1	242
Asa, s. Joseph & Mary, b. Feb. 15, 1760	1	239

	Vol.	Page
WOODWARD, WOODARD, (cont.)		
Isaac, s. [Peter & Althea], b. Aug. 23, 1768	1	242
Isaac, d. Feb. 4, 1800, ae 89	1	246
Ithamer, s. Ephraim & Huldah, b. Jan. 21, 1748/9	1	239
Ithamer, s. Huldah **SHARPE**, Nov. 23, 1773	1	236
James, s. Joseph & Mary, b. Feb. 16, 1749	1	241
James, m. Abigail **HARRIS**, Jan. 14, 1762	1	236
James, m. Sibel **BROWN**, Apr. 16, 1772	1	236
Jared, s. Amos & Anne, b. Apr. 10, 1766	1	241
John, s. Ephraim & Huldah, b. June 10, 1753	1	239
John, s. James & Abigail, b. Oct. 29, 1762	1	245
John, Dea., d. Apr. 1, 1767	1	246
John, s. Enos & Mary, b. Oct. 30, 1769	1	241
Joseph, m. Elizabeth **SYLSBY**, June 24, 1714	1	236
Joseph, s. Joseph & Hannah, b. Feb. 26, 1725/6	1	238
Joseph, d. May 14, 1726	1	246
Joseph, m. Mary **BRADFORD**, May 31, 1748	1	236
Joseph, s. [Sam[ue]l & Margaret], b. July 4, 1767	1	241
Josiah, s. Simeon & Sarah, b. Jan. 17, 1749/50	1	239
Lee, s. Peter & Althea, b. Jan. 15, 1759	1	240
Lee, s. Peter & Mary, b. May 3, 1786(?)	1	244
Loiza, m. Caleb **SANFORD**, of Griswold, Apr. 10, 1842, by		
Rev. Asa King, Westminster	2	74
Lucy, d. [Sam[ue]l & Margaret], b. July 7, 1765	1	241
Lidia, d. Samuel & Margaret, b. Feb. 22, 1758	1	240
Lydia, d. Peter & Deliah, b. May 3, 1786	1	244
Malissia, d. [Bethuel A. & Clarocy], b. June 29, 1812	1	245
Malissa, of Westminster, m. Albert **KIMBALL**, of Scotland,		
Mar. 14, 1831, by Rev. I. G. Rose, of Westminster	2	47
Mary, m. Joseph **CLEVELAND**, June 24, 1725	1	100
Mary, d. Amos Hannah, b. Apr. 13, 1730	1	238
Mary, [twin with Sarah], d. Enos & Mary, b. Jan. 29, 1759	1	240
Mary, d. Joseph & Mary, b. June 26, 1764	1	240
Mary, m. David **MUNROW**, Nov. 30, 1769	1	181
Mary, w. Peter, d. Apr. 17, 1785	1	246
Mary Ann, d. Bethuel A. & Clarocy, b. Mar. 11, 1815	1	245
Mary Ann, m. John **HARTSHORN**, Nov. 17, 1829, by Rev.		
Israel G. Rose, of Westminster	2	40
Mary Anne, of Canterbury, m. Erastus **SMITH**, of Hartford,		
June 27, 1839, by Rev. Charles J. Warren	2	74
Mary Parker, d. Elijah & Aurelia, b. Dec. 13, 1818	1	245
Myriam, d. Simeon & Sarah, b. Nov. 13, 1733	1	238
Miriam, m. James **HIDES**, Dec. 3, 1754	1	155
Noah, s. Richard & Mary, b. Mar. 30, 1718	1	238
Noah, m. Anne **ARMSTRONG**, Nov. 25, 1741	1	236
Noah, s. Noah & Anne, b. Apr. 19, 1744	1	239
Olive, d. Amos & Hannah, b. Feb. 17, 1738	1	238
Olive, d. Mar. 31, 1760	1	246

	Vol.	Page
WOODWARD, WOODARD, (cont.)		
Olive, d. [Amos & Anne], b. July 30, 1768	1	241
Peter, s. Isaac & Elizabeth, b. Aug. 16, 1733	1	238
Peter, m. Althea **ARMSTRONG**, of Norwich, Dec. 24, 1755	1	236
Peter, m. Mary **FROST**, Dec. 23, 1774	1	236
Peter, m. Delilah **BUTT**, Aug. 19, 1785	1	236
Peter, m. Ruth **WHITNEY**, of Pomfret, Mar. 10, 1790	1	237
Phebe, d. Simeon & Sarah, b. May 15, 1747	1	239
Phebe, d. Simeon & Sarah, d. July 21, 1749	1	246
Reuel, s. Richard & Deborah, b. Aug. 13, 1774	1	242
Richard, m. Deborah **DOWNING**, Apr. 30, 1772	1	236
Richard Rufus, s. Richard & Deborah, b. May 11, 1776	1	242
Rufus, s. Jos[eph] & Mary, b. Apr. 21, 1751	1	239
Rufus, s. Joseph & Mary, d. Sept. 11, 1753	1	246
Rufus, s. Joseph & Mary, b. Feb. 15, 1758	1	240
Ruth, d. Rich[ar]d & Deborah, b. Feb. 19, 1773	1	241
Samuel, s. Richard & Mary, b. June 29, 1725	1	238
Samuel, m. Margaret **CLEVELAND**, Jan. 18, 1751	1	236
Sam[ue]l, s. Sam[ue]l & Margaret, b. Oct. 5, 1756	1	240
Samuel, s. [Sam[ue]l & Margaret], b. Jan. 17, 1763	1	241
Sarah, d. Silas & Mary, b. July 26, 1751	1	239
Sarah, m. Will[ia]m **BOND**, Sept. 25, 1754	1	70
Sarah, [twin with Mary], d. Enos & Mary, b. Jan. 29, 1759	1	240
Sarah, d. Enos & Mary, d. Nov. 18, 1760	1	246
Sarah, d. Joseph & Mary, b. May 28, 1768	1	241
Sarah, d. W[illia]m & Zilpha, b. Oct. 20, 1773	1	242
Silas, s. Amos & Hannah, b. Apr. 23, 1728	1	238
Silas, m. Mary **BEDLAKE**, Feb. 28, 1749/50	1	236
Silas, s. Enos & Mary, b. Jan. 17, 1761	1	241
Silas, s. Enos & Mary, d. Mar. 25, 1764	1	246
Silas, s. Enos & Mary, b. May 10, 1765	1	241
Simeon, m. Sarah **BAKER**, Nov. 23, 1732	1	236
Simon, s. Simeon & Sary, b. Jan. 26, 1742/3	1	238
Susanna, d. Joseph & Mary, b. May 13, 1766	1	241
Timothy, s. Samuel & Margaret, b. June 6, 1759	1	240
Ward, s. Ephraim & Huldah, b. Apr. 5, 1751	1	239
Ward, m. Rebecca **PUTNAM**, Oct. 19, 1780	1	236
Wealthian, d. Jos[eph] & Mary, b. Jan. 3, 1756	1	240
We[a]lthian, d. Joseph & Mary, b. Jan. 3, 1756	1	241
Welthen, d. Peter & Althea, b. Feb. 9, 1761	1	240
William, s. Deliver[an]ce & Abigail, b. Sept. 3, 1740(?)	1	240
Will[ia]m, s. Enos & Mary, b. July 14, 1752	1	239
W[illia]m, m. Zilpha **MINARD**, Dec. 10, 1772	1	236
----, an infant child of Peter & Alatheiah, d. Apr. 24, 1763, stillborn	1	246
WORK, Harrison G., of Providence, R. I., m. Frances C. **ENSWORTH**, d. of Nehemiah, of Canterbury, Apr. 5, 1854, by Rev. Robert C. Learned	2	90

	Vol.	Page
WRIGHT, RIGHT, Arunnah, s. [Sam[ue]l & Vienna], b. Apr. 11,		
1783, in Hanover, N. H.	1	243
Cynthia, m. Coddington **DEAN**, b. of Canterbury, Jan. 23,		
1834, by Rev. Otis C. Whiton	2	21
Eben, s. [Sam[ue]l & Vienna], b. July 17, 1786, in		
Hanover, N. H.	1	243
Elizabeth, d. Sam[ue]l & Vienna, b. Oct. 11, 1778	1	242
Esther, of Lebanon, m. Jonas **BOND**, July 26, 1765	1	70
Eunice, d. [Sam[ue]l & Vienna], b. Oct. 23, 1784, in		
Hanover, N. H.	1	243
Lucina, d. Sam[ue]l & Vienna, b. Dec. 23, 1779, in		
Hanover, N. H.	1	243
Lucy, d. [Sam[ue]l & Vienna], b. Feb. 14, 1795	1	243
Olive, d. [Sam[ue]l & Vienna], b. Apr. 9, 1788, in		
Hanover, H. H.	1	243
Phebe, d. [Sam[ue]l & Vienna], b. Oct. 5, 1791	1	243
Samuel, m. Vienna **BOND**, Feb. 16, 1775	1	236
Vienna, d. [Sam[ue]l & Vienna], b. July 10, 1792	1	243
W[illia]m Bond, s. Sam[ue]l & Vienna, b. Sept. 19, 1776	1	242
Zerviah, d. [Sam[ue]l & Vienna], b. Oct. 14, 1781, in		
Hanover, N. H.	1	243
YEARNAM*, Hannah, m. Jonathan **ADAMS**, Mar. 11, 1755		
(*Should be "YEAMAN". See **ADAMS** Genealogy)	1	51
YOUNG, Catharine, m. William **ENSWORTH**, Jr., Oct. 11, 1768	1	133
David, of Norwich, m. Mary E. **HARRIS**, Aug. 29, 1842, by		
Rev. W. Clarke	2	91
Frances S., of Griswold, m. Lydia M. **PELLET**, of Canterbury,		
May 8, 1843, by Rev. W. Clarke	2	91
Jeremiah, m. Nancy **ADAMS**, b. of Canterbury, Nov. 20,		
1831, by Rufus Johnson, J. P.	2	91
Mary, m. Charles **JUSTIN**, Aug. 13, 1830, by Erastus Larned	2	43
Nancy, m. Alvin **BUTTS**, b. of Canterbury, Dec. 18, 1831,		
by Rev. Orrin Catlin	2	9
NO SURNAME		
Abigail, m. James D. **RANSOM**, Dec. 11, 1843, Westminster		
(Entry crossed out)	2	64
Asa, s. Jacob & Abigail, b. June 12, 1777 (Perhaps		
"Asa **FULLER**")	1	144
Cloea, d. [Ketomance & Nance], b. June 4, 1763	1	174
Ephraim, s. Tyxhall & Jerusha, d. June 23, 1749		
(Probably "Ephraim **ENSWORTH**")	1	137
Esther, m. [Nathan **RAYNSFORD**], July 12, 1737	1	210
Harkless, s. Ketomance & Nance, b. Apr. 25, 1761	1	174
Hiram, s. Samuel, [d.] (Perhaps "Hiram **CARTER**")	1	119
John, s. Caleb & Dorkis, [ ]	1	252
Olive, d. [ ]	1	165
Rebeckah, m. Obadiah **JOHNSON**, Sept. 7, 1696	1	167